1837
ARTES
VERITAS
SCIENTIA
LIBRARY OF THE
UNIVERSITY OF MICHIGAN
E PLURIBUS UNUM
TUEBOR
SI QUAERIS PENINSULAM AMOENAM
CIRCUMSPICE

I0837263

Levi Woodbury

# WRITINGS

OF

# LEVI WOODBURY, LL. D.

## POLITICAL, JUDICIAL AND LITERARY.

NOW FIRST SELECTED AND ARRANGED.

IN THREE VOLUMES.

VOL. II.—JUDICIAL.

BOSTON:
LITTLE, BROWN AND COMPANY.
1852.

Stereotyped by
HOBART & ROBBINS,
NEW ENGLAND TYPE AND STEREOTYPE FOUNDERY,
BOSTON.

RIVERSIDE, CAMBRIDGE:
PRINTED BY H. O. HOUGHTON AND COMPANY.

# JUDICIAL.

# JUDICIAL.

## ON STRICT CONSTRUCTION OF POWERS.*

It is essential to the pure and peaceful administration of justice, that all its officers keep carefully within the boundaries of their constitutional powers. Auxiliary to this, but not secondary in importance, is a due knowledge of the leading subjects for their inquiry and decision. Attending to these considerations anxiously, as we all ought, and the judicial tribunals of both the States and the United States are likely to perform their respective functions without jealousy or serious collision; and our beautiful system of double legislatures and double judicatories — of political checks and constitutional balances — can move onward, notwithstanding their complicated machinery, with a regularity and harmony scarcely surpassed by those of the revolutions of the planets. What, then, are the general boundaries for you, as well as this bench, in respect to constitutional power? What are the sacred limits established by the people of the States, beyond which it is usurpation, or, at least, a dangerous dereliction of duty, for any of us to pass?

They are, in brief, that for most internal and domestic objects other courts and other juries have been organized in this country, and offenders in relation to those objects are not amenable to the tribunals of the General Government. In our political system, those other tribunals belong to the several States, act within and for each of them, and any tendency to encroach on their jurisdiction is justly watched over with much jealousy.

Among the reasons for the great sensitiveness which most of our

---

* A Charge to the Grand Jury, delivered in the U. S. Circuit Court, in 1845.

population entertain concerning State rights, on this and all subjects, is the fact that the people, through the States, and not the General Government, are the original source of all power in this country; that they thus made the General Government, and not the General Government them, and that they granted to the General Government only certain limited powers, and expressly retained all others to themselves. The State institutions, including their judicial tribunals, are likewise nearer to the community, and mingled more with their every-day life and business. They also came into existence, generally, at an earlier date, and have been longer tried, and are better known. They relate usually to what is dearer, as well as nearer, to individuals, and more imperative in demands for protection against violence and crime; being private relations of parent and child, master and servant, and that consecrated union of husband and wife, which has, by its improved purity, been one of the greatest instruments in advancing modern civilization. They gather into their embrace, likewise, the altar, no less than the hearth,— the institutions of religion, some of the duties it inculcates and the crimes it forbids, and the rights of freedom of conscience which are here guaranteed. They include, in ordinary affairs, under the State constitutions and State laws, also much of the wide domain of public morals, public education, security in most cases of property as well as person, protection of character, and a vast variety of other topics connected, in that sphere, with the support of political rights and public liberty. In respect to all these, therefore, so far as placed in other hands, we must not, because we ought not to, interfere; but, on the contrary, while forbearing to encroach on the jurisdiction of others, it becomes us to be vigilant over everything clearly intrusted to us by the constitution and laws — over everything which depends chiefly for safety on our labors and our oaths.

What is so intrusted? In a confederated government, like ours, foreign and exterior relations, with the protection of the persons and property embarked under them, can always be more appropriately administered by some general or central power, acting only for the whole, and acting principally on matters which concern the whole. That central power exists in this country, and most of its judicial functions are confided to us. The very nature and object of such a power indicate the extent, no less than the general design, of our duties under it. Within the range of your inquiries, therefore, will be found most of the offences against foreign and exterior business and rights, and also most of the offences against the constitution, laws, government and institutions, formed to protect that business and those rights. Without authority to punish offences against these various institutions of the General Government, as well as the persons and property of our citizens exposed abroad, the whole central authority would become stripped of efficiency and independence. It could not protect the vast foreign commerce placed under its guardianship, or its own rights, or even its own existence. It would become the derision of offenders.

It would not be a government, but a mere appurtenant to a government, and the football of factions. Our fathers were too well read in history to leave so incomplete the great fabric reared here on the ruins of kingly power, after the Revolution. Hence the old Confederation, which was at first sustained by means of the enthusiasm of a civil war, soon, in the calm of peace, developed a want of self-strength and self-support, no less than energy to command respect abroad, that required the additional powers which were afterwards embodied into the general constitution, and under which, and the various acts of Congress since passed, we are now acting. Your duties, then, extend, first, to the protection of the government formed under that constitution; next, to the protection of the people under it, so far as amenable to its provisions; then, with like limitations, of the property under it; and finally, of all the various and important rights shielded by that sacred compact, or by the acts of Congress which have been passed in conformity to it. But, as a grand jury, you are to do this only through the penal code; because civil remedies and redress belong to other ministers of the law than yourselves. You are to yield this protection, also, only so far as that penal code is placed under the jurisdiction of this court; because, in other respects, all proper relief can be had elsewhere. The United States courts have a limited jurisdiction; and hence, according to Chief-justice Ellsworth, instead of presuming all cases within their jurisdiction till the contrary appears, we are to presume "that a cause is without their jurisdiction till the contrary appears."

Such, then, are the general outlines of the boundaries of our constitutional powers. Let me enjoin you to respect the limitations imposed on us, as they come from the great fountain of all power here, whether political or judicial. We are sworn to obey them, and they can be changed or enlarged only by the sovereign sanction of those creating them. At the same time, allow me to enjoin that you sustain in due vigor the grants coming from the same source, as they are equally high in origin, equally important to the whole in certain great exigencies, and are therefore equally to be respected, upheld and enforced.

I do not propose, on this occasion, to enter minutely into a definition and analysis of all the different crimes over which you thus possess cognizance; but it must be manifest that the first duty of every grand jury, in the courts of the United States, is to inquire if the United States themselves have been assailed, and their General Government endangered by any traitorous designs. Not only the existence of this judicial tribunal itself, but all that we hold valuable in war or peace, whether through commerce with foreign nations, or friendly intercourse, harmony and improvement, between almost thirty independent States comprising our vast confederacy, depends much on the preservation of that government with all its rightful powers, and more especially on the vigorous continuance of its hallowed union. Treason against the United States is therefore punished by death. Under the constitution, it "shall consist only in levying war against them, or in adhering to their enemies, giving them aid and comfort." Our ancestors had suffered so much under constructive treasons, and arbitrary persecutions for such felonies, though never meditated, that they hastened, in the constitution itself, to sweep off the whole of them, with all their barbarous confiscations and attainders of innocent blood in their posterity; but still inflicted, as was right, the highest penalty in our system on any overt acts, tending to subvert by violence the very government which helps to protect so much that is dear at home and abroad. I pass by all the details of the kind and quantity of testimony necessary to constitute levying war, or giving aid and comfort to the enemies of the United States, as well as many other particulars bearing on the subject; because you will have the advice on these points of the learned counsel for the government, in case any complaint of treason comes before you, and because the details would be uninteresting, if not useless, when, as now, no such complaint is likely to be presented at this term.

Indeed, it is a cause of much gratitude to Providence that this offence has very seldom been attempted, in any portion of our country. The General Government having been formed with deliberation and full discussion, rather than in haste, and by the people and States themselves, and not by others for them, — having been voluntarily chosen, not imposed by domestic or foreign violence,— having been designed for their interests at large, and not to advance the ambitious ends of a few, whether demagogues or usurpers,— being open to speedy, peaceful, and lawful amendments, instead of resting like an iron incubus on the people, unchanged and unchangeable, for ages,— little justification has ever existed for many alterations in its structure, and none for resorts to violence against its operations. Hence it is, that, in the half-century of its mild and beneficial operation, only one or two instances have occurred of a necessity to rally the public strength against supposed designs to overthrow the government by force.

Not in all of these have the projectors aimed at that catastrophe; and whenever they have, in any case, escaped conviction on technical grounds, the infamy attached to them has been almost equal to what follows plenary conviction; and it is fortunate that, under the purity and patriotism of our population, and their devoted loyalty to republican institutions, the attempted subversion of those institutions in any way, even without violence, is most abhorrent to popular feeling and public opinion, and is generally regarded as little less culpable, in the court of conscience, than actual force against the government, or giving direct aid and comfort to our enemies.

Another like offence consists of misprision of treason, which is the having knowledge of a real treason, and concealing it from public exposure and prosecution. One in some respects similar is the carrying on correspondence with a foreign government to influence it against our own and to defeat its legitimate measures.

The counterfeiting of our public coin is another crime indictable by you; and it is punishable also to pass any debased coin of the kind which is made by law current in the country, or to import any not so made, if in common use, and if imported with an intent to deceive or defraud.

Embezzlement of the public money has, of late years, very properly, been made a crime; and its punishment rigidly enforced against offenders will prove a very great additional security against defalcations.

Robbery of a mail-carrier of any part of the public mail is another aggravated offence. So is the detention, or opening, or destroying, of any letter in the public mail, by a person employed in any part of the post-office establishment. And if any such person take money, or bank-notes, or other writings of value, from any such letter, the offence is of a still deeper dye, and justly punished with greater rigor.

All of these violations of the security of one of the important public institutions of the General Government, and of the sanctity of private correspondence, are offences within your cognizance; and are so hostile to the safety and facilities of epistolary intercourse, whether social, political or commercial, that exemplary punishment should be promptly visited on all offenders of either class. Nor, in this country, under the reign of laws protecting equally low and high, can it be tolerated that the confidence of private correspondence may, in a period of peace, be violated with impunity by those *in power*, under the dangerous plea of *State necessity*, as seems to be countenanced in some other governments, though at the expense, justly, of much public censure, and the scoff and scorn of all that is honorable in private life.

Another crime which it is your province to indict, and which, unhappily blackening the annals of all ages, endangers the *lives* no less than the property of our citizens, is *Piracy*. The unholy lust for money, in uneducated minds, and in others not accustomed to the constant restraints of sound morals and wholesome laws, sometimes overcomes all respects for the right of property, and even the sacredness of life; and when this passion happens to find a theatre for action more protected from punishment by great distance and the lonely waste of oceans, it is apt to exhibit greater depravity, and lead to the darkest tragedies. Hence, in such positions, it is punished with greater severity, in order to check more effectually its outbreaks under those feebler restraints. And hence, what would be robbery only on land, if committed on the high seas, becomes piracy, and is punishable with death. Indeed, it is an offence under the law of nations, independent of particular statutes, and its perpetrators are regarded as the enemies of the whole human race.

Piracy, under our acts of Congress, consists, firstly, in the commission on the high seas — or any waters out of the jurisdiction of any particular State — any offence, which, if committed on land, within a country, would be punished by death. Next, it may be committed by feloniously running away with a vessel, or voluntarily surrendering it to a pirate. So it may amount to piracy, if any seaman lay violent hands on his commander, to prevent his fighting in defence of his vessel; or commit a revolt in the ship.

Finally, with a view to break up the traffic in human blood, and afford an opportunity for education and the arts, Christianity and commerce, to improve the condition at home of the wretched African, as well as leave those in bondage here uncontaminated by new importations of ignorance and paganism from abroad, and thus gradually to be advanced in morals and privileges, under a humane and Christian civilization, till they can be emancipated with safety among ourselves, or returned usefully to gladden the wilderness of their native land, the prosecution of the slave trade has for many years been punished in this country as a piracy. To constitute this last offence, there must be a seizure of some person abroad, negro or mulatto, with a view to make him a slave; or a receipt of such person on board of a vessel with an intent to carry him or her into slavery, or some aid given to confine, or transport, or land, or sell such person as a slave. But, in any of those events, whether the vessel be owned by foreigners or citizens of the United States, the acts are equally culpable, and capitally punished.

All interest or connection with this foreign slave trade is not, however, considered equal in moral turpitude, or evil tendency; and Congress has, therefore, graduated the degree of the crime, and of the punishment, according to the nature of the offence. But, when not a capital offence, it is still unlawful; and indictable by you, and punishable with fine and imprisonment, if any one serves voluntarily on board a vessel of the United States employed to transport slaves from one foreign place to another. So is it to be voluntarily engaged in the slave trade in a foreign vessel. Because both of these acts may tend to increase the trade, and are often so hard-hearted and inhuman in their character as to have been long prohibited by acts of Congress.

The anxiety of our government has been such to suppress this unholy trade, and the dislike of our people is justly such to the degrading search of American ships by foreign powers, that a large armed force, in addition to these severe penalties, is now maintained on the African coast, to coöperate in preventing the trade under the American flag. We had no part or lot in originating a commerce so odious. Our fathers remonstrated against its introduction. Those abroad who censure us most for its evils have offended most in causing them. A large portion of this country has already rid itself of the distasteful fruits of it; and this, not by fanatical rashness, nor by a breach of the spirit or letter of the constitution, but by voluntary and rightful legislation, through each State for itself, and for its own people. In due time, by stopping the fountain-head of slavery, through the power expressly granted to Congress to prohibit further additions to it from abroad, fearlessly and honestly exercised, as this power has been and should continue to be, with other lawful means, which it is not pertinent now to detail, the country will be enabled gradually to purify, as well as diminish, the corrupt waters that have flowed from this fountain, and, it is hoped, ere long to return most of them to their native source.

It will be a lasting glory to our institutions, if all this should be accomplished without violating the sacred compromises of the constitution, or endangering public safety, though by means slow, I admit, and seeming slower here, under the ardent impulses of our free principles, than they really are, when compared with the progress of other ages on like subjects. But they are sure means, and tend neither to subvert the Union,—that holy ark of safety to the republic,—nor alienate brethren who, in revolutions and wars, and adversity of all kinds, no less than in peace and prosperity, have embarked together their destinies, and held on faithfully to the pledge for security to each others' rights — of each others' "fortunes, lives, and sacred honor."

There is another class of offences committed abroad whose punishment is within your jurisdiction. It includes ordinary revolts on board American ships, on the one hand, and, on the other, forcing, with malice, and without justifiable cause, any of our officers or seamen on *shore*, and leaving them behind in any foreign port or place. Great vigilance in ferreting out and punishing both of these crimes is demanded, as well, on the one hand, to protect the hardy and honest seaman from *oppression* while *abroad*, as, on the other, to enable the commanders of vessels to preserve due subordination, and save from shipwreck and destruction the valuable property and lives intrusted to their charge. It includes, likewise, setting on fire our vessels of war, or wilfully casting away ships belonging to citizens of the United States. Outrages of this description, whether committed on the high seas or at home, are alike punishable here.

Without deeming it necessary, at this time, to enter more at large into the character of these crimes, I shall next invite your attention to a catalogue of offences resting on another peculiarity in our political system.

In the multifarious concerns of the General Government, it is obliged to have forts and navy-yards, arsenals and magazines, light-houses, and other similar establishments. Over most of these it has, and must have, exclusive jurisdiction, in order to fulfil efficiently the great ends contemplated in their formation. A like jurisdiction it has over our vessels, whether mercantile or naval, while abroad under the American flag. It follows, then, that, having this jurisdiction, it must punish the various crimes committed within it, or they will be likely to go unavenged, and lead to unbridled and atrocious licentiousness. Hence, for most of the offences committed in such places against the person or property, penalties have been imposed by Congress; and it has become your imperative duty to aid in enforcing them. Thus, murder, or arson, or burglary, larceny or forgery, perpetrated within those places, are crimes; and crimes that, happening within our jurisdiction, will, by you, in the beautiful Saxon idiom of your oath in some States, be inquired of "without fear, favor, affection, or the hope of reward," on the one hand, and, on the other, without the indulgence of either "lucre or malice." Let him, then, who there kills, with malice aforethought, any one who bears impressed on him the Divine image, — who there burns his neighbor's dwelling, in the hours of darkness, — him who there breaks into the sanctuary of one's house, to steal, under the shadow of night, — or feloniously takes property, or resorts to falsifications of writings to obtain what is not his own, — let all such, within reach of your examinations, be made to learn that acts like these are not to escape condign punishment, when committed within the jurisdiction of the United States, any more than when within that of a single State.

There must be, also, under the central government, which collects and disburses so many millions of revenue, numerous officers, and numerous provisions imposing taxes in one form or another. The resistance to those, or other officers of that government, in the due discharge of their duties, as well as the evasion and breach of the revenue laws, may sometimes be of so flagrant a character as to come within your cognizance; and whenever they are, however unpopular such officers sometimes become, and however objectionable, at times, may be some of the legal provisions duty requires them to execute, yet the reign of the laws, and the maintenance of public order, demand that prompt punishment be inflicted. The bribery of any of those officers is another dangerous offence, striking at the root of everything virtuous or just in official life, and poisoning the very fountains of purity, whether in civil, political, or judicial station. Wherever detected, it should receive immediate exposure to public infamy; and this, both in him that gives, and him that takes, the wages of sin.

Extortion in office is another corruption, which should be visited by your reprobation, wherever committed by those who have thus betrayed the confidence reposed in them by the General Government, and perverted official power into the oppression and plunder of the community.

Nor can you do this with success, or we aid you in vindicating the offended majesty of the laws, on any of these violations of public duty, unless our inquiries can be assured of reaching the truth, through the severe prosecution of every species of PERJURY which may be committed in the judicial investigations of any of the tribunals of the General Government. The evils from false swearing can hardly be over-estimated. In vain may you seek to probe guilt, — in vain may we strive to uphold the constitution and laws, and protect innocence, as well as punish crime, — in vain may character and property, and even life, try to exist secure, under the shield of constitutions and laws, — if those who publicly appeal to God for witness to their truthfulness are allowed to commit perjury with impunity, and, unprosecuted and uncondemned, to set that God at defiance, and thus disregard every solemn sanction of religion, as well as of social trust and legal duty.

After these suggestions, gentlemen of the grand jury, I do not deem it useful to detain you longer with remarks on any other portions of the criminal code of the United States. I have said enough to direct your attention to the most important subjects, and, it is hoped, to commend sufficiently to your intelligence, patriotism and integrity, the interests of the government, as connected with the several matters belonging to your cognizance. I am conscious that your zeal to uphold the laws and public order will be found equal to our own, and to any emergency which is likely to arise. Your interests at stake under our system of jurisprudence are great as those of any class among us. Nor have I any doubt, under the educated and moral influences that predominate generally in this country, you will prove as responsible and faithful as any to your official obligations. At the same time, gentlemen, it is not to be concealed, that in a state of society fortunately so equal as ours, and under institutions most of us rejoice to find so liberal, firmness in the cause of truth, and right, and duty, is sometimes wanting. The fears of the good and the judicious often look more to a failure in the administration of justice from timidity, or temporizing with offences, than from ignorance, or wilful infidelity to duty. It is true, also, in connection with these fears, that the Christianity of modern times coöperates with the great extension of commerce and learning and civilization over the world, to produce milder codes of criminal law, and more humane punishments; and Americans, in their rapid as well as reforming progress on all this, are, and should be, the last not to feel duly their genial influences. Yet those influences need not, and should not, disarm us in the punishment of guilt. Reason and experience, enlightened, as here, by our superior systems of teaching and training, and strengthened by the wider diffusion of sound morals and higher responsibilities among citizens, who, like ours, rule so much more than they are ruled in everything around them, will convince all that we must take heed to our peculiar position, and leave no honest effort untried to counteract the evil indulgences and forbearances that might otherwise flow from it. They unite to urge on us the paramount duty in the administration of ours, as of every criminal code, — that the less severe are its penalties, the more invariably and unfalteringly ought they to be enforced, wherever guilt is clear; and that, in the pursuit of such a policy, shall we alone be enabled to make the greater certainty of punishment compensate or atone for its greater lenity.

Impressed duly, I trust, with considerations like these, gentlemen, you will please to retire and enter upon your official inquiries.

## DUTY OF ENFORCING OBJECTIONABLE LAWS UNTIL REPEALED.*

GENTLEMEN OF THE GRAND JURY: — On a former occasion, I took the liberty to invite the attention of your body to some of the excuses or apologies which at times tempt jurors, no less than judges, to be remiss in enforcing the penal code with due certainty. I seize on this opportunity to add a few more illustrations of this subject. For it is only by discussion, only by looking the real evil in the face, that it can be dispelled, or even mitigated. One of the peculiar dangers, not before considered, to which jurors as well as judges are exposed, is the *unpopularity* or *obnoxiousness*, from any cause, of any particular law which has been violated, leading us, at times, on that account, to be timid or unfaithful in enforcing it.

This occurs from the law being out of favor, not merely because of some severe penalty attached to the breach of it, but the subject-matter being a delicate or offensive one — such as the revenue or taxation, or an embargo or post-office regulation. A little reflection must, however, convince all that the duty imposed on both you and us is not to execute the laws of the land as to one subject rather than another, any more than as to one person, or one class of persons, rather than another, or as to those of one creed rather than another, or one color instead of another.

While we, in one sense, in our respective spheres, are holding the scales as well as sword of justice, in humble imitation of the Divine Judge on high, is it possible that we can be justified in pursuing any different course than is believed to govern His all-wise dispensations? — to let law, as law, reign supreme, reign equally over all, and as to all things no less than persons; and, till it is changed by the proper authorities, not to interpose our individual caprices, or fancies, or speculations, to defeat its due course and triumph.

There is also much less justification here than in some countries to disregard laws when disliked; because we can, under the universal suffrage enjoyed here, otherwise help legally to change or annul them by our votes. We thus helped to make them, and they are not forced on us by despotism or minorities, as in some governments. Change them when you please, then, as citizens and legislators, by means of free suffrage, of persuasion and majorities; but as jurors you have sworn to obey them till so changed, and ought to stand by them then faithfully, to the last moment of their existence.

We are safest, in our capacity of public officers, to always walk

---

* Charge to the Grand Jury of the U. States Circuit Court, 1847.

steadfast in the path of our duty to execute the laws as they are, while others, who may make or retain bad laws in the statute-book, are answerable for their own wrong. If they preserve laws on the statute-book which are darkness rather than light and life to the people, theirs is the fault. In some cases, also, where we think the existing laws and punishments are wrong, and hence venture to encourage others in disobedience by neglecting to indict and punish offenders, it should make us pause and halt, when it is remembered, it may turn out that we, ourselves, may not be exactly Solons or Solomons in these respects, nor quite so much wiser than the laws themselves as sometimes we are hastily induced to suppose. It would be a great public misfortune, if these two crimes should be committed, rather than one: the first by the breaker of the obnoxious law, and the second by the public functionary, who allows the real offender to escape unpunished. If, for instance, without looking to the experience of all ages and the necessities of the case, we should not punish a seaman as we ought who piratically runs away with a vessel placed in his trust, or who commits a revolt under the paternal though severe discipline of his commander, or who sets fire to his vessel in the lonely wastes of the ocean, endangering, by example, millions on millions of property, and thousands on thousands of lives, by the most cruel and horrid burning alive which imagination can paint, and this only under some slight provocation as to food and labor,—if we should neglect our sacred and imperative duties, merely because, in our individual opinions, that which is allowed by law is not the most eligible course, and that parents, and those standing in their places, must spare the rod, however disobedient the child; — or, if we hastily believe, because we live under a wise and glorious democracy for adults, there is to be no subordination by minors, or apprentices, or seamen, or soldiers, but all things are to be decided by each for himself, and the child punish the parent, the sailor discipline the captain, the militia-man or soldier issue orders to his general, —and if we attempt to act as if all this was legal, rather than what our fathers and our country and Divine revelation have duly upheld as law, we may learn, too late, that such a course is disorganizing, destructive to all the best interests of society here, and the best hopes hereafter of those who inconsiderately indulge in it.

Notwithstanding this, we may well sympathize, and often must, with suffering in a thousand shapes. We may properly feel indignant at oppression of every kind, mental as well as physical. And no sound principle, human or Divine, requires us, as freemen and as citizens, to approve what our reason and conscience condemn, whether in ordinary cases, individual instances, or in those great struggles of right which have filled history with victims to political oppression, and martyrs to bigotry and intolerance.

But the mode of disapproving, the mode and time of resisting, all we condemn, should be right and legal, and in an appropriate capacity. Extreme measures can be resorted to properly only as citizens, and after all others more moderate and appropriate are first tried and fail. Extreme remedies, too, are justifiable only by citizens or legislators, and for extreme evils, and on occasions suitable. Hence, if a wrong happens to exist in some laws, it can never be a justification, with jurors or judges, to commit another wrong, and much less a crime. On the contrary, considerations like these should be an incentive to us, in our present capacities, to redress every species of offence in our power legally; and to protect those who have suffered, rather than the aggressors, so as to tempt the feeble and poor and oppressed to seek such regular redress here, rather than take the law into their own hands, interested and rash, and become themselves executioners, no less than judges and parties.

Miserable must be the fate of that community where the ministers of the law are themselves disposed to disregard it,—to aid, countenance, and shield its violators. If the agents of the law are to oppose it, unless in justifiable revolutions,—if the great interests of society are to be wounded and sacrificed by those who are appointed to become their sentinels or protectors,—government will become a curse; and justly may we, as a people, instead of being the envy of the world, become the scoff and scorn of all in it that is intelligent, and civilized, and pure; and this, whether such a betrayal of public trust springs from the delusions of false philanthropy or fanatical prejudices, no less than when it arises from unbridled licentiousness.

It is the more unfortunate when the want of steadfastness, uniformity, and fortitude, or unfaltering courage in the execution of the laws, is common: because those qualities are not only necessary to insure an equal administration of the laws, but are indispensable to the general safety of life and property. For instance, everything is exposed, defenceless, unless all who would have self-government respected are not only firm in making the laws rather than caprices govern, and rather than the vagaries of any individual, but carry into judicial life the lion heart in favor of what is established by the people at large, in their constitution and laws. You must be in the court-room neither timid children nor weak women, but act worthy of patriots, or martyrs, and, before being swerved to desert duty and law, must perish at the stake, or die as a Roman senate in your seats. You must despise the clamor which would tempt you to become unjust, and must breast bravely the shock which prejudice or faction may give to unnerve you, and disarm your firmness, and undermine your deliberate judgments.

You will find that your business in the halls of justice is no milk-and-water concern, to be turned away by tremulousness of the nerves, or hysterics, or tales of the nursery. But it is the lofty business of men, high-minded men,—is the great business of life and death, as well as of character and property,—and is to be properly performed only by those who dare do all that does become a man, though in the worst of times.

There is no system nor safety in the administration of justice, except in such certain and inflexible adherence to established laws; established, too, by the people themselves, and not by despots or usurpers. The very idea of the law, in a constitutional republic, involves the requisite that it be a rule, a guide, uniform, fixed and equal, for all, till changed by the same high political power which made it. This is what entitles it to its sovereign weight. And it is such laws, so made and so upheld, which it is our imperative duty to sustain, rather than thwart or disregard. It is to maintain such laws, that all the great sanctions of Christianity and the eternal world urge on us as public officers, would point out with warning dread, and demand from us by all the hopes, as well as terrors, of a future judgment.

There are some minor excuses urged, at times, against executing the laws, which it may be useful to caution you against briefly, before closing.

One is, that the accused belongs to our favorite sect in religion, or our party in politics, or to our own peculiar neighborhood, or our clique in society. But such considerations, however powerful with the affections and passions, should never tempt us to neglect our duties. They never, unless under sudden and strong impulses, can influence the upright to falsify the equal balance of the scales of justice, and screen real guilt from punishment.

On the other hand, the heretic in religion, as we may view him, the opponent in politics, the alien and the unfortunate stranger, cannot ever be entitled to less justice, to less protection, than others, in character and life. It would be a foul reproach to us, if our liberal institutions should not be sustained in shielding as they do equally, in life and property, while performing their duties as good citizens, all reposing under their wings, whether the Catholic or Protestant, the bond or the free, the Jew or the Gentile, the Irishman or the Swiss, the whig or democrat, the abolitionist or friend to the constitution as it is, the man or the brother, whether born on this or the other side of the Atlantic, on this or the other side of the Hudson, or Mississippi, or the Rocky Mountains.

Presumptions of guilt or innocence may sometimes be strengthened or weakened by the place of birth and kind of education and associates a man has grown up with; and good character may at times interpose, and justly save, under suspicion, one who is accused of crime on slight circumstances. And a notorious badness of character, a life unhappily spent among convicts and pirates, may tend to strengthen the presumptions derived from other proof. And both of these are, at times, in evidence in the case. But it is never safe nor legal to rely on them alone, either in indicting or convicting; and much less is it *ever* safe to indict or discharge solely on account of differences or coincidences in faith, or opinion, or profession, of any kind whatever. Remember, that all gaze upon one earth, sun and ocean, — all have one revelation, one God, one judgment hereafter, one hope, one eternity.

All, then, should be equally treated with justice here, as we wish to be treated so ourselves hereafter. Without some such rule, and a steady adherence to it, the rights of each will be measured by the passions and prejudices of others, or by their whims and tyranny. And, in such an event, a single Turkish cadi to try and condemn would be better than two or twelve or twenty such cadis, as it would be much cheaper, and no more oppressive.

Everything would thus become vague, where all should be fixed; everything uncertain, where all should be known and clear. Laws, instead of being written on stone, would be traced in sand; and the guilty would escape, not by *not* being *proved* guilty according to law, but by weakness or wickedness in the judicial tribunals where criminals *are* proved to be guilty, and ought to be so punished.

Again, we must not lay the flattering unction to our souls, that because, by some possibility, there may not be guilt, we can rightfully discharge as if probably there was no guilt; or because, in a few cases among the myriads in the long tracts of time, convictions may have happened from perjury, we can rightly acquit, at any time, without sufficient evidence of perjury.

Under any of the numerous fallacies sometimes urged and yielded to in criminal trials, to say that the accused may possibly be innocent, — that he may possibly be criminated by perjury, — that he possibly may have done the wicked deed when his senses were steeped in forgetfulness by sleep, or peradventure done it from madness rather than badness, under the noxious influence of some sudden insanity, — or that the death may possibly have occurred at the moment by some insurmountable accident, some act of God, rather than by the apparent wrong and malice of the prisoner, — is to say what no juror nor judge can yield confidence to, if the testimony renders a different presumption the most probable. For, it is probability on the testimony and the law that you are to follow, and not loose or fanciful or possible conjectures. The whole business of life is to be governed by probabilities, rather than possibilities, or the world would become a huge lunatic asylum.

Probabilities, and not possibilities, are the general rule of action in society, from the cradle to the grave; and by none other can society move on, in any of its numerous ramifications, so as to insure individual usefulness or public safety. And if we do not punish where guilt is proved to be highly probable, we even abet it, encourage it; we give renewed opportunities and temptations to crime, till desperadoes, buccaneers and pirates, will make land and ocean red with conflagration and blood, and the sun would go down, in clouds and darkness, on all that is glorious in our beloved country.

Again, it is sometimes urged against agreeing to indict or convict, that we have conscientious scruples on the subject. Respect, then, these, by all means, in the proper way and on the proper occasions. One mode is to consider of such scruples before we undertake officially to execute all the laws. We should in advance inform ourselves whether we can conscientiously fulfil what the obligations of our station demand. And if sincere tenderness of conscience presses on the heart and mind against executing some of the laws, it should lead us to decline office, or resign, — not to neglect or disobey, while in office, what we have promised and sworn to perform.

We should, in the outset, request an exemption from fulfilling at all the duties of a station, a compliance with some of which seems to us a sin against God. Or, if a majority prove unaccommodating and inflexible against us, in matters which belong to the conscience, and where we cannot honestly submit, then it behooves those thus differing from them, and thus suffering, not to violate the laws and the exactions of the majority in conformity with the laws, unless by justifiable attempts at a revolution; but rather to withdraw entirely from such a government, and emigrate, instead of doing what seems to us an offence against Heaven, and the well-founded scruples of an enlightened conscience. But, in all such cases, we must take special care not to indulge ourselves in considering an act as a sin which is only disagreeable, or the result of only some prejudice, or caprice, or limited knowledge of the subject. And more especially must we heed this, if the thing to be done be, for instance, like the infliction of capital punishment, one which many of us, including myself, deem ill-judged, but still to be enforced while the laws demand it, considering that our pious forefathers did not hesitate to inflict it in many cases, and when the Scriptures themselves allow it in certain instances, if the community choose to employ it.

Nor can jurors generally be justified in refusing to execute laws from some refined scruples concerning their constitutionality. It is true that laws may sometimes violate the great charter of our liberties. But the presumptions are, that laws sanctioned by such intelligent, numerous and respectable members of society as compose our legislative bodies, are constitutional, and, until pronounced otherwise by the proper tribunal, the judiciary, it is perilous for jurors to disobey them; and it is trifling with their solemn obligations to disregard them in any way, and on any occasion, from constitutional doubts, unless of the clearest and strongest character. Even the bench, whose peculiar province it is to settle such questions, can act only from such doubts, and are culpable if otherwise treating laws as unconstitutional. I propose to say no more, at this time, on these and kindred topics. They are not of the most agreeable character. But, like some unpalatable medicines, they may be none the less useful. Self-study and self-examination are seldom in vain.

It cannot but be good for us, gentlemen, to review, at times, and meditate on, considerations like those connected with our important duties. If done in a proper spirit, it must invigorate our resolves to do right. It helps to enlighten our footsteps some, where we must tread, to check any inadvertent or ill-advised wandering from the true path, and to nerve our minds and hearts for the difficulties of our responsible stations.

Thus shall we, one and all, be more likely to escape any just reproaches in our official career; and, so far as we are concerned in the government and laws of the American people, we shall pursue the best mode to transmit them to our posterity untarnished, and, indeed, in some degree, in a manner worthy the past, the present and the probable future, of our portion of the new world; worthy, I hope, those exalted duties which seem to be allotted to our favored country.

---

## THE ENFORCING OF OBJECTIONABLE LAWS.*

Gentlemen of the Grand Jury: — It often happens, in the discharge of your responsible duties, that some assistance can be given by the court. At times it may be effected by explanations of the crimes within your cognizance, and at times by suggestions as to the general principles and general course of action which should influence your deliberations. To understand these principles and that course of action aright, and to follow them with fidelity, is no less important than to know the extent of your official powers. On those powers, including the offences you are authorized to indict, I have formerly presented such information as seemed to me likely to be useful, and likewise some views concerning the kind of evidence to be required, in your inquiries. On this occasion, I shall take the liberty to add a few remarks on some of the general rules of action most appropriate as your official guides, and on the imperative duty of following where these rules plainly lead. One of these is, that where guilt is clear, jurors should be inflexible in helping to make punishment certain.

In all ages, no less than from Beccaria to Bentham, this has been the constant injunction of every sound jurist as to penal codes. In no other way can the rights of property and life be safe; and, without safety, they are without value. There is no other protection, except the dangerous and doubtful one which a different course, by its uncertainty and license, will compel, for every individual to become his own

---

* A charge to the Grand Jury of the U. S. Circuit Court; delivered in 1848.

avenger — his own juror, judge and executioner, of what he considers proper. If society and government, and their public agents, who are chosen and *paid* to protect the rest, and to avenge the violated majesty of the laws, neglect their trust, and allow the guilty to escape with impunity, what other resource can be left for self-preservation? what security can remain for the hearth or the altar,—for conscience, property, and all political as well as civil rights,—except the arm of each—feeble or strong, as accident may determine? Laws thus become trampled on, society necessarily reverts to anarchy, all lies at the mercy of physical power, and life becomes a state of piracy, or unmitigated tyranny.

To examine briefly some of the lame apologies for such a dereliction of duty, will help, it is hoped, to dissipate them. The most usual excuse for not enforcing the laws with uniform certainty is an opinion sometimes cherished by jurors, and even judges, that in particular cases they are not the best laws which might be made for the subject. But a little reflection must convince men so well educated and so experienced as yourselves, that it is no part of your duty, as grand jurors, to make or to modify the criminal code. You are selected to help to administer or execute that code, not to alter it. And all must be aware that, in a free country, the duty to form or to correct laws is usually, by the constitution, intrusted to a different set of public agents from those who are to execute them. Constitutions, therefore, become vain; political science, checks and balances, are vain; wise divisions and partitions of power, rather than all being monopolized, or despotically vested in one officer or class of officers, are utterly vain; indeed, your solemn oaths to act according to the laws are vain,—if all these are to be disregarded by you, and no indictment found, when an offender is to be punished by a law which you deem, for any cause, inexpedient.

The briefest calm consideration will show how censurable it must be, on account of a mere theoretical opinion like this, to refuse to enforce a binding public law, and allow a notorious criminal to escape, and to repeat with impunity, in still more exaggerated forms, his depredations. By such a refusal, it will be seen, that you would not only neglect a duty which you have voluntarily engaged to perform, but commit at least a moral perjury; for you thus acquit, when the law which you have sworn to enforce condemns. In this way, you would not only become false to the most solemn obligations, both as citizens and public officers, and set a vicious example to the rising generation, but bring disgrace on republican institutions, and on our common country.

We, gentlemen, on this bench, would act alike culpably, were we also to usurp the province of legislators, and amend or unmake obnoxious statutes; or were we to travel out of the path of our duty, and decide what shall be, rather than what now *are*, the laws.

When either juries or judges undertake to depart from the existing statutes, and virtually repeal them in a particular case, the course is to be reprobated, also, on account of its sinister effect on others; because we then commit aggressions on the rights of others, we lawlessly seize on the powers of others; and, in the purest government in the world, we become the most tyrannical,—in one highly moral, we set an example of the greatest theoretical misrule,—and, in the most orderly and peaceful, we open the door to the most flagrant anarchy. If viewed as merely dispensing with a law in a particular case, it is a species of usurpation which helped to bring one of the arbitrary house of Stuart to the block. It is a power, in reality, in its principle, over-ruling not one law, but all laws; and it is not to be exercised, even after indictment and verdict, in the shape of pardon, in a single instance, except by express authority of the constitution, vesting such a power, in extreme cases, not in grand or petit juries, or in this court, but in the chief executive magistrate of the government. Perhaps some of you may deem cautions like these superfluous, and doubt even the possibility of jurors or judges ever falling into errors of so dangerous a tendency.

I regret to be obliged to add, however true it may be, that such conduct must, when viewed face to face, and in its naked deformity, shock most of us, and be shunned with abhorrence; yet occasions are not unknown, where, under one pretence or another, one apology and misrepresentation or another, it is feared that the manifestly guilty are sometimes allowed to escape, under influences of this unfortunate character.

When no other reasons appear to exist, with grand or petit jurors, for acquittals, it is certainly more charitable to presume this than something worse; and it is more just to suppose that such acquittals are at times yielded to from some such calamitous misconception either of power or duty, than from corruption, where the standard of public morals is so high as it really is in this favored country. Nor do I believe that error of opinion as to the proper course in these cases happens often knowingly, any more than corruptly, where intelligence is so widely diffused. But it is done, at times, inconsiderately — almost unconsciously. Being men of like passions, sympathies, frailties and self-deceptions, with other men, we may, occasionally, unless well guarded and repeatedly admonished, slide insensibly into it under temptations or delusions which cannot bear for an instant the scrutiny of sound argument. The danger is not, therefore, that juries or judges will be in a habit of setting up their own wills and opinions openly and avowedly against the existing laws, or refraining to execute them from corrupt motives.

That is a course pursued by some daring Moloch spirits, less considerate about appearances, less scrupulous than others as to forms, and less ingenuous in self-deception; or by some half insane by fanaticism. But the difficulty is, that, when erring in this matter, most of us are hastily seduced into opposition by causes to which we are in some degree blinded, by sympathy, or metaphysical refinements, or over-heated enthusiasm, or long-existing prejudices, or by mere popular clamor. And, under the insidious influence of some of these, we, like St. Paul, while persecuting the disciples of the Saviour, are apt to suppose our course is doing God service, when, at times, it is fatal in its tendency, and full of pitfalls and danger and injustice to the best interests of humanity. Thus, considering the argument a little further, suppose, as individuals, we think a law has some defects. How can this confer on us, as juries or judges, any right to amend or disregard it? If we dislike the fashion of the clothes of a prisoner, or the architecture of the court-room, does that confer on us a power to change them? or is it to influence our opinions on the guilt or innocence of the accused? So as to a law: if it be a law, who has empowered us, from any dislike of its character, to dispense with it? If it be a law, it should continue, till altered, to be our guide, master and sovereign. It is also a presumption that the majority, who should rule on such topics, deem it a good law, or they would cause it to be altered by those whom they select for that purpose. In short, if it be a *law*, no order, or peace, or security, or right, can be maintained, unless we enforce it, till repealed or modified by those whom the constitution authorizes to do it.

Another strong argument for abiding by the law as it is till duly changed, must always be the difference of opinion as to the change most proper, if one is to be made. On this there would often be as many different minds as there are jurors; and differences not reconcilable in such short sessions as yours, and by the large majorities required in your bodies. One person would make the law more strict, another less so. One culprit would be convicted by one jury as the law is, and another, under the same law, be acquitted by another jury; and thus, the result of all trials, independent of the facts, becomes as uncertain as the weather, and as changeable daily as the hours of the ebb and flow of the tides. But, with the uniform test or standard for us as jurors and judges, the law itself, as created and fixed by those authorized to make it, the administration of justice becomes more sure, and punishment certain. In further illustration of the uncertainty of other guides, he whom Burke characterized as having circumnavigated the globe for charity,—he who was the prisoner's friend, and an angel of mercy to the criminal,—still thought, that for murder, arson, and burglary accompanied by cruelty, capital punishment must be inflicted.

At the same time, some of you might desire it in one only, like Sir Thos. Fowell Buxton, in murder; and some in none, and some in more cases than those of Howard. It is not a little remarkable, as to this vacillation or difference in views, that in Michigan, where no capital punishment exists, jurors themselves have lately memorialized the Legislature to restore it in case of murder.* The law, then, till altered, and the law alone, is the only safe anchor and sure guide for us, in our capacities as judges and juries. But, though urging this, I concede there is a wider discretion open to us as citizens, or philanthropists, or legislators. And I thank God that there is; else laws might become

* The criminal statistics of this State in 1850 show more favorable results under the experiment.

as unchangeable and as unimprovable as petrifactions, and society remain little better than a Herculaneum or Pompeii above ground.

In these other capacities, therefore, I would not censure, but encourage, giving full scope to your sympathies. In them, strive, like the great philanthropist Howard, to have the penal laws corrected wherever wrong; strive, by argument, and exhortation, and becoming zeal, and martyr enthusiasm, if you please; but, like him, never *do wrong* yourselves in public office, to attain probable good,—never, in any station or capacity, violate duty and usurp power, for any fancied or imaginary benefit.

Another apology or delusion, at times, is, that, though the law may not be bad, yet the circumstances of the case often require mitigation and mercy towards the accused; and, therefore, the jury neglect to indict, and the court to punish, under its requirements. But this again is encroaching on the powers of the executive, in whom, generally, and not in you or us, is vested the authority to mitigate, or pardon, in full or in part. It is, at the same time, true, that where an indictment may be found either for a mild or more severe crime, or where the court by law can inflict either a milder or more severe punishment, it is justly the right of the jury and the court to select either, according to the circumstances of each case; and it is their duty, and should be their pleasure, then to modify them as those may require. But, when no discretion of that kind is confided to us by law, if we undertake to exercise it, or to pardon, virtually, by not punishing the offender at all, we as much violate our duty as if we ourselves acted as accessories after the fact, and were thus *particeps criminis* in the arson, or revolt, or murder, of which, by the evidence and the law, the accused is guilty. A didactic poet has, therefore, truly said:

"Mercy but murders, pardoning those who kill."

Meaning, of course, those who kill maliciously. If our compassion or sympathy is appealed to, let it be shown in private life, where it rightfully may. Or, if indulged to any extent (and it is justly said, we must be inhuman if entirely without it), is there none due to the ruined or murdered, rather than all to the lawless offender? None to the anguish of bereaved wife and children? none to him who fell among thieves, but all to the thieves themselves? If property is destroyed, is no commiseration to be felt for those suddenly reduced to beggary, and, as sometimes happens, to starvation or the poor-house?

Why should all our kindness, so far as we can and must exercise it, be exhausted on the culprit, rather than a fair portion be exercised in favor of admitted innocence, persecuted, pillaged, defrauded or destroyed? Let us, then, not suppress our humane impulses, but see they be indulged where and how is permissible, and be rightly directed when exercised; and especially, if we are much excited, see that they be kept within their due limits on either side, and obey, as they ever should, rather than frustrate, the decisive commands of justice and law.

It is to be recollected, also, that, by such mistaken courses, beyond our thus rendering aid to the guilty to escape punishment entirely, we encourage others to offend, under the hope of receiving a like sympathy and indulgence. The whole fabric of order and law is thus dangerously undermined; and instead of crime being lessened and prevented by the certainty of punishment, which, rather than vengeance, is the strong argument of Montesquieu, and others, for inflicting it at all, this kind of administration of the laws helps to render them a scoff to evil-doers, and to confound guilt and innocence, by one common fate, and one common license. But, some may say, we deem all kinds of punishment wrong, and consider it the duty of society to educate, teach, and reform all, without inflicting any pain, or unnecessary violence. Yet, till such institutions are established, what is to be done, in the mean time, with offenders? Those confessedly now bad, those not now educated, nor so moral as to refrain voluntarily from crime—they surely are not to be allowed indulgence in it, unlicensed and unpunished, till they can otherwise be made better; nor till the world, by some newly invented system of laws, or new Christian miracle, becomes a Millennium? And if you neglect to punish at all those guilty, will that help to improve mankind, and to hasten a Millennium, through providential secondary causes?—or will it not tend to make bad worse, and to baffle the footsteps of reforming progress, and drive society backward to the anarchy, licentiousness and despotism, of the dark ages?

Beside these general considerations, some of which at one time, and some at another, tend to disarm or unnerve us in strictly executing the laws, there is a specific objection, at times, which, more than any other cause, embarrasses the due enforcement of the penal code. It is, that the punishment inflicted is often believed to be too severe, and more especially if it is death. However much regretted, as citizens or politicians, this defect in a law may sometimes be, yet all will see, on a little reflection, that it furnishes no excuse to us, as jurors or judges, from fulfilling our official oaths to follow faithfully where the law and the evidence lead.

In the capacities of jurors and judges, it has already been shown that we are sworn to enforce the existing laws, whether severe or mild. Neither our oaths nor our duties make any discrimination. It is not our fault, as judges or jurors, that some punishments are too harsh. We did not make the laws, nor is it our fault that prisoners have done wickedly, and exposed themselves to such punishment. It is not our sin, but their own, if they behave so as to suffer with severity. Whatever blame may rest on us is in another capacity, such as citizens and voters, or legislators, in not using due efforts there, where alone we are empowered to use such efforts, to have punishments made milder; here we are tied up—restrained to what exists. In other capacities there is a wider area of freedom, to choose and to change. There is the appropriate field for the labors of the true philanthropist. There compassion and favor are allowed by law to influence us, no less than by nature and Christianity. Instead of denouncing the toils and sympathies of men for their brethren in their lawful sphere,— instead of censuring the good Samaritan for private benevolence and mercy,—let us help him onward there, let us coöperate there, let us crown with ardent praise and gratitude the laborers in that vineyard, such as the Howards, the Frys, the Dwights, of every age and country.

But we must discriminate, or we become unjust. The heavens themselves would return to chaos, and universal ruin reign, if each planet did not keep strictly within its assigned orbit, and each power in nature perform only its own proper function.

In our present official stations, we are authorized to decide merely what is a wrong by the present laws; not what should be wrong on sound principles,— not what those laws ought, in our opinion, to be, in order to become more equal, humane and useful. As to that, in the grand jury room and on the bench, we must pause. There it is our imperative duty to halt. If circumstances of mitigation exist in cases, the power to use it is not only in general vested elsewhere, but, so far from its not being there exercised as often as it ought to be, so as to present an apology for others to interfere, the frequent complaint is, that the pardoning power in this country is exercised too freely. In fact, in one of our States, this very year,—in Missouri,—the grand jury presented the Governor, for using this power too frequently and indiscriminately.

We have sworn to support severe laws till repealed, as well as all others; and though we may dislike capital punishment, as I do myself, yet I have no right to sit here, nor you there, unless we are willing to take the appropriate steps towards enforcing the penalty affixed by the laws in all cases coming within the provisions of the laws. *Think*, we may, with some jurisprudents, and have a right as men to think, that *hanging* is apparently the worst use to which a man can be put. Well may we desire to try an experiment less bloody, and, if not proving successful, return to a more disagreeable severity. In many cases, we may properly wish a milder penalty than the death penalty; we may honestly try to elect legislators who will dispense with what seems in some cases cruel and inhuman. We may petition the executive to commute it for a milder punishment, or pardon it entirely; we may seek to enlighten and persuade the community to wash out entirely its bloody tracks, and abolish their Draco codes, under the genial influences of a wiser civilization, the fruits of wisdom, commerce, and Christianity. Thanks to a benignant Providence, much of this has been accomplished during the past century, though not all desirable. But, while a majority think differently from us, we, as members of the same social community, embodied under the same constitution and laws, shielded in our lives, and fortunes, and honor, and common rights, and common glory, by the same government, — we must rally round that government, and support its constitution and laws, till properly and legally changed, or we become ourselves disorganizers and criminals. In truth, also, this excuse for tampering with our duty, and abolishing a law on account of its severity, by our own arrogant wills, has seldom much reasonable or adequate foundation to rest on in this country.

The tendency of the ameliorated age of the world in which it is our good fortune to live,—the humane influences of an improved literature and higher philosophy,—the religion we profess, so much milder than bloody Paganism,—the softening effects of a liberal interchange of opinions, as well as productions, the world over, by our rapid and enlarging commerce,—and the generous sympathies of our form of government, treating all its citizens as equal, and possessed of sacred rights and immortal souls,—all tend to make our penal code as little severe as any one on the globe. They are not, as once, so very harsh and bloody. The capital offences, in most of our States, have, since the Revolution, been reduced, from fifteen or twenty, to only three or four; and, in some, to one and none. How benignantly does this compare with the two hundred and thirty in England, twenty-five years ago! The most distinguished of philanthropists, as before referred to, did not seek to have capital cases less than three. To use his own language—

"I wish," said he, "that no persons might suffer capitally, *but* for murder, for setting houses on fire, and for house-breaking, attended with acts of cruelty."—(Howard on Penitentiaries, 121.)

This is a vast stride in improvement, to which we have already attained, from times when five hundred a year were executed under Queen Elizabeth, and the same capital punishment was inflicted, in the terse language of the intrepid Buxton, on him who killed his father, or a rabbit in a warren,—on him who was guilty of treason, or wantonly destroying a grape-vine. And, though some of us would fain hasten faster, improve quicker, introduce steam, a railroad, an electric speed in progress, in everything which looks ameliorating, yet we must yield to the greatest number, who hasten more slowly. Because we cannot obtain all we desire, and as speedily as we desire, we must not resist or overturn everything, and thus put an end to hope for what is better, as well as prostrate much of the good which now exists. We should thus, like children, enforce no law, in many cases, because we cannot have the exact law we like.

What wise reformers!—we acquit *entirely*, rather than punish the guilty with what seems to us a little too great severity. What models for our brethren, who are less liberal and sagacious, in other portions of the world!—we become ourselves lawless, and allow the most vicious to continue lawless, in certain cases, rather than stand by what is established, and obey our oaths, till the competent authorities make changes to suit our peculiar notions. The law is thus not only rendered a dead letter, but the whole theory of legislation is violated, and the scientific division of political powers, in all free governments, into legislative, executive and judicial, is utterly disregarded. I fear, too, this may be, at times, with as little true wisdom as right in the result; and with more public danger, by such an example, than with any well-founded hope of public usefulness, in the change. This same principle carried out would justify judicial tribunals in altering or dispensing with laws for civil rights, no less than crimes. We might as well become a Lycurgus, and change or disregard all presented to us there. Thus all fixed and established rules of property, or of action and redress, and rights of every kind, would become nullified. Regular and uniform government — that ordained of God, no less than of man — would give place with us, as judges and jurors, to caprice as a law, prejudice as a law, raw opinion, ignorance, party, anger, or revenge, as a law, and thus universal chaos or violence would reign.

Laws fixed, certain, and uniform, are said to be the distinguishing traits of civilized from savage communities. In these last seldom are any laws, unless it be the arbitrary and uncertain will of the strongest. If laws, then, are useful and indispensable, and indicate civilization, they become so only by their consequences as enforced. A law not enforced is nugatory, and we may as well be destitute of all laws, if the laws that be are not regularly, certainly, and uniformly carried into effect. If it be asked whether we do not thus become mere executive or ministerial officers, without any discretion or judicial capacity, I answer, No. We have discretion, but not a lawless discretion. We have the discretion to see if the facts bring the case within settled principles of law,—to see what is fact, rather than fancy. We have the discretion to follow, in our appropriate sphere, the facts to due conclusions,—to compare and weigh them, and to stand by sound principles and precedents; the discretion to keep within our own jurisdiction, instead of encroaching on the province and rights of others; the discretion to detect fallacies, to expose sophistry and error, to abide by the constitution and the laws, and our duties, but never to *violate* all these with impunity. There is another discretion still, and a wise one, allowed to us by the law itself sometimes. We may, where penalties are capital or very severe, proceed properly with more caution, weigh circumstances with increased care, require really doubtful points to be made more clear. But if enough appear to show guilt, to require a conviction of the accused,— if reasonable doubts are removed, though not all doubts, though not all possibilities of innocence,— if the usual probabilities which justify belief and action in most of the affairs of life appear, though without mathematical certainty,— woe to the juror or judge who then wilfully risks an omission to enforce the law, under whatever pretence, or however high a temptation!

Let us remember, also, that, by neglecting to punish offenders, on account of the severity of punishment, we do not at all enforce, but utterly defeat, our avowed wishes to inflict a milder penalty. We thus inflict no penalty whatever,—the guilty culprit is discharged *entirely*. Whereas, if you indict, and he is convicted, the executive, in his legal attribute of mercy, can mitigate or commute the severe punishment to the milder one which we desire. Beside this, as before suggested, our example in acquitting *entirely* the guilty must so multiply and aggravate offences as to tempt the community, those who would uphold order and law, to introduce new rigors, and to provide for punishing new crimes in public judicial officers, who thus nullify the laws and shield the guilty.

I have much more to say on this subject, but must postpone it to some other occasion. In the mean time, then, gentlemen, as judges and jurors, let us stand firm by the laws as they are; let us all be awakened to enforce them as they are, till constitutionally changed by the proper authorities. Let us complain, if we choose, as citizens, and alter, if we choose, as legislators; but look well to keep in our course, our straight and narrow path, as judicial officers; and then, whatever may betide others, it will not be our official fault. Our footsteps will be those of the faithful, the trustworthy, and the firm in principle and duty.

---

## ON THE PROPER EVIDENCE OF WHAT CONSTITUTES CRIME.*

GENTLEMEN OF THE GRAND JURY: — During my experience with judicial tribunals,— and it has not been a short one, — I have found that juries are less troubled to decide what is a crime than what is the proper and sufficient evidence of it.

On previous occasions, having explained fully to your body the ingredients necessary to constitute most of the offences which come within your cognizance, I shall, for the reason just mentioned, endeavor now to render you some assistance in respect to the evidence that you should require, before subjecting an individual to be arraigned ignominiously, and tried as an offender against the public peace and the majesty of the laws.

The cardinal rule, as to testimony in criminal cases, is, that juries must not convict till all reasonable doubts of the guilt of the accused are removed. It appears to me proper that this should apply with as much force to the finding of indictments by grand juries, as final trials at the bar of the court.

I give you this instruction from what I consider sound reason, as

* Charge to the Grand Jury, District of Massachusetts, October, 1847.

little is said in the books about the principles of evidence which are to govern grand juries. But, as you are to find the charges in the bills of indictment *true*, or dismiss them as "not found," or endorsed "*ignoramus*," it must, of course, be an evidence of some kind after an *inquiry*, by witnesses, either belonging or not belonging to your body. And the great elementary teacher of English law, after saying that the indictment is an accusation, and the grand jury are "to inquire," upon their oaths, whether there be sufficient cause to call upon the party to answer it, justly adds, "*a grand jury ought, however, to be thoroughly persuaded of the truth of an indictment, so far as the evidence goes*, and not to be satisfied merely with remote probabilities — a doctrine that might be applied to very oppressive purposes." (4 Bl. C., 303.)

Hence, it would seem that all reasonable doubts of guilt should be removed, either by the knowledge or evidence of your own body or other persons; else you cannot, under oath, safely declare "*it is a true bill.*" If you find guilt on your own knowledge of the offence and its authors, as may sometimes be done, the truth of the charge is, of course, believed beyond reasonable doubt, or no bill should be returned. Indeed, the case should be clearer in the first instance, to sustain indictments, as the accused is not at liberty to appear before you, and rebut any of the presumptions or proofs exhibited against him. He has an opportunity to do that afterwards, before a petit jury; and if then he is not to be convicted unless clearly criminal, he surely ought not to be called on to defend himself at all, unless the *ex parte* testimony standing alone, and before rebutted, is sufficient to show guilt beyond reasonable doubts.

In short, without as much as this, I am entirely unable to perceive why an accused person, presumed to be innocent before inquiry, should, even temporarily, be subjected to imprisonment, heavy expenses and loss of liberty, and these without being allowed any indemnity from the public to the extent merely of his actual cost, though shown in the end to be not guilty.

It is a ramification of this principle which requires that, in all cases, civil and criminal, the presumptions at first are to be in favor of the respondent. In other words, he is to be presumed innocent till *proved* guilty. The reasons for this are, that special wickedness is a reproach and stain, and hence, not to be supposed to exist, in any one, without strong evidence; and because whoever affirms to guilt in another ought, of course, to prove what he affirms, before the other need go into his defence; and because, usually, a negative as to guilt is incapable of proof. The accused, therefore, is not to be indicted unless the prosecutor goes forward, and not only renders it likely, by legal evidence, that he is guilty,— turns the scales against him,— but removes all well-founded doubts, all "second sober thoughts," which hesitated.

Some caution, however, is necessary, not to carry doubts too far. The true meaning of this rule is, not that grand juries should refrain from finding an indictment, or a petit jury from convicting, because it is possible that the person charged is innocent.

The errors in this respect are of frequent occurrence, and very dangerous to a due administration of justice. Thus, when guilt is distinctly proved, but the accused *may* possibly be innocent, because some of the witnesses may have committed perjury, you are still bound to convict, unless, from the well-known bad character of material witnesses, or from strong contradictory circumstances, you are justified in believing that perjury has taken place in respect to important facts. It is true, that the law-books on evidence furnish some cases where persons have been indicted and convicted on evidence which afterwards turned out to have been false; and these cases are fruitful sources of exhortation, on the part of prisoners, against conviction.

But, while such cases are proper monitions to warn us to be careful in hearings, yet they never show that juries failed in their duty to find indictments, or return verdicts of guilty, where the proofs given were clear and direct, and nothing was introduced to render it probable that the witnesses were perjured. It is as much an abandonment of duty, to act as if witnesses were perjured, where no evidence exists against their veracity, either in irreconcilable contradictions or in their bad characters, as it is to find guilt without any evidence whatever to demonstrate it.

The administration of justice cannot be always infallible. It must be conducted by human means and human confidence, and principles suited to the present condition of the human race; and those means and that confidence are, sometimes, exposed to error, and betrayed, in the business of courts, as in all other human affairs. But still they are least likely to injure or oppress when treated on sound and general principles; and one of the most cardinal of those is to follow where the law and the evidence appear to require, though the law may possibly be misapprehended, or the evidence may possibly be false.

All the affairs of social and political life, no less than judicial, are to be conducted and judged of by probabilities, and not possibilities. Man could not eat or drink, if he trusted to the *possibility* of poison; nor shake hands with a friend, nor visit his workshop, or farm, or store, if relying on the *possibility* of assassination; nor place any representative in power, if deterred by a *possibility* of his unfaithfulness. But take for a guide the test and standard of probabilities, and the affairs of the world can move on, and justice be administered with some equality and uniformity, and with as much freedom from error as human frailty is capable of.

Let this distinction reign and rule, then, whoever may fall.

If mistakes be committed in this way occasionally,—as they sometimes will be in an erring world,—they will be "few and far between." They, also, can often be corrected; while, if happening in most other ways, they are usually irremediable. Thus, in following this course, if a mistake occur in the indictment, it may be corrected in the trial;

or, if not done there, by new trials or pardons; and if, in a few solitary instances, errors are not detected till punishment has been inflicted, the suffering is one of those accidents or sacrifices inseparable from the inestimable benefits of an adherence to sound general rules, and a steady, firm, uniform administration of the laws.

The person who offends by perjury, in such a case, is, likewise, generally made to suffer, if not atone, for the injury he has caused; and if the perjury cannot always be detected in season to save the victim of its wickedness, it is no more an excuse for not following general rules, and general principles, than is the inability of government, or juries, or penal codes, in all cases, to prevent crimes, or, in all cases, to give complete redress to the sufferers by atrocious offences.

It may not be amiss to notice here another and opposite consequence which sometimes happens from this strict adherence to general rules, and that is the escape of the guilty. It is in this view that another remark truly applies, which is often made in respect to the evidence in criminal cases, and which is said to have originated with Sir Matthew Hale,— that it is better for ten guilty persons to escape, than one innocent suffer. If, by a rigid conformity to what the laws and the proof require, ten who are really guilty are not convicted, it is a result which, in a government administered on uniform principles, may, sometimes, occur. These principles must be adhered to for the protection of innocence, prosecuted, as it sometimes is, unjustly; and such a result, however to be deprecated as regards guilt occasionally escaping, is undoubtedly better for society, as a whole, than to punish one innocent person, by a departure from those principles, and from the law and the evidence. It is only saying that the accused is not proved to be guilty by sufficient legal testimony. But it is a perversion of this maxim, if, from compassion, weakness, or more blamable cause, any jury allow the accused to escape, because he may happen possibly to be innocent, when, according to the law and the proof, he ought to be found guilty — quite as much a perversion as to let him escape in such a case, when, in truth, he is both guilty and proved so, and, by the law and evidence, should be found guilty, and suffer the just though painful consequences of good principles disregarded, and the peace of society wantonly disturbed.

The true object, therefore, of this maxim, so often repeated and so much misunderstood, is to enjoin a strict compliance with what the law and evidence require, — though thus the guilty should, at times, be acquitted, — rather than to justify a departure from the law and the evidence in favor of anybody or anything, whether innocence or guilt. Let the law and the evidence, then, have their steady, uniform course; and if the court cannot correct any error afterwards, "the quality of mercy is not strained" in the hands of the executive, where it lawfully resides, and, as before remarked, will be eager to bless abundantly whenever still in its power, and innocence is shown to have suffered by mistake, or accident, or perjury.

I have spoken of what is your duty, in relation to reasonable doubts, chiefly when perjury is not proved by the bad characters of material witnesses. But there are cases where the circumstances or facts developed by witnesses are contradictory; and, trusting to one set of them, or one view of them, all reasonable doubts of guilt are removed; but, trusting to others, they are not removed, and perjury or mistake is reasonably to be inferred.

In such cases, I give it to you in charge, that, if the conflicting circumstances or facts are equally well proved, and are equally strong, it is your duty not to indict. In such case, the scales must always turn, and turn strongly, as before remarked, to prove the guilt, or the innocent view should triumph.

Every citizen should be allowed to dwell secure under his own vine and fig-tree, till thus clearly implicated. There may be cases connected with this branch of the rule which become very perplexing, and are to be solved often by the presumptions that arise from the fact of the good character of the person implicated.

It is then, above all other emergencies here below, that a life well spent brings its great rewards. It then, at times, repels inferences of guilt, rescues victims from conspiracies and false swearing, and brushes away surmises and doubts, and jealousies and envies, and all uncharitableness, as the healthy breeze dissipates miasma and death. Thus, a citizen is charged with a crime, as to which the evidence is contradictory, and not exactly poised, but the weight of it somewhat inclined against him, independent of his character and standing in society. But, let these last have long been good, honest, trustworthy, and be arrayed in addition to other evidence on his side, and they often should turn the scales in his favor. They are facts, and not fancy; they are proofs, and not mere conjecture; and they are proofs which furnish strong grounds, as society is organized, and the human mind and human heart regulated, to show that such men are not likely to become suddenly criminal, and outcasts, or outlaws. That is not the habitual course of wickedness. But the character, though good, may still not be sufficient, in all cases, to countervail what is proved independent of this. It ought not to be, when the evidence of guilt is direct and overwhelming. Hence the benefit of clergy, which once existed, in favor of all who could read and write, and which reduced the punishment, and at times wholly remitted it, has been properly abolished here, as it made learning, rather than good character, the redeeming test. And the absurd rule of the canon law, requiring seventy-two witnesses to convict a cardinal of some offences, has been ridiculed rather than imitated here, as making office or station, rather than individual virtue, repel evidence of guilt. But here, moral character, whether in low or high, a life of integrity, a long obedience to law and order, are, with propriety, allowed often to rebut evidence not entirely decisive as to guilt. They raise some presumptions, friendly to innocence, on principles deeply founded in our natures; not irresistible presumptions — not conclusive — not to be uncontrolled by strong and direct proof, but still entitled in all cases to some weight, and in doubtful ones to decisive weight.

Connected with this direction, and the subject of circumstantial evidence, which is often involved in it, let me caution you next as to the fallacies in vogue respecting circumstantial evidence generally. One is, that circumstantial evidence is weaker, and another that it is stronger, than any other evidence. But the real truth is, that circumstantial evidence differs in no respect from other proof, unless in being less direct. It is matter standing around — *circumstans* — rather than in the thing itself — *in re.* Circumstances, however, are facts, as much as other things. Evidence of circumstances is likewise evidence of facts, and convicting or acquitting on circumstances is doing them on facts.

Thus, in a case of murder, proving a person to be found dead, and bleeding from a recent wound, like that inflicted with a sword, and finding another person near with a sword in his hand, covered with blood, is called a case of circumstantial evidence. But it is a case of proving facts, as much as if you proved any other facts, — as much as if, in that case, you proved the fact of seeing a stab made by the person holding the sword. In the first instance, however, the facts are less direct as to the commission of the murder, and that is the only difference. In both, there may be guilt or innocence, and yet all the facts proved be possibly true.

For instance, — under the first statement, the holder of the sword may have wrenched it from the real murderer, and the latter have escaped; or, he may have picked it up where dropped by the real murderer. Under the last statement, the person seen inflicting the blow may have done it in self-defence, and thus be innocent; or, in defence of his children or wife assailed; or, in a fit of true insanity, caused by the visitation of God.

Hence, it does not answer, in either of these cases, to indict or convict at all events, under a common saying, that circumstances cannot lie; or to acquit in either, under the remark that it is dangerous to convict of any crime upon mere circumstantial evidence.

Circumstances may be not true, as well as any other proved facts, more direct, or more a part of the *corpus delictu.* If they are admitted circumstances, — that is, are conceded to be true on the trial, without proof, — then they cannot lie or mislead; neither can any other admitted or conceded facts. But, when not admitted, and resting on proof as before a grand jury, the same danger exists that they may be untrue, or colored by mistake or perjury, as exists in respect to any other fact attempted to be shown. And if they are admitted or clearly proved, there is no more risk in indicting or convicting upon them, when they are strong enough to remove reasonable doubts of guilt, than to convict or indict on the evidence of any other facts.

The true test, in both cases, if the character of the witnesses be not impeached who furnish the proof, and no counter facts are developed, is to see what is probable — what is fairly and naturally to be *inferred* from all the evidence in each case. And, doing this, if no reasonable doubt remains to operate against the inference of guilt, the duty is imperative to indict and convict, whether the evidence be circumstantial or direct. Thus, in the first case before stated, the material inference from the facts proved, standing entirely alone, is usually that the person near, and having the sword in his hand, inflicted the wound; and this warrants an indictment, when not rebutted. If nothing is proved to vary this case and this inference, in the subsequent trial, it is pretty decisive that nothing could be, when the government allows the prisoner counsel and processes for witnesses.

So, in the last case before stated, like inferences are natural and proper, from such facts standing alone. But when, in either of such cases, other evidence appears, showing a first deadly assault by the person stabbed, — or, showing settled, clear and not feigned nor imaginary insanity, — or, when, in the first case, another person is proved to have been near, having a grudge against the deceased, and was seen running away about that time, — or, when the person holding the sword was on good terms with the deceased, and possessed a good character, and had other sufficient reasons for being at the place at that time, — then the jury might well have reasonable doubts of guilt, and properly refuse to indict.

I have spoken of natural inferences from certain facts proved on this subject. These constitute another most important element in evidence, in criminal cases. Juries must, of necessity, be governed, in reaching many results through inferences from other facts, by certain laws of nature and human reason. They are often obliged to infer one thing from another, and this, whether that other be a fact direct or circumstantial. And, without troubling you with metaphysical distinctions on these matters, no sure guide exists for you in the labyrinth of fraud and crime, as well as of some degree of uncertainty in everything human, where revelation does not exist and apply, but your own experience and the credible experience and investigation of others, as to what are proper inferences. Those teach that the strength of facts or results, inferred from others proved directly, is often little less than that of the others themselves thus proved. As a general rule, it is quite as certain that water placed on the side of a hill, if unobstructed, will run down the hill, as it is that there is a hill, and that there is water. So, as a general rule, it is quite as certain that a disbelief by a witness in the existence of a God, by having less hold on his conscience and fears, impairs the responsibility of an oath, and the confidence to be placed in his testimony, as that he is a witness. So, as a general rule, an individual entertaining malice against another who has been murdered, being near at the time, and carrying deadly weapons, is more likely to have committed the offence than one in a situation the very reverse, and the inference must be more strongly against the former.

Yet, in all cases, notwithstanding such general inferences or presumptions as I have alluded to, and many others that might be enumerated, against persons charged with offences, they may be innocent, and may be proved so even by other circumstances, developed in the testimony on the part of the prosecution before a grand jury. In trials, the respondent may show by evidence facts successfully obviating such general inference against him in his particular case. It is his duty to do this, if they exist; and if not able to do it, neither he, nor his friends, nor society, can complain, if he be convicted under the force of strong general presumptions, from sworn facts. Laws could not otherwise be enforced. Even government could not stand without them, or social intercourse be carried on a single day.

I have just spoken of sworn facts; and this leads me to remind you of another rule of evidence in criminal cases, which deserves consideration from its importance, as well as frequent violation. It is, never to indict, any more than convict, for offences, on what is called mere hearsay evidence. This rule rests on the principle that the fact thus offered to show guilt has never been sworn to. The witness does not testify to the truth of the fact depending on hearsay, but only to the truth that it was told to him by another. Now, although, in every case, the facts proved need not be proved by a witness under oath to the truth of them, yet they must be proved by something nearly equivalent to that.

As a statement or contract in writing, proved by an oath to have been executed by a prisoner, its contents are of course proved by an oath to be his admissions or confessions, and a record against a party; or an entry in a book made against another's interest, and a statement *in articulis mortis*, or under fear of death, and several other facts, may be evidence against a person, — though not under oath, — but yet they must be attended by circumstances which give them weight entirely beyond mere hearsay evidence. So, if a jury make a presentment or indictment of their own knowledge, it must be personal knowledge, and not hearsay; and that is done under the solemnity of their official oaths as to the truth of the charge, if they are not re-sworn as witnesses. The very name of juror — from *juro*, or *jurare*, "to swear" — implies that what they do is done under oath, by themselves as well as others; and your indictments begin with a recital that "the jury on their oaths" present, &c. So that nothing should be found without an oath, or something equivalent to it; and that oath being to the fact itself, and which it proves, and not to the mere hearsay of it from others.

There is another rule of evidence, in relation to crimes, which deserves some attention, before closing these remarks. It is, that no man should be indicted and punished criminally, unless his intentions were criminal. But this principle is often perverted or misunderstood.

It does not mean that substantive and separate evidence must be offered, showing that the accused had, before, or at the time, *avowed* a criminal design. On the contrary, in the entire absence of any such declarations, an intention to commit an offence will generally be inferred from merely doing certain prohibited or unlawful acts. The real difficulty, on this point, is not in agreeing to the principle that the intentions must be criminal, but in agreeing as to what is proper and sufficient evidence that they were criminal. If the acts done were evil in themselves, — *malum in se*, — prohibited by the moral law, and such parts of the common law as are in force, the doing of them is in and of itself sinful, — is, *per se*, wicked, of evil example, and hence punishable. When the accused has been led into their commission by accident or mistake, or any justifiable provocation, as sometimes may happen, it is for him to prove that in his defence. But, without such proof, the natural and legal presumption is that he intended to do wrong when he did what was apparently wrong; and that he intended all the evil and culpable consequences of his acts which usually follow from such acts. He must not, for instance, strike another a heavy blow with a deadly weapon, without its being presumed, from such an act, that he intended to commit murder. So in respect to the presumption that he meant all the usual and natural consequences of his acts. One must not scatter firebrands and death, and say he is in sport. The engineer or commander of a steamboat or locomotive must not put on steam beyond the safe gauge, and crowd onward, reckless of obstacles and perils, till a fatal explosion destroys innocent passengers, and then attempt to shelter himself from responsibility by apologies that he meant only to win a wager with another boat, or a wager against time.

And, on the same principle, your private enemy must not throw ignited matches among combustibles in your dwelling-houses, under the shades of night, without its being presumed, at first, that he intended to commit arson. And, if any justification or extenuation existed, it devolves on him to show it. It is the same in relation to the intent in the commission of crimes which are not so because in themselves immoral, but are made crimes by the statute laws of the government prohibiting them, — or, in technical language, are only *malum prohibitum*. For instance, it happens, in matters peculiarly within your cognizance, that, on account of public reasons, various violations of the revenue laws are made punishable by fine or imprisonment. An intention to do such prohibited acts is by law deemed a criminal intention; that intent is the *malus animus* in this class of cases. Hence, a party committing these acts must be presumed guilty of a criminal intent, without any separate evidence, beyond the mere violation of the law, being adduced to prove such an intent. But if, in truth, facts existed, as they may, which show that an intent to break the law was not entertained, they may be offered by the accused; and then they may, and they should, avail generally to disprove the criminal charge. The liberty to do this in trials is a sacred one; and your power and duty to weigh the excuse, if appearing legally before you, is undoubted, as the prohibited act may have been done from mistake or accident, or from some justifiable motive. The privilege to show such justification constitutes the great safeguard of the liberty of the press, in cases of libel. The excuse may be evident before a grand jury, in what transpires on the part of the prosecution; and, if it shows a justifiable motive, it should exonerate the accused. The law as to this has been much and long perverted in arbitrary governments, and sent many wrongfully to bastiles, dungeons, the scaffold, and dreary exile. The presumption of a criminal intent from certain acts, such as harsh charges against others, in writing or in print, is often right in the first instance; but all should hold that intent to be rebutted, if proof appear that the charges were true. The apology for not holding this was, usually, that the offence consisted in publishing what was likely to lead to breaches of the peace or disrespect to rulers; whereas, in reality, the offence — the gist of it — consists in publishing what is false, and hence, probably, with malice. Publishing the truth from good and useful motives, is the exercise of a right indispensable to free government, and formidable only to wrong-doers. Let grand as well as petit juries, then, throw open the door wide, — throw open their minds and judgments to every just consideration and fact which tend to repel the presumption of bad intentions. Give the accused, fully, the benefit of all rebutting circumstances; and especially, in trials for libel, give him the benefit of showing the truth, the whole truth, and, if the heart appears right, and faithful to duty and veracity, give him the advantage of it, however weak may be the head, or indiscreet the judgment. Such has been the jealousy of some of our people on this subject, that, in the constitution of the State of Maine, in all "indictments for libels," "the jury, after having received the direction of the court, shall have a right to determine, at their discretion, law and the fact." (Revised Statutes of Maine, sec. 4th, p. 8.)

One other consideration connected with the consequences of acts, and the justifications for violence, and I have done with what will be offered at this time on the evidence to prove penal guilt.

In many transactions, apparently crimes, where several are actors, the severity of the law is often visited on one alone, and the others are innocent, and at times even praiseworthy. The line of discrimination is between the first offender and those who afterwards act in self-defence, or in the protection of others, or in support of the public peace. The scrutiny, then, must begin with the inquiry, Who struck the first blow? who was the original wrong-doer? who put the ball of guilt in motion? who kindled the fire which has swollen into a conflagration, and ravaged half a city? Because the law adjudges him to be criminal who begins an affray, rather than the person assailed or injured, though the latter, under excitement of the moment, may exact an eye for an eye, or a tooth for a tooth.

The law goes still further, and justifies not only self-preservation, and all force necessary to insure it, as the first great law of nature, but justifies the father and child, and master and apprentice, under their close and kindly domestic relations, in defending each other with violence, when forcibly attacked. Yea, more, the law upholds any good magistrate, or peace officer, in interfering with reasonable force to arrest offenders or suppress an existing quarrel or riot. Nor should juries be over nice in measuring the exact proportions of violence between the aggressor, in such cases, and the defender of himself or child, or the peace of the community.

But, when the evidence shows clearly an unreasonable excess of force or injury on the part of him first assailed, the latter is and should be answerable for the excess; and the more especially so, if he make a slight assault a cloak to inflict wanton retaliation, or wreak an old grudge with barbarous severity.

Though the scales of justice in such cases are to weigh every attendant circumstance, and make some allowance, as a sort of "tare and tret," for passions, sudden outbreaks, difficulties in preserving exactness of proportions in the heat of violent rencounters, yet her scales are still to be used; and seldom can a discreet and experienced jury mistake as to where the real balance lies.

It is this function of juries, to discriminate between the feigned and the real, to compare and decide on evidence when conflicting, to weigh contradictory arguments, to scrutinize excuses and justifications, and to distinguish between innocent and culpable motives, which gives such high importance to your tribunal, as well as that of petit juries. It not only requires, but helps to cultivate, habits of attention, sagacity and judgment. It demands general intelligence as to affairs of business and human character. It assists to impart it, to make those attached to order more orderly, the friends of law more acquainted with its usefulness, the wise wiser, the firm in duty more firm, and the great mass of society, where resides political power, more powerful, and better able to elicit truth, and act rightfully in judicial no less than political matters. It is a mark as well as aid of superior civilization, no less than good government, when the masses are competent, by acquirements and habits of this kind, to fill the jury-boxes with credit to themselves and benefit to the community.

## ON IMPAIRING AN OBLIGATION OF A CONTRACT UNDER THE CONSTITUTION.*

THE question to be considered in this case is, whether an act of the Legislature of Mississippi, passed February 21st, 1840, impaired *the obligation of any contract* which the State or others had previously entered into with the Planters' Bank.

If it did, the clause in the constitution of the United States expressly prohibiting a State from passing any such law has been violated, and the plaintiffs in error are entitled to judgment.

But, on the contrary, if that act does not impair the obligation of any contract, the judgment below, in favor of the defendants, must be affirmed.

In considering this question, no peculiar liberality of construction in favor of a corporation, so as to render that an encroachment on its rights which is not clearly so, seems to be demanded of us, by any more sacredness in the character of a corporation or its rights than in that of an individual; but rather, that its charter as a public grant is not to be construed beyond its natural import. (8 Peters, 738; 3 Peters, 289; 4 Peters, 168, 514.) The inviolability of contracts, however, and the faithful protection of vested rights, are due to the one no less than the other; and are both involved in the present inquiry, so far as affecting, by way of principle or precedent, all the various and vast interests of this kind existing over the whole Union.

Mr. Madison denounced laws impairing the obligation of contracts, as among those not only violating the constitution, but "*contrary to the first principles of the social compact, and to every principle of sound legislation.*" (Federalist, No. 44.)

Again, in Payne et al. *v.* Baldwin et al., 3 Smedes & Marshall, 677,—one of the cases now before us,—it is truly admitted, that, "in a government like ours, such power is totally out of the range of legislative authority."

At the same time, it is to be recollected that our legislatures stand in a position demanding often the most favorable construction for their motives in passing laws, and they require a fair rather than hypercritical view of well-intended provisions in them. Those public bodies must be presumed to act from public considerations, being in a high public trust; and when their measures relate to matters of general interest, and can be vindicated under express or justly implied

---

* Opinion in case of Planters' Bank *versus* Sharp *et al.* January term S. C. U. S., 1848.

powers, and more especially when they appear intended for improvements made in the true spirit of the age, or for salutary reforms in abuses, the disposition in the judiciary should be strong to uphold them.

Certainly it will be only when they depart from limitations or qualifications of this character, and so use their own rights as to impair the prior rights of others, that a check must be used, however unpleasant to us, by declaring that the constitutional restrictions of the General Government must control a statute of a State conflicting with them, and thus, for harmony and uniformity, make the former supreme, in compliance with the injunctions imposed by the people and the States themselves in the constitution. Governed by such views, we proceed to the examination of the questions arising here, by ascertaining, first, what powers the Legislature of Mississippi granted to the plaintiffs, and then what powers it has taken away from them.

On the 10th of February, 1830, "An act to establish a Planters' Bank in the State of Mississippi" passed; and, among other privileges, in the sixth section, granted that the bank "shall be capable and able, in law, to have, possess, receive, retain, and enjoy, to themselves and their successors, lands, rents, tenements, hereditaments, goods, chattels, and effects, of what kind soever, nature, and quality, not exceeding in the whole six millions of dollars, including the capital stock of said bank, and the same to grant, demise, alien, or dispose of, for the good of said bank."

The seventeenth section gives power, also, "to receive money on deposit, and pay away the same free of expense; discount bills of exchange and notes, with two or more good and sufficient names thereon, or secured by a deposit of bank or other public stock; and to make loans to citizens of the States in the nature of discount on real property, secured by mortgage," &c.

Doing business with these powers, amounting, as it has been repeatedly settled, to a contract in the charter for the use of them (see cases in the West River Bridge, at this term), the bank, on the 24th of May, 1839, took the promissory note on which the present suit was instituted, and, on the 10th day of June, 1842, transferred it to the United States Bank, having first commenced this action on it, the 11th of October, 1841.

But, in the mean time, after the execution of the note, though before its transfer, the Legislature of Mississippi, on the 21st day of February, 1840, passed a law, the seventh section of which is in these words: — "It shall not be lawful for any bank in this State to transfer, by indorsement or otherwise, any note, bill receivable, or other evidence of debt; and if it shall appear in evidence, upon the trial of any action upon any such note, bill receivable, or other evidence of debt, that the same was transferred, the same shall abate upon the plea of the defendant." (See Acts of 1840, p. 15.) This law constitutes the only defence to a recovery in the present case by the plaintiffs. But they contend it is invalid, because, by the constitution, art. 1, § 10, "no State" shall pass any law "impairing the obligation of contracts;" and this law does impair it, in this instance, in two respects. First, in the obligation of the contract in the charter with the State; and secondly, in the obligation of the contract made by the signers of the note declared on with the bank.

To decide understandingly these questions, it will be necessary to go a little further into the true extent of those two contracts under the powers held by the bank, and likewise into the true extent of the subsequent act of the Legislature affecting them.

That promissory notes are to be regarded as either goods, chattels, or effects, within the sixth section of the charter, can hardly be questioned, when it includes these "of what kind soever, nature, and quality." This addition evidently meant to remove any doubt or restriction as to the meaning of those terms, as sometimes employed in connection with peculiar subjects, and to extend the description by them to every kind of personal property belonging to the bank. This construction would go no further than sometimes has been done in England, holding the words *goods and chattels* to include choses in action, as well as other personal property (12 Coke, 1; 1 Atkins, 1182), and by the word *goods* alone, in a bequest, it has been held that a bond will pass (Anonymous, 1 P. Wms. 127).

So, in respect to *effects*, it has been held, when the word is used alone, or *simpliciter*, it means all kinds of personal estate. (13 Ves. 39, 47, note; Michell *v.* Michell, 5 Madd. 72; Hearne *v.* Wigginton, 6 Madd. 119; Cowp. 299.) But if there be some word used with it, restraining its meaning, then it is governed by that, or means something *ejusdem generis*. Here, however, instead of restraining terms being used with it, those most broad and enlarging are added, being "effects of what kind soever, nature, and quality." (Hotham *v.* Sutton, 15 Ves. 326; Campbell *v.* Prescott, 15 Ves. 500; 3 Ves. 212, note.)

The same rule prevailed in the civil law, under the term *bona mobilia*. (1 P. Wms. 267.) And by that law, as well as the common law, promissory notes or choses in action come under the category of movable goods or personal property, as they accompany the person. (2 Bl. Comm. 384, 398.)

The bank was allowed, also, by the seventeenth section, "to discount bills of exchange and notes;" and, in truth, promissory notes usually constitute a large portion of the property of such institutions. Such notes, also, not only by general usage and established forms, are, in most cases, made to run to banks or their order, and must be expected to run so when the banks please; but it is expressly provided, by the twenty-second section of this charter, that "it shall not be lawful for said bank to discount any note or notes which shall not be made payable and *negotiable* at said bank," &c. And, again, by an amendatory act, accepted by the bank, it was provided, on the 9th of

December, 1831, "that such promissory notes shall be made payable and *negotiable* on their face at some bank or branch bank."

But why made negotiable, if no right was to exist to negotiate or transfer them? The bank, then, as the legal holder of such notes, possessed a double right "to dispose" of them; first, from the express grant in the charter itself, empowering them, as to their "goods, chattels, and effects, of what kind soever, nature, and quality," "the same to grant, demise, alien, or dispose of, for the good of said bank" (sixth section); secondly, by an implied authority, incident to its charter and business, and the express requirement that the notes should be "negotiable on their face." We do not refer to the next ground because it is necessary to resort to implication or analogy to establish an authority in the bank, under its charter, to make a transfer of its notes, when it possesses that authority by the very words and spirit of the contract made in the charter by the State.

But, to make the correctness of this conclusion from the specific words of the charter stronger and undoubted, it will be found to be the natural, useful, and proper view of its powers as a bank, under all sound analogy and necessarily implied authority.

To reach this end, it is not indispensable to hold that corporations in modern times possess numerous incidental powers, equal to those of individuals, as was once the doctrine (Kyd on Corp. 108; 2 Kent, Comm. 281, and cases in those treatises); but seems now in some respects overruled. (Earle *v.* Bank of Augusta, 13 Peters, 519, 587, 153; 2 Cranch, 167; 12 Wheat. 64.) But merely to hold, as it often has been in late years, that what is necessary and proper to be done to carry into effect express grants, and which is nowhere forbidden, may in most cases be lawful.

Though such a power as this last to Congress is expressly added in the constitution of the United States, yet it has been considered by some that it would exist as a reasonable incident, under reasonable limitations, without any such express addition. (2 Kent, Comm. 298, and cases there cited.)

Thus a corporation, if once organized, has the implied power to make contracts connected with its business and debts, and through agents and notes, as well as under its seal. (Bank of Columbia *v.* Patterson's Adm'r, 7 Cranch, 299; 8 Wheat. 338; 12 Wheat. 64; 11 Peters, 588.)

So it may hold and dispose of property even in trust, if not inconsistent and unconnected with its express duties and objects. (Vidal et al. *v.* Girard's Ex'rs, 2 Howard, 127.)

Hence, a power to dispose of its notes, as well as other property, may well be regarded as an incident to its business as a bank to *discount notes*, which are required to be in their terms assignable, as well as an incident to its right of holding them and other property, when no express limitation is imposed on the authority to transfer them.

Not that a banking corporation has, under its charter, a constructive power to follow another independent branch of business, such as manufacturing or foreign trade; but merely the business of banking, and to do such acts as are necessary and proper or usual to carry that business into effect, and such as are in harmony with the letter and spirit of its charter.

Nor even that it can adopt any course as an incident, and as necessary and proper, which is merely convenient, or which is expressly forbidden by the charter, or so forbidden by any previously existing laws in the State of a general character.

But, in discounting notes and managing its property in legitimate banking business, it must be able to assign or sell those notes when necessary and proper, as, for instance, to procure more specie in an emergency, or return an unusual amount of deposits withdrawn, or pay large debts for a banking-house, and for any "goods and effects" connected with banking which it may properly own. It is its duty to pay in some way every debt. (6 Gill & Johns. 219.) This court, in the United States *v.* Robertson, 5 Peters, 650, has expressly recognized the authority of a bank to give bonds and assignments to pay its deposit debtors. In that case, "the directors agree to pledge to the government of the United States the entire estate of the corporation as a security for the payment of the original principal of the claim," &c. (p. 648). And such a pledge or transfer was held there to be valid.

It is said, in opposition to this, Why should a bank be considered as able to incur debts? or why to do any business on credit, requiring sales of its notes or other property to discharge its liabilities? Such inquiries overlook the fact, that the chief business and design of most banks—their very vitality—is to incur debts, as well as have credits. All their deposit certificates, or bank-book credits to individuals, are debts of the bank, and which it is a legitimate and appropriate part of its business as a bank to incur and to pay. The same may be said, also, of all its bank-notes, or bills, they being merely promises or debts of the bank, payable to their holders, and imperative on them to discharge. (See Bank of Columbia *v.* Patterson's Adm'r, 7 Cranch, 307; 13 Peters, 593.)

It may, to be sure, independent of justifications like these, not be customary for banks to dispose of their notes often. But, in exigencies of indebtedness, and other wants under pressures like those referred to, it may not only be permissible, but much wiser and safer to do it than to issue more of its own paper, too much of it being already out, or part with more of its specie on hand, too little being now possessed for meeting all its obligations. Indeed, its right to sell any of its property, when not restricted in the charter or any previous law, is perhaps as unlimited as that of an individual, if not carried into the transaction of another separate and unauthorized branch of business. (Angell & Ames on Corp., p. 104, § 9; 4 Johns. Ch.

307; 2 Kent, Comm. 283; 11 Serg. & Rawle, 411.) Both may sell notes to liquidate their debts,—both sell their lands acquired under mortgages foreclosed, or acquired under the extent of executions not redeemed. Both, too, must be able to sell all kinds of their property, when proceeding to close up their business, or find it impracticable. Nor is there any pretence here that any clause in the charter of this bank restricted it from selling its notes or other property under any circumstances, and much less under those, connected with indebtedness and with banking, which have just been referred to. It will be seen, in this way, that all analogies seem to sustain the right which exists, by the express grant in this charter, to "*alien and dispose of*" all its "goods, chattels, and effects, of what kind soever, nature, and quality, for the good of said bank." But, to avoid differences of opinion, we place the right here solely on the express grant. It ought, perhaps, to be added, that the courts of Mississippi once put a more limited construction on this charter. (Baldwin et al. *v.* Payne et al., 3 Smedes & Marshall, 661.)

But, as that very case is now before us for revision, on the ground that it was erroneous, we feel obliged, for that and other reasons, which need not be here enumerated, to put such construction on the charter, and on the law supposed to violate it, as seems right according to our own views of their true intent.

Having thus ascertained the extent of the contract made by the State with the bank in the charter, we proceed next to examine the character and scope of the contract between the maker of the note and the bank.

We have already seen that the bank was not only authorized, but expressly required, to discount notes which were negotiable, or, in other words, which contained a contract or stipulation to pay them to any assignee. Nor is it pretended there was any law of Mississippi, when this charter was given or when this note was taken, which prohibited selling it, and passing to an assignee all the rights, either of property or of bringing a suit in his own name, which then existed with individuals and other banking institutions.

What law existed on this point when the note was actually transferred is not the inquiry, but what existed when it was made, and its obligations as a contract were fixed. The law which existed at the transfer, so far from being the test of the force of a contract made long before, and under different legal provisions, is the violation of it, and the very ground of complaint in the present proceeding.

This contract, then, by the bank with the maker, when executed, enabled the former to sell or assign it, and the indorsee to collect it, not only by its express terms, but by the general law of the State, then allowing transfers of negotiable paper and suits in the name of indorsees. (Howard and Hutchinson's Laws, 373.)

Indeed, independent of the last circumstance, it is highly probable, that, by the principles of the law of contracts and commercial paper, such choses in action may be legally assigned or transferred everywhere, when not expressly prohibited by statute. This was done before the Statute of Anne, in England. And it is done since, as to paper both negotiable and not negotiable, independent of that statute.

If such notes cannot be sued in the name of the indorsee, when running to order, without the help of a statute, they certainly can be sued in the name of the payee, for the benefit of the indorsee, when the transfer is legal in its consideration and form.

The State itself, by passing this law prohibiting the transfer of notes by banks, recognizes the previous right, as well as custom, to transfer them; otherwise, the law would not be necessary to prevent it. Nor is this law supposed to have been founded on any prior abuse of power in negotiating or selling its notes, which, if existing, might obviate the above inference. But it is understood, from the record and opinions of the State court, that the design of the law was to secure another provision of statute not previously existing, but made by the Legislature at the same time, requiring banks to receive their own notes in payment of their debtors, though below par. That design, too, would still recognize the prior authority to sell or transfer.

We are not prepared to say that a State, under its general legislative powers, by which all rights of property are held and modified as the public interest may seem to demand, might not, where unrestricted by constitutions or its own contracts, pass statutes prohibiting all sales of certain kinds of property, or all sales by certain classes of persons or corporations. (14 Peters, 74.) Such has often been the legislation as to property held in mortmain, or by aliens, or certain proscribed sects in religion.

This is, however, very invidious legislation, when applied to classes or to particular kinds of property before allowed to be held generally. Legislation for particular cases or contracts, without the consent of all concerned, is of very doubtful validity. (Merrill *v.* Sherburne et al., 1 New Hamp. 199.) Under our system of government, and the abuses to which in various ways and to various extents that kind of legislation might lead, several of the State constitutions possess clauses prohibitory of such a course where it affects contracts or vested rights; and more especially does the constitution of the United States expressly forbid any such legislation, whenever it goes to impair the obligation of a contract. Hence, the general powers which still exist under other governments, or might once have prevailed here in the States, to change the tenure and rights over property, and especially the *jus disponendi* of it, cannot now, under the federal constitution, be exercised by our States to an extent affecting the obligation of contracts.

The next and final question, then, is, Did the act in question impair the obligation, either of the contract by the State with the bank, or of the contract by the maker of the note with the bank?

We have already ascertained the true extent of both of these contracts before this act passed; that by the State with the bank clearly allowing it to take negotiable notes, and to sell or transfer them, and that with the maker clearly enabling the bank to assign his note, and a recovery to be had on it after a transfer, by the assignee. In this condition of things, with this note taken and held, accompanied by such rights and obligations, the Legislature of Mississippi passed the law already quoted, and now under consideration. It expressly took away the right of the bank to make any transfer whatever of its notes, and virtually deprived an assignee of them of the right to sustain any suit, either in his own name or that of the bank, to recover them of the maker.

The new law, also, conferred in substance on the maker a new right to defeat any action so brought, which he would otherwise have been liable to. These results vitally changed the obligation of the contract between him and the bank, to pay to any assignee of it, as well as changed the obligation of the other contract between the State and the bank in the charter, to allow such notes to be taken and transferred. It is true that this new law might bear a construction, that the transfer was only a voidable act, and not void, and that, if cancelled or waived, a recovery might afterwards be had on the note by the bank; and this seems to have been the view of some of the court in 3 Smedes & Marshall, 681, as well as in Hyde et al. *v.* The Planters' Bank, 8 Robinson, 421. Yet the State court in Mississippi appears finally to have thought it meant otherwise, and to have decided that no suit at all can be sustained on such a note by anybody after a transfer. This was the view which they think influenced the Legislature. (See Planters' Bank *v.* Sharp et al., 4 Smedes & Marshall, 28.) We are disposed to acquiesce in the correctness of this construction, as it seems to conform nearest to the real designs of the Legislature. But this view is not adopted because a decision by a State court on a State statute, though generally governing us, is to control here in the very cases which, on account of that decision, are brought here by appeal or writ of error.

The rights of a party under a contract might improperly be narrowed or denied by a State court, without any redress, if their decision on the extent of them cannot be reviewed and overruled here in cases of this kind; while their decision, if restricting or enlarging the prohibitory act, might more safely stand, as doing no injury in the end, if we hold the act null wherever it is construed by them or us so as to conflict with prior rights obtained under contracts. (See Commercial Bank *v.* Buckingham's Ex'rs, 5 Howard, 317.)

If the State courts of Mississippi should hereafter adopt the dissenting opinion of Judge Sharkey, in 4 Smedes & Marshall, 28, and go back to what they appear to have before held, in 3 Smedes & Marshall, 661,— namely, that the right to sue by the bank, after a transfer, was not taken away, if the plaintiff replied that the transfer had been rescinded, and the interest was now solely in the bank,—and should that construction be adopted here, the force of this new law, as impairing the obligation of the contract, might not be so extensive and clear as now. But still it would seem to impair the contract in some respects; yet whether in such way and extent as to render the obligation itself changed, must be left to be decided definitively when such a case is presented for our decision. In the present instance, however, as before explained, the extent and operation of the prohibitory law being regarded as forbidding any transfer whatever, and, if it takes place, as barring every kind of remedy on the note, the decisive question may be repeated, How can this happen without injury to the plaintiff's contracts? When every form of redress on a contract is taken away, it will be difficult to see how the obligation of it is not impaired. (Green *v.* Biddle, 8 Wheat. 76; 1 Howard, 317; 4 Smedes & Marshall, 507; King *v.* Dedham Bank, 15 Mass. 447.)

If any right or power be left, under the note, by this act, after a transfer is made, it is of no use, when it cannot be enforced and no benefit be derived from it, but an action abated *toties quoties* as often as it is instituted. (8 Wheat. 12; 1 Bl. Comm. 55.) In the mildest view, a new disability is thus attached to an old contract, and its value and usefulness restricted; and these, of course, impair it. (Society for Propagating the Gospel *v.* Wheeler, 2 Gall. 139.)

One of the tests that a contract has been impaired is, that its value has by legislation been diminished. It is not, by the constitution, to be impaired at all. This is not a question of degree or manner or cause, but of encroaching in any respect on its obligation, dispensing with any part of its force. (The Commercial Bank of Rodney *v.* The State of Mississippi, 4 Smedes & Marshall, 507.) So, if the obligation of a contract is to be regarded as the duty imposed by it, here the duty imposed by the State to adhere to its own deliberate grant, and the duty imposed on the signer of the note to make payment to an assignee, as well as to the bank itself, are both interfered with and altered.

In answer to this supposed violation of the contract between the maker of the note and the bank, some objections have been urged which deserve further notice here.

It is sometimes stated, with plausibility, that States may pass insolvent laws, suspending or taking away actions on contracts, where the debtor goes into insolvency, and hence, by analogy, can do it here. But there another remedy is still given on the contract, before the commissioners of insolvency, and a payment is made *pro rata*, as far as means exist. Here there is no other remedy given, or any part payment made. Indeed, it seems that a forfeiture of all right to recover on the note, in any way, is inflicted here as a penalty for making that very transfer which the bank before, by the act of incorporation, as well as by the note itself, was authorized to make. Again, State insolvent laws, if made, like this law, to apply to past contracts and stop suits on them, have been held not to be constitutional, except so far as they discharge the person from imprisonment, or in some other way affect only the remedy. When so restricted, they do not impair the obligation of the contract itself, because the obligation is left in full force and actionable, and future property, as well as present, subjected to its payment, and the body exonerated only as a matter connected merely with the form of the remedy. (Cook *v.* Moffat, 5 Howard, 316, and cases there cited.) The case in 8 Robinson, 421, appears also to have been one on a note executed after the prohibitory law, and not, as here, before. But where future acquisitions are attempted to be exonerated, and the discharge extended to the debt or contract itself, if done by the States, it must not, as here, apply to past contracts, or it is held to impair their obligation. (Ogden *v.* Saunders, 12 Wheaton, 213; Sturges *v.* Crowninshield, 4 Wheaton, 122; 6 Wheaton, 131; 2 Kent, Comm. 392; Bronson *v.* Kinzie, 1 Howard, 311; McCracken *v.* Hayward, 2 Howard, 608; 1 Cowen, 321; 16 Johns. 237; 1 Ohio, 236; Cook *v.* Moffat, 5 Howard, 308, 314.) Congress alone can do this as to prior contracts, by means of an express permission in the constitution to pass uniform laws on the subject of bankruptcy; and which laws, when not restrained by any constitution or clause like this as to States impairing contracts, may in that way be made to reach past obligations.

The misfortune here is, that the Legislature, if meaning merely to insure to bill-holders of the bank, when debtors, the privilege of paying in the bills of the bank (as is supposed, 4 Smedes & Marshall, 1, 90), have not said so, and no more, by providing that promissory notes, though assigned by banks, should still be open to set-offs by their debtors of any of their bills which they then held. This would have been equitable, and no more, probably, than they would be entitled to, on common law principles, if an assignee purchased, as here, after the promissory notes fell due, and perhaps with a knowledge of the existence of such a set-off.

Chief-justice Marshall, in The United States *v.* Robertson, 5 Peters, 659, says, independent of any statute, "every debtor may pay his creditor with the notes of that creditor. They are an equitable and legal tender." Equally just and reasonable would have been a declaratory law as to the allowance of such bills as a set-off, where an assignment had been made collusively between the parties with a view to prevent such a set-off. (8 Robinson, 421.)

But instead of resorting to such measures, the Legislature adopted a shorter and more sweeping mode of attaining the end of preventing assignments which might embarrass or defeat set-offs. They did it by cutting off all assignments whatever, and all remedies whatever upon them. And they accompanied this by another statute, enabling debtors of the bank who held its notes, when their debts fell due, to pay in them, or set them off; and even virtually authorized them to make payment in depreciated bills or notes afterwards bought up for that purpose, and thus to gain an undue advantage over set-offs by other debtors in other matters.

The act as to this last topic was passed the next day after the act prohibiting transfers. (Mississippi Laws, 2 February, 1840, p. 21, sec. 2.) It was in these words:—"All banks above alluded to, and all other banks in this State, shall at all times receive their respective notes at par in liquidation of their bills receivable and other claims due them." These two acts, though undoubtedly well meant, and designed to give an honest preference to bill-holders (see Sharkey's dissenting opinion) as to a paper currency which ought always to be kept on a par with specie, were unfortunately, in the laudable zeal to avert a great apprehended evil, passed without sufficient consideration of the limitations of the powers imposed by the constitution of the Union on the State Legislatures, not to impair the obligation of existing contracts. Nor was it necessary to go so far to secure any legitimate results. Some other laws are referred to, which are upheld and which affect the whole community, and seem to violate some of the important incidents of contracts between individuals, or between them and corporations. But it will usually be found that these are such laws only as relate to future contracts, or, if to past ones, relate to modes of proceeding in courts, to the form of remedy merely, to priority to some classes of creditors (5 Cranch, 298), to the kind of process (9 Peters, 319; 10 Wheat. 51), to the length of the statute of limitations (6 Wheat. 131; 2 Mason, 168; 3 Johns. Ch. 190; 4 Wheat. 200; 1 Howard, 315), to exempting the body from imprisonment (4 Wheat. 200), or tools and household goods from seizure (16 Johns. 244; 1 Howard, 15; 11 Martin, 730), or affecting some privilege attached to the person or territory (Story on Confl. of Laws, 339, &c.), and not to the terms or obligations of any part of the contract itself (Cook *v.* Moffat, 5 Howard, 295; Towne *v.* Smith, 1 Woodb. & Minot, 132; 7 Greenl. 337; 3 Burge on Col. & For. Law, 234, 1046).

And if, in professing to alter the remedy only, the duties and rights of a contract itself are changed or impaired, it comes just as much within the spirit of the constitutional prohibition. (Bronson *v.* Kinzie et al., 1 Howard, 316; 2 Howard, 612; 2 Madison Papers, 1239, 1581.)

Thus, if a remedy is taken away entirely, as here, or clogged "*by condition of any kind, the right of the owner may indeed subsist and be acknowledged, but it is impaired.*" (Green *v.* Biddle, 8 Wheat. 75.) And the test, as before suggested, is not the extent of the violation of the contract, but the fact, that in truth its obligation is lessened, in however small a particular, and not merely altering or regulating the remedy alone. (2 Howard, 612; 8 Wheat. 1.)

Having, it is believed, assigned sufficient reasons to show that the obligation of both of these contracts was impaired, it is now proposed briefly to refer to a few precedents bearing on the correctness of this conclusion, chiefly in respect to the most important of the contracts, — that between the State and the bank. On an examination of the various decisions which have taken place in this court on the violation of the obligation of contracts, it will be found that this case does not come within the principles of any of those where the decision was, that the new laws were no violation; but, on the contrary, is much like several where the decision annulled them as a clear violation. Thus, where a new law has taken the property of a corporation for highways under the right of eminent domain, which reaches all property, private or corporate, on a public necessity, and on making full compensation for it, and under an implied stipulation to be allowed to do it in all public grants and charters, no injury is committed not atoned for, nothing is done not allowed by preëxisting laws or rights, and consequently no part of the obligation of the contract is impaired. (See case of the West River Bridge, and authorities there cited, in 6 Howard, 507.)

So, when the Legislature afterwards tax the property of such corporations, in common with other property of like kind in the State, it is under an implied stipulation to that effect, and violates no part of the contract contained in the charter. (Armstrong *v.* Treasurer of Athens County, 16 Peters, 281. See Providence Bank *v.* Billings, 4 Peters, 514; 11 Peters, 567; 4 Wheat. 699; 12 Mass. Rep. 252; 4 Gill & Johns. 132; 4 Durn. & East. 2; 5 Barn. & Ald. 157; 2 Railway Cases, 23.)

So, when no clause existed in a charter for a bridge against authorizing other bridges near at suitable places, it is no violation of the terms or obligation of the contract to authorize another. (Charles River Bridge *v.* The Warren Bridge et al., 11 Peters, 420.)

Nor is it, if a law make deeds by femes covert good when *bonâ fide*, though not acknowledged in a particular form; because it confirms rather than impairs their deeds, and carries out the original intent of the parties. (Watson *v.* Mercer, 8 Peters, 88.)

Or if a State grant lands, but makes no stipulation not to legislate further upon the subject, and proceeds to prescribe a mode or form of settling titles, this does not impair the force of the grant, or take away any right under it. (Jackson *v.* Lumpkin, 3 Peters, 280.)

Nor does it, if a State merely changes the remedies in form, but does not abolish them entirely, or merely changes the mode of recording deeds, or shortens the statute of limitations. (3 Peters, 280; Hawkins *v.* Barney's Lessee, 5 ib. 457.)

It has been held, also, not only that a Legislature may regulate anew what is merely the remedy, but some State courts have decided that it may make banking corporations subject to certain penalties for not performing their duties,— such as paying their notes on demand in specie,— and that this does not violate any contract. (Brown *v.* Penobscot Bank, 8 Mass. Rep. 445; 2 Hill, 242; 5 Howard, 342.) It is supposed to help enforce, and not impair, what the charter requires. But on this, being a very different question, we give no opinion.

But look a moment at the other class of decisions. Let a charter or grant be entirely expunged, as in the case of the Yazoo claims in Georgia, and no one can doubt that the obligation of the contract is impaired. (Fletcher *v.* Peck, 6 Cranch, 87.)

So, if the State expressly engage in a grant that certain lands shall never be taxed, and a law afterwards passes to tax them. (State of New Jersey *v.* Wilson, 7 Cranch, 164.) Or that corporate property and franchises shall be exempt, and they are then taxed. (Gordon *v.* Appeal Tax Court, 3 Howard, 133.)

So, if lands have been granted for one purpose, and an attempt is made by law to appropriate them to another, or to revoke the grant. (Terrett *v.* Taylor, 9 Cranch, 43; Town of Pawlet *v.* Clark, 9 Cranch, 292.)

Or if a charter, deemed private rather than public, has been altered as to its government and control. (Dartmouth College *v.* Woodward, 4 Wheat. 518.)

Or if owners of lands, granted without conditions or restrictions, have been by the Legislature deprived of their usual remedy for mesne profits, or compelled to pay for certain kinds of improvements, for which they were not otherwise liable. (Green *v.* Biddle, 8 Wheat. 1.)

Or if, after a mortgage, new laws are passed, prohibiting a sale to foreclose it, unless two-thirds of its appraised value is offered, and enacting further that the equitable title shall not be extinguished till twelve months after the sale. (Bronson *v.* Kinzie, 1 Howard, 311; McCracken *v.* Hayward, 2 ib. 608.)

These last cases in Wheaton and Howard are very near in point to the present one, though, in my view, a less strong and decisive encroachment on a previous contract than this is.

So are the cases very near where all remedy whatever is taken away, and it is held that the obligation of the contract is thus impaired. (See some before cited, and 8 Mass. Rep. 430; 2 Gall. 141; 2 Greenl. 294; 1 Howard, 311; 3 Peters, 290; 2 Howard, 608.)

The whole usefulness and value of a note or contract is in this way destroyed, and that without any reference to the contract itself. For these reasons, the judgment below must be reversed.

# ON STATE LICENSE LAWS.*

I CONCUR in the conclusion of my brethren as to the judgment which ought to be pronounced in all the three license cases.

But, differing in some of the reasons for that judgment, and in the limitations and extent of some of the principles involved, and knowing the cases to possess much interest in the circuit to which I belong, and from which they all come, I do not feel at liberty to refrain from briefly expressing my views upon them.

The paramount question involved in all the cases is, whether license laws by the States for selling spirituous liquors are constitutional. It is true that several other points are raised, as to evidence, the power of juries in criminal prosecutions to decide the law as well as the facts, and other questions not connected with the overruling of any clause in an act of Congress, or treaty, or the constitution, which was interposed in the defence. But, confined, as we are, to these last considerations in writs of error to State courts, it would be travelling out of our prescribed path to discuss at all, either the other questions just alluded to, or some which have been long and ardently agitated in connection with this subject; such, for instance, as the expediency of the license laws, or the power of a State to regulate, in any way, the food and drink or clothing of its inhabitants. Fortunately, those questions belong to another and more appropriate forum,—the State tribunals.

But, looking to the relations which exist between the General Government and the different State sovereignties, the question, whether the laws in these cases are within the power of the States to pass, without an encroachment on the authority of the General Government, is one of those conflicts of laws between the two governments, involving the true extent of the powers in each as regards the other, which is very properly placed under our revision. In helping to discharge that duty on this occasion, I carry with me, as a controlling principle, the proposition, that State powers, State rights, and State decisions, are to be upheld when the objection to them is not clear, equally proper as it may be for them, when the objection is clear, to give way to the supremacy of the authorized measures of the General Government. (See Constitution, art. 3.)

It is not enough to fancy some remote or indirect repugnance to acts of Congress,—a "potential inconvenience,"—in order to annul the laws of sovereign States, and overturn the deliberate decisions of State tribunals. There must be an actual collision, a direct inconsistency, and that deprecated case of "clashing sovereignties," in order to

* Opinion in License cases, January term S. C. U. S., in 1847.

demand the judicial interference of this court to reconcile them. (McCulloch *v.* Maryland, 4 Wheat. 316, 487; 1 Story's Com. on Const. 432.)

These cases present two leading facts in respect to the material points, which ought first to be noticed. Neither of them is a prosecution against the importer of spirit or wine from a foreign country; and in neither has a duty been imposed, or a tax collected, by the State from the original defendant, in connection with these articles. From this state of things, it follows, that, however much has been said as to the collision between these license laws and some former decisions of this court, no such direct issue is made up in either of them.

The case usually cited in support of such a proposition is very different. It is that of Brown *v.* Maryland, 12 Wheat. 419, which was a tax or license required, before the sale of an article, from the importer of it from a foreign country; and it was an importer alone who called the constitutionality of the law in question. What do these statutes, then, really seek to do? They merely attempt to regulate the sale of spirit or wine within the limits of States, in regard to the quantity sold at any one time without a license from the State authorities, — as in the cases from Massachusetts and Rhode Island; and in regard to any sale whatever without such license, — as in the case from New Hampshire.

It is true, also, that the quantity allowed to be sold in Massachusetts at any one time, without a license, is not so small as that which is permitted by Congress to be imported in kegs, and in Rhode Island is greater than that which Congress permits to be imported in bottles, and in New Hampshire is no quantity whatever. Yet neither of the laws unconditionally prohibits importations. Indeed, neither of them says anything on the subject of importations. The first inquiry, then, recurs, whether they do not all stand on the same platform in respect to this, and without conflicting in this respect with any act of Congress. My opinion is that they do; as none of them, by prohibiting importations, oppose in terms any act of Congress which allows them, and none seem to me to conflict, in substance, more than form, with entire freedom on that subject. Nor in either case do they, in point of fact, amount to a prohibition of importations in any quantity, however small. Under them, and so far as regards them, importations still go on abundantly into each of those States. It is manifest, also, whether as an abstract proposition or practical measure, that a prohibition to import is one thing, while a prohibition to sell without license is another, and entirely different. The first would operate on foreign commerce, on the voyage. The latter affects only the internal business of the State after the foreign importation is completed and on shore. In the next place, in point of fact, neither of the laws goes so far as to prohibit in terms the sales, any more than the imports, of spirits. On looking at the laws, this will be conceded. But, if such a prohibition existed as to sales, what act of Congress would it come in collision with? None has ever been passed which professes to regulate or permit sales within the States as a matter of commerce. A good reason exists for this, as the subject of buying and selling within a State is one as exclusively belonging to the power of the State over its internal trade, as that to regulate foreign commerce is with the General Government, under the broadest construction of that power.

And what power or measure of the General Government would a prohibition of sales within a State conflict with, if it consisted merely in regulations of the police or internal commerce of the State itself? There is no contract, express or implied, in any act of Congress, that the owners of property, whether importers or purchasers from them, shall sell their articles in such quantities or at such times as they please within the respective States. Nor can they expect to sell on any other or better terms than are allowed by each State to all its citizens, or in a manner different from what has comported with the policy of most of the old States, as well before as since the constitution was adopted. Any other view would not accord with the usages of the country, or the fitness of things, or the unquestioned powers of all sovereign States, and, as is admitted, even of those in this Union, to regulate both their internal commerce and general police. The idea, too, that a prohibition to sell would be tantamount to a prohibition to import, does not seem to me either logical or founded in fact. For, even under a prohibition to sell, a person could import, as he often does, for his own consumption and that of his family and plantations; and, also, if a merchant, extensively engaged in commerce, often does import articles with no view of selling them here, but of storing them for a higher and more suitable market in another State, or abroad. This was the paramount object in the law of Congress, so often cited, as to the importation of kegs of fifteen gallons of brandy, — to have them in proper shape to be reëxported and carried on mules in Mexico, rather than to be sold for use here.

I should question the correctness of this objection, even were it the doctrine in Brown *v.* Maryland, though I do not regard it as the point there settled, or the substantial reason for it. (See Chief-justice Parker's Opinion in The State of New Hampshire *v.* Peirce, in Law Rep. for September, 1845.) That point related rather to the want of power in a State to lay a duty on imports.

But it is earnestly urged, that, as these acts indirectly prohibit sales, such a prohibition of sales is indirectly a prohibition of importations, and importations are certainly regulated by Congress. It is necessary to scrutinize the grounds on which such circuitous reasoning and analogy rest. The sale of spirit being still permitted in all these States, as before remarked, it is first objected, that it is permitted in certain quantities only, except under license, and that this restricts and lessens both the sales and imports. But the leading object of the license is to insure the sales of spirit in quantities not likely to encourage intemperance, and at places and times, and by persons, conducive to the same end. This is the case in New Hampshire, where none can be sold without license; while in the two other States, if no license is granted, the owner may sell in ten or twenty-eight gallons at a time; and in all the three States, the owner may, without license, consume what he imports, or store and reëxport it for a market elsewhere. So the laws of most of the States forbid sales of property on the Sabbath. But who ever regarded that as prohibiting there entirely either their imports or sales?

It is further argued, however, that the license laws accomplish indirectly what is hostile to the policy of Congress, and thus conflict with the spirit of its acts as much as if they prohibited absolutely both importations and sales. But, if effecting this at all, it must be because they tend to lessen, and are designed to lessen, the consumption of foreign spirits, and thus help to reduce the imports and sales of them.

The case from New Hampshire is in this respect less open to objection than the others, the spirit there having been domestic. But, as it came in coastwise from another State, it may involve a like *principle in another view*; and, *in its prohibitory character as to selling* any liquor without license, the New Hampshire statute goes further than either of the others.

Now, can it be maintained that every law which tends to diminish the consumption of any foreign or domestic article is unconstitutional, or violates acts of Congress? For that is the essence of this point. So far from this, whatever promotes economy in the use or consumption of any articles is certainly desirable, and to be encouraged by both the State and General Governments. Improvements of that kind by new inventions and labor-saving machinery are encouraged by patents and rewards. More especially is it sound policy everywhere to lessen the consumption of luxuries, and in particular those dangerous to public morals. So in respect to foreign articles: the disuse of them is promoted by both the General and State Governments in several other ways, rather than treating it as unconstitutional or against the acts of Congress, though the revenue as well as consumption be thereby diminished. Thus, the former orders the purchase of only domestic hemp for the navy, when it can be obtained of a suitable quality and price (Resolution, 18 February, 1843, 5 Statues at Large, 648). And some of the States have often bestowed bounties on the growth of hemp, and of wheat, and other useful articles. An exception like this would cut so deep and wide into other usages and policy well established, as to need no further refutation. But this objection is mixed up with another, — that the operation of these license laws is unconstitutional, because they lessen the amount of revenue which the General Government might otherwise derive from the importation of that which is made abroad. It may be a sufficient reply to this, that Congress itself, by its own revenue system, has, at times, by very high duties on some articles, meant to diminish their consumption, and reduce the revenue which otherwise might be derived from them if allowed to be introduced more largely under a small duty. And in this very article of spirits it has confessedly, from the foundation of the government, made the duties high, so as to discourage their use; and this in the very last tariff of 1846, though considered to be more emphatically a mere revenue measure. So its actual policy for fifteen years has been to lessen the use of spirit in both the army and navy; and by the third section of the act of Aug. 29th, 1842, ch. 267 (5 Statutes at Large, 546), this policy is recognized and encouraged by law.

So, when resorting to internal duties, for a like reason in part, stills and the manufacture of whiskey have been the first resorted to; and, at last, in order to discourage the making of molasses into New England rum, the drawback on the former, when manufactured into spirit and exported, is allowed to stand now on a footing much less favorable than that on sugar when refined and exported.

Again, where States look to the most proper objects of domestic taxation, it is perfectly competent for them to assess a higher tax or excise, by way of license or direct assessment, on articles of foreign rather than domestic growth belonging to her citizens; and it ever has been done, however it may discourage the use of the former, or lessen the revenue which might otherwise be derived from them by the General Government, or tend to reduce imports, as well as restrict the sale of them when considered of a dangerous character.

The ground is, therefore, untenable entirely, that a course of legislation which serves to discourage what is foreign, whether it be by Congress or the States, is, for that reason alone, contrary to the constitution, even if it tend at the same time to reduce the amount of revenue which would otherwise accrue from foreign imports, or from those of that particular article.

Importations, then, being left unforbidden in all of these cases, and the right to sell with a license not being prohibited in any of them, — nor without one prohibited, except qualifiedly in two of them, and in the other absolutely, but not affecting foreign imports at all in that case, as the spirit sold there was of domestic manufacture, — I pass to the next constitutional objection.

It has been contended, that the sum required to be paid for a license, and the penalty imposed for selling without one, are in the nature of a duty on imports, and thus come within the principle really settled in Brown *v.* Maryland, and thus conflict with the constitution. It is conceded, that a State is forbidden "to lay any impost or duties on imports" without the assent of Congress. (Art. 1, § 10.) But neither of these statutes purports to tax imports from abroad of foreign spirits, or imports from another State, either coastwise or by land, of either foreign or domestic spirits. The last mode is not believed to be that referred to in the constitution; and no regulation has ever been made by Congress concerning it when consisting of domestic spirits, as in the case of New Hampshire, except with a view to prevent smuggling. (Act of Congress, Sept. 1, 1789, ch. 11, § 25, and Feb. 18, 1793, ch. 8, § 14; 1 Statutes at Large, 61, 309.)

Nor does either of these statutes purport to tax the introduction of an article by the merchant importing it,—much less to impose any duty on the article itself for revenue, in addition to what Congress requires. Neither of them appears to be, in character or design, a fiscal measure. They do not touch the merchandise till it has become a part of the property and capital of the State, and then merely regulate the disposal of it under license, as an affair of police and internal commerce. They might, then, even tax it as a part of the commercial stock in trade, and thus subject it, like other property, to a property tax, without being exposed to be considered an impost on imports, so as to conflict with the constitution. But the penalty and license in these cases are imposed *diverso intuitu*, and not as a tax of any kind. Hence they operate no more in substance than in form as an impost of the prohibited character.

There is no pretence that the penalty is for revenue; and if the small sum taken for a license should ever exceed the expense and trouble of supervising the matter, and become a species of internal duty or excise, it would operate on spirit made in the State as well as that made elsewhere, and on others as well as importers, and, like any State tax on local property, or local trade, or local business, be free from any conflict with the constitution or acts of Congress. And what seems decisive in these causes as to this aspect of the question is, that neither of the persons here prosecuted was, in fact, an importer of foreign spirit or wines, or set up a defence of that kind as to himself, on the trial, which was overruled in the State courts.

Nor can the proposition, sometimes advanced, be vindicated, that this license, if a tax, and falling at times on persons not citizens, whether they belong to other States or are aliens, is either unjust or unconstitutional. It falls on them only when within the limits of the State, under the protection of its laws, and seeking the privileges of its trade, and only in common with their own citizens. Such taxes are justifiable on principles of international law (Vattel, B. 8, ch. 10, § 132), and I can find no clause in the constitution with which they come in collision.

Again: it has been strenuously insisted on in these cases, and perhaps it is the leading position, that these license laws are virtually regulations of foreign commerce; and hence, when passed by a State, are exercising a power exclusively vested in the General Government, and therefore void. This is maintained, whether they actually conflict with any particular act of Congress or not. But, dissenting from any such definition of that power, as thus exclusive and thus abrogating every measure of a State which by construction may be deemed a regulation of foreign commerce, though not at all conflicting with any existing act of Congress, or with anything ever likely to be done by Congress, I shall not, on this occasion, go at length into the reasons for my dissent to the exclusive character of this power, because these license laws are not, in my opinion, regulations of foreign commerce, and in a recent inquiry on the circuit I have gone very fully into the question. (The United States *v.* New Bedford Bridge, in Massachusetts District.)

My reasons are, in brief, —

1. The grant is in the same article of the constitution, and in like language, with others which this court has pronounced not to be exclusive; e. g., the regulation of weights and measures, of bankruptcy, and disciplining the militia.

2. There is nothing in its nature, in several respects, to render it more exclusive than the other grants; but, on the contrary, much in its nature to permit and require the concurrent and auxiliary action of the States. But I admit that, so far as regards the uniformity of a regulation reaching to all the States, it must in these cases, of course, be exclusive; no State being able to prescribe rules for others as to bankruptcy, or weights and measures, or the militia, or for foreign commerce. A want of attention to this discrimination has caused most of the difficulty. But there is much in connection with foreign commerce which is local within each State, convenient for its regulation and useful to the public, to be acted on by each till the power is abused, or some course is taken by Congress conflicting with it. Such are the deposit of ballast in harbors, the extension of wharves into tide-water, the supervision of the anchorage of ships, the removal of obstructions, the allowance of bridges with suitable draws, and various other matters that need not be enumerated, beside the exercise of numerous police and health powers, which are also by many claimed upon different grounds.

This local, territorial, and detailed legislation should vary in different States, and is better understood by each than by the General Government; and hence, as the colonies under an empire usually attend to all such local legislation within their limits, leaving only general outlines and rules to the parent country at home,—as towns, cities, and corporations, do it through by-laws for themselves, after the State Legislature lays down general principles, and as the war and navy departments and courts of justice make detailed rules under general laws,—so here the States, not conflicting with any uniform and general regulations by Congress, as to foreign commerce, must, for convenience, if not necessity, from the very nature of the power, not be debarred from any legislation of a local and detailed character on matters connected with that commerce omitted by Congress. And to hold the power of Congress as to such topics exclusive, in every respect, and prohibitory to the States, though never exercised by Congress, as fully as when in active operation, which is the opposite theory, would create infinite inconvenience, and detract much from the cordial coöperation and consequent harmony between both governments, in their appropriate spheres. It would nullify numerous useful laws and regulations in all the Atlantic and commercial States in the Union.

If this view of the subject conflicts with opinions laid down *obiter* in some of the decisions made by this court (9 Wheat. 209; 12 ibid. 438; 16 Peters, 543), it corresponds with the conclusions of several judges on this point, and does not, in my understanding of the subject, contradict any adjudged case in point. (5 Wheat. 49; Wilson *v.* Blackbird Creek Marsh Company, 2 Peters, 245; 11 ibid. 132; 14 ibid. 579; 16 ibid. 627, 664; 4 Wheat. 196.)

But, without going further into this question, it is enough here to say, that these license laws do not profess to be, nor do they operate as, regulations of foreign commerce. They neither direct how it shall be carried on, nor where, nor under what duties or penalties. Nothing is touched by them which is on shipboard, or between ship and shore; nothing till within the limits of a State, and out of the possession and jurisdiction of the General Government.

It is objected, in another view, that such licenses for selling domestic spirit may affect the commerce in it between the States, which by the constitution is placed under the regulation of Congress as much as foreign commerce.

But this license is a regulation neither of domestic commerce between the States, nor of foreign commerce. It does not operate on either, or the imports of either, till they have entered the State, and become component parts of its property. Then it has, by the constitution, the exclusive power to regulate its own internal commerce and business in such articles, and bind all residents, citizens or not, by its regulations, if they ask its protection and privileges; and Congress, instead of being opposed and thwarted by regulations as to this, can no more interfere in it than the States can interfere in regulation of foreign commerce. If the proposition was maintainable, that, without any legislation by Congress as to the trade between the States (except that in coasting, as before explained, to prevent smuggling), anything imported from another State, foreign or domestic, could be sold of right in the package in which it was imported, not subject to any license or internal regulation of a State, then it is obvious that the whole license system may be evaded and nullified, either from abroad, or from a neighboring State. And the more especially can it be done from the latter, as imports may be made in bottles of any size, down to half a pint, of spirits or wines; and if its sale cannot be interfered with and regulated, the retail business can be carried on in any small quantity, and by the most irresponsible and unsuitable persons, with perfect impunity.

The apprehension that the States, by these license systems, are likely to impair the freedom of trade between each other, is hardly verified by the experience of a half-century. Their conduct has been so liberal and just thus far on this matter as never to have called for the legislation of Congress, which it clearly has the power to make in respect to the commerce between the States, whenever any occasion shall require its interposition, to check imprudences or abuses on the part of any one of them towards the citizens of another. Some have objected, next, that these laws violate our foreign treaties,—such as those, for example, with Great Britain and Prussia, which stipulate for free ingress and egress as to our ports, as well as for a participation in our interior trade. (See Eight Statutes at Large, 116, 228, 378.) But those arrangements do not profess to exempt their people from local taxation here, or local conformity to license systems, operating, as these State laws do, on their own citizens and their own domestic products in the same way, and to the same extent, as on foreign ones. And neither of those laws in this case forbid access to our ports, or importation into the several States, by the inhabitants of any foreign countries.

In settling the question whether these laws impugn treaties, or regulate either foreign commerce or that between the States, or impose a duty on imports, ordinary justice to the States demands that they be presumed to have meant what they profess till the contrary is shown. Hence, as these laws were passed by States possessing experience, intelligence, and a high tone of morals, it is neither legal nor liberal to attempt to nullify them by any forced construction, so as to make them regulations of foreign commerce, or measures to collect revenue by a duty on foreign imports, thus imparting to them a character different from that professed by their authors, or from that which, by their provisions and tendency, they appear designed for. These States are as incapable of duplicity or fraud in their laws, of meaning one thing and professing another, as the purest among their accusers; and while legitimate and constitutional objects are assigned, and means used which seem adapted to such ends, it is illiberal to impute other designs, and to construe their legislation as of a sinister character, which they never contemplated. Thus, on the face of them, these laws relate exclusively to the regulation of licensed houses, and the sales of an article which, especially where retailed in small quantities, is likely to attract together within the State unusual numbers, and encourage idleness, wastefulness, and drunkenness. To mitigate, if not prevent, this last evil, was undoubtedly their real design.

From the first settlement of this country, and in most other nations, ancient or modern, civilized or savage, it has been found useful to discountenance excesses in the use of intoxicating liquor. And, without entering here into the question whether legislation may not, on this as other matters, become at times intemperate, and reäct injuriously to the salutary objects sought to be promoted, it is enough to say, under the general aspect of it, that the legislation here is neither novel nor extraordinary, nor apparently designed to promote other objects than physical, social, and moral improvement. On the contrary, its tendency clearly is to reduce family expenditures, secure health, lessen pauperism and crime, and coöperate with, rather than counteract, the apparent policy of the General Government itself in respect to the disuse of ardent spirit.

They aim, then, at a right object. They are calculated to promote it. They are adapted to no other. And no other, or sinister, or improper view can, therefore, either with delicacy or truth, be imputed to them.

But I go further on this point than some of the court, and wish to meet the case in front, and in its worst bearings. If, as in the view of some, these license laws were really in the nature of partial or entire prohibitions to sell certain articles within the limits of a State, as being dangerous to public health and morals, or were virtual taxes on them as State property in a fair ratio with other taxation, it does not seem to me that their conflict with the constitution would, by any means, be clear. Taking for granted, till the contrary appears, that the real design in passing them for such purposes is the avowed one, and especially while their provisions are suited to effect the professed object, and nothing beyond that, and do not apply to persons or things, except where within the limits of State territory, they would appear entirely defensible as a matter of right, though prohibiting sales.

Whether such laws of the States as to licenses are to be classed as police measures, or as regulations of their internal commerce, or as taxation merely, imposed on local property and local business, and are to be justified by each or by all of them together, is of little consequence, if they are laws which from their nature and object must belong to all sovereign States. Call them by whatever name, if they are necessary to the well-being and independence of all communities, they remain among the reserved rights of the States, no express grant of them to the General Government having been either proper, or apparently embraced in the constitution. So, whether they conflict or not indirectly and slightly with some regulations of foreign commerce, after the subject-matter of that commerce touches the soil or waters within the limits of a State, is not, perhaps, very material, if they do not really relate to that commerce, or any other topic within the jurisdiction of the General Government.

As a general rule, the power of a State over all matters not granted away must be as full in the bays, ports and harbors, within her territory, *intra fauces terræ*, as on her wharves and shores, or interior soil. And there can be little check on such legislation, beyond the discretion of each State, if we consider the great conservative reserved powers of the States, in their quarantine or health systems, in the regulation of their internal commerce, in their authority over taxation, and, in short, every local measure necessary to protect themselves against persons or things dangerous to their peace and their morals.

It is conceded that the States may exclude pestilence, either to the body or mind, shut out the plague or cholera, and, no less, obscene paintings, lottery tickets, and convicts. (Holmes *v.* Jennison *et al.*, 14 Peters, 568; 9 Wheat. 203; 11 Peters, 133.) How can they be sovereign within their respective spheres, without power to regulate all their internal commerce, as well as police, and direct how, when, and where, it shall be conducted in articles intimately connected either with public morals, or public safety, or the public prosperity? (See Vattel, B. 1, ch. 19, §§ 219, 231.)

The list of interdicted articles and persons is a long one in most European governments, and, though in some cases not very judicious or liberal, is in others most commendable; and the exclusion of opium from China is an instance well known in Asia, and kindred in its policy. The introduction and storage of gunpowder in large quantities is one of those articles long regulated and forbidden here. (New York *v.* Miln, 11 Peters, 102.) Lottery tickets and indecent prints are also a common subject of prohibition almost everywhere. (6 Greenleaf, 412; 4 Blackford, 107. See the tariff of 1842; 5 Stat. at Large, 566, § 28.) And why not cards, dice, and other instruments of gaming, when thought necessary to suppress that vice? In short, on what principle but this rests the justification of the States to prohibit gaming itself, wagers, champerty, forestalling,—not to speak of the debatable cases of usury, marriage brokage bonds, and many other matters deemed either impolitic or criminal?

It might not comport with the usages or laws of nations to impose mere transit duties on articles or men passing through a State; and however resorted to in some places and on some occasions, it is usually illiberal, as well as injudicious. (Vattel, B. 8, ch. 10.) And, if resorted to here, in respect to the business or imports of citizens of other States, might clearly conflict with some provisions of the constitution conferring on them equal rights, and be a regulation of the commerce between the States, the power over which they have expressly granted to the General Government. But the present case is not of that character. Nor would it be, if prohibiting sales within the acknowledged limits of a State, in cases affecting public morals or public health. Nor is there in this case any complaint, either by a foreign merchant or foreign nation, that treaties are broken; or by any of our own States or by Congress, that its acts or the constitution have been violated.

There are additional illustrations of such powers, existing on general principles in all independent States, given in Puffendorf, B. 8, ch. 5, § 30, as well as in various other writers on national law. And those exercised under what he terms "sovereign or transcendental propriety" (§ 7th), and those which we class under the right of "eminent domain," are recognized in the fifth amendment to the constitution itself, and go far beyond this.

Much more is there an authority to forbid sales, where an authority exists both to seize and destroy the article itself, as is often the case at quarantine.

So the power to forbid the sale of *things* is surely as extensive, and rests on as broad principles of public security and sound morals, as that to exclude *persons*. And yet, who does not know that slaves have been prohibited admittance by many of our States, whether coming from their neighbors or abroad? And which of them cannot forbid their soil from being polluted by incendiaries and felons from any quarter?

Nor is there, in my view, any power conferred on the General Government which has a right to control this matter of internal commerce or police, while it is fairly exercised so as to accomplish a legitimate object, and by means adapted legally and suitably to such end alone. New Hampshire has, for many years, made it penal to bring into her limits paupers even from other States; and this is believed to be a power exercised widely in Europe among independent nations, as well as in this country among the States. (New Hampshire Revised Statutes, *Paupers*, 140.)

It is the undoubted and reserved power of every State here, as a political body, to decide, independent of any provisions made by Congress, though subject not to conflict with any of them when rightful, who shall compose its population, who become its residents, who its citizens, who enjoy the privileges of its laws, and be entitled to their protection and favor, and what kind of property and business it will tolerate and protect. And no one government, or its agents or navigators, possess any right to make another State, against its consent, a penitentiary, or hospital, or poor-house farm for its wretched outcasts, or a receptacle for its poisons to health, and instruments of gambling and debauchery. Indeed, this court has deliberately said, "We entertain no doubt whatsoever, that the States, in virtue of their general police power, possess full jurisdiction to arrest and restrain runaway slaves, and remove them from their borders, and otherwise to secure themselves against their depredations and evil example, as they certainly may do in cases of idlers, vagabonds and paupers." (Prigg *v.* Pennsylvania, 16 Peters, 625.)

There may be some doubt whether the General Government or each State possesses the prohibitory power, as to persons or property of certain kinds, from coming into the limits of the State. But it must exist somewhere; and it seems to me rather a police power, belonging to the States, and to be exercised in the manner best suited to the tastes and institutions of each, than one anywhere granted or proper to the peculiar duties of the General Government. Or, if vested in the latter at all, it is but concurrent. Hence, when the latter prohibited the import of obscene prints in the tariff of 1842, it was a novelty, and was considered by some more properly to be left to the States, as it opened the door to a prohibition, or to prohibitory duties, to many articles, by the General Government, which some States might desire, but others not wish to come in as competitors to their own manufactures. But, as previously shown, to prohibit sales is not the same power, nominally or in substance, as to prohibit imports.

It is possible, that, under our system of double governments over one and the same people, the States cannot prohibit the mere arrival of vessels and cargoes which they may deem dangerous in character to their public peace, or public morals, or general health. This might, perhaps, trench on foreign commerce. Nor can they tax them as imports. This might trench on that part of the constitution which forbids States to lay duties on imports. But, after articles have come within the territorial limits of States, whether on land or water, the destruction itself of what contains disease and death, and the longer continuance of such articles within their limits, or the terms and conditions of their continuance, when conflicting with their legitimate police, or with their power over internal commerce, or with their right of taxation over all persons and property under their protection and jurisdiction, seems one of the first principles of State sovereignty, and indispensable to public safety. Such extraordinary powers, I concede, are to be exercised with caution, and only when necessary or clearly justifiable in emergencies, on sound and constitutional principles; and, if used too often, or indiscreetly, would open a door to much abuse. But the powers seem clearly to exist in the States, and ought to remain there; and though, in this instance, they are not used to this extent, but still, as respectable minorities within these three States believe not to be useful, and as some other States do not think deserving imitation, yet they are used as the competent and constitutional power within each has judged to be proper for its own welfare, and as does not appear to be repugnant to any part of the constitution, or a treaty, or an act of Congress. They must, therefore, not be interfered with by this court; and the more especially, as one reason why these powers have been left with the States is, that the subject-matter of them is better understood by each State than by the Union; and the policy and opinions and usages of one State in relation to some of them may be very unlike those of others, and therefore require a different system of legislation. Where can such a power, also, be safer lodged, than with those public bodies, or States, who are themselves to be the greatest sufferers in interest and character by an improper use of it? If it should happen at any time to be exercised injudiciously, that circumstance would furnish a ground for an appeal rather to the intelligence and prudence of the State, in respect to its modification or repeal, than an authority for this court, by a writ of error, to interfere with the well-considered decision of a State court, and reverse it, and pronounce a State law null and void, merely on that account.

Many State laws are such that their expediency and justice may be doubted widely, and by this tribunal; but this confers no authority on us to nullify them; nor is any such authority, for such a cause, conferred on Congress by any part of the constitution.

The States stand properly on their reserved rights, within their own powers and sovereignty, to judge of the expediency and wisdom of their own laws; and while they take care not to violate clearly any portion of the constitution or statutes of the General Government, our duty to that constitution and laws, and our respect for State rights, must require us not to interfere.

## ON MARTIAL LAW IN RHODE ISLAND.*

THE writ in this case charges the defendants with breaking and entering the plaintiff's dwelling-house, on the 29th of June, 1842, and doing much damage.

The plea in justification alleges that, on June 24th, 1842, an assembly in arms had taken place in Rhode Island, to overawe and make war upon the State. And therefore, in order to protect its government, the Legislature, on the 25th of that month, passed an act declaring the whole State to be under martial law. That the plaintiff was assisting in traitorous designs, and had been in arms to sustain them, and the defendants were ordered by J. Child, an officer in the militia, to arrest the plaintiff, and, supposing him within the house named in the writ, to break and enter it for the purpose of fulfilling that order; and, in doing this, they caused as little damage as possible.

The replication denied all the plea, and averred that the defendants did the acts complained of in their own wrong, and without the cause alleged.

To repel the defence, and in vindication of the conduct of the plaintiff, much evidence was offered; the substance of which will be next stated, with some leading facts proved on the other side in connection with it.

The people of Rhode Island had continued to live under their charter of 1663 from Charles the Second, till 1841, with some changes in the right of suffrage by acts of the Legislature, but without any new constitution, and still leaving in force a requirement of a freehold qualification for voting. By the growth of the State in commerce and manufactures, this requirement had for some time been obnoxious, as it excluded so many adult males of personal worth, and possessed of intelligence and wealth, though not of land,—and as it made the ancient apportionment of the number of representatives, founded on real estate, very disproportionate to the present population and personal property in different portions and towns of the State.

This led to several applications to the Legislature for a change in these matters, or for provision to have a convention of the people called, to correct it by a new constitution. These all failing, voluntary societies were formed in 1841, and a convention called by them of delegates selected by the male adults who had resided one year in the State,

* Dissenting opinion in case of Luther *versus* Borden *et al.* January term S. C. U. S., 1849.

with a view chiefly to correct the right of suffrage and the present unequal apportionment of representatives. This, though done without the formalities or recommendation of any statute of the State, or any provision of the charter, was done peacefully, and with as much care and form as were practicable without such a statute or charter provision. A constitution was formed by those delegates, a vote taken on its ratification, and an adoption of it made, as its friends supposed, and offered to prove, by a decided majority, both of the freehold voters and of the male adults in the State.

Political officers for the executive and legislative departments were then chosen under it by those in its favor, which officers assembled on the 3d of May, 1842, and took their respective oaths of office, and appointed several persons to situations under the constitution, and among them the existing judges of the superior court.

After transacting some other business the next day,—but the old officers in the State under the charter not acknowledging their authority, nor surrendering to them the public records and public property,—they adjourned till July after, and never convened again, nor performed any further official duties. Nor did they institute actions for the possession of the public records and public property; but T. Dorr, the person elected governor, at the head of an armed force, on the 25th of June, 1842, in his supposed official capacity, made some attempt to get possession of the public arsenal; but failing in it, he dismissed the military assembled, by a written order, on the 27th of June, and left the State. He stated as a reason for this, "that a majority of the friends of the people's constitution disapprove of any further forcible measures for its support."

In the mean time, the officers under the old charter, having, as before suggested, continued in possession of the public records and property, and in the discharge of their respective functions, passed an act, on the 24th of June, placing the State under martial law. A proclamation was then issued by the governor, warning the people not to support the new constitution or its officers, and another act was passed, making it penal to officiate under it. An application was made to the President of the United States for assistance in quelling the disturbances apprehended, but was answered by him on the 29th of May, 1842, not complying with the request, though with expressions of willingness to do it, should it, in his opinion, afterwards become necessary.

Nothing further seems to have been done by him in the premises, except that, on the 29th of June, the day of the trespass complained of in this action, a proclamation was prepared under his direction, but not issued, denouncing such of the supporters of the new constitution as were in arms to be "insurgents," and commanding them to disperse.

It was next shown by the respondents, that Dorr, the governor elect under the new constitution, was, in August, 1842, indicted for treason against the State, and being apprehended in 1844, was then tried and convicted.

It further appears, that the court, at the trial of the present cause, ruled out the evidence offered by the plaintiff in support of his conduct, and admitted that which went to justify the defendants, and decided that the old charter, and not the new constitution, was in force at the time the act passed declaring martial law, and that this law was valid, and, as pleaded, justified the defendants in their behavior.

Without entering here at more length into details concerning the unhappy controversy which agitated Rhode Island in 1842, it is manifest that it grew out of a political difficulty among her own people, in respect to the formation of a new constitution. It is not probable that the active leaders, and much less the masses, who were engaged on either side, had any intention to commit crimes or oppress illegally their fellow-citizens. Such, says Grotius, is usually, in civil strife, the true liberal view to be taken of the masses. (Grotius on War, B. 3, ch. 11, sec. 6.) And much more is it so, when, in a free country, they honestly divide on great political principles, and do not wage a struggle merely for rapine or spoils. In this instance, each side appears to have sought, by means which it considered lawful and proper, to sustain the cause in which it had embarked, till peaceful discussions and peaceful actions unexpectedly ripened into a resort to arms, and brother became arrayed against brother in civil strife. Fortunately, no lives were destroyed, and little property injured. But the bitterness consequent on such differences did not pass off without some highly penal legislation, and the extraordinary measure of the establishment of martial law over the whole State. Under these circumstances, it is too much to expect, even at this late day, that a decision on any branch of this controversy can be received without some of the leaven of former political excitement and prejudice, on the one side or the other, by those who were engaged in its stirring scenes. Public duty, however, seems to require each member of this court to speak freely his own convictions on the different questions which it may be competent for us to decide; and when one of those members, like myself, has the misfortune to differ in any respect from the rest, to explain with frankness, and undeterred by consequences, the grounds of that difference.

This difference however, between me and my brethren, extends only to the points in issue concerning martial law. But that being a very important one in a free government, and this controversy having arisen in the circuit to which I belong, and where the deepest interest is felt in its decision, I hope to be excused for considering that point fully, and for assigning, also, some additional and different reasons why I concur with the rest of the court in the opinion, that the other leading question — the validity of the old charter at that time — is not within our constitutional jurisdiction. These two inquiries seem to cover the whole debatable ground; and I refrain to give an opinion on the last question, which is merely political, under a conviction that, as a judge, I possess no right to do it, and not to avoid or conceal any views entertained by me concerning them, as mine, before sitting on this bench, and as a citizen, were frequently and publicly avowed.

It must be very obvious, on a little reflection, that the last is a mere political question. Indeed, large portions of the points subordinate to it, on this record, which have been so ably discussed at the bar, are of a like character, rather than being judicial in their nature and cognizance. For they extend to the power of the people, independent of the Legislature, to make constitutions,— to the right of suffrage among different classes of them in doing this,— to the authority of naked majorities,— and other kindred questions, of such high political interest as, during a few years, to have agitated much of the Union, no less than Rhode Island.

But, fortunately for our freedom from political excitements in judicial duties, this court can never with propriety be called on officially to be umpire in questions merely political. The adjustment of these questions belongs to the people and their political representatives, either in the State or General Government. These questions relate to matters not to be settled on strict legal principles. They are adjusted rather by inclination,— or prejudice or compromise, often. Some of them succeed or are defeated even by public policy alone, or mere naked power, rather than intrinsic right. There being so different tastes as well as opinions in politics, and especially in forming constitutions,— some people prefer foreign models, some domestic, and some neither; while judges, on the contrary, for their guides, have fixed constitutions and laws, given to them by others, and not provided by themselves. And those others are no more Locke than an Abbé Sieyes, but the people. Judges, for constitutions, must go to the people of their own country, and must merely enforce such as the people themselves, whose judicial servants they are, have been pleased to put into operation.

Another evil, alarming and little foreseen, involved in regarding these as questions for the final arbitrament of judges, would be, that, in such an event, all political privileges and rights would, in a dispute among the people, depend on our decision finally. We would possess the power to decide against as well as for them, and, under a prejudiced or arbitrary judiciary, the public liberties and popular privileges might thus be much perverted, if not entirely prostrated. But, allowing the people to make constitutions and unmake them, allowing their representatives to make laws and unmake them, and without our interference as to their principles or policy in doing it, yet, when constitutions and laws are made and put in force by others, then the courts, as empowered by the State or the Union, commence their functions, and may decide on the rights which conflicting parties can legally set up under them, rather than about their formation itself. Our power begins after theirs ends. Constitutions and laws precede the judiciary,—and we act only under and after them, and as to disputed rights beneath them, rather than disputed points in making them. We speak what is the law, *jus dicere*, we speak or construe what is the constitution, after both are made, but we make, or revise, or control neither. The disputed rights beneath constitutions already made are to be governed by precedents, by sound legal principles, by positive legislation, clear contracts, moral duties, and fixed rules; they are *per se* questions of law, and are well suited to the education and habits of the bench. But the other disputed points in making constitutions depending often, as before shown, on policy, inclination, popular resolves, and popular will, and arising not in respect to private rights,—not what is *meum* and *tuum*,—but in relation to politics, they belong to politics, and they are settled by political tribunals, and are too dear to a people bred in the school of Sydney and Russel for them ever to intrust their final decision, when disputed, to a class of men who are so far removed from them as the judiciary,—a class, also, who might decide them erroneously as well as right, and if in the former way, the consequences might not be able to be averted except by a revolution,—while a wrong decision by a political forum can often be peacefully corrected by new elections or instructions, in a single month. And if the people, in the distribution of powers under the constitution, should ever think of making judges supreme arbiters in political controversies, when not selected by, nor, frequently, amenable to them, nor at liberty to follow such various considerations in their judgments as belong to mere political questions, they will dethrone themselves, and lose one of their own invaluable birthrights; building up, in this way—slowly, but surely—a new sovereign power in the republic, in most respects irresponsible and unchangeable for life, and one more dangerous, in theory at least, than the worst elective oligarchy in the worst of times. Again, instead of controlling the people in political affairs, the judiciary in our system was designed rather to control individuals, on the one hand, when encroaching, or to defend them, on the other, under the constitution and the laws, when they are encroached upon. And if the judiciary at times seems to fill the important station of a check in the government, it is rather a check on the legislature who may attempt to pass laws contrary to the constitution, or on the executive who may violate both the laws and constitution, than on the people themselves, in their primary capacity as makers and amenders of constitutions.

Hence the judiciary power is not regarded by elementary writers on politics and jurisprudence as a power coördinate or commensurate with that of the people themselves, but rather coördinate with that of the legislature. (Kendall *v.* U. States, 12 Peters, 526.) Hence, too, the following view was urged, when the adoption of the constitution was under consideration: "It is the more rational to suppose that the courts were designed to be an intermediate body between the people and the legislature, in order, among other things, to keep the *latter* within the limits assigned to their authority." (Federalist, No. 77, by Hamilton.) "Nor does the conclusion by any means suppose a superiority of the judicial to the legislative power. It only supposes that the power of the people is superior to both," &c., &c.

But how would this superiority be as to this court, if we could decide finally on all the political claims and acts of the people, and overrule or sustain them according only to our own views? So the judiciary, by its mode of appointment, long duration in office, and slight accountability, is rather fitted to check legislative power than political, and enforce what the political authorities have manifestly ordained. These last authorities are, by their pursuits and interests, better suited to make rules; we, to expound and enforce them, after made.

The subordinate questions which also arise here in connection with the others,—such as whether all shall vote, in forming or amending those constitutions, who are capable and accustomed to transact business in social and civil life, and none others; and whether, in great exigencies of oppression by the legislature itself, and refusal by it to give relief, the people may not take the subject into their own hands, independent of the legislature; and whether a simple plurality in number on such an occasion, or a majority of all, or a larger proportion, like two-thirds or three-fourths, shall be deemed necessary and proper for a change; and whether, if peacefully completed, violence can afterwards be legally used against them by the old government, if that is still in possession of the public property and public records; whether what are published and acted on as the laws and constitution of a State were made by persons duly chosen or not, were enrolled and read according to certain parliamentary rules or not, were in truth voted for by a majority or two-thirds; — these, and several other questions equally debatable and difficult in their solution, are in some aspects a shade less political. But they are still political. They are too near all the great fundamental principles in government, and are too momentous, ever to have been intrusted by our jealous fathers to a body of men like judges, holding office for life, independent in salary, and not elected by the people themselves.

*Non nostrum tantas componere lites.* Where, then, does our power, as a general rule, begin? In what place runs the true boundary-line? It is here. Let the political authorities admit as valid a constitution made with or without previous provision by the Legislature, as in the last situation Tennessee and Michigan were introduced into the Union. (See Federalist, No. 40, and 2 Ell. Deb. 57; 13 Regis by Y. 95, 1164, and Cong. Globe, App. 78, 137, 147.) Let the collected will of the people, as to changes, be so strong, and so strongly evinced, as to call down no bills of pains and penalties to resist it, and no arming of the militia or successful appeals to the General Government to suppress it by force, as none were in some cases abroad as well as in America, and one recently in New York, which might be cited beside those above. (See A. D. 1846, and opinion of their judges.) In short, let a constitution or law, however originating, be clearly acknowledged by the existing political tribunals, and be put and kept in successful operation. The judiciary can then act in conformity to and under them. (Kemper *v.* Hawkins, 1 Virg. Cas., 74, App.) Then, when the claims of individuals come in conflict under them, it is the true province of the judiciary to decide what they rightfully are under such constitutions and laws, rather than to decide whether those constitutions and laws themselves have been rightfully or wisely made.

Again, the constitution of the United States enumerates specially the cases over which its judiciary is to have cognizance, but nowhere includes controversies between the people of a State as to the formation or change of their constitutions. (See Article 3, sec. 2.) Though at first the federal judiciary was empowered to entertain jurisdiction where a State was a party in a suit, it has since been deprived even of that power by a jealous country, except in cases of disputed boundary. (Article 3, sec. 2; Amendment 11th; Massachusetts *v.* Rhode Island, 12 Peters, 755.)

If it be asked, what redress have the people, if wronged in these matters, unless by resorting to the judiciary, the answer is, they have the same as in all other political matters. In those, they go to the ballot-boxes, to the Legislature or executive, for the redress of such grievances as are within the jurisdiction of each, and for such as are not, to conventions and amendments of constitutions. And when the former fail, and these last are forbidden by statutes, all that is left in extreme cases, where the suffering is intolerable and the prospect is good of relief by action of the people without the forms of law, is to do as did Hampden and Washington, and venture action without those forms, and abide the consequences. Should strong majorities favor the change, it generally is completed without much violence. In most States, where representation is not unequal, or the right of suffrage is not greatly restricted, the popular will can be felt and triumph through the popular vote and the delegates of the people in the Legislature, and will thus lead soon, and peacefully, to legislative measures ending in reform, pursuant to legislative countenance, and without the necessity of any stronger collateral course. But when the representation is of a character which defeats this, the action of the people, even then, if by large majorities, will seldom be prosecuted with harsh pains and penalties, or resisted with arms.

Changes thus demanded and thus supported will usually be allowed to go into peaceful consummation. But when not so allowed, or when they are attempted by small or doubtful majorities, it must be conceded that it will be at their peril, as they will usually be resisted by those in power by means of prosecutions, and sometimes by violence, and, unless crowned by success, and thus subsequently ratified, they will often be punished as rebellious or treasonable.

If the majorities, however, in favor of changes, happen to be large, and still those in power refuse to yield to them, as in the English revolution of 1688, or in our own of 1776, the popular movement will generally succeed, though it be only by a union of physical with moral strength; and when triumphant, it will, as on those occasions, confirm by subsequent forms of law what may have begun without them.

There are several other questions, also, which may arise under our form of government, that are not properly of judicial cognizance. They originate in political matters, extend to political objects, and do not involve any pecuniary claims or consequences between individuals, so as to become grounds for judicial inquiry. These questions are decided sometimes by Legislatures, or heads of departments, or by public political bodies, and sometimes by officers, executive or military, so as not to be revisable here. (See Decatur *v.* Paulding, 14 Peters, 497.)

Looking to all these considerations, it appears to me that we cannot rightfully settle those grave political questions which, in this case, have been discussed in connection with the new constitution; and, as judges, our duty is to take for a guide the decision made on them by the proper political powers, and, whether right or wrong according to our private opinions, enforce it till duly altered. But it is not necessary to rest this conclusion on reasoning alone. Several precedents in this court, as well as in England, show the propriety of it.

In Foster et al. *v.* Neilson (2 Peters, 309), where the title to the property depended on the question whether the land was within a cession by treaty to the United States, it was held that after our government, legislative and executive, had claimed jurisdiction over it, the courts must consider that the question was a political one, the decision of which, having been made in this manner, they must conform to. (See, also, 6 Peters, 711, and Garcia *v.* Lee, 12 Peters, 520; 13 Peters, 419.) In The Cherokee Nation *v.* The State of Georgia (5 Peters, 20), the court expressed strong doubts whether it was not a political question, not proper for their decision, to protect the Cherokee Indians in their possessions, and to restrain the State of Georgia and construe and enforce its treaty obligations. Justice Johnson seemed decisive that it was.

In Massachusetts *v.* Rhode Island (12 Peters, 736, 738), it was held that the boundaries between States was a political question *per se*, and should be adjusted by political tribunals, unless agreed to be settled as a judicial question, and in the constitution so provided for. (Garcia *v.* Lee, ib. 520.)

In Barclay *v.* Russel (3 Ves. 424), in respect to confiscations, it was held to be a political question, and a subject of treaty, and not of municipal jurisdiction. (P. 434.)

In Nabob of the Carnatic *v.* The East India Company (2 Ves. jun. 56), the court decided that political treaties between a foreign state and subjects of Great Britain, conducting as a state under acts of

Parliament, are not a matter of municipal jurisdiction, and to be examined and enforced by the judiciary.

Another class of political questions, coming still nearer this, is, which must be regarded as the rightful government abroad, between two contending parties? That is never settled by the judiciary, but is left to the decision of the General Government. (The Cherokee Case, 5 Peters, 50; and Williams *v.* Suffolk Ins. Co., 13 Peters, 419; 2 Cranch, 241; Rose *v.* Himely, 4 Cranch, 268; United States *v.* Palmer, 3 Wheat. 634, and Gelston *v.* Hoyt, ib. 246; The Divina Pastora, 4 Wheat. 64; 14 Ves. 353; 11 Ves. 583; 1 Edw. Ad. 1.)

The doctrines laid down in Palmer's case are as directly applicable to this in the event of two contending parties in arms in a domestic war as in a foreign. If one is recognized by the executive or Legislature of the Union as the *de facto* government, the judiciary can only conform to that political decision. (See, also, The Santissima Trinidad, 7 Wheat. 336, 337.) And, further, that if our General Government recognizes either as exclusively in power, the judiciary must sustain its belligerent rights. (See 3 Sumner, 270.) In the case of The City of Berne *v.* the Bank of England (9 Ves. 348), it was held that "a judicial court cannot take notice of a foreign government not acknowledged by the government of the country in which the court sits." The same rule has been applied by this court in case of a contest as to which is the true constitution, between two, or which possesses the true legislative power in one, of our own States,—those citizens acting under the new constitution, which is objected to as irregularly made, or those under the old territorial government therein. (*Semb.* Scott et al. *v.* Jones et al., 5 Howard, 374.) In that case, we held that no writ of error lies to us to revise a decision of a State court, where the only question is the validity of the statute on account of the political questions and objections just named. It was held, also, in Williams *v.* Suffolk Ins. Co. (3 Sumner, 270), that where a claim exists by two governments over a country, the courts of each are bound to consider the claims of their own government as right, being settled for the time being by the proper political tribunal. And hence no right exists in their judicial authorities to revise that decision. (Pp. 273, 275; S. C., 13 Peters, 419.) "*Omnia rite acta.* It might otherwise happen, that the extraordinary spectacle might be presented of the courts of a country disavowing and annulling the acts of its own government in matters of state and political diplomacy."

This is no new distinction in judicial practice, any more than in judicial adjudications. The pure mind of Sir Matthew Hale, after much hesitation, at last consented to preside on the bench in administering the laws between private parties under a government established and recognized by other governments, and in full possession *de facto* of the records and power of the kingdom, but without feeling satisfied on inquiring, as a judicial question, into its legal rights. Cromwell had "gotten possession of the government," and expressed a willingness "to rule according to the laws of the land,"—by "red gowns rather than red coats," as he is reported to have quaintly remarked. And this Hale thought justified him in acting as a judge. (Hale's Hist. of the Com. Law, p. 14, Preface.) For a like reason, though the power of Cromwell was soon after overturned, and Charles the Second restored, the judicial decisions under the former remained unmolested on this account, and the judiciary went on as before, still looking only to the *de facto* government for the time being. Grotius virtually holds the like doctrine. (B. 1, ch. 4, sec. 20, and B. 2, ch. 13, sec. 11.) Such was the case, likewise, over most of this country, after the declaration of independence, till the acknowledgment of it by England in 1783. (3 Story's Com. on Const. §§ 214, 215.) And such is believed to have been the course in France under all her dynasties and *régimes* during the last half-century.

These conclusions are strengthened by the circumstance, that the Supreme Court of Rhode Island, organized since, under the second new constitution, has adopted this principle. In numerous instances, this court has considered itself bound to follow the decision of the State tribunals on their own constitutions and laws. (See cases in Smith *v.* Babcock, 2 Woodb. and Min.; 5 Howard, 139; Elmendorf *v.* Taylor, 10 Wheat. 159; Bank of U. States *v.* Daniel et al., 12 Peters, 32.) This, of course, relates to their validity when not overruling any defence set up under the authority of the United States. None such was set up in the trial of Dorr, and yet, after full hearing, the Supreme Court of Rhode Island decided that the old charter and its Legislature were the political powers which they were bound to respect, and the only ones legally in force at the time of this transaction; and accordingly convicted and punished the governor chosen under the new constitution for treason, as being technically committed, however pure may have been his political designs or private character. (Report of Dorr's Trial, 1844, pp. 130, 131.) The reasons for this uniform compliance by us with State decisions made before ours on their own laws and constitutions, and not appealed from, are given by Chief Justice Marshall with much clearness. It is only necessary to refer to his language in Elmendorf *v.* Taylor, (10 Wheat. 159.)

Starting, then, as we are forced to here, with several political questions arising on this record, and those settled by political tribunals in the State and General Government, and whose decisions on them we possess no constitutional authority to revise, all which, apparently, is left for us to decide is the other point,—whether the statute establishing martial law over the whole State, and under which the acts done by the defendants are sought to be justified, can be deemed constitutional.

To decide a point like this last is clearly within judicial cognizance, it being a matter of private personal authority and right, set up by the defendants under constitutions and laws, and not of political power, to act in relation to the making of the former.

Firstly, then, in order to judge properly whether this act of Assembly was constitutional, let us see what was the kind and character of the law the Assembly intended, in this instance, to establish, and under which the respondents profess to have acted.

The Assembly says: — "The State of Rhode Island and Providence Plantations is hereby placed under martial law, and the same is hereby declared to be in full force until otherwise ordered by the General Assembly, or suspended by proclamation of his Excellency the Governor of the State." Now, the words "martial law," as here used, cannot be construed in any other than their legal sense, long known and recognized in legal precedents as well as political history. (See it in 1 Hallam's Const. Hist. ch. 5, p. 258; 1 MacArthur on Courts-Martial, 33.) The Legislature evidently meant to be understood in that sense by using words of such well-settled construction, without any limit or qualification, and covering the whole State with its influence, under a supposed exigency and justification for such an unusual course. I do not understand this to be directly combated in the opinion just delivered by the Chief Justice. That they could mean no other than the ancient martial law often used before the Petition of Right, and sometimes since, is further manifest from the fact, that they not only declared "martial" law to exist over the State, but put their militia into the field to help, by means of them and such a law, to suppress the action of those denominated "insurgents," and this without any subordination to the civil power, or any efforts in conjunction and in coöperation with it. The defendants do not aver the existence of any civil precept which they were aiding civil officers to execute, but set up merely military orders under martial law. Notwithstanding this, however, some attempts have been made at another construction of this act, somewhat less offensive, by considering it a mere equivalent to the suspension of the habeas corpus, and another still to regard it as referring only to the military code used in the armies of the United States and England. But when the Legislature enacted such a system "as martial law," what right have we to say that they intended to establish something else and something entirely different? A suspension, for instance, of the writ of habeas corpus,— a thing not only unnamed by them, but wholly unlike and far short, in every view, of what they both said and did? Because they not only said, *eo nomine*, that they established "martial law," but they put in operation its principles; principles not relating merely to imprisonment, like the suspension of the habeas corpus, but forms of arrest without warrant, breaking into houses where no offenders were found, and acting exclusively under military orders, rather than civil precepts.

Had the Legislature meant merely to suspend the writ of habeas corpus, they, of course, would have said that, and nothing more. A brief examination will show, also, that they did not thus intend to put in force merely some modern military code, such as the Articles of War made by Congress, or those under the Mutiny Act in England. They do not mention either; and, what is conclusive on this, neither would cover or protect them, in applying the provisions of those laws to a person situated like the plaintiff. For nothing is better settled than that military law applies only to the military; but "martial law" is made here to apply to all. (Hough on Courts-Martial, 384, note; 27 State Trials, 625, in Theobald Wolfe Tone's case.)

The present laws for the government of the military in England, also, do not exist in the vague and general form of martial law, but are explicitly restricted to the military, and are allowed as to them only to prevent desertion and mutiny, and to preserve good discipline. (1 Bl. Com. 412; 1 MacArthur on Courts-Martial, p. 20.) So, in this country, legislation as to the military is usually confined to the General Government, where the great powers of war and peace reside. And hence, under those powers, Congress, by the act of 1806 (2 Stat. at Large, 359), has created the Articles of War, "by which the armies of the United States shall be governed," and the militia when in actual service, and only they. To show this is not the law by which *other* than those armies shall be governed, it has been found necessary, in order to include merely the drivers or artificers "in the service," and the militia after *mustered* into it, to have special statutory sections. (See articles 96 and 97.) Till mustered together, even the militia are not subject to martial law. (5 Wheat. 20; 3 Stor. Com. Const. § 120.) And whenever an attempt is made to embrace others in its operation, not belonging to the military or militia, nor having ever agreed to the rules of the service, well may they say, we have not entered into such bonds,—*in hæc vinculæ, non veni.* (2 Hen. Bl. 99; 1 Bl. Com. 408, 414; 1 D. & E. 493, 550, 784; 27 State Trials, 625.) Well may they exclaim, as in Magna Charta, that "no freeman shall be taken or imprisoned but by the lawful judgment of his equals, or by the law of the land." There is no pretence that this plaintiff, the person attempted to be arrested by the violence exercised here, was a soldier or militia-man then mustered into the service of the United States, or of Rhode Island, or subject by its laws to be so employed, or on that account sought to be seized. He could not, therefore, in this view of the case, be arrested under this limited and different kind of military law, nor houses be broken into for that purpose and by that authority.

So it is a settled principle even in England, that, "under the British constitution, the military law does in no respect either supersede or interfere with the civil law of the realm," and that "the former is in general subordinate to the latter" (Tytler on Military Law, 365); while "martial law" over-rides them all. The Articles of War, likewise, are not only authorized by permanent rather than temporary legislation, but they are prepared by or under it with punishments and rules before promulgated, and known and assented to by those few who are subject to them, as operating under established legal principles and the customary military law of modern times. (1 East, 306, 313; Pain *v.* Willard, 12 Wheat. 539, and also 19; 1 MacArthur, Courts-Martial, 13 and 215.) They are also definite in the extent of authority under them as to subject-matter as well as persons, as they regulate and restrain within more safe limits the jurisdiction to be used, and recognize and respect the civil rights of those not subject to it, and even of those who are, in all other matters than what are military and placed under military cognizance. (2 Stephen on Laws of Eng. 602; 9 Bac. Abr., *Soldier*, F; Tytler on Military Law, 119.) And as a further proof how rigidly the civil power requires the military to confine even the modified code martial to the military, and to what are strictly military matters, it cannot, without liability to a private suit in the judicial tribunals, be exercised on a soldier himself for a cause not military, or over which the officer had no right to order him; as, for example, to attend school instruction, or pay an assessment towards it out of his wages. (4 Taunt. 67; 4 Maule & Selw. 400; 2 Hen. Bl. 103, 537; 3 Cranch, 337; 7 Johns. 96.)

The prosecution of Governor Wall, in England, for causing, when he was in military command, a soldier to be seized and flogged so that he died, for an imputed offence not clearly military, and by a pretended court-martial without a full trial, and executing Wall for the offence after a lapse of twenty years, illustrate how jealously the exercise of any martial power is watched in England, though in the army itself, and on its own members. (See Annual Register for 1802, p. 569; 28 State Trials, p. 52, Howell's ed.)

How different in its essence and forms, as well as subjects, from the Articles of War was the "martial law" established here over the whole people of Rhode Island, may be seen by adverting to its character for a moment, as described in judicial as well as political history. It exposed the whole population not only to be seized without warrant or oath, and their houses broken open and rifled, and this where the municipal law and its officers and courts remained undisturbed and able to punish all offences, but to send prisoners, thus summarily arrested in a civil strife, to all the harsh pains and penalties of courts-martial or extraordinary commissions, and for all kinds of supposed offences. By it, every citizen, instead of reposing under the shield of known and fixed laws as to his liberty, property and life, exists with a rope round his neck, subject to be hung up by a military despot at the next lamp-post, under the sentence of some drum-head court-martial. (See Simmons' Pract. of Courts-Martial, 40.) See such a trial in Hough on Courts-Martial, 383, where the victim on the spot was "blown away by a gun," "neither time, place, nor persons considered." As an illustration how the passage of such a law may be abused, Queen Mary put it in force in 1558, by proclamation merely, and declared "that whosoever had in his possession any heretical, treasonable, or seditious *books*, and did not presently burn them, without reading them or showing them to any other person, should be esteemed a *rebel*, and without any further delay be executed by the *martial law*." (Tytler on Military Law, p. 50, ch. 1, sec. 1.)

For convincing reasons like these, in every country which makes any claim to political or civil liberty, "martial law," as here attempted, and as once practised in England against her own people, has been expressly forbidden there for near two centuries, as well as by the principles of every other free constitutional government. (1 Hallam's Const. Hist. 420.) And it would be not a little extraordinary, if the spirit of our institutions, both state and national, was not much stronger than in England against the unlimited exercise of martial law over a whole people, whether attempted by any chief magistrate or even by a Legislature.

It is true, and fortunate that it is true, the consequent actual evil in this instance from this declaration of martial law was smaller than might have been naturally anticipated. But we must be thankful for this, not to the harmless character of the law itself, but rather to an inability to arrest many, or from the small opposition in arms, and its short continuance, or from the deep jealousy and rooted dislike generally in this country to any approach to the reign of a mere military despotism. Unfortunately, the Legislature had probably heard of this measure in history, and even at our Revolution, as used by some of the British generals against those considered rebels; and, in the confusion and hurry of the crisis, seem to have rushed into it suddenly, and, I fear, without a due regard to private rights, or their own constitutional powers, or the supervisory authority of the General Government over wars and rebellions.

Having ascertained the kind and character of the martial law established by this act of Assembly in Rhode Island, we ask next, how, under the general principles of American jurisprudence in modern times, such a law can properly exist, or be judicially upheld. A brief retrospect of the gradual but decisive repudiation of it in England will exhibit many of the reasons why such a law cannot be rightfully tolerated anywhere in this country.

One object of parliamentary inquiry, as early as 1620, was to check the abuse of martial law by the king which had prevailed before. (Tytler on Military Law, 502.) The Petition of Right, in the first year of Charles the First, reprobated all such arbitrary proceedings in the just terms and in the terse language of that great patriot as well as judge, Sir Edward Coke, and prayed they might be stopped and never repeated. To this the king wisely replied,—"*Soit droit fait come est desire*,—Let right be done as desired." (Petition of Right, in Statutes at Large, 1 Charles 1.) Putting it in force by the king alone was not only restrained by the Petition of Right early in the seventeenth century, but virtually denied as lawful by the Declaration of Rights in 1688. (Tytler on Military Law, 307.) Hallam, therefore, in his Constitutional History, p. 420, declares that its use by "the commissions to try military offenders by martial law was a procedure necessary within certain limits to the discipline of an army, but unwarranted by the constitution of this country." Indeed, a distinguished English judge has since said, that "martial law," as of old, now "does not exist in England at all," "was contrary to the constitution, and has been for a century totally exploded." (Grant *v.* Gould, 2 Hen. Bl. 69; 1 Hale, P. C. 346; Hale, Com. Law, ch. 2, p. 36; 1 MacArthur, 55.) This is broad enough, and is correct as to the community generally in both war and peace. No question can exist as to the correctness of this doctrine in time of peace. The Mutiny Act itself, for the government of the army, in 36 Geo. 3, ch. 24, sec. 1, begins by reciting, "Whereas, no man can be forejudged of life or limb, or subjected in time of peace to any punishment within the realm by martial law." (Simmons' Pract. of Courts-Martial, 38.)

Lord Coke says, in 3 Inst. 52: — "If a lieutenant, or other that hath commission of martial authority in time of peace, hang or otherwise execute any man by color of martial law, this is murder." "Thom. Count de Lancaster, being taken *in open insurrection*, was, by judgment of martial law, put to death," and this, though during an insurrection, was adjudged to be murder, because done in time of peace, and while the courts of law were open. (1 Hallam's Const. Hist. 260.) The very first Mutiny Act, therefore, under William the Third, was cautious to exonerate all subjects except the military from any punishment by martial law. (Tytler on Military Law, 19, note.) In this manner it has become gradually established in England, that in peace the occurrence of civil strife does not justify individuals, or the military, or the king, in using martial law over the people.

It appears, also, that nobody has dared to exercise it, in war or peace, on the community at large, in England, for the last century and a half, unless specially enacted by Parliament, in some great exigency and under various restrictions, and then under the theory, not that it is consistent with bills of rights and constitutions, but that Parliament is omnipotent, and for sufficient cause may over-ride and trample on them all temporarily.

After the civil authorities have become prostrated in particular places, and the din of arms has reached the most advanced stages of intestine commotions, a Parliament which alone furnishes the means of war, — a Parliament unlimited in its powers, — has, *in extremis*, on two or three occasions, ventured on martial law beyond the military; but it has usually confined it to the particular places thus situated, limited it to the continuance of such resistance, and embraced in its scope only those actually in arms. Thus the "Insurrection Act" of November, 1796, for Ireland, passed by the Parliament of England, extended only to let magistrates put people "out of the king's peace," and subject to military arrest, under certain circumstances. Even then, though authorized by Parliament, like the General Government here, and not a State, it is through the means of the civil magistrate, and a clause of indemnity goes with it against prosecutions in the "king's ordinary courts of law." (Annual Register, p. 173, for A. D. 1798; 1 MacArthur, Courts-Martial, 34.) See also the cases of the invasions by the Pretender, in 1715 and 1745, and of the Irish rebellion in 1798. (Tytler on Military Law, 48, 49, 369, 370, App. No. 6, p. 402, the act passed by the Irish Parl.; Simmons' Practice of Courts-Martial, App. 633.) When speaking of the absence of other and sound precedents to justify such martial law in modern times here, I am aware that something of the kind may have been attempted in some of the doings of the British colonial governors towards this country at the Revolution.

In the Annual Register for 1775, p. 133, June 12th, it may be seen that General Gage issued his proclamation, pardoning all who would submit, except Samuel Adams and John Hancock, and further declaring, "that, as a stop was put to the due course of justice, *martial law* should take place till the laws were restored to their due efficacy."

Though the engagements at Lexington and Concord happened on the 19th of April, 1775, though Parliament had in February previous declared the colonies to be in a state of rebellion (Ibid. p. 247), and though thousands of militia had assembled near Bunker Hill before the 12th of June, — no martial law had been established by Parliament, and not till that day did General Gage, alone and unconstitutionally, undertake, in the language of our fathers, to "supersede the course of the common law, and, instead thereof, to publish and order the use and exercise of martial law." (Ibid. p. 261; Journal of Old Cong. 147, a declaration on 6th July, 1775, drawn up by J. Dickinson.)

Another of these outrages was by Lord Dunmore, in Virginia, November 7th, 1775, not only declaring all the slaves of rebels free, but "declaring martial law to be enforced throughout this colony." (Annual Register for 1775, p. 28; 4 American Archives, 74.) This was, however, justly denounced by the Virginia Assembly as an "assumed power, which the king himself cannot exercise," as it "annuls the law of the land and introduces the most execrable of all systems, martial law." (4 American Archives, 87.) It was a return to the unbridled despotism of the Tudors, which, as already shown, one to two hundred years before, had been accustomed, in peace as well as war, to try not only soldiers under it, but others, and by courts-martial rather than civil tribunals, and by no settled laws instead of the municipal code, and for civil offences no less than military ones. (2 Hen. Bl. 85; 3 Instit. 52; Stat. at Large, 1 Charles 1; Tytler on Military Law, *passim.*)

Having thus seen that "martial law" like this, ranging over a whole people and State, was not by our fathers considered proper at all in peace or during civil strife, and that, in the country from which we derive most of our jurisprudence, the king has long been forbidden to put it in force in war or peace, and that Parliament never, in the most extreme cases of rebellion, allows it, except as being sovereign and unlimited in power, and under peculiar restrictions, the next inquiry is, whether the Legislature of Rhode Island could, looking to her peculiar situation as to a constitution, rightfully establish such a law, under the circumstances existing there in 1842; and, to meet this question broadly, whether she could do it, regarding those circumstances, first, as constituting peace, and next, as amounting to war. In examining this, I shall refrain from discussing the points agitated at the bar, whether the old charter under which it took place was a wise one for a republic, or whether the acts of the Legislature rendering it so highly penal to resort to peaceful measures to form or put into operation a new constitution without their consent, and establishing "martial law" to suppress them, were characterized by the humanity and the civilization of the present age towards their own fellow-citizens. But I shall merely inquire, first, whether it was within the constitutional power of that Legislature to pass such a law as this during peace, or, in other words, before any lawful and competent declaration of war; leaving all questions of mere expediency, as belonging to the States themselves rather than the judiciary, and being one of the last persons to treat any of them with disrespect, or attempt to rob them of any legitimate power.

At the outset, it is to be remembered that, if Parliament now exercises such a power occasionally, it is only under various limitations and restrictions, not attended to in this case, and only because the power of Parliament is by the English constitution considered as unlimited or omnipotent. But here legislative bodies, no less than the executive and judiciary, are usually not regarded as omnipotent. They are in this country now limited in their powers, and placed under strong prohibitions and checks. (8 Wheat. 88; 3 Smedes & Marshall, 673.)

This court has declared that "the Legislatures are the creatures of the constitution. They owe their existence to the constitution. They derive their powers from the constitution. It is their commission; and therefore all their acts must be conformable to it, or else they will be void." (Vanhorne's Lessee *v.* Dorrance, 2 Dall. 308; Vattel, ch. 3, sec. 34.) In most of our Legislatures, also, as in Rhode Island in A. D. 1798, by a fundamental law, there has been incorporated into their constitutions prohibitions to make searches for papers or persons without a due warrant, and to try for offences except by indictment, unless in cases arising in the army or navy or militia themselves.

The genius of our liberties holds in abhorrence all irregular inroads upon the dwelling-houses and persons of the citizen, and with a wise jealousy regards them as sacred, except when assailed in the established and allowed forms of municipal law. Three of the amendments to the constitution of the United States were adopted, under such influences, to guard against abuses of power in those modes by the General Government, and evidently to restrict even a modified "martial law" to cases happening among military men, or the militia when in actual service. For one of them, amendment fourth, expressly provides, that "the right of the people to be secured in their persons, houses, papers, and effects, against unreasonable searches and seizures, shall not be violated; and no warrants shall issue but upon probable cause, supported by oath or affirmation, and particularly describing the place to be searched, and the persons or things to be seized." The others are amendments third and fifth. And who could hold for a moment, when the writ of habeas corpus cannot be suspended by the Legislature itself, either in the General Government or most of the States, without an express constitutional permission, that all other writs and laws could be suspended, and martial law substituted for them over the whole State or country, without any express constitutional license to that effect, in any emergency? Much more is this last improbable, when even the mitigated measure, the suspension of the writ of habeas corpus, has never yet been found proper by Congress, and, it is believed, by neither of the States, since the federal constitution was adopted. (3 Story's Com. on Const. § 1325.)

Again, the act of June 24th, 1842, as an act of legislation by Rhode Island, was virtually forbidden by the express declaration of principles made by the Rhode Island Assembly in 1798, and also by the views expressed through the delegates of their people upon adopting the federal constitution, June 16th, 1790. These may be seen in 1 Elliott's Deb. 370, declaring, in so many words, "that every person has a right to be secure from all unreasonable searches and seizures of his person, his papers, or his property," and warrants to search without oath, and seizures by general warrant, are "oppressive," and "ought not to be granted."

But, as these views were expressed in connection with the constitution of the General Government, though avowed to be the principles of her people generally, and as the doings in 1798 were in the form of a law, and not a constitution, it was subject to suspension or repeal; and hence it will be necessary to look into the charter to Rhode Island of 1663, her only State constitution till 1842, to see if there be any limitation in that to legislation like this, establishing martial law.

So far from that charter, royal as it was in origin, permitting an unlimited authority in the Legislature, it will be found expressly to forbid any laws "contrary and repugnant unto" "the laws of this our realm of England," and to require them to be, "as near as may be, agreeable" to those laws. (See Document, p. 12.)

This, so far from countenancing the establishment of martial law in Rhode Island, contrary to the Petition of Right in England and her Bill of Rights, regulated it by the same restrictions "as near as may be." Nor did our Revolution of A. D. 1776 remove that restraint, so far as respects what was then the body of English laws. For, although Rhode Island chose to retain that charter with this restriction after the Revolution, and made no new constitution with other limitations till 1842 or 1843, yet probably "the laws of England" forbidden to be violated by her Legislature must be considered such as existed when the charter was granted in 1663, and as continued down to 1776. After that, her control over this country *de jure* ceasing, a conformity to any new laws made would not be required. But, retaining the charter as the sole guide and limit to her Legislature until she formed a new constitution, it seems clear that her Legislature had no right, on the 25th of June, 1842, to put the whole State under martial law by any act of Parliament in force in England in 1663 or in 1776, because none such was then in force there, nor by any clause whatever in her charter, as will soon be shown, nor by any usages in her history, nor by any principles which belong to constitutional governments or the security of public liberty.

To remove all doubt on this subject, the charter does expressly allow "martial law" in one way and case to be declared, and thus impliedly forbids it in any other. *Expressio unius est exclusio alterius.* But so far from the martial law allowed by it being by permission of the Legislature and over the whole State, it was to be declared only in war waged against a public enemy, and then by the "military officer" appointed to command the troops so engaged; and then not over their whole territory and all persons and cases, but he was to "use and exercise the law martial in such cases only as occasion shall necessarily require." (P. 15.)

Even this power, thus limited, as before shown, related to the troops of the State, and those liable to serve among them in an exigency, and when in arms against an enemy. They did not touch opponents, over whom they could exercise only the municipal laws if non-combatants, and only the law of nations and belligerent rights when in the field, and after war or rebellion is recognized as existing by the proper authorities. Again, it would be extraordinary indeed, if in England the king himself is restrained by Magna Charta, and by the Petition as well as Declaration of Rights, binding him to these limits against martial law since the revolution of 1688 (4 Bl. Com. 440; 2 Peters, 656), and yet he could grant a charter which should exonerate others from the obligations of Magna Charta and the general laws of the kingdom, or that they could be exonerated under it as to the power of legislation, and do what is against the whole body of English laws since the end of the sixteenth century, and what Parliament itself, in its omnipotence and freedom from restrictions, has never, in the highest emergencies, thought it proper to do without numerous limitations, regulations and indemnities, as before explained.

Beside this, it may well be doubted whether, in the nature of the legislative power in this country, it can be considered as anywhere rightfully authorized, any more than the executive, to suspend or abolish the whole securities of person and property at its pleasure; and whether, since the Petition of Right was granted, it has not been considered as unwarrantable for any British or American legislative body, not omnipotent in theory like Parliament, to establish in a whole country an unlimited reign of martial law over its whole population; and whether to do this is not breaking up the foundations of all sound municipal rule, no less than social order, and restoring the reign of the strongest, and making mere physical force the test of right.

All our social usages and political education, as well as our constitutional checks, are the other way. It would be alarming enough to sanction here an unlimited power, exercised either by legislatures, or the executive, or courts, when all our governments are themselves governments of limitations and checks, and of fixed and known laws, and the people a race above all others jealous of encroachments by those in power. And it is far better that those persons should be without the protection of the ordinary laws of the land who disregard them in an emergency, and should look to a grateful country for indemnity and pardon, than to allow, beforehand, the whole frame of jurisprudence to be overturned, and everything placed at the mercy of the bayonet.

No tribunal or department in our system of governments ever can be lawfully authorized to dispense with the laws, like some of the tyrannical Stuarts, or to repeal, or abolish, or suspend the whole body of them ; or, in other words, appoint an unrestrained military dictator at the head of armed men.

Whatever stretches of such power may be ventured on in great crises, they cannot be upheld by the laws, as they prostrate the laws and ride triumphant over and beyond them, however the Assembly of Rhode Island, under the exigency, may have hastily supposed that such a measure in this instance was constitutional. It is but a branch of the omnipotence claimed by Parliament to pass bills of attainder, belonging to the same dangerous and arbitrary family with martial law. But even those have ceased to succeed in England under the lights of the nineteenth century, and are expressly forbidden by the federal constitution; and neither ought ever to disgrace the records of any free government. Such laws (and martial law is only still baser and more intolerable than bills of attainder) Mr. Madison denounces, as "contrary to the first principles of the social compact, and to every principle of sound legislation." (Federalist, No. 44.)

In short, then, there was nothing peculiar in the condition of Rhode Island as to a constitution in 1842, which justified her Legislature in peace, more than the Legislature of any other State, to declare martial law over her whole people; but there was much in her ancient charter, as well as in the plainest principles of constitutional liberty, to forbid it. Considering this, then, and that some cases already cited show that domestic violence is still to be regarded, not as a state of war, giving belligerent rights, but as conferring only the powers of peace in a State, through its civil authorities, aided by its militia, till the General Government interferes and recognizes the contest as a war, this branch of our inquiries as to martial law would end here, upon my view of the pleadings, because the defendants justify under that law, and because the State Legislature alone possessed no constitutional authority to establish martial law, of this kind and to this extent, over her people generally, whether in peace or civil strife. But some of the members of this court seem to consider the pleadings broad enough to cover the justification, under some rights of war, independent of the act of the Assembly, or, as the opinion just read by the Chief Justice seems to imply, under the supposed authority of the State, in case of domestic insurrection like this, to adopt an act of martial law over its whole people, or any war measure deemed necessary by its Legislature for the public safety.

It looks, certainly, like pretty bold doctrine in a constitutional government, that, even in time of legitimate war, the Legislature can properly suspend or abolish all constitutional restrictions, as martial law does, and lay all the personal and political rights of the people at their feet. But bolder still is it to justify a claim to this tremendous power in any State, or in any of its officers, on the occurrence merely of some domestic violence.

We have already shown that, in this last event, such a claim is entirely untenable on general principles, or by the old charter of Rhode Island, and was denounced as unlawful by our fathers, when attempted against them at the Revolution, and has in England been punished as murder when exercised to kill one, though taken in open arms in an insurrection. (See cases, *ante.*)

The judgment which the court has pronounced in this case seems to me, also, to be rested, not on any right of this kind in peace, but, on the contrary, to uphold the act of martial law only as a war measure. But the grounds have not been shown, to my conviction, for supposing that war and war measures, and the rights of war, existed legally in Rhode Island when this act passed. And, finally, it seems to me that the insurrection then existing was not in a stage of progress which would justify any mere belligerent rights; but if any, it was such rights in the General Government, and not in the Legislature of the State, obtained, too, by mere implication, and, as to so formidable a measure as this, operating so loosely and recklessly over all its own citizens.

It is admitted that no war had duly been declared to exist, either by Rhode Island or the United States, at the time this war measure was adopted, or when the trespass under it was committed. Yet, had either wished to exercise any war powers, they would have been legalized in our political system, not by Rhode Island, but the General Government. (Constit. Art. 1, sec. 8; 3 Story's Com. on Constit. §§ 215, 217; 1 Bl. Com. by Tucker, App. p. 270.)

It may not be useless to refresh our minds a little on this subject. The constitution expressly provides that "the Congress shall have power to declare war." (Art. 1, sec. 8.) This is not the States, nor the President, and much less the Legislature of a State. Nor is it foreign war alone that Congress is to declare, but "war," — war of any kind existing legitimately or according to the law of nations. Because Congress alone, and not the States, is invested with power to use the great means for all wars,— "to raise and support armies," "to provide and maintain a navy," "to provide for calling forth the militia to execute the laws of the Union, suppress insurrections, and repel invasions," and "to provide for organizing, arming, and disciplining the militia." The largest powers of taxation, too, were conferred on Congress at the same time, and in part for this cause, with authority to borrow money on the credit of the Union, and to dispose of the public lands. But the States, deprived of these means, were at the same time properly relieved from the duty of carrying on war themselves, civil or foreign, because they were not required to incur expenses to suppress even "domestic violence," or "insurrections," or "rebellions." By a provision, (sec. 4, art. 3), "the United States shall guarantee to every State in this Union a republican form of government, and shall protect each of them against invasion, and, on application of the Legislature (or of the executive when the Legislature cannot be convened), against domestic violence." This exclusiveness of the war power in Congress in all cases, domestic or foreign, is confirmed, too, by another authority given to Congress, not only to organize and discipline the militia, no less than to have regular armies and navies, but "to provide for calling forth the militia" "to suppress insurrections." (Sec. 8, art. 1.) And, lest it might be argued that this power to declare war and raise troops and navies was not exclusive in the General Government, as is the case with some other grants to it deemed concurrent, about weights and measures, bankrupt laws, &c. (see cases cited in Boston *v.* Norris, 7 Howard, 283), the reasons for this grant as to war, and an express prohibition on the States as to it, both show the power to be exclusive in Congress. Thus, the reasons as to the power itself are cogent for having it exclusive only in one body, in order to prevent the numerous and sudden hostilities and bloody outbreaks in which the country might be involved, with their vast expenses, if thirty States could each declare and wage war under its own impulses. (1 Bl. Com. by Tucker, App. p. 270.) And, to remove all doubt on that point, the constitution proceeded expressly to provide, in another clause, a prohibition on the States (sec. 10, art. 1),—that "no State shall, without the consent of Congress," "keep troops or ships of war in time of peace," "or engage in war, unless actually invaded, or in such imminent danger as will not admit of delay."

This accorded with the sixth and ninth articles of the old confederation, which vested in it exclusively the power to declare war, and took the power of waging it from the States, unless in case of sudden attacks by Indians or pirates, or unless actually invaded by enemies, or in such imminent danger of it that time cannot be had to consult Congress. (1 Laws of U. S. 15, 16, Bioren's ed.)

No concurrent or subordinate power is, therefore, left to the States on this subject, except by occasional and special consent of Congress, which is not pretended to have been given to Rhode Island; or unless "actually invaded" by some enemy, which is not pretended here; or unless "in such imminent danger as will not admit of delay," which manifestly refers to danger from a foreign enemy threatening invasion, or from Indians and pirates. Another circumstance to prove this, beside the language itself being used in connection with foreign invasions and the danger of them, and not insurrections, is the like clauses in the old confederation being thus restricted. One of those (article 9th) declares that "the United States in Congress assembled shall have the *sole and exclusive* right and power of determining on peace and war, except in the cases mentioned in the sixth article." (1 Laws of U. S. 16, Bioren's ed.) And the sixth article, after providing against foreign embassies, troops, and vessels of war by a State, adds: — "No State shall engage in any war unless such State be actually invaded by enemies, or shall have received certain advice of a resolution being formed by some nation of Indians to invade such State, and the danger is so imminent as not to admit of delay till the United States in Congress assembled can be consulted." Nor, by an additional provision, could a State grant commissions to ships of war or letters of marque, "except it be after a declaration of war by the United States," and only against the kingdom or state against whom the war had been declared, "unless such State be infested by pirates, in which case vessels of war may be fitted for that occasion," &c. (1 Laws of U. S. 15, Bioren's ed.)

It is impossible to mistake the intention in these provisions, and to doubt that substantially the same intention was embodied by restrictions in the present constitution, similar in terms, though not entering into so great details. What is, however, decisive as to this intent in the constitution, is the action on it by the second Congress, only a few years after, and of which some were members who aided in framing the constitution itself. That Congress, May 2d, 1792, authorized force to be used by the President to aid in repelling the invasions here referred to in the constitution, and they are described in so many words, as "shall be invaded, or be in imminent danger of invasion from any foreign nation or Indian tribe." (1 Stat. at Large, 264.) So again in the act of Feb. 28, 1795 (1 Stat. at Large, 424), and still further sustaining this view, the power to aid in suppressing insurrections in a State is given in a separate section, showing that they were not deemed the invasions and the "imminent danger" of them expressed in different sections of the act of Congress as well as of the constitution. If, however, this "imminent danger" could, by any stretch of construction, be considered broader, it did not exist here so as to prevent "delay" in applying to the President first;

because, in truth, before martial law was declared, time had existed to make application to Congress and the President, and both had declined to use greater force, or to declare war, and the judicial tribunals of the State were still unmolested in their course. Besides this, at the time of the trespass complained of here, the few troops which had before taken up arms for the new constitution had been disbanded, and all further violence disclaimed.

Whoever, too, would justify himself under an exception in a law or constitution, must set it up and bring his case within it, neither of which is attempted here as to this exception; but the justification is, on the contrary, under this head, placed by the defendant and the court on the existence of war, and rights consequent on its existence.

Some mistake has arisen here, probably, from not adverting to the circumstance that Congress alone can declare war, and that all other conditions of violence are regarded by the constitution as but ordinary cases of private outrage, to be punished by prosecutions in the courts; or as insurrections, rebellions, or domestic violence, to be put down by the civil authorities, aided by the militia, or, when these prove incompetent, by the General Government, when appealed to by a State for aid, and matters appear to the General Government to have reached the extreme stage, requiring more force to sustain the civil tribunals of a State, or requiring a declaration of war, and the exercise of all its extraordinary rights. Of these last, when applied to as here, and the danger has not been so imminent as to prevent an application, the General Government must be the judge, and the General Government is responsible for the consequences. And when it is asked, what shall a State do, if the General Government, when applied to, refrains to declare war till a domestic force becomes very formidable, I reply, exert all her civil power through her judiciary and executive, and if these fail, sustain them by her militia, coöperating, and not independent, and if these fail, it is quite certain that the General Government will never hesitate to strengthen the arm of the State when too feeble in either of these modes to preserve public order. And how seldom this will be required of the General Government, or by means of war, may be seen by our unspotted, unbroken experience of this kind, as to the States, for half a century, and by the obvious facts, that no occasion can scarcely ever, in future, arise for such interference, when the violence, at the utmost, must usually be from a minority of one State, and in the face of the larger power of the majority within it, and of the coöperation, if need be, of the whole of the rest of the Union.

Carry these constitutional provisions with us, and the facts which have existed, that there had been no war declared by Congress, no actual invasion of the State by a foreign enemy, no imminent danger of it, no emergency of any kind, which prevented time or delay to apply to the General Government, and remember that, in this stage of things, Congress omitted or declined to do anything, and that the President also declined to consider a civil violence or insurrection as existing so as to justify his ordering out troops to suppress it. The State, then, in and of itself, declared martial law, and the defendants attempted to enforce it. In such a condition of things, I am not prepared to say that the authorities of a State alone can exercise the rights of war against their own citizens; persons, too, who, it is to be remembered, were for many purposes at the same time under the laws and protection of the General Government. On the contrary, it seems very obvious, as before suggested, that in periods of civil commotion, the first and wisest and only legal measure to test the rights of parties and sustain the public peace under threatened violence, is to appeal to the laws and the judicial tribunals. When these are obstructed or over-awed, the militia is next to be ordered out, but only to strengthen the civil power in enforcing its processes and upholding the laws. Then, in extreme cases, another assistance is resorted to, in the suspension of the writ of habeas corpus. And, finally, if actual force, exercised in the field against those in battle array, and not able to be subdued in any other manner, becomes necessary, as *quasi* war, whether against a foreign foe or rebels, it must first, as to the former, be declared by Congress, or recognized and allowed by it as to the latter, under the duty of the United States "to protect each of them against invasion" and "against domestic violence." (Art. 4, sec. 4.) When this is not done in a particular case by Congress, if then in session, it is done by the President, in conformity to the constitution (Art. 1, sec. 8), and the act of Congress of February 28, 1795 (1 Stat. at Large, 424), "to provide for calling forth the militia to execute the laws of the Union, suppress insurrections, and repel invasions."

Under all these circumstances, then, to imply a power like this declaration of martial law over a State as still lawfully existing in its Legislature, would be to imply what is forbidden by all constitutional checks, forbidden by all the usages of free governments, forbidden by an exclusive grant of the war power to Congress, forbidden by the fact that there were no exceptions or exigencies existing here which could justify it, and, in short, forbidden by the absence of any necessity in our system for a measure so dangerous and unreasonable, unless in some great extremity, if at all, by the General Government, which alone holds the issues of war and the power and means of waging it.

Under these views and restrictions, the States have succeeded well, thus far,—over half a century,—in suppressing domestic violence in other ways than by martial law. The State courts, with the aid of the militia, as in Shays' rebellion and the Western insurrection, could, for aught which appears, by help of the *posse comitatus*, or at least by that militia, have in this case dispersed all opposition. They did this in both of those instances, so much more formidable in numbers, and made no resort to martial law. (See before, and Minot's History, 163, 178.) In one of them, not even the writ of habeas corpus was suspended by the State, and never by the United States, though empowered to do that in dangerous emergencies. (2 Kent's Com. 24; 2 Story's Com. on Const. § 1335.) But if civil process, aided by the militia, should fail to quell an insurrection against State laws, which has never yet happened in our history, then an appeal lies, and is appropriate, to the General Government for additional force, before a resort can be had to supposed belligerent rights, much less to any exploded and unconstitutional extremes of martial law.

As before shown, such an appeal had been made here, but not complied with, because, I presume, the civil authority of the State, assisted by its own militia, did not appear to have failed to overcome the disturbance. How, then, let me ask, had the State here become possessed of any belligerent rights? how could it in any way be possessed of them, at the time of the passage of the act declaring martial law, or even at the time of the trespass complained of? I am unable to discover. Congress, on this occasion, was in session, ready to act when proper and as proper, and it alone could, by the constitution, declare war, or, under the act of May 2d, 1792, allow the militia from an adjoining State to be called out. (1 Stat. at Large, 264.) But Congress declared no war, and conferred no rights of war. The act of February 28th, 1795 (1 Stat. at Large, 424), seems to be made broader as to the power of the President over *all* the militia, and, indeed, over the regular troops, to assist on such an occasion, by another act of March 3d, 1807. (2 Stat. at Large, 443.) But the President, also, did nothing to cause or give belligerent rights to the State. He might, perhaps, have conferred some such rights on the militia, had he called them out, under the consent of Congress; but it would be unreasonable, if not absurd, to argue that the President, rather than Congress, was thus empowered to declare war, or that Congress meant to construe such insurrections, and the means used to suppress them, as wars; else Congress itself should in each case pronounce them so, and not intrust so dangerous a measure to mere executive discretion. But he issued no orders or proclamations. Had he done so, and marched troops, though the action of the executive under the standing law is not waging war, yet, I concede, it is attempting to suppress domestic violence by force of arms, and in doing it, the President may possess and exert some belligerent rights in some extreme stages of armed opposition. It is he, however, and those acting under his orders, who, it will be seen, may possibly then, at times, use some such rights, and not the State or its organs. Nor is it till after the President has interfered that such rights arise, and then they arise under the decision and laws and proceedings of the General Government. Then the organs of that government have come to the conclusion that the exercise of force independent of the civil and State authorities has become necessary. (Federalist, No. 29.) The President has been considered the paramount and final judge as to this, whether in invasion or rebellion, and not the governors or Legislatures of States. This was fully settled during the war of 1812 with England. (3 Story's Com. on Const. § 1206; 11 Johns. 150.) He may then issue his proclamation for those in insurrection to disperse, and, if not dispersing, he may afterwards call out the militia to aid in effecting it. (Martin *v.* Mott, 12 Wheat. 30.) But not till then do any belligerent rights exist against those even in arms, and then only by or under him. It is a singular coincidence, that, in England, it is held to be not "lawful" for the chief magistrate to order out the militia in case of "rebellion and insurrection," without "the occasion being first communicated to Parliament, if sitting, and, if not sitting, published by proclamation." (1 MacArthur, 28; 12 Statutes at Large, 432, 16 George 3, ch. 3; 8 Stat. at Large, 634, sec. 116.) And here, under the act of 1793, the President himself could not call out the militia from another State to assist, without consulting Congress, if in session, much less could he declare war. (1 Stat. at Large, 264, sec. 2.)

When the President issues his orders to assemble the militia to aid in sustaining the civil authorities of the State to enforce the laws, or to suppress actual array and violence by counter force, obedience to those orders by the militia then undoubtedly becomes a military duty. (12 Wheat. 31.) So in England. (8 Stat. at Large, sec. 116; 11 Johns. 150; 4 Burrows, 2472; 12 Johns. 257.) And a refusal to obey such a military summons may be punished in due form, without doubt, by a court-martial. (Houston *v.* Moore, 5 Wheat. 1, 20, 35, 37; 3 Story's Com. on Const. § 120.) When such troops, called out by the General Government, are in the field on such an occasion, what they may lawfully do to others, who are in opposition, and do it by any mere belligerent rights, is a very different question. For now I am examining only whether any belligerent rights before this even existed, on the part of the State, as matters then stood, commensurate with this strong measure of putting martial law in force over the whole State. The precedents, as well as the sound reasons and principles just adverted to, are all, in my view, the other way.

Under our present constitution, the first, if not nearest, precedent in history as to the course proper to be followed in any State insurrection is Shays' rebellion in Massachusetts. Having occurred in 1787, before the formation of the federal constitution, and having been suppressed by the State alone under its own independent authority (Minot's History of Shays' Insurrection, p. 95), it was untrammelled by any of the provisions now existing about war and insurrections in that constitution. But the course pursued on that occasion is full of instruction and proof as to what was deemed the legal use of the militia by the State, when thus called out, under the old confederation, and the extent of the rights of force incident to a State on a rebellion within its limits. We have before shown that the provisions in the old confederation as to war were much the same in substance as in the present constitution. Now, in Shays' rebellion the resort was not first had at all to the military, but to civil power, till the courts themselves were obstructed and put in jeopardy. And when the militia were finally called out, the whole State, or any part of it, was not put under martial law. The writ of habeas corpus was merely suspended for a limited time, and the military ordered to aid in making arrests under warrants, and not by military orders, as here. They were directed to protect civil officers in executing their duty, and nothing more, unless against persons when actually in the field obstructing them. (Ibid. 101.)

The language of Governor Bowdoin's orders to Major-General Lincoln, January 19th, 1787, shows the commendable caution deemed legal on such an occasion: — "Consider yourself in all your military offensive operations constantly as under the direction of the civil officer, saving where any armed force shall appear and oppose your marching to execute these orders."

This gives no countenance to the course pursued on this occasion, even had it been attempted to be justified in the pleadings as a right of war, though in a domestic insurrection, and not yet recognized as existing so as to require countenance and assistance through the interposition of force by the General Government. Even General Gage did not, though illegally, venture to declare martial law in 1775 till the fact occurred, as he averred, that the municipal laws could not be executed. Much less was it unlikely here that these laws could not have been executed by the civil power, or at least by that assisted by the militia, when the judges of the Supreme Court of Rhode Island had been appointed their own judges, and been approved by those who were considered in an insurrectionary condition.

In substantial accordance with these views was, likewise, the conduct of the General Government in the insurrection against its own laws in the only other case of rebellion of much note, except the controverted one of Burr's, in our national history. It was in Western Pennsylvania, in 1793, and where the rebellion, or violent resistance, and even treason, as adjudged by the courts of law in The United States *v.* The Insurgents of Pennsylvania (2 Dallas, 335), were committing against the government of the United States.

So far, however, from martial law having then been deemed proper or competent to be declared by Congress, and enforced anywhere, or even the writ of habeas corpus suspended, the troops were called out expressly to coöperate with the civil authorities, these having proved insufficient. (Findley's Hist., App. 316, 317.) But that of itself did not seem to be considered as *per se* amounting to war, or as justifying war measures. The government, therefore, neither declared war, nor waged it without that declaration, but did what seems most humane and fit on such occasions, till greater resistance and bloodshed might render war measures expedient; that is, marched the troops expressly with a view only to "cause the laws to be duly executed."

Nor was this done till Judge Peters, who officiated in that district in the courts of the United States, certified that he had issued warrants which the marshal was unable to execute without military aid. (1 American State Papers, 185.) The acts of Congress then required such a certificate, before allowing the militia to be called out. (1 Stat. at Large, 264.) The marshal also wrote, that he needed "military aid." (1 Am. State Papers, 186.) The additional force, authorized by Congress, was expressly for that same purpose, as well as to suppress such combinations. (1 Stat. at Large, 403.) And though with these objects, so fully did it seem proper to reach this last one by means of the first, the orders in the field were to a like effect, and the arrests made were by authority of the civil officers, and those seized were carried before those authorities for hearing and trial. (Findley, 181.)

The secretary of war, likewise, issued public orders, in which, among other things, it is stated, that "one object of the expedition is to assist the marshal of the district to make prisoners," &c. "The marshal of the district of Pennsylvania will move with you and give you the names of the offenders, their descriptions, and respective places of abode, who are to be made prisoners under criminal process." And so exclusively did Congress look to the laws of the land for a guide, that special sessions of the Circuit Court nearer the place of offence were allowed (March 2d, 1793, 1 Stat. at Large, 324) to be called, when necessary, to try offenders.

The President, throughout the excitement, evinced the characteristic moderation and prudence of Washington, constantly enjoined a subordination of the military to the civil power, and accompanied the troops in person to see that the laws were respected. (Findley's History of the Western Insurrection, p. 144.) "He assured us," says Findley (p. 179), "that the army should not consider themselves as judges or executioners of the laws, but as employed to support the proper authorities in the execution of them." That he had issued orders "for the subordination of the army to the laws." (P. 181.) This was in accordance with the course pursued in England on some similar occasions. (1 MacArthur on Courts-Martial, 28.) And though some arrests were to be made, they were to be in a legal civil form, for he said, "Nothing remained to be done by them but to support the civil magistrate in procuring proper subjects to atone for the outrages that had been committed." (Findley, 187.) The orders or warrants executed seem to have emanated from the federal judge of the Pennsylvania district. (Pp. 200, 201, 204, ch. 16.)

The arrests in 1805 and 1806, in what is called Burr's conspiracy, furnish another analogy and precedent. They were not made till an oath and warrant had issued, except in one or two cases. And in those the prisoners were immediately discharged, as illegally arrested, as soon as writs of habeas corpus could be obtained and enforced. By the constitution (Art. 3, sec. 9), "the privilege of the writ of habeas corpus shall not be suspended unless when, in cases of rebellion or invasion, the public safety may require it."

And Congress then declined to suspend that writ, much less to declare martial law, even where the supposed rebellion existed. Nor was the latter done by the States, in the rebellions of 1787 and 1794, as before explained, but merely the writ of habeas corpus suspended in one of them. It is further characteristic of the jealousy of our people over legislative action to suspend the habeas corpus, though expressly allowed by the constitution, that, after a bill to do it in 1807 seems to have passed the Senate of the United States, through all its readings in one day, and with closed doors, the House of Representatives rejected it, on the first reading, by a vote of 113 to 19. (See the Journals of the two Houses, 25th and 27th Jan., 1807.) And this, although the bill to suspend the habeas corpus provided it should be done only when one is charged *on oath* with treason or misdemeanor affecting the peace of the United States, and imprisoned by warrant on authority of the President of the United States, or the Governor of a State or Territory. It was not deemed prudent to suspend it, though in that mild form, considering such a measure at the best but a species of dictatorship, and to be justified only by extreme peril to the public safety. And Mr. Jefferson has left on record his opinion, that it was much wiser, even in insurrections, never even to suspend the writ of habeas corpus. (2 Jefferson's Cor. and Life, 274, 291.) But what would have been thought then of a measure of "martial law," established over the whole country, acting too without oath or warrant, and under no grant by the constitution, instead of a mere suspension of a writ, and which suspension was permitted by the constitution in certain exigencies? Again, if only to repeal or suspend the habeas corpus requires a permissive clause in the constitution, how much more should the repeal or suspension of all municipal laws? Indeed, the Mutiny Act itself, as, for instance, that of 53 George 3, ch. 18, sec. 100, does not allow the military to break open a house to arrest so bad a culprit as a deserter without a warrant and under oath. (38 Stat. at Large, 97.)

So, though a rebellion may have existed in Burr's case in the opinion of the executive, and troops had been ordered out to assist in executing the laws and in suppressing the hostile array, this court held that an arrest by a military officer of one concerned in the rebellion, though ordered by the executive, was not valid, unless he was a person then actually engaged in hostilities, or in warlike array, or in some way actually abetting those who then were so. (Bolman and Swartout's case, 4 Cranch, 75, 101, 126; 1 Burr's Tr. 175.) And if an arrest was made without an order of the commander-in-chief, the court would discharge at once. (Alexander's case, 4 Cranch, 75, 76, in note.) It should also be by warrant, and on oath; and, in most cases, these were then resorted to by General Wilkinson. (Annual Register for 1807, p. 84.) And so jealous were the people then of abuses, that a neglect by him of obedience to the requisitions of the habeas corpus, in some respects, led to a presentment against his conduct by the grand jury of New Orleans. (Annual Register for 1807, p. 98.) But here no actual arrest was made, though attempted, and, what was less justifiable, without oath or warrant, the house was broken into; and hence, any justification by martial law failing which might be set up for the former, would seem more clearly to fail for the latter. Certainly it must fail unless the latter was proper in this way, under all the circumstances, though no one was there liable to be arrested, and none actually arrested.

This doctrine of their failing is familiar in municipal law in breaking houses to seize persons and property on legal precept, when none are found there liable to be seized. (5 Coke, 93, *a;* Bac. Abr. *Execution*, W.)

In civil dissensions, the case stands very differently from foreign ones. In the latter, force is the only weapon, after reason and negotiation have failed. In the former, it is not the course of governments, nor their right, when citizens are unable to convince each other, to fly at once to arms and military arrests and confiscations. The civil power can first be brought to bear upon these dissensions and outbreaks through the judiciary, and usually can thus subdue them.

All these principles, and the precedents just referred to, show that the course rightfully to be pursued on such unfortunate occasions is that already explained; first resorting to municipal precepts, next strengthening them by coöperation of the militia if resisted, and then, if the opposition are in battle array, opposing the execution of such precepts, to obtain further assistance, if needed, from the General Government, to enforce them, and to seize and suppress those so resisting in actual array against the State.

But affairs must advance to this extreme stage through all intermediate ones, keeping the military in strict subordination to the civil authority, except when acting on its own members, before any rights of mere war exist or can over-ride the community, and then, in this country, they must do that under the countenance and controlling orders of the General Government. Belligerent measures, too, must come, not from subordinates, but from those empowered to command, and be commensurate only with the opposing array,—the persons, places and causes where resistance *flagrante bello* exists of the reckless character justifying violence and a disregard of all ordinary securities and laws. It is not a little desirable that this doctrine should prove to be the true one, on account of its greater tendency to secure orderly and constitutional liberty instead of rude violence, to protect rights by civil process rather than the bayonet, and to render all domestic outbreaks less bloody and devastating than they otherwise would be.

There having been, then, no rights of war on the part of the State when this act of Assembly passed, and certainly none which could justify so extreme a measure as martial law over the whole State as incident to them, and this act being otherwise unconstitutional, the justification set up under it must, in my opinion, fail. If either government, on the 24th of June, possessed authority to pass an act establishing martial law to this extent, it was, of course, that of the United States,— the government appointed in our system to carry on war and suppress rebellion or domestic violence when a State is unable to do it by her own powers. But as the General Government did not exercise this authority, and probably could not have done it constitutionally in so sweeping a manner, and in such an early stage of resistance, if at all, this furnishes an additional reason why the State alone could not properly do it.

But if I err in this, and certain rights of war may exist with one of our States in a civil strife like the present, in some extreme stage of it, independent of any act of Congress or the President recognizing it, another inquiry would be, whether, in the state of affairs existing at this time, such rights had become perfected, and were broad enough, if properly pleaded, to cover this measure of martial law over the whole State, and the acts done under it, in the present instance. The necessities of foreign war, it is conceded, sometimes impart great powers as to both things and persons. But they are modified by those necessities, and subjected to numerous regulations of national law, and justice, and humanity. These, when they exist in modern times, while allowing the persons who conduct war some necessary authority of an extraordinary character, must limit, control, and make its exercise under certain circumstances and in a certain manner justifiable or void, with almost as much certainty and clearness as any provisions concerning municipal authority or duty. So may it be in some extreme stages of civil war. Among these, my impression is that a state of war, whether foreign or domestic, may exist, in the great perils of which it is competent, under its rights and on principles of national law, for a commanding officer of troops under the controlling government to extend certain rights of war, not only over his camp, but its environs and the near field of his military operations. (6 American Archives, 186.) But no further, nor wider. (Johnson *v.* Davis et al., 3 Martin, 530, 551.) On this rested the justification of one of the great commanders of this country and of the age, in a transaction so well known at New Orleans.

But in civil strife they are not to extend beyond the place where insurrection exists. (3 Martin, 551.) Nor to portions of the State remote from the scene of military operations, nor after the resistance is over, nor to persons not connected with it. (Grant *v.* Gould et al., 2 Hen. Bl. 69.) Nor, even within the scene, can they extend to the person or property of citizens against whom no probable cause exists which may justify it. (Sutton *v.* Johnston, 1 D. & E. 549.) Nor to the property of any person without necessity or civil precept. If matters in this case had reached such a crisis, and had so been recognized by the General Government, or if such a state of things could and did exist as to warrant such a measure, independent of that government, and it was properly pleaded, the defendants might, perhaps, be justified within those limits, and under such orders, in making search for an offender or an opposing combatant, and, under some circumstances, in breaking into houses for his arrest.

Considerations like these show something in respect to the extent of authority that could have been exercised in each of these cases as a belligerent right, had war been properly declared before and continued till that time (6 American Archives, 232), neither of which seems to have been the case. It is obvious enough that, though on the 24th of June, five days previous, Luther had been in arms at Providence, several miles distant, under the governor appointed under the new constitution, in order to take possession of some of the public property there, and though in the record it is stated that the defendants offered to prove he was at this time in arms somewhere, yet, the fact not being deemed material under the question of martial law, on which the defence was placed, it does not seem to have been investigated. How it might turn out can be ascertained only on a new trial. But to show it is not uncontroverted, the other record before us as to this transaction states positively that Mrs. Luther offered to prove there was no camp nor hostile array by any person in the town where this trespass was committed, on the 29th of June, nor within twenty-five miles of it in any part of the State, and that Dorr had, on the 27th instant, two days previous, published a statement against "any further forcible measures" on his part, and directing that the military "be dismissed."

The collection which had there happened, in relation to the disputed rights as to the public property, under the new constitution, seems to have been nothing, on the evidence, beyond a few hundreds of persons, and nothing beyond the control of the courts of law, aided by the militia, if they had been wisely resorted to,—nothing which, when represented to the executive of the United States, required, in his opinion, from its apprehended extent or danger, any war measures,—the calling out of the militia of other States, or aid of the public troops, or even the actual issue of a proclamation; and the persons who did assemble had, it appears, two days before the trespass, been disbanded, and further force disclaimed, without a gun being fired, or blood in any way shed, on that occasion.

Under the worst insurrections, and even wars, in our history, so strong a measure as this is believed never to have been ventured on before by the General Government, and much less by any one of the States, as within their constitutional capacity, either in peace, insurrection, or war. And if it is to be tolerated, and the more especially in civil feuds like this, it will open the door, in future domestic dissensions here, to a series of butchery, rapine, confiscation, plunder, conflagration, and cruelty, unparalleled in the worst contests in history between mere dynasties for supreme power. It would go in practice to render the whole country — what Bolivar at one time seemed to consider his — a *camp*, and the administration of the government a *campaign*.

It is to be hoped we have some national ambition and pride, under our boasted dominion of law and order, to preserve them by law, by enlightened and constitutional law, and the moderation of superior intelligence and civilization, rather than by appeals to any of the semi-barbarous measures of darker ages, and the unrelenting, lawless persecutions of opponents in civil strife which characterized and disgraced those ages.

Again, when belligerent measures do become authorized by extreme resistance, and a legitimate state of war exists, and civil authority is prostrate, and violence and bloodshed seem the last desperate resort, yet war measures must be kept within certain restraints in all civil contests in all civilized communities.

"The common laws of war, those maxims of humanity, moderation, and honor," which should characterize other wars, Vattel says (B. 3, ch. 8, sec. 294 and 295), "ought to be observed by both parties in every civil war." Under modern and Christian civilization, you cannot needlessly arrest or make war on husbandmen or mechanics, or women and children. (Vattel, B. 3, ch. 8, sec. 149.) The rights of war are against enemies, open and armed enemies, while enemies, and during war, but no longer. And the force used then is not to exceed the exigency,— not wantonly to injure private property, nor disturb private dwellings and their peaceful inmates. (Vattel, B. 3, ch. 8, sec. 148.) Much will be allowed to discretion, if manifestly exercised with honesty, fairness, and humanity. But the principles of the common law, as opposed to trials without a jury, searches of houses and papers without oath or warrant, and all despotic invasions on private personal liberty,— the customary usages to respect the laws of the land except where a great exigency may furnish sufficient excuse, — should all limit this power, in many respects, in practice. (2 Stephens on Laws of England, 602.) The more especially must it be restrained in civil strife, operating on our own people in masses and under our system of government in distributing authority between the States and the Union, as the great powers of war are intrusted to the latter alone, and the latter is also to recognize when that which amounts to a rebellion exists, and interfere to suppress it, if necessary, with the incidents to such interference. Under the right of war the defence must also rest, not only on what has been alluded to, but, as before suggested, on the question whether the insurrection at the time of this trespass was not at an end. For if one has previously been in arms, but the insurrection or war is over, any belligerent rights cease, and no more justify a departure from the municipal laws than they do before insurrection or war begins. If any are non-combatants, either as never having been engaged in active resistance, or as having abandoned it, the rights of civil warfare over them would seem to have terminated, and the prosecution and punishment of their past misconduct belongs then to the municipal tribunals, and not to the sword and bayonet of the military.

The Irish Rebellion Act, as to martial law, was expressly limited "from time to time during the continuance of the said rebellion." (Tytler on Military Law, 405.) And in case of a foreign war it is not customary to make prisoners and arrest enemies after the war has ceased and been declared abandoned, though the terms of peace have not been definitely settled. And if any of them voluntarily, like Bonaparte, abandon the contest, or surrender themselves as prisoners, the belligerent right to continue to imprison them after the war is at an end, much less to commit violence, as here, on others, with a view to capture them, is highly questionable, and has been very gravely doubted. (Vattel, B. 3, ch. 8, sec. 152, 154.) Circumstances like these make the rule of force and violence operate only to a due extent and for a due time, within its appropriate sphere, and secure beyond that extent and time the supremacy of the ordinary laws of the land. Much more in a social or civil war, a portion of the people, where not then in arms, though differing in opinion, are generally to be treated as non-combatants, and searched for and arrested, if at all, by the municipal law, by warrant under oath, and tried by a jury, and not by the law martial.

Our own and English history is full of such arrests and trials, and the trials are held, not round a drum-head or cannon, but in halls of justice and under the forms of established jurisprudence. (See State Trials, *passim.*) The writ of habeas corpus, also, unless specially suspended by the Legislature having power to do so, is as much in force in intestine war as in peace, and the empire of the laws is equally to be upheld, if practicable. (Ibid. 532; 4 Cranch, 101; 2 Hen. Bl. 69.)

To conclude, it is manifest that another strong evidence of the control over military law in peace, and over these belligerent rights in civil strife, which is proper in a bold and independent judiciary, exists in this fact, that whenever they are carried beyond what the exigency demands, even in cases where some may be lawful, the sufferer is always allowed to resort, as here, to the judicial tribunals for redress. (4 Taunt. 67, and Baily *v.* Warder, 4 Maule & Selw. 400. See other cases before cited.)

Bills or clauses of indemnity are enacted in England, otherwise officers would still oftener be exposed to criminal prosecution and punishment for applying either belligerent rights or the military law in an improper case, or to an excess in a proper case, or without probable cause. (1 MacArthur on Courts-Martial, 33, 34; Tytler on Military Law, 49 and 489; see last act in Appendix to Tytler and Simmons.) And when in an insurrection an opponent or his property is treated differently from what the laws and constitution, or national law, sanction, his remedy is sacred in the legal tribunals. And though the offender may have exposed himself to penalties and confiscations, yet he is thus not to be deprived of due redress for wrongs committed on himself.

The plaintiff in one of these records is a female, and was not at all subject to military duty and laws, and was not in arms as an opponent supporting the new constitution. And if the sanctity of domestic life has been violated, the castle of the citizen broken into, or property or person injured, without good cause, in either case the jury of the country should give damages, and courts are bound to instruct them to do so, unless a justification is made out fully on correct principles. This can and should be done without any vindictive punishment, when a party appears to have acted under a supposed legal right. And, indeed, such is the structure of our institutions, that officers, as well as others, are often called on to risk much in behalf of the public and of the country in time of peril. And if they appear to do it from patriotism, and with proper decorum and humanity, the Legislature will, on application, usually indemnify them by discharging from the public treasury the amount recovered for any injury to individual rights. In this very case, therefore, the defence seems to be by the State, and at its expense. It shows the beautiful harmony of our system, not to let private damage be suffered wrongfully, without redress, but, at the same time, not to let a public agent suffer, who, in a great crisis, appears to have acted honestly for the public, from good probable cause, though in some degree mistaking the extent of his powers, as well as the rights of others. But whether any of the rights of war, or rights of a citizen in civil strife, independent of the invalid act of the Assembly declaring martial law over all the State, have here, on the stronger side against the feebler, been violated, does not seem yet to have been tried. The only point in connection with this matter which appears clearly to have been ruled at the trial, was the legality or constitutionality of that act of Assembly. I think that the ruling made was incorrect, and hence that there has been a mis-trial.

The judgment should, in this view, be reversed; and though it is very doubtful whether, in any other view, as by the general rights of war, these respondents can justify their conduct on the facts now before us; yet they should be allowed an opportunity for it, which can be granted on motion below to amend the pleas in justification.

## ON TAXES BY STATES ON PASSENGERS IN VESSELS FROM ABROAD, TO SUPPORT PAUPERS.*

In relation to the case of Turner *v.* Smith, from New York, I wish merely to express my non-concurrence with the opinions pronounced by the majority of this court. But standing more intimately connected with the case of Norris *v.* Boston, by my official duties in the First Circuit, I feel more obliged to state, in some detail, the reasons for my opinion, though otherwise content to acquiesce silently in the views expressed by the Chief Justice; and though not flattering myself with being able, after the elaborate discussions we have just heard, to present much that is either novel or interesting.

The portion of the statute of Massachusetts which in this case is assailed, as most questionable in respect to its conformity with the constitution, is the third section. The object of that is to forbid alien passengers to land in any port in the State, until the master or owner of the vessel pays "two dollars for each passenger so landing." The provisions in the other sections, and especially the second one, requiring indemnity for the support of lunatics, idiots, and infirm persons on board of vessels before they are landed, if they have been or are paupers, seem admitted by most persons to be a fair exercise of the police powers of a State.

This claim of indemnity is likewise excused or conceded as a power which has long been exercised by several of the Atlantic States in self-defence against the ruinous burdens which would otherwise be flung upon them by the incursions of paupers from abroad, and their laws are often as stringent against the introduction of that class of persons from adjoining States as from foreign countries. (Revised Statutes of New Hampshire, ch. 67, § 5; 5 Howard, 629.)

Such legislation commenced in Massachusetts early after our ancestors arrived at Plymouth. It first empowered the removal of foreign paupers. (See Colonial Charters and Laws, 1639, p. 173, and 1692, p. 252.) It extended next to the requisition of indemnity from the master, as early as the year 1701. (See Statute of 13 Wm. III., ibid. 363.) But while it embraced removals of paupers not settled in the colony, and indemnity required from the master for the support of foreigners introduced by sea, I do not think it assumed the special form used in the third section of this statute until the year 1837,

* Dissenting opinion in case of Norris *v.* City of Boston and Smith *v.* Turner. January term S. C. U. S., 1849.

after the decision in the case of the City of New York *v.* Miln, 11 Peters, 107. I shall not, therefore, discuss further the provisions in the second section of the statute; for, at all events, the requisitions of that section, if not by all admitted to be constitutional, are less objectionable than those of the third; and if the last can be vindicated, the first must be, and hence the last has constituted the burden of the arguments on both sides.

It will be remembered that this third section imposes a condition on landing alien passengers, or, in other words, levies a toll or fee on the master for landing them, whether then paupers or not, and that the present action is to recover back the money which has been collected from the master for landing such passengers.

After providing, in the following words, that, "when any vessel shall arrive at any port or harbor within the State, from any port or place without the same, with alien passengers on board, the officer or officers whom the mayor and aldermen of the city, or the selectmen of the town, where it is proposed to land such passengers, are hereby authorized and required to appoint, shall go on board such vessel and examine into the condition of said passengers," the third section of the statute declares that "no alien passenger, other than those spoken of in the preceding section, shall be permitted to land, until the master, owner, consignee, or agent of such vessel shall pay to the regularly appointed boarding officer the sum of two dollars for each passenger so landing; and the money so collected shall be paid into the treasury of the city or town, to be appropriated as the city or town may direct for the support of foreign paupers."

It is conceded that the sum paid here on account of "alien passengers" was demanded of them, when coming in some "vessel," and was collected after she arrived at a "port or harbor within the State." Then, and not till then, the master was required to pay two dollars for each before landing, "to be paid into the treasury of the city or town, to be appropriated as the city or town may direct for the support of foreign paupers."

By a subsequent law, as the foreign paupers had been made chargeable to the State treasury, the balances of this fund in the different towns were required to be transferred to that treasury.

After careful examination, I am not satisfied that this exercise of power by a State is incapable of being sustained as a matter of right, under one or all of three positions.

1st. That it is a lawful exercise of the police power of the State to help to maintain its foreign paupers.

2d. If not, that it may be regarded as justified by the sovereign power which every State possesses to prescribe the conditions on which aliens may enjoy a residence within, and the protection of, the State.

3d. Or it may be justified under the municipal power of the State to impose taxes within its limits for State purposes. I think, too, that this power has never been ceded to the General Government, either expressly or by implication, in any of the grants relied on for that purpose, such as to lay duties on imports, or to prohibit the importation of certain persons after the year 1808, or to regulate commerce.

Under the first ground of vindication for the State, the whole statute was most probably enacted with the laudable design to obtain some assistance in maintaining humanely the large number of paupers, and persons likely soon to become paupers, coming to our shores by means furnished by the municipal authorities in various parts of Europe. (See 3 Ex. Doc. of 29th Congress, 2d Session, No. 54.) Convicts were likewise sent, or preparing to be sent, hither from some cities on the Continent. (Ibid.)

A natural desire, then, would exist, and would appear by some law, to obtain, first, indemnity against the support of emigrants actually paupers, and likely at once to become chargeable; and, secondly, funds to maintain such as, though not actually paupers, would probably become so, from this class of aliens.

It is due to the cause of humanity, as well as the public economy of the State, that the maintenance of paupers, whether of foreign or domestic origin, should be well provided for. Instead of being whipped or carted back to their places of abode or settlement, as was once the practice in England and this country in respect to them; or, if aliens, instead of being re-shipped over a desolate waste of ocean, they are to be treated with kindness and relieved or maintained. But still, if feasible, it should, in justice, be at the expense of those introducing them, and introducing the evils which may attend on them. This seems to have been the attempt in this statute, and as such was a matter of legitimate police in relation to paupers.

But those persons affected by the third section not being at the time actual paupers, but merely alien passengers, the expediency or right to tax the master for landing them does not seem so clear, in a police view, as it is to exact indemnity against the support of those already paupers. Yet it is not wholly without good reasons, so far as regards the master or owner who makes a profit by bringing into a State persons having no prior rights there, and likely in time to add something to its fiscal burdens and the number of its unproductive inhabitants. He who causes this danger, and is the willing instrument in it, and profits by it, cannot, in these views, object to the condition or tax imposed by the State, who may not consider the benefits likely to arise from such a population a full counterbalance to all the anticipated disadvantages and contingencies. But the aspect of the case is somewhat different, looking at the tax as falling wholly on the passenger. It may not be untrue, generally, that some portion of a burden like this rests eventually on the passenger, rather than the master or owner. (Neil *v.* State of Ohio, 3 Howard, 741—743.) Yet it does not always; and it is the master, and the owners through him, who complain in the present action, and not the passengers; if it fell on the latter alone, they would be likely, not only to complain, but to go in vessels to other States, where onerous conditions had not been imposed. Supposing, however, the burden, in fact, to light on them, it is in some, though a less degree, and in a different view, as a matter of right, to be vindicated.

Were its expediency alone the question before us, some, and among them myself, would be inclined to doubt as to the expediency of such a tax on alien passengers in general, not paupers or convicts. Whatever may be their religion, whether Catholic or Protestant, or their occupation, whether laborers, mechanics, or farmers, the majority of them are believed to be useful additions to the population of the New World, and since, as well as before our Revolution, have deserved encouragement in their immigration by easy terms of naturalization, of voting, of holding office, and all the political and civil privileges which their industry and patriotism have in so many instances shown to be usefully bestowed. (See Declaration of Independence; Naturalization Law; 1 Lloyd's Debates, Gales and Seaton's ed., p. 1147; Taylor *v.* Carpenter, 2 Woodbury & Minot.) If a design existed in any statute to thwart this policy, or if such were its necessary consequence, the measure would be of very questionable expediency. But the makers of this law may have had no such design, and such does not seem to be the necessary consequence of it, as large numbers of emigrants still continue to arrive in Massachusetts, when they would be likely to ship for ports in other States where no such law exists, if this operated on them as a discouragement, and, like other taxes, when felt, or when high, had become in some degree prohibitory.

The conduct of the State, too, in this measure, as a matter of right, is the only question to be decided by us, and may be a very different one from its expediency. Every sovereign State possesses the right to decide this matter of expediency for itself, provided it has the power to control or govern the subject. Our inquiry, therefore, relates merely to that power or right in a State; and the ground now under consideration to support the exercise of it is her authority to prescribe terms, in a police view, to the entry into her boundaries of persons who are likely to become chargeable as paupers, and who are aliens.

In this view, as connected with her police over pauperism, and as a question of mere right, it may be fairly done by imposing terms which, though incidentally making it more expensive for aliens to come here, are designed to maintain such of them and of their class as are likely, in many instances, ere long to become paupers in a strange country, and usually without sufficient means for support, in case either of sickness, or accident, or reverses in business. So it is not without justification that a class of passengers from whom much expense arises in supporting paupers should, though not at that moment chargeable, advance something for this purpose, at a time when they are able to contribute, and when alone it can with certainty be collected. (See New York *v.* Miln, 11 Peters, 156.) When this is done in a law providing against the increase of pauperism, and seems legitimately to be connected with the subject, and when the sum required of the master or passenger is not disproportionate to the ordinary charge, there appears no reason to regard it as any measure except what it professes to be,—one connected with the State police as to alien passengers, one connected with the support of paupers, and one designed neither to regulate commerce nor be a source of revenue for general purposes. (5 Howard, 626.)

The tax is now transferred to the State treasury, when collected, for the reason that the support of foreign paupers is transferred there; and this accords with an honest design to collect the money only for that object.

The last year, so fruitful in immigration and its contagious diseases of ship-fever and the terrific cholera, and the death of so many from the former, as well as the extraordinary expense consequent from these causes, furnish a strong illustration that the terms required are neither excessive nor inappropriate.

There are many other reasons showing that this is legitimately a police measure, and, as such, competent for the State to adopt. It respects the character of those persons to come within the limits of the State,—it looks to the benefits and burdens deemed likely to be connected with their presence,— it regards the privileges they may rightfully claim of relief, whenever sick or infirm, though on shipboard, if within the boundaries of the State,— it has an eye to the protection they will humanely receive if merely *in transitu* through the State to other governments, and the burdens which, in case of disease or accidents, without much means, they may thus throw upon the State. And the fund collected is expressly and wholly applied, after deducting the expenses of its collection, to "the support of foreign paupers."

A police measure, in common parlance, often relates to something connected with public morals; and in that limited view would still embrace the subject of pauperism, as this court held in 16 Peters, 625. But in law, the word *police* is much broader, and includes all legislation for the internal policy of a State. (4 Bl. Com. ch. 13.)

The police of the ocean belongs to Congress and the admiralty powers of the General Government; but not the police of the land or of harbors. (Waring *v.* Clarke, 5 Howard, 471.)

Nor is it any less a police measure because money, rather than a bond of indemnity, is required as a condition of admission to protection and privileges. The payment of money is sometimes imposed in the nature of a toll or license fee, but it is still a matter of police. It is sometimes demanded in the nature of charges to cover actual or anticipated expenses. Such is the case with all quarantine charges. Substantially, too, it is demanded under the indemnity given by the second section, if the person becomes chargeable; and if that be justifiable, so must be this; the fact that one is contingent and the other absolute cannot affect their constitutionality. Neither is it of consequence that the charge might be defrayed otherwise, if the State pleased, as from other taxes or other sources. This is a matter entirely discretionary with the State. This might be done with respect to quarantine expenses or pilotage of vessels; yet the State, being the sole judge of what is most expedient in respect to this, can legally impose it on the vessel, or master, or passengers, rather than on others, unless clearly forbidden by the federal constitution. And it can be none the less a police measure than is a quarantine charge, because the master or owner is required to pay it, or even the passengers, rather than the other people of the State by a general tax.

Even to exclude paupers entirely has been held to be a police measure, justifiable in a State. (Prigg *v.* Pennsylvania, 16 Peters, 625; 5 Howard, 629.) Why, then, is not the milder measure of a fee or tax justifiable in respect to those alien passengers considered likely to become paupers, and to be applied solely to the support of those who do become chargeable from that class? And why is not this as much a police measure as the other? If such measures must be admitted to be local, are of State cognizance, belong to State interests, they clearly are among State rights.

Viewed as a mere police regulation, then, this statute does not conflict with any constitutional provision. Measures which are legitimately of a police character are not pretended to be ceded anywhere in the constitution to the General Government in express terms; and as little can it be argued that they are impliedly to be considered as ceded, if they be honestly and truly police measures. Hence, in all the decisions of this tribunal on the powers granted to the General Government, either expressly or by implication, measures of that character have been regarded as not properly to be included. (License Cases, 5 Howard, 624; Baldwin's Views, 184, 188; cases cited in The United States *v.* New Bedford Bridge, 1 Woodb. & Min. 423.)

Thus viewed, the case also comes clearly within the principles settled in New York *v.* Miln, 11 Peters, 102, and is fortified by the views in the License Cases, 5 Howard, 504. The fact that the police regulation in the case of Miln was enforced by a penalty instead of a toll, and in the License Cases by a prohibition, at times, as well as a fee, does not alter the principle, unless the mode of doing it in the present case should be found, on further examination, before closing, to be forbidden to the States.

But if this justification should fail, there is another favorable view of legislation such as that of the third section of the statute of Massachusetts, which has already been suggested, and which is so important as to deserve a separate consideration. It presents a vindication for it different from that of a mere police regulation, connected with the introduction or support of aliens, who are or may afterwards become paupers, and results from the power of every sovereign State to impose such terms as she pleases on the admission or continuance of foreigners within her borders. If this power can be shown to exist, and it is in its nature and character a police power also, then we have already demonstrated that the States can rightfully continue to exercise it. But if it be not such a power, and hence cannot be ranked under that title, and enjoy the benefit of the decisions exempting police powers from control by the General Government, yet if it exists as a municipal rather than a police power, and has been constantly exercised by the States, they cannot be considered as not entitled to it, unless they have clearly ceded it to Congress, in some form or other.

First, then, as to its existence. The best writers on national law, as well as our own decisions, show that this power of excluding emigrants exists in all States which are sovereign. (Vattel, B. 1, ch. 19, § 231; 5 Howard, 525, 629; New York *v.* Miln, 11 Peters, 142; Prigg *v.* Pennsylvania, 16 Peters, 625; and Holmes *v.* Jennison, 14 Peters, 565.)

Those coming may be voluntary emigrants from other nations, or travelling absentees, or refugees in revolutions, party exiles, compulsory victims of power, or they may consist of cargoes of shackled slaves, or large bands of convicts, or brigands, or persons with incendiary purposes, or imbecile paupers, or those suffering from infectious diseases, or fanatics, with principles and designs more dangerous than either, or under circumstances of great ignorance, as liberated serfs, likely at once, or soon, to make them a serious burden in their support as paupers, and a contamination of public morals. There can be no doubt, on principles of national law, of the right to prevent the entry of these, either absolutely, or on such conditions as the State may deem it prudent to impose. In this view, a condition of the kind here imposed, on admission to land and enjoy various privileges, is not so unreasonable, and finds vindication in the principles of public law the world over. (Vattel, B. 1, ch. 19, §§ 219, 231, and B. 2, ch. 7, §§ 93, 94.)

In this aspect it may be justified as to the passengers, on the ground of protection and privileges sought by them in the State, either permanently or transiently, and the power of the State to impose conditions before and while yielding it. When we speak here or elsewhere of the right of a State to decide and regulate who shall be its citizens, and on what terms, we mean, of course, subject to any restraint on her power which she herself has granted to the General Government, and which, instead of overlooking, we intend to examine with care before closing.

It having been, then, both in Europe and America, a matter of municipal regulation, whether aliens shall or shall not reside in any particular State, or even cross its borders, it follows that, if a sovereign State pleases, it may, as a matter of clear right, exclude them entirely, or only when paupers or convicts (Baldwin's Views, 193, 194), or only when slaves, or, what is still more common in America, in free States as well as slave States, exclude colored emigrants, though free. As further proof and illustration that this power exists in the States, and has never been parted with, it was early exercised by Virginia as to others than paupers (1 Bl. Com. by Tucker, pt. 2, App. p. 33), and it is now exercised, in one form or another, as to various persons, by more than half the States of the Union. (11 Peters, 142; 15 ib. 516; 16 ib. 625; 1 Brockenbrough, 434; 14 Peters, 568; 5 Howard, 629.)

Even the old Congress, September 16th, 1788, recommended to the States to pass laws excluding convicts; and they did this, though after the new constitution was adopted, and that fact announced to the country. "Resolved, That it be, and it is hereby, recommended to the several States to pass proper laws for preventing the transportation of convicted malefactors from foreign countries into the United States." (Journal of Congress for 1788, p. 867.)

But the principle goes further, and extends to the right to exclude paupers, as well as convicts, by the States (Baldwin's Views, 188, 193, 194); and Mr. Justice Story, in the case of New York *v.* Miln, 11 Peters, 56, says, as to the States,—"I admit that they have a right to pass poor-laws, and laws to prevent the introduction of paupers into the States, under like qualifications."

Many of the States also exercised this power, not only during the Revolution, but after peace; and Massachusetts especially did, forbidding the return of refugees, by a law in 1783, ch. 69. Several of the States had done the same as to refugees. (See Federalist, No. 42.)

The first naturalization laws by Congress recognized this old right in the States, and expressly provided that such persons could not become naturalized without the special consent of those States which had prohibited their return. Thus in the first act:—"Provided, also, that no person heretofore proscribed by any State shall be admitted a citizen as aforesaid, except by an act of the Legislature of the State in which such person was proscribed." (March 26, 1790, 1 Stat. at Large, 104. See a similar proviso to the third section of the act of 29th January, 1795, 1 Stat. at Large, 415.)

The power given to Congress, as to naturalization generally, does not conflict with this question of taxing or excluding alien passengers, as acts of naturalization apply to those aliens only who have already resided here from two to five years, and not to aliens not resident here at all, or not so long. (See acts of 1790, 1795, and 1800.)

And it is not a little remarkable, in proof that this power of exclusion still remains in the States rightfully, that while, as before stated, it has been exercised by various States in the Union,—some as to paupers, some as to convicts, some as to refugees, some as to slaves, and some as to free blacks,—it never has been exercised by the

General Government as to mere aliens, not enemies, except so far as included in what are called the Alien and Sedition Laws of 1798. By the former, being "An act concerning aliens," passed June 15th, 1798 (1 Stat. at Large, 571), power was assumed by the General Government, in time of peace, to remove or expel them from the country; and that act, no less than the latter, passed about a month after (Ibid. 596), was generally denounced as unconstitutional, and suffered to expire without renewal; on the ground, among others assigned for it, that, if such a power existed at all, it was in the States, and not in the General Government, unless under the war power, and then against alien enemies alone. (4 Elliott's Deb. 581, 582, 586; Virginia Resolutions of 1798.)

It deserves special notice, too, that, when it was exercised on another occasion by the General Government, not against aliens, as such, but slaves imported from abroad, it was in aid of State laws passed before 1808, and in subordination to them. The only act of Congress on this subject before 1808 expressly recognized the power of the State alone then to prohibit the introduction or importation "of any negro, mulatto, or other person of color," and punished it only where the States had. (See act of Feb. 28, 1803, 2 Stat. at Large, 205.) In further illustration of this recognition and coöperation with the States, it provided, in the third section, that all officers of the United States should "notice and be governed by the provisions of the laws now existing in the several States, prohibiting the admission or importation of any negro, mulatto, or other person of color, as aforesaid; and they are hereby enjoined vigilantly to carry into effect said laws," i. e., the laws of the States. (See 1 Brockenbrough, 432.)

The act of March 2d, 1807, forbidding the bringing in of slaves (2 Stat. at Large, 426), was to take effect on the first of January, 1808, and was thus manifestly intended to carry into operation the admitted power of prohibition by Congress, after that date, of certain persons contemplated in the ninth section of the first article, and as a branch of trade or commerce which Congress, in other parts of the constitution, was empowered to regulate. That act was aimed solely at the foreign slave-trade, and not at the bringing in of any other persons than slaves, and not as if Congress supposed that, under the ninth section, it was contemplated to give it power, or recognize its power, over anything but the foreign slave-trade. But of this more hereafter.

It will be seen also in this, that the power of each State to forbid the foreign slave-trade was expressly recognized as existing since, no less than before, 1808, being regarded as a concurrent power, and that by this section no authority was conferred on Congress over the domestic slave-trade, either before or since 1808.

If the old Congress did not suppose it was right and proper for the States to act in this way on the introduction of aliens, after the new constitution went into operation, why did they, by their resolution of

1787, recommend to the States to forbid the introduction of convicts from abroad, rather than recommend it to be done by Congress under the new constitution?

It is on this principle that a State has a right, if it pleases, to remove foreign criminals from within its limits, or allow them to be removed by others (Holmes *v.* Jennison, 14 Peters, 568); though the obligation to do so is, to be sure, an imperfect one, of the performance of which she is judge, and sole judge, till Congress make some stipulation with foreign powers as to their surrender (11 Peters, 391); and if States do not surrender this right of affixing conditions to their ingress, the police authorities of Europe will proceed still further to inundate them with actual convicts and paupers, however mitigated the evil may be at times by the voluntary immigration, with the rest, of many of the enterprising, industrious, and talented. But if the right be carried beyond this, and be exercised with a view to exclude rival artisans, or laborers, or to shut out all foreigners, though persecuted and unfortunate, from mere naked prejudice, or with a view to thwart any conjectural policy of the General Government, this course, as before suggested, would be open to much just criticism.

Again: considering the power to forbid as existing absolutely in a State, it is for the State where the power resides to decide on what is sufficient cause for it,—whether municipal or economical, sickness or crime; as, for example, danger of pauperism, danger to health, danger to morals, danger to property, danger to public principles by revolutions and change of government, or danger to religion. This power over the person is much less than that exercised over ships and merchandise under State quarantine laws, though the General Government regulates, for duties and commerce, the ships and their cargoes. If the power be clear, however others may differ as to the expediency of the exercise of it as to particular classes or in a particular form, this cannot impair the power.

It is well considered, also, that if the power to forbid or expel exists, the power to impose conditions of admission is included as an incident or subordinate. Vattel (B. 2, ch. 8, § 99) observes, that, "since the lord of the territory may, whenever he thinks proper, forbid its being entered, he has, no doubt, a power to annex what conditions he pleases to the permission to enter." (Holmes *v.* Jennison, 14 Peters, 569, 615, Appendix.)

The usage in several States supports this view. Thus the State of Maryland now, of Delaware since 1787, of Pennsylvania since 1818, if not before, and of Louisiana since 1842, besides New York and Massachusetts, pursue this policy in this form. (7 Smith's Laws of Pennsylvania, 21; 2 Laws of Delaware, 167, 995; 1 Dorsey's Laws of Maryland, 6, 10.) And though it is conceded that laws like this in Massachusetts are likely, in excited times, to become of a dangerous character, if perverted to illegitimate purposes, and though it is manifestly injudicious to push all the powers possessed by the States to a harsh extent against foreigners any more than citizens, yet, in my view, it is essential to sovereignty to be able to prescribe the conditions or terms on which aliens or their property shall be allowed to remain under its protection, and enjoy its municipal privileges. (Vattel, B. 1, ch. 19, §§ 219, 231.)

As a question of international law, also, they could do the same as to the citizens of other States, if not prevented by other clauses in the constitution reserving to them certain rights over the whole Union, and which probably protect them from any legislation which does not at least press as hard on their own citizens as on those of other States. Thus, in article fourth, section second: — "The citizens of each State shall be entitled to all privileges and immunities of citizens in the several States." And the old Confederation (article fourth) protected the ingress and egress of the citizens of each State with others, and made the duties imposed on them the same.

Such is the case of Turner *v.* Smith, considered in connection with this, collecting the same of its own citizens as of others; and to argue that States may abuse the power, by taxing citizens of other States different from their own, is a fallacy, because Congress would also be quite as likely to abuse the power, because an abuse would reäct on the State itself, and lessen or destroy this business through it, and because the abuse, instead of being successful, would probably be pronounced unconstitutional by this court, whenever appealed to.

With such exceptions, I am aware of no limitations on the powers of the States, as a matter of right, to go to the extent indicated in imposing terms of admission within their own limits, unless they be so conducted as to interfere with some other power, express or implied, which has been clearly granted to Congress, and which will be considered hereafter.

The last ground of vindication of this power, as exercised by Massachusetts in the third section, is under its aspect as imposing a tax.

Considering this, the inquiry may be broad enough to ascertain whether the measure is not constitutional, under the taxing power of the State generally, independent of its authority, already examined, as to a police, over the support of paupers, and as to municipal regulations, over the admission of travellers and non-residents.

It deserves remark, in the outset, that such a tax, under the name of a toll or passport fee, is not uncommon in foreign countries on alien travellers when passing their frontiers. In that view it would be vindicated under long usage and numerous precedents abroad, and several in this country, already referred to.

It requires notice, also, that this provision, considered as a license fee, is not open to the objection of not being assessed beforehand at stated periods, and collected at the time of other taxes. When fees of a specific sum are exacted for licenses to sell certain goods, or exercise certain trades, or exhibit something rare, or for admissions to certain privileges, they are not regarded so much in the light of common taxes as of fees or tolls. They resemble this payment required here more than a tax on property, as they are not always annual, or collected at stated seasons; they are not imposed on citizens only, or permanent residents, but frequently are demanded as often as an event happens, or a certain act is done, and at any period, and from any visiter or transient resident. But fees or tolls thus collected are still legitimate taxes.

Another view of it as a tax is its imposition on the master of the vessel himself, on account of his capital or business in trade, carrying passengers, and not a tax on the passengers themselves. The master is often a citizen of the State where he arrives with a cargo and passengers. In such a case, he might be taxed on account of his business, like other citizens; and so, on other general principles, might masters of vessels who are not citizens, but who come within the limits and jurisdiction and protection of the State, and are hence, on that account, rightfully subjected to its taxation, and made to bear a share of its burdens. It is customary in most countries, as before named, to impose taxes on particular professions and trades or businesses, as well as on property; and whether in the shape of a license or fee, or an excise or poll-tax, or any other form, it is of little consequence, when the object of the tax is legitimate, as here, and its amount reasonable.

States, generally, have the right also to impose poll-taxes, as well as those on property, though they should be proportionate and moderate in amount. This one is not much above the usual amount of poll-taxes in New England. Nor need they require any length of residence before a person is subject to such a tax; and sometimes none is required, though it is usual to have it imposed only on a fixed day.

The power of taxation, generally, in all independent States, is unlimited as to persons and things, except as they may have been pleased, by contract or otherwise, to restrict themselves. Such a power, likewise, is one of the most indispensable to their welfare, and even their existence.

On the extent of the cession of taxation to the General Government, and its restriction on the States, more will be presented hereafter; but in all cases of doubt, the leaning may well be towards the States, as the General Government has ample means ordinarily by taxing imports, and the States limited means, after parting with that great and vastly increased source of revenue connected with imposts. The States may, therefore, and do frequently, tax everything but exports, imports, and tonnage, as such. They daily tax things connected with foreign commerce as well as domestic trade. They can tax the timber, cordage, and iron of which the vessels for foreign trade are made; tax their cargoes to the owners as stock in trade; tax the vessels as property, and tax the owners and crew per head for their polls. Their power in this respect travels over water as well as land, if only within their territorial limits.

It seems conceded, that, if this tax, as a tax, had not been imposed till the passenger had reached the shore, the present objection must fail. But the power of the State is manifestly as great in a harbor within her limits to tax men and property as it is on shore, and can no more be abused there than on shore, and can no more conflict there than on shore with any authority of Congress as a taxing power not on imports as imports. Thus, after emigrants have landed, and are on the wharves, or on public roads, or in the public hotels, or in private dwelling-houses, they could all be taxed, though with less ease; and they could all, if the State felt so disposed to abuse the power, be taxed out of their limits as quickly and effectually as have been the Jews in former times in several of the most enlightened nations of modern Europe.

To argue, likewise, that the State thus undertakes to assess taxes on persons not liable, and to control what it has not got, is begging the question, either that these passengers were not within its limits, or that all persons actually within its limits are not liable to its laws and not within its control. To contend, also, that this payment cannot be exacted, on the ground that the great correction of excessive taxation is its oppression on the constituent, which causes a reäction to reduce it (4 Wheat. 316, 428), and in this case the tax does not operate on a constituent, is another fallacy, to some extent. For most taxes operate on some classes of people who are not voters, as, for example, women, and especially resident aliens; and if this reasoning would exempt these passengers, when within the limits of the State, it would also exempt all aliens, and others not voters, however long resident there, or however much property they possess.

It seems likewise well settled, that, by the laws of national intercourse, and as a consequence of the protection and hospitality yielded to aliens, they are subject to ordinary reasonable taxation in their persons and property by the government where they reside, as fully as citizens. (Vattel, B. 2, ch. 10, § 132, p. 235; Taylor *v.* Carpenter, 2 Woodbury & Minot.) But I am not aware of the imposition of such a tax in this form, except as a toll or a passport; it being, when a poll-tax, placed on those who have before acquired a domicile in the State, or have come to obtain one *animo manendi.* Yet, whatever its form, it would not answer hastily to denounce it as without competent authority, when imposed within the usual territorial limits of the State.

In short, the States evidently meant still to retain all power of this kind, except where, for special reasons at home, neither government was to tax exports, and, for strong reasons both at home and abroad, only the General Government was to tax imports and tonnage.

Having explained what seem to me the principal reasons in favor of a power so vital to the States as that exercised by Massachusetts in this statute, whether it be police or municipal, regulating its residents or taxing them, I shall proceed to the last general consideration, which is, whether this power has in any way been parted with to Congress entirely, or as to certain objects, including aliens.

It is not pretended that there is *eo nomine* any express delegation of this power to Congress, or any express prohibition of it to the States. And yet, by the tenth amendment of the constitution, it is provided, in so many words, that "the powers not delegated to the United States by the constitution, nor prohibited by it to the States, are reserved to the States respectively, or to the people." If, in the face of this, Congress is to be regarded as having obtained a power of restriction over the States on this subject, it must be by mere implication, and this either from the grant to impose taxes and duties, or that which is usually considered a clause only to prohibit and tax the slave-trade, or that to regulate commerce. And this statute of Massachusetts, in order to be unconstitutional, must be equivalent to one of these, or conflicting with one of them.

In relation, first, to the most important of these objections, regarding the statute in the light of a tax, and as such supposed to conflict with the general power of taxation conferred on Congress, as well as the exclusive power to tax imports, I would remark, that the very prohibition to the States, in express terms, to tax imports, furnishes additional proof that other taxation by the States was not meant to be forbidden in other cases and as to other matters. *Expressio unius, exclusio est alterius.* It would be very extraordinary, also, that, when expressly ceding powers of taxation to the General Government, the States should refrain from making them exclusive in terms, except as to imports and tonnage, and yet should be considered as having intended, by mere implication, there or elsewhere in the instrument, to grant away all their great birthright over all other taxation, or at least some most important branches of it. Such has not been the construction or practical action of the two governments for the last half-century, but the States have continued to tax all the sources of revenue ceded to Congress, when not in terms forbidden. This was the only safe course. (Federalist, No. 32.)

One of the best tests that this kind of tax or fee for admission to the privileges of a State is permissible, if not expressly forbidden, is the construction in two great cases of direct taxes on land imposed by Congress, in 1798 and 1813. The States, on both of those occasions, still continued to impose and collect their taxes on lands, because not forbidden expressly by the constitution to do it. And can any one doubt, that, so far as regards taxation even of ordinary imports, the States could still exercise it if they had not been expressly forbidden by this clause? (Collet *v.* Collet, 2 Dallas, 296; Gibbons *v.* Ogden, 9 Wheat. 201.) If they could not, why was the express prohibition made? Why was it deemed necessary? (Federalist, No. 32.)

This furnishes a striking illustration of the true general rule of construction, that, notwithstanding a grant to Congress is express, if the States are not directly forbidden to act, it does not give to Congress exclusive authority over the matter, but the States may exercise a power in several respects relating to it, unless, from the nature of the subject, and their relations to the General Government, a prohibition is fairly or necessarily implied. This power in some instances seems to be concurrent or coördinate, and in others subordinate. On this rule of construction there has been much less doubt in this particular case as to taxation, than as a general principle on some other matters, which will hereafter be noticed under another head. The argument for it is unanswerable, that, though the States have, as to ordinary taxation of common subjects, granted a power to Congress, it is merely an additional power to their own, and not inconsistent with it.

It has been conceded by most American jurists, and, indeed, may be regarded as settled by this court, that this concurrent power of taxation, except on imports and exports and tonnage (the last two specially and exclusively resigned to the General Government), is vital to the States, and still clearly exists in them. In support of this may be seen the following authorities: — McCulloch *v.* State of Maryland, 4 Wheat. 316, 425; Gibbons *v.* Ogden, 9 Wheat. 1, by Chief Justice Marshall; Providence Bank *v.* Billings, 4 Peters, 561; Brown *v.* State of Maryland, 12 Wheat. 441; 4 Gill & Johns. 132; 2 Story's Com. on Const. § 437; 5 Howard, 588; Weston *v.* City of Charleston, 2 Peters, 449; Federalist, No. 42.

Nor is the case of Brown *v.* Maryland, so often referred to, opposed to this view. It seems to have been a question of taxation, but the decision was not that, by the grant to the General Government of the power to lay taxes and imposts, it must be considered, from "the nature of the power," "that it [taxation generally] should be exercised exclusively by Congress." On the contrary, all the cases before and hereafter cited, bearing on this question, concede that the general power of taxation still remains in the States; but in that instance it was considered to be used so as to amount to a tax on imports, and, such a tax being expressly prohibited to the States, it was adjudged there that for this reason it was unconstitutional. Under this head, then, as to taxation, it only remains to ascertain whether the toll or tax here imposed on alien passengers can be justly considered a tax on imports, as it was in the case of Brown *v.* Maryland, when laid on foreign goods. If so considered, it is conceded that this tax has been expressly forbidden to be imposed by a State, unless with the consent of Congress, or to aid in enforcing the inspection laws of the State. Clearly it does not come within either of those last exceptions, and therefore the right to impose it must depend upon the question, whether it is an "impost," and whether passengers are "imports," within the meaning of the constitution. An *impost* is usually an *ad valorem* or specific duty, and not a fee like this for allowing a particular act, or a poll-tax like this,—a fixed sum per head. An *import* is also an article of merchandise, goods of some kind,—property, "commodities." (Brown *v.* Maryland, 12 Wheat. 437. See McCulloch's Dict. *Imports;* 5 Howard, 594, 614.) It does not include persons unless they are brought in as property,—as slaves, unwilling or passive emigrants, like the importation referred to in the ninth section of the first article of the constitution. (New York *v.* Miln, 11 Peters, 136; Case of the Brig Wilson, 1 Brock. 423.)

Now there is no pretence that mere passengers in vessels are of this character, or are property; otherwise they must be valued, and pay the general *ad valorem* duty now imposed on non-enumerated articles. They are brought in by no owner, like property generally, or like slaves. They are not the subject of entry or sale. The great objection to the tax in Brown *v.* Maryland was, that it clogged the sale of the goods. They are not like merchandise, too, because that may be warehoused, and reëxported or branded, or valued by an invoice. They may go on shore anywhere, but goods cannot. A tax on them is not, then, in any sense, a tax on imports, even in the purview of Brown *v.* Maryland. There it was held not to be permitted until the import in the original packet or cask is broken up, which it is difficult to predicate of a man or passenger. The definition there, also, is "imports are *things* imported," not persons, not passengers; or they are "*articles* brought in," and not freemen coming of their own accord. (12 Wheat. 437.) And when "imports" or "importation" is applied to men, as is the case in some acts of Congress, and in the ninth section of the first article of the constitution, it is to men or "persons" who are property and passive, and brought in against their will or for sale as slaves,—brought as an article of commerce, like other merchandise. (New York *v.* Miln, 11 Peters, 136; 15 Peters, 505; 1 Bl. Com. by Tucker, pt. 2, App. 50.)

But, so far from this being the view as to free passengers taxed in this statute,—that they are merchandise or articles of commerce, and so considered in any act since 1808, or before,—it happens that, while the foreign import or trade as to slaves is abolished, and is made a capital offence, free passengers are not prohibited, nor their introduction punished as a crime. (4 Elliott's Deb. 119.) If "importation" in the ninth section applied to one class of persons, and "migration" to another, as has been argued, then allowing a tax by Congress on the "importation" of any person was meant to be confined to slaves, and is not allowed on "migration," either in words or spirit, and hence it confers no power on Congress to tax other persons (see Iredell's remarks, 4 Elliott's Deb. 119); and a special clause was thought necessary to give the power to tax even the "importation" of slaves, because "a duty or impost" was usually a tax on things, and not persons. (1 Bl. Com. by Tucker, App. 231.)

Indeed, if passengers were "imports" for the purpose of revenue by the General Government, then, as was never pretended, they should and can now be taxed by our collectors, because they are not enumerated in the tariff acts to be admitted "free" of duty, and all *non-enumerated* imports have a general duty imposed on them at the end of the tariff; as, for instance, in the act of July 30, 1846, section third, "a duty of twenty per cent. *ad valorem*" is laid "on all goods, wares and merchandise imported from foreign countries, and not specially provided for in this act."

To come within the scope of a tariff, and within the principle of retaliation by or towards foreign powers, which was the cause of the policy of making imposts on imports exclusive in Congress, the import must still be merchandise or produce, some rival fruit of industry, an article of trade, a subject, or at least an instrument of commerce. Passengers, being neither, come not within the letter or spirit or object of this provision in the constitution.

It is, however, argued, that, though passengers may not be imports, yet the carrying of them is a branch of commercial business, and a legitimate and usual employment of navigation.

Grant this, and still a tax on the passenger would not be laying a duty on "imports" or on "tonnage;" but it might be supposed to affect foreign commerce at times, and in some forms and places, and thus interfere with the power to regulate that, though not with the prohibition to tax imports and tonnage. Consequently, when hereafter considering the meaning of the grant "to regulate commerce," this view of the objection will be examined.

But there seems to be another exception to this measure, as conflicting with the powers of the General Government, which partly affects the question as a tax, and partly as a regulation of commerce. It is, that the tax was imposed on a vessel before the passengers were landed, and while under the control of the General Government. So far as it relates to the measure as a tax, the exception must be regarded as applying to the particular place where it is collected, in a vessel on the water, though after her arrival within a port or harbor. It would seem to be argued, that, by some constitutional provision, a State possesses no power in such a place. But there is nothing in the taxing part of the constitution which forbids her action in such places on matters like this. If forbidden at all, it must be by general principles of the common and of national law, that no State can assess or levy a tax on what is without the limits of its jurisdiction, or that, if within its territorial limits, the subject-matter is vested exclusively by the constitution in the General Government.

It will be seen, that, if the first exception be valid, it is not one connected with the constitution of the United States, and hence not revisable here. It was not, and could not properly be, set up as a defence in the court of a State, except under its own constitution, and hence not revisable in this court by this writ of error. But as it may be supposed to have some influences on the other and commercial aspect of the objection, it may be well to ascertain whether, as a general principle, a vessel in a port, or its occupants, crew, or passengers, are in fact without the limits and jurisdiction of a State, and thus beyond its taxing power, and are exclusively, for all purposes, under the government of the United States. One of the errors in the argument of this part of the cause has been an apparent assumption that this tax—considered as a tax—was collected at sea, before the voyage ended, and was not collected within the limits and jurisdiction of the State. But, *ex concesso*, this vessel then was in the harbor of Boston, some miles within the limits of the State, and where this court itself has repeatedly decided that Massachusetts, and not the General Government, has jurisdiction. First, jurisdiction to punish crimes. (See in Waring *v.* Clarke, 5 Howard, 441; Ibid. 628; Coolidge's case, 1 Wheat. 415; Bevans' case, 3 Wheat. 336; 1 Woodbury & Minot, 401, 455, 481, 483.) Next, the State would have jurisdiction there to enforce contracts. So must she have to collect taxes, for the like reason (5 Howard, 441); because it was a place within the territorial limits and jurisdiction of the State. Chief Justice Marshall, in 12 Wheat. 441, speaks of "their [the States'] acknowledged power to tax persons and property within their territory." (Ibid. 444.)

The tax in this case does not touch the passenger *in transitu* on the ocean, or abroad,—never till the actual arrival of the vessel with him in port. An arrival in port, in other acts of Congress using the term, is coming in, or anchoring within, its limits, with a view to discharge the cargo. (2 Sumner, 419; 5 Mason, 445; 4 Taunton, 662, 722; Toler *v.* White, Ware, 277.)

For aught that appears, this vessel, before visited, had come in and was at anchor in the port. The person so going into port abroad is considered to have "arrived," so as to be amenable to his consul, and must deposit his papers. He has come under or into the control of shore power, and shore authority, and shore laws, and shore writs, and shore juries; at least concurrently with other authorities, if not exclusively. In common parlance, the voyage, for this purpose at least, is not interrupted; for then it has ended, and the State liabilities and powers begin, or the State becomes utterly imbecile. Hence, speaking of a country as distinguished from the sea, and of a nation as a State, Vattel (B. 1, ch. 23, § 290) says: — "Ports and harbors are manifestly an appendage to, and even a part of, the country, and consequently are the property of the nation. Whatever is said of the land itself will equally apply to them, so far as respects the consequences of the domain and of the empire." If the ports and harbors of a State are *intra fauces terræ*, within the body of a country, the power of taxation is as complete in them as it is on land, a hundred miles in the interior. Though on tide waters, the vessels are there subject for many purposes to State authority rather than federal, are taxed as stock in trade, or ships owned, if by residents; the cargo may be there taxed; the officers and crew may be there taxed for their polls, as well as estate; and, on the same principle, may be the master for the passengers, or the passengers themselves. Persons there, poor and sick, are also entitled to public relief from the city or State. (4 Metcalf, 290, 291.) No matter where may be the place, if only within the territorial boundaries of the State, or, in other words, within its geographical limits. The last is the test, and not whether it be a merchant-vessel or a dwelling-house, or something in either, as property or persons. Unless beyond the borders of the State, or granted, as a fort or navy-yard within them, to a separate and exclusive jurisdiction, or used as an authorized instrument of the General Government, the State laws control and can tax it. (United States *v.* Ames, 1 Woodb. & Minot, 76, and cases there cited.)

It is true there are exceptions as to taxation which do not affect this question; as where something is taxed which is held under the grants to the United States, and the grants might be defeated if taxed by the State. That was the point in McCulloch *v.* Maryland, 4 Wheat. 316; Weston *v.* City of Charleston, 2 Peters, 449; Dobbins *v.* Commissioners of Erie County, 16 Peters, 435; Osborn *v.* Bank of the United States, 9 Wheat. 738. But that is not the question here, as neither passengers nor the master of the vessel can be considered as official instruments of the government.

In point of fact, too, in an instance like this, it is well known that the general jurisdiction of the States for most municipal purposes within their territory, including taxation, has never been ceded to the United States, nor claimed by them; but they may anchor their navies there, prevent smuggling, and collect duties there, as they may do the last on land. But this is not inconsistent with the other; and this brings us to the second consideration under this head,—how far such a concurrent power in that government, for a particular object, can, with any propriety whatever, impair the general rights of the States there on other matters.

These powers exist in the two governments for different purposes, and are not at all inconsistent or conflicting. The General Government may collect its duties, either on the water or the land, and still the State enforce its own laws without any collision, whether they are made for local taxation, or military duty, or the collection of debts, or the punishment of crimes. There being no inconsistency or collision, no reason exists to hold either, by mere construction, void. This is the cardinal test.

So the master may not always deliver merchandise rightfully, except on a wharf; nor be always entitled to freight till the goods are on shore; yet this depends on the usage, or contract, or nature of the port, and does not affect the question of jurisdiction. (Abbott on Shipping, 249; 4 Bos. & Pul. 16.) On the contrary, some offences may be completed entirely on the water, and yet the State jurisdiction on land is conceded. (United States *v.* Coombs, 12 Peters, 72.)

So a contract with the passenger may or may not be completed on arriving in port, without landing, according as the parties may have been pleased to stipulate. (Brig Lavinia, 1 Peters, Adm. 126.)

So the insurance on a cargo of a ship may not in some cases terminate till it is landed, though in others it may, depending on the language used. (Reyner *v.* Pearson, 4 Taunton, 662, and Levin *v.* Newnham, ib. 722.) But none of these show that the passengers may not quit the vessel outside the harbor, in boats or other vessels, and thus go to the land, or go to other ports. Or that, if not doing this, and coming in the same vessel within the State limits, they may not be subject to arrests, punishments, and taxation or police fees, or other regulations of the State, though still on board the vessel. Nor do any of them show that the vessel and cargo, after within the State limits, though not on the shore, are not within the jurisdiction of the State, and liable, as property of the owner, to be taxed in common with other stock in trade.

I will not waste a moment in combating the novel idea, that taxes by the States must be uniform, or they are void by the constitution on that account; because clearly that provision relates only to taxes imposed by the General Government. It is a fallacy, also, to argue that the vessels, crews, and passengers, when within the territory of a State, are not amenable to the State laws in these respects, because they are enrolled as belonging to the United States, and their flag is the flag of the United States. For though they do belong to the United States in respect to foreign nations and our statistical returns and tables, this does not prevent the vessels at the same time from being owned by citizens of the State of Massachusetts, and the crew belonging there, and all, with the passengers, after within her limits, from being amenable generally to her laws.

If taking another objection to it as a tax, and arguing against the tax imposed on the vessel, because it may be abused to injure emigration and thwart the General Government, it would still conflict with no particular clause in the constitution or acts of Congress. It should also be remembered that this was one objection to the license laws in 5 Howard, and that the court held unanimously they were constitutional, though they evidently tended to diminish importations of spirituous liquor and lessen the revenue of the General Government from that source. But that being only an incident to them, and not their chief design, and the chief design being within the jurisdiction of the States, the laws were upheld.

It is the purpose which Mr. Justice Johnson thinks may show that no collision was intended or effected. "Their different purposes mark the distinction between the powers brought into action, and while frankly exercised they can produce no serious collision." (Gibbons *v.* Ogden, 9 Wheat. 235.) "Collision must be sought to be produced." "Wherever the powers of the respective governments are frankly exercised, with a distinct view to the end of such powers, they may act on the same subject, or use the same means, and yet the powers be kept perfectly distinct." (P. 239. See 1 Woodbury & Minot, 423, 433.)

The next delegation of power to Congress, supposed by some to be inconsistent with this statute, is argued to be involved in the ninth section of the first article of the constitution. This they consider as a grant of power to Congress to prohibit the migration from abroad of all persons, bond or free, after the year 1808, and to tax their importation at once and forever, not exceeding ten dollars per head. (See 9 Wheat. 230, by Mr. Justice Johnson; 15 Peters, 514.) The words are:—"The migration or importation of such persons as any of the States now existing shall think proper to admit shall not be prohibited by the Congress, prior to the year 1808; but a tax or duty may be imposed on such importation, not exceeding ten dollars for each person." But it deserves special notice, that this section is one entirely of limitation on power, rather than a grant of it; and the power of prohibition being nowhere else in the constitution expressly granted to Congress, the section seems introduced rather to prevent it from being implied except as to slaves, after 1808, than to confer it in all cases. (1 Brockenbrough, 432.)

If to be implied elsewhere, it is from the grant to regulate commerce, and by the idea that slaves are subjects of commerce, as they often are. Hence, it can go no further than to imply it as to them, and not as to free passengers.

Or if to "regulate commerce" extends also to the regulation of mere navigation, and hence to the business of carrying passengers, in which it may be employed, it is confined to a forfeiture of the vessel, and does not legitimately involve a prohibition of persons, except when articles of commerce, like slaves. (1 Brockenbrough, 432.) Or, finally, however far the power may extend under either view, it is still a power concurrent in the States, like most taxation and much local legislation as to matters connected somewhat with commerce, and is well exercised by them when Congress does not, as here, legislate upon the matter either of prohibition or of taxation of passengers. It is hence that if this ninth section is a grant of the power to prevent the migration or importation of other persons than slaves, it is not an exclusive one, any more than that to regulate commerce, to which it refers; nor has it ever been exercised so as to conflict with State laws, or with the statute of Massachusetts now under consideration. This clause itself recognizes an exclusive power of prohibition in the States, until the year 1808. And a concurrent and subordinate power on this by the States, after that, is nowhere expressly forbidden in the constitution, nor is it denied by any reason or necessity for such exclusiveness. The States can often use it more wisely than Congress in respect to their own interests and policy. They cannot protect their police, or health, or public morals, without the exercise of such a power, at times and under certain exigencies, as forbidding the admission of slaves and certain other persons within their borders. One State, also, may require its exercise, from its exposures and dangers, when another may not. So it may be said, as to the power to tax *importation*, if limited to slaves, the States could continue to do the same when they pleased, if men are not deemed "imports."

But to see for a moment how dangerous it would be to consider a prohibitory power over all aliens as vested exclusively in Congress, look to some of the consequences. The States must be mute and powerless.

If Congress, without a coördinate or concurrent power in the States, can prohibit other persons as well as slaves from coming into States, they can of course allow it, and hence can permit and demand the admission of slaves, as well as any kind of free persons, convicts or paupers, into any State, and enforce the demand by all the overwhelming powers of the Union, however obnoxious to the habits and wishes of the people of a particular State. In view of an inference like this, it has therefore been said that, under this section, Congress cannot admit persons whom a State pleases to exclude. (9 Wheaton, 230; Justice Johnson.) This rather strengthens the propriety of the independent action of the State, here excluding conditionally, than the idea that it is under the control of Congress.

Besides this, the ten dollars per head allowed here specially to be collected by Congress on imported slaves is not an exclusive power to tax, and would not have been necessary or inserted, if Congress could clearly already impose such a tax on them, as "imports," and by a "duty" on imports. It would be not a little extraordinary to imply by construction a power in Congress to prohibit the coming into the States of others than slaves, or of mere aliens, on the principle of the alien part of the Alien and Sedition Laws, though it never has been exercised as to others permanently, but the States recommended to exercise it, and seventeen of them now actually doing it. And equally extraordinary to imply, at this late day, not only that Congress possesses the power, but that, though not exercising it, the States are incapable of exercising it concurrently, or even in subordination to Congress. But beyond this, the States have exercised it concurrently as to slaves, no less than exclusively in respect to certain free persons, since as well as before 1808, and this as to their admission from neighboring States no less than from abroad. (See cases before cited, and Butler *v.* Hopper, 1 Wash. C. C. 500.)

The word "migration" was probably added to "importation" to cover slaves when regarded as persons rather than property, as they are for some purposes. Or if to cover others, such as convicts and redemptioners, it was those only who came against their will, or in a *quasi* servitude. And though the expression may be broad enough to cover emigrants generally (3 Madison State Papers, 1429; 9 Wheat. 216, 230; 1 Brockenbrough, 431), and some thought it might cover convicts (5 Elliott's Deb. 477; 3 Madison State Papers, 1430), yet it was not so considered by the mass of the convention, but as intended for "slaves," and calling them "persons" out of delicacy. (5 Elliott's Deb. 457, 477; 3 ib. 251, 541; 4 ib. 119; 15 Peters, 113, 506; 11 ib. 136; 1 Bl. Com. by Tucker, App. 290.) It was so considered in the Federalist, soon after, and that view regarded as a "misconstruction" which extended it to "emigration" generally. (Federalist, No. 42.) So afterwards thought Mr. Madison himself, the great expounder and framer of most of the constitution. (3 Elliott's Deb. 422.) So it has been held by several members of this court (15 Peters, 508); and so it has been considered by Congress, judging from its uniform acts, except the unfortunate Alien Law of 1798, before cited, and which, on account of its unconstitutional features, had so brief and troubled an existence. (4 Elliott's Deb. 451.)

In the constitution, in other parts as in this, the word "persons" is used, not to embrace others as well as slaves, but slaves alone. Thus, in the second section of the first article, "three-fifths of all other *persons*," manifestly means slaves; and in the third section of the fourth article, "no *person* held to service or labor in one State," &c., refers to slaves. The word *slave* was avoided, from a sensitive feeling; but clearly no others were intended in the ninth section. Congress so considered it, also, when it took up the subject of this section in 1807, just before the limitation expired, or it would then probably have acted as to others, and regulated the migration and importation of others as well as of slaves. By forbidding merely "to import or bring into the United States, or territories thereof, from any foreign kingdom, place, or country, any negro, mulatto, or person of color, with intent to hold, sell, or dispose of such negro, mulatto, or person of color, as a slave, or to be held to service or labor," it is manifest that Congress then considered this clause in the constitution as referring to slaves alone, and then as a matter of commerce; and it strengthens this idea, that Congress has never since attempted to extend this clause to any other persons, while the States have been in the constant habit of prohibiting the introduction of paupers, convicts, free blacks, and persons sick with contagious diseases, no less than slaves; and this from neighboring States as well as from abroad.

There was no occasion for that express grant, or rather recognition, of the power to forbid the entry of slaves by the General Government, if Congress could, by other clauses of the constitution, for what seemed to it good cause, forbid the entry of everybody, as of aliens generally; and if Congress could not do this generally, it is a decisive argument that the State might do it, as the power must exist somewhere in every independent country.

Again: if the States had not such power under the constitution, at least concurrently, by what authority did most of them forbid the importation of slaves from abroad into their limits between 1789 and 1808? Congress has no power to transfer such rights to States. And how came Congress to recognize their right to do it virtually by the first article and ninth section, and also by the act of 1803? It was because the States originally had it as sovereign States, and had never parted with it exclusively to Congress. This court, in Groves *v.* Slaughter, 15 Peters, 511, is generally understood as sustaining the right of States, since 1808 no less than before, to prohibit the bringing into their limits of slaves for sale, even from other States, no less than from foreign countries.

From the very nature of State sovereignty over what is not granted to Congress, and the power of prohibition, either as to persons or things, except slaves after the year 1808, not being anywhere conferred on, or recognized as in the General Government, no good reason seems to exist against the present exercise of it by the States, unless where it may clearly conflict with other clauses in the constitution. In fact, every slave State in the Union, long before 1808, is believed to have prohibited the further importation of slaves into her territories from abroad (Libby's Case, 1 Woodb. & Min. 235; Butler *v.* Hopper, 1 Wash. C. C. 499); and several, as before stated, have since prohibited virtually the import of them from contiguous States. Among them may be named Kentucky, Missouri, and Alabama, as well as Mississippi, using, for instance, as in the constitution of the last, such language as the following: — "The introduction of slaves into this State as merchandise, or for sale, shall be prohibited from and after the first day of May, 1833." (See Constitutions of the States, and 15 Peters, 500.)

Coming by land or sea to be sold, slaves are equally articles of commerce, and thus bringing them in is an "importation or migration of persons;" and if the power over that is now exclusive in Congress, more than half the States in the Union have violated it. If a State can do this as to slaves from abroad or a contiguous State, why not, as has often been the case, do it in respect to any other person deemed dangerous or hostile to the stability and prosperity of her institutions? They can, because they act on these persons when within their limits, and for objects not commercial, and doing this is not disturbing the voyage, which brings them in as passengers, nor taxing the instrument used in it, as the vessel, nor even the master and crew, for acts done abroad, or anything without her own limits. The power of the State in prohibiting rests on a sovereign right to regulate who shall be her inhabitants,—a right more vital than that to regulate commerce by the General Government, and which, as independent or concurrent, the latter has not disturbed, and should not disturb. (15 Peters, 507, 508.)

But the final objection made to the collection of this money by a State is a leading and difficult one. It consists in this view, that, though called either a police regulation, or a municipal condition to admission into a State, or a tax on an alien visiter, it is, in substance and in truth, a regulation of foreign commerce, and the power to make that being exclusively vested in Congress, no State can properly exercise it.

If both the points involved in this position could be sustained, this proceeding of the State might be obliged to yield. But there are two answers to it. One of them is, that this statute is not a regulation of commerce; and the other is, that the power to regulate foreign commerce is not made exclusive in Congress.

As to the first, this statute does not *eo nomine* undertake "to regulate commerce," and its design, motive, and object were entirely different.

At the formation of the constitution, the power to regulate commerce attracted but little attention, compared with that to impose duties on imports and tonnage; and this last had caused so much difficulty, both at home and abroad, that it was expressly and entirely taken away from the States, but the former was not attempted to be. The former, too, occupies scarce a page in the Federalist, while the latter engrosses several numbers. A like disparity existed in the debates in the convention, and in the early legislation of Congress. Nor did the former receive much notice of the profession in construing the constitution till after a quarter of a century; and then, though considered in the case of Gibbons *v.* Ogden (9 Wheaton, 1) as a power clearly conferred on Congress, and to be sustained on all appropriate matters, yet it does not appear to have been held that nothing connected in any degree with commerce, or resembling it, could be regulated by State legislation; but only that this last must not be so exercised as to conflict directly with an existing act of Congress. (See the text, and especially the mandate in 9 Wheat. 239, 240.) On the contrary, many subjects of legislation are of such a doubtful class, and even of such an amphibious character, that one person would arrange and define them as matters of police, another as matters of taxation, and another as matters of commerce. But all familiar with these topics must know, that laws on these by States for local purposes, and to operate only within State limits, are not usually intended, and should not be considered, as laws "to regulate commerce." They are made entirely *diverso intuitu.* Hence, much connected with the local power of taxation, and with the police of the States as to paupers, quarantine laws, the introduction of criminals or dangerous persons, or of obscene and immoral prints and books, or of destructive poisons and liquors, belongs to the States at home. It varies with their different home policies and habits, and is not, either in its locality or operation, a matter of exterior policy, though at times connected with, or resulting from, foreign commerce, and over which, within their own borders, the States have never acted as if they had parted with the power, and never could with so much advantage to their people as to retain it among themselves. (9 Wheaton, 203.) Its interests and influences are nearer to each State, are often peculiar to each, better understood by and for each, and, if prudently watched over, will never involve them in conflicts with the General Government or with foreign nations.

The regulation and support of paupers and convicts, as well as their introduction into a State, through foreign intercourse, by vessels, are matters of this character. (New York *v.* Miln, 11 Peters, 141; License Cases, 5 Howard; Baldwin's Views, 184.) Some States are much exposed to large burdens and fatal diseases and moral pollution from this source, while others are almost entirely exempt. Some, therefore, need no legislation, State or national, while others do, and must protect themselves when Congress cannot or will not. This matter, for instance, may be vital to Massachusetts, New York, Louisiana, or Maryland; but it is a subject of indifference to a large portion of the rest of the Union, not much resorted to from abroad; and this circumstance indicates, not only why those first-named States, as States, should, by local legislation, protect themselves from supposed evils from it, where deemed necessary or expedient, but that it is not one of those incidents to our foreign commerce in most of the Union which, like duties, or imposts, or taxes on tonnage, require a uniform and universal rule to be applied by the General Government.

A uniform rule by Congress not being needed on this particular point, nor being just, is a strong proof that it was not intended Congress should exercise power over it; especially when paupers, or aliens likely to become paupers, enter a State that has not room or business for them, but they merely pass through to other places, the tax would not be needed to support them or help to exclude them; and hence such a State would not be likely to impose one for those purposes. But, considering the power to be in Congress, and some States needed legislation, and that being required to be uniform, if Congress were to impose a tax for such purposes, and pay a ratable proportion of it over to such a State, it would be unjust. If, to avoid this, Congress were to collect such a tax, and itself undertake to support foreign paupers out of it, Congress would transcend the powers granted to her, as none extend to the maintenance of paupers, and it might as well repair roads for local use, and make laws to settle intestate estates, or, at least, estates of foreigners. And if it can do this because passengers are aliens and connected with foreign commerce, and, this power being exclusive in it, State taxes on them are therefore void, it must follow that State laws are void also in respect to foreign bills of exchange, a great instrument of foreign commerce, and in respect to bankrupt laws, another topic connected with foreign commerce,—neither of which, but directly the reverse, is the law.

"To regulate" is to prescribe rules, to control. But the State, by this statute, prescribes no rules for the "commerce with foreign nations." It does not regulate the vessel or the voyage while in progress. On the contrary, it prescribes rules for a local matter, one in which she, as a State, has the deepest interest, and one arising after the voyage has ended, and not a matter of commerce or navigation, but rather of police, or municipal, or taxing supervision.

Again: it is believed that in Europe, in several instances of border states, so far from the introduction of foreigners who are paupers, or likely soon to be so, being regarded as a question of commerce, it is deemed one of police merely; and the expenses of alien paupers are made a subject of reclamation from the contiguous government to which they belong.

This view, showing that the regulation of this matter is not, in substance more than in words, to regulate foreign commerce, is strengthened by various other matters, which have never been regarded as regulating commerce, though nearer connected in some respects with that commerce than this is. But like this, they are all, when provided for by the States, regulated only within their own limits, and for themselves, and not without their limits, as of a foreign matter, nor for other States. Such are the laws of the States which have ever continued to regulate several matters in harbors and ports where foreign vessels enter and unload. (Vanderbilt *v.* Adams, 7 Wendell, 349.) The whole jurisdiction over them when within the headlands on the ocean, though filled with salt water and strong tides, is in the States. We have, under another head, already shown that it exists there exclusively for most criminal prosecutions, and also for all civil proceedings to prosecute trespasses and recover debts of the owners of the ship or cargo, or of the crew or passengers, and whether aliens or citizens. And though the General Government is allowed to collect its duties and enforce its specific requirements about them there, as it is authorized to do, and does, under acts of Congress, even on land (Gibbons *v.* Ogden, 9 Wheat.; United States *v.* Coombs, 12 Peters, 72), yet it can exercise no power there, criminal or civil, under implication, or under a construction that its authority to regulate commerce there is exclusive as to matters like these. No exclusive jurisdiction has been expressly ceded to it there, as in some forts, navy-yards, and arsenals. Nor is any necessary. Not one of its officers, fiscal or judicial, can exert the smallest authority there, in opposition to the State jurisdiction, and State laws, and State officers, but only in public vessels of war, or over forts and navy-yards ceded, or as to duties on imports, and other cases, to the extent specifically bestowed on them by constitutional acts of Congress. And to regulate these local concerns in this way by the States is not to regulate foreign commerce, but home concerns. The design is local; the object a State object, and not a foreign or commercial one; and the exercise of the power is not conflicting with any existing actual enactment by Congress.

The States also have and can exercise there, not only their just territorial jurisdiction over persons and things, but make special officers and special laws for regulating there in their limits various matters of a local interest and bearing, in connection with all the commerce, foreign as well as domestic, which is there gathered. They appoint and pay harbor-masters, and officers to regulate the deposit of ballast and anchorage of vessels (7 Wendell, 349), and the building of wharves;

and are often at great expense in removing obstructions. (1 Bl. Com. by Tucker, 249.)

These State officers have the power to direct where vessels shall anchor, and the precautions to be used against fires on board; and all State laws in regard to such matters must doubtless continue in force till conflicting with some express legislation by Congress. (1 Bl. Com. by Tucker, 252.) I allude to these with the greater particularity, because they are so directly connected with foreign commerce, and are not justified more perhaps, under police, or sanatory, or moral considerations, than under the general principle of concurrent authority in the States on many matters granted to Congress,— taking care not to attempt to regulate the foreign commerce, and not to conflict directly and materially with any provision actually made by Congress,— nor to do it in a case where the grant is accompanied by an express prohibition to the States, or is in its nature and character such as to imply clearly a total prohibition to the States of every exercise of power connected with it. To remove doubts as to the design to have the power of the States remain to legislate on such matters within their own limits, the old confederation, in article ninth, where granting the power of regulating "the trade and managing all affairs with the Indians, not members of any of the States," provided that "the legislative right of any State, within its own limits, be not infringed or violated." The same end was meant to be effected in the new constitution, though in a different way; and this was, by not granting any power to Congress over the internal commerce, or police, or municipal affairs of the States, and declaring expressly, in the tenth amendment, that all powers not so granted were reserved to the people of the States.

It follows from what has been said, that this statute of Massachusetts, if regarded as a police measure, or a municipal regulation as to residents or visiters within its borders, or as a tax or any local provision for her own affairs, ought not to be considered as a regulation of commerce; but it is one of those other measures still authorized in the States, and still useful and appropriate to them. Such measures, too, are usually not conflicting with that commerce, but adopted entirely *diverso intuitu*, and so operating.

Conceding, then, that the power to regulate foreign commerce may include the regulation of the vessel as well as the cargo, and the manner of using the vessel in that commerce, yet the statute of Massachusetts does neither. It merely affects the master or passengers after their arrival, and for some further act than proposed to be done. And though vessels are instruments of commerce, passengers are not. And though regulating the mode of carrying them on the ocean may be to regulate commerce and navigation, yet to tax them after their arrival here is not. Indeed, the regulation of anything is not naturally or generally to tax it, as that usually depends on another power. It has been well held in this court, that, under the constitution, the taxing of imports is not a regulation of commerce, nor to be sustained under that grant, but under the grant as to taxation. (Gibbons *v.* Ogden, 9 Wheat. 201.) Duties may, to be sure, be imposed at times to regulate commerce, but oftener are imposed with a view to revenue; and therefore, under that head, duties as taxes were prohibited to the States. (9 Wheat. 202, 203.)

It is a mistaken view to say, that the power of a State to exclude slaves, or free blacks, or convicts, or paupers, or to make pecuniary terms for their admission, may be one not conflicting with commerce, while the same power, if applied to alien passengers coming in vessels, does conflict. Slaves now excepted, though once not entirely, they are all equally and frequently passengers, and all oftener come in by water, in the business and channels of ocean commerce, than by land. But if the transit of persons coming into the States as passengers, by water, is a branch of commerce, so is their coming in by land; and this, whether from other nations on our land frontier, or from other States. And if Mississippi and Ohio can rightfully impose prohibitions, taxes, or any terms to such coming by land or water from other States, so may Massachusetts and New York, if thus coming from foreign nations by water. Congress, also, has like power to regulate commerce between the States, as between this country and other nations, and if persons coming in by water as passengers belong to the subject of commerce and navigation on the Atlantic, so do they on the lakes and large rivers; and if excluding or requiring terms of them in one place interferes with commerce, so it does in the other.

Again: if any decisive indication, independent of general principles, exists as to which government shall exercise the taxing power in respect to the support of paupers, it is that the States, rather than the General Government, shall exercise it (9 Wheat. 206, 216); and exercise it as such a power, and not, by a forced construction, as a power "to regulate commerce." The States have always continued to exercise the various powers of local taxation and police, and not Congress; and have maintained all paupers. And this, though the general authority to regulate commerce, no less than to lay taxes, was granted to Congress. But police powers and powers over the internal commerce and municipal affairs of States were not granted away; and under them, and the general power of taxation, States continued to control this subject, and not under the power to regulate commerce. Nor did Congress, though possessing this last power, ever attempt to interfere, as if to do so was a branch of that power, or justifiable under it, because in terms using language connected with commerce. Thus, in the Kentucky constitution, and substantially in several others, it is provided that the Legislature "shall have full power to prevent slaves from being brought into this State as merchandise," and Congress sanctioned that constitution, and the rest, with such provisions in them.

These affairs are a part of the domestic economy of States, belong to their interior policy, and operate on matters affecting the fireside, the hearth, and the altar. The States have no foreign relations, and need none, as to this. (1 Bl. Com. by Tucker, App. 249.)

The fair exercise of such powers rightfully belonging to a State, though connected often with foreign commerce, and indirectly or slightly affecting it, cannot therefore be considered, in any point of view, hostile, by their intent or origin, as regulations of such commerce. (See in point, Gibbons *v.* Ogden, 9 Wheat. 203; 11 Peters, 102.)

In this view, it is immaterial whether this tax is imposed on the passenger while in the ship, in port, or when he touches the wharf, or reaches his hotel. All these places, being within the territory, are equally within the jurisdiction of the State for municipal purposes such as these, and not with a view to regulate foreign commerce; it being conceded that a tax may be imposed on a passenger after quitting the vessel and on the land, why may it not before, when he is then within the limits of the State? In either instance, the tax has no concern with the foreign voyage, and does not regulate the foreign commerce; whereas, if otherwise, it might be as invalid when imposed on land as on water.

Much of the difficulty in this case arises, I apprehend, from a misconception, as if this tax was imposed on the passenger at sea, and before within the territorial limits of the State. But this, as before suggested, is an entire misapprehension of the extent of those limits, or of the words and meaning of the law.

If, then, as is argued, intercourse by merchants in person, and by officers in their vessels, boats, and wagons, is a part of commerce, and the carrying of passengers is also a branch of navigation or commerce, still the taxing of these after the arrival in port, though Congress there has power to collect its duties as it has on land, is not vested at all in Congress; or, if at all, not exclusively.

Who can point to the cession to the United States of the jurisdiction, by Massachusetts or New York, of their own ports and harbors for purposes of taxation, or any other local and municipal purpose?

So far from interfering at all here with the foreign voyage, the State power begins when that ends, and the vessel has entered the jurisdictional limits of the State. Her laws reach the consequences and results of foreign commerce, rather than the commerce itself. They touch not the tonnage of the vessel, nor her merchandise, nor the baggage or tools of the aliens; nor do they forbid the vessels carrying passengers. But as a condition to their landing and remaining within the jurisdiction of the State, enough is required by way of condition or terms for that privilege, and the risk of their becoming chargeable, when aliens (though not chargeable at the time), to cover in some degree the expenses happening under such contingency. This has nothing to do with the regulation of commerce itself,— the right to carry passengers to and fro over the Atlantic Ocean,—but merely with their inhabitancy or residence within a State, so as to be entitled to its charity, its privileges, and protection. Such laws do not conflict directly with any provision by the General Government as to foreign commerce, because none has been made on this point, and they are not in clear collision with any made by that government on any other point. When, as here, they purport to be for a different purpose from touching the concerns of the General Government,—when they are, as here, adapted to another local and legitimate object,—it is unjust to a sovereign State, and derogatory to the character of her people and Legislature, to impute a sinister and illegitimate design to them, concerning foreign commerce, different from that avowed, and from that which the amount of the tax and the evil to be guarded against clearly indicate as the true design. Hence, as before remarked, Mr. Justice Johnson, in the same opinion which was cited by the original defendants, says the *purpose* is the test; and if that be different, and does not clash, the law is not unconstitutional.

So Chief Justice Marshall, in 9 Wheat. 204, says, that Congress for one purpose and a State for another may use like means and both be vindicated. And though Congress obtains its power from a special grant, like that of the power "to regulate commerce," the State may obtain it from a reserved power over internal commerce, or over its police. Hence, while Congress regulates the number of passengers to the size of the vessel, as a matter of foreign commerce, and may exempt their baggage and tools from duties, as a matter of imposts on imports, yet this is not inconsistent with the power of a State, after passengers arrive within her limits, to impose terms on their landing, with a view to benefit her pauper police, or her fiscal resources, or her municipal safety and welfare. And the two powers, thus exercised separately by the two governments, may, as Mr. Justice Johnson says. "be perfectly distinct." So, in the language of Chief Justice Marshall, "if executed by the same means," "this does not prove that the powers themselves are identical."

The measures of the General Government amount to a regulation of the traffic, or trade, or business, of carrying passengers, and of the imposts on imports; but those of the States amount to neither, and merely affect the passengers or master of the vessel after their arrival within the limits of a State, and for State purposes, State security, and State policy.

As we have before explained, then, if granting that the bringing of passengers is a great branch of the business of navigation, and that to regulate commerce is to regulate navigation, yet this statute of Massachusetts neither regulates that navigation employed in carrying passengers, nor the passengers themselves, either while abroad in foreign ports, or while on the Atlantic Ocean, but merely taxes them, or imposes conditions on them, after within the State. These things are done, as Mr. Justice Johnson said, in another case, "with a distinct view." And it is no objection that they "act on the same subject" (9 Wheat. 235); or, in the words of Chief Justice Marshall, "although the means used in their execution may sometimes approach each other so nearly as to be confounded." (P. 204.) But where any doubt arises, it should operate against the uncertain and loose, or what the late Chief Justice called "questionable power to regulate commerce" (9 Wheat. 202), rather than the more fixed and distinct police or taxing power.

In cases like this, if, amidst the great complexity of human affairs, and in the shadowy line between the two governments over the same people, it is impossible for their mutual rights and powers not to infringe occasionally upon each other, or cross a little the dividing line, it constitutes no cause for denouncing the acts on either side as being exercised under the same power or for the same purpose, and therefore unconstitutional and void. When, as is seldom likely, their laws come in direct and material collision, both being in the exercise of distinct powers, which belong to them, it is wisely provided, by the constitution itself, and consequently by the States and the people themselves, as they framed it, that the States, being the granting power, must recede. (9 Wheat. 203; License Cases, 5 Howard; United States *v.* New Bedford Bridge, 1 Woodb. & Minot, 423.) Here we see no such collision.

There are other cases of seeming opposition which are reconcilable, and not conflicting, as to the powers exercised both by the States and the General Government, but for different purposes. Thus, hides may be imported under the acts of Congress taxing imports and regulating commerce; but this does not deprive a State of the right, in guarding the public health, to have them destroyed if putrefied, whether before they reach the land or after. So as to the import of gunpowder by the authority of one government, and the prohibition by the other, for the public safety, to keep it in large quantities. (4 Metcalf, 294.) Neither of these acts by the State attempts to interfere with the commerce abroad, but after its arrival here, and for other purposes, local and sanatory, or municipal.

In short, it has been deliberately held by this court, that the laying a duty on imports, if this was of that character, is an exercise of the taxing power, and not of that to regulate commerce. (Gibbons *v.* Ogden, 9 Wheat. 201, by Chief Justice Marshall.) And if, in Brown *v.* Maryland, 12 Wheat. 447, the tax or duty imposed there can be considered as held to violate both, it was because it was not only a tax on imports, but provided for the treatment of goods themselves, or regulated them as imported in foreign commerce, and while in bulk.

But if the power exercised in this law by Massachusetts could, by a forced construction, be tortured into a regulation of foreign commerce, the next requisite to make the law void is not believed to exist in the fact that the States do not retain some concurrent or subordinate powers, such as were here exercised, though connected in certain respects with foreign commerce. Beside the reasons already assigned for this opinion, it is not opposed to either the language or the spirit of the constitution in connection with this particular grant. Accompanying it are no exclusive words, nor is the further action of the States, or anything concerning commerce, expressly forbidden in any other way in the constitution. But both of these are done in several other cases, such as "no State shall coin money," or no State "engage in war," and these are ordinary modes adopted in the constitution to indicate that a power granted is exclusive, when it was meant to be so.

If this reasoning be not correct, why was express prohibition to the States used on any subject where authority was granted to Congress? The only other mode to ascertain whether a power thus granted is exclusive, "is to look at the nature of each grant, and if that does not clearly show the power to be exclusive, not to hold it to be so." We have seen that was the rule laid down by one of the makers and great expounders of the instrument. (Federalist, No. 82. See also 14 Peters, 575.)

It held out this as an inducement to the States to adopt the constitution, and was urged by all the logic and eloquence of Hamilton. It was, that a grant of power to Congress, so far from being *ipso facto* exclusive, never ousted the power of the States previously existing, unless "where an exclusive authority is in express terms granted to the Union, or where a particular authority is granted to the Union, and the exercise of a like authority is prohibited to the States; or where an authority is granted to the Union, with which a similar authority in the States would be utterly incompatible."

This rule has been recognized in various decisions on constitutional questions by many of the judges of this court. (2 Cranch, 397; 3 Wheat. 386; 5 Wheat. 49; Wilson *v.* Blackbird Creek Marsh Company, 2 Peters, 245; Prigg *v.* Pennsylvania, 16 Peters, 627, 655, 664; New York *v.* Miln, 11 Peters, 103, 132; Groves *v.* Slaughter, 15 Peters, 509; Holmes *v.* Jennison, 14 Peters, 579.) So by this court itself, in Sturges *v.* Crowninshield, 4 Wheat. 193. And also by other authorities entitled to much respect. (4 Elliott's Deb. 567; 3 Jefferson's Life, 425—429; 3 Serg. & Rawle, 79; Peck's Trial, 86, 87, 291—293, 329, 404, 434, 435; Calder *v.* Bull, 3 Dall. 386; 1 Kent's Com. 364; 9 Johns, 568.)

In other cases it is apparently contravened. (9 Wheat. 209; 15 Peters, 504, by Mr. Justice McLean, and 511, by Mr. Justice Baldwin; Prigg *v.* Pennsylvania, 16 Peters, 543; New York *v.* Miln, 11 Peters, 158, by Mr. Justice Story; The Chusan, 2 Story, 465; Golden *v.* Prince, 3 Wash. C. C. 325.)

But this is often in appearance only, and not in reality. It is not a difference as to what should be the true rule, but in deciding what cases fall within it, and especially the branch of it as to what is exclusive by implication and reasoning from the nature of the particular grant or case; or, in the words of Hamilton, "where an authority is granted to the Union, with which a similar authority in the States would be utterly incompatible."

Thus, in the celebrated case of Sturges *v.* Crowninshield, the rule itself is laid down in the same way substantially as in the Federalist; namely, that the power is to be taken from the State only when expressly forbidden, or where "the terms in which a power is granted to Congress, or the nature of the power, require that it should be exercised exclusively by Congress." (4 Wheat. 122, 193, by Chief Justice Marshall; Prigg *v.* Commonwealth of Pennsylvania, 16 Peters, 626, by Chief Justice Taney, and 650, by Mr. Justice Daniel.)

And Chief Justice Marshall on another occasion considered this to be the true rule. That was in the case of Wilson *v.* Blackbird Creek Marsh Company, 2 Peters, 245, though a commercial question. And Judge Story did the same in Houston *v.* Moore, 5 Wheat. 49,—a militia question. So many of the other grants in this same section of the constitution, under like forms of expression, have been virtually held not to be exclusive; such as that over weights and measures; that over bankruptcy (Sturges *v.* Crowninshield, 4 Wheat. 122); that over taxation (see cases already cited); that to regulate the value of foreign coins; that to discipline the militia (Houston *v.* Moore, 5 Wheat. 1; 3 Stor. Com. on Constitution, § 1202; 15 Peters, 499; Rawle on the Constitution, ch. 9, p. 111); that "to provide for the punishment of counterfeiting coin" (Fox *v.* State of Ohio, 5 How. 410); and robbing the mail, when punished as highway robbery (5 Wheat. 34). Why, then, hold this to be otherwise than concurrent?

There are still other grants, in language like this, which never have been considered exclusive. Even the power to pass uniform naturalization laws was once considered by this court as not exclusive (Collet *v.* Collet, 2 Dallas, 296); and though doubt has been flung on this since by the United States *v.* Villato, 2 Dall. 372, Chirac *v.* Chirac, 2 Wheat. 269, and by some of the court in 5 Howard, 585, and Golden *v.* Prince, 3 Wash. C. C. 314; and though these doubts may be well founded unless the State naturalization be for local purposes only in the State, as intimated in Collet *v.* Collet, and more favorable than the law of the United States, and not to give rights of citizenship out of the State (1 Bl. Com. by Tucker, App. 3, 4, 255, 296), which were the chief objections in 3 Wash. C. C. 314; yet this change of opinion does not impugn in principle the ground for considering the local measure in their case as not conflicting with foreign commerce. The reasoning for a change there does not apply here.

So, it is well settled that no grant of power to Congress is exclusive, unless expressly so, merely because it may be broad enough in terms to cover a power which clearly belongs to the State; e. g., police, quarantine, and license laws. They may relate to a like place and subject, and by means somewhat alike, yet, if the purposes of the

State and of Congress are different and legitimate for each, they are both permissible and neither exclusive. (See cases before cited, 4 Wheat. 196; 3 Ell. Deb. 259; Baldwin's Views, 193, 194.)

This very grant of the power "to regulate commerce" has also been held by this court not to prevent bridges or ferries by the States where waters are navigable. (Wilson *v.* Blackbird Creek Marsh Company, 2 Peters, 245.) So elsewhere. (Corfield *v.* Coryell, 4 Wash. C. C. 371; 1 Woodb. & Min. 417, 424, 425; 9 Wheat. 203. See also Warren Bridge Case, 11 Peters, 420; 17 Conn. 64; 8 Cowen, 146; 1 Pick. 180; 7 N. Hamp. 35.) And it has been considered elsewhere not to confer, though in navigable waters, any right or control over the fisheries therein, within the limits of a State. (4 Wash. C. C. 383. See also Martin *v.* Waddell, 16 Peters, 367; 3 Wheat. 383; Angell on Tide Waters, 105.) So the States have been accustomed to legislate as to pilots, and Congress has concurred in it. But if the acts of the States alone as to pilots are not valid, on the ground of a concurrent power in them, it is difficult to see how Congress can transfer or cede to the States an authority on this which the constitution has not given to them. (Chief Justice Taney, in 5 Howard, 580.) The real truth is, that, each possessing the power in some views and places, though not exclusively, Congress may declare it will not exercise the power on its part, either by an express law or by actual omission, and thus leave the field open to the States, on their reserved or concurrent rights, and not on any rights ceded to them by Congress. This reconciles the whole matter, and tends strongly to sustain the same view in the case now under consideration.

Nor has it ever been seriously contended, that, where Congress has chosen to legislate about commerce and navigation on our navigable waters as well as the sea-coast, and to introduce guards against steam explosions and dangers in steam vessels, the law is not to be enforced as proper under the power to regulate commerce, and when not in conflict with any State legislation. This power in Congress is at least concurrent, and extends to commerce on rivers, and even on land, as well as at sea, when between our own States or with foreign countries. Whether this could be done as to vessels on waters entirely within any one State, is a different question, which need not be here considered. (See Waring *v.* Clarke, 5 Howard, 441.)

As a general rule of construction, then, the grants to Congress should never be considered as exclusive, unless so indicated expressly in the constitution by the nature or place of the thing granted, or by the positive prohibition usually resorted to when that end is contemplated, as that "no State shall enter into any treaty," or "coin money," &c.; "no State shall, without the consent of Congress, lay any imposts or duties on imports," &c. (Art. 1, § 9. United States *v.* New Bedford Bridge, 1 Woodb. & Min. 432.)

It is also a strong argument, after using this express prohibition in some cases, that, when not used in others, as it is not here, it is not intended. Looking at the nature of this grant, likewise, in order to see if it can or should be entirely exclusive, we are forced to the same conclusions.

There is nothing in the nature of much which is here connected with foreign commerce that is in its character foreign, or appropriate for the action of a central and single government; on the contrary, there is matter which is entirely local,—something which is seldom universal, or required to be either general or uniform. For though Congress is empowered to regulate commerce, and ought to legislate for foreign commerce as for all its leading incidents, and uniform and universal wants, yet "to regulate commerce" could never have been supposed by the framers of the constitution to devolve on the General Government the care of anything except exterior intercourse with foreign nations, with other States, and the Indian tribes. Everything else within State limits was, of course, to be left to each State, as too different, in so large a country, to be subjected to uniform rules, too multifarious for the attention of the central government, and too local for its cognizance over only general matters.

It was a difference between the States as to imposts or duties on imports and tonnage which embarrassed their intercourse with each other and with foreign nations, and which mainly led to the new constitution, and not the mere regulation of commerce. (9 Wheat. 225.) It was hence that the States, in respect to duties and imposts, were not left to exercise concurrent powers, and this was prevented, not by merely empowering Congress to tax imports, but by expressly forbidding the States to do the same; and this express prohibition would not have been resorted to, or been necessary, if a mere grant to Congress of the power to impose duties or to "regulate commerce" was alone deemed exclusive, and was to prevent taxation of imports by the States, or assessing money by them on any kind of business or traffic by navigation, such as carrying passengers.

Congress, in this way, resorted to a special prohibition where they meant one (as to taxes on imports); but where they did not, as, for example, in other taxation, or regulating commerce, they introduced no such special prohibition, and left the States to act also on local and appropriate matters, though connected in some degree with commerce. Where, at any time, Congress had not legislated or preöccupied that particular field, the States acted freely and beneficially, yielding, however, to Congress when it does act on the same particular matter, unless both act for different and consistent objects. (Gibbons *v.* Ogden, 9 Wheat. 204, 239.) In this way much was meant to be left in the States, and much ever has been left, which partially related to commerce; and an expansive, and roving, and absorbing construction has since been attempted to be given to the grant and the power to regulate commerce, apparently never thought of at the time it was introduced into the constitution. When I say much was left, and meant to be left, to the States in connection with commerce, I mean, concerning details and local matters, inseparable in some respects from foreign commerce, but not belonging to its exterior or general character, and not conflicting with anything Congress has already done. (Vanderbilt *v.* Adams, 7 Wendell, 349; New Bedford Bridge Case, 1 Woodb. & Min. 429.) Such is this very matter as to taxation to support foreign paupers, with many other police matters, quarantine, inspections, &c. (See them enumerated in the License Cases, 5 Howard.)

The provisions in the State laws in 1789, on these and kindred matters, did not therefore drop dead on the adoption of the constitution, but only those relating to duties expressly prohibited to the States, and to foreign and general matters which were then acted on by Congress. Chief Justice Marshall, in Sturges *v.* Crowninshield (4 Wheat. 195), considered "the power of the States as existing over such cases as the laws of the Union may not reach."

So far as reasons exist to make the exercise of the commercial power exclusive, as on matters of exterior, general, and uniform cognizance, the construction may be proper to render it exclusive, but no further, as the exclusiveness depends in this case wholly on the reasons, and not on any express prohibition, and hence cannot extend beyond the reasons themselves. Where they disappear, the exclusiveness should halt. In such case, emphatically, *cessante ratione, cessat et ipsa lex.*

It nowhere seems to have been settled that this power is exclusive in Congress, so that the States can enact no laws on any branch of the subject, whether conflicting or not with any acts of Congress. But, on the contrary, the majority of the court in the License Cases (5 Howard, 504) appear to have held that it is not exclusive as to several matters connected in some degree with commerce. The case of New York *v.* Miln (11 Peters, 141) seems chiefly to rest on a like principle, and likewise to hold that measures of the character now under consideration are not regulations of commerce.

Indeed, besides these cases, and on this very subject of commerce, a construction has at times been placed, that it is not exclusive in all respects, as will soon be shown, and if truly placed, it is not competent to hold that the State legislation on such incidental, subordinate, and local matters, is utterly void when it does not conflict with some actual legislation by Congress. For the silence of Congress, which some seem to regard as more formidable than its action, is, whether in full or in part, to be respected and obeyed only where its power is exclusive, and the States are deprived of all authority over the matter. The power must first be shown to be exclusive before any inference can be drawn that the silence of Congress speaks, and a different course of reasoning begs the question attempted to be proved. In other cases, when the power of Congress is not exclusive and that of the States is concurrent, the silence of Congress to legislate on any mere local or subordinate matter within the limits of a State, though connected in some respects with foreign commerce, is rather an invitation for the States to legislate upon it,—is rather leaving it to them for the present, and assenting to their action in the matter,— than a circumstance nullifying and destroying every useful and ameliorating provision made by them.

Such, in my view, is the true rule in respect to the commercial grant of power over matters not yet regulated by Congress, and which are obviously local. In the case of Wilson *v.* The Blackbird Creek Marsh Co., Chief Justice Marshall not only treated this as the true rule generally, but held it applicable to the grant to Congress of the power "to regulate commerce," and that this grant was not exclusive nor prohibitory on the action of the States, except so far as it was actually exercised by Congress, and thus came in conflict with the laws of the States. These are some of his words: — "The repugnancy of the law of Delaware to the constitution is placed entirely on its repugnancy to the power to regulate commerce with foreign nations, and among the several States, a power which has not been so exercised as to affect the question." (2 Peters, 252.)

The Chief Justice in another case held that a power being vested in Congress was not enough to bar State action entirely, and that it did not forbid by silence as much as by action. He says,— "It is not the mere existence of the power, but its exercise, which is incompatible with the exercise of the same power by the States. It is not the right to establish these uniform laws, but their actual establishment, which is inconsistent with the partial acts of the States." (Sturges *v.* Crowninshield, 4 Wheaton, 195, 196.) And in 16 Peters, 610, Justice Story admits "that no uniform rule of interpretation can be applied to it [the constitution], which may not allow, even if it does not positively demand, many modifications in its actual application to particular clauses."

Hence, if the power "to regulate commerce" be regarded by us as exclusive, so far as respects its operations abroad, or without the limits of the country, because the nature of the grant requires it to be exclusive there, and not exclusive so far as regards matters consequent on it which are within the limits of a State, and not expressly prohibited to it nor conflicting with anything done by Congress, because the nature of the grant does not require it to be so there, we exercise then what appears to be the spirit of a wise conciliation, and are able to reconcile several opinions elsewhere expressed, some as to the concurrent and some as to the exclusive character of the power "to regulate commerce." It may thus be exclusive as to some matters and not as to others, and everything can in that aspect be reconciled and harmonious, and accord, as I have before explained, with the nature and reason of each case, the only constitutional limits where no express restrictions are imposed. I am unable to see any other practical mode of administering the complicated, and sometimes conflicting, relations of the federal and State governments, but on a rule like this. And thus deciding the cases as they arise under it, according to the nature and character of each case and each grant, some indicating one to be exclusive, and some indicating another not to be exclusive; and this, also, at times, as to different kinds of exercise of power under one and the same grant. (See Justice Johnson, 9 Wheat. 235—239.) There is another view of this question which leads to like results. If the opposite opinions mean only that the States cannot, after express grants to the General Government, legislate on them for and in behalf of the General Government, and not simply for themselves in local matters,—cannot legislate for other States without their own limits, *extra territorium*, or as to general uniformity, general conduct, or the subject-matter over the whole country, like naturalization and bankruptcy,—then there is no difference between the spirit of those opinions and my own. But if they are construed to mean, that after such a grant, with no express prohibition on a State to act for itself alone on the matter, and none implied from their relations to the General Government and the nature of the subject, a State cannot make such regulations and laws for itself, and its own people, and local necessities, as do not violate any act of Congress in relation to the matter, I do not think they are supported either by sound principle or precedents.

Necessities for a different course have existed, and ever must exist, in the complex movements of a double set of legislators for one and the same people.

They may crowd against each other in their measures slightly and doubtingly, but that, as before shown, is not sufficient to annul and override those of the States, as there must be for that disagreeable consequence a direct conflict, a plain incompatibility. (3 Stor. Com. on Const. 434; New Bedford Bridge Case, 1 Woodb. & Min. 417, 418; 9 Wheaton, 238.)

This circumstance shows, also, that the argument to avoid State legislation is not sufficient when it discovers some different spirit or policy in the general measures of the States from that in the General Government. The States have a right to differ in opinion,—some are very likely often to differ. But what clause in the constitution makes such an instance of independence a nullity, or makes a different object an illegitimate one? To be a nullity, it must oppose what has been actually done or prescribed by Congress, and in a case where it has no reserved power to act differently from Congress. We have already seen that an indirect reduction of the revenue of the General Government by the license laws, when passed under a legitimate power, and with a different legitimate view, did not render them unconstitutional, nor does this, under like circumstances, though it may indirectly operate in some measure against emigration.

If it did, a law by a State to favor the consumption of its own products would be pronounced void, and so would be a high tax by a State on wharves or stores, as all these would somewhat embarrass and render more expensive the business connected with foreign commerce.

So this condition imposed on passengers after their arrival might in some degree affect the business and commerce of carrying them to that State, when the alien passengers are taxed before they are permitted to land.

There are two classes of grants to which this rule now under consideration is applicable, and the force of it will be more striking when they are examined separately. One includes grants where Congress has acted, and continues to act, in relation to them; and the other, where it has never acted, or, if it has once acted, has ceased to do so.

Now the vindication for the States to act in the last class is, that, unless each State is considered authorized still to legislate for itself, the subject-matter will be without any regulation whatever, and a lawless condition of things will exist within the heart of the community, and on a matter vital to its interests. Such is now the case as to weights and measures, Congress never having legislated to produce uniformity concerning them, though the power is expressly granted to it in the constitution.

Now, on the construction that such a grant of power is exclusive, and, whether exercised or not, it is unconstitutional for any State to legislate on the subject for itself; and, moreover, that Congress does in truth regulate by its silence as much as by its action, and when doing nothing about it virtually enacts that nothing shall be done about it by any of the States, it will follow that not only all the legislation by the States on weights and measures since 1789 is illegal and void, but all their legislation now existing on matters of bankruptcy, and in respect to the disciplining of the militia, and imposing taxes on land, is also void. For the powers over all these are expressly ceded tc Congress, and are not now regulated by any existing acts of Congress, though all except weights and measures once have been. The argument alluded to, if sound, would thus be strong, that Congress, having once acted on these and ceased to, means that nothing more shall be done.

On this exclusive principle, though the action of the States on them is not forbidden expressly in the constitution, nor impliedly beyond what grows out of any express grant, all the States in the Union are disarmed from any action whatever on such matters, and all their laws on these topics, so essential to their domestic industry and trade, their public security and political existence by means of revenue, are to be considered null and void.

The catastrophe which would follow on such a construction has led this court, as heretofore explained, to hold that the States still possess a concurrent power to act on matters of bankruptcy, the discipline of the militia, taxation of land, and some subjects of commerce; and like considerations would undoubtedly lead them, when the cases arise, to hold, that, notwithstanding such grants, the laws of the States, not conflicting with any passed by the General Government, on many other such topics, must be considered valid. Indeed, it seems conceded by some of the members of the court in this case, that the States are, by some power coördinate or subordinate, rightfully legislating on weights and measures, pilots, bankruptcy, the militia, &c. But if they have not this power without any grant or license by Congress, they cannot have it by any such grant, because Congress is not empowered by the constitution to grant away powers vested in it by the people and the States; and how can it hereafter, by legislation, give any power to them over this subject if not having it now?

Again, in the other class of cases, where Congress has already legislated, and still legislates, some time elapsed before it passed laws on any subject, and years before it acted at all on some of them; and in almost the whole, its first legislation was only a beginning and in part, doing more and more from time to time, as experience and the exigencies of the country seemed to require. It is not necessary to repeat here several detailed illustrations and cases on this collected in the case of the United States *v.* New Bedford Bridge, 1 Woodb. & Min. 430. In the mean time, the States continued to exercise their accustomed powers, and have ever since done it on all matters not forbidden expressly in the constitution, not exclusive in their nature, and not conflicting with actual provisions in relation to them already made under the General Government. (14 Peters, 594.)

To show, further, that these grants of power are not always and necessarily exclusive, and that legislation on them by Congress to any extent is not as prohibitory on the States where it is silent as where it enacts, the States have not only continued to punish crimes which Congress could punish, but they have, in numerous instances, regulated matters connected, locally at least, with commerce abroad, and between the States, and with the Indians.

In so large a territory as the jurisdiction of the General Government embraces, in so many and so diversified topics as come before it, and in the nature of its supervisory powers on certain subjects, requiring action only on what is general and foreign, and to produce uniformity merely as to that, it becomes almost inevitable that many local matters and details must be left to be regulated by some local authorities. Yet, as explained in the License Cases, like the by-laws of corporations, made by them and not the Legislature, they must not conflict with the general regulations or laws prescribed by the paramount power. But, so far from being exclusive, even while it is exercised, and much less while it is dormant or unexercised, the paramount power summons to its aid, in order to be effective, the contemporaneous and continued action of others. Thus not only moneyed corporations, but towns and cities, must make numerous by-laws in order to enforce the general provisions laid down by the legislation of the State. Thus, too, this court must make numerous rules to carry into effect the legislation of Congress in respect to it; and the war and the navy departments must compile and enforce volumes of regulations of a like kind and for a like purpose, taking care, as all subordinate power in such cases must, not to violate any general law prescribed on the subject. (See 1 Woodb. & Min. 423.)

The condition of this whole country when colonies of England furnishes another illustration of the relation and character of such powers. The parent government at home was sovereign, and provided general regulations, either in acts of Parliament or charters, but still left the several colonies (and surely our States have as much power as they) to legislate as to details, and introduce any regulations suited to their own conditions and interests, not conflicting with the general provisions made by the paramount power at home. (1 Bl. Com. by Tucker, App. 109, 110.)

Indeed, what becomes of the whole doctrine of concurrent powers on this hypothesis of exclusiveness in all mere grants, and of the usage that the States may act in such concurrent cases or local matters till their measures conflict directly with those of Congress? (Ibid. 179.) Where is the line of distinction between a measure by the State which is void, whether it conflict or not, and one which is not void till it comes into actual collision with some law passed by the General Government? What becomes of the idea, that the power to regulate foreign commerce is exclusive, and Congress may prohibit the introduction of obscene prints under it, and yet the States may do the latter also, but touch nothing connected with commerce? Is not the introduction of these connected with it? Cannot the States, too, patronize science and the arts in various ways, though a like power is conferred on Congress by means of patents and copyrights? (Livingston *v.* Van Ingen, 9 Johns. 572.)

Nor do I understand the words of Mr. Justice Johnson, in the case of Gibbons *v.* Ogden, in the sense attributed to them by some. "The practice of our government," says he, "has been, on many subjects, to occupy so much only of the field open to them as they think the public interests require." (9 Wheat. 234.) It is argued that this means to exclude State action, where Congress has not occupied the field, as well as where it has. Yet it seems plainly to be inferred, from other words connected, that he considers "the power of the States must be at an end so far as the United States have by their legislative act taken the subject under their immediate superintendence." This means the subject then under consideration. But where have they so taken the subject of the admission of alien passengers into States, and the terms of it, "under their immediate superintendence"? They may have regulated the manner of their coming here, but where their maintenance here when sick or poor, or likely to be poor; where their taxation here?

They have regulated also their naturalization in this country, but not under the grant of the power "to regulate commerce," or impose imposts on imports; but, knowing it was not involved in either, a separate and express grant was wisely inserted in the constitution to empower Congress to make uniform rules on this subject.

It will be seen, that, where Congress legislates about foreign commerce or passengers as connected with it, that legislation need not, and does not, forbid the States to legislate on other matters not conflicting. Thus all will harmonize, unless we interpolate, by mere construction, a prohibitory clause either in the law or in the constitution. You may, if you please, call the power so exercised by Congress exclusive in one sense or to one extent, but it is not in others. It may be considered as exclusive so far as it goes, and still leave the rest of the field concerning them open to the States. Thus the right to regulate the number of passengers in vessels from abroad in proportion to the tonnage has been exercised by Congress, and may be deemed the use of a legitimate authority. (3 Statutes at Large, 448; 9 Wheat. 216.) So has it been exercised to exempt their personal "baggage" and "tools" from *imposts*, not, as some seem to suppose, their *goods* or *merchandise.* (1 Statutes at Large, 661.) But this statute of Massachusetts conflicts with neither. So Congress provides for uniform naturalization of aliens, but this statute does not interfere with that. So Congress does not forbid passengers to come from abroad; neither does this statute.

Again, Congress nowhere stipulates or enacts, or by the constitution can do it, probably, as before suggested, that passengers shall not in their persons be taxed on their arrival within a State, nor terms be made as to their residence within them. Again, the objection to this view involves another apparent absurdity,—that, though the regulation of commerce extends to passengers, it is not entirely exclusive in the General Government if they come with yellow fever and the cholera, and that they are then subject to State control and its quarantine expenses and fees; but are not, if they come with what the State deems equally perilous. That is, if they endanger the health of the body, the power over them is not exclusive in Congress, but if they endanger only the police of the State, its pauper securities, and its economy, morals, and public peace, the power is exclusive in Congress, and goes to strip the State of all authority to resist the introduction of either convicts, slaves, paupers, or refugees. If these last only come in the tracks of commerce in vessels from abroad, and are enrolled as passengers, the States cannot touch them, but may seize on them at once if their bodies are diseased. It would be useful to have that clause in the constitution pointed out which draws such a novel line of discrimination.

In holding this measure to be a regulation of commerce, and exclusive, and hence void, wherever the power of Congress over commerce extends, a most perilous principle is adopted in some other respects; for that power extends over the land as well as water, and to commerce among the States and with the Indian tribes, no less than to foreign commerce. (See art. 1, § 8.) And if it can abrogate a tax or terms imposed by States in harbors over persons there, it may do so whenever the power over commerce goes into the interior, and as to matters connected with it, and also between States.

On this reasoning, passengers there in vessels, boats, wagons, stages, or on horseback, are as much connected with commerce as if they come in by sea; and they may consist of paupers, slaves, or convicts, as well as of merchants or travellers for pleasure and personal improvement; and thus all the laws of Ohio, Mississippi, and many other States, either forbidding or taxing the entrance of slaves or liberated blacks, will be nullified, as well as those of almost every Atlantic State, excluding paupers coming in from without their limits.

Congress has sanctioned at least five constitutions of States exercising a power to exclude slaves, and the introduction of them as merchandise and for commerce. And how can this be reconciled by those who would reverse the judgments below, on the ground that the commercial power is exclusive in Congress, and not either concurrent in one view or independent in another, in some particulars, in the States?

Another consequence from the opposite doctrine is, that, if Congress by regulating commerce acts exclusively upon it, and can admit whom it pleases as passengers, independent of State wishes, it can force upon the States slaves or criminals, or political incendiaries of the most dangerous character. And furthermore, that it can do this only by admitting their personal baggage free, as doing that, it is argued here by some, shows the owner must come in free, and neither be excluded nor taxed by the State after within her limits.

This makes the owner of the personal baggage a mere incident or appurtenant to the baggage itself, and renders, by analogy, any legislation as to taxing property more important than taxing the person, and, indeed, overruling and governing the person as subordinate and inferior. So, if Congress by making baggage free exonerates passengers from a State tax, it exonerates all the officers and crews of vessels from State taxes; for their personal baggage is as free as that of passengers. They, too, are as directly connected with commerce as the passengers; and by a parity of reasoning, the absurdity follows, that, by admitting American vessels free of tonnage duties, the owners of them are also made free from State taxes.

Every person acquainted with the tariff of the General Government knows that specially declaring a box or chest of apparel "free" does not exonerate anything else or any other article, much less can it any person, if taxed by a State law. On the contrary, all things not specially taxed, nor specially declared "free," have a duty imposed on them by Congress as non-enumerated articles, and so would passengers, if imports, and if Congress had a right to tax them. And if saying nothing about passengers would imply that they were free from taxes of the United States, much more of the States, why is it necessary to declare in terms any article "free," when silence would make it so? The real truth rather is, that Congress has no right to tax alien friends, or exclude them, and hence the silence. This statute, then, contravenes no act of Congress on this matter of passengers.

And while all the legislation of Congress as to passengers operates on them at sea during the voyage, except imposts being forbidden on their baggage, which is solely within the jurisdiction of Congress, all the legislation of Massachusetts operates on them after their arrival in port, and without any attempt then to impose any duty on their baggage. The former legislation by Congress, regulating their number in proportion to the tonnage, is, as it should be, *extra territorium;* the latter, as it should be, *infra territorium;* and thus both are proper, and the jurisdiction over either is not exclusive of that exercised by the other, or conflicting materially with it.

Having considered the different general grounds which can be urged in support of this statute, and the objections made in opposition to them, I shall proceed, before closing, to submit a few remarks on some miscellaneous topics relied on to impeach its provisions. One is a supposed conflict between this statute and some treaties of the General Government.

I am aware that a tax or fee on alien passengers, if large, might possibly lead to collision with those foreign governments, such as Great Britain and Prussia, with whom we have treaties allowing free ingress and egress to our ports. (See 8 Stat. at Large, 116, 228, 378.) But neither of them complains in this instance, and I do not consider this law as conflicting with any such provisions in treaties, since none of them profess to exempt their people or their property from State taxation after they arrive here.

If such a stipulation were made by the General Government, it would be difficult to maintain the doctrine, that, by an ordinary treaty, it has power to restrict the rights and powers of the several States any further than the States have by the constitution authorized, and that this has ever been authorized. But it has not here been attempted; and these particular treaties are subject to the ordinary laws of the States, as well as of the General Government, and enable the citizens of those countries merely to have free ingress and egress here for trade (see Treaty of 1794, art. 3; 8 Stat. at Large, 117), having no relation to their coming here as passengers to reside or for pleasure. Nor can they apply in the present case at all, as the record now stands, finding only that the master was a British subject or his vessel British, but not that his passengers belonged to Great Britain.

The Prussian treaty does not appear to contemplate anything beyond the establishment of reciprocal duties, and a treatment in other respects like "the most favored nations." (8 Stat. at Large, 164.)

And who ever thought that these treaties were meant to empower, or could in any moral or political view empower, Great Britain to ship her paupers to Massachusetts, or send her free blacks from the West Indies into the Southern States or into Ohio, in contravention of their local laws, or force on the States, so as to enjoy their protection and privileges, any persons from abroad deemed dangerous, such as her felon convicts and the refuse of her jails? Again, so far as regards the liberty of commerce secured to British subjects in Europe by the fourteenth article of the treaty of 1794, it does not apply to those coming from the British Provinces in America, as did this vessel (8 Stat. at Large, 124), and by the eighteenth article of that treaty was to last only ten years. (P. 125.) And while it did last, it was expressly made "subject always, as to what respects this article, to the laws and statutes of the two countries respectively." (P. 124.)

Besides this, the whole of the treaty of 1794, including the third article, probably was suspended by the war of 1812, and exists now only as modified in that of 1815, which gives to British subjects no higher rights than "other foreigners." (Art. 1; 8 Stat. at Large, 228.) The old articles of confederation contained a clause which indicated in a different form like views as to what was proper in treaties, and indicates a wise jealousy of power exercised in hostility to the policy of a State. That policy is never intended to be thwarted by any arrangements with foreign nations by reciprocal treaties, as they relate merely to the imposts on tonnage and cargoes by the national governments, requiring them to be equal, and do not concern the port and harbor fees or expenses imposed by the local authorities for local purposes. The best security that these fees and taxes will never be unreasonably high and injurious to foreigners is the tendency they would then have to drive trade to other ports or countries contiguous, where they might be lower.

The same right exists also in States to impose conditions on the selling of certain articles by foreigners and others within their limits, as a State may prefer to encourage its own products, or may deem the use of some foreign articles of bad influence in other respects. (Grotius on the Rights of Peace and War, B. 2, ch. 2, § 20; License Cases, 5 Howard.)

Nor can I see, as has been urged, any collision between this statute and the act of Congress to carry into effect our commercial arrangement of 1830 with Great Britain. (4 Stat. at Large, 419.) The intention of that act does not in any respect seem to go beyond that of the treaties just referred to, and in some respects is to have matters stand as they did before. Each side imposed charges and duties. They existed in England and her colonies, as well as with us; but this arrangement sought only to have them not unequal nor prohibitory of trade, and not to discriminate against each other by general legislation. (See 1 Commerce and Navigation, State Papers, 158; 4 Stat. at Large, 419.)

A few remarks as to some objections urged against the large amount and the motive of this tax, and I have done.

If the payment was to be vindicated under the general taxing power alone, it is clear that the amount could not affect the question of the constitutionality of the tax. And if it was very high, considering its professed object "for the support of foreign paupers," and was applied in part to other objects, that is a matter within the discretion of the State, and if it proved oppressive, and thus diverted this kind of business to the ports of other States, it would, like all high taxes, react, and be likely in time to remedy, in a great degree, the evil. But viewed as a police measure, the amount of the payment and the application of it may, in my view, have an important bearing.

Thus a State is authorized to impose duties on imports sufficient to defray the expenses of her inspection laws, but not an amount disproportionate to them, nor to apply the money thus collected to other purposes.

It would seem that the same rule would govern her assessments to enforce the quarantine laws, and it could hardly be tolerated, under the right to enforce them and demand sufficient to defray their charges, that they should be justified to collect enough more for other purposes, and thus apply the quarantine funds to make roads or maintain schools.

In such events in these cases, either this court would be obliged to declare void assessments which were clearly perverted and improperly collected and applied, or Congress could direct the excess to be paid into the treasury of the General Government. (3 Elliott's Deb. 291.) Congress is in the constitution expressly empowered to revise and control the sums collected by the States to defray the expenses of their inspection laws. (Art. 1, § 10.)

A mere pretext in a law colorably for one object, but really for another, as in condemning lands for public purposes when the true object was different, though not to be presumed to be done by any sovereign State, must, if clearly proved, be difficult to uphold. (West River Bridge *v.* Dix, 6 Howard, 548.) But here the amount of the tax, compared with the burden flung on the State by foreign paupers, does not look so much like a wish to prohibit entirely the entrance of alien passengers, and thus disclose a covert design, hostile to the policy of the General Government, as like a wish to obtain enough to cover the expenses and trouble of maintaining such of them as, though not paupers, are likely to become so in the ordinary course of human events. This is a highly important consideration in judging whether the law throughout looked really to the subject of pauperism, and not to hostility towards emigration, nor, under the third section, to revenue from foreign commerce, independent of the pauper system. It is unjust to regard such provisions as intended to conflict with foreign commerce, when there is another and local matter which they profess to reach, and can and do honestly reach.

It is, therefore, too broad in some cases to say that the object and motive of the State in requiring the payment, or the amount demanded, is of no importance; because, though the great question is a question of power, yet the object and motive may bring it within some existing power, when a different object or motive would not. The different purpose in a State often shows that there is no collision or wrong, and justifies the measure. (4 Wheat. 196; 9 Wheat. 335; Baldwin's Views, 193.)

So, as to the amount demanded, it might be sufficient only for a legitimate State object, and hence might be constitutional, as, for instance, to pay the expenses of inspection laws, when a much larger amount would not be permissible, if too much for the particular object deemed constitutional. But in this case, as no excess is shown on the record, a conclusive opinion on this point is necessary.

This construction of the constitution, upholding concurrent laws by a State where doubts exist and it is fairly open for adoption, has much to commend it in this instance, as the States, which singly become feebler and weaker daily as their number and the whole Union increase, being now thirty to one, instead of thirteen to one, will not thus be rendered still feebler, and the central government, daily becoming more powerful and strong, will not thus be rendered still stronger. So the authority of the latter will not thus, by mere construction, be made to absorb and overwhelm the natural and appropriate rights of sovereign States, nor mislead them by silence. Leaving this matter also to each will not conflict with any existing action of the General Government, but promote and sustain the peaceful operations of both in their appropriate spheres.

It will operate justly among the States, no less than between them and the General Government, as it will leave each to adopt the course best suited to its peculiar condition, and not leave one helplessly borne down with expenses from foreign sources while others are entirely free, nor draw the General Government, in order to remedy such inequalities, into a system of police and local legislation, over which their authority is doubtful, as well as their ability to provide so well for local wants as the local governments, and those immediately interested in beneficial results.

A course of harshness towards the States by the General Government, or by any of its great departments,— a course of prohibitions and nullifications as to their domestic policies in doubtful cases, and this by mere implied power,— is a violation of sound principle, will alienate and justly offend, and tend ultimately, no less than disastrously, to dissolve the bands of that Union, so useful and glorious to all concerned.

> "Libertas ultima mundi,
> Quo steterit, ferienda loco."

In conclusion, therefore, I think that, in point of law, the conduct of the State in imposing this condition or payment on alien passengers can be vindicated under its police rights to provide for the maintenance of paupers, and under its authority as a sovereign State to decide on what conditions or terms foreigners, not citizens of any of the United States, shall be allowed to enjoy its protection and privileges, and under its concurrent powers of taxation over everything but imports and tonnage. I think, too, that this power in the State is not taken away by the authority ceded to Congress, either to tax imports and tonnage, or to prohibit the importation of persons (usually limited to slaves), or to regulate commerce.

---

## ON ADMIRALTY JURISDICTION.*

On most of the facts involved in this libel, little controversy exists. It is certain that the respondents took the property of the plaintiffs on board their steamboat, the Lexington, to carry it, on her last calamitous voyage, the 13th of January, 1840, from New York to Stonington. It is equally certain that it was lost on that voyage, in Long Island Sound, at a place where the tide ebbed and flowed strongly, and several miles from shore, and probably without the limits of any State or county. It is certain, likewise, that the property was lost in consequence of a fire, which broke out in the boat in the night, and consumed it, with most of the other property on board. The value of it is also sufficiently certain, and that it was put on board, not by an officer of the bank, but by Harnden, a forwarding agent for the community generally, and under a special contract between Harnden and the respondents, that the latter were not to run any risk, nor be responsible for any losses of property thus shipped by him.

But some other facts are not so certain. One of that character is, whether the fire occurred by accident, without any neglect whatever by the respondents and their agents, or in consequence of some gross neglect by one or both. It would not be very material to decide this last fact, controverted as it is and in some degree doubtful, if I felt satisfied that the plaintiffs could recover anywhere, and more especially in admiralty, on the contract made by Harnden with the respondents, for the breach of the contract to carry and deliver this property.

---

* Opinion in case of New Jersey Steam Navigation Company *v.* Merchant's Bank. January term S. C. U. S., 1848.

The first objection to such a recovery on the contract anywhere is, that it was made with Harnden, and not with the bank. (Butler *v.* Basing, 2 Car. & Payne, 613; 15 Mass. 370; 2 Story, 32.) Next, that he was acting for himself, in this contract, on his own duties, liabilities, and undertakings, and not for them; and that the bank, so far as regards any contract, looked to him and his engagement with them, and not to the respondents or their engagement with him. (6 Bingh. 131.) Next, that the articles, while on board the boat, were to be in the care and control of Harnden, and not of the master or owners; and hence no liability exists on the contract even to him, much less the bank. (Story on Bailments, p. 547, § 582.) And this same conclusion is also urged, because Harnden, by his contract, made an express stipulation, that the property carried should be at his risk, as well as in his care. (See 5 East. 428; 1 Ventris, 190, 283.) It is contended further, that, if the bank can sue on Harnden's contract made with the respondents, it must be on the principle of his acting in it as their agent, and not for himself alone; and if so, and they, by suing on it, adopt its provisions, they must be bound by the stipulation in it made by him, not to hold the respondents liable for any risk or loss.

It is, however, doubted, whether, with such a stipulation, the respondents are not, by public policy, to be still liable on a contract like this, in order to insure greater vigilance over all things intrusted to their care (Gould *v.* Hill, 2 Hill, 623), and on the ground that the parties could not mean by the contract that the carriers were to be exonerated for actual misbehavior, but only for accidents otherwise chargeable on them as *quasi* insurers. (Atwood *v.* Reliance Insurance Company, 9 Watts, 87; 2 Story, 32, 33.)

It is insisted, next, that, as the unusual nature of the property carried, in this case, was not made known to the carriers, nor a proportionate price paid for its transportation, the owner cannot recover beyond the usual value of common merchandise of such a bulk. (Citizen's Bank *v.* Steamboat Nantucket, 2 Story, 32; 25 Wend. 459; Gibbon *v.* Paynton, 4 Burr. 2301.)

But, giving no decisive opinion on the validity of any of these objections, as not necessary in the view hereafter taken, yet they are enumerated to show some of the difficulties in sustaining a recovery on this contract, notwithstanding their existence.

Another important objection remains to be considered. It is, that no jurisdiction exists over this contract in a court of admiralty where these proceedings originated. The contract was made on land, and of course within the body of the county of New York. It was also not a contract for a freight of goods abroad, or to a foreign country, the breach of which has been here sometimes prosecuted in courts of admiralty. (Drinkwater et al. *v.* The Spartan, Ware, D. C. 149, by a proceeding *in rem* (155); De Lovio *v.* Boit, 2 Gall. 398; The Volunteer, 1 Sumner, 551; Logs of Mahogany, 2 Sumner, 589;

6 Dane's Abr. 2, 1, *Charter-parties.* See a case, *contra*, in the records of Rhode Island, A. D. 1742.)

But the law of England is understood to be, even in foreign charter-parties, against sustaining such suits, *ex contractu*, in admiralty. (3 D. & E. 323; 2 Lord Raym. 904; 1 Hag. Ad. 226, and cases cited in 12 Wheaton, 622, 623.)

By agreement of the judges in A. D. 1632, admiralty was not to try such cases, if the charter-party was contested. (Dunlap's Adm. 14; 4 Instit. 135; Hobart, 268.)

It seems, however, to be doubted by Browne (2 Browne's Civ. and Adm. Law, 122, 535), whether the libellant may not proceed in admiralty, if he goes to recover freight only, and not a penalty. It is also believed, that, in this country, contracts to carry freight between different States, or within the same State, if it be on tide-water, or at least on the high seas, have sometimes been made the subject-matter of libels in admiralty. (Dunlap's Adm. 487; 1 Sumner, 551; 3 Am. Jur. 26; 6 Am. Jur. 4; King et al. *v.* Shepherd, 3 Story, 349, in point; Gilp. D. C. 524; Conkling, Pra. 150; De Lovio *v.* Boit, 2 Gall. 448.) I am inclined to the opinion, too, that, at the time the constitution of the United States was adopted, and the words "cases of admiralty and maritime" were introduced into it, and jurisdiction over them was subsequently given in civil proceedings, in the act of 1789, to the District Courts, the law in England had in some degree become changed in its general principles in respect to jurisdiction in admiralty over contracts. Their courts had become inclined to hold, that the place of performance of a contract, if maritime in its subject, rather than the place of its execution, was the true test as to its construction and the right under it. This conformed, also, to the analogy as to contracts at common law. (See cases in Towne *v.* Smith, 1 Woodbury & Minot, 135.)

It is not unusual for the place to which the parties look for fulfilling their duties to be not only different from the place of making the contract, but for the parties to regard other laws and other courts, applying to the place of performance, as controlling and as having jurisdiction over it. (Bank of the United States *v.* Donally, 8 Peters, 361; Wilcox *v.* Hunt, 13 Peters, 378; Bell et al. *v.* Bruen, 1 Howard, 169.)

Hence, for a century before 1789, Lord Kenyon says, admiralty courts had sustained jurisdiction on bottomry bonds, though executed upon the land; because, "if the admiralty has jurisdiction over the subject-matter, to say that it is necessary for the parties to go upon the sea to execute the instrument borders on absurdity." (See Menetone *v.* Gibbons, 3 D. & E. 267—269; 2 Lord Raym. 982; 2 H. Bl. 164; 4 Cranch, 328; Paine's C. C. 671.) On this principle, the admiralty has gradually been assuming jurisdiction over claims for pilotage on the sea, both the place of performance and the subject-matter being there usually maritime. (10 Wheat. 428; 7 Peters,

324; 10 Peters, 108; 11 Peters, 175; 1 Mason, C. C. 508.) Because, on the general principle just referred to, as to the object of the contract, if "it concerned the navigation of the sea," and hence was in its nature and character a maritime contract, it was deemed within admiralty jurisdiction, though made on land. (Zane *v.* The Brig President, 4 Wash. C. C. 454; 4 Mason, C. C. 380; The Jerusalem, 2 Gall. 191, 465, 448; The Sloop Mary, Paine, C. C. 671; Gilp. D. C. 184, 477, 429; 2 Sumner, 1.)

This is the principle, at the bottom, for recovering seamen's wages in admiralty. (Howe *v.* Nappier, 4 Burr. 1944.)

Not that the consideration merely was maritime, but that the contract must be to do something maritime as to place or subject. (Plummer *v.* Webb, 4 Mason, C. C. 380; Berni *v.* The Janus et al., 1 Baldw. C. C. 549, 552; "A New Brig," Gilp. D. C. 306.) But we have already seen there are several direct precedents in England against sustaining these proceedings in admiralty on the contract, such as a charter-party or bill of lading, and strong doubts from some high authorities against it in this country. Chancellor Kent seems to think a proceeding in admiralty, on a charter-party like this, cannot be sustained, except by what he calls "the unsettled doctrine laid down in De Lovio *v.* Boit." (3 Kent, Comm. 162. See likewise Justice Johnson's opinion to the like effect in Ramsey *v.* Allegre, 12 Wheat. 622.)

Looking, then, to the law as held in England in 1789, and not considering it to be entirely clear in favor of sustaining a suit in admiralty on a charter-party like this, and that it is very doubtful whether any more settled or enlarged rule on this subject then prevailed in admiralty here, or has since been deliberately and generally adopted here, in respect to charter-parties or bills of lading, I do not feel satisfied in overruling the objection to our jurisdiction which has been made on this ground.

The further arguments and researches since Waring *v.* Clarke (5 How.) tend also, in my view, to repel still more strongly any idea that admiralty jurisdiction had become extended here, at the Revolution, in cases either of contracts or torts, more broadly than in England.

But it is not necessary now to go into the new illustrations of this cited in the elaborate remarks of the counsel for the respondents, or discovered by myself, in addition to those quoted in the opinion of the minority in Waring et al. *v.* Clarke, and in The United States *v.* The New Bedford Bridge, 1 Woodbury & Minot. Among mine is the declaration by Lord Mansfield himself, December 20th, 1775, that the colonies wished "that the admiralty courts should never be made to extend there," instead of wishing their powers enlarged (6 American Archives, 234; Annual Register for 1776, pp. 99, 100); and there is likewise the protest of the friends of America, the same year, in the House of Lords, that the increase of admiralty power by some special acts of Parliament was a measure favored at home rather than here, and was not acceptable here, but denounced by them as an inroad on the highly prized trial by jury. (6 American Archives, 226.) Among those cited is the conclusive evidence, that in some of the colonies here before the Revolution the restraining statutes of Richard II., as to the admiralty, were *eo nomino* and expressly adopted, instead of not being in force here. (See in South Carolina, 2 Statutes at Large, 446, in 1712, and in Massachusetts, Dana's Defence of New England Charters, 49—54; in Virginia, "the English Statutes" passed before James I., 9 Hening's Statutes, 131, 203; Commonwealth *v.* Gaines, 2 Virg. Cases, 179, 185; in Maryland, 1 Maryland Statutes, Kilty's Report, 223; and in Rhode Island, her records of a case in 1763, at Providence.)

But I pass by all these, and much more, because, notwithstanding the course of practice here the last half-century in some districts, and the inattention and indifference exhibited in many others as to the true line of discrimination between the jurisdiction belonging to the common law courts and that in admiralty, enough appears to induce me, as at present advised, not to rest jurisdiction in admiralty over a transaction like this on contract alone. I shall not do it, the more especially when a ground less doubtful in my apprehension exists and can be relied on for recovering all the loss, if the damage was caused by a tort.

I have turned my attention to ascertain whether the facts in this case exhibit any wrong committed by the respondents of such a character as a tort, and in such a locality as may render our jurisdiction in admiralty clear over it, looking to the principles of admiralty law in England, and also in this country, so far as can now be discovered to have existed at the time of our Revolution.

First, as to this, it is argued, that, in point of fact, gross negligence existed in the transportation of this property. If so, this conduct by the respondents or their agents may be sufficient to justify a proceeding *ex delicto* for the nonfeasance or misfeasance constituting that neglect, and causing the loss of this property, entirely independent of the contract or its form, or the risks under it, or the want of notice of the great value of the property. Particularly might this be sufficient, if the injury was caused in a place, and under circumstances, to give a court of admiralty undoubted jurisdiction over it as a marine tort.

The question of fact, then, as to neglect here, and the extent of it, may properly be investigated next, as in one view of the subject it may become highly important and decisive of the right to recover, and as it is our duty to settle facts in an admiralty proceeding, when they are material to the merits.

As before intimated, it is here virtually conceded that the property of the plaintiffs, while in charge of the respondents as common carriers on the sea, was entirely lost, by the burning of the boat in which it was transported.

The first inference from these naked facts would be, that the fire was produced by some cause for which the owners were responsible, being generally negligence, and that *primâ facie* they were chargeable. (6 Martin, 681; Story on Bailments, §§ 533, 538.)

Indeed, the common carrier who receives property to transport, and does not deliver it, is always held *primâ facie* liable. (Abbott on Ship., ch. 3, § 3; 1 Ventris, 190; 6 Johns. 169; 8 Johns. 213; 19 Wendell, 245; Story on Bailments, § 533; 3 Kent, Comm. 207, 216; 3 Story, 349, 356; 5 Bingh. 217, 220; 4 Bingh. 218.)

If they would have this inference or presumption changed, so as to exonerate themselves, it must be done by themselves, and not the plaintiffs, and by proof removing strong doubts; or, in other words, turning the scales of evidence in their favor in this attempt. This idea is fortified by the express provision establishing a presumption, by the act of Congress, in case of damages by explosions of steam. (5 Stat. at Large, p. 305, § 13.)

Independent of this presumption, when we proceed to examine the evidence on both sides as to the contested points of fact connected with the loss, it is found to be decidedly against the conduct of the respondents and their agents; and, so far from weakening the presumption against them from the actual loss, it tends with much strength to confirm it. There had, to be sure, been recent repairs, and certificates not long before obtained of the good condition of the boat. But, on the proof, she does not seem to have been in a proper state to guard against accidents by fire when this loss occurred. Her machinery was designed at first to burn wood, and had not long before been changed to consume anthracite coal, which created a higher heat. And yet there was a neglect fully to secure the wooden portions of the boat, near and exposed to this higher heat, from the natural and dangerous consequences of it. So was there an omission to use fire-brick and new sheet-iron for guards, nigh the furnace. On one or two occasions shortly before this accident, the pipe had become reddened by the intense heat so as to attract particular attention; and shortly before, the boat actually caught fire, it is probable, from some of those causes, and yet no new precautions had been adopted.

In the next place, the act of Congress (5 Stat. at Large, pp. 304, 305) requires the owners of steamboats "to provide, as a part of the necessary furniture, a suction-hose and fire-engine and hose suitable to be worked in said boat, in case of fire, and carry the same upon each and every voyage in good order." (Sec. 9.) And it imposes also a penalty of $500 for not complying with any condition imposed by the act. (Sec. 2.)

The spirit of this requisition is as much violated by not having the hose and engine so situated as to be used promptly and efficiently, as by not having them at all, or not having them "in good order."

The hose and engine were not kept together, and hence could not be used on that fatal night. One was stowed away in one part of the boat, and the other elsewhere, so as not to be in a situation to be brought promptly into beneficial use.

Again, it was an imperative provision in the act of Congress before referred to (sec. 9),—and the neglect of it was punished by a fine of $300, on the owner as well as master,—"that iron rods or chains shall be employed and used in the navigating of all steamboats, instead of wheel or tiller ropes." Yet this was not complied with, and renders their conduct, in this respect, not only negligent, but illegal.

Though, in fact, this accident may not have proved more fatal than otherwise from this neglect, the non-compliance with the provision was culpable, and throws the burden of proof on the owners to show it did not contribute to the loss. (Waring et al. *v.* Clarke, 5 Howard, 463.) It is true, that Congress, some years after, March 30, 1845, dispensed with a part of this provision (5 Stat. at Large, 626), under certain other guards. Yet in this case even those other guards were wholly omitted.

Nor does there appear to have been any drilling of the crew previously, how to use the engine in an emergency, or any discipline adopted, to operate as a watch to prevent fires from occurring, or, after breaking out, to extinguish them quickly. Indeed, the captain, on this occasion, checked the efforts of some to throw the ignited cotton overboard, so as to stop the flames from spreading, by peremptorily forbidding it to be done.

The respondents, to be sure, prove that several buckets were on board. But the buckets, except in a single instance, were not rigged with heaving-lines, so as to be able to draw up water, and help to check promptly any fire which might break out. And in consequence of their fewness or bad location, some of the very boxes containing the specie of the plaintiffs were broken open and emptied, in order to hold water. Lastly, when discovered, the officers and crew do not appear generally to have made either prompt or active exertions to extinguish the fire, or to turn the vessel nearer shore, when this property, and the passengers, would be much more likely to be preserved, eventually, than by remaining out in the deep parts of the Sound.

The extent and nature of the liability thus caused are well settled at law. The property of the plaintiffs was destroyed by fire, through great neglect by the defendants and their agents. Common carriers are liable for losses by fire, though guilty of no neglect, unless it happen by lightning. (1 D. & E. 27; 4 D. & E. 581; 3 Kent, Comm. 217; 5 D. & E. 389; Gilmore *v.* Carman, 1 Smedes & Marsh, 279; King et al. *v.* Shepherd, 3 Story, Rep. 360; 2 Brown, Civ. and Adm. Law, 144; 2 Wend. 327; 21 Wend. 190.) These respondents were common carriers, in the strictest and most proper sense of the law. (King et al. *v.* Shepherd, 3 Story, Rep. 349. See other cases, *post.*)

They would, therefore, be liable in the present case without such neglect, if this view of it applied to a recovery on the ground of a tort as well as of a contract. But, as it may not, the next inquiry is if the facts disclosed a breach of duty, a culpable neglect, either by the officers or owners of the vessel, amounting to a tort, and for which the defendants are responsible.

It is well settled that a captain is bound to exercise a careful supervision over fires and lights in his vessel, ordinarily. (Malynes, 155; The Patapsco Ins. Co. *v.* Coulter, 3 Peters, 237, 228, 229; Busk *v.* The Royal Ex. Ass. Co., 2 Barn. & Ald. 82.)

He is required in all things to employ due diligence and skill (9 Wend. 1; Rice's R. 162), to act "with most exact diligence" (1 Esp. Ca. 127), or with the *utmost care* (Story on Bailm. § 327.) But how much more so in a steamboat, with fires so increased in number and strength, and especially when freighted with very combustible materials, like this,—chiefly with cotton!

His failure to exert himself properly to extinguish any fire amounts to barratry. (*3 Peters, 228, 234*; Waters *v.* Merch. Louisville Ins. Co., 11 Peters, 213; 10 Peters, 507.) And if the property be insured against barratry, the owners may then recover.

To be sure, in one case, the owners of a steamboat were exonerated from paying for a loss by fire. But it was only under the special provision of the local laws, rendering them exempt, if the fire occurred "by accidental or uncontrollable events." (See Civil Code of Louisiana, 63d article; Hunt *v.* Morris, 6 Martin, 681.)

So the written contract for freight, as well as that for insurance, sometimes does not cover fire, but specially exempts a loss by it. (3 Kent, Comm. 201, 207.)

In such case, there may be no liability for it on the insurance, and doubtfully on the charter or bill of lading, unless it was caused by gross neglect, *crassa negligentia.* But in case of such neglect, liability exists even there. (3 Kent, Comm. 217; 3 Peters, 238; 1 Taunton, 227.) In this view, the owners seem liable for all damages which they or their servants could have prevented by care. (8 Serg. & Rawle, 533.) As an illustration of what are meant by such damages, they are those which happen, if on land, from unskilful drivers, "from vicious and unmanageable horses, or when occasioned by overloading the coaches, as these would imply negligence, or want of care." (Beckman *v.* Shouse, 5 Rawle, 183.)

From the above circumstances, the conclusion is almost irresistible, that what constitutes a gross neglect by the respondents and their agents, as to the condition of the boat and its equipments, existed here, and by the deficiencies and imperfection of them contributed much to the loss of this property; and beside this, that want of diligence and skill on board, after the fire broke out, as well as want of watchfulness and care to prevent its happening or making much progress, was manifest.

If any collateral circumstance can warrant the exaction of greater vigilance than usual, on occasions like these, or render neglects more culpable, it was, that the lives of so many passengers were here exposed by them, and became their victims. This last consideration is imperative, in cases of vessels devoted both to freight and passengers, to hold the owners and their servants responsible for the exercise of every kind of diligence, watchfulness and skill, which the principles of law may warrant. Beside the great amount of property on board on this occasion, they had in charge from one to two hundred passengers, including helpless children and females, confiding for safety entirely to their care and fidelity. All of these, except two or three, were launched into eternity, during that frightful night, by deaths the most painful and heart-rending. Had proper attention been devoted to the guards against fire, such as prudence and duty demanded, or due vigilance and energy been exercised to extinguish it early, not only would large amounts of property probably have been saved, but the tragic sufferings and loss of so many human beings averted.

In view of all this, to relax the legal obligations and duties of those who are amply paid for them, or to encourage careless breaches of trusts the most sacred, or to favor technical niceties likely to exonerate the authors of such a calamity, would be of most evil example over our whole sea-board, and hundreds of navigable rivers and vast lakes, where the safety of such immense property and life depends chiefly on the due attention of the owners and agents of steamboats, and is, unfortunately, so often sacrificed by the want of it. To relax, also, when Congress has made such neglect, when followed by death, a crime, and punishable at least as manslaughter, would be unfaithfulness to the whole spirit of their legislation, and to the loudest demands of public policy.

Their enactment on this subject is in these words (see statute before cited, sec. 12): — "That every captain," &c., "by whose misconduct, negligence, or inattention to his or their respective duties, the life or lives of any person on board said vessel may be destroyed, shall be deemed guilty of manslaughter," &c.

Showing, then, as the facts seem to do here, wrongs and gross neglect by both the owners and officers of the boat, the next step in our inquiries is, whether any principles or precedents exist against their being prosecuted in admiralty as a tort, and by a proceeding which sounds *ex delicto*, and entirely independent of any contract.

The recovery, in cases like this, on the tort, counting on the duty of the carrier and its breach by the negligent loss of the property, is common, both in this country and abroad, in the courts of common law.

Whether it be redressed there in trespass or case, when suing *ex delicto*, is immaterial, if, when case is brought, the facts, as here, show neglect or consequential damage, rather than those which are direct and with force. And if case lies at common law on such a state of facts, there seems to be no reason why a libel in admiralty may not lie for the wrong, whenever, as here, it was committed on the sea, and clearly within admiralty jurisdiction over torts. For the admiralty is governed by like principles and facts, as to what constitutes a tort, as prevail in an action at law for damages, and its ingredients are the same, whether happening on land or water. But case will lie at law, on facts like those here, for reasons obvious and important in the present inquiry. Indeed, on such facts the ancient action was generally in case, and counted on the duty of the carrier to transport safely the property received, and charged him with tortious negligence in not doing it. (1 Price, 27; 2 Kent, Comm. 599; 3 Wend. 158.) In such proceedings at common law, the difference was in some respects, when *ex delicto*, more favorable to the owners, as then some neglect, or violence, or fraud, or guilt of some kind, must be shown, amounting to a breach of public duty by the carrier or his servants. (Hinter *v.* Dibdin et al., 2 Adol. & Ell., N. S. 646; 2 New R. 454; 2 Chit. R. 4.) While in the action of assumpsit, more modern, but by no means exclusive, the promise or contract alone need be shown, and a breach of that, though without any direct proof of neglect, as carriers are, by their duties, in law, insurers against all losses except by the king's enemies and the act of God. (3 Brod. & Bingh. 62, 63; 19 Wend. 239; Forward *v.* Pittard, 1 D. & E. 27; 1 Esp. Ca. 36; 2 Chit. R. 1; Ashmole *v.* Wainwright, 2 Adol. & Ell., N. S. 663.)

So it is well settled that these rules of law, and all others as to common carriers by land, apply to those by water, and to those boats carrying freight, as this one did. (10 Johns. 1; 1 Wils. 281; 3 Esp. Ca. 127; 2 Wend. 327; 3 Story, 349.)

What, then, in principle, operates against a recovery?

Some would seem to argue that a proceeding *ex delicto* must be trespass, and that case is not one. But when it proceeds, as here, for consequential damages, and those caused by gross neglect, and not a mere breach of contract, it sounds *ex delicto* as much as trespass itself. (1 Chit. Pl. 142; 3 East, 593; 2 Saund. 47, *b.*)

The misconduct complained of here amounted to a tort, as much as if it had been committed with force. A tort means only a wrong, independent of or as contradistinguished from a mere breach of a contract. The evidence here, in my apprehension, shows both misfeasance and nonfeasance, and a consequential loss from them, which it is customary to consider as tortious. It was here, to be sure, not a trespass *vi et armis*, and perhaps not a conversion of the property so as to justify trover, though all the grounds for the last exist in substance, as the plaintiffs have lost their property by means of the conduct of the defendants, into whose possession it came, and who have not restored it on demand, nor shown any good justification for not doing it.

It is altogether a mistake, as some seem to argue, that force and a direct injury are necessary to sustain proceedings in tort, either at law or in admiralty, for damages by common carriers. So little does the law regard, in some cases, the distinction between nonfeasance and misfeasance, in creating a tort and giving any peculiar form of action for it, that in some instances a nonfeasance is considered as becoming misfeasance; such as a master of a vessel leaving his register behind, or his compass, or anchor. (3 Peters 235.) And "torts of this nature," as in the present case, may be committed either by "nonfeasance, misfeasance, or malfeasance," and often without force. (4 D. & E. 484; 1 Chit. Pl. 151; Bouvier's Dict., *Tort.*) And even where *mala fides* is necessary to sustain the proceeding, gross negligence is evidence of it. (4 Adol. & Ell. 876; 1 Howard, 71; 1 Spence's Eq. Jur. 425; Jones on Bailments, 8; Story on Bailments, §§ 19, 20.) The action in such case is described as "upon tort," and arises *ex delicto.* (2 Kent, Comm. 599.) In most instances of gross negligence, misfeasance is involved (2 Cromp. & M. 360); as a delivery to a wrong person, or carrying to a wrong place, or carrying in a wrong mode, or leaving a carriage unwatched or unguarded. (2 Cromp. & M. 360; 8 Taunt. 144.) Where case was brought for damage by overloading and sinking a boat, it was called an action "for a tort," and sustained, though the injury was wholly consequential. (1 Wils. 281.)

Again: it has been argued, that if direct force be not a necessary ingredient to recover in this form of action, it must in some degree rest on the contract which existed here with Harnden, and be restrained by its limitations. But the books are full of actions on the case where contracts existed, which were brought and which count entirely independent of any contract, they being founded on some public duty neglected, to the injury of another, or on some private wrong or misfeasance, without reference to any promise or agreement broken. (12 East, 89; 4 Howard, 146; Chit. Pl. 156; Forward *v.* Pittard, 1 D. & E. 27; 2 N. Hamp. 291; 2 Kent. Comm. 599; 3 East, 62; 6 Barn. & Cres. 268; 5 Burr. 2825; 6 Moore, 141; 9 Price, 408; 5 Barn. & Cres. 605—609.) Some of the cases cited of this character are precisely like this, being for losses by non-delivery of property by common carriers, and sued for as torts thus committed. (5 D. & E. 389.) They go without and beyond the contract entirely.

Nor is intent to do damage a necessary ingredient to sustain either case or trespass. (2 New R. 448.) Though the wrong done is not committed by force or design, it is still treated as *ex delicto* and a tort, if it was done either by a clear neglect of duty, by an omission to provide safe and well-furnished carriages or vessels, by carelessness in guarding against fires and other accidents, by omitting preparations and precautions enjoined expressly by law, or by damages consequent on the negligent upsetting of carriages, or unsafe and unskilful navigation of vessels. (See cases of negligent defects in carriages and vessels themselves, 2 Kent, Comm. 597, 607; 6 Jurist, 4; The Rebecca, Ware, D. C. 188; 10 East, 555; 1 Johns. Cas. 134; 5 East, 428. Or in machinery, Camden and Amboy Railroad *v.* Burke, 13 Wend. 611, 627; 5 East, 428; 9 Bingh. 457.) Even if the defect be latent. (3 Kent, Comm. 205. See those of careless attention, The Rebecca, Ware, D. C. 188. See those of non-conformity to legal requisitions, as hose and engine here not in good order, Waring et al. *v.* Clarke, 5 Howard. See those consequent on negligent driving, 4 Barn. & Cres. 223; Bretherton *v.* Wood, 3 Brod. & Bingh. 54.) If damage or loss happen by neglect or wrong of a servant of a common carrier, the principal is still liable. (13 Wend. 621; Story on Partnership, § 489; Dean et al. *v.* John Angus, Bee's Adm. 369, 239; Story on Bailments, § 464; 2 Browne, Civ. and Adm. Law, 136.) This is necessary to prevent fraud; if such neglect be not evidence of fraud or misfeasance. The owner should be liable for employing those negligent. (Story on Agency, § 318 and note.)

There is another important consideration connected with this view of the subject, and relieving it entirely from several objections which exist to a proceeding founded wholly on a contract rather than a tort. It is this: Where the injury is caused by a tort or fraud, no question arises as to any special agreement or notice, as with Harnden here, not to assume any risk. In short, the agreement, of that kind here, does not exonerate, if "malfeasance, misfeasance, or gross negligence," happens by owners or their servants. (13 Wend. 611; 19 Wend. 234, 251, 261; 5 Rawle, 179, 189; 2 Crompt. & M. 353; 2 Kent, Comm. § 40; Brooke *v.* Pickwick, 4 Bingh. 218; 3 Brod. & Bingh. 183.) Because the wrong is then a distinct cause of action from the breach of the contract, and the exception in it as to the risk was intended to reach any loss not happening through tortious wrong. "Even with notice, stage-proprietors and carriers of goods would be liable for an injury or loss arising from the insufficiency of coaches, harness, or tackling, from the drunkenness, ignorance, or carelessness of drivers, from vicious and unmanageable horses, or when occasioned by overloading the coaches, and these would imply negligence or want of care." (3 Rawle, 184.) It is further settled, in this class of cases, that the principle of not being liable for jewels, money, and other articles of great value, unless notice was given of it and larger freight paid in consequence of it, does not apply. (4 Bingh. 218; 5 Bingh. 223; 2 Crompt. & M. 353.) Because here the liability is not that of an insurer against many accidents and many injuries by third persons of the property carried, and which it may be right to limit to such values as were known and acted upon in agreeing to carry. But it is for the wrong of the carrier himself, or his agents; their own misfeasance or nonfeasance, and hence gross neglect, renders them responsible for the whole consequential damages, however valuable the property thus injured or lost. (2 Barn. & Ald. 356; 8 Taunt. 174; 4 Binn. 31; 2 Adol. & Ell. 659; 5 Barn. & Ald. 341, 350; 16 East, 244, 245.)

Some think the neglect in such case, so as to be liable for valuables, must amount to misfeasance. (2 Adol. & Ell. 659; 2 Myl. & Craig, 358.) It must be "misfeasance or gross negligence." (2

Kent, Comm. 607, note; 13 Price, 329; 12 B. Moore, 447; 5 Bingh. 223—225; 8 Mees. & Wels. 443.) By a recent statute in England, under William IV., though the carrier has been exonerated from the liability and care of valuables, without notice, yet he cannot be if gross neglect happens. (2 Adol. & Ell. 646.)

All this being established at law, what is there to prevent this wrong from being deemed a tort, in connection with maritime matters, — or, in other words, "a maritime tort," — and subject to be prosecuted in admiralty? I am not aware that a marine tort differs from any other tort in its nature or incidents, except that it must be committed, as this was, on the high seas. (See cases cited in Waring et al. *v.* Clarke, 5 Howard.) These it was held sufficient to constitute a marine tort, and one actionable in admiralty, if the wrong was committed only on tide-water.

We have already suggested, also, as to the gist of the wrong, that gross neglect, the elements and definition of it, are the same on the water as on land, and consequential or direct damages by a wrong are regarded in the same light on both. The actions of case, as well as trespass, at common law, in illustration of this, are numerous, as to torts on the water. (See *ante.*)

Force, too, is no more necessary to constitute this kind of tort at sea than on land, or in admiralty than in a common law court. (3 Story, 349.) That is the gist of this branch of the case. It is true that most of the libels in admiralty for torts are for such as were caused by force, like assaults and batteries (4 Rob. Adm. 75); or for collision between ships on the sea, to the injury of person or property (2 Browne's Civ. and Adm. Law, 110; Dunlap's Adm. 31; Moore, 89); or for wrongful captures (10 Wheat. 486; Bee's Adm. 369; 1 Gall. 315; 3 Cranch 408); or for carrying off a person *in invitum* (Dunlap's Adm. 53); or for any "violent dispossession of property on the ocean" (1 Wheat. 257; L'Invincible, 1 Wheat. 238; 3 Dall. 344.) And though, where trespass is brought at common law, or a tort is sued for in admiralty as "a maritime trespass," there must usually have been force and an immediate injury (1 Chit. Pl. 128; 11 Mass. 137; 17 Mass. 246; 1 Pick. 66; 8 Wend. 274; 3 East. 293; 11 Wheat. 36, *argu.;* 4 Rob. Adm. 75), yet it need not be implied or proved in trespass on the case at law, or in a libel in admiralty for consequential damages to property. Such a libel lies as well for a tort to property as to the person, on the sea (2 Browne's Civ. and Adm. Law, 109, 202; Doug. 594, 613, note; 4 Rob. Adm. 73—76; Martin *v.* Ballard et al., Bee's Adm. 50, 239); and for consequential injury by a tort there, as well as direct injury. (Sloop Cardolero, Bee's Adm. 51, 60; 3 Mason, 242; 4 Mason, 385—388; 2 Browne's Adm. 108; 2 Story, 188; 2 Sir Leoline Jenkins, 777.) It was even doubted once, whether, for such torts at sea, any remedy existed elsewhere than in admiralty. (2 Browne's Civ. and Adm. Law, 112.) Indeed, 1 Browne's Civ. and Adm. Law, 397, shows, that, beside rights arising from contract, there were "obligations or rights arising to the injured party from the torts or wrongs done by another." And these were divided into those arising *ex delicto* and those *quasi ex delicto;* and the former included "damage" to property, as in this case. It meant injury to property by destroying, spoiling, or deteriorating it, and implied "faultiness or injustice" (491), but not necessarily force. Either trespass or case sometimes lies for a marine tort, even in the collision of vessels, where at times the only force is that of winds and tides, and the efforts of the master were to avoid, rather than commit, an injury. (1 Chit. Pl. 145; 2 Story, 188; 11 Price, 608; 3 Car. & Payne, 554.) Damages by insufficient equipments, ropes, &c., must be paid by the owners of the vessel to the merchant, even by the laws of Oleron (art. 10). (See Laws, 136; Laws of Wisby, art. 49.) And nothing is more consequential, or less with force, than that kind of injury.

Finally, the principles applicable to the definition of the wrong or tort being here in favor of a recovery in admiralty, and there being no precedents in opposition, but some in support of it, the inference is strong that this destruction of the property of the plaintiffs may well be regarded and prosecuted in admiralty as a marine tort.

Though I admit there are no more cases in point abroad, in 1789, for sustaining a suit for a consequential injury by a carrier as a tort, than on the contract, in admiralty, yet the principles are most strongly in favor of relying on the tort, without any opposing decision, as there is to a libel on the contract. Beside this, other difficulties are avoided, and more ample justice attained, by the libel here for the tort, than by one for the contract.

A moment to another objection,—that the libel in this case does not contain allegations in proper form to recover damages in admiralty, as if for a maritime tort.

This libel is in several separate articles, rather than in a single count. In none of them is any contract specifically set out, though in one of them something is referred to as "contracted." The libel avers, that the respondents were common carriers; that a public duty thus devolved on them; that they received the property on board to transport it, and so negligently conducted, it was lost. The breach is described throughout, not of what had been "contracted" or promised, but as a wrong done, or tort, and specifies several misdoings. It is in these words:

"Yet the respondents, their officers, servants, and agents, so carelessly and improperly stowed the said gold coin and silver coin, and the engine, furnace, machinery, furniture, rigging, and equipments of the said steamboat were so imperfect and insufficient, and the said respondents, their officers, servants, and agents, so carelessly, improperly, and negligently managed and conducted the said steamboat Lexington, during her said voyage, that by reason of such improper stowage, imperfect and insufficient engine, furnace, machinery, furniture, rigging, and equipments, and of such careless, improper, and negligent conduct, the said steamboat, together with the gold coin and silver coin to the libellants belonging, were destroyed by fire on the high seas, and wholly lost."

Where contract and tort, in the forms of declaration at common law in actions of the case, are with difficulty discriminated, the general test adopted is, if specific breaches are assigned, sounding *ex delicto*, it is case on the tort. (Jeremy on Carriers, 117.) Here this is done.

The same technical minuteness is not necessary in a libel as in a declaration at common law. (5 Rob. Adm. 322; Dunlap, Adm. 438, 439; Ware, D. C. 51.) Only the essential facts need be alleged, without regard to particular forms, either in contract or tort. (Hall's Prac. 207, 138; Dunlap, Adm. 427.)

And in the same libel between the same parties, unlike the rule at common law, it is held by some that both contract and tort may be joined, though it is proper to state them in separate articles in the libel, like separate counts. (*Semble* in 3 Story, R. 349; Dunlap, Adm. 89.) And in some cases it is clearly better not to unite them. (Ware, D. C. 427.) Here, if the libel is considered as but separate paragraphs of one article, it is a good one in tort. (Dunlap, Adm. 114, 115; 4 Mason, C. C. 541.) And if as separate articles, one of them is valid in tort.

The forms of libels for maritime torts include those which caused only consequential damages, as well as those which caused direct damages. Dunlap, Adm. 49; 3 Story, R. 349, one count seems to be for the wrong.

There are cases of this kind merely for improper usage to passengers, by bad words and neglect; but no force existed, or was alleged. (3 Mason, C. C. 242.)

Others are libels for seducing or carrying away a minor son of the plaintiff to his damage, like the actions on the case at common law. (Plummer *v.* Webb, 4 Mason, C. C. 380.) Yet they are called, as they are in law, "tortious abductions."

So a libel lies for loss of goods "carelessly and improperly stowed." (Ware, D. C. 189.)

But if the libel here was less formal in tort, the liberality practised in admiralty pleadings, recording the substance chiefly, as in the civil law, would allow here any necessary amendments. (Dunlap, Adm. 283; 4 Mason, C. C. 543; 3 Wash. C. C. 484.) Or would allow them in the court below, by reversing the judgment, and sending the case back, with directions to permit them there. (4 Wheat. 64, 63; 4 Howard, 154; 1 Wheat. 264, 13; 9 Peters, 483.)

The amount of damages which can be awarded in admiralty, in a case like this, has been agitated by some of the court, but was not argued at the bar. It is not without difficulty, but can in a minute or two be set right. By the ancient practice in admiralty, in case of contracts of freight made by the master, it is true that the owners were liable, whether *ex contractu* or *ex delicto*, and whether *in personam* or *in rem*, for only the value of the vessel, or the capital used in that business. (Dunlap, Adm. 31.) And if the vessel was lost, the remedy against the owners was entirely lost in admiralty. (Ware,

D. C. 188.) Yet it is a conclusive answer, that here, as well as abroad, the rule of the civil and common law is to give the whole loss. (2 Kent, Comm. 606; 3 Kent, Comm. 217.) And that this rule of full damage in a libel in admiralty has been adopted here after much consideration. Livingston, Justice, in Paine, C. C. 118, says, that "it had long been regarded as a general principle of maritime law" to make the owners liable for a tort by the master, and that now the whole injury was the measure of damage, without reference to the value of the vessel and freight. (See also, Del Col *v.* Arnold, 3 Dall. 333; The Appollon, 9 Wheat. 376; 3 Story, R. 347; 2 Story, R. 187.)

This is modified by some State laws, under certain circumstances. (See The Rebecca and Phebe, Ware, D. C.) And in England, by 53 Geo. III. ch. 99.

But even there the owner is still liable beyond the value of the vessel and freight, if the damage or neglect was "committed or occasioned" with "the fault or privity of such owner." (See Statutes at Large of that year; Phebe, Ware, D. C. 269. See, for this and other statutes, 2 Bro. Civ. and Adm. Law, 45, excusing owners if the pilot alone is in fault. See 6 Geo. IV. ch. 125, § 55; 1 Wm. Rob. 46; 1 Dod. Adm. 467.) So the whole injury must be paid now on the contract, and the owners cannot escape by abandoning the vessel which did the wrong. (2 Bro. Civ. and Adm. Law, 206, note.)

On principle, also, this is the right rule in admiralty, clearly, where the owners themselves at home, and not the master abroad, made the contract, or where they were guilty of any neglect in properly furnishing the vessel, and not he. (Phebe, Ware, D. C. 269, 203—206.)

The principle of his binding them only to the extent of the property confided to him to act with, or administer on, does not apply to that state of facts (Abbott on Ship. 93), but only to his doings abroad.

The contracts made abroad are usually in his name, as well as by him, and not by the owners, and he only to sue or be sued. (Abbott on Ship., pt. 2, ch. 2, § 5.)

In Waring et al. *v.* Clarke, which was a tort by the master at home, in a collision of two boats, the whole amount of the injury was awarded. (See also 1 Howard, 23; 3 Kent, Comm. 238.) So principle, no less than precedent, requires it now, in admiralty as well as common law, when the master is usually not a part-owner, but a mere agent for the owners, and doing damage, as here, by unskilfulness or neglect, and not by wilful misconduct. (Ware, D. C. 208; 1 East, 106.) For this, surely, those should suffer who selected him *respondet superiori.* (1 East, 106; Abbott on Ship., pt. 2, ch. 2, § 9; 2 Kent, Comm. 218.)

It is a mistake, likewise, to suppose, as some have, that the rule of damage is thus higher in admiralty than at common law, or when counting on the tort rather than contract. The only difference is, that in admiralty, if counting on the contract, doubts exist whether a recovery can be had on the precedents, while, if counting on the tort, no doubt exists, the place of the tort being clearly on the sea, and within admiralty jurisdiction. Nor do I see any sound reason for not sustaining this case in admiralty, when jurisdiction exists there over the subject, because this proceeding is *in personam* and not *in rem.* (6 Am. Jur. 4; 2 Bro. Civ. and Adm. Law, 396; 2 Gall. 461, 462; Hard. 173.)

The jurisdiction is one thing, the form of proceeding another; and it is only when the vessel itself is pledged, and no personal liability created, so as to lay a foundation for an action at law, that the form of proceeding seems to help to give jurisdiction in admiralty, where alone the libel *in rem* in such case can be followed. (3 D. & E. 269.)

But even then, I apprehend, the subject-matter must be proper for admiralty, or it could not be prosecuted there *in rem*, because, if the subject-matter is a carriage or horse, rather than a ship or its voyage, or something maritime, admiralty would get no jurisdiction by the thing itself being pledged, or to be proceeded against. (The Fair American, 1 Peters, Adm. 87; Duponceau on Jurisdiction, 22, 23.)

Indeed, the rule in England to this day seems to be adverse to proceeding in admiralty at all, even *in rem*, to recover freight. (Abbott on Ship. 170.) King et al. *v.* Shepherd et al., 3 Story, 319, was a libel, *in personam*, against a common carrier by water, and held that the liability was the same as on land, and an act of God to excuse must be immediate, and that the burden of the excuse rests on the respondents, and they are not discharged by a wreck, but must attend to the property till safe or restored.

So it has been adjudged by this court to be proper to prosecute in admiralty for marine torts, *in personam* as well as *in rem.* (Manro *v.* Almeida, 10 Wheat. 473; The Appollon, 9 Wheat. 362; Bee, Adm. 141; The Cassius, 2 Story, R. 81; 14 Peters, 99.) See also the rules of this court (1845), for admiralty practice, to 14th, 15th, 16th, and 17th (3 Howard, 7, Preface), and which expressly allow in libels for freight proceedings *in rem* or *in personam*, and in some trespasses to property either mode.

I concur, therefore, in the judgment of the court, affirming the decree for full damages, but on the ground of a recovery for the wrong committed as a marine tort, rather than on any breach of contract which can be prosecuted by these plaintiffs, and in admiralty.

# ON ADMIRALTY JURISDICTION.*

It is important to notice in the outset some unusual features in this case. The Supreme Court is called upon to try the facts as well as the law in it, and to decide them between parties in interest who belong to the same State, and as to a transaction which happened, not on the high seas, as is usual in torts under admiralty jurisdiction, but two hundred miles above the mouth of the Mississippi river, within the limits of a county, and in the heart of the State of Louisiana. A question of jurisdiction, therefore, arises in this, which is very important, and must first be disposed of. It involves the trial by jury as to trespasses of every kind happening between the ocean and the head of tide-waters in all the numerous rivers of the United States, as well as the rights of the citizens near them, in such disputes with their neighbors, to be tried by their own local tribunals and their own laws, rather than be subject to the great inconvenience and expense of coming hither, at such a distance, and under a different code, to vindicate their just claims. These interesting considerations in the case, and my differing in opinion on them from the majority of the court, will, it is hoped, prove a sufficient apology for justifying that difference in some detail.

A great principle at the foundation of our political system applies strongly to the present case, and is, that, while supporting all the powers clearly granted to the General Government, we ought to forbear interfering with what has been reserved to the States, and, in cases of doubt, to follow where that principle leads, unless prevented by the overruling authority of high judicial decisions. So, under the influence of kindred considerations, in case of supposed improvements or increased convenience by changes of the law, it is an imperative duty on us to let them be made by representatives of the people and the States, through acts of Congress, rather than by judicial legislation. (Paine's C. C. 75.) Starting with these views, then, what is the character of the adjudged cases on the facts here to which they are to be applied?

Those to be found on the subject of torts through the collision of vessels are mostly of English origin, coming from a nation which is not only the source of much of our own jurisprudence, but entitled by her vast commerce to great respect in all matters of maritime usage and admiralty law. No principle appears to be better settled there than

* Dissenting opinion in case of Waring et al. *v.* Clarke.

that the court of admiralty has not jurisdiction over torts, whether to person or property, unless committed on the high seas, and out of the limits of a county. (3 Bl. Com. 106; 4 Instit. 134; Doug. R. 13; 2 East's Crown Law, 803; Bac. Abr., *Courts of Admiralty*, A; 5 Rob. Ad. 345; Fitzh. Abr. 192, 416; 2 Dod. 83; 4 Rob. Ad. 60, 73; 2 Browne's Civ. and Ad. Law, 110, 204; 2 Hag. Ad. 398; 3 D. & E. 315; 3 Hag. Ad. 283, 369; 4 Instit. 136; Chamberlain et al. *v.* Chandler, 3 Mason's C. C. 244.) This is not a doctrine which has grown up there since the adoption of our constitution, nor one obsolete and lost in the mist of antiquity; but it is laid down in two acts of Parliament as early as the fourteenth century, and has been adhered to uniformly since, except where modified within a few years by express statutes. (The Public Opinion, 2 Hag. Ad. 398; 6 Dane's Abr. 341.)

The first of these acts, the thirteenth of Richard II., declared that the admiralty must "not meddle henceforth of anything done within the realm, but only of a thing done upon the sea." (3 Hag. Ad. 282; 1 Statutes at Large, 419.) Then, in two years after, to remove any doubts as to what was meant by the *realm* and the *sea*, came the fifteenth of Richard II., ordering that of "things done within the bodies of counties by land or water, the admirals shall have no cognizance, but they shall be tried by the law of the land." (2 Pickering's Statutes, 341.) This gave to the common law courts there, and forbade to the admiralty, the trial of all collisions between vessels when not on the high seas, and not out of the body of a county, though on waters navigable and salt, and where strong tides ebbed and flowed. (2 Hag. Ad. 398; Selden on Dominion of the Sea, B. 2, ch. 14.) And it did this originally, and continued to do it, not only down to the eighteenth century, but to our Revolution, and long since; because it was necessary to secure the highly-prized trial by jury, rather than by a single judge, for everything happening where a jury could be had from the vicinage of the occurrence within a county, and because it secured a decision on their rights by the highly-prized common law, inherited from their fathers, and with which they were familiar, rather than by the civil law or any other foreign code, attempted to be forced upon the commons and barons by Norman conquerors or their partisans.

Among the cases in point as to this, both long before and since our Revolution, one of them (Velthasen *v.* Ormsley, 3 D. & E. 315) happened in A. D. 1789, the very year the constitution was adopted. (See also Violet *v.* Blague, Cro. Jac. 514; 2 Hag. Ad. 398; 4 Instit. 134—148; 6 Dane's Abr. 341, *Prohibition.*) And one of the most strenuous advocates for admiralty jurisdiction in Great Britain admits, that for damages done by the collision of ships, "if done at sea, remedy can be had in the admiralty, but not if it happen within the body of a county." (2 Browne's Civ. and Ad. Law, 111.)

Since then, on his complaint, an express statute has been passed

(1 and 2 George IV., ch. 75, § 32), that any damage done by a foreign ship, "in any harbor, port, river, or creek," may be prosecuted either in admiralty or common law courts. (The Christiana, 2 Hag. Ad. 184; 38 British Statutes, ch. 274.) And, later still, a like change is considered by some to be made concerning injuries by domestic ships, under the 4 and 5 Victoria, ch. 45. (See it in the Statutes at Large.) But till these statutes, not a case of this kind can probably be found sustained in admiralty, even on the river Thames, at any place within the body of a county, though yearly covered with a large portion of the navigation of the world. (See cases before cited, and 1 Dod. Ad. 468; 1 Wm. Rob. 47, 131, 182, 316, 371, 391, 474; Curtis' Admiralty, tit. *Collision.*)

Nor is this a peculiarity in the admiralty system of that country confined to torts alone. But the same rule prevails as to crimes, and has always been adhered to, with a single exception, originally made in the statute itself of Richard, as to murder and mayhem committed in great vessels in the great rivers below the first bridges. (Com. Dig. *Admiralty*, E, 5, note; Hale's History of Common Law, 35; 3 Rob. Ad. 336; 4 Inst. 148; 1 Hawk. P. C., ch. 37, § 36; Palmer's Practice in House of Lords, 371, note.)

The next inquiry is, if this distinction, confining the jurisdiction in admiralty over torts to such as happen on the high seas without the limits of a county, rested on such important principles as to be adopted in this country? Some seem disposed to believe it of so little consequence as hardly to have been worth attention. But this is a great mistake. The controversy was not in England, and is not here, a mere struggle between salt and fresh water,—sea and lake,—tide and ordinary current,—within a county and without,—as a technical matter only.

But there are imbedded beneath the surface three great questions of principle in connection with these topics, which possess the gravest constitutional character. And they can hardly be regarded as of little consequence here, and assuredly not less than they possessed abroad, when they involve, (1.) the abolition of the trial by jury over large tracts of country, (2.) the substitution there of the civil law and its forms for the common law and statutes of the States, (3.) and the encroachment widely on the jurisdiction of the tribunals of the State over disputes happening there between its own citizens.

Without intending to enter with any minuteness into the origin and history of admiralty jurisdiction abroad, it will be sufficient, in order to illustrate the vital importance of this question of locality, to say that the trial by jury and the common law, so ardently adhered to by the Anglo-Saxons, was soon encroached on after the Conquest by the Norman admirals claiming jurisdiction over certain maritime matters, not only on the ocean, and trying them without a jury, and on principles of their favorite civil law, but on the waters within the body of a county, and where a jury could easily be summoned, and where the principles of the common law had ever in England been accustomed to prevail. A struggle, therefore, of course, soon sprung up in respect to this, as their monarchs had begun to organize an admiral's court within a century after the Conquest, but without any act of Parliament now found to vindicate it. (See the Statutes at Large, and 3 Reeves' History of the English Law, 197.) And laying down some regulations as to its powers by ordinances, as at Hastings, under Edward the First, but not by any acts of Parliament consulting the wishes of the barons and the commons. Whether this was constitutional or not, it was sufficient to make them look on the admiralty as a foreign and odious interloper. Reeves says (3 Reeves' Hist. of English Law, 137),—"The office of admiral is considered by the French as a piece of state invented by them." And whether it was imported thence by the conquerors, or originated with the Rhodians, or Romans, or Saracens, rather than the French or English, its principles seem to have been transplanted to western Europe from the Mediterranean, the cradle of commerce for all but the Asiatic world; and it was regarded by the commons and barons of England as an intruder into that realm, and without the sanction of Parliament.

In the course of a few years, that same sturdy spirit, which in Magna Charta was unwilling to let the laws of England be changed for a foreign code, proceeded, by the 13th and 15th of Richard II., to denounce and forbid the encroachments of the admirals, and their new forms and code of the civil law, into the bodies of counties and the local business of the realm. It produced those two memorable acts of Parliament, never since departed from in torts or crimes except under express statutes, and fixing the limit of jurisdiction for them at the line between the counties and the high seas. And they have ever since retained it there, except as above named, from the highest principles of safety to the common law, English liberties, and the inestimable trial by jury,— principles surely no less dear in a republic than a monarchy.

If the power of the admiral was permitted to act beyond that line, it was manifestly without the apology which existed thus far on the ocean, of there being no jury to be called from the vicinage to try the case. (Prynne's Animadversions, 92, 93; Fitzh. Abr. 192, 216.) And if the act, by an alias and a fiction, was alleged to be done in the county, when, in fact, it happened at a distance, on the seas, the jury would be less useful, not in truth residing near the place of the occurrence, not acquainted with the parties or witnesses, and the case itself not being one happening where the common law usually operated, and with which the people and the judges were familiar.

This last circumstance furnished another reason why the admiralty court was allowed there, and should be here, to continue to exercise some jurisdiction, beside their military and naval power, over the conduct of seamen and the business of navigation when foreign. Because such matters were connected with the ocean, with foreign intercourse, foreign laws, and foreign people, and it was desirable to have the law as to them uniform, and administered by those possessing some practical acquaintance with such subjects; they being, in short, matters extra-territorial, international, and peculiar in some degree to the great highway of nations. It is when thus confined to that great highway and its concerns, that admiralty law deserves the just tribute sometimes paid to it of expansive wisdom and elevated equity.* Then only there is an excellence in such regulations as to navigation over those for rights and duties on land; the last being often more for a single people, and their limited territory, while the former are on most matters more expanded, more liberal,—the gathered wisdom of and for all maritime ages and nations. They are also what has been approved by all, rather than a few, and for the territory of all in common. And hence that beautiful tribute paid to them by Antoninus, and just as beautiful, that he was "lord of the world, but Law the lord of the sea." (2 Browne's Civ. and Ad. Law, 38.)

The sea being common to all nations, its police and the rights and duties on it should be governed mainly by one code, known to all, and worthy to be respected and enforced by all. This, it will be seen, indicates in letters of strong light the very line of boundary which we have been attempting to draw, on grounds of deep principle, here as well as in England. It is the line between State territory and State laws on the one hand, and the ocean, the territory of all nations, and the laws of all nations, the admiralty and sea laws of all nations, on the other hand, leaving with those, for instance, residing within local jurisdictions, and doing business there, the local laws and local tribunals, but with those whose home and business are on the ocean, the forms and laws and tribunals which are more familiar to them. This line being thus a certain and fixed one, and resting on sound principles, has in England withstood the shock of ages. It is true, that some modifications have been recently made there, but only by express statutes, and carefully guarded so as not to innovate on the common law and the trial by jury. That this line of distinction was, in fact, appreciated quite as highly here as in England, is shown by various circumstances that need not be repeated; but, among them were solemn resolutions of the old Congress against acts concerning trade and revenue, extending the power of admiralty courts beyond their ancient limits, and thus taking away the trial by jury. (1 Journal, 19, 20.) And as a striking evidence of the dangerous importance attached to this outrage, it was remarked in the convention of North Carolina, that "the Stamp Act and the taking away of the trial by jury, were the principal causes of resistance to Great Britain." (4 Elliott's Deb. 157.) Indeed, this same jealousy of the civil law, and its mode of proceeding without a jury, led, in the first legislation by Congress, to

* And the vice-admiral is hence quaintly called "the justice of the peace for the sea," by Sir Leoline Jenkins; but who ever supposed him the justice of the peace two hundred miles inward from the sea?

forbid going into chancery at all, if relief at law is as ample and appropriate. (See sixteenth section of Judiciary Act, 1 Statutes at Large, 83.) So as to admiralty, a statute of Pennsylvania, passed during the Revolution, allowed it only in cases "not cognizable at common law." (1 Dall. 106.) And our fathers never could have meant, that parties, for matters happening within a county or State, should be dragged into admiralty any more than equity, if as full a remedy, and of as good a kind, existed in courts of law, where they could enjoy their favorite code and mode of trial. (1 Bald. C. C. 405.) This would leave much to admiralty still, as well as to equity, and more especially in the former, by proceedings *in rem*. And when it became convenient to vest additional power in the same court, or power over a wider range of territory, as it might in the progress of society and business, it could be done here by express statute, as it has been in respect to the lakes, under the power to regulate commerce, and allowing a trial by jury if desired.

In short, instead of less, much additional importance should be attached to this line of distinction here, beyond what exists in England; because it involves here not only all the important consequences it does there, but some which are new and peculiar. Instead of being, as it once was there, a contest between courts of one and the same government, it may become here a struggle for jurisdiction between courts of the States and courts of the United States, always delicate, and frequently endangering the harmony of our political system. And while the result there, in favor of the admiralty, would cause no additional inconvenience and expense, as all the courts sit in one city, such a result here compels the parties to travel beyond their own counties or States, and in case of appeal to come hither, a distance sometimes of a thousand or fifteen hundred miles.

Admitting, then, as we must, that the doctrine I have laid down as to torts was the established law in England at our Revolution, and was not a mere technical doctrine, but rested on great principles, dear to the subject and his rights and liberties, should it not be considered as the guide here, except where altered, if at all, by our colonial laws or constitutions, or acts of Congress, or analogies which are binding, or something in it entirely unsuitable to our condition? The best authorities require that it should be. (1 Peters' Ad. 116, 236, note; 1 Peters' C. C. 104, 111, 114; 1 Paine's C. C. 111; 2 Gall. 398, 471; 3 Mason, 27; Bemis *v.* The Janus et al., 1 Baldwin's C. C. 545; 12 Wheat, 638; 1 Kent's Com. 377; 4 Dall. 429; 4 Wash. C. C. 213.) Yet this is contested in the present case.

Some argue that the constitution, by extending the judicial power to "all cases of admiralty and maritime jurisdiction," meant cases different from those recognized in England as belonging to the admiralty at the Revolution, or those as modified by ourselves when colonies. These jurists stand prominent, and their views seem to-day adopted by a portion of this court. (See the argument in De Lovio *v.* Boit, 2 Gall. 398.)

The authorities which I have cited against this position seem to me overwhelming in number and strength; and some of them come from those either engaged in making the constitution, or in construing it in the earliest stages of its operation. Let me ask, What books had we for admiralty law, then, as well as common law,—both referred to in the constitution,—but almost exclusively English ones? What had the profession here been educated to administer,—English or French admiralty? Surely the former. The judges here were English, the colonies English, and appeals, in all cases on the instance side of the court, lay to the English admiralty at home.

What "cases of admiralty," then, were most likely to be in the minds of those who incorporated those words into the constitution?—cases in the English reports, or those in Spain, or Turkey?—cases living and daily cited and practised on both in England and here, or those in foreign and dead languages, found in the assizes of Jerusalem near the time of the Crusades?

It is inferred by some, from 6 Dane's Abr. 352, 353, that cases in admiralty are to be ascertained, not by English law at the Revolution, but by principles of "general law." And Judge Washington held, it is said, we must go the general maritime law of the world, and not to England alone. (Dain et al. *v.* Sloop Severn, 4 Hazard's Penn. Reg. 248, in 1828.) But the whole tenor of Mr. Dane's quotations and reasons, in respect to admiralty jurisdiction, is to place it on the English basis; and Judge Washington, in several instances, took it for his guide, and commended it as the legal guide. In the United States *v.* Gill, 4 Dall. 429, he says:—"But still the question recurs, Is this a case of admiralty and maritime jurisdiction within the meaning of the constitution? The words of the constitution must be taken to refer to the admiralty and maritime jurisdiction of England, from whose code and practice we derived our systems of jurisprudence, and, generally speaking, obtain the best glossary." (See also 4 Wash. 456, 457.)

Neither of these eminent jurists was ever likely to go to the laws of continental Europe as guides, unless in cases not well settled either here or in England; and then, as in the common law courts and in chancery, they might probably search all enlightened systems of jurisprudence for suggestions and principles to aid. Chancellor Kent, also, with his accustomed modesty, yet with clearness, supporting a like doctrine with that just quoted from Judge Washington, observes,—"But I apprehend it may fairly be doubted, whether the constitution of the United States meant, by admiralty and maritime jurisdiction, anything more than that jurisdiction which was settled and in practice in this country under the English jurisprudence when the constitution was made." (1 Kent's Com. 377.) Another strong proof that this was the opinion prevailing here at that time is, that a court of admiralty was established in Virginia, in 1779, under the recommendation of Congress to all the States to make prize courts; and, by the act of Assembly, it is expressly provided that they are to be "governed in their proceedings and decisions by the regulations of the Congress of the United States of America, by the acts of the General Assembly, by the laws of Oleron, and the Rhodian and Imperial laws, so far as they have been heretofore observed in the English courts of admiralty, and by the laws of nature and nations." (10 Hening's Stat. 98.) They thus, after our own laws, State and national, made England the guide.

It is said by others, appealing to feelings of national pride, that we are to look to our own constitution and laws, and not to England, for a guide. So we do look to our own laws and constitution first, and when they are silent, go elsewhere. But what are our own laws and constitution, unless those in England before our Revolution, except so far as altered here, either before, or then, or since, and except such in England then as were not applicable to our condition and form of government? This was the guide adopted by this court in its practice as early as August 8th, 1791 (1 Howard, 24); and as late as January, 1842, it treated the practice in England as the rule in equity, where not otherwise directed; and in Gaines et al. *v.* Relf et al., 15 Peters, 9, it decided that when our own "rules do not apply, the practice of the Circuit and District Courts must be regulated by the practice of the court of chancery in England." (See, also, Vattier *v.* Hinde, 7 Peters, 274.) And most of its forms and rules in admiralty have been adopted in our District and Circuit Courts. (See Rule XC., in 1 How. 66, Pref.) And this court has again and again disposed of important admiralty questions, looking to England alone, rather than the Continent, as a guide, when they differed.

Thus the Continental law would carry admiralty jurisdiction over all navigable streams. Yet this court has deliberately refused to do it, in The Thomas Jefferson, 10 Wheat. 428. Had it not so refused, in repeated instances, there would have been no necessity for the recent act of Congress as to the lakes and their tributaries. So, the civil law gives a lien for repairs of domestic ships; but this court has not felt justified in doing it without a statute, because not done in England. (7 Peters, 324.) And in Hobart *v.* Drogan et al., 10 Peters, 122, this court felt bound to follow the English decisions as to salvage, though in some respects harsh. (See, also, 3 Howard, 568.)

So, when the constitution and the acts of Congress speak, as they do in several instances, of the "common law," do they not mean the English common law? This court so decided in Robinson *v.* Campbell, 3 Wheat. 223, adhering, it is said, "to the principles of common law and equity, as distinguished and defined in that country, from which we derive our knowledge of those principles." Why not, then, mean the English admiralty law when they speak of "cases of admiralty and maritime jurisdiction"? They of course must, by all analogous decisions and by established usage, as well as by the opinions of eminent jurists. The English decisions furnish, also, the most natural, appropriate, uniform, and well-known principles, both for action and judicial decision.

It would be extraordinary, indeed, for this court to undertake to exercise a legislative power as to this point, and without warrant to search the world over and select, for the trial of private rights, any law they may prefer. On the contrary, its duty rather is to declare the law which has already become ours, which we inherited from our ancestors or have enacted ourselves, and which is not vagrant and uncertain, but to be found in our own judicial history and institutions, our own constitution, acts of Congress, and binding precedents. Congress also might, in many instances, perhaps, make the law better than it is, and mould it so as to meet new exigencies in society, and suit different stages of business and civilization; and, by new laws as to navigable waters, judicial tribunals, and various other matters, is yearly doing this. But does this court possess that legislative power? And if Congress chooses to give additional jurisdiction to the District Court on the lakes, or tide-waters, or navigable streams between them, and allow jury trials when desired, under its power to regulate commerce and collect a revenue, will this not answer every valuable purpose, and supply any new want or fancied improvement in a more satisfactory and more constitutional manner than for courts to do it without consulting Congress?

That Congress possess the power to do this cannot be plausibly questioned. The late law as to jurisdiction over the lakes, which is given to the District Court, but not as an admiralty case under the constitution, and with a jury when desired, is a strong illustration of legislative opinion being the way we contend.

Any expansion or enlargement can be thus made, and, by withdrawing in part the jurisdiction now conferred on the District Courts in any matters in admiralty, Congress can also abridge the exercise of it as experience and time may show to be wise. For this reason, we are unable to see the force of the argument just offered by four members of this court, that if the English admiralty law was referred to in the expression of "all cases of admiralty and maritime jurisdiction," no change in it could be made, without being at the trouble and expense of altering the constitution.

But, in further answer to this, let me ask if the constitution, as they contend, was meant to include cases in admiralty as on the continent of Europe rather than in England, could the law as to them be more easily altered than if it was only the law of England? And would it not take the interpretation of the admiralty law as much from the courts in one case as in the other?

It is conceded, next, that legislation has, in some respects, in England, since 1789, changed and improved her admiralty proceedings;

but this only furnishes additional evidence that the law was different when our constitution was framed, and that these changes, when useful and made at all, should be made by legislation and not by judicial construction, and they can rightfully have no force here till so made. (United States *v.* Paul, 6 Peters, 141.) The difference, too, between a change by Congress and by this court alone is, furthermore, that the former, when making it, can and doubtless will allow a trial by jury, while we are unable to do this, if we make the change by construing the case to be one legitimately of admiralty jurisdiction.

Finally, then, the law, as it existed in England at the time of the Revolution, as to admiralty jurisdiction over torts, is the only certain and safe guide, unless it has been clearly changed in this respect, either by the constitution, or acts of Congress, or some colonial authority. We have already seen that the constitution has not used words which are fairly open to the idea that any such change was intended. Nor has it made any alteration in terms as to torts. And no act of Congress has introduced any change in respect to torts, having in this respect merely conferred on the District Courts cognizance of "all civil cases" in admiralty, without in a single instance defining what shall be such cases in connection with torts. The next inquiry, then, is, whether the colonies changed the law as to the locality of torts, and exercised jurisdiction over them in admiralty, though committed within a county, and not on the high seas.

I am compelled to go into these details more than would otherwise be done, considering their tediousness, on account of the great reliance on them in one of the opinions just read. In order to operate on the point under consideration, it will be seen that any colonial change must have been so clear and universal as to have been referred to in the constitution and the act of Congress of 1789, and to be the meaning intended by their makers to be embraced in the expression of "cases of admiralty and maritime jurisdiction," rather than the meaning that had usually been attached to them by the English language and the judicial tribunals of England, for centuries. And this change, likewise, must have been clearly meant to be referred to and adopted, notwithstanding its great encroachment in torts on the boasted trial by jury, and which encroachment they were denouncing as tyranny in other cases, and notwithstanding its natural consequences would be new collisions with the powers of the State tribunals, which they were most anxious to avoid. I have searched in vain to find acts of assembly in any of the thirteen colonies, before 1776, making such a change, much less in a majority or all of them. Nor can I find any such judicial decisions by vice-admiralty courts in any of them, much less in all. Nor is it pretended that any acts of Parliament or judgments in the courts in England had prescribed a different rule in torts for the colonies from what prevailed at home.

It would be difficult, then, to show that a law had become changed in any free country, except by evidence contained in its legislation, or constitutions, or judicial decisions. But some persons, and among them a portion of this bench, have referred to commissions of office to vice-admirals as evidence of a change here; and some, it is feared, have been misled by them. (1 Kent's Com. 367, note; 2 Gall. 373.)

These commissions, in the largest view, only indicated what *might* be done, not what was actually afterwards done under them. In the next place, all must see, on reflection, that a commission issued by the king could not repeal or alter the established laws of the land.

Beside the forms of some of these commissions, referred to in De Lovio *v.* Boit (2 Gall. 398), an entire copy of one of them is in Stokes, and another in Duponceau on Jurisdiction, p. 158, and in Woodcock's Laws of the British Colonies, p. 66. It will be seen that they are much alike, and though there are expressions in them broad enough to cover all "fresh waters" and "rivers," and even "banks of any of the same" (Woodcock, 69), yet tide-waters are never named as the limit of jurisdiction; and, over and paramount to the whole, the judge is required to keep and cause to be executed there "the rights, statutes, laws, ordinances, and customs, anciently observed." Where anciently observed? In England, of course; and thus, of course, were to comply with the English statutes and decisions as to admiralty matters.

This limitation is inserted several times, from abundant caution, in the commission in Woodcock, 66, 67, 69.

But, beside these conflicting features in different parts of them, the commissions of vice-admirals here seem, in most respects, copies of mere forms of ancient date in England (Woodcock's Brit. Col. 123), and, of course, were never intended to be used in the colonies as alterations of the laws, and were, as all know, void and obsolete in England when differing from positive statutes. So virtually it was held in the colonies themselves. (The Little Joe, Stewart's Ad. R. 405; and The Apollo, 1 Hag. Ad. 312; Woodcock's Laws and Const. of the Colonies, 123.) These commissions, also, if they prove anything here actually done different from the laws in England, except what was made different by express statute, as to matters connected with breaches of the laws of revenue and trade, and not as to torts, prove quite too much, as they go above tide-water, and even on the land.

But it is not believed that they led to any practices under them here different from the laws at home in respect to torts. None can now be found stated, either in reports of cases or contemporaneous history. Probably in the colonies the same rules as at home prevailed on this, for another reason; because no statute was passed as to torts here, and appeals to the admiralty at home existed, on the instance side of the court, till a recent change, so as to preserve uniformity in the colonies and at home. (Bains *v.* The James Baldw. 549; Woodcock, 242.) A case of one of those appeals is reported in 2 Rob. 248, 249, The Fabius. There the enlarged powers conferred on vice-admiralty courts by the 6 and 7 of William III., as to seizures and prosecutions for breaches of the laws of trade and revenue, are not, as I understand the case, considered admiralty powers, and we all know they were not so *per se* or *proprio vigore.* A looser practice in the colonies, but no difference of principle, except under statute, appears to have been tolerated. (Woodcock's Laws, &c., 273.)

In accordance with this, Tucker, in his Appendix to Part I. of 1 Black. Com. 432, after a careful examination of charters and other documents, comes to the conclusion, that the laws at home before emigration, both statute and common law, so far as applicable to the condition of the colonies, and in favor of life, liberty, and property of the subject, "remained in full force therein until repealed, altered, or amended by the legislative authority of the colonies respectively, or by the constitutional acts of the same when they became sovereign and independent States." (See, also, to this effect, Montgomery *v.* Henry, 1 Dall. 49; 1 Chalmers' Op. 195; Woodcock, 156.) But what seems to settle this inquiry is the treatise of a colonial judge, giving some data on this very subject, and of course well informed on the subject. Stoke's View of Constitution of British Colonies (p. 270) contains an account of the admiralty jurisdiction in the colonies before the Revolution.

Two things are clearly to be inferred from him: — 1st. That admiralty and maritime cases extended only to matters "arising on the high seas;" and, 2d. That the practice and rules of decision in admiralty were the same here as in England.

Thus, in chapter 13, page 271, he says: — "In the first place, as to the jurisdiction exercised in the court of vice-admiralty in the colonies, in deciding all maritime causes, or causes arising on the high seas, I have only to observe, that it proceeds in the same manner that the High Court of Admiralty in England does." "The only book that I have met with, which treats of the practice of the High Court of Admiralty in England, is Clarke's Praxis Admiralitatis, and this is the book used by the practitioners in the colonies."*

In connection with this, all the admiralty reports we have of cases before the Revolution, and of cases between 1776 and 1789, seem to corroborate the same view, and are worth more to show the actual jurisdiction here than hundreds of old commissions containing obsolete powers never enforced. There is a manuscript volume of Auchmuty's decisions made in the vice-admiralty court in Massachusetts, about 1740. (See Curtis' Merchant Seamen, 348, note.) It will

* Woodcock on the British Colonies is equally explicit, that the vice-admiralty courts in the colonies were called so because in fact subordinate to the admiralty at home, and with like jurisdiction, except where altered by positive statute. Thus, speaking of "the jurisdiction of the admiralty over subjects of maritime contract," he says, — "With respect to this authority it may be only necessary to observe, that in such matters the admiralty court in the colonies holds plea agreeably to the course of the same court in England." (p. 272.)

be difficult to find in them, even in one colony, much more in the thirteen, clear evidence of any change here, before the Revolution, in respect to the law concerning the locality of torts.

The very first case, of Quitteville *v.* Woodbury, April 15, 1740, is a libel for a trespass. But it is carefully averred to have taken place "at the Bay of Honduras, upon *the open sea*, on board the ship King George."

No other case of tort is printed; and on a careful examination of what has not been printed, no case is found varying the principle. There is one for conversion of a vessel and cargo, July 30th, 1742, tried before George Cradock, deputy judge in admiralty, Farrington *v.* Dennis. But the conversion happened on the high seas, or what in those days was often termed the "*deep sea.*" So a decision in the State of Delaware, in 1788, reported in the Introduction to 4 Dall. 2 (last edit.); the judge seems to concede it to be law in that colony, that all cases, except prize ones, must happen "on the high seas," in order to give the admiralty jurisdiction over them.

So a few cases before the adoption of the constitution are reported in Bee's Admiralty Decisions, though they are mostly on contracts. But they all make a merit of conforming to the course in the English admiralty, rather than exhibiting departures from and enlargements of its jurisdiction. See one in A. D. 1781, Bee's Adm, 425, and another in the same year (p. 419), and another in 1785 (p. 369). But the most decisive of all is a case in A. D. 1780, in the High Court of Appeals in Pennsylvania, Montgomery *v.* Henry et al., 1 Dall. 49.

It was a proceeding in admiralty, regarded by some as sounding in tort, and by some in contract; but as to the line of jurisdiction, this having happened, as averred, on the river Delaware, the court say, through Reed, their president,—"But it appears to us, that from the 13th and 15th Richard II., the admiralty has had jurisdiction on all waters out of the body of the county. There has been great debate as to what is meant by high seas. A road, haven, or even river, not within the body of the county, is high sea in the idea of civilians. Therefore, if the river Delaware is out of the body of any county, we think it clear that it is within the admiralty jurisdiction."

In short, as to this matter, the first principles of English jurisprudence, as applicable to her colonies, show that there could be no difference here on a matter of this kind, unless authorized by express statute at home, extending to the colonies, or by acts of assembly here, expressly sanctioned at home.

Blackstone says,—"For it hath been held, that if an uninhabited country be discovered and planted by English subjects, all the English laws then in being, which are the birthright of every subject, are immediately there in force." (1 Bl. Com. 108; 2 P. Wms. 75.) Exceptions, of course, exist as to matters not applicable to their condition, but none of them reach this case, and require consideration.

Were not we then British colonies, and beginning here in an uninhabited country, or, what is equivalent, tenanted by a people not having any civilized laws? Why, then, were not the principles of English admiralty law in force here in the vice-admiralty courts, as much as the English common law in other courts,—and which has been declared by this tribunal to have been the basis of the jurisprudence of all the States in 1789? (3 Peters, 444.) Indeed, any laws in the plantations contrary to or repugnant to English laws were held to be void, if not allowed by Parliament at home. (3 Bl. Com. 109, App. 380, by Tucker.)

What is left, then, for the idea to rest on of a change in respect to the locality of torts here, to give admiralty courts jurisdiction over them different from what existed in England in 1776? We have already seen that there is nothing in the constitution, nothing in any acts of Congress, nothing in any colonial laws, or colonial decisions in the vice-admiralty courts. Some venture to infer it merely from analogies. But, denying the competency for courts of limited jurisdiction, like ours, to do this, if impairing jury trials and encroaching on State jurisdictions, without any express grant or authority to that effect, let me ask, what are the analogies? The only ones which can be imagined are cases of crimes, contracts, and seizures for breaches of laws of revenue and trade. But the decisions as to crimes prove directly the reverse.

In respect to them, no change whatever on this point has occurred, and the rule recognized in this country as the true one concerning their locality is, like that in England, if tried in admiralty as being crimes by admiralty law, they must have been committed without the limits of a county or State. (4 Mason, C. C. 308; 5 ibid. 290; 1 Dall. 49; 3 Wheat. 336, 371; 5 ibid. 76, 379; 12 ibid. 623; 4 Wash. C. C. 375; Baldw. C. C. 35.)

And all crimes on the waters of the United States made puinshable in the courts of the United States, by acts of Congress, with few or no exceptions, if connected solely with admiralty jurisdiction, are scrupulously required to have been committed on the sea or the high seas, "out of the jurisdiction of any particular State."

In all criminal cases in admiralty in England, the trial has also been by jury, by an express act of Parliament, ever since the 32 Henry VIII. (Com. Dig., *Admiralty*), and so far from the same principle not being considered in force here, the constitution itself, before any amendments, expressly provided for all criminal trials of every kind being by a jury. (Art. 3, § 2, and Federalist, No. 81.)

So, the old Confederation (Article 9th) authorized Congress to provide courts for the trial "of piracies and felonies committed on the high seas." (1 Laws, Bioren's edit., p. 16.) And when Congress did so, they thought it expedient to adopt the same mode of trial for acts "on the sea" as on the land, and "according to the course of the common law;" and under a sort of mixed commission, as under the 28

Henry VIII., to try these offences, consisting of the justices of the Supreme Court in each State, united with the admiralty judge, they imperatively required the use of a jury. (7 Journ. of Old Cong. 65; Duponceau on Juris. 94, 95, note.)

Finding, then, that any analogy from crimes directly opposes, rather than favors, any change as to torts, let us proceed to the case of contracts. It will be necessary, before they can be allowed any effect, for their friends to show that the locality of contracts has been changed here, and then that such change should operate on torts. Contracts, in one aspect of the subject, did not differ as to their locality from torts and crimes before Richard II. any more than after.

But, as the question in relation to the locality of contracts here is still undecided, and is before this court awaiting another argument, on account of divisions of opinion among its members in respect to it, no analogy can be drawn to govern other questions from what is itself thus uncertain; and it is not deemed decorous by me to discuss here the moot question as to contracts, or, till the other action pending in relation to them is itself settled, to draw any inference from what I may suppose to be, or not to be, their locality.

Without, then, going further into the subtilties as to the locality or want of locality of contracts within admiralty jurisdiction, so fully discussed in 2 Gallison, 475, by Judge Story, on the one hand, and in 12 Wheaton, 622, by Justice Johnson, on the other, as well as in the case of the Lexington, at this term, it is enough to say, that is not the question now under consideration. It is, at the nearest, but collateral, and differently situated. For in trespass it was always a test, not only that it happened on the sea, instead of merely tide-water, but out of the body of a county.

And above all this, those very writers who contend that locality does not govern the jurisdiction over contracts admit that it controls, and always has controlled, the right to try both torts and crimes (with the exceptions before named, and not influencing this question), during all the fluctuations and struggles about contracts during the last four hundred years.

In the resolutions said to have been prepared by the judges in 1632, with a view to arrange differences concerning jurisdiction, no change or modification is made as to torts. (Dunlap's Prac. 13, 14; Bevans' case, 3 Wheat. 365, note.)

Nor was there any in the mutual arrangement between the different courts in 1575. (See it in 3 Wheat. 367, note; Prynne's Animadversions, 98, 99.) And in Crowell's Ordinance of 1648, on the jurisdiction of the admiralty, so much relied on by those friendly to the extension of it, and by some supposed to have been copied and followed in this country, damages by one ship to another were included, but it was meant damages on the sea, being described as "damages happening thereon, or arising at sea in any way." (Dunlap's Ad. 16.)

Hence, even in admiralty writers and admiralty courts, it is laid down repeatedly, "in torts, locality ascertains the judicial powers." And again, "in all matters of tort, locality is the strict limit." (2 Bro. Civ. and Ad. Law, 110.) So, in The Eleanor, 6 Rob. Ad. 40, Lord Stowell said, "the locality is everything," instead of holding it to be an obsolete or immaterial form.

Lastly, in respect to analogies in seizures for breaches of the laws of revenue and trade, it is claimed that some change has occurred there, which should influence the jurisdiction over torts. But these seizures are not for torts, nor has the change in relation to the trial of them happened on any principle applicable to torts. Moreover, it has been made as to seizures only under express statutes, and the construction put on those statutes; and if this is to be followed by analogy, no change can be made as to torts except by express statutes.

But there has never been any such statute as to them, and if without it the change was made by analogy, tide-waters would not be the test, as is here contended, but, like cases of seizures, any waters navigable by a boat of ten tons burden. It is even a matter of very grave doubt, whether a mistake was not committed in refusing a trial by jury in cases of seizure, under our Judiciary Act, whenever desired, or, at least, whenever not made on the high seas. Kent, Dane, and several others, think the early decisions made on this, and which have since been merely copied, were probably erroneous. (1 Kent's Com. 376; 6 Dane, 357.)

So thought Congress, likewise, when, Feb. 13th, 1801 (sec. 11th), it conferred on the Circuit Court jurisdiction over "all seizures on land or water, and all penalties and forfeitures made, arising, or accruing under the laws of the United States." This was original cognizance, though not in a court of admiralty, and properly treated seizures on water as on land, and to be all, of course, tried by a jury. (2 Stat. at Large, 92.) This was a change made by Congress itself, aided by some of the first lawyers in the country. But, as the whole statute was repealed, on account of the obnoxious circumstances as to the judges under which it was passed, all the changes fell with it.

The admiralty in England did not exercise any jurisdiction over seizures for revenue, though on the ocean. (8 Wheat. 396, note.) But it was in the court of exchequer, and was devolved on admiralty courts in the colonies for convenience, as no court of exchequer existed there. (Duponceau's Jurisdiction, 139, and note.) This additional jurisdiction, however, was not an admiralty one, and ought to have been used with a jury, if desired, as in the exchequer. Powers not admiralty are, for convenience, still devolved on admiralty courts; and it was a great grievance, complained of by our ancestors here, that such a trial was not allowed in such cases before the Revolution. Undoubtedly it was the expectation of most of those who voted for the act of 1789, that the trial by jury would not be here withheld in cases of seizures for breach of laws of the revenue, which they had always insisted on as their constitutional right as Englishmen, and, *a fortiori*, as Americans.

They had remonstrated early and late, and complained of this abridgment of the trial by jury even in the Declaration of Independence, and as one prominent cause and justification of the Revolution. (1 Journal of Old Congress, 45; 6 Dane's Abr. 357; Baldw. C. C. 551.) As plenary evidence of this, it is necessary to quote here but a single document, as that was drawn up by John Jay, afterwards the chief-justice of this court. It is the address by the old Congress, October 21st, 1774, to the people of Great Britain, and among other grievances says,—"It was ordained, that whenever offences should be committed in the colonies against particular acts imposing duties and restrictions upon trade, the prosecutor might bring his action for the penalties in the *courts of admiralty;* by which means the subject lost the advantage of being tried by an honest, uninfluenced jury of the vicinage, and was subjected to the sad necessity of being judged by a single man,—a creature of the crown,—and according to the course of a law (civil) which exempts the prosecutor from the trouble of proving his accusation, and obliges the defendant either to evince his innocence or to suffer."

Now, after these reprobations of such a practice,—after two specific amendments to the constitution to secure the trial by jury in cases before doubtful,—and after three clauses in the Judiciary Act expressly allowing it in all proper cases,—who can believe that they intended in the ninth section of that very act to use language which ought to be construed so as to deprive them entirely of a jury trial in that very class of cases where the refusal of it had long been denounced by them as oppressive, unlawful, and one of the grounds for a revolution? Should we thus brand them with duplicity, or tyranny?

As a single illustration that their views in the act of 1789 have probably been misconstrued or misapprehended, if seizures for breaches of the laws of revenue and trade were in reality "cases of admiralty and maritime jurisdiction," as meant in the constitution, then no statute was necessary, like a clause in that of 1789, to make them so, and to make them so not at the line of tide-water, which is here contended for, but wherever a boat of twenty tons could go from the ocean. And if they were not such cases to that extent and in that manner without a statute, but were common law and exchequer cases, then it is certain a statute would not make them "admiralty cases," but might devolve their trial on the District Court, allowing a jury, as that trial was expressly reserved by the amendment to the constitution in all common law cases. Stokes discloses the derogatory reason assigned for such a violation of our forefathers' rights by some of the British statutes before the Revolution (Stokes on Constitution of

Colonies, 360). With much *naïveté*, he says,—"In prosecutions in the courts of vice-admiralty in the colonies for the breach of any act of Parliament relating to the trade and revenue of the colonies, all questions as well of *fact* as of law are decided by a judge alone, without the intervention of a jury; for such was the inclination of the colonists in many provinces to carry on a contraband trade, that to try the fact of an information by a jury would be almost equivalent to the repealing of the act of Parliament on which such information was grounded. In other respects, I apprehend the proceedings should be conducted as near as may be to the practice of the Court of Exchequer in England." And the reason said to have been assigned by Judge Chase for the construction first put on the Judiciary Act—that seizures for violation of the laws of revenue and trade were meant by Congress to be treated as cases in admiralty, and tried without a jury, though they never had been so tried in England till the encroaching statutes, and never here except as our fathers declared to be illegally—is almost as harsh, and more derogatory on our fathers themselves, as being an act done by themselves, in saying it was to avoid "the great danger to the revenue if such cases should be left to the caprice of juries." (The United States *v.* Betsy, 4 Cranch, 446, note.)

Whoever could conjecture, for such a reason, that a statute was intended to have such a construction, seems to have forgotten the remonstrances of our fathers against the odious measures of England corresponding with such a construction; and to have overlooked the probable difference in the feelings of juries towards laws made by themselves or their own representatives, and those made by a Parliament in which they were not represented, and whose doings seemed often designed to oppress, rather than protect them. And what presumption is there that an exclusion of juries from trials as to trade and revenue, for causes like these, was meant to be extended to torts?

The reason is totally inapplicable, and hence the presumption entirely fails. What a stretch of presumption, without sufficient data, is it to infer that this resisted case of seizures is first strong evidence of a larger jurisdiction in admiralty established here, and likely to be adopted under the constitution by those who had always ardently opposed it, and next is evidence of a larger jurisdiction in other matters, disconnected entirely with that, and all the reasons ever urged in support of it!

The last inquiry on this question of jurisdiction is, What have been the decisions concerning the locality of torts in admiralty in the courts of the United States since the constitution was adopted?

It is the uncertainty and conflict concerning these which has in part rendered it necessary to explore with so much care how the law was here, when our present system of government went into operation.

It is a matter of surprise, on a critical examination of the books, to see upon how slight foundations this claimed departure from the established law in force in England as to torts rests, when looking to precedents in this country. I do not hesitate to concede to the advocates of a change, that the doctrine has been laid down in two or three respectable compilers. (Curtis on Merchant Seamen, 362; Dunlap's Ad. 51.) But others oppose it; and we search in vain for reasons assigned anywhere in its favor. The authorities cited from the books of reports in favor of a change here are not believed, in a single instance, to be in point, while several appear to maintain a contrary doctrine.

They are sometimes mere *dicta*, as the leading case of De Lovio *v.* Boit, in 2 Gall. 467, 424, that having been a case of a contract and not a tort; or as in 1 Mason, C. C. 96, that having occurred on the high seas. So Thomas *v.* Lane, 2 Sumner, 1; Ware 75, 96; 4 Mason, C. C. 380. Or they are cases cited, such as Montgomery *v.* Henry, 1 Dall. 49, which relate to contracts alone. (See, also, case by Judge Conkling, in New York Leg. Ob., Oct. 1846; The Mary, 1 Paine's C. C. 673.) Or they happened, as was averred in 1 Dall. 53, on waters out of any county. Or they are cases of seizure for breaches of the laws of trade, and navigation, and revenue, depending on express *statute alone.* (The Vengeance, 3 Dall. 297; The Betsy, 4 Cranch, 447; Wheelan *v.* The United States, 7 ibid. 112; Conkling's Pr. 350; 1 Paine's C. C. 504; Gilp. 235; 1 Wheat. 920; 8 ibid. 391.) And are, as before explained, probably misconstrued.

The parent of many of these mistaken references, and of the decisions as to seizures, is the case of The Vengeance, in 3 Dall. 297, a case which Chancellor Kent, in his Commentaries, justly says "was not sufficiently considered" (vol. 1, p. 376). It was not a case of tort, as some seem to suppose; nor even a seizure, under the act of 1789, for a breach of the laws as to revenue and trade. But it was an information for exporting arms, prohibited by a special act, passed 22d May, 1793.

Some of the references, likewise, are to cases of prize, which in England as well as here never depended on locality, like the high seas, but might be even on land, and were at first conferred on the admiralty courts by special commission, and were not originally a part of its permanent jurisdiction. (10 Wheat. 315; 5 ibid. 120, App.; 4 Dall. 2; Doug. 613, note; 1 Kent's Com. 357.) Where any of the references in the books here are to printed cases of tort, they uniformly appear to have been committed on the high seas, or without the body of a county and State. (Burke *v.* Trevitt, 1 Mason, 96, 99, 360; Manro *v.* The Almeida, 10 Wheat. 474, 486, 487; The Josefa Segunda, ibid. 315; Thomas *v.* Lane, 2 Sumner, 1; The Appollon, 9 Wheat. 368; Plummer *v.* Webb, 4 Mason's C. C. 380, and Ware, 75; Steele *v.* Thatcher, Ware 96.) If the act happened in foreign countries, in tide-waters, there may well be jurisdiction, as being not within the body of any county here. (Thomas *v.* Lane, 2 Sumner, 9.) Such was the case of The Appollon, 9 Wheat. 368, not being a case within tide-waters and a county in this country.

There is an expression in 12 Peters, 76, which is supposed by some to sanction a change. But it is only a *dictum*, that having been a case of crime; and the idea and the expression are, not that torts or crimes could be tried in admiralty, when committed within a county, on tide-water therein, but that in no case, if committed on land or above tide-water, could they be tried there as admiralty offences, but only as offences defined and punished by acts of Congress under the power to regulate commerce. (United States *v.* Coombs, 12 Peters, 76.) This may be very true, and yet in torts, as well as crimes, they may not be punishable without a statute, and as mere admiralty cases, unless committed on the ocean.

During this session I have for the first time seen a case decided in one of our circuits, which holds that the tide-waters of the Savannah river are within the jurisdiction of the admiralty, as to collisions between boats. (Bullock *v.* The Steamboat Lamar, 1 Western L. J. 444.) But as the learned judge seems to have taken it for granted that the question of jurisdiction had been settled by previous decisions, he does not go into an examination of its principles, and cites only one authority (7 Peters, 324), which will be found to be a case of contract, and not tort. So that, with this single exception, so far as it be one, not a single reported case is found, and only one manuscript case referred to (Dunl. Adm. 51), where a tort was committed within one of our counties, though on tide-water, which was adjudged to be within admiralty jurisdiction, since the country was first settled, or of a like character in England, unless by recent statutes, for the last four centuries.

On the contrary, in Bee's Admiralty Reports and Peters', in Gilpin's and Ware's, cases for torts are found, but all arising on the high seas, unless some doubt exists as to one in the last, partly overruled afterwards in the Circuit Court. So, whatever may be the *obiter dicta*, it is the same as to all in Paine, Washington, Baldwin, and even Gallison, Mason, Sumner, and Story. Indeed, this result accords with what was rightfully to be anticipated from the rule laid down in the first elementary law-book in the hands of the profession at the time of the Revolution, that "admiralty courts" (3 Bl. 106) had cognizance of what is "committed on the high seas, out of the reach of our ordinary courts of justice." And "all admiralty causes must be, therefore, causes arising wholly upon the sea, and not within the precincts of any county." (3 Bl. Com. 106.)

Moreover, as to American authorities directly against these supposed changes as to torts, it is hardly possible to find anything stronger than the absence we have just referred to, almost entire, of any attempt in actions to sustain the jurisdiction in admiralty over torts, unless happening on the high seas, and the uniform settled decisions in England, that it exists only there. But, beside this, there is the absence likewise of any colonial statutes or colonial decisions to bring in question at all the adjudged cases at home, which governed this question here no less than there. There is next the remark by Chancellor Kent, that if tides ebb and flow in a county, a recovery cannot be had for a tort there, on the principles of the common law courts. (1 Kent's Com. 365, note; 3 Hag. Ad. 369.)

And no one can read the learned Digest of Dane, without seeing that in torts he considers the trial by jury proper, wherever they occur within the body of any county. (6 Dane's Abr. *Prohibition.*) And it is laid down generally, in several other instances in this country, that the locality of torts must be on "the sea," in order to confer jurisdiction on the admiralty. (Thackery et al., Gilp. 524, 529; 3 Mason, 243; Baldw. C. C. 550—554. So in Adams *v.* Haffards, 20 Pick, 130.) See also the colonial case before cited from 1 Dall. 53, Montgomery *v.* Henry et al., directly in point, that the line of the county was the test, and not tide-water, unless without the county. This was in 1780, and is most conclusive proof that no colonial enlargement of mere admiralty jurisdiction as to this matter had occurred here in practice, either under the words of commissions to vice-admiralty judges, or any difference of circumstances and condition.

But, beside this, one resolve of the old Congress shows that they considered the line of the county as the true one; and hence its violation in cases of trade and revenue, under statutes passed to oppress them, caused their remonstrances that the vice-admiralty courts had transgressed the ancient limits of the bodies of counties. (1 Journal of Old Con. 21—23.) How unlikely, then, is the inference from this, that the framers of the constitution regarded this encroachment as the true line, and, when protesting against it, not only meant to adopt it, but extend it to cases of torts!

It is not a little remarkable, too, that, in maturer life, Judge Story himself, in speaking of the jurisdiction over torts (3 Com. on Constit. 1659), says, — "The jurisdiction claimed by the courts of admiralty as properly belonging to them extends to all acts and torts done upon the high seas, and within the ebb and flow of the sea." That means, at common law, outside of a county.

Thus, says Coke, in 4 Inst. 134: — "So as it is not material whether the place be upon the waters *infra fluxum et refluxum aquæ;* but whether it be upon any water within any county." (Sea Laws, 234.) Again, the ebb and flow of tide, to give jurisdiction to the admiral, means on the coast outside. (Fortescue, De Laudibus L. Ang. 68, note.) So, in 2 Madison Papers, 799, 800, it will be seen that Judge Wilson deemed the admiralty jurisdiction to relate to what the States had not exercised power over, and to the sea. So, in The Federalist, No. 80, cases arising on the high seas are said to be those embraced.

Indeed, the departure from the settled line of jurisdiction as to torts here, so far as it may have gone in theory or speculation, seems likely to have begun in mistake rather than in any old commission or adjudication, founded on any statute or any well-settled principle. It is likely to have commenced either by omitting to discriminate between torts and contracts, or between torts depending on general principles and seizures for violating laws of revenue and trade, which depended on the words of a special statute, and the construction given to those words; or from a supposed but unfounded analogy to the rules as to prizes, with which our fathers were very familiar in the Revolution, and taking cognizance of them in admiralty here, as in England, if captured anywhere, not only on tide-water or "below high-water mark," but even on land. (4 Dall. 2; 2 Bro. Civ. and Adm. Law, 112; 5 Wheat., App. 120.) Or it may have occurred,—and that probably was oftenest the case,—from various general expressions in the English books and cases as to the admiralty jurisdiction being coëxtensive with tide-waters, when that expression means, in all the adjudged cases in England as to torts and crimes,—and must, on principle, as before shown, mean, in order to secure the trial by jury and the common law,—the tide-waters on the sea-coast, the flux and reflux of the tide, out of the body of a county.

There is a similar expression in Judge Story's Commentaries on the Constitution (vol. 3, § 1667), as to crimes, in speaking of the existence of admiralty jurisdiction over them in creeks "and bays within the ebb and flow of tide;" but he takes care to add, very properly, "at least in such as are out of the body of any county in a State." Probably the true origin of the whole error was by looking to expressions about tide-water, or the ebb and flow of tide, without noticing further that the act must be in such tide-waters as "are out of the body of any county in a State," and that this was indispensable to be observed, in order to protect the invaluable principles we have been discussing.

The power of the General Government and its courts over admiralty matters was doubtless conferred on account of its supervision over foreign trade and intercourse with other nations, and not to regulate boats like these, far in the interior, and never going to any foreign territory, or even adjoining State,—much less touching the ocean. Nothing can be more significant of the correctness of this limitation to matters on the ocean, than the remarks of Chief Justice Jay, in Chisholm *v.* Georgia, 2 Dall. 475, that the judicial power of the Union was extended to "cases of admiralty and maritime jurisdiction, because, as the seas are the joint property of nations, whose rights and privileges thereto are regulated by the laws of nations and treaties, such cases necessarily belong to national jurisdiction."

Our forms of proceeding, also, in admiralty, and which are founded on substance, count usually on the transaction as having happened on "the high seas," knowing full well that they are the great theatre and territory for the exercise of admiralty law and admiralty power; and being obliged to make such an allegation in England in order to gain jurisdiction. (Ross *v.* Walker, 2 Wils. 265.)

Half the personal quarrels between seamen in the coasting trade and our vast shore fisheries, and timber-men on rafts, and gundalo men, and men in flat-boats, workmen in the sea-coast marshes, and half the injuries to their property, are where the tide ebbs and flows in our rivers, creeks, and ports, though not on the high seas. But they never were thought to be cases of admiralty jurisdiction when damages are claimed,—much less when prosecuted for crimes; never in creeks, though the tide ebbs and flows there through half of our sea-board towns,—never in rivers. All is within the county, and is usually tried before State officers and by State laws.

It has just been remarked by one of my brethren, as to torts and crimes, as has been before said by some in controversies as to contracts, that the statutes of Richard the Second were not in force in the colonies. (See 2 Gall. 398, 473; 1 Peters' Ad. 233; Ware, 91; Hall's Ad. Pract. 17, Pref.) I cheerfully concede it may well be doubted whether any portion of the common law or English statutes, passed before the settlement of this country, became in force here, unless suited to our condition, or favorable to the subject and his liberties. But these statutes were both. They were suited to the condition of those attached to the common law and jury trial in the colonies, no less than at home, and they were in favor of the rights and liberties of the subject, to be tried by his own and not foreign laws, and by a jury for all matters happening within the realm, and not on the high seas. And so far from ancient statutes of that character not having any force here, they had as much as those parts of the common law which were claimed, Oct. 14, 1774, by Congress, among the "indubitable rights and liberties to which the respective colonies are entitled." (1 Journal of Congress, 28.) They came here with them, as a part of their admiralty law, as much as came any portion of the common law, or the trial by jury. They came as much as Magna Charta or the Bill of Rights, and they should exist here now, in respect to all matters, with all the vigor that characterized them at home at the time of our Revolution. (Baldw. C. C. 551; Ramsey *v.* Alleyne, 12 Wheat. 638. So decided virtually in Montgomery *v.* Henry, 1 Dall. 53; Talbott *v.* The Three Briggs, 1 Dall. 106.)

The principles, dear to freemen of the Saxon race,—preferring the trial by jury, and the common law, to a single judge in admiralty, and the civil law,—which were involved in those statutes, could be no less highly prized by our American fathers than their English ancestry, especially when we look to their numerous resolutions on this subject, both before and during the Revolution, cited in other portions of this opinion.*

* They are so numerous as to remind one of the zeal and perseverance in favor of

One of our soundest jurists has said, long since,—"The common law of England, and every statute of that country made for the benefit of the subject before our ancestors migrated to this country, were, so far as the same were applicable to the nature of their situation, and for their benefit, brought over hither by them; and wherever they are not repealed, altered, or amended, by the constitutional provisions or legislative declaration of the respective States, every beneficial statute and rule of the common law still remains in force." (Tucker, in Part II. of Bl. Comm. App. 99; 2 Chalm. Op. 75; Woodcock, 159.)*

Whether the 13 and 15 of Richard II. were in affirmance of what was the true limit of admiralty jurisdiction at first in England, or otherwise, is not very material. But it is certain that it was likely to be but declaratory of that, as the people were so devoted to the common law trials by jury. The extraordinary idea, that these statutes were not in force here, was first broached in A. D. 1801, and then in a District Court, in direct opposition to the views expressed in 1 Dall. 53. The point then decided under that novel notion was, that a lien existed for repairs of a domestic ship, without the aid of any statute, and has been since expressly overruled by this court in The General Smyth, 4 Wheat. 413. And why overruled by this court, but on the principle that the admiralty jurisdiction here was what it had been in England before our constitution, and not elsewhere,—not that of France before the Norman conquest, or that of Holland now?

Indeed, Justice Story, as a commentator in respect to other clauses of the constitution no more open to such a construction than this, concedes that they are to be "understood" "according to the known distinction in the jurisprudence of England, which our ancestors brought with them upon their emigration, and with which all the American States were familiarly acquainted." (3 Story's Com. on the Constitution, 506, § 1639.)

Nor let it be again offered in extenuation, that the power being concurrent in the common law courts, the plaintiff from choice goes into the admiralty; because the other party, who is often prosecuted only to be vexed and harassed, and who has rights as well as the plaintiff, may be thus forced into admiralty, rather than the common law, much against his choice. Nor let it be said further, as an apology, that the trial by admiralty is better and more satisfactory, when our ancestors,

---

the great charter, which was such as to require it to be read twice a year in each cathedral, and to have it ratified anew over thirty times, when put in peril by encroaching monarchs. (1 Stat. at Large [English], 274, ch. 3; also p. 1, note.)

* Thus people who go to form colonies "are not sent out to be slaves, but to enjoy equal privileges and freedom." (Grotius, De Jure Belli, B. 2, ch. 9, § 10.) Or "the same rights and privileges as those who staid at home." Or, as in the charter of Elizabeth to Raleigh, "enjoy all the privileges of free denizens, or persons native of England." (Part I. of Tucker's Bl., vol. 1, p. 383, App.)

both English and American, have resisted it, and excluded it in all common law cases, for reasons most vital to public liberty and the authority of the local tribunals. Such an enlargement of a power so disliked by our fathers is also unnecessary; because, if desirable to have the United States courts try such cases, rather than those of the States, they can be enabled to do it by express provisions, under the power to regulate foreign commerce and collect revenue, as is now done on the lakes (12 Peters, 75; 5 Statutes at Large, 726; Act of February 26th, 1845); and reserving, as in that case, the right of trial by jury.*

I have thus examined this question in all its various aspects, and endeavored to answer all which has been suggested in favor of a change here as to the line of admiralty jurisdiction in the case of the collision of vessels, as well as other marine torts.

Among my remarks have been several, showing that there was nothing in our condition as colonists, or since, and nothing in the nature of the subject and the great principles involved, which should render the same line of jurisdiction not proper in America which existed in England, but in truth some additional reasons in favor of it here. I do not now, in conclusion, propose to dwell much on this peculiar condition of ours, though some members of this court have just urged it earnestly as a reason why the same line does not apply, as they have why the statutes of Richard II. did not apply. But the idea is as untenable in respect to the principle generally, looking to our condition, as we have already shown it to be in respect to those statutes. Thus, in that condition, what reason was there ever for a change? None. And, if otherwise believed, when we were colonies, would not the change have been made by acts of assembly approved at home, or an act of Parliament? And if not done when colonies, but supposed to be proper after the Revolution, would not the framers of the constitution, or of the Judiciary Act, have known it as quickly and fully as this court? and was it not more proper for them to have made such a change than this court? If our political institutions or principles required it, did not they know, and should not they have attended to that rather than we? If such a change had already happened in the then thirteen colonies, and was too well known and acquiesced in, as to torts and crimes, to need any written explanation or sanction, why cannot it be pointed out in colonial laws, or in judi-

* As some evidence that the makers of this last law did not suppose it settled that the District Courts could, as admiralty courts, have any jurisdiction as to torts, because committed on tide-waters within a State, when they felt obliged to pass a special law to confer it on the lakes, it was not conferred there as exercised on "tide-waters," which would have been sufficient, if so settled, but on "the high seas, or tide-waters within the admiralty and maritime jurisdiction," &c. This statute is also scrupulous to save the trial by jury when desired, and thus avoids treating it as an admiralty power got in torts, unless on the high seas, by a construction contrary to the political opinions and prejudices of our ancestors, and to the whole spirit of our institutions.

cial records, or at least in contemporaneous history of some kind? And if such a change was required and intended, as some insist, by resorting to other than English law for a guide as to what were admiralty cases within the meaning of the constitution, because something less narrow, geographically or otherwise, as it has been argued, something on a grander scale, and in some degree commensurate in length and breadth with our mighty rivers and lakes, was needed,—as if a system which had answered for trade over all the oceans of the globe was not large enough for us,—then why not extend it at least over all our navigable waters, and not halt short at the doubtful, and fluctuating, and pent-up limits of tide-water? And was a change so much required to go into the bodies of numerous counties and States, to the jeopardy of jury trials, by any increased dislike to them among our jealous fathers? Were they wishing, by mere construction, to let more and more go into the cognizance of the admiralty and be tried without a jury, and without the principles of the common law, when they had been so indignantly remonstrating against any and every the smallest encroachment by England on that sacred trial? And is this guarantee of a jury trial in such cases to be considered of subordinate moment in the views of those living at the era of the formation of the constitution, and the passage of the act of 1789, when their eagerness was such to guarantee it fully, that two of the only twelve amendments ever made to it relate to additional safeguards for this trial? And in the Judiciary Act of 1789, there are introduced, *ex industria*, three separate provisions to secure jury trials.

Indeed, so far from there being anything in our condition as colonists, or in public opinion at the Revolution, which demanded a change enlarging admiralty forms and jurisdiction, the old Congress specially resolved, November 25th, 1775, when recommending to the colonies to institute courts to try captures, or devolve the power on those now existing, that they "provide that all trials in such case be had by a jury," which was going further in their favor, instead of short of what had ever been done in England. And, in 1779, Virginia established admiralty courts, under recommendation of the old Congress, and expressly allowed a jury in all cases where either party desired it, if both were citizens. (10 Hening's Stat. 101.) The same is understood to have been done in several other States. (See The Federalist, No. 83.) In Massachusetts, under the old charter, as long ago as 1673, the court of admiralty was expressly authorized to allow a jury when it pleased. (Ancient Charter and Laws, 721, App.) Iredell says, also, in the North Carolina Convention (4 Elliot's Deb. 155): "There are different practices in regard to this trial in different States. In some cases they have no juries in admiralty and equity cases; in others, they have juries in them, as well as in suits at common law."

And to the objections made against adopting the constitution, because the trial by jury might be restricted under it and suitors be compelled to travel far for a hearing in ordinary cases (1 Gales' Debates in First Congress), it was argued that Congress would possess the power to allow juries even in cases in admiralty (The Federalist, No. 83), and afterwards, by the original amendments to the constitution, it was made imperative to allow them in all "cases at common law." Yet now, by considering torts within a county as triable, or as "cases in admiralty," which was not done by the common law, nor when the constitution was adopted, either in England or here, we produce both the great evils deprecated,—an abridgment of the jury trial from what prevailed both here and in England, and the forcing of citizens to a great distance from their State tribunals, to defend their rights under a different forum and a different system of laws.

After these additional proofs of the caution of our ancestors to check the usual admiralty power of trial without a jury, and more especially to prevent any extension of it, could they for a moment, when so jealous of the General Government and its overshadowing powers, wish to extend them further than ever before, either here or in England? * Did they mean to relinquish their time-honored and long-cherished trial for torts on water within a county, and take for a model despotic France, for instance, which knew no trial by jury in any case, and where the boundaries between the admiralty and other courts were almost immaterial, being equally under the civil law, and equally without the safeguard of their peers? And would they be likely to mean this, or wish it, when every such extension of admiralty jurisdiction was at the expense of the State courts, and transferring the controversies of mere citizens of one State to distant jurisdictions, out of their counties and in certain events to the remote seat of the General Government, and then to be tried there, not by the common law, with whose principles they were familiar, but by the civil, and when a full remedy existed at home and in their own courts? Much less could they be supposed willing to do this when the trial of facts in this court was not to be by their peers from the vicinage, or on oral testimony, so that the witnesses could be seen, scrutinized and well compared, but by judges, who, however learned in the law, are less accustomed to settle facts, and possess less practical acquaintance with the subject-matter in controversy. And what are the urgent and all-controlling reasons which exist to justify the new line urged upon us, in such apparent violation of the constitution, and with so inauspicious a departure from anything required by our condition, or

* Indeed, in England, it has been controverted whether the power in admiralty to punish torts anywhere ever existed, even before Richard II. (3 Mason's C. C. 244), except through a jury, used to settle the facts and assess the damages. (See 4 Rob. Ad. 60, note to Rucker's case.) The Black Book of the Admiralty, art. 12, p. 169, is cited as speaking of the use of a jury twice in such cases. (See also Roughten, De Of Admiralis, 69, note.) And at this day, in England, in this class of torts, as hereafter shown, the masters of Trinity House act virtually as a jury.

from what seem to have been the principles and precedents at the Revolution?

It is not the line of the civil law, any more than of the common law. If this innovation had extended admiralty jurisdiction over all navigable waters, it would have been, at least, less vague, and found some vindication in its analogy to the civil code. (Digest, 43, tit. 12, 13; Code Napoleon, B. 2, ch. 2, tit. 556; Zouch's Elements of Jurisp. 382.) But the rule of tide-water within a county, and not on the sea, conforms to no code or precedent; neither marching boldly over all which is navigable, nor halting where the ocean meets the land; neither shunning to make wide inroads into the territories of juries, nor pushing as far as all which is nautical and commercial goes. The only plausible apology for it, which I can find, is in a total misconception, before adverted to, of the ancient and true rule, which was tide-water, but, at the same time, tide-water without the body of the county, on the high seas. But, instead of the flux and reflux of the tide on the high seas, and without the body of the county or State, and to support which line stood the great pillars of a jury trial and the common law, have been attempted to be substituted, and that without authority of any statute or clause in the constitution, as to torts, the impulses from the tides at any and every distance from the ocean, sometimes encroaching from one to two hundred miles into the interior of counties and States, and prostrating those great pillars most valuable to the people of the States. And what, let me repeat the inquiry, is gained by such a hazardous construction? Not an adherence to old and established rules; not a respect for State rights; not strengthening the Union or its clear powers where assailed, but weakening by extending them to doubtful, irritating, and unnecessary topics; not an extension of a good system, allowing the admiralty to be one for all nautical matters, to all navigable waters and commercial questions, but falling short, in some of our vast rivers or inland seas, near one thousand miles from the head of navigation, and cutting off several cities with twenty, thirty, and even forty thousand population. The late act of February 26th, 1845 (5 Statutes at Large, 726), was intended to remedy this, but does not include any cases above tide-water on the Mississippi, or Cumberland, or Ohio, and many others, but only those on the lakes and their tributaries, and very properly even there reserves, with scrupulous care, not only the right to either party of a trial by jury, but any remedy existing at common law or in the States.

So, looking to results, if we disclaim jurisdiction here, what evil can happen? Only that our citizens in this class of cases will be allowed to be tried by their own State courts, State laws, and State juries. While, if we do the contrary, the powers of both States and juries will be encroached on, and just dissatisfaction excited, and the harmonious workings of our political system disturbed. So, too, if our national views have become actually changed so greatly, that a trial by a single judge, and in admiralty, is preferred to a trial by jury in the State tribunals or the Circuit Courts, then our overruling the jurisdiction in this case will only leave Congress to declare the change, and provide for it, rather than this tribunal.

So the excuse for trying such cases in admiralty rather than in courts of common law, which some have offered, on the ground that the rules of decision are much the same, appears very ill-considered, when, if the civil law in this instance does not differ essentially from the common law, the rules of evidence by it do, depriving us, as triers, of the sight of the witnesses, and their apparent capacity and character, and depriving the defendant of the invaluable trial by jury, and stripping him of the right of being tried, and the State courts of the right of trying controversies between their citizens, in the neighborhood where they occur. "All controversies directly between citizen and citizen will still remain with the local courts," said Mr. Madison, in the Virginia convention. (3 Elliott's Deb. 489.)

Now, after all this caution exercised in England not to extend nor change admiralty jurisdiction there without the aid of express statute and a reservation of common law remedies,— after a refusal to do it here recently as to the lakes and their tributaries, except in the same way, and preserving the trial by jury,— after all the sensitiveness of our fathers in not doing it as to seizures for breach of revenue and navigation laws, except by express statute,— after their remonstrances and cautions in various ways against abridging the trial by jury,— after the jealousy entertained when the constitution was adopted, that this court might absorb too much power from the State tribunals, and the respect and forbearance which are always justly due to the reserved rights of the States,— it certainly seems much wiser in doubtful cases to let Congress extend our power, than to do it ourselves, by construction or analogy.

So far from disturbing decisions and rules of property clearly settled, I am, for one, strongly disposed to uphold them, *stare decisis*, and hence I am inclined in this case to stand by the ancient landmarks, and not set everything afloat,— to stand, in fine, by decisions, repeated and undoubted, which govern this jurisdiction, till a different rule is prescribed by Congress.

The first doubt as to the jurisdiction in admiralty over the present case is thus sustained, but, being overruled by a majority of the court, I proceed briefly to examine the next objection. It is one founded in fact. It denies that the tide did in truth ebb and flow at Bayou Goula, the place of this collision, in ordinary times.

There is no pretence that the water there is salt, or comes back from the ocean, or that the tide there sets upward in a current, or ever did, in any stage of the water in the Mississippi. Yet this is the ordinary idea of the ebb and flow of the tide. I concede, however, that it has been settled, by adjudged cases, that the tide is considered in law to ebb and flow in any place where it affects the water daily and regularly, by making it higher or lower in consequence of its pulsations, though no current back be caused by it. (Rex *v.* Smith, 2 Doug. 441; The Planter, 7 Peters, 343; Hooker *v.* Cummings, 20 Johns. 98; Angell on Tide-waters, 637.) Yet this, of course, must be a visible, distinct rise and fall, and one daily caused by the tides, by being regular, periodical, and corresponding with their movements. Amidst conflicting evidence on a point like this, it is much safer to rely on collateral facts, if there be any important ones admitted, and on expert or scientific men, who understand the subject, than on casual observers. The sea is conceded to be two hundred and three miles distant; and the current of the Mississippi so strong as to be seen and felt far out to sea, sometimes quite forty miles. The tides on that coast are but eighteen or twenty inches high. The velocity of the current of the river is ordinarily three to four miles an hour in high water, and the river is two hundred feet deep for one hundred miles above New Orleans. (Stoddard's Hist. of Louisiana, 158.) It therefore becomes manifest, that, on general principles, such a current, with its vast volume of water, could not only never be turned back or overcome by the small tides of eighteen inches, as the fact of its influence forty miles at sea also demonstrates, but would not probably, in ordinary times, be at all affected in a sensible and regular manner two hundred and three miles distant, and weakened by all the numerous bends in that mighty river. From New Orleans to St. Louis the bends are such, that a boat must cross the stream 390 times. (Stoddard's Hist. of Louisiana, 374.)

Again, the descent in the river from the place of this collision to the ocean is quite a foot and a half, all the usual rise of the tide on the coast; and hence, at a low stage of water in the river, much more at a high one, thirty feet above the lowest, no tides are likely to be felt, nor would they probably be during the whole season of a full river, from November to June.

In the next place, several witnesses testify as to their observations in respect to the tides, and confirm what might be expected from these collateral facts. The most scientific among them took frequent observations for two years, at or nigh Jefferson College, thirty-seven miles nearer the sea than the place of this collision, to ascertain this very fact, and testifies that no regular daily influence is felt there from the tides. Oscillations may occur, but not regularly, nor as tides. They happen in that way even near the foot of the Falls of Niagara, but of course are produced by causes entirely disconnected from the tides of the ocean. So they happen, from other causes, on most of our interior lakes.

Sometimes continued winds in one direction make a great difference in the rise of the water at different places; and sometimes the emptying in near of large tributary streams, changeable in their size, at different seasons. Both of these are testified to occur in the Mississippi in its lower parts. At high water, which prevails over half the year, from rains and the dissolving of snow, it also deserves notice that the fall of the river towards the ocean is near one and two-thirds of an inch per mile; and the difference between high and low water mark near Bayou Goula is, also, as before noticed, from thirty to thirty-three feet.

From all this, it is easy to see, that, during more than half the year, it is hardly possible that a regular tide from the ocean should be felt there, though it is admitted that, in conflict with this, some witnesses testify to what they consider such tides there, and, indeed, as high up as Bayou Sarah. But their evidence is insufficient to overcome, in my mind, the force of the other facts and testimony on this subject.

In connection with this point, it seems to be conceded, also, that, in order to give admiralty jurisdiction, the vessels must be engaged in maritime business, as well as the collision have occurred where the tide ebbs and flows. There might be some question, whether the main business of either of these boats was what is called maritime, or touching the sea, — *mare*, — so as to bring them and their business within the scope of admiralty power. If, to do that, they must be employed on the high seas, which is the English rule, neither was so engaged in any part of its voyage or business. Or if, for that purpose, it is enough, as may be contended in this country, that they be engaged exclusively on tide-waters, neither was probably so employed in this instance. And it is only by holding that it is enough for one end of the voyage to be in tide-water, however fresh the water or slight the tide, that their employment can be considered maritime.

In The Thomas Jefferson, 10 Wheat. 428, the court say, the end or beginning of the employment may be out of tide-water, if "the service was to be substantially performed on the sea or tide-water." So in The Phœbus, 11 Peters, 183. But in the case of the Thomas Jefferson, as well as the Phœbus, the service, being, in fact, chiefly out of tide-waters, was not considered as maritime.

In the case of The Planter, 7 Peters, 324, the whole service performed was in tide-waters, and was a contract, and hence deemed maritime. Here the boats were employed in the trade between New Orleans at one point, and Bayou Sarah at the other, a distance of one hundred and sixty-five miles. If the tide ebbs and flows as high as Bayou Goula, or ninety-seven miles above New Orleans, which we have seen is doubtful, it is only a small fraction above half the distance, but not enough above half to characterize the main employment of the vessel to be in tide-waters, or to say that her service was substantially on the sea, or even tide-water. The De Soto made trips still higher up than Bayou Sarah, to Bayou Tunica, twenty-seven miles further from New Orleans. The testimony is, also, that both these boats were, in their construction, river, and not sea boats; and the De Soto was built for the Red river trade, where no tides are pretended to exist, and neither was ever probably on the ocean, or within a hundred miles of it.

It is doubtful if a vessel, not engaged in trade from State to State, or from a State abroad, but entirely within a State, comes under laws of the General Government as to admiralty matters or navigation. It is internal commerce, and out of the reach of federal jurisdiction. Such are vessels on Lake Winnipiseogee, entirely within the State of New Hampshire. In the Luda and De Soto, they were engaged in internal commerce, and not from State to State, or from a State to a foreign country. (1 Tucker's Bl. Com. 250, note.)

In most cases on the Mississippi, the boats are engaged in the coasting trade from one State to another, and hence are different, and assume more of a public character. So on the lakes the vessels often go to foreign ports, as well as to other States, and those on the seaboard engaged in the fisheries usually touch abroad, and are required to have public papers. But of what use are custom-house papers or admiralty laws to vessels in the interior, never going from State to State, nor from a State to a foreign country, as was the situation and employment at the time of these two boats?

These are strong corroborations that this is a matter of local cognizance, — of mere State trade, — of parties living in the same county, and doing business within the State alone, — and should no more be tried without a jury, and decided by the laws of Oleron and Wisbuy, or the Consulat del Mare, or the Black Book of Admiralty, than a collision between two wagoners in the same county.

The second objection, then, as a whole, is in my view sustained; and, being one of mere fact rather than law, it is to be regretted that the court could not have agreed to dismiss the libel on that ground, without settling the other points, and without prejudice to the rights of either party in a trial at common law. The plaintiff would then be enabled to have all the facts on the merits examined and adjudicated by a jury from the valley of the Mississippi; much more skilful than this court, from their residence and experience, in judging upon accidents and negligences in navigation on that great thoroughfare.

The only good reason that the admiralty judge was ever intrusted with the decision of facts, rather than a jury, was, that originally he was but a deputy of the admiral, and often a nautical man, — acquainted with nautical matters, and acting only on them; and now, in England, he calls to his aid on facts the experienced nautical officers or masters of the Trinity House, — "a company," says Coke, "of the chiefest and most expert masters and governors of ships." (4 Inst. 149.) He takes their opinion and advice on the facts as to collisions of vessels, before he himself decides. (2 Bro. Civ. and Ad. Law, 112; 6 D. & E. 766; The Celt, 3 Hag. Ad. 327.) The case is often fully argued before them first. (1 Wm. Rob. 133—135, 273, 314; Hall's Ad. Pr. 139; 5 Rob. Ad. 347.) But everything here is so different, and so much against the skill of judges of this court in settling such facts, that in cases of doubt we are very likely, as has now happened, to disagree, and it is far better they should be examined by a jury in the vicinage of the collision.

Perhaps it was a consideration like this that led to the doctrine, both abroad and here, in favor of the common law courts having concurrent jurisdiction in these cases of collision, even when they happen on the high seas. (1 Chit. on Pl. 152, 191; 15 Mass, 755; 3 East, 598; Percival *v.* Hickey, 18 Johns. 257; 15 Johns. 119; 14 Johns. 273; Curtis' Merch. Seamen, 367; 9 Johns. 138; Smith *v.* Condry, 1 Howard, 36; Gilp. 483; 4 Mason, C. C. says it is claimed; 2 Gall. 343 on precedent.)

Indeed, the laws of Louisiana are quoted as pertaining to and regulating the conduct of boats when passing on the Mississippi within that State. (1 Bullard & Curry's Dig. § 794.) But, so far from their being a guide to us in admiralty, if having jurisdiction in that way over these boats at this place, the rights of parties, as before seen in such questions, are to be settled by the laws existing in some undescribed part of the world, but not England in A. D. 1776 or A. D. 1789, or Louisiana in A. D. 1845. If England, this case would not be tried at all in admiralty, as we have seen; and if Louisiana, then the case would not be settled by admiralty law, but by the laws of Louisiana, and in the State tribunals.

Again, whoever affirms jurisdiction to be in the courts of the United States, must make it out, and remove all reasonable doubts, or the court should not exercise it. (Bobyshall *v.* Oppenheimer, 4 Wash. C. C. 483; 7 Peters, 325; Peters' C. C. 36.) Because these courts are courts of limited jurisdiction, and acting under express grants, and can presume nothing beyond the grant; and because, in respect to admiralty power, if anything is presumed when not clear, it is presuming against the trial by jury, and the State tribunals, and their reserved rights. Where a jurisdiction is of a limited nature, "they [claiming it] must show that the party was brought within it." (1 East, 650.) And where a case is in part dependent on common law, and in part on admiralty, it must be tried in the courts of the former. (Bee's Ad. 470.)

But, the second objection to our jurisdiction being also considered by the court untenable, this case is to be examined on the merits; and as to these it seems to me not free from difficulty, though in my view indicating some fault in both the boats.

From the very nature of navigation, — as vessels cannot be always turned quick, and as a constant lookout is hardly practicable both night and day, — collisions on rivers with frequent bends in them, like the Mississippi, and during darkness, are occasionally almost inevitable, and often are attended by no blame. The danger and injury to both vessels is so great in almost every case,— one or both not unseldom going down, with all on board, — that the strongest motives exist with all to use care and skill to avoid collisions. The want of them, therefore, is never to be presumed, but is required to be clearly proved. To presume otherwise, would be to presume men will endanger their own lives and property, as well as those of others, without any motive of gain or ill-will.

Hence our inquiries must start with the probability that, in such collisions, accident and misconception as to courses and distances caused the injury, rather than neglect or want of skill. Indeed, in these cases it is laid down as a rule, by Sir Christopher Robinson, in The Ligo, 2 Hag. 356, that "the law requires that there shall be *preponderating* evidence to fix the loss on the party charged, before the court can adjudge him to make compensation." (2 Dod. 83.) I am unable to discern any such clear preponderance in this case in favor of the Luda. It is true that some allowance must be made as to the testimony of the officers and men in each boat. In both they would naturally be attached to her character or interests, and desirous in some degree of vindicating themselves or friends. And it happens that, from such or some other cause, those on each side usually testify more favorably as to the care and skill with which the boat was conducted in which they were employed at the time. Hence, resort must be had to some leading and admitted facts as a guide, when they can be distinctly ascertained, to see whether the collision was from any culpable misconduct by either. For like reasons, we should go to witnesses on shore and passengers, where they had means of knowledge, rather than to the officers and crews implicated on either side. Taking these for our guidance chiefly, and so far as it is possible here to decide with much accuracy, most of the case looks to me, on the facts, quite as much like one of accident, or one arising from error of judgment and mutual misapprehension, as from any culpable neglect on the part of the officers of the De Soto alone.

It is to be remembered, that this collision occurred in the night; that neither of the regular captains were on the deck of either boat, though both pilots were at their stations; that, being near a landing, the De Soto supposed the Luda was going to stop there, and hence pursued a different course from what she would if not so supposing; and that the Luda supposed the De Soto would not stop there, and hence did not pursue the course she would if believing she was about to stop. That both boats in the darkness seemed, till very near, to believe each other further off than they in truth were, and hence did not use so early the precautions they otherwise might have done. It is to be remembered, also, that not one of the usual sources of blame in the adjudged cases existed here clearly on the part of the De Soto. Some witnesses swear to the De Soto's having her light hung out, and several, including a passenger, that if the Luda had not changed her course unexpectedly, and when near, she would not have been struck by the De Soto; and that the De Soto, if changing hers, and going lower down than her port, did so only to round to and lay with her head up in the customary manner. Nor was there any racing between rivals, to the peril of the vessels and life, which led to the misfortune, and usually deserves condign punishment. Nor was any high speed attempting for any purpose; and the movement of the De Soto, though with the current, is sworn to have been slowest, and hence she was less bound to look out critically. (The Chester, 3 Hag. Ad. 319.) Nor is there any law of admiralty requiring a descending boat on a river to lie still till an ascending one approaches and passes, though an attempt was made to show such a usage on the Mississippi, which was met by counter evidence. Again, the Luda was not at anchor, so as to throw the duty on the De Soto to avoid her, as is often the case on the sea-coast. (The Girolamo, 3 Hag. Ad. 169; The Eolides, ibid. 369.) Nor was the Luda loaded and the other not, but in ballast and with a wind, and hence bound not to injure her. (The Baron Holberg, 3 Hag. Ad. 244; The Girolamo, ibid. 173.) Nor was one moved by steam and the other not, and hence the former, being more manageable, obliged to shun the latter. (The Shannon, 2 Hag. Ad. 173; The Perth, 3 Hag. Ad. 417.) Nor is there a rule here, as in England, issued by the Trinity House in 1840, and to be obeyed or considered bad seamanship, that two steamboats approaching, and likely to hit, shall put their helms to port, though the principle is a sound one on which it rests. (1 Wm. Rob. 274, 275; 7 Jurist, 380, 999.) Under considerations like these, if any blame rests on the De Soto,— and there may be some,— certainly quite as much seems to belong to the Luda. Neither put the helm to port. Both boats were, in my view, too inattentive. Both should have stopped their engines earlier, till the course and destination of each other were clearly ascertained; and both should have shaped their courses wider from each other, till certain they could pass without injury. (7 Jurist, 380; 8 ibid. 320.) The Luda certainly had more conspicuous lights, though the De Soto is sworn not to have been without them, and is admitted to have been seen by the Luda quite half a mile off, though in the night. On the contrary, the movements of the De Soto were slowest, which is a favorable fact in such collisions (7 Jurist, 381), though she did not lie by, as she should have done, under the law of Louisiana, if that was in force, and she wished to throw all the risk on "the ascending boat;" for throwing that risk so is the only gain by conforming to the statute. (1 Louis. Dig. 528, Art. 3533, by Grimes.)

But I do not propose to go more fully into this, as it is not the point on which I think the case should be disposed of. I merely refer to enough to show it is a question of difficulty and doubt whether the injury did not result from casualty, or mutual misapprehension and blame, rather than neglect, except in particulars common to both, or at least in some attached to the plaintiffs, if not so great as those in respect to which the original defendants erred. Any fault whatever in the plaintiffs has, it is said in one case, been held to defeat his action. (Vanderplank *v.* Miller, Moody & Malk. 169.) But, in any event, it must influence the damages essentially. For though, when one vessel alone conducts wrongfully, she alone must pay all damages to the extent of her value (5 Rob. Ad. 345), and this agrees with the laws of Wisbuy if the damage be "done on purpose" (2 Peters' Ad. 84, 85, App.), and with the laws of Oleron (2 ibid. 28), yet if both vessels were culpable, the damage is to be divided either equally between them (3 Hag. Ad. 328, note; 4 Adolph. & Ell. 431; 9 Car. & P. 613; Reeves *v.* The Constitution, Gilpin, 579), or they are to be apportioned in some other more appropriate ratio, looking critically to all the facts. (The Woodrop-Sims, 2 Dod. Ad. 85; 3 Scott, N. R. 336; 3 Man. & G. 59; Curtis' Admiralty, 145, note.) So in England, though no damages are given, when there is no blame on the part of the defendant. (The Dundee, 1 Hag. Ad. 120; Smith et al. *v.* Condry, 1 Howard, 36; 2 Browne's Civ. and Ad. Law, 204.) Yet, by the laws of Wisbuy, 1 Peters' Ad. 89, App., — "If two ships strike against one another, and one of them unfortunately perishes by the blow, the merchandise that is lost out of both of them shall be valued and paid for *pro ratâ* by both owners, and the damage of the ships shall also be answered for by both according to their value." (Sea Laws, 141.) This is now the law in Holland, and is vindicated by Bynkershoek, so as to cover cases of doubt and equalize the loss. (2 Browne's Civ. and Ad. Law, 205, 206.) So now on the Continent, where a collision happened between vessels in the river Elbe, and it was not the result of neglect, the loss was divided equally. (Story's Conflict of Laws, 423; Peters et al. *v.* Warren Ins. Company, 14 Peters, 99; 4 Adolph. & Ell. 420.)

Hence, whether we conform to the admiralty law of England on this point, though refusing to do it on other points, or take the rule on the Continent for a guide, the amount of damages allowed in this case is erroneous, if there was any neglect on the part of the original plaintiffs, or if the collision between the boats was accidental.

# ON BRIDGES OVER NAVIGABLE WATERS GRANTED BY STATES, AND ADMIRALTY JURISDICTION AS TO IT, AS WELL AS WANT OF JURISDICTION BY THE FEDERAL COURTS, WITHOUT A SPECIAL ACT OF CONGRESS.*

THIS motion has been argued on both sides with a fulness and ability suited to the importance of some of the questions involved in it.

I have taken time to examine those questions, and shall now proceed to dispose of them with as much brevity as is consistent with their difficulty and number, and the wide interests connected with them.

They include national and constitutional considerations of great moment, and a decision on them involves results which affect practically most of the States in the Union.

Most of them have authorized bridges to be built over navigable waters, and several of them have done it within the ebb and flow of the tides of the sea, and at, if not below, the limits of some ports of entry as well as delivery, and to the obstruction in some degree, and generally to the delay, of all navigation above them. Their power to do this, in the progress of internal improvements, and of turnpikes, canals and railroads, with a view to advance internal commerce and travel, is to be considered, on the one hand, as well as the authority of the General Government, on the other hand, to check, prevent or suppress such works, whether bridges, aqueducts, or viaducts, whenever injurious to that foreign commerce of the country which is placed under its regulation, and whenever impeding the navigation between the States as well as foreign navigation, and whenever conflicting with the full use of the ports of entry or delivery within the United States by other nations in friendly alliance with us.

In considering the jurisdiction of this Court to punish the respondents for doing what is alleged against them in this indictment, and which is the sole question presented by the motion now under consideration, it may be proper to notice, in the outset, that the acts done by the defendants are justified under authority from the State of Massachusetts as early as 1795, and have thus been allowed not merely for the private gain of the stockholders, but for facility to public travel, and the internal trade and intercourse of that portion of the State and Union.

---

* Opinion in case of United States *v.* The New Bedford Bridge, October Term Circuit Court U. S., for the 1st District, 1846.

The acts of the respondents, then, are not wanton acts of wrong, nor conduct undertaken merely for the purpose of private emolument. They are virtually the acts of the State. The respondents, in substance, justify under the State; and the merits of the case are the same as if the parties were the United States against the State of Massachusetts herself. Consequently, the respondents are not to be punished by this or any other proceeding, unless their acts were authorized originally by the State without constitutional power; or unless their acts now come in collision with some subsequent and lawful legislation by Congress; or unless, in the lapse of time, what was done at first, without affecting injuriously public navigation, has caused accumulations of sand and a shoalness in the channel, so as to obstruct passing and repassing with vessels; or, unless, by the increased size of vessels and steamboats, the draw of the bridge has become too narrow for them to go through, or the large additions to their number prevent them from being accommodated within more restricted limits, and in passing through a single draw.

Such being the grounds on which alone the respondents could be convicted, the general inquiry is, if this Court possesses authority to sustain an indictment against them for the acts done.

The motion, in excepting to the jurisdiction of this Court to try a case like the present, specifies, as the ground of it, the omission or refusal by Congress to have such acts as are charged in the indictment declared to be an offence against the United States.

And if, for that or any other reason, it should appear to this Court a question of real doubt whether it possesses any jurisdiction in such a case over the subject-matter, it will be its duty not to proceed further in the trial. (2 Gall. 325.)

Because, being a court of limited jurisdiction, it cannot transcend those limits, though the parties make no objection, but is bound, itself, to pause. (2 Cranch, 126; 12 Pet. 719; 1 Peters, C. C. 36.) And in any stage of the case. (4 Wash. C. C. 84; Davison *v.* Champlin, 7 Conn. 244; Perkins *v.* Perkins, 7 Conn. 559.)

Whereas, in England, their higher courts have general jurisdiction, and proceed till it is excepted to; and the presumptions are not, as here, that a case is without their jurisdiction, till the affirmative is clearly shown. (4 Dall. 11, Ch. J. Ellsworth; 5 Cranch, 185.)

In the courts of the United States, jurisdiction must be derived from the constitution itself, or treaties, or acts of Congress, and the question here relates first to jurisdiction by the United States over the subject-matter, as a crime, in the place of this transaction; and next, whether that jurisdiction is vested in this court, if it exists over the subject.

Though the motion speaks only of no act of Congress giving us jurisdiction, yet the argument in its favor proceeds on the ground, that, in order to give to this court jurisdiction, there must be some clause in the constitution, or a treaty, or an act of Congress, making proceedings like those by the respondents an offence, and conferring on this court the trial and punishment of it, and that there is no clause of that kind in either.

While, on the other hand, on the part of the government, doubting whether any such special legislation is necessary, it is contended that the constitution and treaties, as well as several acts of Congress, make such conduct as that of the respondents illegal, and devolve the punishment of it on this court. The conduct of the defendants being permitted by the State, as described in this indictment, can hardly be deemed a crime on its face.

All sovereignties, bordering on the sea-shore, have a right to exercise jurisdiction over the waters adjoining. (Vattel, B. 1, ch. 231; Bevans' case, 3 Wheat. 337; Pollard's Lessee *v.* Hagan, 3 How. 212; Justin. Inst. B. 2, Tit. 1, § 294.)

This usually does not extend outside of capes and ports, and beyond low water on the open coasts, except as hereafter explained, for revenue, fishing, &c., and as to foreigners, sometimes a cannon-shot from shore. (Vattel, B. 1, ch. 23, § 281—295.)

It has been settled, however, in Massachusetts, that power over those waters, or obstructions in them by bridges, can be authorized by the State, but cannot be authorized by commissioners of roads, or any power short of the State itself, through legislation. (Vattel's L. of Nat. 43, ch. 9, B. 1; 12 Pick. 467; 4 ibid. 460; 2 Mass. 492; Inhabitants of Arundel *v.* McCulloch, 10 ibid. 70; 2 Pick. 344; 5 ibid. 199; Commonwealth *v.* Charlestown, 1 ibid. 180; Angell on Tide-waters, 45, 46, 128; 15 Wend. 113; case of Georgetown Corp. *v.* Alex. Canal Co. 12 Pet. 91; State *v.* Hampton, 2 N. Hamp. 22.)

Where a stream, as here, is within the limits of a State in its whole course, I see no reason, as a general principle, why that State might not obstruct its navigation, or suspend it.

In The King *v.* Montague, 4 Barn. & Cres. 598, it was held, that a right to navigate in a river or creek might be taken away by act of Parliament, or by the Commissioners of Sewers, or by natural causes, *e. g.* filling up, or the recess of the sea. (Vooght *v.* Winch, 2 Barn. & Ald. 670.)

If a road exists there now, courts may presume that the right to navigate was extinguished before, if no proof is given where or how it was done.

Before the federal constitution existed, it is, therefore, not to be doubted, that each State, as sovereign, could govern, within its own limits, roads, ferries, bridges, regulations of quarantine and health, ports of entry, navigation and commerce, internal and external.

When forming that constitution, they conferred the power to regulate commerce with foreign nations and between States, and to collect revenue from imports, on the General Government, retaining still the powers over the other matters as before, and not to be restricted in them unless their exercise should in some case conflict with the due exercise of the paramount powers granted to Congress. (3 Wheat. 387; 14 Pet. 617.)

The States, then, can, of course, continue forever to regulate and punish what they have not delegated to the General Government. (2 Dall. 432—435; 4 Cranch, 75; 3 Pet. 201; 12 ibid. 524; Pollard's Lessee *v.* Hagan, 3 How. 212.) Besides this, they can continue, probably, to do the same as to what they have delegated, but not exclusively (and where they are not expressly forbidden to act), until Congress legislate in respect to it, in such a manner as to supersede their action. But of this last proposition more hereafter.

Under these views of the relations between the States and the General Government, since the constitution was formed, it has been held, that navigable rivers themselves, for some purposes, and the soil under them, as well as the tide-waters within the capes and counties, still belong to the States where they are situated. (3 Wheat. 383; 16 Pet. 410; 3 How. 212.)

So all other rights over her waters, not ceded for navigation merely, remain in a State; *e. g.* as to fisheries; and hence she can continue to regulate them in subordination to the other. (Angell on Tide-waters, 105; 3 Wheat. 383.)

Regulations of rights of property in lands and fishing on the coasts of a State are not regulations of commerce, and do not conflict with the constitution, or any act of Congress. (4 Wash. C. C. 380.)

States may regulate ferries, roads, inspections, &c., without violating the grant over commerce to Congress (though in some degree and indirectly affecting commerce), if it does not come in clear and direct conflict with some legislation by Congress. (Ibid. 379; 2 Pet. 245.) But the *jus privatum* in the State must be so exercised as not to impair or obstruct the higher *jus publicum* in the United States and the people at large. (4 Wash. C. C. 379; 3 How. 230; 1 Story, Comm. on Const. 432; Pierce *v.* New Hampshire, 5 How. 504; 15 Wend. 113.) And it was laid down generally, in United States *v.* Bevans, 3 Wheat. 337, 389, that admiralty and maritime jurisdiction, ceded to the General Government, did not pass the waters where that jurisdiction exists, or any territory; and hence, no general jurisdiction over them, but only over that specific matter of admiralty jurisdiction, the rest remaining in the State contiguous. A bay or haven, however, must be out of the jurisdiction of a State, to make an offence punishable there under many of the acts of Congress, as Congress has not, if it can, extended powers over waters in a State always concurrent with the State, and made offences there punishable. If Congress can punish them under any ceded power, it has not yet. I think it may punish obstructions or nuisances, if necessary to regulate foreign commerce, preserve buoys and breakwaters, or collect revenue, but perhaps only what is necessary to enforce that grant, and others as to maintaining a navy, &c. (3 How. 230.)

A State retains the powers before named, because not granted away, and the exercise of them by Congress is invalid, because not granted to it, on the same ground that its exercise of others is valid only because they are granted to it.

Hence, on the subject of roads, a State, thus sovereign and unlimited in its own constitution, could, as to its own citizens and powers, pass a law to stop up any of its public roads or navigable rivers, or to erect bridges and viaducts over them without draws or with insufficient draws. (Ibid. 212, 229; 16 Pet. 410.) It would rest in its discretion, to make the interests of those concerned immediately in the coasting and foreign trade to yield to those engaged in interior commerce.

So, on the subject of floating logs on those rivers, it is a local species of business, if it be commerce, and may be regulated by a State; and clearly so, till Congress act on it differently. (Scott *v.* Willson, 3 N. Hamp. 321.)

It has been customary, therefore, for all the sea-board States to authorize bridges across navigable streams, under certain limitations, connected with common highways, turnpikes and railroads.

In Massachusetts alone there have been, since Charles River Bridge, in 1785, fourteen or fifteen special licenses and acts of incorporation of that kind. (See 1 Special Laws, p. 93 and onward; 2 ibid. to 7th vol.) This, without objection till now, is strong evidence of the right. (Briscoe *v.* Bank of Kentucky, 11 Pet. 257, 318.)

The Legislature has always been in the habit of thus promoting its domestic or internal commerce and convenience in travelling, when of an opinion that its people would gain more by the bridge than the navigation under it without the bridge. (1 Pick. 180.)

But, not forgetting navigation, they seldom, if ever, allow such an obstruction without a draw of sufficient width to accommodate navigation and ship-building, and vessels wishing to pass through.

Incorporations of bridges in such places have frequently been recognized, by State judiciaries, as suitable exercises of power by States. (17 Conn. 64; 8 Cow. 146; 1 Pick. 180; 7 N. Hamp. 35.)

In the States within what was governed by the ordinance for the North-western Territory, perhaps, this could not be done, as that ordinance declares that all navigable rivers within it shall continue to be "common highways." (3 Ohio, 496; 1 McLean, 351; 3 How. 224.) But I speak of States without any such restriction, or any in their own constitutions, or in the assent to their admission given into the Union by Congress. (Pollard *v.* Hagan, 3 How. 212.) Or where no treaty by the General Government, like that of 1783 and 1794, stipulated for the free navigation of a river like that one of the Mississippi. "The navigation of the river Mississippi, from its source to the ocean, shall forever remain free and open to the subjects of Great Britain and the citizens of the United States." (Art. 8 of

Treaty of 3 Sept. 1783, 8 Stat. at Large, 83.) "The river Mississippi shall, however, according to the treaty of peace, be entirely open to both parties." (Art. 3d of Treaty of 1794, 8 Stat. at Large, 117.)

It is yet unsettled, whether, if a river navigable above one State then runs into another before it joins the ocean, the lower State may not obstruct it, or exact tolls. This point was not started, nor decided, though it would arise in 12 Pet. 97; nor need it be settled here, as all this stream is in one State. The free navigation of the Mississippi, or of the Florida rivers, however, was never yielded to us, while Spain, a foreign State, owned the territory at their outlets. Nor is that of the St. Lawrence or of the St. Johns, owned by the British, yielded, except by treaty, and for a *quid pro quo.*

The arguments in favor of their freedom in such cases, though plausible, have never yet been admitted as rendering the question a settled one, in national law, in their favor. (1 Am. State Papers, Foreign Relations, 252, 253, 260; 3 ibid. 341; Jour. of Old Cong. 1787; 1 Lyman, Dip. of U. States, 239, 267; 2 For. Rel. 101.)

Even the sound duties in the Baltic, for passing through an arm of the sea, are acquiesced in by most nations, though it is rather to defray the expense of keeping it lighted, as light-money is paid on other coasts, and to remove and replace buoys yearly, as the ice forms and disappears, and keep the passage free from piracies, than any departure from the general principle that the sea is free to all, however rivers may be, as the sea is the great highway of nations, rather than of one nation; and the outlet usually is not enclosed by the territory of any one government.

The case of the Black Sea may be an exception, at the straits, as there that is preserved a close sea by Turkey, and its passage obstructed and regulated as if a navigable river, entirely within her territory, though resisted, and at times successfully, by other nations. (See on these, Vattel, B. 1, ch. 23, § 281—295.)

But that not being this case, nor this being an obstruction by an individual, without a claim of authority from the State, I feel compelled to admit that the State itself may set up her State rights to legislate concerning the waters where this bridge exists clearly within her limits, and partially obstruct them, if she thinks it beneficial, till her acts conflict with some law of Congress connected with foreign commerce, or that between the States. (Kellogg *v.* The Union Company, 12 Conn. 7.)

But, while conceding such rights to States over their navigable waters, I think that corresponding duties are imposed on them to treat wanton or careless obstructions in them by individuals as offences, and to punish or remove them as nuisances. This is the doctrine of both the common and the civil law. (1 McLean, 380; City of Georgetown *v.* Alex. Canal Co., 12 Pet. 91; Bac. Abr. Nuisance, B.; 2 Ld. Ray. 1163; 10 Mass. 70; Coop. Just. 68, and note, 455;

Angell on Tide-waters, 15, 16; Vattel, B. 1, ch. 22; 20 John. R. 98; 17 ibid. 195; 3 Caines, R. 319; 2 Conn. 481.)

The passing upon such rivers belongs to the public or people at large, as public highways, and can be obstructed only by acts of Parliament in England, or the States here; or, perhaps, in some cases by Congress, when under the execution of some of its special powers. (Martin *v.* Waddell, 16 Pet. 367, 410; Hale, De Jure Maris, 11; Commonwealth *v.* Ruggles, 10 Mass. 391.) Thus, in England, while the king owns the soil between high and low water, the sea and navigable waters are open to be used in common by the people, whether for navigation or fishing, unless the former is stopped by the sovereign power before named, or the fishing is in fresh water owned by an individual on both sides. There is a *jus privatum* and a *jus publicum.* (Angell on Tide-waters, 16, 19, 109; 5 Com. D. 102; 10 Coke, 141; 1 Salk. 357; 1 Mod. 105; Rex *v.* Smith, 2 Doug. 441; 5 Coke, 107.)

And if fishing, as one public right, should conflict with navigation, another, the former, as of minor importance, must yield, and the parties take in their seines. (Angell on Tide-waters, 32, 95; Post *v.* Munn, 1 South. 61.)

In Massachusetts, the province or colony so changed the common law principle on this subject, that the soil on the sea-shores belonged to the contiguous owners rather than the king [or the Province, and afterwards the State], for one hundred rods, when the tide ebbed out so far. (1 Pick, 180; 6 Mass. 153, 435.) And, by some usage or common law, it has been held, that the owner may build houses or wharves on the flats one hundred rods, and thus obstruct the navigation there, but leaving it open beyond. (Angell on Tide-waters, 154, 155; Austin *v.* Carter, 1 Mass. 231; Adams *v.* Frothingham, 3 ibid. 252.)

It is otherwise, if not left open beyond. (Angell on Tide-waters, 157; 2 Davis' Abr. 697.) But in Respublica *v.* Caldwell, 1 Dall. 150, it is held, that one cannot build a wharf encroaching on navigable water, though room enough beyond is left for navigation. (So in England, *semb.* 2 Starkie, 511; S. C. 3 Serg. & Lowber, 453.)

Generally, however, whether the soil under the tide and under navigable rivers is owned by individuals or the States, it is, till changed by special legislation, subject to the public easement of passing over it as a water highway. (Angell on Tide-waters, 53, 109; Adams *v.* Frothingham, 3 Mass. 352.) Such right was expressly reserved in the Mass. Charter, p. 1, and 148.

And if an individual owns the soil on both sides of a navigable river or arm of the sea, he cannot erect a bridge across, so as to impede or injure the *jus publicum* for navigation. (Commonwealth *v.* Charlestown, 1 Pick. 180.)

If done by an individual, or any persons without authority from the

State, such obstacles to navigation are and should be punishable, and usually are under the local government.

Without going into discriminations as to different kinds of obstruction and the different modes of redress, whether the former be by bridges, or ballast, or sunken ships, or the latter by a suit for damages, or an injunction or indictment, information or abatement as of a nuisance, it is sufficient here to refer to the following cases. (Russell on Crimes, 485; 1 Cowp. 86; Angell on Tide-waters, 29, 31, 45, 101; 10 Mass. 70; Hargrave's Tr. 36. See appropriations by Congress to remove obstructions in the Mississippi and other rivers, and in harbors, as in New Bedford, and especially sunken ships near Savannah and Baltimore; and 5 Co. 101; 2 Salk. 459; 3 Bl. C. 5; Nabob of the Carnotic *v.* East India Co., 1 Ves. Jr. 371; 5 Barn. & Ald. 268, and cases cited, *post;* Malynes' Lex Mercat. See cases before cited. 6 Barn. & Cres. 566; Leach, Cr. L. 388; 2 Leach, C. C. 1093; 3 Wheat. 366, note; 2 Pet. 245; East, C. L. 773; Bac. Abr. "Injunction," B.; Rose *v.* Groves, 5 Mann. & Grang. 613; 1 Es. C. 148; Cro. El. 664; 2 New Ca. 281; Willes, 74; 4 Maule & Selw. 101; 2 Scott, 446.)

So, in England, a grant of land, covered by the sea, does not justify the grantee in putting up obstructions to the free navigation. (10 Price, 350, 378. See *post*, Angell on Tide-waters, 141, 150; 8 Brow. T. R. 18.)

The public rights to navigate, &c., go to ordinary high water (Angell on Tide-waters, 67; 2 John. R. 337; Commonwealth *v.* Charlestown, 1 Pick. 180); while private rights begin at the same place. (Ibid.)

From all this it is manifest, that the place where this bridge is situated, and the subject-matter of it, and of nuisances in the river there, are within the scope of State authority to punish or permit, till Congress legislate, for some of the objects within its sphere, in such a way as to come in collision with the action of the State.

If it be asked, then, whether the State laws make these acts a crime, it may be answered, from what has been stated, that, but for their special legislation, allowing this bridge, those acts doubtless would be a nuisance, and punishable as a crime in the State courts as at common law.

But an obstruction of a public highway within the limits of the State, by its own permission, probably could not be punished as a crime there, if the act of incorporation by the State permitting it be constitutional. (15 Wend. 114; 2 Pet. 245; Inhabitants of Dover *v.* The Portsmouth Bridge, N. Hamp. Sup. Ct., Strafford County, 1846.)

It would be difficult to regard that as an offence against State laws which has been done in conformity to them, under an act of incorporation from them. She is, perhaps, the best judge on all local matters, all sections and interests being represented in her public councils; and at least, if she, for public considerations, authorizes a bridge, under certain restrictions and limitations, which she deems safe, it would be an anomaly for her herself to consider its erection a crime.

If she authorizes it injudiciously, and injures navigation to her ports more than she benefits interior travel and trade, she is the chief sufferer.

Such being the condition of State powers, State rights and State laws, on this subject, without reference to the constitution of the United States, the next inquiry is, how have these been affected by that constitution, either by prohibitions to the States, or by the grants to the General Government before referred to, and the legislation which has taken place under them?

After the federal constitution was adopted, if a law by a State on this subject violated any prohibitory clause in it, or any act of Congress, duly enforcing any grant of power from the States, it would, of course, be unconstitutional; but whether it would then be a crime, under the Federal Government, and punishable by indictment in this Court, as legislation now stands, depends on still other considerations, which will soon be examined.

Before deciding what part, if any, of the constitution, the acts done by the respondents violated in any degree, we must ascertain what authority in respect to such subjects the States parted with.

The powers not granted by the States remained as before; that is, they were reserved to the States or the people, as either may have exercised them before. Thus, in Miln *v.* New York, 11 Pet. 102, 139, it is held that the powers reserved to the States are usually unaffected by the federal constitution.

Again, the States may continue to legislate for internal commerce, for police, for roads, ferries, canals, &c., and regulate all, and "the use of them, where such regulations do not interfere with the free navigation of the waters of the State for purposes of commercial intercourse, nor with the trade within the State, which the laws of the United States permit to be carried on." (Corfield *v.* Coryell, 4 Wash. C. C. 371.)

Three kinds of commerce are confided to the General Government —foreign, between the States, and with the Indians. Hence, Congress possesses the power to regulate them, over those navigable waters, and to punish offenders in public vessels sailing upon those waters. (3 How. 230; 3 Wheat. 387.)

In this instance, it is contended that the doings by and under the State interfere with and obstruct foreign commerce and that between the States.

But this is not done *eo nomine*, nor was such the avowed design; for Massachusetts was regulating domestic or internal commerce, and hence acting on a subject not granted at all to Congress, but among those reserved. (Brown *v.* Maryland, 12 Wheat. 419, 452, J Thompson; Gibbons *v.* Ogden, 9 ibid. 1, 194.) And the only ground of complaint in such a case is, that the State has so exercised her power over that reserved subject as to impair the rights of the public and the General Government as to foreign commerce, or that between the States.

Do the acts, authorized to be done by Massachusetts, violate, then, anything delegated to the General Government over foreign commerce, or that between the States? And if so, is such a violation made a crime by the General Government, and the trial of it devolved on this court?

In order to consider a State law as void, because conflicting with one of the United States, it must not only affect the subject-matter, have some influence over it, but be directly incompatible or repugnant,—an extreme inconvenience to it. (1 Story, Comm. on Const. 432.)

Then must interpose, but not till then, the supremacy of the laws of the General Government, within its proper sphere, prevailing over those of the States, when so using their own as to encroach on others.

If "clashing sovereignties" come before us,—if one claims a right to set up what the other claims a right to pull down, or one to use powers of taxation so to abuse them, and violate what is confided to the General Government,—then we must decide which is right; and if the General Government is, then its laws must be paramount and prevail.

Holding the laws of the State to be subordinate when in conflict, is not giving to the United States any odious supremacy; but merely saying, that when the States have parted with certain powers to Congress, they shall not so continue to exercise what are reserved as to impair the grant and use of those they have, for paramount public objects, confided elsewhere. *Verba fortius accipiuntur contra proferentem.*

The exercise of reserved powers by the State, when conflicting with legitimate acts of Congress, must yield, if so used as to be repugnant, as must the exercise of concurrent powers by the States, when becoming repugnant. Otherwise, the General Government could not move on, and its constitution and laws be paramount even within their proper sphere. (11 Pet. 103, 137, 147, 156; Gibbons *v.* Ogden, 9 Wheat. 1, 195, 209; 12 Wheat. 419, 446; 6 Pet. 515; Commonwealth *v.* Kimball, 24 Pick. 359, 365; United States *v.* Hart, Peters' C. C. 390; Holmes *v.* Jennison, et al., 14 Pet. 540, 574.) This is necessary by the constitution itself. (Art. 6th.)

"This constitution, and the laws of the United States which shall be made in pursuance thereof, and all treaties made, or which shall be made, under the authority of the United States, shall be the supreme law of the land; and the judges in every State shall be bound thereby, anything in the constitution or laws of any State to the contrary notwithstanding."

So clearly was it supposed, when the constitution was adopted, that the acts of Congress under it would prevail over conflicting State laws, that the only objection was, they would ride over the State constitutions also.

But Mr. Madison, in the 44th number of the Federalist, shows clearly that they must prevail over State constitutions, also, when conflicting; or there would be no uniformity of laws in operation over all the Union, but some would be nullified in one State by its constitution, but be in full force in others.

In 4 Wash. C. C. 378, 379, in speaking of the power to regulate commerce invested in the General Government, the judge says: it "comprehends the use of a passage over the navigable waters of the several States," and further, it "renders these waters the public property of the United States for all the purposes of navigation and commercial intercourse, subject only to Congressional regulation."

Hence, I cannot doubt that the power to regulate commerce abroad and between the States, conferred on Congress, authorizes it to keep open and free all navigable streams, from the ocean to the highest ports of delivery or entry, if no higher, and protect the intercourse between two or more States, on all our tide-waters. (2 Gall. 398; 3 How. 230; Gibbons *v.* Ogden, 9 Wheat. 1; New York *v.* Miln, 11 Pet. 102, 135; Angell on Tide-waters, 50.) Congress may remove unauthorized obstructions, or punish them by acts of Congress; and it may punish injuries on land, if they tend to interfere with foreign commerce and navigation; or those between different States, though mere admiralty powers may not go above the sea. (United States *v.* Coombs, 12 Pet. 72. See, in detail, Miln *v.* New York, 11 Pet. 102, 155, by J. Story.)

In the recent case of Waring *v.* Clarke, 5 How. 441, it has been settled, that jurisdiction in admiralty exists over torts, by collision of vessels, committed above the sea or tide-water, however far it flows into the body of a county. But this is not the English law; and it is to be hoped will never be extended in this country to crimes, the subject we are now considering. The powers of Congress, however, embrace much wider matters than those of mere admiralty, on account of its authority over our foreign relations, and the regulation of our commerce, not only with foreign nations, but between the States. And, as one evidence that the framers of the constitution meant that the latter should cover matters on land often, as well as at sea, power was given to Congress, not only "to define and punish felonies committed on the high seas," but "offences against the law of nations." These last happen as often on land as water; as do offences against the revenue, and the purity of our coin, and the security of the mails, and of all public property. Mere admiralty authority is much more restricted. By that, also, as well as by the authority to regulate commerce, no soil may pass. The right to the soil is one thing, the right to navigation in the water over it another; and is vested elsewhere, for some purposes, in our government, as well as in other governments.

It seems that now, in England, where a grant is made to a town or city of lands between high and low water mark, it is not to be construed as giving a right to obstruct free navigation, carried on by any or all people under general rights of trade, such as are enjoyed under our General Government. And where obstructed, a bill may be filed in the Exchequer by the Attorney General, to restrain and abate the obstruction as a nuisance. (Attorney General *v.* Burridge, 10 Price, 350; Attorney General *v.* Parmenter, 10 Price, 378.)

If towns here claim jurisdiction over waters navigable below low water, they have no right to the water, nor any to the soil below high water. (Palmer *v.* Hicks, 6 Johns. R. 133.)

For purposes of foreign commerce, and of that from State to State, the navigable rivers of the whole country seem to me to be within the jurisdiction of the General Government, with all the powers over them for such purposes [whenever they choose to exercise them] which existed previously in the States, or now exist with Parliament in England.

So, by the Civil Law, "navigable rivers," "the sea and its shores," are destined to common use (1 Domat, Lib. 8, § 1, art. 1), and the common use here for conveyance is with the Union. They are a species of highway, and, therefore, cannot be appropriated to private use, except temporarily, either by individuals or corporations. (New Orleans *v.* United States, 10 Pet. 662, 724, 729.) Certainly not, in a permanent manner, unless authorized by the paramount government, which supervises and controls them as highways.

There is a very instructive case on this subject in 10 Price, 350,—The Attorney General *v.* Burridge,—which seems to have escaped the research of the counsel.

It was an information by bill, praying that the defendants might be restrained from obstructing Portsmouth harbor, "so that the sea may again flow and reflow over the piece or parcel of ground mentioned in the bill."

The obstruction was by buildings on piles over navigable portions of the harbor, and it was justified under a grant of the soil from the king.

It seemed to be conceded, that the king may own the shore between high and low water, and grant any private interest in it. (See pages 369 and 401.) Such is the doctrine as to the States. (3 Wheat. 383.)

But it was also held, that the people, or, in other words, the public, have a right to the navigation, and an interest in all ports. (10 Price, 372. Hale, De Portibus Maris, Part 2, ch. 7.)

The king or his grantees have the soil, *jus privatum*, but subjects generally, and alien friends, have a right to navigate the water, a *jus publicum;* and hence, if the buildings are a nuisance, they can abate them, 373, 378; as if on a public highway, 2 Anstr. 603. Individuals must use their own so as not to injure others. (10 Price, 378.) *Sic utere tuo, ut non alienum lædas.*

What does encroach on or straiten the harbor, or lessen the depth of water and navigation, is a fact, *questio facti*, 374. But when done, it is an offence against the power which supervises the general commerce of the country. (Hale, De Portibus Maris, 35, 84. See also next case, Attorney General *v.* Parmenter, 10 Price, 378, 412; Attorney General *v.* Richards, 2 Anstr. 603, 608.)

But though Congress is enabled to make laws, keeping navigable rivers and navigation unobstructed, as high up at least as the ports of entry and delivery, if not as high up as the waters are navigable, and impose punishments for such obstructions as crimes, yet, if it has not been so done, can we punish it as a crime? If we cannot, this stands in the threshold against sustaining the present indictment in a court of the United States, and the act of incorporation by the State, allowing the bridge to be built, stands in the way of punishing the obstruction by it as a crime in the State courts.

Some hold, that a grant being made to Congress to regulate foreign commerce, and extend its judicial power to all cases in admiralty, and collect a revenue from imports, and maintain a navy, those grants alone, without any action on them, by the General Government, as to bridges and other obstructions, divest the States of all authority to make laws in connection with navigable waters, and that hence such an act of incorporation as exists in this case is unconstitutional and void, and is to be put out of the case, as if not existing.

While others contend, that as the States have not granted the power to Congress over their internal commerce, that remains exclusively in the States; and that, under this, they may erect bridges connected with that internal commerce, without being amenable to any supervision or check by the General Government; and certainly not, unless the legislation conflicts in point of fact with some which has actually taken place under Congress. My own views do not accord exactly with either of these general positions. I think (1), that the power is, by the grants above referred to, vested in Congress over navigable waters connected with our foreign and coasting trade, and for purposes of revenue, but does not by those grants prevent the States from continuing their former legislation over them, and especially as to reserved objects, till it conflicts with some laws passed by Congress under those grants, or some treaties made, or some express provisions of the constitution. (14 Pet. 594.)

And (2), that when the States exercise the powers reserved, as to their internal commerce and police, they may do it with impunity, while not in conflict with anything before done on the part of the General Government. But when in conflict, the express grant to Congress, and the action on it properly by the paramount government, must overrule and control all which is done repugnant to it by the State. (12 Conn. 7.)

If it was necessary to admit that the State here, as contended by the prosecution, was exercising a power to regulate that foreign commerce, such as is confided to the General Government in the constitution, its conduct was perhaps still valid, till it conflicted with some act passed by Congress, or some duty or right under its federal relations. (11 Pet. 103; 15 Pet. 574.)

But it would hardly be necessary in this case to go into that, if all admitted that a State might do this act of empowering a bridge to be erected here, under its reserved rights as to internal commerce. For then, of course, it would be valid, till conflicting with some paramount act of Congress under its conceded authority to regulate foreign commerce and that between the States. (2 Pet. 245.)

Yet this, as before remarked, being contested, and it being considered by some vital against the constitutionality of the State laws, if affecting a matter of foreign commerce, or that between the States, though not conflicting with any act yet passed by Congress, I shall make a few remarks on it here, and refer to others made by me in Peirce *v.* New Hampshire, 5 How. 554, 618.

I think it the safer and sounder opinion, that a mere naked power, unexercised and dormant in the General Government, with no prohibition, express or implied, to the States, to act on the same matter, could not make the State legislation upon it nugatory or unconstitutional, much less render acts crimes which are done under State laws of that description. (Willson *v.* The Black Bird Creek Company, 2 Pet. 245.) Such are laws as to weights and measures. Beside these, as to disciplining the militia, and on bankruptcy, and regulating the army. (Groves *v.* Slaughter, 15 Pet. 449.) The subject under consideration now, as to roads and bridges, was, however, never of that mere doubtful character, but was among the powers supposed to be reserved to the States, where it before belonged. (9 Wheat. 203.)

It was always to continue to be exercised by them for domestic or interior commerce within each State, that branch of commerce not having been granted at all to the General Government. And, as hereafter explained, it could never be questioned in its exercise till it impaired or encroached on some power over foreign commerce, or that between the States, which had been confided to all the States united.

If the States can and will, till special legislation by Congress, punish such acts as they deem injurious to the public interests, and do it either under their reserved or concurrent powers, no necessity exists for any forced construction to enable this Court to act, in order to prevent such wrongs from going unprosecuted.

If done under their reserved powers, and able to be vindicated under them, their right is clear. But if done as a concurrent power, and relating to some local matter, connected with foreign commerce, either allowing or punishing it, their right is less clear, but, in my view, can be successfully vindicated.

Supposing that I have not succeeded in showing this act of incorporation, and the conduct of the defendants under it, to be legal under the reserved powers of the States; it seems to me legal, as before intimated, under a concurrent right in the States to legislate on local matters connected with foreign commerce, till coming in actual and serious collision with some measures by Congress. My reasons for this opinion are these: The States were the great fountains of legislation, the bulwarks of social and civil rights. Where they had acted before the constitution, they would be likely to continue to provide as to local matters within their own limits, till Congress got ready to provide for them, when the power was granted to Congress. This would especially be the case as to such pressing and interesting matters as commerce. The constitution, when not expressly forbidding the States to act longer on the matter, nor forbidding it by necessary implication, seems to allow it, and the continuance of some local State cognizance over it is often requisite for the public peace and safety.

Hence, it has become the more prevailing doctrine among jurists and statesmen in these cases of powers bestowed on Congress, and not expressly, or from the nature of the case, prohibited to the States, that till Congress find it expedient to make specific laws under them, the authority of the States must be regarded as still continuing, in order to preserve order and the public tranquillity, and to regulate and punish, or license and uphold, local measures, according to the views of each State, or the interests of the community within its boundaries.

Because, otherwise, there could be no punishment for some of the most flagrant outrages; and because the makers of the constitution well knew that Congress could not at once and forthwith provide for the full exercise of all its clear powers, if it wished, and would find it expedient not to use some, till time and occasion might develop the necessity of using what had been confided to it, and then would provide for the emergency by further and specific legislation.

In the mean time, considering the States as still legally entitled to preserve the public interests and peace within their limits, and punish violations of them, in cases where they did it before, would not be derogatory to the General Government, nor strip it of any legitimate authority; it would treat the continued exercise of such powers by the States as only concurrent, or rather subordinate, till the General Government found it expedient to legislate; and then, of course, the concurrent or subordinate authority of the States yielding to the exercise of the same authority by the General Government which it had been empowered to use, and whose exercise of it, where once commenced, would be paramount.

The following books and cases sustain this course of reasoning. (4 Elliott's Deb. 367; 3 Jeff. Sp. 425—429; Peck's Trial, 401, 434, 435; 2 Cra. 397; 3 Serg. & R. 179; 4 Wheat. 196, 198. See others, *post*, and in Houston *v.* Moore, 5 Wheat. 1, 49; Sturges *v.* Crowninshield, 4 Wheat. 196; Willson *v.* The Black Bird Creek

Company, 2 Pet. 245; Prigg *v.* Pennsylvania, 16 Pet. 539, 627, 655, 664; 9 John. R. 568; Miln *v.* New York, 11 Pet. 103, 132, by Thompson, J.; 3 Wheat. 386; Calder *v.* Bull, 3 Dall. 386; 1 Kent, C. 364.)

This view is not limited to that class of cases where the States have not granted to the General Government any power, though bordering closely on express grants, as in case of the fisheries. They still retain the power to regulate these on their rivers and on their coasts as before, and have never parted with the power over them. (4 Wash C. C. 383; Martin *v.* Waddell, 16 Pet. 367.)

So, as to quarantine laws, police regulations, ferries, and roads and bridges, the States retain the general power over them all. (Miln *v.* New York, 11 Pet. 102, 141, 142, 151.) So, in respect to pilots, they continue to legislate by the express assent of Congress; and it is not, in my view, a truth that the States and the people have not granted power to Congress, which may affect ferries, roads and bridges, in certain cases, by granting authority to the General Government to regulate commerce, foreign and between the States; but probably that, till Congress act on the subject, the States should continue to act, for reasons before stated, and when Congress have legislated on a part only, should afterwards continue to act so far as Congress have not come in collision with the State laws.

The cases of the militia, and of bankrupt laws, weights and measures, taxation of land, &c., have been before referred to, and are familiar cases, where the States have continued for half a century to act, when Congress did not conflict with them, though they are powers clearly and expressly granted to the General Government, in the same language and article with those as to commerce, but not seeming to be exclusive in their character. And in numerous other instances, since the first years of the operations of the government, the courts of the United States have, for the first time, been specially empowered to try for offences in cases where previously they possessed no such authority to do it, and where previously even the acts complained of were not offences by any laws in force under the government of the United States. (See many cases as to crimes, in the Act of March, 1825.)

It is, at the same time, conceded, that the courts of the United States have felt indisposed to decide cases on this ground, when able to dispose of them on other grounds.

Hence, in Miln *v.* New York, 11 Pet. 102, the judgment was rendered on the ground that the State was exercising a reserved right; and so in Groves *v.* Slaughter, 15 Pet. 509; and so a part of the Court in Holmes *v.* Jennison, 14 Pet. 540, 580.

But Thompson, J., in the former, held this doctrine, and Ch. J. Taney seemed to do it in the latter, though he said (15 Peters, 509), it was not yet decided, nor was it necessary to decide, whether a State law was not good as to foreign commerce, till it conflicted with some act by Congress.

In the recent decision in what are called the license cases (5 How. 504), some members of the Court went into this question, and held that if the license laws were regulations affecting our commerce abroad or between the States, they were defensible as local measures, not intended to encroach on the acts of Congress, and not, in fact, impugning any of their provisions to produce uniformity, and regulate generally the trade or navigation of the country.

They were like colonial laws in respect to a parent country, or by-laws of cities, towns and corporations, as compared with their charters, or rules of the navy and war departments, and of courts under general provisions organizing them. All are permissible, yet all subordinate; and none are void till repugnant and inconsistent. (See the license cases, 5 How. 504.)

Thus, for illustration, Congress has made no provision for keeping many of our ports and harbors free from sand-bars and deposits of mud, so as to enable vessels engaged in the foreign or coasting trade to enter and depart under the general regulations of commerce for that purpose; and some have deemed it unconstitutional for Congress to expend money on such objects. But cannot the States remove those bars and deposits? States and cities have often done this. Because Congress has made the place a port of entry, can the States do nothing in relation to it, under the idea that the power of Congress is exclusive? Cannot the States and cities under them, also, appoint harbor-masters to regulate ballast, and the place of anchorage of the foreign vessels?

Cannot they make or authorize wharves, at which the vessels can unload? or prescribe how their fires shall be extinguished or guarded while in port, so as to prevent conflagration to the shipping and the town?

It is not mere quarantine or health laws, or inspection laws, or police laws, or pauper laws, or bridges and roads, or laws as to internal commerce within the State, all of which may be considered as reserved, and the power over them never granted; but much as to the improvement and regulation of harbors and vessels in port in other respects, the loading and unloading, and various minutiæ, some as to pilotage, and some as to the crews, all connected with the vessels engaged in foreign navigation, as well as others, but not directing anything in respect to them which conflicts with any actual existing legislation by Congress.

In 14 Peters, 579, the chief-justice and a majority of the Court held, that unless the power was exclusive in the General Government, a State might continue to exercise it, if she had done it before the constitution; and that it was not exclusive, unless expressly forbidden to the States, or in its character one which should be exercised alone by the General Government, and implies an exclusion of the States entirely; *e. g.* legislation over the District of Columbia, p. 589. On such principles, if, says Justice Barbour, "they can be construed as being exclusive," "then the necessary consequence is, that the States cannot exercise them, whether the General Government shall or shall not think proper to exercise them. If, on the contrary, they are not exclusive, but concurrent, then the States may rightfully exercise them, and no question of repugnancy can ever arise whilst the power remains dormant and unexecuted by the General Government."

As some powers are expressly prohibited to the States, this raises a presumption that all are which it was meant should be. And as these local powers in connection with foreign commerce are not expressly forbidden to the States, they were not to be so considered, and have not been in practice for the last half-century.

The advocates of the exclusiveness of this power in Congress will no more allow the States to act, where Congress has not acted, than where it has.

They hold, that the power is gone from the States entirely, and that Congress, by its silence, as emphatically speaks that nothing shall be done, as, by its legislation, that something shall be. (The Chusan, 2 Story, 415, 465; Golden *v.* Prince, 3 Wash. C. C. 313, 322; Prigg *v.* Pennsylvania, 16 Pet. 539, 618; 9 Wheat. 209; Groves *v.* Slaughter, 15 Pet. 504, by McLean, J., and 511, by Baldwin, J.; Miln *v.* New York, by Story, J., 11 Pet. 158; 5 Wheat. 1, 21, 22; 12 Wheat. 438.)

But how does this tally with the fact that the General Government, under the new constitution, went into effect March 3d, 1789? (Owens *v.* Speed, 8 Wheat. 420.)

Most of the important laws as to imposts, ports of entry, and the judiciary, did not pass for some months after. (See 1 Laws by Litt. & Br., 24, 27, 72.)

Hence, on this theory, it is obvious that an entire interregnum of law has existed, and must exist in many cases, till Congress legislate expressly on matters that have been confided to it.

I am not here going into the powers expressly reserved to and left with the States, but those which are granted, though in their nature not granted exclusively in every respect, local or otherwise, and not exercised in hostility, but in allegiance and subordination, to the General Government. (2 Cranch, 297; 9 John. R. 507; 3 Serg. & R. 179.)

A regulation by a State may aid or coöperate with an act of Congress,—be a friend, and not an enemy; and though it is not a police one, yet, if within the legislative scope of the action of a sovereign State, it may move on till impinging against something actually prohibited to the States, or actually and legitimately done by Congress contrary to it. (See case Prigg *v.* Pennsylvania, 16 Pet. 539, 657, views of the minority.)

The idea that, because Congress can act on the matter, but have not, all State action, though favorable and assisting the object, is *ipso facto* void, seems to me entirely untenable. (Daniel, J., p. 657, and Thompson, J., p. 635.)

And it is equally void in the views of some, if the action of the State coincides and aids any exercise of powers by Congress, as if conflicting with it. (Prigg *v.* Pennsylvania, 16 Pet. 651.)

All permitted to the General Government is not enjoined to be done, and at once, but only when necessary, useful or required by public exigencies; *e. g.* to declare war, to borrow money, to lay and collect taxes, as well as to regulate commerce.

And when some loans are needed, or some taxes, or some regulations of commerce, it does not follow that all are, or all these powers at once are to be acted on and exhausted; or that the States cannot continue to borrow money, or collect taxes, or pass any local laws concerning commercial matters, when not expressly prohibited, and not conflicting with those by Congress for general and uniform purposes. (4 Dall. 11; 5 Cranch, 61.)

All the powers have never yet been legislated on which are given to Congress in the constitution. (7 Cranch, 504; 1 Wash. C. C. 235; 4 Wash. C. C. 383; Paine's C. C. 51; 4 Dall. 10; 3 Wheat. 387.)

The constitution has merely empowered Congress to regulate certain matters, when its members please. But till they please to do it, and in all which Congress do not please to touch at any time, the States may usefully continue to regulate the subject within their respective limits, till Congress finds it expedient and a duty to act for the whole. (See cases before cited.)

In one part of the constitution, art. 1, § 10, the States are at once and absolutely prohibited longer to do certain things, and then, of course, there is no concurrent power; as, for instance, "no State shall declare war," "no State shall make anything but gold and silver a tender," "no State shall emit bills of credit," &c.

But, in other places, and especially as to the regulation of commerce, it is not so. It is not "no State shall longer regulate commerce," but "Congress shall have power" "to regulate commerce, or foreign," &c., and so is the grant. That is, Congress shall have power to regulate it whenever and to whatever extent it pleases; but, in the mean time, till it chooses to regulate it, and in all it leaves unregulated of a local character, the States are not prohibited to do what they before had a right to do. Congress may in terms, also, be at times invested exclusively with a power, or its further exercise by a State may be inconsistent, incompatible, or absurd. Such is the government of the District of Columbia, or of the navy. They stand, of course, like prohibitions, and are governed accordingly. (Houston *v.* Moore, 5 Wheat. 49.)

It is not a little singular, that amidst so high-toned and broad constructions as Hamilton generally adopted, he still acquiesced in this system of construction concerning the grants of judicial power to the

General Government, and held them never to oust that of the States before existing, unless clearly contradictory. In No. 82 of the Federalist, he says: "But, as the plan of the convention aims only at a partial union or consolidation, the State governments would clearly retain all the rights of sovereignty which they before had, and which were not, by that act, exclusively delegated to Congress. This exclusive delegation, or rather this alienation of State sovereignty, would only exist in three cases: where the constitution in express terms granted an exclusive authority to the Union; where it granted, in one instance, an authority to the Union, and in another prohibited the States from exercising the like authority; and where it granted an authority to the Union, to which a similar authority in the States would be absolutely and totally contradictory and repugnant."

But can it be pretended, that the action by a State on mere local matters of a commercial character, and about which Congress has not yet legislated, is contradictory or repugnant? Certainly not, till Congress do something concerning this particular matter; and then, as before shown, its laws and regulations must be considered paramount. (15 Pet. 509.)

The chief importance, in settling the true construction of grants like these, to be such as not to prevent the State Courts and State Legislatures from continuing to act till Congress legislates, is, that it takes away any apology for forced and broad constructions, and a resort to common and admiralty law analogies and aids, without acts of Congress evidently and clearly made in order to punish offences. For, without such a dangerous construction and resort, they can be punished by the States, if the States please.

But, if they could not be either so punished or allowed, how would the argument stand? An act would merely go unpunished till Congress choose to denounce it as a crime, and provide what court should try it.

And, for this reason, can limited courts like this, under a limited government like that of the United States, assume, that because the people and the States have empowered Congress to regulate commerce, and define piracies and felonies committed on the high seas, and given to its courts authority over all cases of admiralty and maritime jurisdiction, the offences connected with these matters are sufficiently defined in the constitution itself? Surely not.

The next question to be examined in detail, and with the care its deep interest to the State and the General Government deserves, is, whether the conduct described in this indictment, though at a place where the powers of Congress may reach for commercial purposes, can be regarded as a crime by this Court, unless it has been clearly so declared by the constitution, or a treaty, or an act of Congress, and its trial devolved on us?

Various decisions have been made, which hold that some act of Congress, or at least the constitution or a treaty, must expressly define a crime, and grant jurisdiction over it to the Circuit Court, before the latter can sustain an indictment for any conduct supposed to violate the public rights or public peace.

And, in accordance with these, it has been further held, that a matter must be presented to a court of the United States in some authorized form, before it becomes a case under the constitution or laws. (Osborn *v.* The Bank of the United States, 9 Wheat. 738; 1 Pet. 511.)

The decisions above referred to proceed upon the ground, that the General Government itself is one of limited powers, and hence possesses no authority to punish conduct, beyond what is expressly granted to it, or is necessary and proper to carry into effect what is expressly granted. That it hence follows, no conduct can be declared a crime by Congress, which does not come within such power. That the constitution, being an organic instrument and form of government for general purposes, does not usually establish courts, and limit their jurisdiction, and parcel out among them and define various offences, but leaves that duty to Congress. The definition of treason, in the 3d article and 2d section, is almost the only exception.

It is furthermore held, that if Congress does not declare particular acts to be offences, and prescribe the extent of punishment and place of trial, though the subject-matter is within the powers granted to the General Government, no particular court has any right to try a person for doing these acts, or affix any punishment to them, as every court under the General Government is limited to the trial and punishment of such matters, and such only, as Congress has been pleased to confide to it. (3 Wheat. 389; 4 ibid. 407; Rhode Island *v.* Massachusetts, 12 Pet. 657, 721; 3 Kent, C. 333, 341, 364; 1 Kent, C. 363.)

It has been repeatedly held, that though certain powers are granted to the General Government, it is considered that no acts done against them can usually be punished as crimes without specific legislation. Thus, it is said, "The legislative authority of the Union must first make an act a crime, affix a punishment to it, and declare the court that shall have jurisdiction of the offence." (See United States *v.* Hudson & Cowdin, 7 Cranch, 34, Johnson, J.; 4 Dall. 10, in note to Stanly *v.* Bank of North America.)

And again, that acts of Congress, as well as the constitution, must generally unite to give jurisdiction to a particular court. (1 Kent, C. 294; 4 Dall. 8; Clarke *v.* Bazadone, 1 Cranch, 212; McIntire *v.* Wood, 7 Cranch, 504.)

The Circuit Courts cannot act, unless the power is conferred by Congress. (4 Wash. C. C. 383; Barry *v.* Mercein, 5 How. 103.) It is unlike the king in England, who has divided all his judicial power among his several courts.

So, generally, it is not enough to constitute an act a crime, that it is opposed to some law or the constitution, unless they declare it to be criminal or punishable. It often is but a civil injury or wrong. (Evans *v.* Foster, 1 N. Hamp. 374.) Though in many cases, from the nature of the opposition or violation of a law, it may be criminal on common law principles, in other cases it would not be.

Is it, then, an offence under the constitution, by construction and a resort to any common law principle? In *Ex parte* Bollman & Swartwout, 4 Cranch, 75, 93, the true guide in answering this question is given. "Courts which originate in the common law possess a jurisdiction which must be regulated by the common law, until some statute may change their established principles; but courts which are created by written law, and whose jurisdiction is defined by written law, cannot transcend that jurisdiction." (Marshall, Ch. J., and p. 102, Johnson, J.)

Treason is defined in the constitution; but when cases are not clearly within it, courts will leave them to "receive such punishment as the Legislature in its wisdom may provide." (p. 127.)

It may also be deemed an exception to the requirement of a specific act of Congress in every case, and for all purposes, if the constitution or a treaty should define a crime with precision, as the former does treason, and the latter do at times the crimes where surrenders shall be made, and in the latter the matter should also be within the authority of the treaty-making power. (See the Extradition treaties with France and England.) But unless they went further, and in the constitution or treaty, or elsewhere, designated the court or magistrate to try or examine the offence, that must still be done by legislation, or the jurisdiction in any particular court could not be sustained. (See case of the British Prisoners, *ante*, p. 66.) For all the courts of the United States being, as before explained, formed under a constitution of limited powers, and being courts of limited jurisdiction, a case must come within what is confided to any one of them before they can try it. The grant in the constitution of judicial power does not vest it in any court. But by another clause it is vested in the Supreme Court, and such inferior courts as Congress may from time to time establish.

Congress, therefore, must say how much or what shall vest in one inferior court, and what in another; and how much by one act, and when the residue.

In Livingston *v.* Van Ingen, 1 Paine, 45, the Court holds, that when an action at law is given in Circuit Courts, it does not follow that it may enjoin on the equity side, as no such express grant of jurisdiction is made; but it has been given since by act of Congress, in 1819. There is no power, even in civil matters, in this Court, to take cognizance of them, unless an act of Congress has given it. (1 Paine, 48, 49.) If so limited in civil cases, it is *a fortiori* in criminal cases.

Courts, when established, get only what is conferred on them by Congress, and not what is in the constitution given to Congress, except some jurisdiction which is there given to the Supreme Court, and will soon be referred to in detail. Much power remains dormant in Congress, which it is not expedient to exercise at particular periods, or about which Congress have not yet agreed how to legislate. (1 Paine, 51; 4 Wash. C. C. 383.)

To enable this Court to act, a case must not only fall within the judicial power of the United States, as conferred by the constitution, but jurisdiction over it must have been conferred on the Circuit Court by some act of Congress. (Conkling, Prac. 69, 88.) Such cases alone are those described in the Judiciary Act, as "cognizable under the authority of the United States." (2 Dall. 297.)

The same doctrine prevails as to a mandamus, except in the District of Columbia. (McIntire *v.* Wood, 7 Cranch, 504; 12 Pet. 524.)

So as to suits by the first United States bank, the act of incorporation being silent. (Bank of United States *v.* Devereaux, 5 Cranch, 61. So as to crimes, The United States *v.* Hudson, 7 Cranch, 32; The United States *v.* Bevans, 3 Wheat. 336; United States *v.* Wiltberger, 5 Wheat. 76; United States *v.* Smith, ibid. 153, 157; 5 Mason, C. C. 300; 12 Pet. 73; 4 Dall. 10; 3 Kent, C. 363.)

It continues in this way till Congress calls into action its otherwise dormant powers, which, as before remarked, it evokes slowly, but seldom fully. (5 Wheat. 115, note; Conk. Pr. 70, 71; 10 Wheat. 190.)

Indeed, we must look entirely to the constitution, treaties, and acts of Congress, to see what constitutes an offence in this Court.

The United States has no unwritten code to give it jurisdiction, though the common law, as before remarked, may be resorted to for analogies and definitions, where jurisdiction is conferred.

Over civil cases in admiralty, jurisdiction is expressly given to the District Courts by Congress by a general grant, and to Circuit Courts an appeal in them; but not over criminal cases in admiralty, either to the District or Circuit Courts. Jurisdiction cannot be exercised over the last, except as parcelled out and granted by particular acts of Congress, or by some general transfer to this Court of all cases of a criminal character in admiralty. (Conk. Prac. 82, 83; 5 Wheat. 76; 3 ibid. 387.)

The only cases contrary to this are The United States *v.* Coolidge, 1 Gall. 488, 496, overruled in 1 Wheat. 415; and dicta in De Lovio *v.* Boit, 2 Gall. 388, 470; and remarks in the note to 5 Wheat. 115, and in 4 Dall. 429, by Justice Washington. If concurrent jurisdiction is given to State courts in some cases, then the exclusive jurisdiction in the Circuit Courts is thus far modified. (Houston *v.* Moore, 5 Wheat. 29.) And a judgment in either is probably a bar to a suit in the other. (Ibid.; 11 John. 519.) But a mere arrest is not a bar. (1 Gall. 1.)

So a Circuit Court has no cognizance of military offences, that being by law conferred on courts martial. (Ibid.; 3 Kent, C. 341.) That is, probably, if happening on the high seas. (1 Kent, C. 362. Opinion of Attorney General, 114, 120.)

I acquiesce in these principles and in this course of reasoning, as the safest and soundest in our complicated system of government, and one which has the sanction not only of the contemporaneous construction to this effect placed on it by some of the framers of the constitution, afterwards seated on the bench of the Supreme Court, but of succeeding times, and of many of the statesmen and jurists of the last half-century.

It is an exception to a part of this reasoning for the previous action of Congress, where the constitution itself provides for a Supreme Court, and declares some of the matters which shall belong to its jurisdiction, and hence takes from Congress any power to dispense with such a tribunal, or to confer the trial of those specified topics on any other tribunal. (See article 3, § 1, 2.)

Thus, "The judicial power of the United States shall be vested in the Supreme Court, and in such inferior courts as the Congress may from time to time ordain and establish." (Sec. 1.)

And, "In all cases affecting ambassadors, other public ministers and consuls, and those in which a State shall be a party, the Supreme Court shall have original jurisdiction. This last has been amended. (Amendment 11.) In all the other cases before mentioned, the Supreme court shall have appellate jurisdiction, both as to law and fact, with such exceptions and under such regulations as the Congress shall make." (Sec. 2.)

This prevents Congress from conferring original, or any but appellate jurisdiction, on the Supreme Court, in any cases except those specified. (Marbury *v.* Madison, 1 Cranch, 137, 173; 3 Cro. 75; 7 Wheat. 42; 3 Dall. 17.)

And it is another exception, or perhaps, more properly speaking, an incident to the establishment of such a court and other inferior courts under the constitution, that they, like the legislative bodies of the Senate and House of Representatives, possess authority to punish for contempts in the transaction of the business intrusted to them.

It is considered an authority inherent in such bodies, appurtenant and indispensable, never necessary under any other governments to be conferred by particular laws, though open as this has been to subsequent legislation, modifying and regulating it, as was done after Judge Peck's impeachment, in respect to courts. (See Anderson *v.* Dunn, 6 Wheat. 204; 7 ibid. 45; Act 3d, March, 1831; 4 John. R. 317; 9 John. R. 395; United States *v.* Hudson & Goodwin, 7 Cranch, 33, 34; 6 John. R. 357; 14 East, 1; 5 Dow, P. R. 165; 4 Cranch, 94.)

Having thus seen that this indictment cannot be sustained in this Court, unless some law of the United States has declared it to be a crime, and given to this Court jurisdiction over it, a necessity exists in the next place to examine whether any portions of the constitution, or treaties, or acts of Congress, have in fact done this; whether any of them have really prohibited as crimes such acts as those of the respondents, and empowered this tribunal to punish them.

It is more convenient often, and therefore I am inclined to consider these last questions together, as they depend on like principles and precedents. I do not understand it to be contended that any part of the constitution, or treaties, or acts of Congress, specifically declares the placing such obstructions as those in navigable tide-waters, like those at New Bedford, to be a nuisance, or any other offence against the United States, and punishable by fine or otherwise in this court. But the reliance is chiefly on general provisions and principles involved in them, supposed to be comprehensive enough to include this case.

The discussion on this branch of the case has taken a very wide range, and will receive, as it requires, some detail in its consideration, in order to cover the whole ground.

I am not aware of any clauses in the constitution relied on so much for this purpose as that in section 8th, article 1st, which provides that "Congress shall have power" "to regulate commerce with foreign nations, and among the several States, and with the Indian tribes;" and that in the second section of article 3d, declaring that "the judicial power shall extend to all cases in law or equity arising under this constitution, the laws of the United States, and treaties made, or which shall be made, under their authority," and "to all cases of admiralty and maritime jurisdiction."

We will, therefore, examine the effect of these clauses first. It will be seen that both of them relate to the powers conferred on Congress by the people of the States, and not to the powers conferred by Congress on any of the courts of the United States.

They merely prescribe the extent to which Congress may go in legislating as to commerce; and instead of themselves providing for details in the constitution, they wisely leave to Congress to make such regulations as to commerce as it shall deem useful and proper, to define what shall be crimes against it, and declare how they shall be punished, and in what courts. (United States *v.* Coombs, 12 Pet. 72.)

They proceed, also, to authorize Congress in express terms "to define and punish piracies and felonies committed on the high seas, and offences against the law of nations" (8th section), but do not attempt it in the constitution itself.

It will be manifest from all the expressions, no less than from the character of the instrument as a more general frame of government, and not one filling up and providing for details of legislation, that these clauses lay down rules as to the powers of Congress, rather than the powers of this Court and its jurisdiction.

It leaves the latter powers as they should be left, to the discretion of Congress and the public necessities and welfare, as these may from time to time require Congress, within the scope of the authority thus conferred on it, to define and parcel out for trial whatever it may deem unlawful, and properly punishable by the judicial tribunals of the United States.

Judge Chase says, in a note to Stanley *v.* The Bank of North America, 4 Dall. 10, "The notion has frequently been entertained, that the federal courts derive their judicial power immediately from the constitution; but the political truth is, that the disposal of the judicial power, except in a few specified instances, belongs to Congress. If Congress has given the power to this Court, we possess it, not otherwise; and if Congress has not given the power to us or any other court, it still remains at the legislative disposal;" and concludes it is not best for Congress at once to go as far as it may. (3 Wheat. 387. See cases before.)

And such would seem to be the conclusion as to crimes by the admiralty law, by like analogies and reasons, except for the expression before referred to in the constitution, saying that the judicial power shall extend "to all cases of admiralty and maritime jurisdiction."

But that is only one of the enumerated subjects, like that "to regulate commerce," which before belonged to the sovereign control of each State, and which by the constitution it was provided should be thereafter placed under the control of the General Government, and be acted on by its judicial tribunals. Ch. J. Marshall says, in Bevan's case, 3 Wheat. 387, "It proves the power of Congress to legislate in this case, not that Congress has exercised the power." After that provision, it was still necessary, in order to enable one of its tribunals to try cases of admiralty and maritime jurisdiction, whether civil or criminal, to confer such authority on them to try all such cases, or to try only that portion of them which Congress might then choose to legislate on, and define and intrust to such tribunals.

The same necessity existed for the action of Congress in this respect, as in respect to another enumerated grant to the judicial power over controversies "between citizens of different States." No court, after being created by Congress, could have ventured to try such a case, under that grant merely in the constitution, without some legal provision, conferring that particular power on that court.

And so as to "all cases in law or equity arising under this constitution," "the laws of the United States, and treaties made, or which shall be made, under their authority," though placed within the judicial power of the Union, rather than of the States, not one of those cases, whether of a civil or criminal character, could be tried by any particular court of the United States, till an act of Congress empowered that court in particular to try it, with the exception before alluded to, of cases affecting "ambassadors, other public ministers and consuls, and those in which a State shall be a party," and which, with appeals, are, by the constitution itself, conferred on the Supreme Court.

The Convention knew that admiralty power under the Confederation had been exercised by each State, except at times as to prizes. (1 Mad. Pap. 91, 105; 2 ibid. 712.) They knew that, in order to produce uniformity and regulate commerce, the power should thenceforward be exercised by the General Government. Hence, in the early drafts of the constitution, to the Supreme Court was given jurisdiction over "all cases of admiralty and maritime jurisdiction" (2 Mad. Pap. 743, 744); and it was to be original there at first.

The Convention was at first opposed to having any courts but State tribunals and a Supreme Court of the United States; and, after letting the former try all cases, permitted appeals to the Supreme Court. It, therefore, at first gave also to that Supreme Court admiralty and maritime jurisdiction, as being a matter not suitable for the State tribunals; and at one time struck out entirely any power in Congress to establish "inferior courts." (Ibid. 729.) At last it restored inferior courts, and gave to the Supreme Court still jurisdiction over admiralty cases, and others now in the constitution granted to the judicial power. But it provided that in other cases, except the trial of the President when impeached, jurisdiction might be devolved on inferior tribunals. (2 Mad. Pap. 1238.) Towards the close (p. 1556) it assumed the present form, and the jurisdiction of "the judicial power" was extended to admiralty cases, rather than that of the Supreme Court.

But, what is decisive that, in doing this, they did not mean to adopt the whole admiralty code, criminal and civil, and confer jurisdiction over it on any particular court, but leave that to Congress, as it might find it expedient to define or adopt parts of it from time to time, it proceeded in another clause expressly to authorize Congress to make definitions of piracies and maritime felonies. This would have been unnecessary and improper, if the whole admiralty code as to crimes had already been adopted.

The reasons for this were, that different punishments in different States existed for these felonies; and as they were under admiralty power, and refer to foreign commerce, and are vague at common law, it was best to enable Congress to make them more certain. 3 Mad. St. Pa. 1348, 1349, and in the Federalist, No. 42, it is also said, "But neither the common nor the statute law of that [Great Britain] or any other nation ought to be a standard for the proceedings of this, unless previously made its own by legislative adoption." (No. 42, by Madison.)

When all the powers, not expressly granted to Congress, or not necessary and proper to carry those granted into effect, are reserved cautiously to the people and the States, it would hardly answer to enlarge the powers of courts by a very broad construction.

If the immediate delegates of the people were to be strictly restrained, much more should be their delegates in the judiciary, whose members are not subject to reëlections and short terms of office.

These causes, then, not seeming to grant these powers to this Court, but rather to Congress, can they be aided so as to make out the definition of a crime in this case, and confer the trial of it on this Court, by a resort to any other clause of the constitution or to the common law, or the admiralty law in connection with the constitution?

Looking for a constitutional definition of the present offence, and the power conferred on this Court over it, and nothing being found done or completed in either of the great and leading clauses on this subject that have already been considered, it was not likely to have been done in any other clauses, if not accomplished in those already examined, so important and so germane to the subject. It belonged to topics of commerce and admiralty jurisdiction, and to the power of courts, rather than other matters, unless we were justified in expecting the unqualified adoption of some whole code of laws in a constitution. Had there been a provision in it like that of our ancestors at Plymouth Rock, respecting the Mosaic code, directing the laws of any country or sovereign to be in force till Congress could make better ones, and offences under them to be prosecuted in any courts created by Congress, the difficulty in this case would have been cured, if the conduct of the respondents should amount to an offence under those laws. Or, had there been a provision of a like tenor, adopting the common law, or the civil law, or the admiralty law, as a whole, and placing the execution of them in charge of this Court, then our jurisdiction would be clear, if the acts complained of were made an offence under and by them.

But no such clause exists, and none was likely to exist, for reasons, some of which have already been alluded to, and others that will occur to every reflecting mind.

Beside the circumstance that a constitution is generally designed to regulate the legislative department, as well as others, rather than to make the laws themselves, it is obvious, from the great extent of territory, and different systems of jurisprudence, and numerous people to be operated upon by laws of the United States, that their agents could not find time in one convention to make a constitution and code of laws also, or consider how much of any existing code it was best to adopt absolutely. That they were not delegated to meet for the latter purpose; that, therefore, they did not attempt it; and consequently, instead of doing it, or adopting any general code as a guide, they merely empowered Congress within certain limits to legislate on certain topics, and, with a view to prevent an interregnum, left, of course, the State laws in force till Congress should do this, except where prohibiting expressly, or by strong implication, the further action of the States on certain subjects.

Nor was the convention which formed that instrument ripe and ready to adopt absolutely even the common law, much less the civil or admiralty law, with all their details, and with many uncertainties, and much vagueness as to their extent at different dates, and discriminating from which date they should be regarded as taking effect. (5 Wheat. 182, by Livingston.) The different States had conducted differently as to each of them: some introducing the common law as existing when their ancestors first emigrated hither; some as existing at the Revolution; and some, with large exceptions from it at both periods, of what did not accord with our situation and habits and new form of government.

Again, some had adopted much of the civil law in their courts of equity and courts of probate; and others but little, and that only as an appurtenant to their common law tribunals and jurisdiction; and some, from their interior position, had adopted nothing of the admiralty law, and others little, if any, of it as existing peculiarly on the continent of Europe, and others more or less, perhaps, of what prevailed in England at the time of our Revolution.

Hence it was wise not to wrangle and divide, as they must, by attempting to introduce, by means of the constitution, the common law of England, or of any one State, or of all the States, so far as it might be in force in all. The uncertainty as to its extent, the difficulty of fixing it in cases of doubt, and the specific or general exclusion of all parts of it not suitable to our condition, were matters too formidable to be encountered in connection with their other great labors. It is also very inconvenient to adopt in any constitution any code as a part of the law of the land, without at the same time proceeding to make it alterable, by legislation alone, as the interests and wants and experience of society might require. Otherwise, the smallest change, however urgent, could not be effected, but with all the delay, expense, and formality, of amending a constitution, or the whole organic form of government for a great people.

Hence the common law of England has been considered as not put in force, directly or indirectly, by means of any clause in the constitution of the United States, so as to create, make, or help to make, anything an offence, which has not been made so by the constitution itself, or acts of Congress passed under it. Duponceau on Jur. of Courts of United States, p. 9, says: "The common law of the United States is no longer the source of power or jurisdiction, but the means or instrument through which it is exercised." (See also Wheaton *v.* Peters, 8 Pet. 591, 658; United States *v.* Worral, 2 Dall. 384; 1 Tucker's Black. 378, notes; Serg. on Const. Law, 274; Federalist, No. 42; 1 McLean, C. C. 464; 2 McLean, C. C. 433; 2 Burr's Trial, 437, 482; Dorr's case, 3 How. 103, 105; 1 Wheat. 415; Duponceau on Jur. of C. of United States, Pref. 14; Goodenough on Am. Juris. 276; 1 Kent, Com. 318, 319; 1 Story, Com on Const. 132, 137, 141; 4 Cranch, 75; 7 Cranch, 32; 9 Cranch, 333; 2 Brock. 477; 2 Pet. 144, 446; 11 Pet. 175; 12 Pet. 524. *Contra*, The Regulus, 1 Pet. Admiralty, 213; ibid. 229, note; 4 Dall. 429, Justice Washington.)

And, however courts may properly resort to the common law to aid in giving construction to words used in that constitution and those laws (United States *v.* Palmer, 3 Wheat. 610, e. g. "robbery"), the body of the common law, as such, does not alone give jurisdiction in any case, and enable the Court to declare any acts to be offences under the United States and to try them, where the constitution and the acts of Congress have been silent concerning them. (7 Cranch, 32; 1 Wheat. 415; 3 Wheat. 336; 5 Wheat. 76.)

At the same time, in deciding on private rights in civil cases, which must often be according to the laws of the respective States, the common law will govern us so far as it is in force in each State. (1 McLean, C. C. 464; United States *v.* Lancaster, 2 ibid. 431; 10 Wheat. 158.) But it will be as the law of that State, rather than of the United States.

So as to the admiralty law, as a code in civil or criminal matters, it is not adopted and put in force in this Court by any part of the constitution. But Congress is merely authorized to confer jurisdiction on its Courts in cases arising under that law, though it has not yet done so, except to the District Court in civil cases, as we have already shown.

There being no definition of this particular offence as a crime in the constitution, and no right to aid it in such a definition by the common or the admiralty law, and there being also no grant in the constitution to this Court to exercise jurisdiction over it, but only a grant to Congress to legislate upon such matters, the next inquiry is, has this defect been supplied by any provision in any treaty made in pursuance to the constitution?

A treaty being, by the 6th article of the constitution itself, declared to be "the supreme law of the land," it will govern this case, if full and detailed upon it.

Sometimes treaties may require no appropriations to carry them into effect, or any change of existing laws, being minute enough and explicit enough to be enforced without any new or additional provision; and in such case it may be the duty of the judicial tribunals to execute them without any act of Congress. (See British Prisoners, *ante*, p. 66.)

In other cases, and generally, modified, or at least declaratory, laws will be first necessary. (Ibid.)

But there is no pretence here that any treaty between this country and any other stipulates that obstructions like the bridge of the respondents, and its consequences, shall be deemed an offence, and be punished by this Court on account of its injury to alien friends and their vessels in entering and departing from our ports and harbors.

Such obstructions, however, may be prejudicial to foreigners, and to their rights under treaties, if allowing trade and navigation here to be interrupted, whether the obstructions be temporary or permanent.

But it would be difficult to try them as crimes, when nowhere declared to be so, or to try them by this Court, unless jurisdiction over them is in some appropriate manner clearly conferred on it. Such an obstruction seems to violate the spirit of the treaty of November

19th, 1794, article 3d, with England. It stipulated for each party "freely to pass and repass, by land or inland navigation, into the respective territories and countries of the two parties on the continent of America," "and to navigate all the lakes, rivers, and waters thereof, and freely to carry on trade and commerce with each other." (8 Stat. at Large, 116.)

It did not admit vessels "into sea-ports, harbors, bays, or creeks, of his majesty's said territories, nor into such ports of the rivers in his majesty's said territories, as are between the mouth thereof and the highest port of entry from the sea," except in small vessels between Quebec and Montreal, nor yield the admission of British vessels from the sea into rivers of the United States beyond the highest ports of entry for foreign vessels from the sea.

But it meant to permit such free navigation up to the highest port of entry here for foreign vessels from the sea; yet no clause has been found in this or any other treaty, making obstructions like these crimes, if placed within the limits of such ports or below them, and giving this Court cognizance of them.

Whether a civil action would not lie in such case for delay and damage by an alien friend, against the respondents, or by one of our own citizens, without any further legislation, and under existing treaties and existing laws, is a different question, and one to which some attention will be given before I close.

The only other legitimate source of power by this Court over this case is some act of Congress. (Conk. Prac. 57.)

None giving it, *eo nomine*, has been referred to; none is pretended to exist.

The one most relied on in support of it substantially is that of 1789, which in section 11th gives to this Court jurisdiction "of all crimes and offences cognizable under the authority of the United States, except where this act otherwise provides, or the laws of the United States shall otherwise direct." (1 Stat. at Large, 79.)

But this seems to relate rather to the power of the Circuit Court to try this case, if a crime, than to make it a crime.

Though it is contended by the counsel for the government that it is an adoption and grant to this Court of jurisdiction over all offences which exist under admiralty and maritime law, because all such are "cognizable" under the constitution, and hence "under the authority of the United States," and that the acts now in question are crimes by admiralty law. But if the words "cognizable under the authority of the United States" were meant here to embrace all offences over which the judicial power was extended by the constitution, it would cover all other offences under that constitution or treaties, without any acts of Congress being necessary to define them, and confer jurisdiction over them on this Court.

Again, "cognizable under the authority of the United States," used here as applied to a Court, means, of course, "triable," or placed under its jurisdiction by the constitution, or treaties, or laws of the United States. (See Kendall *v.* United States, 12 Pet. 524, 637, 648.)

The word is so used by Blackstone in speaking of "injuries cognizable by the Courts Maritime or Admiralty Courts." (2 Bl. C. 106.)

So Bayley, J., says, "I think the true construction of this statute is to restrain the operation of the 4th section to cases cognizable in the Superior Courts." (King *v.* Crisp, 1 Barn. & Ald. 282, 287.)

This act might mean that the Circuit Court should exercise jurisdiction over all matters which were made crimes by the constitution or laws, when no particular court was otherwise designated that should try them.

But it still leaves the question open, What is a crime by that constitution or those laws? And till the acts complained of in this case are declared to be crimes by the constitution or laws, this Court, though having cognizance of all crimes which exist under them, cannot pronounce any acts to be crimes within their purview.

A different construction, if competent under the words of this act of Congress, does not seem to accord with its spirit, or cotemporaneous construction by Congress and the courts.

It was early seen that a different course would leave the whole criminal code vague, loose, undefined and uncertain, where certainty in all countries is most desirable.

That specific legislation, under the general grant in the constitution, would be much safer to property, liberty and life.

And, finally, that the construction limiting the expression, "cognizable under the authority of the United States," to what was made cognizable as a crime by any part of the constitution or by any act of Congress, was more in unison with the strictness belonging to all criminal codes.

Accordingly, under this view, specific legislation at once commenced defining special offences, which otherwise would have been unnecessary.

Besides this, the courts of the United States at once held, as before shown, that this kind of legislation was first proper and necessary, in order to make even ordinary offences "cognizable under the authority of the United States," so as to be tried by this Court. Other considerations tended to sustain the idea that this expression as to "authority" referred to what was implicitly enacted by Congress, or expressly declared in the constitution, to be crimes, rather than all which might possibly be done by Congress under the constitution.

Again, had Congress declared that all acts criminal by admiralty and maritime law should be so here (and certainly, if going further, had said also that they should be tried by this Court, as offences under the constitution of the United States), then, probably, they might have been cognizable by us under its "authority," in the same way that, Congress having conferred the trial of all civil cases in admiralty on the District Courts, they are all triable there. Similar provisions would probably have been made in both cases, if the course meant to be pursued was the same in both; and if nothing was said as to the kind of punishment, it might perhaps be as the punishment was in admiralty generally (or possibly by fine and imprisonment), and be prosecuted by indictment. For, whatever the law declares to be a crime, it is said, must be prosecuted here by indictment, unless a remedy by information is specially given. (1 Gall. 3, 177; 7 Cranch, 285.)

But, considering the jealousy of our ancestors as to courts of admiralty, on the ground that, except on confession, for which torture was once used, the proof must be equal to two witnesses, and that no trial by jury was allowed till the 28th of Henry VIII., with other reasons hereafter alluded to, the framers of the constitution would not be very likely to mean to adopt its criminal code *en masse.* Under 28th Henry VIII., the definition of crimes remained, but not the rules of evidence or trial without a jury. (5 Dane's Abr. 342.) And though some of the ancient objections to the admiralty are obviated here by trial in crimes by jury, yet those in respect to its system of proofs in criminal cases might remain, and the prejudices on this subject prevented the exercise of much admiralty power over crimes before the Revolution in any of the thirteen Provinces, and still less on any matter during the Revolution, and afterwards till the adoption of the constitution, except as connected with subjects of prize. (Bains *v.* The James & Catharine, 1 Baldw. 544, 565.)

Perhaps I ought to except revenue matters, as, by 7 and 8 William III., admiralty courts were allowed to control those here, and punish in a King's Court, rather than in a colonial one, in order to deprive the colonists of trial by jury when enforcing obnoxious laws of trade. (6 Dane's Abr. 342.)

If this was in one sense acquiesced in after much resistance, as hopeless to be remedied (see 3 Wheat. 384, 385, *arguendo* the history of it), it was considered a great grievance in principle, as will be hereafter shown, and a topic of loud, long and most indignant remonstrance, till ended by the Revolution. (See on this the opinion of the minority of the Court in Waring *v.* Clarke, 5 How. 441.)

To the illustrations there given, may be added the express provision in the bill of rights in the constitution of New Hampshire (Art. 20), that the trial of jury shall be sacred in all cases, except those happening "on the high seas," and "seamen's wages."

It is true, at the same time, that when forming a General Government, whose chief duty was in respect to foreign affairs and foreign commerce, and its regulation not only abroad, but between the States, the sagacious framers of the constitution saw that it should be invested with all the admiralty and maritime powers which might be proper to be exercised within our own territory.

Hence, they conferred the exercise of them on that government, but still left that government in its legislation to bestow at once, or gradually, all or a part of the civil powers in admiralty on such courts as it deemed most appropriate, and all or a part of the criminal powers in admiralty in a like manner, under such limitations and restrictions of every kind as it might think useful.

Hence, likewise, Congress, in order to carry on at once the ordinary business in admiralty, connected with commerce and navigation, bestowed all power "in civil cases" on the District Courts. But it saw and knew the difference between the clause in the constitution and their own legislation, and instead of copying it so as to embrace "all classes in admiralty," limited the power given to only "civil cases" in admiralty.

Now, if Congress intended to reserve the criminal cases in admiralty, and bestow a jurisdiction over them generally on the Circuit Court, it would probably have proceeded to do so in terms *ipsissimis verbis.* But, instead of that, it then and since merely selected out particular cases of admiralty offences, defined them, and conferred jurisdiction on this Court over them under certain limitations, and without specifying whether it exercised power over them as crimes in admiralty, or under its authority to regulate commerce, or under some other constitutional grant. Indeed, it is hardly to be presumed that Congress intended by the act under consideration to confer power on this Court to try, as a crime, anything which might be made a crime, but which had not been made nor defined to be one, either in the constitution itself or any law, when such caution was used in defining some crimes, and imposing restrictions and limitations as to others.

The act of March 3d, 1825, which defines so many, and makes them, like others enumerated in the act of 1790, specifically punishable in the Circuit Court, generally does not give jurisdiction to this Court, unless the offence is defined and its punishment prescribed, if on the water, as committed on the "seas," or "upon the high seas, or in any arm of the sea, or in any river, haven, creek, basin, or bay, within the admiralty and maritime jurisdiction of the United States, and out of the jurisdiction of any particular State." (See sections 4 and 6.)

Generally, too, cases of crimes come to this Court only where a State has no jurisdiction. (5 How. 441.) Such was the definition by Blackstone of the Admiralty Court, to try cases without the jurisdiction of the common law courts on the seas. It is a wise policy to leave as much with the States as may be, though Congress has the power to go further in some cases, if it pleases. (4 Dall. 11; 5 Cranch, 61; Baïns *v.* The James & Catharine, 1 Baldw. 544, 565; 12 Pet. 721; 1 Wheat. 326; 4 ibid. 407; 3 ibid. 389.)

Another forcible reason why Congress did not mean to have any criminal cases in admiralty "cognizable" as such by this Court, originally, was, that this was not the admiralty and maritime court created by Congress under the constitution. (1 Bee's Adm. 11.) That was the District Court. (3 Dall. 6.) And had Congress intended to confer general criminal jurisdiction in such cases on any court, it would have been likely to have given it to that court, as it did the civil cases, and allowed the trials in the former to be by jury there, as they must have done under the sixth amendment of the constitution, as well as under a provision in the body of it. (Art. 3, § 2.)

Appeals in cases criminal, as well as in civil, could have been allowed to this Court; but, without an express allowance, this Court never has got any jurisdiction by general grant or implication as a court of admiralty, because it was not such a court originally, and was never converted into one since. (The Vrow Magdalen, Bee's Adm. 11.)

It is another decisive objection to a construction of the act of 1789, which would, under the words "cognizable under the authority of the United States," embrace all admiralty crimes as existing here or abroad at the Revolution, that this branch of our criminal code would thus be left very uncertain as to the crimes themselves thus intended to be embraced.

Laws defining crimes should be precise and clear, so that all men may know easily what they are to avoid. (United States *v.* Sharp, 1 Pet. C. C. 119.) And it is most dangerous, by mere construction, to convert that into an offence which is otherwise permitted. By the opposite view, it would be left uncertain at what era and place the admiralty law as to crimes was meant to be adopted, and thus doubtful whether this very offence, described in this indictment, was intended to be embraced, and questionable whether the kind of punishments in any case, where the punishments happened to vary, was to be affixed according to Rhodian or Roman law, the assizes of Jerusalem or the Consular system, the Danish, French, or English codes, or those of some other period and people since the voyage of the Argonauts.

It is a matter of some regret that Congress had not been a little slow, cautious, and discriminating, when they conferred jurisdiction in all civil cases, and had not either enumerated what it considered properly as civil cases in admiralty, specifying subjects and places, or referred to some era, or code, or country, as to its civil admiralty jurisdiction, as a guide. *Misera est servitus ubi lex est vaga aut incerta.*

For now in that, as we should be obliged to do in crimes, had power over them been given, one judge thinks he ought to go to the Rhodian laws for the test, another to the Consulato del Mare, another to the laws of Oleron, another to those of Wisby, another to the era before Richard II., another to the black book of the admiralty, another to the 13th and 15th of Richard II., another to the act of Parliament of 28th Henry VIII., and others to periods still later. (See 5 How. 441.) Some trace the power which is to be the standard to Saxon, some to Norman, some to Saracen or Carthaginian, some to Roman, and some to Turk or Crusader.

Again, one judge gets admiralty jurisdiction both criminal and civil by the locality of the act, as if on the ocean at all; another, if on it where the tide ebbs and flows; another, if on it without the limits of a county; another, if on great rivers navigable below their bridges, though not salt; another, by the subject-matter, if maritime or not; another, by the parties, if seamen or landsmen. (See cases in the precedent last cited.)

This same uncertainty exists about what are maritime contracts, as may be seen by the order of the Supreme Court at the same session for a reärgument in the Merchants' Bank *v.* The New Jersey Company, in a libel on a domestic charter party in admiralty, where the court was supposed to be equally divided as to jurisdiction. Such vagueness and uncertainty, even in civil cases, have agitated the courts of the United States the whole half-century of their existence; and it may have been foreseen, as still more objectionable in respect to the crimes punishable in admiralty, and probably this helped to lead to a refusal to legislate in the same general way as to them. As to them, they have selected out particular and urgent cases for punishment, within careful limits as to the places where they occurred, and made them punishable in such cases only, leaving the others to the State tribunals, till some failure of justice, or emergency for new power to prevent guilt from escape, should justify and require further provisions for punishment by the courts of the General Government.

That these are no imaginary uncertainties, which stand in the way of supposing such a code was meant to be adopted in cases where life and liberty were at stake, some judges have deliberately held that we should go to the continent of Europe to ascertain what our admiralty law is, and not to England. (See cases in the precedent just referred to.) Others, that we must go to England alone. (See ibid.)

They differ vitally, also, as to eras of the admiralty, when its laws and practice are in force here, whether civil or criminal, and going only to England for the law, as most do. (United States *v.* McGill, 4 Dall. 426.) Some hold that the constitution referred to the admiralty law as existing in England before the important legislation of the 13th and 15th of Richard II. (See in 5 Wheat. 114, note; Conk. Prac. 145; 1 Paine, 111—117.)

And again and again it is insisted that these statutes, the great landmarks of admiralty law in England, are not in force here at all. (See The Jerusalem, 2 Gall. 345, and De Lovio *v.* Boit, ibid. 398, 467, 473; Hall's Prac. 17 Pref.; The Sandwich, 1 Pet. Adm. 233; Ware's Adm. R. 91; 5 How. 411.)

While others maintain that they involved the inestimable trial by jury, and the highly-prized principles of the common law against the civil code of a foreign conqueror, and came here with our fathers as much as Magna Charta itself, and were in as full force in Maine and Georgia as in the county of Kent or Bristol in England. (See 5 How. 441. Opinion of minority.)

Others hold the admiralty law throughout to be as it was in England, when our ancestors emigrated here. (Ramsay *v.* Allegre, Johnson, J., 12 Wheat. 612; 1 Kent Comm. 337; Conk. Prac. 155.)

Others limit it as in use in America at the time of our Revolution, and thus collecting it rather from the obscurity and darkness of colonial practice than any other more certain sources. (2 Gall. 398, 471; 1 Pet. Adm. 116 and 236, note; 1 Paine, 111—114; 3 Mason, 27; Bains *v.* The James and Catherine, 1 Baldw. 545; 12 Wheat. 638, Johnson, J.)

Others modify the time to the period of the adoption of the constitution, which is much the same in effect. (1 Kent Com. 377; 3 Pet. 446.) The sounder opinions seem to me those which incline to these last eras. (4 Dall. 429, and cases in 5 How. 441.)

And if a foreign code be thus adopted in the grant of power to Congress over it, or in the act of Congress as to civil admiralty cases in the District Courts, it must probably be considered the code as then existing, and not as at some prior period. (Kendall *v.* United States, 12 Pet. 524.)

Thus, in England, the control and curtailments which had been exercised by the common law courts were recognized as proper and obligatory, according to some; and the admiralty courts had at last submitted in England to the claims of the common law courts, and the contest was at rest. (1 Law Jour. 425; Hall's Adm. Pr.)

But the Supreme Court (5 How. 441) has recently, by five to three of its members, given a judgment in a case of collision of vessels on the Mississippi, two hundred miles above the ocean, and where it is very doubtful whether the influence of the tides is felt at all, and within the heart of a county in Louisiana, for reasons entirely different from some which have been suggested by me as the true test of what admiralty law ought to prevail here.

But, those reasons being dissented from by four to four of the Court, I do not undertake to state or adopt them, though the judgment of the Court on the point then in controversy is binding, and will be respected by me till changed.

But that judgment is confined to maritime torts, not embracing the subject of crimes now under consideration.

In short, then, if we look to English decisions as to crimes, being those referred to in "cases of admiralty" in the constitution, and in the act of 1789, the English precedents are to control us.

There the admiralty court is governed by the civil law, the law marine and law merchant, unless where those laws are controlled by the statute law of the realm, or by the authority of the municipal courts, which unquestionably possess a superintending power, and might restrain that court, should it overstep the just limits of its jurisdiction. (Neptune, 3 Hag. Adm. 129, 136. See "Prohibitions,"

3 Bl. Com. 112; Curtis on Merch. Sea. 344; 4 Wash. C. C. 456; 6 Dane's Abr. 350, "Prohibitions.")

Except in prize admiralty jurisdiction, these powers must extend or contract as "authorized usage and established authority" require; but not go beyond these, as it is a suspected jurisdiction, not being exercised with juries. (2 Hag. Adm. 55.)

In fine, then, according to such views, the maritime laws of England, in force or existing at our Revolution, must be the chief guide. Few admiralty decisions were then reported, and we must go to common law courts for cases and rules as to them, when in collision. (1 Pet. Adm. 229, 230, 113.)

Next, the Roman and civil law, where no English cases or statutes are to be found. (Ibid. 149.)

We must include in English the laws of Oleron, &c., except as by statute overruled and disused in case of punishments harsh and barbarous. (1 Pet. Adm. 142; Com. Dig. "Adm. E. 112;" Percival *v.* Hickey, 18 John. R. 257, 292.)

Courts of admiralty do not proceed according to the law of nations, except in cases of prize. (Ibid. 271, arg.)

Or, unless suits are brought in admiralty under the law of nations, on the instance side of the court. (Ibid. 279, arg.; Doug. 648.)

There, if the common law is resorted to for a definition of principles, it covers the law of nations, as whatever is penal by the law of nations is by the common law. (5 Wheat. 176, note.)

But, to show still further uncertainties in the admiralty law, if adopted *en masse* as to crimes, some others, in the teeth of all this, hold that the decisions of the common law courts in England, restraining and limiting the admiralty jurisdiction, though well settled before A. D. 1776, are not to be respected and enforced here. (The Jerusalem, 2 Gall. 345; *Ex parte* Lewis, ibid. 483; Plummer *v.* Webb, 4 Mason, 380, 387.)

Those who hold these doctrines, and go to ages before the 13th of Richard II., and to the continent of Europe, for guides on points well settled in England by statutes and decisions before our Revolution, make everything vague, and afloat on a sea of uncertainty.

If we go to those early ages, to the birthplace of admiralty law in the Mediterranean, where Consular Courts may have preceded those called Admiralty, and where those of the "Fisc" may have embraced some admiralty as well as revenue powers, and where, under different nations, different forms of government, and in different advances of civilization, different punishments and crimes, and rules of admiralty law, clearly did prevail on many points, which are we to be governed by?

If we were to take the admiralty law as in force here about crimes, and "cognizable under the authority of the United States" by this Court, and as it existed elsewhere than in England, or here at the Revolution, which is insisted on in this case, as in many others (5

How. 441, and cases cited), all would be uncertain, not only on this, but still other accounts.

In Holland, the care of mounds and dikes was confided to the admiralty; in Denmark and Sweden, of the marine; in England, of the navy; in France, of the fisheries. (2 Pet. Adm. 234, note.)

It was of little consequence, comparatively, on the continent, to preserve any settled lines between the admiralty and other courts, as all of them followed the civil law, and had no trials by jury.

But when an attempt was made to transfer admiralty courts and powers to England, in which the common law and not the civil prevailed, and the barons, as in Magna Charta, avowed that they were unwilling the laws of England should be changed, *nolumus leges Angliæ mutari, quæ hujuscunque usitatæ sunt et approbatæ*, it soon became important to protect themselves in the enjoyment of the common law and of the trial by jury, to limit admiralty jurisdiction, as was done by 13th and 15th Richard II., and again, as further modified, in 28th Henry VIII.

It is just as important in this country as in England to discriminate between what really belongs to the admiralty system and courts as admiralty, and what not, and what has of late been conferred on them by statute, which did not belong to them on mere admiralty principles. Indeed, it is more important here, on account of State laws and State rights; because in the last, as in other things not theirs, not belonging to courts of admiralty at our Revolution, the trial of jury is still a right of the people, and the course of the common law in evidence, and a court composed of more than one judge, and a trial by neighbors in their own State tribunals and by their own laws, rather than at a distance and by a different code.

Finally, these conflicts and uncertainties as to what belonged to the admiralty as such, even in civil cases, is one of the strongest reasons for not adopting by a forced construction merely of the constitution, under the act of 1789, the still more vague and doubtful code of admiralty as to crimes.

But there are stronger objections to the idea that our fathers intended by the act of 1789 to confer on this Court a cognizance of all the admiralty crimes that existed in England or on the continent in the fourteenth century.

A brief reference to the establishment and curtailment of the admiralty power in England will demonstrate this.

The admiralty court was considered by the people of England as an intruder from abroad, not tolerated in its large claims for a single half-century, and more and more obnoxious here, as well as in England, to the very moment of the Revolution; and hence its powers were not likely to be extended or enlarged here, or hastily adopted and enforced as to crimes.

Even the word *Admiral* or Admiralty, however long existing in France, or Turkey, or the Mediterranean, or in Arabia (5 Wheat.

106, note), appears in the English language but seldom before the fourteenth century, and then Edward III. first organized the admiralty court as a court. (Note to 5 Wheat. 113; 2 Bl. C. 64, 69; Bac. Abr. " Court of Adm.")

All the records and commissions before King John, if any existed, are said to be lost. (Com. Dig. " Admiralty " Court; Selden, Mare Clausum, B. 2, ch. 14.)

But it is very probable that the whole regular establishment of the admiralty did not exist two generations before the 13th and 15th of Richard II., the immediate successor of Edward III., limited and checked by the Parliament, as it deprived the barons of some privileges as to wrecks, and introduced new laws, as the civil, and new modes of trial, as not by jury, and new kinds of evidence, by forced confession or two witnesses. (See 28th Henry VIII.)

The practice before Richard II. had been for admiralty without juries, certainly in contracts, and by rules of the civil law, to extend jurisdiction so far, that more than half of the commercial jurisprudence of the realm was absorbed in it. (12 Wheat. 616, Johnson, J.)

Its power was not, perhaps, so much an usurpation on what was practised in other courts on the continent, all of whose tribunals were governed chiefly by the civil law and without juries; and hence, magnifying and enlarging admiralty power did not encroach on the rights of parties there and rules of decision, and on judicatories governed by different laws.

But in England it was a deep and sudden inroad on the former laws of the realm and rights of the people, and was strenuously resisted. The Conqueror was regarded in the eleventh century as prostrating English liberties (Thompson on Magna Charta, p. 1), and one of the new instruments for it, under his successors, was the court of admiralty.

One of the great engines by the barons and the people, to protect themselves, was the first charter about the year 1100, under Henry I.; and again the Great Charter, towards the close of that century, under King John, and in which, in article 25th, it was expressly guaranteed that thereafter persons be tried "according to the judgment of their peers in the king's courts." (Thompson's Charter, p. 54, and also p. 55 in article 29.)

And, after the continued breaches of these charters, so as to require from thirty to forty compulsory renewals and confirmations of them, a further resort was had to acts of Parliament of a more stringent and precise character, against the encroachments by the admiralty courts.

The nature as well as cause of the curtailment then made of its general claims as to criminal jurisdiction is nowhere so well embodied as in the terse and pointed language of the acts of Parliament itself, the 13th of Richard II.

"CHAPTER 5.

"What things the Admiral and his Deputy shall meddle.

"*Item.*—Forasmuch as a great and common clamor and complaint hath been oftentimes made before this time and yet is, for that the Admirals and their deputies hold their session within divers places of this realm as well within franchise as without, accroaching to them greater authority than belonged to their office, in prejudice of our Lord the King and the common law of the realm, and in diminishing of divers franchises and in destruction and impoverishing of the common people, it is accorded and assented, that the Admirals and their deputies shall not meddle from henceforth of anything done within the realm, but only of a thing done upon the sea, as it hath been used in the time of the noble Prince, King Edward, Grandfather of our Lord the King that now is." (1 Stat. at Large, 385, Ruffhead.)

To remove any evasions by the general expressions here used of the *realm* or the *sea*, this was followed, in two years, by another statute. (Title 15 Richard II., 1391.)

"In what places the Admiral's jurisdiction doth lie."

There had been complaints of his encroachments and injuries to king and cities, and is herewith "established that all manner of contracts, places and all other things rising within the bodies of the counties, as well by land as by water, and also of wreck of sea, the admiral's court shall have no manner of cognizance, power nor jurisdiction," but shall be tried "by the laws of the land."

"Nevertheless of the death of a man and of a mayhem done in great ships being and hovering in the main stream of great rivers only beneath the bridges of the same rivers nigh to the sea, and in none other places of the same rivers the Admiral shall have cognizance."

This, it will be seen, first limited the criminal as well as civil jurisdiction to acts not done within the body of a county, whether on land or water, except in great ships on great rivers, murder and mayhem, and thus excluded the present case.

This is still the law in respect to crimes, in England. (Co. Litt. 260; 2 Br. Civ. and Ad. L. 487; 2 Gall. 398; La Caux *v.* Eden, Doug. 594; 4 Coke, 137.)

If the exception there, *beneath*, that is, *below* the bridges, used the word *pountz*, in Norman French, which meant points or capes of the land, and not *pons*, bridges, as some contend (Owen, 122; 1 Dall. 106, note; 3 Rowe's Hist. of E. L. 198, note), then the places below them were deemed a species of haven outside of the county, and was in keeping with the rest of the act. But no similar provision exists in our legislation about crimes; and if it enlarged admiralty power any in England, we have in this respect shown a disposition to limit or narrow it more than even in the 13th of Richard II.

In the struggles of the two following centuries, further curtailments, rather than enlargements, took place in England, in respect to crimes.

Hence, after passing first the 13th and then the 15th of Richard II., throwing the common law jurisdiction over most offences, instead of admiralty, and especially within the body of counties, though on navigable water, next came the 28th of Henry VIII., bringing under the cognizance of common law judges in part, and of juries and of common law principles, all the crimes before left for trial in the admiralty courts, and committed even on the high seas, and without the body of a county. (2 Bro. Cr. and Ad. L. 458; 5 Wheat. 76 and 115, note. See the whole statute in 4 Pick. Stat. 441, and interesting matters connected with it. 3 Instit. 111; 6 Dane's Abr. 350; 1 Baldw. 553.)

It was under this statute that the notorious Captain Kidd was tried at the Old Bailey in 1701, for offences committed in India and elsewhere, charged to be "in admiralty jurisdiction," and by a commission partly of common law judges, "to execute the office of Lord High Admiral." (14 How. St. Tr. 230, 297.)

It is said in some books (see cases before cited, and Hall's Prac. 17 Pref.) that these two statutes do not extend to the colonies in terms. This is true, because these colonies did not then exist. And, in The Sandwich (1 Pet. Ad. 233), Judge Winchester thinks those statutes as construed in England did not apply here. (So Ware, R. 91, and 2 Gall. 398.) But, in all these, the remarks concerning them are in connection with contracts, and not crimes.

Our fathers had grown up under those statutes, were attached to their principles and that of 28th Henry VIII.; came here so, and continued so, as regard crimes. (See fully 5 How. 441.) Why not, then, take admiralty law as in England at our Revolution, and not as before Richard II., as respects crimes, except as changed in England in the form of trial before our Revolution, by the 28th Henry VIII.?

All these statutes, when enacted, extended to all Englishmen, English rights and English liberties; and they have been carried with them, when emigrating to every quarter of the globe, as their birthright. All such statutes, as well as the common law, when not inapplicable to our condition (Halsey *v.* Whitney, 4 Mason, 206, 213), were insisted on as a part of our colonial and inestimable privileges. (See the case of Waring *v.* Clarke, 5 How. 441, and cases cited there, and Mayo *v.* Wilson, 1 N. Hamp. 53, 58; Houghton *v.* Page, 2 ibid. 42; State *v.* Rollins, 8 ibid. 550; 1 Story, Com. on Con. 140, note; 8 Pet. 688.)

They were conformed to in most of the colonies, and their vice-admiralty courts, as regards the limits of counties, the common law, and juries as to crimes committed within them, till the Revolution, and even to the adoption of the constitution, so far as any traces of such trials can be found here. (12 Wheat. 638, *semb.;* 1 Baldw. 551.)

And crimes never appear, in our colonial existence, to have been tried here in admiralty courts, or on admiralty principles, and by the civil law in force there, without juries; except under two express statutes, under William III. and George I., passed to tyrannize over the colonies, crimes were sometimes attempted to be tried by commissioners in vice-admiralty courts without a jury. In such a case, in 1769, that court held it had the power to try in Massachusetts a seaman who had killed a lieutenant for attempting to impress him. But, under a vehement public indignation, he was acquitted. (Hutch. Hist. of Mass. Bay, p. 236.)

The admiralty, likewise, was none the less liked by our fathers, because it was one of the instruments used at home, as well as here, to enforce impressments. (Com. Dig. Adm. G.)

Beside this, by the 7th and 8th of William III., the admiralty courts were made the instruments to punish violations of the laws of trade and navigation in the colonies, and the appointment of their judges was taken by the crown from the Lord High Admiral (3 Hag. Adm. 279), and penalties were prosecuted there, and our fathers stripped of jury trials in such cases, and subjected to vexatious forms of proof, the burthen being flung on the claimants, in case of seizures, rather than the government, and the informer shielded from costs.

This was resented nowhere more highly than in Massachusetts; and, instead of being acquiesced in gradually, was resisted till the Revolution itself.

Thus, the Massachusetts House of Representatives, in the preliminary contest some years before the Revolution, passed the following resolve. (State Papers of Mass., p. 51, from 1768 to 1770.)

"13. *Resolved*, That the extension of the powers of the Court of Admiralty within this province is a most violent infraction of the right of trials by juries; a right which this House, upon the principles of their British ancestors, hold most dear and sacred; it being the only security of the lives, liberties, and properties of his Majesty's subjects here." (See Ware, p. 91.)

A volume of similar expressions of censure on the admiralty encroachments here on jury trials, and other rights of the colonies, might be presented. In the old Congress, in 1774, it was declared to be a special and great grievance to be tried in admiralty for acts "arising within the body of a county." (1 Baldw. 551.)

In the Declaration of Independence, too, one grievance was "for depriving us in many cases of the benefit of trial by jury." (See more fully on this, Waring *v.* Clarke, 5 How. 441, opinion of the minority.)

Beside what is stated there, it is not a little curious that our forefathers, in only three years after landing at Plymouth Rock, "Ordained, 17th December, 1623, by the Court then held, that *all* criminal facts, and also all matters of trespass and debts between man and man, should be tried by the verdict of twelve honest men, to be empanelled by authority in the form of a jury on their oaths." (Russell's Guide to Plymouth, 169, note.)

It is shown fully in 5 How. 441, how tenaciously our fathers insisted that they brought with, and continued in force in the colonies, all laws and rights favorable to the subject, and as to them were stern as the barons of old, in Magna Charta, against changes and encroachments. So, unless by positive statutes at home, admiralty power continued here unenlarged, and rather restricted from what it then was in England, than widened, as many have conjectured.

Probably the admiralty in England submitted at first to curtailment with more grace, as the Lord High Admiral, whose "deputy" the judge in admiralty is (2 Bro. Civ. and Adm. L. 457), was still allowed to hold naval courts martial in fleets and ships, for trying all naval offences, and thus keeping up a police, and preserving the public peace, not only in ships-of-war, but on the great highway of nations. (Ibid. 487.)

And the odium attached to capital trials and punishments by courts martial without a jury would have been such as tending to abolish them, if the parties had not, by the terms of enlistment, voluntarily stipulated for such trials by military peers, and the exigencies of war did not often render their speedy and summary mode of procedure almost indispensable.

In the mutiny act of 22d George II., a special proviso is introduced, that the powers of naval courts martial shall not extend to any matters still left to admiralty jurisdiction. (1 McArthur on Courts Martial, 174; 3 Wheat. 360, note.)

And an additional reason, corroborating all this, is, that the admiralty court had not for two centuries in England as an admiralty court, but only through a commission, including other judges and a trial by jury, had any jurisdiction over felonies; and it was doubted whether it had any over misdemeanors at all. Indeed, another strong illustration of the strength of public sentiment in England against trials in the admiralty for any offences whatever is, that though the 28th of Henry VIII. is in terms relating, not to misdemeanors, but only felonies, yet, since its passage, no crimes whatever, whether misdemeanors or felonies, are tried in the court of admiralty by the judge of admiralty alone; but they are all tried by a jury, and all prosecuted in the courts of common law, or under a commission, or under special statutes. (2 Bro. Civ. and Adm. L., No. 3 App. 519; 2 Black. Com. by Chitty; Corfield *v.* Coryell, 4 Wash. C. C. 371, 383.)

In truth, the better opinion is, that admiralty courts, at the time our constitution was adopted, did not punish misdemeanors; and hence there must be an act of Congress to punish such misdemeanors, or no jurisdiction over them exists in the Circuit Courts. (4 Wash. C. C. 383.)

In accordance with this view, by 29th George III., it was enacted that all other offences than felonies, committed on the high seas, be tried by a commission, as by the 28th Henry VIII. (Russ & Ry. 1, note.) And so far from there being any disposition evinced here to depart from such restraints, that the framers of the constitution, in giving Congress a power to define "piracies and felonies committed on the high seas," undoubtedly meant to go as far as had been gone by the 28th of Henry VIII., and cover all offences tried in the admiralty since then, and leave nothing to loose and general construction, as to what was and what was not an offence merely by admiralty law.

They meant further, by the 4th and 6th amendments of the constitution, to secure the use of a grand jury in all cases of crimes formerly tried otherwise in admiralty, and a "trial by an impartial jury," and by witnesses face to face. (1 Tr. Bl. 72, 73.) And the legislation since (Baldw. C. C. 554), from the start to the present moment, has corresponded, by saying, in almost every crime committed on water, that, to give the courts of the United States jurisdiction over them, they must, as by the 15th of Richard II., be committed out of the body of a county, or, in other words, "out of the jurisdiction of any State."

They do not except even those in great ships on the great rivers below the bridges, if within any part of a State.

It is doubtful whether many of the framers of the constitution thought of any criminal jurisdiction, in extending judicial powers to cases in admiralty.

It was "civil cases." It was those that belonged to commerce. It was a separate grant to define and punish piracies and felonies committed on the high seas, and probably thinking that power had not been embraced in giving authority over cases in admiralty.

When Congress came to legislate about cases in admiralty, it did, in order to prevent any doubt, confer on the admiralty court jurisdiction over civil cases only. And it gave cognizance of crimes in admiralty neither to that court nor any other, as over crimes in admiralty, but gave cognizance of several specified offences to the District Court, and of several to this Court.

It is most important to have as much as possible granted by Congress, under the power to regulate commerce, &c., rather than by admiralty merely; as in the last case no jury is allowed by the constitution, but in others one is, and the trial is also by the State laws, or those of Congress, and not by a foreign code.

The whole leaning of this court, therefore, in case of any doubt, should be towards obtaining jurisdiction over commercial questions, or crimes against navigation and trade, by special legislation of Congress, rather than by broad constructions of any grants of mere admiralty power. Because, there a jury can be used, under the power to regulate commerce.

The only prominent attempt to revive here the ancient admiralty jurisdiction over crimes by construction, when committed on the water, within the jurisdiction of a State, has been in Coolidge's case (1 Gall. 496).

This has been overruled in 1 Wheat. 415. Some others have been noticed as to revenue seizures and torts, in the case of Waring *v.*

Clark, 5 How. 441. And though some have supposed that the word "maritime," added in the constitution after the word "admiralty," might be construed as extending the present meaning of the word admiralty (2 Gall. 471; 3 Story's Com. on Const. 527, and note to 5 Wheat. 113), yet it would seem to me to raise an implication that it was restrictive, and if anything had got into admiralty which was not strictly maritime, or happening on the seas (*mare*), it was not to be embraced, as the cases must be as admiralty and maritime jurisdiction, that is, of both, must be of things on the sea maritime as well as called admiralty. (See, also 10 Wheat. 429 and 418; 11 Pet. 175; Gilp. 526.) At the utmost, "maritime" and "admiralty" courts are treated as the same, and the expression a pleonasm in Selden on Fleta, and Federalist, No. 8, p. 531. (See also "Courts Maritime or Admiralty Courts," 3 Bl. C. 106 and 68.)

Again, in another view, the difference now is merely nominal between admiralty and maritime, since the admiralty court has ceased to be military. (1 Pet. Adm. 233, note.) Hence, maritime in the constitution may be to show that no military or naval power is granted in it, but only maritime; and thus, too, it is restrictive, rather than enlarging.

Now, after all this, to suppose that our ancestors intended in any statute, like that of 1790 or 1789, unless their language was more clear and explicit to that effect, to grant a power to this Court to try and punish everything as an offence in particular places which was one in admiralty in England or on the continent in the fourteenth century, though never since, or on the continent in 1789, is presuming against what was probable from the whole subject-matter, and the history of ourselves no less than our ancestors, both legal and political.

Showing, then, that an act like this was prosecuted in admiralty in England, in the fourteenth century, is not enough to make it a crime now, unless such continued to be the law and usage there at the time of the adoption of our constitution.

The references have been very full, by the counsel for the government, to prove that the admiralty courts on the continent of Europe formerly, and in England before Richard II., exercised a power over such subjects. And it may not be disputable, that, for a brief period, they did, if looking to the ancient commissions and inquisitions, and the usages in France, and some parts of the Mediterranean. But the conflicts which quickly arose in respect to the exercise of this and other criminal jurisdiction by the admiralty court in England led, as before seen, to the restraining statutes of 13th and 15th of Richard II.

The struggle was afterwards only occasionally renewed, till it led to a still more restraining, and, in some views, more important, statute of 28th Henry VIII., A. D. 1520, which took from the court of admiralty, as such, all important criminal jurisdiction, and devolved it on a commission, composed of judges at common law, as well as in doctors commons, and required all the trials of crimes to be by a jury.

Hence, if Congress, in the act of 1789, had expressly conferred on this Court jurisdiction to try all criminal cases in admiralty, as it did on the District Court to try all civil ones, and had declared that what was criminal by admiralty laws should be so considered and punished by this Court, this would have made a stronger case. (5 Wheat. 153.) But still doubt would exist whether the acts of the respondents amounted to an offence in admiralty. Certainly they would not, if the correct test as to such an offence be what was understood to be one in England or here, when the constitution was adopted, however little doubt might exist if we looked to what was a crime in admiralty before the 13th and 15th of Richard II. in England, or since on the continent of Europe.

This will be seen in what has already been stated in respect to the boundary of admiralty jurisdiction, before and after those celebrated curbs on its encroachments.

But, beyond this, to render it very improbable that many matters, before treated as crimes in admiralty, continued to be so treated, many will doubtless remember the long struggle between the court of admiralty and courts of common law in the thirteenth and fourteenth centuries, for jurisdiction over offences, as well as civil cases, on navigable waters within the body of a county, and which led to the restraining statutes of Richard II., and was one with many other quarrels, which terminated in the hanging of some of the judges on both sides. The Chief Justice Tresilian seems to have headed one party, and Arundel, the Lord High Admiral, the other. (1 Henry's Hist. of Eng. 258, 263; 1 Hargrave's State Trials, 1.)

After such a warning, the admiralty court would not be very likely to encroach again soon into the bodies of counties, and punish as crimes in admiralty there what the common law courts and Parliament itself, by the restraining statutes of Richard, considered as offences to be tried only in the latter tribunals, and which it was afterwards made penal to prosecute in admiralty. Though some of the old commissions to the admirals may have retained their old forms, as to an inquiry into nuisances by seines and weirs for fishing, and rubbish, obstructing navigation, as quoted by Sir Lionel Jenkins and others. (See Zouch's Adm. 92; Clarke's Pr. 99; 7th Article of the Practice of the Ct. of Adm. in the Black Book; Bracton, p. 12, § 6; Spelman's Relics of Adm. 286; Constable's case, 5 Coke, 106; 2 Hale's P. C. 11—20; Richard I.; Edward III.; Richard II.; Henry VIII., in Ruffhead's edit., p. 6, 260, 329, 424, 448; 2 Bro. Civ. & Adm. L. 463, 465, 474.) Yet in many cases the inquiries were limited to places below or beneath the lowest bridges. See before, and Zouch's Adm. 92, usually "below" them, or only up to them from the sea. (Lex Mercatoria, p. 88; 2 Hale P. C. 18.)

They seldom, if ever, extended into the body of a county, unless sometimes on salt water when the tide was in. (2 Bro. Civ. & Adm. L. 30; Bac. Abr. "Court of Admiralty;" Constable's case, 5 Coke, 106.) And the common law courts had concurrent jurisdiction as to those crimes in rivers. (2 Hale, P. C. 16, 54; 1 Starkie, R. 16.)

Or, unless the collection of gravel or rubbish actually obstructed navigation or perilled ships and life in great rivers in fresh or "sweet" waters towards the sea below the bridges (Clerke's Prac. p. 119); and this was all before 15th Richard II., or violated that statute, if the rivers were in the body of the county. (See Black Book, ch. 34, p. 109. See, also, the Inquisition of Queensboro', in Hall's Adm. Prac. 20, Pref.) See the articles drawn up under James I., as to the power of the court of admiralty. (Pref. of Hall's Adm. Prac. 24; 2 Bro. Civ. & Adm. L. 79; 2 Hale's P. C. 16 and 118; Dunlap's Adm. Prac. 7.)

It is true that the Inquisition of Queensboro' was in Edward III., 49th (A. D. 1376). (Zouch's Adm. 34; 4 Partesue Col. 200.) But this was before the 15th of Richard II., and centuries before our Revolution.

As before remarked, Sir Lionel Jenkins also attempted to revive the ancient jurisdiction, and in his charges went nearly as far as before Richard II. He says, inquire of "all such as have cast ballast, rubbish or filth, into our navigable rivers below the bridges next the sea," or stones for lighters to fasten to, and not laid a yard deep in the ground, so harbors not become "choaked up." (341 Ap. 530 and 532 in Curtis' Adm.)

Strictly speaking, he might mean to confine these inquiries to the sea and below bridges, as he says, "all nuisances and abuses upon our salt waters and navigable rivers beneath those bridges which are next the sea" (540), and hence not like the present case.

But, if he did not mean to confine himself to the high seas, or to the era before Richard II., as to offences, his views are a departure from express statutes, and the actual jurisdiction exercised in admiralty as well as common law. (12 Wheat. 635, Johnson, J.)

If he meant to go as far as the words in the ancient and obsolete forms of commissions, as shown in the Black Book of Admiralty, in Clerke's Practice, he meant to violate express acts of Parliament, unless keeping below the bridges.

The old inquest or inquiry run (14th Article in Clerke's Prac. translated into Latin) into "*alias causas quascunque super mare, et infra quoscunque rivos, aquas seu rivulos maris,*" but takes care to add, "*usque ad primum pontem emergentes terminare.*" So in a note to the 14th article in felonies, "*felonias spoliationes,*" the power run to sweet or fresh waters, "*aquis dulcibus*" as well as "*super mare;*" but it was only in them "*ubi dominus magnus admirallus Angliæ habet aut habere consuevit auctoritatem sive jurisdictionem,*" i. e., below the first bridges in cases of murder and mayhem.

The same attempt was made, by construction of old phrases and otherwise, to depart from the true limits of admiralty jurisdiction,—that is, "the high seas,"—in Massachusetts, when a colony, and was resisted in a remonstrance by the House of Representatives, in 1770, as first in the list of their grievances, and by a committee, of which John Hancock and Samuel Adams were members. "We have seen of late, innumerable encroachments on our charter; courts of admiralty, extended from the high seas, where, by the compact in the charter, they are confined, to numberless important causes upon land;" followed by a list of other grievances. (Mass. State Papers, p. 47.)

The modern commission or patent to the judge of admiralty includes several things as of old, but not now by law in his power. (1 Hag. Adm. 312.) Indeed, a great part of the powers given by the terms of the commission are totally inoperative. (Ibid. See, also, Little Joe, Stewart's Adm. R. 407.)

Again, by the resolutions of the judges (4 Feb. 1632), an attempt was made to revive the ancient jurisdiction of the admiralty concerning obstructions in rivers. This was placed, not on any ground except to try mayhem and murders there in great vessels below the bridges, but, as to the admiral, it was said, that "by exposition and equity thereof, he may inquire of and redress all annoyances and obstructions in those rivers that are an impediment to navigation, or passage to or from the sea," and not be prohibited. (See Dunlap's Adm. Prac. 14; 3 Wheat. 367, note; Hall's Adm. Prac. 24, 25, Pref.)

But, beside this being probably below only, and not at or above the bridges, those resolutions were not laws, could not abrogate the laws, and were disavowed afterwards as assented to by several of the judges. (Hall's Adm. Prac. 26, Pref.; T. Raymond's R. 3; 12 Wheat. 617; Bee's Adm. 420.) They do not appear ever in this respect to have been practised on. (Bac. Abr. "Court of Admiralty, A.")

Again, this was an exception in a statute of only murder and mayhem in great ships; and it would be most extraordinary to consider an exception expressed as a good reason for making other exceptions not expressed. On the contrary, the sound legal maxim is *expressio unius est exclusio alterius.*

So of many other matters cited in old books as admiralty powers. They were such as are now obsolete since Richard II., and with the growth of cities and distribution of such powers among municipal officers and other courts.

Thus, when an inquiry in admiralty was ordered as to the anchorage of vessels and their injury to each other in port (Zouch's Adm. p. 97), it related to a maritime matter, and was before Richard II., and hence took place in admiralty. So as to the demeanor of seamen and ferrymen, and to repress their uncivil names, it related to maritime men, and was previous to that statute. (Zouch's Adm. 91; Lex Mercat. p. 77.)

The admiral, at first, merely governed and punished seamen by a sort of naval rather than commercial code. After the navy was separated, and merely protected the mercantile marine, he continued to settle disputes as to matters happening anywhere on the sea flood, out of the body of counties, as the county magistrates and juries did not exist there, and it seemed to be the appropriate theatre of his power. (2 Bro. Civ. & Adm. L. 30.)

Though restrained within the counties, he was powerful without; and the claim of the king to the four narrow seas, and his ancient admiralty jurisdiction over them, were never relaxed. They were beyond the *corpus comitatus*. (See Selden's Right and Domain of the Sea, "Ownership of the Sea," 384; Hale, De Portibus Maris, p. 85, 86.) All nations were in them for a time made to "veil the bonnet." (2 Bro. Civ. & Adm. L. 469, 470.)

Shutting the admiralty court, then, out of all criminal jurisdiction since the 13th and 15th of Richard II., and certainly since Henry VIII., in England, as to matters happening within a county, how could the framers of the constitution or the authors of the act of 1789 mean to use language broad enough to make the present case "cognizable" in admiralty — a case happening several miles within a county? I will not undertake to say that some of the members of the Supreme Court, in the recent case in 5 How. 441, have not gone far enough to make the admiralty law, as existing in England in the most remote ages, and as on the continent in more modern times, the true rule for deciding what are or are not within the jurisdiction of admiralty courts here in certain civil cases. The decision will speak for itself.

But, believing that a majority have not said so, if any of them mean so, as to crimes, I do not feel justified in regarding as guides in this instance anything which was not deemed proper matter for admirálty cognizance in England at our Revolution, unless made so here by colonial changes, or made so since by our constitution and acts of Congress. (See more fully on this my dissenting opinion, and the cases there cited.)

Look a moment to the facts in the present indictment.

Though the acts complained of were committed on salt water, within the ebb and flow of the tide, and where the river was navigable, yet the obstruction is not below, but above, and at the bridge, and is within the body of the county. Where is the instance in England of treating one of the bridges on the great rivers as itself a nuisance, either since or before Richard II.? But there is no doubt that such an act unauthorized, if an obstruction to navigation, whether by throwing in rubbish or timber, would be a nuisance at common law, and punishable not only there, but in most of the State courts for the trial of crimes and questions at law, rather than of equity or admiralty. (See cases, *post.*)

As strong proof that the admiralty has not for many centuries punished any nuisances, all the cases reported of prosecutions for nuisances are either in common law courts or in the exchequer by a bill for an injunction. None are found in admiralty, though Sir Lionel Jenkins (1 Zouch, 88, 96) claimed the power in ports and navigable rivers. (Com. Dig. Adm. E. 13.)

But where is the case of its undisputed exercise in admiralty since Richard II.? Where at the time of our Revolution? "The water, banks, &c., within ports and havens, are within the power of the Commissioner of Sewers." (Com. Dig. "Navigation, D." Col. 38.)

A penalty for throwing ballast into them is imposed by 19 George II., and is a fine collected before a magistrate, and not in admiralty. (Ibid.)

The city of London has, by patent or grant, charge of the Thames, as well as the soil under it, and assesses taxes to repair wharves and remove rubbish. (Calthrop's Cases, p. 122, 123.)

We have, also, already shown, that the admiralty courts in England punished no misdemeanors when our Revolution took place; and that all their criminal jurisdiction was probably intended by the framers of the constitution to be parcelled out, and, indeed, conferred on Congress, to grant to its courts under other heads, and not as mere admiralty offences.

But, to consider that an offence in admiralty, which was committed within a port, within the *fauces terræ*, the promontories of it, within the jurisdiction of a State, within the body of a county, within the reach of State laws and the State courts, not on board a public ship, or in a fort or lighthouse or navy-yard under the exclusive jurisdiction of the United States, not in any ship whatever,— and yet, in this age, or that of the framers of the constitution, to be regarded as clearly within the cognizance of an admiralty court merely as such, and having no aid from specific acts of Congress otherwise reaching and punishing the act as injurious to commerce, or to some other subject like revenue or navigation, placed under its regulation and protection,— that, I think, would be a pretty bold stride, whatever may have been the law in England at the time of the Crusades, or in the Mediterranean, where the pliable principles of the civil law, rather than those sturdy and jealous ones of the common law, predominate. Seeing all this difficulty as to what powers of admiralty, at what era and in what country, are in force here, and the doubts even in some civil cases not yet removed (5 How. 441), it is perhaps fortunate that Congress adopted a different course as to criminal cases, and, instead of conferring all power over them in the gross on this or any other court, merely granted it in detail, in particular cases, from time to time, as the public exigencies and obvious expediency required Congress to act.

In this way, Congress did not disturb the colonial prejudices against such a broad jurisdiction in admiralty as we and our ancestors had for so many centuries been opposing, and especially in criminal matters. In this way, also, the prejudices in favor of trials in the common law courts, or courts acting on their law side, and on common law principles, and in common law forms, were acquiesced in, and left to the tribunals in each State, without any action on them by Congress, or the offences specially defined by acts of Congress; and the jurisdiction over them specially given to the Circuit Court, and given to it, not as a court of admiralty, but as a law court.

In this way, they avoided collision with the States, the State courts, State jealousies, State jurisdiction and State rights; selecting only for offences acts committed without State jurisdiction, or on the high seas, or in places expressly ceded to the United States.

Having shown, from this cursory view of the history of the curtailment of admiralty jurisdiction in England, that the construction claimed by the prosecution as to what is "cognizable under the authority of the United States," in the act of 1789, could not, on any fair grounds, be intended by its makers, as it thus would become necessary to ride back, and ride over all changes in admiralty since the beginning of the fourteenth century,— and having shown that a transaction like this, an obstruction in any waters within a county, has not for centuries been deemed a crime cognizable in admiralty in England or in this country, however exceptionable and punishable it once was in admiralty, or may at times be now in the courts of common law,— I might stop as to this. But it is very doubtful whether the place of this offence, even were the act a crime in some places and cognizable in admiralty, was within the criminal jurisdiction of admiralty courts in England, or here at the time of the Revolution. An act may be a crime in one place against admiralty law, which is not, if done in another place.

This act was not done on the high seas, nor out of the body of a county, though within tide-water.

Locality in crimes, as in torts, has ever been considered the chief test of admiralty jurisdiction. The very acts of Congress which punish crimes connected with maritime affairs usually require, in express terms, that they shall have been committed out "of the jurisdiction of a State;" but the bridge and the nuisance, if any in this case, are confessedly within the body of a county; and though over tide-water, are not on the high seas, nor on a narrow arm of the sea or harbor without the boundaries of a county.

This question is in some aspects like the last, but in others is different; and fortifies it, because developing the local boundaries of all criminal jurisdiction in admiralty, whether for nuisances in public waters or other offences, to be without the *locus in quo* here.

I shall, under this head, say nothing of the character and locality of this particular offence as charged in the indictment, except by showing that all jurisdiction of all crimes in admiralty, with a single exception before named, was in England, both in 1776 and 1789, excluded from a place like this.

The general rule is, that the admiralty jurisdiction in crimes, after the 15th of Richard II., was only on the sea without the body of a county. (Com. Dig. "Admiralty, E. 5, note;" 4 Wash. C. C. 375; Corfield *v.* Coryell, 3 Wheat. 371; 2 Bro. Adm. & C. L. 465, 475; Hall's Adm. Prac. 19; 5 Mason, C. C. 298. *Super mare altum*, Com. Dig. Adm. E. 1; 5 Wheat. 76, 379; 12 ibid. 623, 627, by Johnson, J.; Hale's Hist. of C. L. p. 35, ch. 2; 3 Story, Com. p. 534.) That this included the sea thus situated, to high-water mark, though some say only to low-water mark. (1 Baldw. C. C. 35; 3 Wheat. 336; 3 Instit. 113; 1 Mason, C. C. 147, 152; Ware's R. 95. See cases above.) That it embraced even ports, havens and creeks, if so situated without the county. (Montgomery *v.* Henry, 1 Dall. 49.) There they are considered "the high sea" or "main sea," and so also when without the capes. (United States *v.* Grush, 5 Mason, C. C. 298; 3 Rob. Adm. 336; Hargrave's Tracts, 88.)

But they are usually *infra corpus comitatus*, within the *fauces terræ*, landlocked, and then admiralty criminal jurisdiction ceases, and, of course, that of the United States founded on it. (12 Pet. 72; Com. Dig. "Navigation, K. & Admiralty, E. 5;" 4 Instit. 148; 1 Story, 259; 1 Bl. C. 110; 5 Wheat. 99, 184; 1 Mason, C. C. 360; 1 Hawk. ch. 37, § 36; United States *v.* Grush, 5 Mason, C. C. 240; United States *v.* Robinson, 4 ibid. 308; 3 Wheat. 336.) To show the application of this to the present facts, this is the law in the river Thames. (Com. Dig. "Admiralty, F. 2;" 4 Instit. 139; 1 Roll. 539.) And in other rivers, however salt, or strong their tides. (3 Wheat. 94.) So in most roadsteads. (1 Rob. Adm. 233.)

But not so in an open roadstead in a foreign country. (5 Wheat. 200; 1 Gall. 524, 624; 2 Sumn. 482.) So an "arm of the sea" may be within a county, as the mouths of many rivers are regarded in England. (5 Mason, C. C. 300.) So most creeks are within the county. (10 Price, 401; Hale, De Port. Mar. 46—48.)

Hence a creek is said not to be a port or a haven, or to have this privilege. (Com. Dig. "Navigation, C.;" Bac. Abr. "Courts of Admiralty.") Certainly not, if fresh water, or within the county. (5 Wheat. 76, note.) And, it is hence, as hereafter explained, probably, that, in the Black Bird Creek case, Ch. J. Marshall says nothing of the dam across it violating the rights to go to any port of delivery, or to sail upwards to the highest ports. (See *post.*)

The acts of Congress concerning the fisheries give a bounty when "employed at sea for the term of four months," and this has been construed to mean out of the ports and harbors of the sea-coast. (Schooner Harriet Boynton, 1 Story, C. C. 251.)

The space between capes of the main sea, or high seas, or ocean, is usually so wide, that one cannot see what is done across, and the coroner, sheriff or people, not be able to see and know an act done. (Angell on Tide-waters, 13 Pref. and cases.)

In cases of doubt, the county acts, more especially if it has been the usage for it to act there. (2 East, P. C. 804; 6 Dane's Abr.

341, 346; 1 Com. Dig. "Admiralty, F. 2;" Angell on Tide-waters, 300—301; 4 Instit. 140.)

Such cases must arise often, as the state of the air would make a great difference as to the distance things could be seen distinctly. The Arabs in the north of Africa consider it a mile when so far as not to be able to distinguish a man from a woman.

The punishment of crimes, without such limits, Congress may impart to such courts as are thought most proper. (4 Elliott's Deb. 290, 291; 1 Kent, Com. 319; 3 Wheat. 356, arg.)

So, if a crime be committed on the high seas, but in a foreign vessel, we have no jurisdiction of it. A gun fired, and killing, the act is done where the vessel is on board of which occurs the killing. (United States *v.* James Davis, 2 Sumn. 482; 1 Leach, C. C. 432.)

That may be on the high seas, if outside, and the vessel is afloat, though the ground is bare there at low tide.

If in a foreign vessel, we have no jurisdiction. (2 Sumn. 485.) It is, *pro tanto*, foreign territory. (United States *v.* The Pirates, 5 Wheat. 197; United States *v.* Kessler, 1 Baldw. C. C. 25.)

Piracy being an offence against the law of nations, as well as our own laws, may be punished here wherever committed, on the sea, if not in a vessel of some foreign power. (United States *v.* Klintock, 5 Wheat. 152.)

A revolt, under the statute of April 30th, 1790, need not be on the high seas, as the statute does not say, in this crime, it must be out of the jurisdiction of the State, or on the high seas, but only in some ship. (United States *v.* Hamilton, 1 Mason, C. C. 443; 1 Bro. Laws, 113.)

But Congress makes this a crime within the body of a county, not by its power over admiralty matters, as those matters in crimes do not arise within the county. It is rather by its power to regulate commerce, and punish offences committed in the prosecution of it, and in vessels. This may be done on land as well as water in several cases, as Congress governs the commerce between the States, often wholly on land. (12 Wheat. 446.) The revised act of March 3d, 1835, punishes a revolt, if "on the high seas, and in their admiralty jurisdiction," but does not say, out of the limit of a county. (4 Bro. L. 776.) Hence its meaning in this respect is to be settled, though in other cases the high seas have been held to be the unenclosed ocean. (See before, 5 Mason, 290.)

Confining a captain on board an American ship, if in port, is punishable. (United States *v.* Storer, 4 Wash. C. C. 548.) Yet it is not an admiralty case, but one under the power to regulate commerce.

I should have much confidence in this view as to the locality of crimes, in order to give admiralty jurisdiction over them; and that this indictment must fail on this account alone, if on no others, had it not been equally strong as to a like locality of maritime torts being necessary to give admiralty jurisdiction over them; and the Supreme

Court recently, in 5 How. 441, held that locality in the latter, to confer such jurisdiction, need not be on the ocean, or outside of a county. They held it might be anywhere on tide-water, though two hundred miles in the interior of a State, and in the centre of one of its counties.

To be sure, the decision is carefully confined to the case of collision between vessels, and does not in terms extend to other torts, or to contracts or crimes.

But I must confess that my opinion is weakened in respect to this ground concerning crimes.

And I abandon all analogies, which had before been relied on by me, on account of a like rule in torts generally. The cases in respect to them may be seen, however, in 5 How. 441, collected in the dissenting opinion.

So also may be seen there the reply as to any contrary reasoning or analogy derived from the locality of contracts, and of cases of seizures for breaches of the laws of revenue and trade on the water.

In other matters, more than crimes, connected with admiralty jurisdiction, it may be important at times to discriminate between the sea and the high sea, a river navigable and not navigable, whether the tide ebbs and flows at a particular place or not, and whether jurisdiction does not extend for some purposes to other than our own vessels, beyond the sea-shore.

But I apprehend that in crimes, "the seas," or "the high seas," or "the ocean," mean much the same (6 Dane's Abr. 348), and that in other matters "the ebb and flow of tide," "the flood mark," or "the sea flood," were often much the same, though not always. (2 Gall. 402.)

So, when it becomes material to decide what is navigable or not, as in the act for revenue seizures on streams navigable from the sea by boats of ten tons burthen, the act of Congress in this way itself virtually defines what is meant by the term navigable for that purpose.

There may be many places, also, where the tide ebbs and flows, which are not navigable. (Mayor of Lynn *v.* Turner, Cowp. 86.) Or, if navigable, are not public. (Ibid.; 5 Taunt. 86.) They may be not public, though the tide ebbs and flows, if made navigable by expense of the owners, and the use by them has been exclusive. (Miles *v.* Rose, ibid. 705.)

But I shall not go into this inquiry, though an interesting one, it not being necessary, to dispose of the present motion. Some of the leading cases on it are, Hooker *v.* Cummins, 20 John. R. 98; The People *v.* Platt, 17 ibid. 195; 3 Caines, R. 319; 2 Conn. 481; 4 Burr. 2162; Davies' R. 149; Angell on Tide-waters, 63, 91; Rex *v.* Smith, 2 Doug. 441; The Steamboat Planter, 7 Pet. 343.

So, looking to foreigners and other purposes, the territorial limits of the United States extend a marine league from shore, a cannon-shot. (Vattel, B. 1, ch. 21; 4 Cranch, 234; 2 ibid. 187, 234;

Church *v.* Hubard, 1 Gall. 62; The Ann, 3 Wheat. 630; Act of 1798 and 1820; United States *v.* Kessler, 1 Baldw. C. C. 34, 35; Angell on Tide-waters, 12 Pref.)

Sometimes further it is said (1 Baldw. 35), to keep foreigners from fighting and smuggling. (The Apollo, 9 Wheat. 370; 5 ibid. 201; App. 123.)

But the details on this are not material to the present inquiries, and will not be pursued. The leading views on them may be seen in Bee's Adm. R. 206, 207; Jennings *v.* Carson's Ex'rs, 1 Pet. Adm. 29, note; 1 Azuni, 195; 8 Geo. I., ch. 12; 3 Hag. Adm. 289.

A provision making acts like those of the respondents a crime, and intrusting the trial of them to this Court, not being found in the act of Congress of 1789, in express words, nor the power being embraced in or under it, by any clear reference to any admiralty code of any age or people, as meant to be adopted by it, nor being likely to be meant as included, from its vagueness, and the exclusion of an offence like this within a county, from the English admiralty code since Richard II., and admiralty jurisdiction over offences generally not reaching a place like this in England, either in 1776 or 1789, it may next be asked, if this matter was acted on in admiralty in this country, while we were colonies, and has thus, by any implication connected with the act of 1789 and the constitution, become a crime?

It seems to be contended, and perhaps ought to be conceded, that if the admiralty code in England had been departed from here, by any voluntary law, or general and uniform usage in this or other matters freely adopted, so as to be likely to be well known and recognized, at the time the constitution was adopted, such modification might be supposed to be adopted by implication.

But such an usage on any point in any one of the thirteen Colonies, not recognized or acted on in the residue of the thirteen, could not be regarded as thus operating in the minds of the framers of the constitution.

This matter, however, has in all its ramifications been examined by me, so far as any means exist in relation to our colonial history, colonial reports, and colonial statutes, in the case in 5 How. 441.

And it will be only necessary to refer to these here, and to say that, in my opinion, notwithstanding the broadness of commissions, copied from old and obsolete forms, the doings under them prove clearly a very close conformity by the vice-admiralty courts in the British colonies to the admiralty jurisdiction and principles at home, except where in one or two instances altered by express acts of Parliament, to harass and oppress them. And, if the feelings prevalent here before the Revolution in respect to admiralty powers are evidence of what was meant in the constitution by "cases in admiralty," or in subsequent acts of Congress, no doubt can exist, that a restriction, rather than enlargement beyond the English practice, even as then existing, was desired, and the trial by jury meant to be more widely secured.

There is not a more striking illustration that Massachusetts refused to tolerate or approve any of the enlargements and encroachments of admiralty jurisdiction, which in some respects were forced on them while Colonies, by statutes at home, than the indignant remonstrances she so often put forth on the subject, emanating from some of her most intelligent patriots. (See one specimen before given.)

This view would not prevent Congress, under its power to regulate commerce, and allowing a trial by jury if desired, expressly to invest the District Court, or this Court, with jurisdiction over both torts and crimes within the body of a county on tide-waters, as it has already invested it with jurisdiction in cases of seizures for breaches of the laws of trade and revenue. But this was never possessed in England by the court of admiralty. It belonged there to the Exchequer, and was made an appurtenant here to the admiralty, both before and since the Revolution; because no court of exchequer existed here, and not because it ever was or ever can be in its nature an admiralty power, when the seizure is not only above the ocean, and above tide-water, but as far into the interior as a boat of ten tons' burthen can be floated. (See 5 How. 441.)

In a like manner, Congress, under that power to regulate commerce, has conferred on the District Court jurisdiction over maritime matters on the tideless lakes in our interior, but not as belonging to it by means of its admiralty jurisdiction; else this specific grant would have been unnecessary, the court before having cognizance of all civil cases in admiralty, and else the allowance given of a trial by jury would not have been in symmetry.

And how much better it is that new powers should thus be conferred, and doubtful ones invested in it with certainty, than to force them within it by construction only of grants not specifically embracing them, will be strikingly manifest, when, if thus expressly conferred, the inestimable trial by jury exists, and the principles of evidence applied may generally be those of the common law; while in the other grant no trial by jury is allowed,—certainly none in civil cases,—and they are tried by a different code of law and evidence from what we and our fathers have been much accustomed.

Many things look now as if belonging to the admiralty jurisdiction, which do not in modern times belong to it here or in England.

Such are lighthouses.

But they were granted to the Trinity House, and placed in their charge, as early as Henry VIII. (Bac. Abr. "Court of Admiralty.")

So buoys and beacons, once in charge of the admiralty (1 Siderfin, 158), have not been of late, except by a patent or grant from Parliament. And whoever dreamed here that the expenditure of the vast sums which have been appropriated in this country for the improvements of rivers and harbors, and the removal of snags, and sawyers, and sand-bars, belonged to the care of the District Courts, as courts of admiralty, in all civil cases?

On the contrary, here and in England these have ever been matters of special legislation and general supervision, entirely under other legislative powers. (McCulloch's Dict. "Buoys and Beacons.")

Though lighthouses and beacons have at times, under a special patent, been erected by the admiralty, the duties collected on them and the charge of them belonged to the Trinity House, long before the Revolution. (See 8th Elizabeth; 4 Instit. 149; Com. Dig. Navigation, H. Beacon and T. 3.)

The powers exercised here by the General Government over commerce, and matters and waters connected with it, are not all of admiralty origin and character, but much wider.

So, when Congress erects lighthouses, and builds breakwaters and a navy, and goes far beyond the admiralty in England at the Revolution, in removing snags and sand-bars, and making moles and piers, and marine hospitals. (Bac. Abr. "Court of Admiralty, B.") Many of the offences connected with these are new, and not of admiralty origin, and are within capes and headlands, and some within the body of counties, and on the land. In truth, with the power to regulate commerce, and carry on our foreign relations, and build forts, and navy-yards, and lighthouses, maintain a navy, &c. &c., a code of criminal law has grown up connected with these powers, and for their protection, which belongs to the whole matter, and not to admiralty alone. (See *post.*)

What they then were in England, and since have been till 1776 or 1789, are the guides as to what must now be understood as the extent of the criminal jurisdiction meant to be allowed to Congress to confer on the courts of the United States, as mere admiralty powers, or as being, *per se*, admiralty powers. The learning and labor of the counsel for the government, as to earlier periods, have been interesting, and shed much light on the antiquity of different kinds of admiralty power. But the practices in such remote ages, and under governments so different from that of England, cannot control the present case, under the laws as existing when the constitution was adopted, with the modifications and additions since made by acts of Congress.

And, as the growth of the country is developed, and national exigencies arise, the further exercise of its just powers will often be called for, entirely independent of any grants of admiralty jurisdiction, and leaving more and more doubtful what parts, if any, as to crimes, were ever meant to rest merely on those grants. (Stanly *v.* The Bank of North America, 4 Dall. 10, note.)

It is by no means certain, if the grant of admiralty jurisdiction had been omitted entirely in the constitution, that the other grants, to regulate commerce, maintain a navy, declare war, and collect a revenue from imposts, and establish courts, &c. &c., would not have enabled it to confer on those courts all the criminal jurisdiction, if not the civil, which they now possess, connected with maritime affairs.

The admiralty code of criminal law was also one in some respects too bloody for us and this age; as, for example, death to remove a buoy. (Curtis' Adm. 544; Jenkins' Works.)

As the ground has been taken, I shall next proceed to inquire briefly if the acts complained of in this indictment are made punishable by the force of any other act of Congress than that of 1789, either directly or by construction. In examining any other acts, we are met not only by the presumption that Congress would not mean to do indirectly or circuitously what ample reasons showed they would be inclined to do directly, and which they did not do directly, but by the impropriety of holding that to be an offence, and prosecuting it as such, which is so only by construction, or inference, or implication.

The act chiefly relied on, as being violated indirectly by this obstruction, and rendering it illegal, is that making New Bedford a port of entry. (See it in 1 Stat. at Large, 629.) It is made to "include all the waters and shores within the towns of New Bedford, Dartmouth," &c.

This bridge is within the limits of that port, as a "port" would usually be defined, i. e., the waters within the gate, or door, or outlet towards the sea.

This port is allowed by Congress to be a place for shipping produce to foreign countries or other domestic ports, and for introducing merchandise from abroad for home consumption. It is an encroachment on it to place bridges across it without draws sufficiently wide for all vessels to pass and repass, or to throw stone and gravel into its bed so as to make parts of the channel too shoal for navigation.

It is a very important port, possessing over one hundred thousand tons of shipping,— equal in that respect to any in England or America except four in each of them, and superior to any whatever in France. Its freedom from improper obstructions ought, therefore, to be carefully watched over and preserved.

And it is contended, that any encroachment on it, or violation of the rights existing when it was made a port of entry, ought to be considered a crime or misdemeanor.

But, supposing that it should be, can it be considered as made a crime or offence by this act of Congress? This act merely allows exports and imports there, but does not punish any obstruction in its waters. In England, many important and exclusive privileges have been conferred on certain ports, as the Cinque ports, and the ports of London and Hull.

But here no preference can, by the constitution, be given to one port over another (Art. 1, § 9), and whatever power properly belongs to Congress, in regulating commerce and establishing ports of entry and delivery, to protect them by penalties from encroachments and obstructions by wharves, buildings and bridges, it is in this case sufficient to say that Congress has not yet exercised that power. But, if wharves or bridges are so made as to obstruct a port, or any navigable waters, they are undoubtedly illegal under the laws of Massachusetts, unless authorized by the city, or State, or General Government, which may possess authority over this matter.

Whether illegal, so as to constitute a crime, or only a civil wrong, must depend on the laws of the government possessing jurisdiction over the place and subject. If made a crime by that government, they may be criminally prosecuted, as the laws shall specify, in those courts having jurisdiction over the place and subject.

The State of Massachusetts possesses the jurisdiction over this place for many purposes, though navigable water, as before shown; and can and would punish an obstruction as a nuisance in a highway, if she had not herself authorized it.

Such bridges and wharves, when built out of the territory over which Congress exercises exclusive legislation, such as the District of Columbia, are erected by State authority, and regulated entirely by State laws, or are constructed at individual pleasure and responsibility. They are, as here, within the limits of the State, and one of its counties; and though, in regulating commerce, Congress might probably make laws which would render penal any obstructions to foreign navigation, whether placed there with or without State permission, yet, till Congress do this, can such an obstruction be said to violate this act of Congress, merely creating the port of New Bedford into a port of entry? Much more, can it be a crime under that act?

The officers of such a port are usually State officers,—its warden, its health officers, its harbor-masters. The General Government usually places no person there except for purposes of revenue, such as the collector and his subordinates. If there be lighthouses or forts near, then there are other officers, in connection with them, rather than the port as a port.

In ancient times, when some harbors or ports were secured by chains, and the chain-master, or master of the key, opened it for vessels to pass, and collected revenue or tolls, he may have had authority to look into and prosecute such matters; and in France he was required to report offences of this kind to the admiralty. (French Laws, B. 4, Title 2. See Laws, 254—257, 340.) Though in some instances he was appointed probably by the city authorities, rather than by the central government or the admiralty. Such is the case here, usually, as before remarked, as to wardens of ports, harbor-masters, &c. Those who commanded the forts at the entrance, as well as the navy for defending the port, were public officers of the government, but they never had, and cannot here have, any concern with the domestic or civil police, and erection of bridges and wharves within the harbor.

It is difficult, then, to hold, from the express words of the act creating the port of New Bedford to be a port of entry, or by implication from analogies and usages elsewhere, that the punishment of obstructions, like this bridge, belongs to the General Government or any of its officers.

On the contrary, it belongs usually to the local authorities; and, though Congress may be authorized under the constitution to regulate and punish them, yet, till done by specific laws for that purpose, its courts cannot regard such acts as an offence against the United States, however they may be in some cases crimes and private injuries under the State or local laws.

The free ingress and egress of our people to all ports of entry in the Union is necessary; and the obstructing navigation in one of them, and especially one so important as New Bedford, is not to be countenanced when done by individuals without authority, and could effectually be punished as nuisance in the State courts. Nor can it be shut up in part, or entirely, as the port of Boston was by the Boston Port Bill before the Revolution, without working inequality and partiality, whether it be done by a license or order from the State, or the United States, and by force of a law, or by rocks, wood, or chains across its mouth, by individual and private speculation.

And, if a wrong or injustice has been perpetrated, under color of law, and cannot be prosecuted in the State courts while that law remains in full force, and cannot be redressed as a crime in the United States' courts, till some further legislation occurs defining or declaring it to be a crime, and empowering them to try it, yet it is a misfortune which might soon be obviated by Congress, and one which now might, perhaps, as will soon be examined further, be relieved against in a civil remedy by damages to the person aggrieved specially by it, so as at an early day to correct the evil, provided this conduct delays, or interrupts, or injures the navigation of the country. (See *post.*)

But it is next contended, that if no jurisdiction over the matter is obtained by the act making this port a port of entry, it is conferred by force of the acts appointing custom-house officers there, and collecting revenue. (See 2d section, act of March 2, 1799, ch. 22, 1 Stat. at Large, 627.)

The like reasoning applies to this position as to that concerning the port as a port of entry, except that the officers to collect the revenue are officers of the General Government, and the revenue also belongs to that government.

All which they are authorized to do may, therefore, be connected with the federal power and federal supervision, and any obstruction to their rightful acts may be an offence punishable in the federal courts. Such is the course of some of the laws on this subject, and such have been the decisions where such specific laws have existed, but not without.

Here, however, no clause in any of them is pointed out which makes obstructions like these a violation of any revenue law.

It is true that the tendency of such obstructions may be to lessen the amount of business and revenue at New Bedford; but it will increase them probably at other ports, to which business may be thus diverted, and hence not injure the revenue of the country as a whole.

So it is argued that the "Force-Bill," as it has been called, conferred larger powers on custom-house officers to remove custom-houses when the collection of revenue at them was obstructed, and gave to this Court wider jurisdiction to punish them. But it was only where the obstructions were not to the navigation by stone, or gravel, or timber, but by the interference of the State authorities, or of unauthorized individuals, to prevent the entry of foreign merchandise, and the payment of duties thereon. That law was passed March 2d, 1833. (4 Stat. at Large, 999.) It was passed entirely *diverso intuitu*, as all know who were actors in those scenes, and never contemplated the punishment of obstructions like these.

It was against "unlawful obstructions, combinations or assemblages of persons" (section 1). The additional jurisdiction there given to the Circuit Court was to try in civil cases persons guilty of such assemblages, and injuries by them (section 2), and to try offences against the revenue laws, where jurisdiction has not been already conferred. This was all.

The act authorizing coasting licenses, and for regulating the same, is also supposed to be violated by this obstruction. (See the act of February 18, 1793, 1 Stat. at Large, 395, and March 2, 1819, 3 ibid. 493.)

It is certain that this act was meant to empower such vessels to go and trade in all the navigable waters of the United States, and on its coasts, and that any prevention of this would violate the spirit of those acts. (9 Wheat. 1.)

It speaks of the going on "sea-coasts" and "navigable rivers." Hence, in the case of Gibbons *v.* Ogden (9 Wheat. 1), it was held that a law of New York, excluding steamboats with such licenses from navigating the Hudson river, or giving an exclusive right to certain boats to do it, was deemed unconstitutional and void. And, for aught I see, an obstruction placed in navigable waters by an individual, without constitutional authority, would violate such license, and be a ground for civil redress in damages.

It disturbs navigation; and navigation is one branch of commerce, and a law of Congress covering it is thus violated. (See 9 Wheat. 1.)

It is, perhaps, this idea, in connection with the right which belongs to vessels to go to ports of entry and delivery unimpeded and undelayed, that the counsel in The People *v.* Saratoga & Rensellaer Railroad Co. (15 Wend. 113, 121) conceded that a bridge, though with a draw, if below a port of entry, was unconstitutional.

If so at all, it must be because it restricts and curtails, in some degree, the full privileges of licensed and registered vessels to egress and ingress, as to all parts of such ports, in the pursuit of their lawful business. It also violates the rights before alluded to, by some of our treaties, given to foreigners to visit such ports, and these considerations may confer a power on the General Government to remove obstructions below such ports that do not exist above. (See the Maysville Road Veto.) I do not understand the Court, in 15 Wendell, to hold that any bridge at or above a port of entry like New Bedford, with a draw in it, is unconstitutional, if only somewhat incommoding navigation, but only when it stops or cuts off some of it entirely. (P. 132; New York *v.* Miln, 11 Pet. 102.)

But the same difficulty exists here as in the other acts of Congress, in regarding the obstruction as a crime against the United States, without some clause in the constitution or in an act of Congress declaring it to be one.

The acts complained of in the indictment being then authorized by the State, and hence not a crime under its laws,—the States having power to authorize them till conflicting with some provision in the constitution, or a treaty, or an act of Congress,—and there being no such conflict with any, that makes these acts a crime, or confers power on this Court to punish it, the conclusion follows, that we have no jurisdiction to sustain the indictment.

I am strengthened in this conclusion, till Congress legislate further, by the consideration that even now any individual, suffering by this obstruction in his rights to free navigation, is not probably without redress.

The power, then, in the State of Massachusetts, to incorporate the New Bedford bridge with a draw to allow vessels to pass, existed in 1795; and this exercise of it violates no prohibition in the federal constitution, no treaty, and no act of Congress enforcing the granted powers under it to the General Government, unless it be that giving coasting licenses.

It violates that, perhaps, only as to vessels which, from their size, cannot pass through the draw, or as high up the harbor, from deposits, as they used to; and the owners of such, when actually obstructed and delayed by means of this bridge, might probably have redress in damages, or by way of injunction against it in chancery. (Spooner *v.* McConnell, 1 McLean, 338; The People *v.* Saratoga & Rensellaer Railroad Co. 15 Wend. 113, and p. 135.)

But even they could not prosecute the bridge as for a crime, in the federal courts, when no clause in the federal constitution or the acts of Congress declares such an obstruction to be a crime.

No prosecution for a crime can now be sustained anywhere, even in the State courts, for reasons already given, unless the act of incorporation to the defendants should be held void by those courts, as trenching on the powers of the General Government, or on the rights of coasters under acts of Congress. How that might be, they must decide for themselves when appealed to.

Civil redress, however, in the cases before described, seems obtainable in the courts both of the States and United States, notwithstanding the decision in 2 Pet. 253, as there it does not appear that any port of entry existed above, and here it does; and that the stoppage of some navigation to some parts of it is as entire as the State prohibition in Gibbons *v.* Ogden, 9 Wheat. 1, 221.

We may say, with Chief-justice Hall, when we agree that one hath a right, "If so, then they must have some remedy to come at it," in The King *v.* Hornby, 5 Mad. 87; 1 D. & E. 512; 2 Ld. R. 953; *ubi jus ibi remedium.* And the "judicial powers should be coëxtensive with the legislation, so far at least as they are to be enforced by judicial proceedings." (Kendall *v.* United States, 12 Pet. 527.) But the question of a right is first to be settled, and then where the remedy is to be sought. At law; or in equity; before courts martial; or in admiralty; or before the Legislature; and in State courts and Legislatures, or in the United States?

Though there is then no part of the constitution, or treaties, or acts of Congress, appearing on their face to make such an obstruction a crime, there is no necessity to give a forced construction to bring the case within those acts in order to punish it, there being full redress, without doing this, to such individuals as specially suffer by it.

We have already shown that, in the absence of legislation by Congress, making acts crimes, which may be within some of the constitutional grants of power to Congress, such as the regulation of commerce and cases in admiralty, the States possess concurrent or subordinate authority over such matters, till the paramount action by Congress takes place, if it choose to make the acts crimes; but, if not, then to give civil redress, if the acts be contrary to its own laws, or those of the United States.

The establishment of courts of the United States did not in many cases divest the State courts of any jurisdiction before exercised. It would seldom do it, unless on matters vested exclusively in the General Government as crimes against it, or in its jurisdiction, and forbidden to the States. (See Federalist, No. 82.)

And it is every day's practice for a citizen, though able to sue in the federal courts, to prosecute his rights in the State courts. For some acts on navigable waters, redress may be had in either. (4 Wash. C. C. 383.)

Congress, in the act of February, 1838, granting admiralty jurisdiction over the lakes, specially reserved all concurrent rights in State courts and at common law. (See before.)

In Alabama, their Supreme Court has entertained a libel against a steamboat for wages. (9 Porter, 112, 181.)

Yet the better opinion seems to be, that when an exclusive power, like that in admiralty, is conferred on the courts of the United States, no concurrent remedy, except a common law one, exists in the State courts. (3 Story's Com. on Con. 534, note, and 553, note. See, also, 1 Kent, Com. 351 and 377, note; Rawle on Con. 202; The

American Ins. Company *v.* Canter, 1 Pet. 512, 546; 1 Wheat. 337; Gelston *v.* Hoyt, 3 ibid. 246, 312, 313; 2 Story, 465.)

I have added several cases connected with this question, without stopping to enter into the consideration of their bearing in detail.

If the act of incorporation in this case should be held void, as contrary to some acts of Congress, it is obvious, that then both the old civil and criminal remedies might exist in the State courts, for such an obstruction of navigable waters, but only a civil remedy in this Court, from the want of some law making the obstruction a crime against the United States, and punishable in this Court.

The objection against treating as a crime what has not been made so by any clause in the constitution or an act of Congress, does not apply to a civil suit.

For, by the 34th section of the judiciary act, private rights and civil remedies are to be governed by the laws of the States, if none exist of the United States, even when tried in the federal courts, in cases where the latter have jurisdiction over the question and the parties. (See before.)

And though that could not be deemed a private wrong or civil injury, any more than a crime, which a State law authorized, in conformity to its constitution and that of the United States, yet it might be considered criminal under the State laws, as to highways and nuisances, if considering the act of incorporation under which it was done as unconstitutional, it being then in conflict with some power or law of Congress; and might be open to a civil action in the federal courts, as being illegal both under such State laws as are valid, and also by the laws of the United States.

In the course of the argument, it has been asked, if a State can with impunity levy and collect duties on tonnage and imports, or forbid entries of vessels into a port?

The reply is now obvious, that it cannot; and any such act by a State, conflicting with any rights under existing acts of Congress, would be actionable, and civil redress be had in this Court, and civil, if not criminal, in the State courts. Such virtually was the case of Gibbons *v.* Ogden. States may continue to use old and concurrent powers on these matters till Congress legislate on them, when the States must yield. (McCulloch *v.* The State of Maryland, 4 Wheat. 316; 14 Pet. 535; Commissioners of Erie *v.* Dobbins, 16 ibid. 435.)

There is little doubt that laws enough now exist to protect in this Court, by appropriate civil suits, all the rights and interests of the United States in any lands within them, or any personal property, or any easements on land or water, or any franchises.

So they can try the rights of others in these, where the parties reside, so as to give us jurisdiction in that respect. Full civil jurisdiction to that extent is conferred by the 34th section of the judiciary act, before quoted.

On the civil remedies and rights of this character, in such cases, in behalf of the United States, this Court has recently given its views at length, in the United States *v.* Ames, *ante*, p. 76.

But no law or section confers on this Court all jurisdiction in such cases to punish acts considered as crimes by the admiralty, or maritime laws, or by common law; nor is there any such section or act, that makes an obstruction in navigable waters a nuisance, or other crime, and gives jurisdiction over it to this Court.

The 34th section of the judiciary act has been thought by some to be broad enough to give relief here. It is: "That the laws of the several States, except where the constitution, treaties, or statutes of the United States, shall otherwise require or provide, shall be regarded as rules of decision in trials at common law, in the courts of the United States, in cases where they apply."

It might be inferred by some, from the face of this, that we could get from the State laws some common law jurisdiction and principles, if not statute law, to give us authority to punish in this case. (Duponceau on Jur. 43, 44.)

But there are several objections to that view. We must first obtain jurisdiction by the constitution, or acts of Congress, over a crime or civil suit, before we can apply in the trial the laws, statute or common, of a State. (The Orleans *v.* Phœbus, 11 Pet. 175; The Planter, 7 ibid. 324, 337.) And that jurisdiction we have not yet got, as yet ascertained, over this as a crime.

In the next place, after getting jurisdiction, the application of the State laws to the trial of the case is only where it is a civil and not a criminal case. (2 Burr's Trial, p. 180, App.) Otherwise the court might entertain jurisdiction over most of the crimes in most of the States in the Union. (1 Kent, Com. 398.)

Cases in Chancery are in doubt also in this respect, whether the State laws can be applied in equity trials by this Court, as they and the practice in them rest on general principles of the civil law and usage in England, applicable here, and are not "trials at common law." (See Rhode Island *v.* Massachusetts, 12 Pet. 657, 697.)

And, finally, if the State laws, after we got jurisdiction, were to govern in the trial, they would prevent our punishment of this act complained of, though open to be done usually. For here it has been authorized by the State, in incorporating the respondents, and allowing them to erect this bridge, and must be conformed to, unless the measures of the State, and of the respondents under them, are void, for repugnancy to some act of Congress.

Under these doubts as to the validity of the various grounds urged in support of this indictment, I feel compelled to dismiss it. In all questionable cases, in courts like this, of limited jurisdiction, instead of leaving so much to construction by courts, and leaving so many uncertainties and conflicts, both in civil and criminal cases in admiralty, it seems to me wise for Congress to legislate freely, as difficulties may appear, regulating the future, and removing that vagueness as to the law which is so great a curse to the community.

As the country increases in wealth and population, and the interior commerce and travel may outgrow its foreign and preponderate in the State Legislatures, and lead to bridges for turnpikes, or viaducts for railroads, and aqueducts for canals, obstructing seriously the navigation of our great rivers and arms of the sea, and, as in this case, not requiring draws suitable to the dimensions and passage of modern steam vessels, it may become necessary for Congress to exercise more of its powers to regulate commerce.

It may be proper to protect the foreign trade, and that between State and State, by water, against inroads upon its freedom by those looking more to land travel and land freights.

And, though obstructions in navigable waters, by State authority or without, may injure some of the towns and some of the business of that State more than the business of other portions of the Union, or of alien friends trading here, yet other portions and other business of the State may reap more than a proportional benefit, and hence, as a State measure, it may, on the whole, be useful.

But, when looking at its influence on other parts of the Union and their citizens, who trade thither only by water, and treating it, as must be done under the government of the Union, as a national matter, and its influence as on the whole nation, it may be an unmitigated and uncompensated evil to many other States, and, in respect to some alien friends under treaties, be a measure wholly unjustifiable. In such case, on looking to such events, and in the rapid multiplication of such bridges and obstructions, it may become necessary for Congress to wake up more of its dormant powers to regulate commerce, and provide relief and redress, criminal and civil, in all cases of this kind clearly within its authority, and clearly requiring punishment or redress.

I should be one of the last to desire to see such legislation take place prematurely or hastily, or at first with severity, as the subject is one possessing much delicacy, and many ramifications of deep interest.

But it is more and more exciting public attention; and an era is approaching, if not come, when the general powers of the central government for the whole, on matters connected with the interests of the whole, may be called for to protect private rights and remote privileges, and overcome local combinations of wealth and influence, seeking their own profit, rather than looking to national duties and rights in respect to others; and, likewise, to correct errors of State Legislatures in granting unlimited powers as to time to keep up a bridge over a navigable river, which by a change of business may have become a great public evil; or limited and unchangeable powers as to time, and the width of a draw for vessels to pass, which last, by an unexpected change in the size of vessels, has become useless, and a total obstruction to that class of ships; or powers, supposed not injurious to the river below, or at the bridge for navigation, but which have unexpectedly been followed by accumulations of sand and mud, obstructing most seriously and permanently the whole commerce of a large river.

In some cases, the legislation of Congress might not require the bridge itself to be removed, but only draws widened, so as not to damage the commerce between States or abroad, if the States themselves cannot and will not correct them by legislation or otherwise. In some cases it might require the obstructions collected in deposits of stone, gravel or mud, to be removed; and in others, the whole bridge to give way for a ferry, if the injury to navigation was great, and could in no other mode be obviated.

As the States have exercised this power of erecting bridges across navigable streams over half a century, and in numerous cases over navigable waters, where the tide ebbs and flows, in Maine, New Hampshire, Connecticut, New York, Pennsylvania, Delaware, &c., and Congress have followed their example in the District of Columbia, any new and restrictive legislation by the General Government would be unjust, if not suited to the exigencies of the case, and, of course, go no further than is necessary to discharge its duties in relation to the powers confided to it for the benefit of the States and the people as a whole. Its true attitude is one not seeking collision, or being punctilious as to trifles, nor acting with harshness, where a fair exercise of ancient powers and usages has been indulged in, and where, by a double government, and some concurrent powers over like subjects, some difficulties are unavoidable, and are to be met always in a charitable, conciliatory and compromising spirit.

It must act only in cases worthy the government of the whole Union, and in a manner becoming the government of the whole Union, *dignus vindice nodus.*

After such legislation, there would need be no grounds of jealousy or distrust as to its effect; as the laws will be made by our own delegates in the General Government, under our own constitution, the cases tried, as in the States, by juries, rather than without, and by our own jurors, before our own judges, under our own ameliorated codes of law, and the punishments be as mild, and suited to modern notions of civilization in the States.

But, in doing this, it would not be enough, as before suggested, for Congress to vest jurisdiction in this Court in all cases of mere admiralty and maritime crimes, even if enumerating and defining them when misdemeanors as well as felonies, because the power of Congress over commerce is much broader, as to both territory and subjects, than what belongs to admiralty courts as such.

It is unrestricted as to commerce between the States as well as abroad, and is increased by the powers to maintain a navy, and defend the country by forts, and improve harbors, and make breakwaters and hospitals, and collect revenue on imports. Hence, it can extend to numerous cases which in England were under the jurisdiction of other courts than the admiralty, and can well be intrusted to the Circuit Court, as are most of its other powers, not as admiralty ones, except appeals from the district tribunals.

Nor will it be necessary, in any of these cases, to make the jurisdiction exclusive of the State courts, except where the power that is executed by it is exclusive in its nature.

In all other cases, the rights, and remedies, and duties and liabilities, of our people, can be taken care of in the State courts, except where the laws of the latter may conflict with those of Congress on the same subject.*

---

## ON STATE RIGHT TO CONDEMN A FRANCHISE.†

In the decisions of this Court on constitutional questions, it has happened frequently that, though its members were united in the judgment, great differences existed among them in the reasons for it, or in the limitations on some of the principles involved. Hence it has been customary in such cases to express their views separately. I conform to that usage in this case the more readily, as it is one of the first impression before this tribunal, very important in its consequences, as a great landmark for the States as well as the General Government, and, from shades of difference and even conflicts in opinion, will be open to some misconstruction.

I take the liberty to say, then, as to the cardinal principle involved in this case, that, in my opinion, all the property in a State is derived from, or protected by, its government, and hence is held subject to its wants in taxation, and to certain important public uses, both in war

* This opinion was mostly prepared before the decision in the case of Waring *v.* Clarke (5 How. 441), although it was not delivered until after.

† Opinion in the case of the West River Bridge Co. *v.* Dix et al. January Term S. C. U. S., 1848.

and peace. (Vattel, B. 1, ch. 20, § 244; 2 Kent, Com. 270; 37 Am. Jurist, 121; 1 Bl. Com. 139; 3 Wils. 303; 3 Story on Const. 661; 3 Dallas, 95.) Some ground this public right on sovereignty. (2 Kent, Com. 339; Grotius, B. 1, ch. 1, § 6.) Some, on necessity. (2 Johns. Ch. 162; 11 Wend. 51; 14 Wend. 51; 1 Rice, 383; Vanhorne's Lessee *v.* Dorrance, 2 Dallas, 310; Dyer *v.* Tuscaloosa Bridge, 2 Porter, 303; Harding *v.* Goodlett, 3 Yerger, 53.) Some, on implied compact. (Raleigh & Gaston Railroad Co. *v.* Davis, 2 Dev. & Bat. 456; 2 Bay, 36, in S. Car.; 3 Yerger, 53.) Where a charter is granted after laws exist to condemn property when needed for public purposes, others might well rest such a right on the hypothesis that such laws are virtually a part and condition of the grant itself, as much as if inscribed in it, *totidem verbis.* (Towne *v.* Smith, 1 Woodbury & Minot, 134; 2 Howard, 608, 617; 1 Howard, 311; 3 Story on Const. §§ 1377, 1378, *quære.*)

But, however derived, this eminent domain exists in all governments, and is distinguished from the public domain, as that consists of public lands, buildings, &c., owned in trust exclusively and entirely by the government (3 Kent, Com. 339; Memphis *v.* Overton, 3 Yerger, 389), while this consists only in the right to use the property of others, when needed, for certain public purposes. Without now going further into the reasons or extent of it, and under whatever name it is most appropriately described, I concur in the views of the Court, that it still remains in each State of the Union in a case like the present, having never been granted to the General Government, so far as respects the public highways of a State; and that it extends to the taking for public use for a road any property in the State, suitable and necessary for it. (Tuckahoe Canal case, 11 Leigh, 75; 11 Peters, 560; 20 Johns. 724; 3 Paige, Ch. 45; 7 Pick. 459.) But whether it could be taken without compensation, where no provision exists like that in the fifth amendment of the constitution of the United States, or that in the Vermont constitution, somewhat similar, is a more difficult question, and on which some have doubted. (4 D. & E. 794; 1 Rice, 383; 3 Leigh, 337.) I do not mean to express any opinion on this, as it is not called for by the facts of this case. But compensation from the public in such cases prevails generally in modern times, and certainly seems to equalize better the burden. (2 Dallas, 310; Pisc. Bridge *v.* Old Bridge, 7 N. Hamp. 63; 4 D. & E. 794; 1 Nott & McCord, 387; Stokes et al. *v.* Sup. Ass. Co., 3 Leigh, 337; 11 Leigh, 76; Hartford Bridge, 17 Conn. 91; Vattel, B. 1, ch. 20, § 244; 3 Paige, Ch. 45; 2 Dev. & Bat. 451; 2 Kent, Com. 339, note; Lex. & Oh. Railroad case, 8 Dana, 289.)

Nor shall I stop to discuss whether it is on this principle of the eminent domain alone that private property has always been taken for highways in England, on making compensation, so as to be a precedent for us. This was done there formerly, not as here, but by a writ *ad quod damnum*, and it was for ages issued before the grant of any new franchise by the king, whether a road, ferry, or market; and the inquiry related to the damage by it, whether to the public or individuals. (Fitz. N. B. 221; 3 Bac. Abr., *Highways*, A.)

Nor were alterations in roads, or even the widening or discontinuing of them, allowed without it. (Thomas *v.* Sorrel, Vaughan, 314, 348, 349; Cooke, ch. 267; 6 Barn. & Ald. 566.)

But in modern times Parliament, by various laws, have authorized all these, after inquiry, and compensation awarded by certain magistrates. (1 Burr. 263; Camp. 648; Cro. Car. 266, 267; 5 Taunt. 634; Domat, B. 1, t. 8, § 2; 7 Adol. & Ellis, 124.)

And thus, notwithstanding the theoretical omnipotence of Parliament, private rights and contracts have been in these particulars, about compensation and necessity for public use, as much respected in England as here.

So as to railroad companies, as well as turnpikes, under public trustees, and as to common highways; the former are often authorized there to erect bridges, and carry their roads over turnpikes and other highways; but it is on certain conditions, keeping them passable in that place or near, and on making compensation. (Kemp *v.* L. & B. Railway Co., 1 Railway Cases, 505, and Attorney-General *v.* The L. & S. Railroad, 1 ibid. 302, 224; 2 ibid. 711; 1 Gale & D. 324; 2 ibid. 1; 4 Jurist, 966; 5 ibid. 652; 9 Dowling, P. C. 563; 7 Adol. & Ellis, 124; 3 Maule & Selw. 526; 11 Leigh, 42.)

But I freely confess that no case has been found there by me exactly in point for this, such as the taking of the road or bridge of one corporation for another, or of taking for the public a franchise of individuals connected with them. Though, at the same time, I have discovered no prohibition of it, either on principle or precedent, if making compensation and following the mode prescribed by statute.

The peculiarity in the present case consists in the facts, that a part of the property taken belonged to a corporation of the State, and not to an individual, and a part was the franchise itself of the act of incorporation.

I concur in the views, that a corporation created to build a bridge like that of the plaintiffs in error is itself, in one sense, a franchise. (2 Bl. Com. 37; Bank of Augusta *v.* Earle, 13 Peters, 596; 4 Wheat. 657; 7 Pick. 394; 11 Peters, 474, 454, 472, 490, 641, 645; 11 Leigh, 76; 3 Kent, Com. 459.) And, in another sense, that it possesses franchises incident to its existence and objects, such as powers to erect the bridge and to take tolls. (See same cases.)

I concur in the views, also, that such a franchise as the incorporation is a species of property. (7 N. Hamp. 66; Tuckahoe Canal Co. *v.* Tuckahoe & Camb. Railroad Co., 11 Leigh, 76.) It is a legal estate vested in the corporation. (4 Wheat. 700; 11 Peters, 560.) But it is often property distinct and independent of the other property in land, timber, goods, or choses in action, which a corporation, like a body not artificial, may own. (3 Bland, 449; 11 Leigh, 76.)

It is also property subject to be sold, sometimes even on execution (*Semb.*, 4 Mass. 495; 11 Peters, 434), and may be devised or inherited. (17 Conn. 60.) And while I accede to the principle urged by the counsel for the bridge, that the act of incorporation in this case was a contract, or in the nature of one, between the State and its members (1 Mylne & Craig, 162; 4 Peters, 514, 560; Lee *v.* Nailer, 2 You. & Coll. 618; King *v.* Pasmoor, 3 D. & E. 246; Woodward *v.* Dartmouth College, 4 Wheat. 628; 7 Cranch, 164; Terrett *v.* Taylor, 9 Cranch, 43, 52; 9 Wend. 351; 11 Peters, 257; Canal Co. *v.* Railroad, 4 Gill & Johns. 146; 3 Kent, Com. 459; Enfield Toll-bridge case, 17 Conn. 40; 1 Greenleaf, 79; 8 Wheat. 464; 10 Conn. 522; Peck, 269; 1 Alabama, 23; 2 Stewart, 30), I concur in the views of the Court, that this or other property of corporations may be taken for the purpose of a highway, under the right of eminent domain, and that the laws of Vermont authorizing it are not in that respect and to that extent violations of the obligation of any contract made by it with the corporation. (Bradshaw *v.* Rodgers, 20 Johns. 103, 742; The Trust. of Belf. Ac. *v.* Salmond, 2 Fairf. 113; Enfield Bridge case, 17 Conn. 40, 45, 61; 3 Paige, Ch. 45; Charles River Bridge *v.* Warren Bridge, 7 Pick. 394, 399; S. C., 11 Peters, 474; 1 Bland, 449; Bellona Co. case, 3 Bland, 449.)

Because there was no covenant or condition in the charter or contract, that the property owned by it should not be liable to be taken, like all other property in the State, for public uses in highways. (7 N. Hamp. 69; 4 Wheat. 196; Jackson *v.* Lamphire, 3 Peters, 289.)

Because, without such covenant, all their property, as property, must be liable to proper public uses, either by necessity, or the sovereignty of the State over it, or by implied agreement.

And because, on a like principle, taxes may be imposed on such property, as well as all other property, though coming by grant from the State, and may be done without violating the obligation of the contract, when there is no bonus paid or stipulation made in the charter not to tax it. This is well settled. (5 Barn. & Ald. 157; 2 Railway Cases, 17 arg. 23; 7 Cranch, 164; New Jersey *v.* Wilson, 4 Peters, 511; Providence Bank *v.* Billings, 11 Peters, 567, Shaw, C. J., in Charles River Bridge *v.* Warren Bridge; Gordon *v.* Appeal Tax Court, 3 Howard, 146; 12 Mass. 252; 4 Wheat. 699; 4 Gill & Johns. 132, 153; Williams *v.* Pritchard, 4 D. & E. 2.) The grantees are presumed to know all these legal incidents or liabilities, and they being implied in the grant or contract, their happening is no violation of it. (8 Peters, 281, 287; 11 Peters, 641, 644; 3 Paige, 72.)

Vattel says,—"The property of certain things is given up to the individuals only with this reserve." (B. 1, ch. 20, § 244.)

In England anciently, when titles of land became granted with immunities from numerous ancient services, it was still considered that such lands were subject by implication, under a certain *trinoda necessitas*, to the expenses of repair of bridges as well as forts, and of repelling invasion. (Tomlins, Dict., *Trinoda Necessitas*; 3 Bac. Abr., *Highways*, A.)

Even the right to a private way is sometimes implied in a grant, from necessity. (Cro. Jac. 189; 8 D. & E. 50; 4 Maule & Selw. 387; 1 Saund. 322, note.)

It is laid down, also, by Justice Story, that "a grant of a franchise is not in point of principle distinguishable from a grant of any other property." (Dartmouth College *v.* Woodward, 4 Wheat. 699, 701.)

I concur, therefore, in the further views, that the corporation as a franchise, and all its powers as franchises, both being property, may, for these and like reasons, in proper cases, be taken for public use for a highway. (Pierce *v.* Somersworth, 10 N. Hamp. 370; 11 N. Hamp. 20; Piscat. Bridge *v.* N. Hamp. Bridge, 7 N. Hamp. 35, 66; 8 N. Hamp. 398, 143; 11 Peters, 645; Story, J., in Warren Bridge *v.* Charles River Bridge; 2 Kent, Comm. 340, note; 2 Peters, 658; 5 Paige, Ch. 146; 1 Rice, 383; 2 Porter, 296; 7 Adol. & Ellis, 124; 3 Yerger, 41; 2 Fairf. 222; 23 Pick. 360; J. Bonaparte *v.* C. Railroad, Baldw. C. C. 205; Tuckahoe Canal Co. *v.* The T. & J. River Railroad Co., 11 Leigh, 42; Enfield Bridge Co. *v.* Hartford & New Haven Railroad, 17 Conn. 40; Armington *v.* Barnet, 15 Vermont, 745, and 16 Vermont, 446, this case; 3 Cowen, 733, 754; 11 Wendell, 590; Lex. & Oh. Railroad case, 8 Dana, 289; 18 Wend. 14.)

It must be confessed that some surprise has been felt to find this doctrine so widely sustained, and in so many of the States, and yet no exact precedent existing in England.

But, in relation to it here, I am constrained, in some respects, to differ from others, and, as at present advised, agree to the last proposition, concerning the taking of the franchise itself of a corporation, only when the further exercise of the franchise as a corporation is inconsistent or incompatible with the highway to be laid out.

It is only under this limitation as to the franchise itself that there seems to be any of the necessity to take it which, it will be seen in the positions heretofore and hereafter explained, should exist. Nor do I agree to it with that limitation, without another,—that it must be in cases where a clear intent is manifested in the laws that one corporation and its uses shall yield to another, or another public use, under the supposed superiority of the latter and the necessity of the case. (4 Gill & Johns. 108, 150; Barbour *v.* Andover, 8 N. Hamp. 398.)

Within these limitations, however, the acts of incorporation and all corporate franchises appear to me to possess no more immunity from reasonable public demands for roads and taxes than the soil and freehold of individuals.

The land may come by grant or patent from the State, as well as the corporation, and both the grant and corporation may be contracts. But they are contracts giving rights of property, held, and of course understood to be held, subject to those necessary burdens and services and easements to which all other property is liable. And it is neither inconsistent with the grant of them, nor a violation of the contract contained in them, to impose those burdens and easements, unless an express agreement has been made to the contrary by the State in the act of incorporation or grant, as is sometimes done in respect to taxation. But where the corporation as a franchise, or its powers as franchises, can still be exercised usefully or profitably, and the highway be laid out as authorized, I see no reason why these franchises should then be condemned or taken. The property owned by a banking or manufacturing corporation may, for instance, be condemned for highways, necessarily, where situated on a great line of travel; but why should their franchises be, if their continued existence and use may be feasible and profitable, and one not inconsistent with the taking and employment of their other property for a public highway?

In this instance, however, as a fact, the franchise was established, and seems to be useful, only in one locality. The continuance of it elsewhere than at this spot would be of no benefit to individual members or the public. If the bridge itself and land of the corporation at that place were taken, it was better for the latter that the franchise should be taken with them, if enhancing the damages any; because, unlike a bank or manufacturing company, the corporation could not do business to advantage elsewhere, even within the limited four miles, as there was no road elsewhere within their grant. The law of Vermont, too, was clear, that the toll-bridge might be made to give way for a free highway. It is, therefore, only under the particular circumstances and nature of this case, that, in my apprehension, the taking of the franchise itself was not a violation of the contract. For, under different circumstances, if a franchise be taken and condemned for a highway, when not connected locally with other property wanted, when it can be exercised on ordinary principles elsewhere, when not in some respects incident to, or tied up with, the particular property and place needed, I am not now prepared to uphold it. I am even disposed to go further, and say, that if any property of any kind is not so situated as to be either in the direct path for a public highway, or be really needed to build it, the inclination of my mind is, that it cannot be taken against the consent of the owner. Because, though the right of eminent domain exists in some cases, it does not exist in all, nor as to all property, but probably as to such property only as, from its locality and fitness, is necessary to the public use. (*Semb.*, 4 Mylne & Craig, 116; Webb *v.* Manch. & Leeds Railway Co., 1 Railway Cases, 576.)

It may be such, not only for the bed of the road, but perhaps for materials in gravel, stone, and timber, to build it with. Yet even then it must be necessary and appropriate as incidents. (2 Dev. & Bat. 462; 13 East, 200.)

And also, for aught I now see, circumstances must, from its locality and the public wants, raise an urgent necessity for it. "The public necessities" are spoken of usually as the fit occasion to exercise the power, if it be not derived from them in a great degree, and the reason of the case is confined to them. (See cases before.)

The ancient *trinoda necessitas* extended to nothing beyond such necessity.

Indeed, without further examination, I fear that even these limitations may not be found sufficient in some kinds of public highways,— such as railroads, for instance. And I must hear more in support of this last position before acquiescing in their right to take, *in invitum*, all the materials necessary to build such roads,—as the timbers on which their rails are laid, or the iron for the rails themselves.

Nor do I agree that, in all cases of a public use, property which is suitable or appropriate can be condemned. The public use here is for a road, and the reasoning and cases are confined chiefly to bridges and roads, and the incidents to war. But the doctrine, that this right of eminent domain exists for every kind of public use, or for such a use when merely convenient, though not necessary, does not seem to me by any means clearly maintainable. It is too broad, too open to abuse. Where the public use is one general and pressing, like that often in war for sites of batteries, or for provisions, little doubt would exist as to the right. *Salus populi suprema est lex.* So as to a road, if really demanded in particular forms and places to accommodate a growing and changing community, and to keep up with the wants and improvements of the age,—such as its pressing demands for easier social intercourse, quicker political communication, or better internal trade,—and advancing with the public necessities from blazed trees to bridle-paths, and thence to wheel-roads, turnpikes, and railroads.

But when we go to other public uses, not so urgent, not connected with precise localities, not difficult to be provided for without this power of eminent domain, and in places where it would be only convenient, but not necessary, I entertain strong doubts of its applicability. Who ever heard of laws to condemn private property, for public use, for a marine hospital or state-prison?

So a custom-house is a public use for the General Government, and a court-house or jail for a State. But it would be difficult to find precedent or argument to justify taking private property, without consent, to erect them on, though appropriate for the purpose. No necessity seems to exist which is sufficient to justify so strong a measure. A particular locality as to a few rods in respect to their site is usually of no consequence; while as to a light-house, or fort, or wharf, or highway between certain termini, it may be very important and imperative. I am aware of no precedents, also, for such seizures of private property abroad, for objects like the former, though some such doctrines appear to have been advanced in this country. (3 Paige, 45.) Again, many things belonging to bridges, turnpikes, and railroads, where public corporations for some purposes, are not, like the land on which they rest, local and peculiar and public, in the necessity to obtain them by the power of the eminent domain. Such seem to be cars, engines, &c., if not the timber for rails, and the rails themselves. (Gordon *v.* C. & J. Railway Co., 2 Railway Cases, 809.)

Such things do not seem to come within the public exigency connected with the roads which justifies the application of the principle of the eminent domain. Nor does even the path for the road, the easement itself, if the use of it be not public, but merely for particular individuals, and merely in some degree beneficial to the public. On the contrary, the user must be for the people at large,— for travellers, — for all,— must also be compulsory by them, and not optional with the owners,— must be a right by the people, not a favor,— must be under public regulations as to tolls, or owned, or subject to be owned, by the State, in order to make the corporation and object public, for a purpose like this. (3 Kent, Comm. 270; Railroad Co. *v.* Chappell, 1 Rice, 383; Memphis *v.* Overton, 3 Yerger, 53; King *v.* Russell, 6 Barn. & Cres. 566; King *v.* Ward, 4 Adol. & Ellis, 384.)

It is not enough that there is an act of incorporation for a bridge, or turnpike, or railroad, to make them public, so as to be able to take private property constitutionally, without the owner's consent; but their uses, and object, or interests, must be what has just been indicated,— must in their essence, and character, and liabilities, be public within the meaning of the term "public use." There may be a private bridge, as well as private road, or private railroad, and this with or without an act of incorporation.

In the present instance, however, the use was to be for the whole community, and not a corporation of any kind. The property was taken to make a free road for the people of the State to use, and was thus eminently for a public use, and where there had before been tolls imposed for private profit and by a private corporation so far as regards the interest in its tolls and property.

And the only ground on which that corporation, private in interest, was entitled in any view originally to condemn land or collect tolls was, that the use of its bridge was public,— was open to all, and at rates of fare fixed by the Legislature and not by itself, and subjected to the revision and reduction of the public authorities.

It may be, and truly is, that individuals and the public are often extensively benefited by private roads, as they are by mills, and manufactories, and private bridges. But such a benefit is not technically nor substantially a public use, unless the public has rights. (1 Rice, 388.) And in point of law it seems very questionable as to the power to call such a corporation a public one, and arm it with authority to seize on private property without the consent of its owners.

I exclude, therefore, all conclusions as to my opinions here being otherwise than in conformity to these suggestions; though when, as in the present case, a free public use in a highway and bridge is substituted for a toll-bridge, and on a long or great and increasing line of public travel, and thus vests both a new benefit and use, and a more enlarged one, in the public, and not in any few stockholders, I have no doubt that these entitle that public for such a use to condemn private property, whether owned by an individual or a corporation. (Boston W. P. Co. *v.* B. & W. Railroad Corp., 23 Pick. 360.) And it is manifest that unless such a course can be pursued, the means of social and commercial intercourse might be petrified, and remain for ages, like the fossil remains in sandstone, unaltered, and the government, the organ of a progressive community, be paralyzed in every important public improvement. (2 Dev. & Bat. 456; 1 Rice, 395; 8 Dana, 309.)

I exclude, also, any inference that, in assenting to the doctrine that an act of incorporation for a toll-bridge is a contract, giving private interests and rights as well as public ones, and thereby not allowing a State to take the private ones or alter them, unless for some legitimate public use, or by consent, as laid down in 4 Wheat. 628, I can or do assent to the doctrine of some of the judges there in respect to public *offices* being such contracts as not to be changed or abolished by a State on public considerations, without incurring a violation of the contract.

I should be very reluctant to hold, till further advised, that public offices are not, like public towns, counties, &c., mere political establishments, to be abolished or changed for political considerations connected with the public welfare. (9 Cranch, 43.) The salaries, duration, and existence of the offices themselves seem to be exclusively public matters, open to any modification which the representatives of the public may decide to be necessary, whenever no express restriction on the subject has been imposed in the constitution or laws. (*Quære.* Hoke *v.* Henderson, 4 Dev. 1.)

This would seem the implied condition of the office or contract, as much as that it may be taxed by the government under which it is held, though not by other governments, so as to impair or obstruct it. (See, as to the last, McCulloch *v.* Maryland, 4 Wheat. 316; Weston *v.* The C. C. of Charleston, 2 Peters, 449; Dobbins *v.* Comm. of Erie City, 16 Peters, 435.)

Finally, I do not agree that even this franchise, as property, can be taken from this corporation without violating the contract with it, unless the measure was honest, *bonâ fide*, and really required for what it professed to be, beside being, as before remarked, proper, on account of the locality and nature of this property, to be condemned for this purpose.

And though I agree that, for most cases and purposes, the public authorities in a State are the suitable judges as to this point, and that the judiciary only decide if their laws are constitutional (2 Kent, Comm. 340; 1 Rice, 383); that the Legislature generally acts for the public in this (2 Porter, 303; 3 Bl. Comm. 139, note; 4 D. & E. 794, 797); that road agents are their agents, under this limitation (1 Rice, 383); yet I am not prepared to agree, that if, on the face of the whole proceedings,— the law, the report of commissioners, and the doings of the courts,— it is manifest that the object was not legitimate, or that illegal intentions were covered up in forms, or the whole proceedings a mere "pretext," our duty would require us to uphold them. (Ibid.; Rice, 391.) In England, though this power exists, yet if used maliciously or wantonly, it is held to be void. (Boyfield *v.* Porter et al., 13 East, 200.)

In this case, however, while the fairness of it is impeached by the plaintiffs in error, yet on the record the object avowed is legal. It was to make travel free where it was before taxed; and the bridge, though remote from the changes desired in the old road, was still situated on the great line of travel over it, and not merely by color and finesse connected, and, from increases in population and business, seemed proper to be made free at the expense of the town or county.

Nor on the face of the record do the proceedings seem void, because the assessment may have been without a jury, when it was made by the legal officers, appointed for that purpose. (3 Peters, 280; 2 Dev. & Bat. 451, 460; Beekman *v.* Sar. Railroad, 3 Paige, Ch. 45.) Nor void as made by the commissioners without notice, when the return states notice, and when there was a full hearing enjoyed by all before the Court on the report.

Nor void because the compensation was too small to the corporation,— as it was assessed in conformity to law,— or too burdensome to the town alone to discharge, though the last might well have been flung on a larger number, like a county. (10 N. Hamp. 370; Tomlins, Dict., *Ways*, 2; 1 Rice, 392.) Nor because the commissioners take a fee instead of an easement, when the Legislature provide for a fee as more expedient. (2 Dev. & Bat. 451, 467.) Nor because some of the property condemned was personal, when it was mixed with the real, and when real or personal, if needed and appropriate, may at times be liable. (1 Rice, 383.)

With these explanations, I would express my concurrence in the judgment of the Court.

# CHARGE IN THE CASE OF ADAMS & HAMMOND *vs.* EDWARDS & HOLMAN.*

YOUR duties thus far, gentlemen, have been of a very laborious character, and I am sorry to say that they are not yet ended. The counsel for the different parties having finished their comments on the testimony, it becomes your difficult task, under the directions of the Court in relation to the points of law, to apply these facts to the law; and according as the evidence and the law is, so to find for the plaintiffs or defendants.

I do not think, gentlemen, it is necessary, on either side, to refer to anything which is foreign to the law or the evidence, before a Massachusetts jury, and to caution them against it; for they are too intelligent and too experienced in these matters to be influenced by any extraneous considerations; they know well the responsibility of their oaths, and they know well their duties under those oaths.

But, gentlemen, although this responsibility belongs to you, yet the law, as you will perceive, which is applicable to the case, must be given to you by the Court, and under the responsibility of its station and knowledge. It will be necessary to discriminate properly and carefully what the law is, and what the position of the case is, and all the different points arising in it.

Now, gentlemen, there are nominally two actions before you, on the part of Mr. Adams, against the defendants. They both, however, involve but one set of points, so far as regards the defendants. One action is the claiming of damages prior to January 16, 1847, for the infringement of certain patent privileges to the defendant; and on that you can give no damages subsequent to January 16, 1847. But there is another action, commenced at an after period, for damages between

---

* This was an action before the Circuit Court of the United States, Boston, Nov. 6, 1848, founded upon a patent, dated June 1, 1843, and granted to Daniel Fitzgerald, and by him assigned to Enos Wilder, who assigned to Daniel S. Wilder. The invention related to the making of fire-proof iron safes, and the nature of the invention consisted in interposing plaster of Paris between the inner and the outer chests, after the manner described in the specification. Many of the points arising in the case are very interesting and important to the profession. The trial was very long, and ably conducted by the distinguished counsel. S. P. Staples, of New York, and B. R. Curtis, of Boston, for the plaintiffs. R. Choate, of Boston, Dana and Jewell, do., for the defendants.

the 16th of January, 1847, where the other ends, to the 11th of November, 1847, a period of something like ten months.

Having settled the merits of the question, if you find for the plaintiffs, you will merely discriminate, in the verdict, the damages in the first action from those in the second,— giving the first for the time from the first infringement of the patent down to the 16th of January, 1847, and the last for the time included between January, 1847, and November, 1847.

Having shown you the position of these two suits, and that it will be necessary to apportion the damages in the way that I have stated, I will proceed to explain to you, in brief, how this question arises; for the length of the trial has been so great that you may not be able to discriminate exactly the position of the case in the outset.

The plaintiffs sue on a patent, which they say was taken out in 1843, by Daniel Fitzgerald, and assigned to the plaintiffs in that year, —passing from the hands of Fitzgerald to Enos Wilder, but getting to the plaintiffs as a patent,—and the patent of 1843. Discriminate that, if you please, from every other patent (as many have on the trial been mentioned), in order to understand the case thoroughly, — a patent issued in 1843, and assigned to them by Benj. G. Wilder, who obtained it from Enos Wilder, and who acted as the agent of B. G., and Enos having obtained it from Fitzgerald.

Now, that patent being obtained in 1843, and assigned to the plaintiffs, no person has a right to use what is described in it without their permission, or paying them a compensation. They say that they did not give any permission to the defendants to use it, but that the defendants did use it from 1843 to 1847; and the claim they lay before you is for damages for this use.

Now, in order to see what is in controversy, you will start with the fact that a patent was taken out in June, 1843.

The next point is, that the defendants have used, manufactured and sold safes similar to those described in this patent. That is not in controversy. It is proved by several witnesses, and is not in dispute, that they have manufactured such safes for three or four years.

Now that, gentlemen, in point of law, would entitle the plaintiffs to recover for the damages they have sustained, prima facie. They bring here a public document or grant made correctly in point of law. The patents are not now issued indiscriminately; and on the face it is, therefore, good, if there is nothing shown against it, and there cannot be made out a prima facie case against it.

You perceive, then, gentlemen, that the case becomes narrowed down very much by the defence, which rests on two great points. This defence is, that notwithstanding the defendants have used it, yet, for various reasons, they had a right to use it. And secondly, even though they had not a right to use it under the law, yet they used it under such circumstances that there should not be any damages given. This defence you must look into.

Had the defendants a right to use this patent? For, if they had, they should not be responsible; if they had not, they should.

Now, gentlemen, as a general principle of law, although a patent thus obtained, and thus offered in evidence, as I have said, is prima facie evidence for the plaintiff to recover, yet it is competent for the defendant to show that he has a right to use this; and he may sustain this defence on various points. He may show that he had a license to use it from the party who obtained the patent, and in such a form that he had a right to use the patent. He may show that he had purchased the right,— that is, supposing the patent is good; or he may show something to prove that the patent is not good, — as by showing that some other person is the inventor, and not the patentee, — or by showing that it had been in public use for two years before the patent was applied for; or by showing that it had been on sale for two years before, with his consent; or by proving that from patriotism, generosity, or in despair, or from some other cause, he had abandoned it, — so that the other party has a right to use it, and any one may take it up, as a sort of waif, or derelict property. And I mention these points because they are all relied on for the defence, and, being relied on for the defence, you must start with the principle of law, that the defendant should, on these, make out his defence, just as you originally started with the principle that the plaintiff must make out his position a prima facie case.

If the defendant impugns the testimony, which the plaintiff offers, as to the legality or correctness of the patent, concerning this particular testimony you must see how the scale preponderates.

* * * * * *

The first argument to show that this patent is bad is, because it is of a matter not considered patentable. Now, gentlemen, in order to judge of that, we must first inquire what it is for, before you can see whether it is for a matter patentable, or not patentable. I shall instruct you, as a matter of law, that such things are patentable as the discoverer undertakes to apply in combination or separately, so as to produce new and beneficial results. We must make some broad and general distinctions of that kind.

It need not be a new material.

It need not be an entire new machine.

It need not be wholly or throughout a new application.

But it must, when it is a combination as it is here, it must bring some new features into the combination, and produce new and beneficial results. And if it does that, it is of no matter how slight is the change. If there is a novelty in the application and in the machine, and if it produces new results and valuable results, it is patentable, whether only the combination is new, or only an important part is new. There must be something new in relation to it, and it must produce better results than what were produced before. *And when you get novelty in parts or in combination, and novelty in results, and beneficial ones, you get what the constitution and laws were enacted to protect, that is, something new invented which benefits mankind.* It must not be a frivolous object, like the invention of an improvement in making playing-cards, which has been driven out of court because the object was bad. But here the object was laudable, — to insure safety to the most valuable articles of property. The security, then, was patentable, if a new and useful change. Next, then, did it produce beneficial and new results? It must be more useful, it must have some superior advantages to what existed before, or it could not produce such results, — as ever have proved to resist severe fires, and such as consumed former safes and their contents, without injuring these. Now, gentlemen, in testing what is a new combination, as I have said, you may not have a new material, but you must have something different in form or system from what was used before in this way, and so different as to cause new and better results. Now, as I understand it, safes have long existed before; and such as are called double safes. There had long been some opening between two chests, at some times to be occupied by air, and at other times by substances supposed to be non-conductors of various kinds, — some without the application of it to the doors, and some with the application of it to the doors.

But what Fitzgerald claims here to be new, if I understand it, is not the use of plaster of Paris to repel fire entirely, in some modes and in some articles, but that it had not been used before in combination with these double chests for the purpose of repelling fire to the thickness with which he used it, in both the doors and sides, and in the liquid state. He says, in the patent, it may be used dry or liquid; but what he expressly relies upon, and describes in detail, is the liquid state, and of a certain thickness. As you will see, this has an important bearing upon the results, — that he uses it for the doors too, as well as for the sides.

The patent, then, is that the safe shall be constructed, under his invention, so as to have a space of two or three inches, — you will see the description in the patent, — a wider space than has been generally employed before. Two or three inches! The preparation shall not be put on merely as a wash, or nailed on like a sheet of mica or zinc, but it shall be poured in, in a liquid state, to that thickness. I have the impression that this pouring in, in a liquid state, in accordance with the answer to a question which I put to a scientific gentleman on the stand, is a peculiarity in filling all the holes and cracks better, which is essential. For, those acquainted with fires, and their operation upon safes, are aware that one great danger of burning up papers is in consequence of the external heated air being through some small fissures of joints communicated, — not the flame. And that one great means of preventing fire destroying the papers inside is by reducing the preparation to the liquid form, and pouring it in as a thin paste, so as to be more sure of filling the smallest spaces between the two chests.

There may be some advantage from the moisture which comes out during the melting, which may serve to protect the same from the fire. But it strikes my mind that this result has been brought about, under this invention, not only by having plaster of Paris used,—which is a good non-conductor, and imbibes, after calcined, much water,—but by having it used in this liquid state, so as to fill up all the crevices, being more perfectly tight, and hardening quick, swells or expands some, so as to fit still closer; and by having it so very thick, instead of as in the safes which existed before, which you have seen described, and some of which you have seen here, having a mere coat of plaster half an inch thick, instead of two or three inches, as Fitzgerald had it, and as his specification details.

You will at once know, from remembering your experience, that a coat of two or three inches of matter thus non-combustible will resist the progress of a fire much more than a mere wash, or a mere coating of half an inch or a quarter of an inch. However that may be, he claims it of a certain thickness. He describes the moist state particularly for its use, and he applies it to the doors, as well as to the other parts.

If the doors are not secured, as well as the other parts, it renders the contents quite unsafe. It is therefore this new combination of plaster for this purpose, in this thickness, in the moist state, which seems to constitute the gist of this discovery,—and applied all around, to the doors as well as to the other parts; producing such different results as have been shown here,—of resisting the largest fires,—it could hardly be justifiable, I think, for the Court to say that it is not patentable, for want either of importance, apparent novelty, or usefulness. I shall soon, however, suggest something more for and against its novelty, when considering the special testimony against it under that aspect. I may have said enough as to what is meant by a patent being useful. It must not be frivolous or unimportant. I hardly need dwell upon this. It is a question of fact, what is useful, after instructing you as a question of law that the patent must be useful. And a jury have no great difficulty about that. If they find it introduced extensively into use, they will conclude that it is useful; for the people will not throw away old articles, when old ones are as useful as new, and particularly for the protection of such valuable articles as papers and money. The utility comes home, therefore, to everybody, if the extensive use is made out. If this does resist fire best, you will judge whether it is not useful both in its object and results, by whomsoever planned and matured.

Passing by these, you come to the next important part of the defence, and the evidence in relation to which has occupied the greater portion of the trial. And that is, was the improvement, as I have described it to you from this patent as patentable and useful,—was this improvement made by Fitzgerald originally, or by some other person? This is the special defence, just referred to, against its novelty. Was there such a machine, of the description contained in his specification,—was there such a machine invented or matured before he did it? If there was, the law says, and says properly, that he cannot succeed. Because the world then had the benefit of it,—if it pleased,—another person was entitled to protection on account of it, and to aid the invention it was not necessary to issue a patent here. But, in order to test this point, the prior invention must have existed before with these qualities, with this combination, with this description substantially. So far as it refers to the subject-matter in Fitzgerald's patent, it must be substantially the same. And I do not say, as one of my brethren upon the bench has said, that there is no definite signification to the word *substantial.* When we say a thing is substantially the same, we mean it is the same in all important particulars. It must be of the same material, when the material is important; it must be of the same thickness, when thickness is important; it must be applied in the same way, condition, and extent, to the doors as well as the sides, when either of these circumstances makes an essential difference. If some other machine had all this, as in Fitzgerald's, then it was substantially the same. It is not a matter of moment to make the chest itself of one substance or another, if there is no difference in the period at which they melt, and if they are alike impenetrable to heated air. It may be made of tin, or iron, or brass. It is of no consequence whether it is in form a square or a parallelogram, or whether there is a small mixture with the plaster, which neither vitiates nor improves it. But it must be the same in power to resist heat and exclude heated air, and then, in this particular, it is *substantially* the same.

I mean, by change of form not being material, when the form does not contribute toward the new result. When it does, the forms must be alike in all important particulars. As other inventions must have been not only substantially like this, but prior in time, in order to vitiate it, it will be necessary for you to find when Fitzgerald invented this, in order to determine whether they or he invented it first. The law means, by invention, not maturity. It must be the idea struck out, the brilliant thought obtained, the great improvement in embryo. You must have that; but if he has that, he may be years improving it—maturing it. It may require half a life. But in that time he must have devoted himself to it as much as circumstances would allow. But, if he strikes out the plan which he afterwards patents, that is the time of the invention—that is the time when the discovery occurs. And we are speaking now of the invention, and not of the application. The date of the invention is the time, if it is followed up.

Now, it is contended, on the part of the respondents, that there were discoveries like this, even earlier than 1830. But in 1830 some of their witnesses say, and others in 1831 and '32, that there were clear discoveries of using this plaster in this way, and before Fitzgerald started this idea, which he afterwards matured and patented.

Now, gentlemen, fixing the time of Fitzgerald's invention, you will see whether there were any of that description or not. The plaintiffs contend that this time was in 1830, and they give you a whole history of it from various sources, and among others from the patentee upon the stand. What led him to the discovery,— the experiments he made, the progress in his own mind,— and what disabled him,— the want of means,— from maturing his ideas, has been detailed to you. But his attempts continued, after making the discovery. By various experiments on the power of plaster in this way, — applied in this form, put on moist by balls, more in the form of plaster than of paste,— he found that it would stand fire better than anything else. And in this one of his brothers unites with him, and the testimony shows that he thought early of using it with a safe. He certainly, in 1831, not only made these experiments, but made them with a small box; and he speaks of thinking then that he would get a patent as soon as he could get some person who would assist him. And another brother unites in testifying to what took place in 1831, and Mr. Loring unites with them in the same.

In 1832 he tried it with larger boxes or safes, with the idea of safes in his mind. And Post, the son,— the witness of that name who testified upon the stand,— confirms what has been said by others in what took place at his father's at that time. It was exhibited at the office or house of his father, in New York, in 1832; to Ireland and Yerrick, in 1833, who testify, with regard to the facts then occurring, of Fitzgerald desiring aid, and wanting to get it, in obtaining a patent. In 1834, Mr. Kelsey testifies to experiments, and also in 1835. He says that he made experiments in 1836. And especially, early in 1836, after the great fire, he went on more extensively in tests, and tried to get persons to unite with him. Mr. Sherwood united with him on that occasion, and did make experiments, which he has detailed here, under oath, with great clearness. The question is then presented, on this evidence, did he strike out this idea, which he afterwards got patented, as early as 1831, and did he follow it up to 1836, till maturity, and follow it up too in various ways, and with reasonable diligence, considering his means? If you believe that he did, then the question will recur, whether there was anything earlier of this kind, and to this extent, by others.

The first thing that is offered to prove this is the Conner safe. And here you come at once to the thickness of the material used. You will see its thickness in that safe here before you, and can judge whether it is as well calculated to confer security against fire; and you will next go to the door of it, and see if the door was at all secured against fire; and if neither of these securities existed, as in Fitzgerald's, and that was as early as 1830, you will determine whether this would be all the improvement which Fitzgerald accomplished by thickening the material three-fold, and applying it to the doors, as well as the sides. But there is another objection to this. It was not until October, 1830, and Fitzgerald made his experiments previously, in that year; some witnesses say that it was not complete until 1831 or '32.

Passing from these to the French safes,—nobody swears that they were here before 1832; some do not swear that the French safes were in this country before 1833 or '4. The evidence proves them to look ten years old at that time. Although, according to the appearance of them, they may have been made some years before, were they in fact, or only much exposed at sea? And were they the same in substance? Were they the same, is the important inquiry on the point now under consideration. It is very important, under the other head, to consider whether their previous use occurred abroad or in this country,—looking at the similitude, or difference. Were not the nails driven through them,—through the plaster and all? Again, as to the substance between the chests,—was it plaster? And was it as thick as this? And were the doors secured like this? All these are considerations which affect the question at issue, and must be made reasonably clear and certain. And that is the reason why you are to decide what Fitzgerald's invention was. For others cannot compete with it, unless they were like it substantially, and had similar qualities.

I then suggest to you the safe of Marr, in England. That was not in existence in 1834. And, gentlemen, is there any evidence that Marr's was used with plaster? It was spoken of, in the specification, with feathers, and cotton, and almost every non-conductor in existence. If he placed no more reliance upon it than upon feathers and cotton, it would hardly be an invention like this. But it is for you to say whether it was the same, and whether it was used with plaster liquid or powdered, or ever used with plaster at all. That is a question for you to decide, which I leave entirely in your hands.

I do not know of any other safes which it was contended interfered with Fitzgerald's, till you come down to where I stop in the examination, to 1836. And then, if you believe he made an application for this patent which was not afterwards abandoned, no other invention would deprive him of priority, made after 1836, or within the two previous years. But if he had made an invention which he abandoned utterly, and did not try to get a patent for, after once rejected, and did not resume the attempt after the first trial by a new application, then his priority fails, by the first application; and you must look to other applications which were duly followed up, and to other inventions within two years of them. What did he do, under these circumstances? For there must be an invention by others before his application,—there must be a discovery by some other person before he applied,—in order to destroy his originality. You have it in evidence how he did apply in 1836, and what his specifications were. And then you have in evidence,—which has been commented on so much,—how his first application was rejected in 1836 or '7, and why it was rejected; how he renewed it again in 1837; how he applied also for the Desk Safe, and succeeded in 1838; and how, after a second rejection of the present claim, he applied again a third time, and how he failed; how it was continued in 1839, and was amended and kept up, till he finally, by an appeal, obtained his patent in 1843. The great question is, whether he made an application in 1836, by a specification which was afterwards substantially embodied in this patent of 1843; and whether he ever meant to abandon it, after his original application?

I instruct you, in point of law, with reference to the rejection, that the proof of abandonment of his application would depend upon two circumstances: whether he meant to give it up,—to give all up with regard to it,—or whether, being needy, he gave up during a short time, for want of funds. You would not trip up a man of genius, who had made a discovery, in consequence of a want of means to prosecute his labors to their final consummation, if you thought he intended to persevere. And even if the application was withdrawn, if he kept it up in his own mind, and if he meant to keep it up before the Patent Office, if you think he did not intend to abandon it, and did not, but merely suspended operations till he could get means, then all the other inventions would apply only, and must have been, two years before 1836. But if he did not then reasonably persevere, nor then mean to, they would apply to two years before 1839, when he had his specification corrected, and persisted in on the records till he obtained the patent.

I proceed now to the next branch of the defence; it is one admissible by law, and often a very important one to the community; and that is, that this invention of Fitzgerald, although original, and important, and valuable, and applied for in 1836, and persisted in till 1843, and not meant to be abandoned during that time, yet he did allow it to be in public use without taking out a patent, or without applying for one, for two years before 1836.

Now, gentlemen, you will perceive that the law, as to this, depends upon two questions: What is a public use? and what is two years before the application? If you consider the application of 1836 as never having been abandoned, except for a few months, not renewed from want of means to assist in prosecuting his claim, then the public use must be for two years before 1836. But if you suppose that application was abandoned, then the public use must be two years before it was renewed, so as to avail under the principles already laid down. A "public use" is this. Public use is opposed to private use. If a man has an invention, and uses it privately, and nobody knows of it, then the use of it cannot debar another person from an invention or patent of it. What is the evidence of a public use, as opposed to a private one? It need not be a general use by the community. It must be used, however, and used openly, so that the structure and *modus operandi* are apparent. But, gentlemen, one evidence of a public use is the manufacture of an article publicly and openly for sale; not universally, but still publicly,— not by one person alone, and for his own private use; it is the manufacture of it publicly,— it is the offering of it for sale publicly.

Now, if a machine had been offered for sale, or had been manufactured, or had been used by various persons publicly, two years before he applied, his patent would fail. You can easily see the reason for it. A man is not to lie by and let the public — several persons — use his invention, without objection. He is not to lie by and let persons manufacture the articles for sale, as if not to be patented; because he thus misleads them. He is not to lie by and let them be sold in that way in public stores. But, gentlemen, there must be a public use for two years, and a use, too, of the same machine in all essential particulars. Now, was there any use of such a machine before 1836, similar in substance as to the material parts and arrangements: its liquid state,— the mode in which it was applied to the sides and to the doors,— the thickness of it, and all that? Or, if you will fix upon some later period than 1836 for the commencement of his valid application, was any other machine in use two years before that later period? The law of 1839, in respect to two years, was passed after the first application. But I instruct you that the law of 1839 applies, on all trials since, to previous cases as well as to subsequent cases. The law has come in, and given two years use and sale, without being barred so as to cover experiments and trials of machines to improve them. What next are the previous public uses relied on? The only ones which have any bearing upon this question are the Conner and French safes, which have been already considered partially.

Was the use public in these cases, is one chief ingredient under this head. Was such a safe as Conner's used by the community? Was it actually sold in the stores? If there is evidence of it, you will refer to it.

But if one man alone kept it,— made it for himself, kept it in his counting-room or in his cellar,— it would be for private use. Next, was Conner's substantially the same as this? On that enough has been heretofore suggested. And the French safes,— as to the use of them, you will judge how the evidence is: whether there was any evidence that they were used in this country, or made in this country, or sold in this country,— if they were like this in all essentials,— is another question for you to decide.

The provision in the defence which I shall next advert to is, that if he allowed these safes to be on sale for two years before his first application, the patent is invalid. There is justice in that. He thus would virtually extend his term for the patent to run. But did Fitzgerald give permission to any others than himself or his agents to use them, or were they on sale in the market before he made his first application? You will see. What is the evidence on that subject? If there be none, or none satisfactory, it cannot operate against this patent. There is one other circumstance in the defence, and that is, that this invention was described in books before the discovery of Fitzgerald. I think this must, by the act of Congress, be before the "discovery," and not before the application. One of the acts of 1836 speaks of the description in books as being necessarily before the discovery, and the use or sale before the application. In the description in books, in express terms it says that it must be before the "discovery." If I am not wrong, there are books referring to Marr's patents, though that is clearly after this invention or discovery, and referring to the use of plaster as a non-conductor. But do they describe this invention of Fitzgerald's, in all its material combinations? If they do that, they are no bar to the validity of this invention.

And not to delay any further upon these things. I would say, finally, that if Fitzgerald, after all this,—if he succeeds and overcomes all this, yet if he, or they under him, abandon this invention to the public, from patriotism, generosity, or any other cause, then they should not trip up any person for using it afterwards; for a parent does not often abandon his own child. An inventor does not abandon the fruits of his genius, except from some great cause. Was there any great cause which induced Fitzgerald or Wilder to abandon this? Have they acted as though they intended to hold on to it? Have they, in fact, held on to get the benefits of it; or have they utterly given it up, and abandoned it?

Something has been said on the opinions of the plaintiffs concerning the validity of their patent. I would state to you, as a question of law, that any admissions of facts made by the plaintiffs they are bound by, — unless they were made under a mistake,— unless the plaintiff shows that he was entrapped into a confession, or that he labored under some gross error concerning the facts. But opinions given with regard to the law by parties do not hold them in this way. Suppose a person thinks he is not entitled to a legacy; it makes no difference with the law. Many persons come here with great confidence about the legality or illegality of certain questions; it often turns out that they were very much mistaken. But when a party states a fact, and he does not show that he is under a mistake, we hold him to it; otherwise, the opposite party is deceived, or misled.

The final question on which I wish to say a few words is the question of damages. On the one side is the claim of your giving nominal damages, and on the other of giving full damages. And it is perfectly competent for you to give only nominal damages, if you think that the plaintiffs have not been injured any, or if you think that the plaintiffs have conducted in such a manner that the defendants have been misled.

On the other hand, gentlemen, if the defendants have not been misled, but meant to get the use of this safe without paying anything for it, it would be a circumstance for the jury to give full damages, but not vindictive damages. And I sometimes instruct a jury to give damages, not only to pay for the injury, but, beside the taxable costs of the suit, to remunerate the plaintiff for the extra counsel-fees and necessary incidental expenses in undertaking it. If the defendants are not inventors, and have not bought of inventors, it is one of those cases where larger damages ought to be given. But if they have been misled by the plaintiffs, it is a case for smaller damages.

In relation to the additional points which have been submitted, for instruction, by the defendants, it has been said that the claim in 1839 and 1843 does not extend to the degree of thickness which was laid down by me as embraced in the patent of 1843. On that point I would instruct you that he says, at the close, in these words: "I claim the application of plaster of Paris in the construction of all iron safes in the manner above described, or in any other manner substantially the same." What he says, "above described," as to the thickness, is this. It is of a "space between the inner and outer safe of about three inches, which space may be varied a little, but should be the same all round, and in every direction." I would instruct you, in point of law, that the reference is to that,— to three inches. I had supposed it was only two or two and a half inches; but it is still thicker. He describes it as liquid, too, and then says it may be in that or some other way. The words are these: "I then take plaster of Paris, or gypsum, and having boiled it, or baked it in an oven, and calcined it, and reduced it to a powder, I mix it with water till it is about the consistency of cream or thin paste, so fluid as that it may readily be poured into the space left as above to receive it." He does not merely say that he wishes to use it in this way. He describes the process which he actually performs as in the liquid one — as the doors, he says, "the inner and outer doors are prepared in the same way." And, "where one door is used, it should be made in the same manner, leaving a like space between the inner and outer crust or face of the door; and, for a like purpose, should be fitted to the chest or safe with great accuracy." Also, "the sides and openings of the doors are to be neatly finished, as in other chests."

The question of law is, that when he refers to the "manner above described;" he refers to the thickness: to the liquid paste, especially: and to the filling of the doors, as well as the rest of the chest.

As to the application of 1836, the request says that this claim was not in substance there. We must compare this application, and see. In 1836 he used water, but it was with a plaster, rather than a paste; and he says: "Within this is a coat of a peculiar plaster (to be hereinafter described), one inch and a half in thickness; next within this, is a lining of any kind of wood about three-fourths of an inch thick: next, another coating of the plaster two inches thick; the whole is then lined with wood covered with sheet-iron, upon which the shelves and apartments are fixed. These various proportions may be varied to suit the size of the chest, and other circumstances; more or less of the plaster being used, according to the liability of the chest to be subjected to very great heat, in case of fire." He says that the thickness is a very important ingredient, and that it is important when the situation is such that the fire is likely to be a large one. Here is gypsum,— and water with it, so as to form a plaster,— and two inches thick in one place, and one and a half inches in another. It is also said, that if the specification describes this under Marr, it is sufficient, even if he had made, as he swears, no practical machine with plaster. In his testimony, he says twice, that he never did make one with plaster. If he describes gypsum, he must describe its use like this. But he says nothing of its being used as a plaster, or of its being poured in as a paste, and nothing of the thickness.

It is also said that, if Fitzgerald was three years before '36 in inaction, it would imply that he had thrown it up. But you will judge, from the evidence, whether in 1835, 1834 and 1833, he did not make direct experiments, and apply to persons for aid.

Another word as to Mathews. He did not use the word plaster at all, and says nothing of thickness. He speaks of "soap-stone, Roman cement, alum, or glue." I should hold them to be different from plaster, though they might be non-conductors; and that a patent for them did not cover one for plaster of Paris, to be used in the peculiar form and extent described by Fitzgerald.

You will retire, gentlemen, and settle the facts in dispute, and then apply them to the points in controversy, under the principles of law, as explained by the Court for your guide.

# CHARGE IN THE CASE OF SAMUEL COLT *vs.* THE MASSACHUSETTS ARMS COMPANY.*

You have already understood, gentlemen of the jury, that the claim of the plaintiff against the defendants is founded upon a supposed violation by the defendants of the patent-right of the plaintiff. I trust you come to the consideration of this case with a due regard to the rights and privileges of both sides. They both claim under patents. They both have a right to have these patents protected, so far as they can be without conflicting with each other; and when they conflict with each other, the more recent, of course, is to give way to the elder, because the one who patents an invention first is entitled to the protection of the principle in it over everybody else that patents it afterwards. In the nature of things and common sense, this must be so. But that does not preclude — and that is the source of the difficulty in this case — any person subsequently from making an improvement on that patent, by way of addition to it, or making it better and more useful. But all that the person who does that — who makes an improvement — can protect under his letters-patent, his subordinate patent, is that which is new, that which he has added; because if, by making an addition or improvement to an old patent, a party could get possession of the old patent itself, and use it without paying for it, no patent which was of any value would last a year, — for such is the progress of science and of the arts, that some kind of improvement or other can be made upon everything. A party has a right to make an improvement, but all that he can patent is that which he improves, — his own invention. He, therefore, must be careful, before using an addition, to get the license of the old patentee to use the old patent in combination with his improvement; otherwise, he must use his improvement alone, if he can, or, as he may often do with great

* This was an action before the Circuit Court for Massachusetts, brought by Samuel Colt, of Hartford, Conn., the inventor of the Repeating Fire Arms, usually known as "Revolvers," or "Six Shooters," against the Massachusetts Arms Company, located at Chicopee, Mass., for an infringement of his patent-right, by manufacturing arms in which were embodied several of the improvements already secured by letters-patent to him. The trial of this cause was very long, and many questions of law, of great importance, as regards the law of patents, as well as the questions of fact in the cause, are embodied in the charge. A full report of the cause was made for the plaintiff, and this charge was revised by his honor Judge Woodbury. The counsel for the plaintiff were G. T. Curtis, of Boston, E. Dickerson, of New Jersey, and Charles Levi Woodbury, of Boston; and for the defendants, R. Choate, of Boston, R. A. Chapman and Hon. George Ashmun, of Springfield, Mass.

safety, wait a year or two, until the old patent expires, when he would be free to use it in connection.

I recommend you, gentlemen, to commence the investigation of this controversy, looking at this aspect of it, with a feeling of no hostility or prejudice against the defendants, because they happen to be a corporation, or happen to be a probable overmatch for any single individual; and you should not let your sympathies go beyond the rule of law and duty, because the plaintiff stands alone, and because he has evidently been struggling for fifteen or twenty years on this subject, to do something which might confer a benefit upon his country, and reward his own exertions. He can properly recover a verdict, if he is entitled to it; but if he is not entitled, he cannot, however great may have been his sacrifices. You, therefore, should have no prejudices on the one side, or sympathies on the other, which could divert you from doing what is just and legal between these parties.

In the first instance, the plaintiff must make out his right, — that he has a patent for a particular subject, which, he says, the defendants have violated; and then he must make out the violation of that patent by the defendants. In order to do that, he has laid before you letters from the Patent Office, dated as early as February, 1836, in which he undertakes to describe a certain improvement which he has made by several combinations. At a subsequent time, in 1848, he amended his specification so as to describe his improvement with more clearness or fulness, but the same invention; and then again, in 1849, he applied for and obtained an extension of seven years. The reason for conferring extensions generally by the officers of the government, who are authorized to do it, is to reward the party in some degree for his skill and genius, when he has not, to appearances, been already rewarded. It should not be granted, except in cases of valuable patents, useful to the country, and where the parties have been unfortunate, and not reaped from them the advantage they anticipated. The government first authorize some officers connected with the Patent Office to make the extension, and then Congress interferes and makes further extensions, when they think the party has not been sufficiently rewarded. That is the whole controversy in relation to extensions, about which you have heard so much. An extension being granted whenever the party appears to have a valuable improvement and has not realized from it sufficient to indemnify him, parties may object to that first, on notice being given. The controversy, then, is, whether the patentee has or has not realized what is sufficient to constitute a reward.

In this case, the plaintiff amended his specification, and he has had it extended, so that it prima facie covers the time when this infringement is alleged to have taken place. I speak of this making out a prima facie case, notwithstanding any proof that on the records of the country there is a subsequent patent for a similar subject to the defendants. The plaintiff's patent overrides the defendants' entirely, when they are for the same subject, because it was granted earlier by the government, and therefore no one who comes afterwards, and gets a patent for the same thing, can take away his rights. The government, by giving another patent, cannot take away that of a prior patentee. They can no more take it away, than you can take away the property of your neighbor. He has vested rights in it until the term expires; and, therefore, the government, when they give a subsequent patent which may cover a prior one, cannot, in law, take away the rights under the prior patent, whatever may have been the accident or mistake in granting it; and although it may have covered other things which belong to a prior patent, yet the prior patent stands until the term expires: otherwise, the government might take away any private property which exists, which a man had acquired, and give it to some person afterwards, by a mere arbitrary transfer. But that would not do. When a man obtains a grant from the government, he holds it as much as when he gets a grant or a deed from an individual; and, by a subsequent grant, unless he assents to it, he cannot be divested of it. Therefore, the law says, when a prior patent is offered, — as in this case, — it prima facie covers what it describes, and must stand, notwithstanding a subsequent patent may have been granted, which covers a portion of the same thing. It stands for what it is worth,— for what it covers.

But there is another step to be taken in this case; and that is, notwithstanding the plaintiff's patent, so far as it goes, is to continue in full force until it expires, and until the extension expires, yet he cannot recover of the defendants, unless it contains a principle which they have encroached upon. They may have done a great many other things, they may have made a great many other improvements, but the plaintiff must show that his contains a principle which the defendants, among other things, have adopted and used. He has put a great many experts on the stand, and some who may not be called exactly experts in scientific matters, though they may be experts in the use of fire-arms, and proved by them that theirs does contain a principle, among other things, which is involved in his. I do not propose to go into details of the evidence, but you will recollect several testified to the effect that the operation of the defendants' and plaintiff's pistols is the same in substance. It is conceded that they differ in form, in proportions, and in what are called mechanical equivalents. You understand what that means as well as the Court; it has been explained to you by experts. I can only tell you, as a principle of law, that where the difference is only in form or proportion to bring about similar results, or where it is only by using a mechanical equivalent instead of what is used by the other, there is, in point of law, not that considerable difference in principle, or in operation, or in results, which the law holds as not being a violation of what preceded it; but if it differs in something beyond mechanical equivalents, — if it differs in something beyond form and proportions,— if the difference in the parts where it is charged is very considerable,— the liability exists on the part of the plaintiff not to claim that as similar to his.

Look a little at this in a practical point of view, and as practical men. Although there may be, for instance, in a subsequent patent, two things which differ from the prior patent in something beyond mechanical equivalents, form, and proportions,— and though they may be improvements, and, therefore, are not to be treated as violations of the other,— yet, at the same time, it is to be considered, that if there is a third thing introduced in the defendants' which is covered by the plaintiff's patent, the party is liable for that third, although not for the other two. Therefore it becomes important, in considering this subject throughout, that you consider these five different claims of the plaintiff. They are separate combinations. They are not five things combined into one. They are five, constituting one patent, but each of them is a separate combination, as you will see in the patent. If they were all one combination simply, and not set out as, and not in substance, different combinations, the defendants, in order to infringe, would have to violate the combination as a whole. But where there are five separate combinations, as there are in this case, the first may be violated, the second may be violated, but the third need not; *because they are for separate combinations*, and the language of the claims is, first *combining the rotating chambered breech*, &c., second, combining the breech with the lock, &c., third, placing the nipples, &c. They are each distinct, and not all going to form a whole as a combination. I am requested to instruct you to consider them separately, and I do so. If the defendants use one of them, it is enough; and it is of no consequence to this result whether they use more than one, or more than two, except in respect to damages. When you come to that subject, it may be of some importance to discriminate how many of them they violate, because, according to the importance of that one combination, and according to the various combinations they may encroach upon, may be the amount of damages to be recovered.

I have said that I am going on to see how far the plaintiff first makes out his prima facie case, because the defendants have offered the testimony of experts, who swear that theirs is unlike the plaintiff's in principle, and that, in their opinion, it does not encroach. All that is to be considered when you come to make up your verdict. But, if the plaintiff has shown a patent which the Court considers legal; if he has shown an extension which is prima facie valid; if he has shown, by other experts, that the defendants' machine, patented ten or eleven years after his, however much more it may cover in some particulars, encroaches upon his, and that his machine is useful, — he lays the foundation for damages, prima facie. As to the utility, which is the only other point to be considered under this aspect of the case, there has been but one opinion expressed upon both sides,— that Colt's fire-arms have been regarded by those most skilful in the use of them, for many years since 1836, as very valuable and very effective; that their utility, in this respect, has not only been tried in different wars and different services, but it has been examined by the government and favorably acted upon; and that, in a controversy between the defendants, or the person under whom they claim, and Colt, where the former interposed against the plaintiff's having a contract for a considerable number of these arms, the most experienced and intelligent officers reported decidedly in favor of the utility of the plaintiff's arm. If the prima facie case is thus made out, all that will remain on that prima facie case would be the damages; and, as I remarked to you, they would be influenced by the number of the combinations violated, and their importance.

[Mr. Curtis remarked that the question of damages was not to be considered by the Jury.]

That is so much easier, gentlemen, for you and for me. The question of damages the parties have settled among themselves; it is much better that they should be so settled. I was about to repeat, what I had occasion to say lately in this very district, in relation to damages: that I am determined, so far as regards myself, that if a party has clearly violated the patent of another, he shall not pay less than he would if he had contracted to use the machine during the time he had been using it. The idea cannot be tolerated in a civilized community, that a man, by trespass, shall use a machine for a less sum than he would have to pay for its license.

Notwithstanding all this, the defendants say, and they have a right to say, that, conceding their patent to be of more recent date than the plaintiff's, and, therefore, bound to yield to it, as between them, on the records of the Patent Office, yet that the plaintiff was not the original inventor of those improvements which he has covered by his patent. It is true they are right in thinking that, if they support it by facts; and it is true that although the government gives the patentee a patent which they suppose is original, it is open, by the act of Congress of 1836, and all other acts which preceded it, to be impugned and impeached. A patentee is exposed to have his patent shown not to be the first in date of that character; and then, however wrong or right the defendant is in his course, yet the foundation is struck from under the feet of the plaintiff as having been the original inventor, if the defendant is able to show that there were prior machines used, containing in substance the principle involved in the plaintiff's. It is no matter whether those prior inventions were patented or not, if they existed, if they were discovered, if they were used. The only effect of patenting, as regards this aspect of the question, is, that it rather evinces an idea on the part of the person who made this invention that there was something in it, that it was valuable, and that he did not mean to abandon it to the community; therefore, he protects it by a patent; supposing it valuable, he intends to reap some benefit from it. Whereas, if he set up an invention many years ago, and did not patent it, but let the world use it, there is some indication that he supposed he had nothing very valuable or important. But it goes as far to impeach the plaintiff's machine, if it existed, as if it existed and was patented. And it is of no consequence, if it existed, that the party does not choose to prosecute. In some respect of the patent law, it might be important to show that it had been abandoned; that is, when the party undertakes to rely on priority of use to defeat the plaintiff. But here the reliance is not on prior use; therefore it is of no consequence whether it is abandoned or not, but whether it was the prior invention. When I say "it," I mean a machine involving the same or a similar principle.

A great many other considerations have been pressed in connection with this view of the subject, but I believe there is no way in which you will be able to comprehend more clearly whether there was a prior invention, similar in substance to Colt's, than to see what Colt's was, before you compare it with others, or compare the others with Colt's. What did Colt do? He undertook, undoubtedly, from all that appears in the case, and from the specification, to get the power, through a revolver, of having more discharges in a short space of time than by a single barrel. That is one great essence of all this principle of revolving fire-arms. He introduced revolvers, undoubtedly, which might be fired oftener within the same space of time. Another object which he seems to have developed in his specification is, that he should do this with as much safety as possible, by means of nipples, placed between partitions, or in recesses, so that the fire should not communicate from one barrel to the other. In doing all this, you will perceive, as revolvers cannot be had conveniently, without a pretty large magazine and barrel besides, for a pistol it would necessarily make the arm heavy; — one of the general objects connected with a revolver would be to have it no heavier than was necessary for security. With five or six barrels, it would be necessary to have more weight than with one or two. He must attend, therefore, as a general principle, to make these arms effective, that they contain weight and strength enough for security, but at the same time that they should not be more cumbersome than necessary to accomplish the object pointed out. All those general principles Mr. Colt seems, from his specification, to claim. He seems to have sought, in his combination, some way to cock, uncock, turn the revolver, and hold it in its place, while the discharge was going off. If he could not do that, although he had the cylinder with six chambers, it would be a mere child's toy. He, therefore, sets out, in his first claim, that he combines the breech with the lock, so that by lifting the hammer to cock the lock, the cylinder shall be turned; and he goes on to enlarge upon that in the second claim; the cylinder must be held firm for a time, in order to effect the discharge; and then, after the discharge, he wants to turn it again, and therefore there must be some way to liberate it, which is the second combination. These are the two leading combinations that he sets out in his specification; then there is a third, in regard to the nipples and partitions; the fourth and fifth are subordinate matters.

The first inquiry, after seeing what his combinations are, is whether there were any arms, preceding his, which involve and unite these different improvements which he sets out he had made, and were the same in principle. A great deal has been said here about methods in the specifications. The patent is not for a method, merely, but for a machine operating in that method, or mode, or form, which the patent covers. Now, was there a former fire-arm which contained this first combination in substance, and the second in substance, and the third? or, was there one which contained any one of them? If there was a machine which contained one of them, it would precede him on that one, but only on it. If there is any one of the five which did not exist before him in that form, he is entitled to recover on that. You are now prepared to take up the different fire-arms which, it is said, existed before, and were similar in substance to the plaintiff's.

The only gun, according to my minutes, which is contended to have been of an earlier date than Colt's invention, provided he made it in 1831, as he contends he did, is what is called the French or Coolidge gun, about which you have had a good deal of testimony,— some from the person who manufactured it and sold it pretty extensively, and was interested in the use of it. That was patented abroad about 1818, and published in 1825, so that it is early enough in date; and the only question is, whether the combination and the machinery used there to effect the object was the same in substance or principle with that in Mr. Colt's. It is contended, on the one hand, that it was similar, and experts have been put on the stand to prove it, some of whom speak of a spring in it for revolving the chambers, as different from the common spring which is used in fire-arms, being acted upon, and making a movement by that action, and by the inherent power of the spring; in other words, it was a coil spring, wound up by the hand. On the part of the plaintiff, experts say that this kind of a spring, and the mode of operating it, was different in substance from the mode of operating in Colt's, by drawing up the hammer, and in that way causing the chamber to revolve without any coil spring. On that subject I am requested to charge you whether in point of law that coil spring is the same with the common spring which is often put into fire-arms. I must confess my inability to do it, unless you first find the fact for me, and that fact I submit to you. Whether it is the same in substance or principle, depends on whether it is the same kind of an instrument or not, and whether it acts in the same way in substance, and produces the same result in substance. If it does, you may consider it, in law, the same in principle. But, on the contrary, although called a spring, if it operates on a principle different from springs usually employed, if the results are not the same, if it does not act in the same manner, if it is to be wound up by hand in order to make it continue to operate, I should tell you it is not the same in point of law. Things may go by the same name, and not be the same in substance or principle. We talk about the main-spring of a watch, but it is a very different thing from some springs; yet it is a spring. Whether it is like others in substance or not, is a question for the jury to determine, and not the Court; it is a question of fact.

But I would recommend you to look at this question, as to the similarity of the French or Coolidge gun, in another view. Was that gun or rifle made so that it could operate as Colt's does? is the hand used no more in it than in Colt's? In Colt's the hand is used to draw the hammer and cock the piece, and for nothing else, so that you can go on revolving it *ad infinitum;* of course, some one must use the hand to reload. Did the Coolidge gun operate in that way? Must you, or must you not, in that gun, use the hand to wind up the spring, as well as to draw back the hammer, before you can turn the cylinder? Must you not use the hand there again, and wind up the spring?

But there is another consideration connected with this which possesses some importance, and that is,—whether it was different or not,—did it succeed like this of Colt's? If it was the same in substance,—if it was the same in principle,—would it not have succeeded as well, and did it succeed as well? On that you must go to the testimony of Mr. Collier. He said, that after making a small number, compared with the whole, he became satisfied, as all others who used the arm did, that this spring was inefficient and unnecessary in his gun, and that it was flung aside entirely, and the barrels have ever since been turned by the hand at every discharge. These are considerations to be weighed in connection with the opinion of experts. If you believe that that spring was the same in substance as Colt's,—that it operated as well as Colt's, that it was not flung aside, and still continues to operate,—if you believe it could be used originally with no more employment of the hand in connection with it than in Colt's, you are at liberty, and ought, probably, to come to the conclusion, that it contained in substance all that is in Colt's. But, if you do not believe these things, if you believe the reverse was true, then this should not be considered as taking away from Mr. Colt his merits as the original inventor.

I say this is the only gun which is pressed upon you earlier than 1831, the supposed date of Colt's invention. As to that date, however, there seems to be some conflict, to a certain extent. As I stated, in your hearing, in the progress of the case, while the testimony was putting in, the date of the invention is the date of the discovery of the principle involved, and the attempt to embody that in some machine,—not the date of the perfecting of the instrument. It was on that account that I did not consider it pertinent to go into the testimony as to the progress of the perfecting of the machine. If the invention was made,—if it was set forth in a machine which would and did discharge a fire,—that is all which is necessary to constitute the invention. But the party cannot get a patent until he perfects it in some sense of the word,—that is, until he goes on and makes improvements to render it practical and useful,—for it is one element of a machine, necessary to sustain a patent, that it is useful. It is a very different thing to sustain a patent, when it is attacked by another patent, from what it is to show the invention compared with a prior invention; that invention is the discovery of the main principle of the machine, and embodying it in wood or iron, or of whatever it is to be composed, and making it act. Perhaps I go quite too far in requiring all these things; but such is the state of society, and such is the pirating principle which governs many, that it is necessary. I have tried a case here in which, when a party was perfecting a machine, another man stole into the workshop, examined the principle, got the dimensions, and pirated the principle before the inventor had an opportunity to perfect the machine in any sense of the word. He could not get out his patent until he got his machine made, and so that it would work; but he could protect himself against a pirate who encroached upon him.

In order to settle the point of invention here, before you go any further, you have the testimony not only of Mr. Chase, but some half-a-dozen who saw this invention, and saw two specimens in iron or steel, as early as 1831. Those specimens and drawings are produced, and the witness (Mr. Chase) swears that they have been in his possession ever since, until a few months ago. To contradict that, I do not remember any testimony. There are some circumstances which ought to be weighed, as far as they should be, against this positive proof, coming from a variety of sources. One is, that although Mr. Colt considered his machine then perfected so as to entitle him to a patent for it, and he started for Washington with drawings and models, he did not get it patented until 1836; and that this delay is a circumstance which would go to raise some probability that he had not made his invention perfect. If there was no positive testimony that he had made it, this would be entitled to some consideration; as it is, you must give it such weight as it deserves. For, in addition to this, the plaintiff produces the testimony of Mr. Elliot, that in 1832 Mr. Colt went to Washington with his fire-arm, and with drawings, for the purpose of taking out a patent. In 1831 the transaction took place at Hartford, and the invention in 1832 had made such progress as that he thought he was entitled to take out his patent; and Mr. Elliot then thought it a beautiful machine, and that it would be useful, and recommended the delay, in one sense of the word showing that the circumstance about the delay is not entitled to the weight it usually might be. Mr. Elliot recommended the delay, and that he should go to Europe and take out a patent abroad, because fire-arms are unfortunately needed all the world over, and needed more in Europe than here, although we use them pretty freely sometimes; and also that he should file a caveat here, setting out, substantially, his claims, and warning the Patent Office against issuing a patent to anybody else for a like thing; that caveat, they say, was burned in the Patent Office in 1836.

If you believe that the plaintiff's invention was made in 1831 or '32, all the others, except the French gun, seem to be of a subsequent date. The Smith gun, which is the one pressed most strongly as to date, was not finished, according to the mass of the testimony, until 1833,— some considered that it was in 1834,— but it was not finished, so as to be an operative piece, until 1833; and if so, it is wholly immaterial to go into any consideration as to how near it resembles the plaintiff's, for if it was of subsequent date, it does not impair or impeach his. Mr. Colburn admits that his gun was not made until 1833; his patent is dated '33. It had a double trigger. But, if it was not until 1833, there is no use of going over these various considerations, travelling to Michigan, to Auburn and back again, and seeing all these processes and contrivances alleged to have been resorted to, to color and rust up and fit the gun for the trial, and the explanation which has been made why this was done, and that no fraud was contemplated, and no improper agency was exerted about it; all these are of no consequence, if it was as late as 1833, and Colt's was invented in 1831 or '32.

You see why the point of invention is so important, and not patenting; because, if Colt's was invented in 1831 or '32, and was known to several persons in Hartford, although he attempted to keep it as quiet as he could, he was probably pirated upon by these persons, rather than they pirated upon by him, especially if Colburn was at Hartford. The importance of showing these other improvements and machines, similar to Colt's, before, is, that if they existed before, he may have copied them; but if all which were similar in principle existed after, he did not copy from them, but they were likely to have copied from him. But it often happens that they do not copy at all; that they are a sort of independent original inventors; yet such is the law that the date of the invention becomes very material, because it is the earliest in date that is then to succeed.

The Ohio gun was as late as 1834 or '35; and if you believe it was several years after Colt's, it is not important to go into the differences.

I do not propose to say anything more on this subject, except to have you put to your brethren, Mr. Foreman, when you return to your room, after reviewing the evidence, this general consideration: Did any of these guns succeed as the plaintiff's did? If they did, it raises a strong presumption, in addition to any testimony, that they were similar. As I said about the French gun, did they operate as Colt's did? as successfully? did they continue to operate? If they were the same in principle, another question occurs in connection with that fact, and which you will consider and give it its due weight, and no more: whether you have heard on the stand, in the progress of this case, or anywhere else, of the power and effectiveness of Smith's rifles in the world; have they crossed the Atlantic, or penetrated the wilds of America? Coolidge's guns, used now without anything to turn them but the hand, — do you hear and read of them as circulated through both hemispheres? The Ohio gun, — the Colburn gun, — have they succeeded? are they known? do the experts, the men of science here, speak of them as displaying something new, beautiful, and successful? That is to be considered.

On the other hand, it is true, things may fail for a time, and not eventually — not entirely; the parties may not choose to patent them, even if they contain something valuable. But what is the presumption? If these great improvements were made before Colt made them, what became of them? why did they disappear any more than his, if they were the same in principle and in substance? That is to be considered and weighed with the other testimony, and that importance given it which seems rational under all the circumstances of the case.

I hasten to another consideration connected with this subject — as to the extension, in the procurement of which, the defendants aver that there was some moral fraud, and that it should, therefore, vitiate a recovery here by the plaintiff. As you heard in the course of the trial, the commissioner, in acting on this subject, acts under a law of Congress; and it is his business to conform to the law; it is his business not to make the extension until he is satisfied that the party has not been sufficiently rewarded: and when he is so satisfied, it is his duty to grant the extension making it in conformity to the law. It is not the case of a suit between A and B. It is a proceeding pending between a patentee and the government; but, with abundant caution, the government says, in its law, that when this application is made, the commissioner shall give notice to the world, that they may come in and show why it should not be extended. In this case, notice was given, and a certain time fixed for the purpose. Nobody appeared. Probably some opposition was expected, from the adjourning of it; the adjournment may have been made for the purpose of receiving other testimony, the testimony not having been prepared until it was ascertained whether there would be opposition testimony as to expenditures and receipts, to see how the balance stood. Notice of the day had been given in Court; anybody disposed to make opposition could do so; no one chooses to go: I do not know that the commissioner does wrong, after that, whenever he has evidence that the party was not remunerated, in making an extension. It ought to be made seasonably, that the party may know whether he is to have seven years more; and I do not know that anybody has a right to complain, if he does not choose to go there and make opposition, at the time mentioned. But, whether he did right or wrong, the extension is legal; it is valid as regards the original patentee, and nobody has a right to complain, in a moral or any other point of view, who got notice and did not choose to go and attend to it, whether because he did not intend to show that Mr. Colt had made a great deal out of it at that time, or because he thought it more liberal to let the extension take place, or that it was very likely to take place if he did oppose it, on account of the great merit of the machine. Whatever may have been the cause, he did not appear at the proper time, and the commissioner made the extension; it is, therefore, in point of law, valid, and I see in it no evidence of fraud. If there was any fraud at all, it would be in the commissioner, rather than anybody else. The jury cannot find fraud, without evidence.

It is said, too, there was an assignment, and therefore Mr. Colt could not recover. Counsel have not dwelt upon it, in the close, on either side. It appeared, in a subsequent stage of the case, that the interest which was assigned has been reässigned, in conformity with the laws of New Jersey; and therefore he is entirely justified in recovering, if he makes out his case in other respects. I would not instruct you that the agreement produced here would, of itself, revest the title in Mr. Colt; because I think that the meaning of the agreement is, that if the Patent Arms Company ceased to make these arms, they licensed Mr. Colt to go on and make them, instead of themselves. It is rather a license than a revesting of the interest. But I do instruct you that this reässignment is, in law, valid, and is enough without going to the other.

There is one other consideration which has been suggested in the progress of the trial,—that the plaintiff claims all modes for doing the thing, and therefore he claims too much. In point of law, the claim must be construed to mean the modes which he points out for his operations, and not any and all modes. It is true the operation of the law is such that any mode which is equivalent to the one he points out, which is similar, is covered by his patent, when he claims a particular mode; but he does not in his patent claim only what he points out, and that covers all which are similar and analogous, which vary only in form. Having made this suggestion, I come now to the last consideration, which is considered by the defendants of considerable importance,—the point of infringement.

I have already suggested to you what are the leading principles which would govern in an infringement. The defendants' patent must use something which is one of the combinations of the plaintiff's, in order to infringe; they must have taken some one of the combinations, and used it. Adding and infringing as much as they may, if they have taken one, they are liable for the use of that one. It is true that there may be a distinction of another kind; if a defendant does not add, but makes a change,—merely improves one part of the machinery used,—he may do that, and not be liable in the common acceptation of the term, and it might not be considered as a separate and additional improvement, but a change which is made by itself. If they be improvements, for instance, of the bevel gear and ratchet, that has nothing to do with Mr. Colt's mode of moving the cock, and fastening the revolver, and all that. There is a cog put in there which is new; it is there, in and of itself, whether it is an improvement or not. If it is an improvement, it can be protected as such; but it does not enable them to use other portions of Mr. Colt's patent — other portions, which they never invented, and never got a license to use.

Experts throw some light upon this point, as to whether the defendants' pistol does not use in substance what is in Colt's. It may use them more or less in some particulars, but does it use what Colt's uses, and what he invented in substance, — some efficient part of the machinery? Messrs. Mapes and Blanchard swear that it uses in substance the same as Mr. Colt's, with a variation of form, and of mechanical equivalents. On the contrary, witnesses on the part of the defendants seem positive that it is not similar in substance.

There is another consideration in connection with this,— and where you can find general considerations to advert to, perhaps they are safer than contradictory testimony,— Do you, or do you not, believe that Wesson invented the machine or pistol,— whether he would ever have made it, if he had not seen and profited by Colt's in doing it? and was he not trying to defeat the renewal of Colt's patent in 1850? He was there, by his counsel. He had had Colt's to see for twelve years, or more; — could he have made his unless he had seen and profited by it? Does not that raise the presumption? That is for you to consider. If not, why did he want to defeat the extension of Colt's? Why, if Colt's had not been extended, it would have expired, and he and everybody else could have used it with impunity!

I do not know that there is much in the consideration pressed on the one side or the other about which is superior. That is not the question; it is whether they operate upon a similar principle. Though on that subject, if you think right to advert to it, you can take not only the testimony upon both sides, but that of the Board of Ordnance, which examined both, to see which was superior, and decided, for reasons which have been laid before you, that Colt's was superior to the defendants'. I do not consider that a question of great magnitude; though, if the jury choose to go into it in connection with other matters, they have a right to do it.

I believe I have suggested to you everything which is proper for me to say on the subject. Doubtless other considerations will occur to yourselves. I have no wish, in this case, but that you should examine it carefully, and render such a verdict as the sense of the jury dictates.*

---

* The jury rendered the following verdict:

"The jury, in the case of Colt *vs.* the Massachusetts Arms Company, find, in the plaintiff's gun, a new and novel combination to produce the effect described in his patent, *not found* in any other fire-arm prior to his invention; and the jury further find the defendants have infringed the first three claims of the plaintiff's patent, and assess damages in the sum of one dollar, according to the agreement."

# CHARGE TO THE JURY IN THE CASE OF WILLIAM W. WOODWORTH, AS ADMINISTRATOR, &c., *vs.* RODOLPHUS C. EDWARDS ET AL.*

It must be gratifying to your feelings, Gentlemen of the Jury, that this cause is so far concluded, although your final duty, and an arduous one, soon begins.

The details have been so full upon both sides, that I apprehend there will be no difficulty about your deciding aright. The differences, gentlemen, which arise in patent cases, spring frequently from parties misunderstanding the law, and, at other times, from ignorance of each other's facts. It is important, therefore, that you properly understand the law, and apply it to the real facts now under consideration. I shall not go over the testimony in detail. But, in order to understand what is in dispute, and what you are to try, you should recollect that the plaintiff in this suit moved for an injunction on the equity side of this court, against the defendants, to restrain them from infringing, by use of the Brown machine, the rights of the plaintiff under the Woodworth patent; which restraining power the court, without a jury, possesses under the act of Congress. After hearing arguments, the court came to the conclusion that there had been an infringement, and granted the injunction. They considered that the defendants had no more right to use the machine, if truly belonging to the plaintiff, than they had to use his horse, or any other property; and my associate judge and myself, after most mature deliberation, granted the injunction. Brown, himself, who is the patentee of the machine in use by the defendants, had been enjoined in the Circuit Court of the United States for the District of Vermont, and that, too, previous to the decision here. The question may be asked, then, how the present action came here. The Court of Chancery does not use a jury, unless the facts are difficult in its own view, or the title of the plaintiff is denied. Then the court may wish in the first instance, and the defendants may claim in the second instance, and the court consent to order an inquiry before a jury. Although the plaintiff may have been using Woodworth's machine, and, either by himself or his assignees, had been in possession of the right for nearly a quarter of a century, and recovered in various cases, yet he had not recovered against the defendants. They had the right, therefore, to have the

* This case was tried at Boston, — commenced March 27th, and given to the jury April 16th, 1848.

title tried at law, with themselves, in my view; and, in coming to that conclusion, I had great respect for the opposite view of one of my associates in New York. Yet I preferred to send it to a jury,— of whose judgment, as to facts, I have a high opinion,— although other courts have declined. I told the parties then, gentlemen, that although Woodworth was prima facie the inventor, and his patent had been repeatedly sustained, with others, yet, if the defendants in this case should make an affidavit stating that they did not believe Woodworth was the inventor of the planing machine, and should offer to try the issue before a jury, if the plaintiff did not accept the offer, and bring an action at law, I would dissolve the injunction.

You will, then, try the question, "Is Woodworth the inventor?" If that turn out to be true, and the defendants have used a machine like his in principle, they should respond in damages. What are the objections to Woodworth's title? I say objections, because his title is made out, prima facie. He has a public authority in his favor. He has a patent. He has had his patent renewed by a Board of Commissioners, under the 18th section of the act of Congress approved July 4th, 1836; again, by an act of Congress, and afterwards reïssued by the Commissioner of Patents, upon a surrender for a defective specification. In addition, the counsel for the plaintiff has read to you various judicial decisions in his favor. Woodworth has long been in possession, and has made sales to a large amount; and, if I am not in error, the patent has never been defeated in a trial on the merits. The counsel for the defendants said that there was a verdict at Albany; but that was on a collateral question, since cured by a disclaimer; and something was said of another in Pennsylvania. But where is the evidence of any other? If there is any evidence, give it its weight. But everything in doubt is to be construed in favor of the inventor. Twenty years have nearly elapsed since the patent issued at first. The title is thus almost as strong, gentlemen, as the titles under which you hold your lands, unless disproved by the respondent.

The defendants contend (1) That the original patent granted to William Woodworth, on the 27th day of December, 1828, has expired, and that the extension, obtained under the 18th section of the act of Congress, is fradulent and void; (2) That the reïssued specification is different from the specification of 1828, and for a different machine; (3) That it is not only void for the causes named, but that Daniel Dunbar, and not William Woodworth, was the original inventor; (4) That the invention of the planing machine is clearly indicated in the writings of General Bentham, in the fifth volume of the Repertory of Arts; and also in the 10th volume of the Repertory of Arts, a work published in England, and known in this country; also by Malcom Muir, in Scotland, whose patent bears date the 1st day of June, 1828; also by the Hill machine, which was said to have been in use in 1827 and 1828, at Woburn, in this State; by the Hale machine, patented by John Hale, the 21st day of June, 1828; and lastly, by Uri Emmons. If they make out to your satisfaction any one of these, then the defence is complete; or, if they shall satisfy you that the renewal or extension of the patent was obtained of the board by fraud, or that the reïssued specification by the Commissioner of Patents was applied for and obtained by fraud. You see, then, gentlemen, what you are to try: first, the claim of the plaintiff; and, second, the defence on the part of the respondents, denying the plaintiff's title; and that denial is the chief reason why the case goes to you. They have a right to make such denial, if they believe in its truth.

It is a rule in this country, that mind, as well as business, is open to competition, provided the competition does not injure the rights of others. Hence this machine, patented to Brown, should be used, if it can be without injury to the rights of others.

But it does not matter that it is the rights of others as patentees; these rights are rights of property as much as their wheat which is growing in the field. This is not doing injustice to the community. If the machine is invented by an individual, by his talents and toils, other persons have no right to take the idea or the machine away from him. I know, gentlemen, that a patent is sometimes considered odious, and there is much talk about monopolies. But a patent is not one in that sense; it is a right that is guaranteed by the constitution. In section eighth of that instrument, you will find an exclusive use allowed to be guaranteed to a patentee, in order to encourage science and the arts. This is not a monopoly of what belongs to others; it is merely securing his own property, as perfected by him, and not discovered before. But if pretended to have been discovered before, then it is to be shown. The respondents urge that the questions shall be tried as if they had not been tried before. If we had not ruled so, in one sense of the term, the case would not have come before you. But, on the other side, the facts and circumstances are far different from what they must have been at the first trial. Now, the plaintiff has a right to lay before you evidence, beside his patent; such as twenty years of possession, a large amount of sales, two renewals or extensions, and several recoveries, some in chancery and some at law. All these, therefore, tend to show more strongly that he has a title. All are to be weighed by you, and should, of course, prevail, unless you are satisfied that there is, prior to this, or in his renewal or surrender, something to defeat his right.

So far from falling short of England in liberality, in most of our principles, we ought, at least, to keep pace with her. It is now a familiar English rule of patent law, that, where there is a doubt, the inclination should be in favor of the patentee; because the design is to encourage improvements, and where a party has taken out a patent and made a mistake, he has, and should have, a right to correct it. In England it is incorporated now into the English patent itself; and I asked for one, the other day, if it could be obtained, to show the fact, that if there is a doubt, it is to be taken most strongly in favor of the patentee. The forms may be seen in Godson and Webster.

Under these rules, gentlemen, proceed to the first objection. It is, that the patent was defective. If so, it may be surrendered, and the mistake corrected. The commissioner has the right, upon that surrender, to cause a new patent to be issued for the unexpired term. But the allegation is, that this amendment was done to deceive, and included, through fraud or otherwise, what was not originally invented. If so, the new specification ought not to be upheld. Now, look at the patent itself. The old law did not in terms allow a correction, but the courts held that it was proper; and when the patent law of 1793 underwent a revision in 1836, a section was incorporated authorizing the patentees to surrender the patent, and take out a new and amended patent, in case of an error in it, through inadvertence or mistake. There are two points, gentlemen, about which there can be no doubt. First, the respondents do not deny that the patent can be surrendered, if insufficient; and, secondly, that the commissioner is the judge, if surrendered, of a mistake. The law makes it so, and his decision is evidence that there was a mistake or inadvertence, unless fraud was practised on him. It is said that the mistake must have been a fatal one. I do not so understand it. If the patent was infringed, and some expression was of doubtful construction, leading to litigation, lessening the value of the right, and rendering it in some degree inoperative, that would be sufficient. That was the case with this patent. The specification was defective as to pressure rollers, and was surrendered; and I instruct you, gentlemen, that the administrator of William Woodworth had a right to surrender the original patent, and that the Commissioner of Patents had a right to cause a patent to be issued with an amended specification, including pressure rollers, if they were a part of the original invention, and omitted by inadvertence; and that the patent, thus reïssued, is good and valid in law, unless it is shown to have been obtained fraudulently.

Now, gentlemen, what is brought against the fairness of this amendment? Why, what occurred at Hudson in the summer of 1828, showing that no such rollers existed there. This we will examine hereafter. It is also said that there is a difference in the language of the two patents; that the new patent had something different, and which is not in the original patent. I mentioned, the other day, the case of amending a writ or plea. You could not wish to amend a writ, if the same language is to be used. If amended, it must be for the same cause of action, but not in the same language. It is so with the patent. It must be for the same invention; the language is different; and in a writ the language would be different. Why get out an amended writ or patent, even in substance in the same language? Of what use?

Next, as to the Hudson machine. The true inquiry here is, to see if the matters covered by the amended language had been used by

Woodworth in December, 1828, when he took out his patent. The testimony given at Hudson goes back to what existed in the summer of 1828, and not December. That is one species of evidence. The machine built at Hudson in the summer of 1828, and which was afterwards taken to the dry dock, in the city of New York, is to be considered; and Dunbar swears that it did not contain pressure rollers. But new machines, with alterations, were afterwards built at the dry dock, before December. Morse, a respectable citizen, says that he saw one there in October, with such rollers. Between the summer of 1828 and October, what Woodworth added, we cannot tell, except by the evidence. It is agreed and proved, that at the dry dock there were several new machines which were undertaken, and that some of them were not useful. But the great change is the pressure rollers, which were used to carry forward the material, to keep it down, and to aid in reducing it to an equal thickness. The question, then, is, Did pressure rollers exist in the original machine at the dry dock, before December, or did Woodworth borrow them afterwards from Emmons? Beside the oath of Mr. Morse, just referred to, who was at the dry dock, and saw the machine, in October, 1828, swearing that there were pressure rollers then, Mr. Wells testifies to the same point, and Mr. Strong, who drew the specification, that he knew then of the pressure rollers. It is for you to pass upon this evidence. The machine of Dunbar, with his evidence, might be prima facie against this. But it may all be true, as matters were at Hudson in the summer of 1818, and yet Woodworth might afterwards have added them, before December, 1828; for his witnesses testify, positively, that in October pressure rollers had been introduced by Woodworth, and before he took out his patent.

As to the point of fraud, that is settled by the previous decision in favor of his actual use of the pressure rollers, before taking out the patent. There is no evidence of fraud, gentlemen, except that growing out of the new specification, and, as is argued, its averring too much. If you believe, however, that the rollers were there before December, 1828, then that ends this inquiry. Fraud is nothing slight; it must be shown by no equivocal evidence; it must be fully made out. But it is also said, that there was fraud practised before the Board of Commissioners; and that is the next point. There was a witness on the stand who had objections to the renewal, and who went to Washington to oppose the renewal upon other grounds; as an assignee, and not on the ground of Woodworth's not being the inventor. But, after a conference with Mr. Wilson, he was satisfied as to the assignment. It is said, also, that there is evidence of fraud in the accounts,— that there were several hundred thousand dollars received, though not so much cleared. But the amount received is unimportant, if little was realized. Was the amount stated fairly? This is a question for you. If the truth was exhibited, then it would not appear that any fraud was practised. These are all the objections as to the letters patent themselves.

Next, —Was the invention original? Before you go into the question of other similar and prior machines, you will ask yourselves what principles does Woodworth's machine contain? What was it for? It was an improved machine for planing, tonguing, and grooving, plank and boards. It is not for any new element, different from that which before existed, or for a new wheel or cylinder alone, but for a new combination of parts. Now, this is just as common as getting out a patent for a new part; and it is as patentable, if a new combination, as if he had invented a new machine.

One of Arkwright's inventions was for a new combination, rather than for new parts. A new combination requires genius, labor and expense, and is often as useful as a new part. What did Woodworth profess to combine in his machine? Why, to combine knives upon a cylinder or wheels with pressure rollers, according to the specification of 1845, so as to plane, tongue and groove, if necessary, at one operation. Anything else? The cylinder was to have a movable head.

When you commence your inquiry, you will ask the question, whether the machine was so constructed; and whether, if so, it would answer a valuable purpose. It has been properly said, that a description which you cannot understand is not to be depended upon. But this machine worked well in October and December, 1828; one witness said, better even than now. It would be taking you too far to show you slight differences between this and prior inventions. All the great discoveries have proceeded gradually, little by little. Take the art of printing: it was approaching for one or two centuries; the clergy and nobility, each man, had his seal, and the letters or insignia were there, and stamped. But it was not a type, —it was not printing. Blocks had been known for stamping articles, but they were not types; and when printing was discovered, when movable letters were used, and applied to multiply manuscripts, that was the great invention that perfected it. So with the mariner's compass. For ages, the nearest approach was to float the needle in a bowl of water, stuck in a straw. But some lucky genius discovered that it might be fixed on the centre, and thus revolve better. The change was slight, but the great object was accomplished. So with the introduction of steam. I have seen the original printed patent granted to Rumsey, by the laws of Maryland. The patent says nothing about steam, but moving boats against a current. He wanted something of that kind secured: and although steam was doubtless his agent, and steam had been known abroad, as powerful to move machinery, in Spain, and by the Marquis of Worcester, by Watt, and many others, by Fitch and others here, yet it was not successful in this way until the time of our own Fulton. Before Fulton, it was three miles an hour in navigation; afterwards, it went up, until it reached a useful speed of fifteen to twenty miles, and far greater than could have been originally attained. There was a novelty and utility in this which has proved incalculable.

Now, gentlemen, we are prepared to pass to the other machines, and see if they are, in all important particulars, like the machine of Woodworth at the dry dock. *First*, I will recur to the testimony of Dunbar, about his model for his machine. All that he testifies about took place twenty years ago. He says that all at Hudson was suggested by him to Woodworth; and the defendants have produced Riesdorph and Ray, and one or two others, to confirm him. It is further alleged, that Woodworth became involved in disposing of his second machine, of 1836; and he said to one of the witnesses, at that time, that the patent of 1828 was not his invention. You will look at the testimony, and say what there is to meet this. This is a mere declaration of Woodworth, after he had chiefly sold out, and not under oath. Against it, is the oath of Woodworth, when he applied for his patent, and the two oaths of his attached to the proceedings in chancery, which had been laid before the court in the case wherein John Gibson was plaintiff, and Woodworth and Russells were defendants. There Woodworth swears, again and again, that he is the inventor. There is also Riesdorph's own letter to Wilson, of like tenor; and the testimony of Beekman, and Morse, and Wells, and Strong, to show that Woodworth was really the inventor of what was most useful, the pressure rollers combined with the rest. And Dunbar swears that he was working under Woodworth and Strong when making his suggestions. Then Mrs. Atherton, the daughter of Woodworth, speaks of her father's confinement, when his hand was injured,— of his making drawings, and that the invention was the theme of his conversation. Then, gentlemen, we have the testimony of Mr. Blanchard, one of the most ingenious men this country has produced, as to conversations with Woodworth on the subject of a planing machine, and previous to the application to Dunbar by Woodworth. It is urged, also, with much force, that Dunbar did not even ask for a patent, and that for twenty years he did not try to defeat the application of Woodworth, any more than in 1828. There is evidence, also, that Woodworth alone did originally apply for and try to support this patent. It is to be weighed, likewise, gentlemen, that Woodworth, or his representatives, went forward to get a renewal of it. If Dunbar had been the inventor, would he not have told of it then? — although that would not have been conclusive. Again, Congress, supposing that Woodworth was the inventor, granted a second extension to his heirs; and it is said, plausibly, that it would not have showered upon Woodworth, or his heirs, such a fortune, without proper inquiry, and without objection by Dunbar, if he was the true inventor. Woodworth, gentlemen, is dead. Dunbar is not heard of until after Woodworth sleeps in his grave, unable to reply or explain.

After you have examined this, then I will ask you to consider another point, — whether Dunbar does really conflict so much as is supposed. What is it Dunbar claims to be his suggestion, and what is it that Woodworth did invent, in the end? You are to ask whether the machine at the dry dock was not materially different from Dunbar's model? Did it not receive a new and important alteration there? The defendants say that the machine which went to the dry dock was worthless, and that, until after Emmons' patent was issued, it was of no use. But if you believe that the new dry dock machine became practical, and if what was added at the dry dock was practical, then, whatever Dunbar did do at Hudson, you are to ask whether he did enough, on his own admission, to amount to this new and useful machine. It is not pretended that Emmons' patent was taken out until 1829, and after Woodworth's was in successful operation at the dry dock, with pressure rollers. There is no pretence that Woodworth had been at Syracuse to pirate them, or that Dunbar had invented these rollers.

What is the next prior invention set up? It is contended that Emmons had, as early as 1824, attempted to plane at Syracuse. I do not intend to go into the evidence on this. It has been insisted that the machine at Syracuse would not work. Gifford, for whom, and at whose cost, it was made, swears it would not work. Upon the principle which I have laid down, it must, in order to defeat the patent of Woodworth, have been the same thing in principle, and suited to effect the same object. He must have perfected, also, something useful. It is conceded, on both sides, that it did not satisfactorily work; and it was abandoned, and taken to pieces. You will look at the after doings of Emmons in 1829, and see whether you must not believe there were sinister purposes in them. You have heard it said that there had been a piracy on Woodworth, and that certain persons had applied to Emmons, who, for a consideration, undertook to get a patent for his former machine; and that the papers were prepared, and an application made to Dr. Jones, who was then at the head of the patent office, who agreed to issue a patent on Emmons' oath that it was invented early in 1824.

Woodworth poor and thus harassed, there was a compromise made, which, standing alone, would be much, but, with all the explanations, may have little weight. So Emmons' own confession, before his death, satisfied Woodworth's opponents that he did not really invent, in 1824, what he patented in 1829.

You will see whether, on the other proof, Emmons' patent planed the same way, and tongued and grooved the same way. If not, then, what it was, and what was its modus operandi, and whether unlike Woodworth's, I will leave for your consideration. If it had succeeded well, and in 1824 Emmons had operated it, he would have been prior to Woodworth; but if he did not, and he and Twogood and others, in 1829, had designed to do wrong, he could go to the Patent Office and copy from Woodworth, as I have before said. Is it proved that he ever put a machine in successful operation, even in 1829?

I will proceed next to Muir's machine. That is earlier in date, and if the same, though a foreign patent, must prevail. It appears that, three or four years after his first patent had been issued, Muir took out a new patent, combining Woodworth's improvements. I would recommend you to see what the planing was at first done with; whether stationary knives planed the surface of the board, and whether it was like the machine of Woodworth, which does not work with stationary knives, but with revolving knives. The principle is entirely different. Woodworth operates by an adze cut, while in Muir's machine the knives are stationary, and the board is shoved over.

I will then recommend you to go to Bentham, and see whether he describes a machine like Woodworth's;—not separate and detached parts of a machine, but did he have an actual machine like this, or describe this? It is put as a description, and not as of a practical machine. I do not think that is sufficient, unless it describe something which did or would operate in the same way.

You will examine the Bramah machine in a like way. Then I will call your attention to the machine of Hill, which was not patented. The test is, did the Hill machine succeed? Because, if they were alike, it would succeed as well as this. You have boards planed in it before you. The Hill machine principally planed boards for boxes. Did it reduce to an equal thickness, or did it discharge well its shavings? These are important elements.

You will then go to Hale's. Did Hale's succeed? And, if it did, was it calculated to effect the same object? Would it reduce to an uniform thickness? Would not the clamps, or teeth, which dragged the board through, injure the face of the board?

I next call your attention to the Smith machine. Did his patent succeed? Some of the witnesses say it could not succeed. But did it plane? What did he do with it? What kind of a wheel had he? If it planed at all, did it not plane with knives put on the side or disc of the wheel?

I shall not detain you any longer, gentlemen, by detailing the testimony. After going through it all, and deciding upon the credibility of the several witnesses, you are to say whether Woodworth was the inventor. And if he was the inventor, then you are to inquire as to the infringement and the damages.

You will first inquire about the infringement. Mr. Adams has said, in two affidavits filed in this court, that the principle of the Woodworth machine, and the principle of the Brown machine, are the same. And if you look at Mr. Brown's patent, you will find that he describes rather an improvement as his, than the whole machine. Now, if he has invented an endless carriage, as an improvement, Woodworth cannot use it. If he buys of Woodworth the right, he can use the original machine, and, in addition, his improvement of the carriage;

and nobody else can use the carriage, without his consent. That his machine is an infringement, is not only proved here, but has been before in chancery, against both Brown and the defendants.

Finally, upon the question of damages, if you see nothing on the part of the respondents but an honest wish to test the title of the plaintiff, I do not think that, in questions of this kind, smart money should be given. I do not see anything in the case to call for vindictive damages, if they are ever proper. The plaintiff should be made whole, and no more.

It is not the profit alone that is to be accounted for; it is also the extra cost to sustain the right, which has been expended. It is proper that lawyer's fees should be allowed; the untaxable cost of obtaining testimony from abroad and at home. I have always had the fullest confidence in the jury-box. Jurors will bring sound common sense to aid them in their deliberations. I have always thought that a jury would know how to act on all matters of fact, better than the court could; and so far as regards facts, would be inclined to do what would be right in these cases. I, therefore, gentlemen, leave the case with you, on these matters, with entire confidence.

The counsel for the defendants requested the court further to charge the jury, as it did in writing, on the following points, though some of them had been before embraced in the charge.

1. Whether the new patent of 1845 be substantially for a different invention from the patent of 1828, is a question for the jury on the evidence. (4 Howard, 403.)

*Answer.* It is subject to the rules of evidence in respect to it, stated by the court.

2. The eighth question certified up to the Supreme Court, in Wilson *v.* Rousseau, is in these words: "Whether the court can determine as matter of law, upon an inspection of the said two patents, and their respective specifications, that the said new patent of the 8th July, 1845, is not for the same invention for which the said patent of 1828 was granted."

"The question involved in the eighth point propounded does not present any question of law which this court can answer." (4 Howard, 688.)

*Answer.* None, except as charged to the jury.

3. Instruct the jury that if the mere changing the keyed rollers were only such an alteration or addition as any mechanic of ordinary skill would naturally make, then the mere change of those rollers was not the subject of a patent.

*Answer.* It was not, unless it introduced a new principle, and answered a new end.

4. That if the jury are satisfied that Dunbar invented the cutter wheel, represented in his model, and described in the plaintiff's patents of 1828 and 1845, such invention negatives Woodworth's

right to such a cutter wheel; that the plaintiff has never claimed any other wheel; so that the defendants have either combined a cutter like Dunbar's, with his feeding apparatus, a combination in which, and in each element of which, the plaintiff has no right, or else have used a cutter substantially unlike the plaintiff's, and have therefore committed no infringement.

*Answer.* In such case, he could not patent the cutter wheel alone, but only in combination with something else, not before combined together.

5. That if Hale's machine contains the same elements and the same combination claimed by the plaintiff, then, although said machine had not operated successfully, so as to be permanently employed, the plaintiff had not a right to adopt Hale's elements and combination, and claim to hold them as his own patentable invention.

*Answer.* The plaintiff has no right to patent exactly such a combination as some one had invented before; and a prior invention is not a bar, if it was useless, and abandoned.

6. That the words in Woodworth's specification of 1845, "employment of rotating planes substantially such as herein described," limit his invention to such rotating planes as he has expressly described in his preceding specification; and that if the cylinder used by the defendants substantially differs from those rotating planes, such use is no infringement of the plaintiff's rights.

*Answer.* If it differ in principle from them,— not without.

7. That the plaintiff, in his patent of 1845, claiming the combination of his cutter with certain rollers, "as described," is limited by his previous description; and if, from said previous description, it appears that the rollers used by the plaintiff were feeding rollers, and used for that purpose, and if the jury find that the defendants do not use rollers for feeding, as described by the plaintiff, but feed by a substantially different arrangement of means, such use is not an infringement of the plaintiff's rights.

*Answer.* The rollers may be used for pressure, as well as feeding, and the use of the combination of the cutter knives with them is not affected by changing the mode of feeding by some mechanical equivalent or analogous device.

8. That simply changing the form or the proportions of any machine, in any degree, is not a patentable invention.

*Answer.* Unless so changed as to introduce a new principle, or new material results.

9. That a change of form which produces a difference in the degree of the result, but not in the kind of result, does not, because of such difference, constitute a patentable invention.

Same answer.

10. That if the patent of December 27, 1828, was not, at the time of its surrender, inoperative or invalid by reason of a defective or insufficient description or specification, or by reason of the patentee claim-

ing in his specification as his own invention more than he had a right to claim as new, then the surrender was unlawful, and the new patent of July 8, 1845, is void.

*Answer.* The decision of the Commissioner is prima facie binding as to that, but may be rebutted.

11. That a patent is valid and operative in law, when it has been found so by the verdict of a jury, trying its validity, sanctioned by the judgment of the court; and when the patentee and his assigns obtain injunctions restraining the unlicensed use of any machine described or indicated by the specification and drawings.

*Answer.* This question does not arise, as there is no evidence of a former trial where this objection was taken.

12. That if the specification of December 27, 1828, was defective, yet, if the defect did not arise by inadvertence, accident, or mistake, but from a fraudulent and deceptive intention, the patent is void.

*Answer.* Yes, but the finding of the commissioners is prima facie the other way.

13. That if said patent of December 27, 1828, was invalid or inoperative, by reason of a defective or insufficient description or specification, yet, if the patentee did not, within a reasonable time, specify anew to cure such defect, that is a circumstance which the jury may take into consideration to determine whether the defect, if there was any, arose from fraud.

*Answer.* No such point is made. But the jury may consider it, as to fraud, or not.

14. That if the patentee, in his patent of November 15, 1836, fully described any of the operating parts of the machine now claimed as of the invention of 1828, and made oath that the operating parts of the machinery itself, in the two machines of 1828 and 1836, were unlike, and dissimilar, and bore no resemblance to one another, and that the machine patented in 1836 was not an infringement upon or in addition to the machinery patented in 1828, that is conclusive evidence that no part of the machine of 1836 was embraced in the machine or covered by the patent of 1828.

*Answer.* This is not exactly pertinent, probably; but may be considered, though it is not conclusive.

15. That if the Hill machine actually did exist, and was used, as testified to by the Hills and Gilson, and actually did embrace the combination now claimed by the plaintiff, as testified to by Adams and Coney, and if Woodworth only made an improvement upon said machine, and has claimed the whole machine, or the whole combination, instead of his improvement only, then his patent is void for having claimed too much.

*Answer.* No; unless Hill's was earlier, and worked well, and was not abandoned.

16. That if the cutting cylinder in the defendant's machine is not

substantially the same as that described and included in the claim of Woodworth, then the defendants have not infringed.

*Answer.* The two machines are to be compared, and the jury are to decide if the last contains the important principles in the first, though it may also contain some additions or changes.

17. That the application of rotating knives such as were before known, and used for planing gun-stocks and other materials, to the planing of boards, is not a substantial patentable invention.

*Answer.* There is no such question here as that. The patent is not for a new part, but for a new combination. But it would not be patentable if the object was merely changed, and there was no change in the machine.

18. That if the substituting a solid cylinder with knives attached to longitudinal flanges, instead of a cutting-wheel with knives attached to its head by screws, produces a rotary cutter containing a new principle,—to wit, a firm and continued support for the blades,—and thereby performing better work, and so materially affecting the result, such a solid cylinder is patentable as a substantive new invention, and the use of it is not an infringement upon a patent right to use the double-headed wheel with the detached knives.

*Answer.* No such question arises, or has been argued. But it alone might be patentable, if different in principle, though it would not justify using with it any old and useful combination, which had before been patented.*

---

* The jury found a verdict for the plaintiff of five hundred dollars.

# ON THE POWER OF THE LEGISLATURE AS TO PUBLIC MATTERS, WITHOUT IMPAIRING CONTRACTS.*

THIS is a writ of error, under the 25th section of the judiciary act, brought to reverse a judgment rendered by the Supreme Court of the State of Connecticut.

It is claimed by the plaintiff that the clause in the constitution of the United States against impairing the obligation of contracts was set up there in defence to certain proceedings which had been instituted against that corporation by virtue of rights derived from legislative acts of that State, and which acts the plaintiff insisted had impaired the obligation of a contract existing in behalf of East Hartford.

It being manifest, from the record, that such a defence was set up, and that the court overruled the objection, so that jurisdiction exists here to revise the case, we proceed to examine, whether, on the facts of the case, any such contract appears to have existed, and to have been violated by the State legislation, which was drawn in question.

It will be seen that the point before us is one of naked constitutional law, depending on no equities between the parties, but on the broad principle in our jurisprudence, whether power existed in the Legislature of Connecticut to pass the acts in 1818 and 1841, which are complained of in this writ of error.

The supposed contract claimed to have been impaired related to certain rights in a ferry, which were alleged to have been granted by the State across the Connecticut river. This grant is believed to have been made to Hartford as early as the year 1680, and half of it transferred to East Hartford in 1783. But no copy of the first grant being produced, nor any original referred to, or found, it is difficult to fix the terms or character of it, except from the nature of the subject, and the subsequent conduct of the parties, including the various acts of the Legislature, afterwards passed, regulating this matter.

From these it is manifest that two leading considerations arise, in deciding, in the first place, whether by this grant a contract like that contemplated in the constitution can be deemed to exist. They are, first, the nature of the subject-matter of the grant, and next, the character of the parties to it.

---

* Case of the Town of East Hartford, plaintiff in error, *vs.* the Hartford Bridge Company. Supreme Court of the United States. December term, 1850.

As to the former, it is certain that Connecticut passed laws regulating ferries, in 1695; and Massachusetts began to grant ferries as early as 1644 (Col. Charter, 110 p.), and to exercise jurisdiction over some even in 1630. (Charles River Bridge *v.* the Warren Bridge, 11 Peters, 430.) In 1691, she provided that no one should keep a ferry, without license from the Quarter Sessions, and under bonds to comply with the duties and regulations imposed. (280 p.)

In the rest of New England it is probable that a similar course was pursued, by the Legislatures making, as a general rule, the tolls and exercise of the franchise entirely dependent on their discretion. But in some instances the owners of the lands, on the banks of small rivers, opened ferries upon them, and claimed private interests therein. And in still other cases of public grants to private corporations or individuals, a similar interest has been claimed.

It is highly probable, too, that, in some instances, public corporations, like the plaintiff in this case, may have set up a like interest, claiming that the subject-matter granted was one proper for a contract, or incident to some other rights, like private interests owned on the bank of a river.

Supposing, then, that a ferry may, in some cases, be private property, and be held by individuals or corporations under grants in the nature of contracts, it is still insisted here that the ferry across a large navigable river, and whose use and control were entirely within the regulation of the colonial Legislature, and came from it, would be a mere public privilege or public license, and a grant of it not within the protection of the constitution of the United States, as a matter of contract.

But it is not found necessary for us to decide finally on this first and more doubtful question, as our opinion is clearly in favor of the defendants in error on the other question, namely, that the parties to this grant did not, by their character, stand in the attitude towards each other of making a contract by it such as is contemplated in the constitution, and as could not be modified by subsequent legislation. The Legislature was acting here on the one part, and public municipal and political corporations on the other. They were acting, too, in relation to a public object, being virtually a highway across the river, over another highway up and down the river. From this standing and relation of these parties, and from the subject-matter of their action, we think that the doings of the Legislature, as to this ferry, must be considered rather as public laws than as contracts. They related to public interests. They changed as those interests demanded. The grantees, likewise,—the towns,—being mere organizations for public purposes, they were liable to have their public powers, rights and duties, modified or abolished, at any moment, by the Legislature.

They are incorporated for public, and not private objects. They are allowed to hold privileges or property only for public purposes. The members are not shareholders, nor joint partners in any corporate estate, which they can sell or devise to others, or which can be attached and levied on for their debts.

Hence, generally, the doings between them and the Legislature are in the nature of legislation, rather than compact, and subject to all the legislative conditions just named; and, therefore, to be considered as not violated by subsequent legislative changes.

It is hardly possible to conceive the grounds on which a different result could be vindicated, without destroying all legislative sovereignty, and checking most legislative improvements, as well as supervision and amendments over its subordinate public bodies.

Thus, to go a little into details, one of the highest attributes and duties of a Legislature is to regulate public matters, with all public bodies, no less than the community, from time to time, in the manner which the public welfare may appear to demand.

It can neither devolve these duties permanently on other public bodies, nor permanently itself suspend or abandon them, without being usually regarded as unfaithful, and, indeed, attempting what is wholly beyond its constitutional competency.

It is bound, also, to continue to regulate such public matters and bodies, as much as to organize them at first. Where not restrained by some constitutional provision, this power is inherent in its nature, design and attitude; and the community possesses as deep and permanent an interest in such power remaining in and being exercised by the Legislature, when the public progress and welfare demand it, as individuals or corporations can, in any instance, possess in restraining it. (See Taney, J., in 21 Peters, 548—7.)

In Gosler *v.* the Corporation of Georgetown, 6 Wheaton, 596—8, it was held, that a city, with some legislative power as to bye-laws, streets, &c., could, after establishing a graduation for its streets, and after individuals had built in conformity to it, change materially its height. This case appears to settle the principle that a legislative body cannot part with its powers, by any proceeding, so as not to be able to continue the exercise of them. It can and should exercise them again and again, as often as the public interests require, and though private interests may intervene; and then should not be injured, except on terms allowed by constitution. Yet, public interests in one place or corporation may be affected injuriously by laws without any redress, as legislation on public matters looks to the whole, and not a part, and may, for the benefit of the whole to the injury of a part, change what is held under it by public bodies for public purposes. The Legislature, therefore, could not properly divest itself of such control, nor devolve it on towns or counties; nor cease, from any cause, to exercise it on all suitable occasions. (Clark *v.* Corp. of Wash. 12 Wheat. 54.)

Its members are made by the people agents or trustees for them on this subject, and can possess no authority to sell or grant their power over the trust to others. (Presby. ch. *v.* City of New York, 5 Cowan, 542. Fairtille *v.* Gilbert et al., 2 D. and E. 169.)

Nor can the public be estopped by such attempts, since the acts of their agents are to be for the public and for its benefit, and not for themselves individually, and are under a limited authority or jurisdiction, so as to be void if exceeding it.

Looking to the subject when, as here, the grantees, as well as the grantors, are public bodies, and created solely for municipal and political objects, the continued right of the Legislature to make regulations and changes is still clearer.

Perhaps a stronger illustration of this principle than any yet cited exists in another of our own decisions.

In the State of Maryland *v.* Baltimore & Ohio Railroad (3 Howard 551) this court held that a grant by the Legislature to a County of a sum forfeited could be dispensed with by the Legislature afterwards, as it was made for public, not private purposes, and to a public body.

There is no private interest or property affected by this course, but only public incorporations and public privileges. It may be otherwise in case of private bodies, or individuals, or of private property granted or acquired. The Legislature might not be justified to revoke, transfer or abolish them, on account of the private character of the party or the subject. (Paulet *v.* Clarke, 9 Cranch 292; Tennet et al. *v.* Taylor et al. 48—5.) But every thing here is public.

While maintaining the exemption of private corporations from legislative interference, Justice Washington, in 4 Wheaton, 659, in the Dartmouth College case, still admits that corporations for "*public government*,"—such as a "town or city,"—are under the control of legislation; whereas private corporations are governed by the statutes of their founders, or by their charters (660, 661). He remarks further, that the members of such a public corporation "accepted the charter for the public benefit alone; and there would seem to be no reason why the government, under proper limitations, should not alter or modify such a grant, at pleasure." (661, 663.) And Justice Story concurs with him, by saying:

"It may also be admitted that corporations for mere public government, such as towns, cities and counties, may, in many respects, be subject to legislative contract." (4 Wheat. 694.)

When they are wished to be not in some respects so subject, but to act exclusively, it should be expressed so in the constitutions of their States. What is exclusive in them would there appear expressly; and when it is not, a legislative provision, if made for the purpose of rendering it exclusive, is, for the reasons before stated, doubtful in its validity.

The public character of all the parties to this grant, no less than its subject-matter, seems, therefore, to show that nothing in the nature of a contract, with terms to be fulfilled or impaired like private stipulations, existed in this case, so as to prevent subsequent interference with the matter by the Legislature, as the public interests should appear to require.

But, in order to justify the plaintiff in what he set up below, there must not only have been a contract, or quasi contract, but a violation of its obligation. It will, therefore, be useful to follow out further the nature and conditions of this supposed contract, in order to throw more light on both the questions, whether this grant was such a contract as the constitution contemplates, and whether it has been at all impaired. The authority of a Legislature may probably supersede such a ferry as is public, and across a great public highway of a navigable river, by allowing a bridge over the same place, as has before been virtually held by this court. (11 Peters, 422, and 6 Howard, 507.) It could, also, alter or abolish wholly the public political corporation to which the grant was made, as this is yearly done in dividing towns and counties, and discontinuing old ones. It is therefore clear that, whatever in the nature of a contract could be considered to exist in such a case, by a grant to a town of some public privilege, there must be implied in it a condition that the power still remained, or was reserved in the Legislature to modify or discontinue the privilege in future, as the public interest might, from time to time, appear to require. (Charlestown Bridge et al. *v.* Warren Bridge et al., 11 Peters, 421; West River Bridge *v.* Dix et al., 6 Howard, 507.)

Accordingly, it is admitted, in this case, that the Legislature, as early as 1695, in fact, regulated the tolls of this ferry, and continued to do it until 1783, when it granted to East Hartford one-half of the privilege, and that only "during the pleasure of the Assembly." All concerned in the privilege, therefore, became thus estopped to deny that this ferry was to be used by the town as a mere public license, and to be used in conformity with the views of the Legislature, as to what in future might be deemed most useful to the community at large.

Because the old town of Hartford acquiesced in this regulation of tolls, and in this transfer of half to East Hartford in this limited or conditional manner, and the latter acquiesced in the acceptance of it, on the terms expressed, to hold it during "the pleasure of the Assembly."

Such being, then, the public character of the subject, and parties of the grant, and such the terms and conditions of it,— rather than being one of private property, for private purposes, to private corporations or individuals, and absolutely rather than conditionally,— in what respect has it been violated by the Legislature?

No pretence is made that it has been, unless by the discontinuance of the ferry in 1818 and in 1841. The former act of the Legislature was passed under the following circumstances: A bridge had been authorized over the river, near the ferry, as early as 1808; and no provision was then made as to the ferry, probably from a belief it would, after the bridge was finished, fall into disuse, and be of no importance to anybody.

No objection was made, or could be sustained, to the constitutionality of this incorporation in this way. (11 Peters, 420; 4 Pick. 463.) But when the bridge became damaged greatly in 1818, and the company was subjected to large expenses in rebuilding, the Legislature deemed it proper to provide, in its behalf, that the ferry should not be kept up afterwards, except when the bridge became impassable.

The words were, that "after the company shall have repaired the bridge, &c., the ferries by law established between the towns of Hartford and East Hartford shall be discontinued, and said towns shall never thereafter be permitted to transport passengers across said river," &c.

This bridge corporation, being the present defendants in error, proceeded therefore to rebuild and keep up their bridge in a more costly manner, and beneficially and safely to the community. They were a private pecuniary body, and were aided much by the suspension or discontinuance of the ferry, in their additional charter.

The Legislature, in making the discontinuance, did only what it supposed was advantageous to the public, by securing a better, quicker, and surer method of passing the river on the bridge; and they thus appear to have violated no condition or terms of any contract or quasi contract, if it had made any with the plaintiff. (11 Peters, 542.)

On the contrary, as before suggested, the Legislature merely acted within its reserved rights, and only passed a new law on a public subject, and affecting only a public body But, beside the implied powers continuing in the Legislature, as heretofore explained, and which warrant all it did in 1818, and the exercise of which cannot be regarded as impairing any contract, we have seen that there was an express provision in the grant to East Hartford, limiting the half of the ferry transferred to it, "during the pleasure of the Assembly."

The legislative pleasure, expressed in 1818, that the ferry should cease, came, then, directly within this condition; and the permission to exercise that pleasure in this way was not only acquiesced in from 1818 to 1836, but was treated as the deliberate understanding, on both sides, from 1783 to 1836.

The statute-books of Connecticut are full of acts regulating ferries, including this, and modifying their tolls from 1783 downwards, and in many instances imposing new and onerous duties. (See 1 Stat. of Conn. 314 to 327.)

And to show how closely the power of the Legislature was exercised to regulate this matter, without being regarded as impairing, in that way, any contract or obligation, it appears that when Hartford was incorporated into a city, about 1820 (Rev. Stat. 110), it was expressly provided:

"But said city shall have no power to regulate or affect the fisheries in or *the ferry upon said river*," — Connecticut.

Well, too, might East Hartford, in 1783, be not unwilling to take her charter and half the ferry, subject to this suspension; as her own existence at all, then and thereafter, depended on legislative pleasure; and, as all the property or privileges of the old town would remain with the old one, when a new was carved out of it, unless otherwise expressly provided. (4 Mass. 384; 2 N. H. 20.)

Our inquiries would terminate here, as this legislation, in 1818, is the supposed violation of a contract that was chiefly relied on below, had there not been several other acts of legislation as to this ferry in 1836, 1841 and 1842, some of which are claimed to have impaired contracts made with the plaintiffs, either then or in 1783.

But the act of 1836, about which much has been said in the argument here, and much was, very probably, urged in the court below, simply repealed that part of the act of 1818 discontinuing the ferry. It thus affected the bridge company deeply and injuriously, but did not impair any supposed contract with East Hartford; was not hostile to its rights, and is not, therefore, complained of by that town, nor open to be considered as a ground for revising the judgment below, under this writ of error.

On this, see Satterlee *v.* Mathewson, 2 Peters, 413; Jackson *v.* Lamphire, 3 Peters, 289, 7 Peters, 243, 11 Peters, 540; Strader *v.* Graham, 10 Howard.

The State court, however, pronounced it unconstitutional, and had jurisdiction to do it; and if they had not arrived at such a result, they could not have sustained some of their other conclusions.

This decision of theirs, being founded on their own constitution and statutes, must be respected by us, and, in this inquiry, must be considered prima facie final. (Luther *v.* Bender, 7 Howard, 1, and cases there collected.)

We shall, therefore, not revise the legal correctness of that decision, but refer only to a few of the facts connected with the repeal of 1836, and with the decision on it below, so far as is necessary to explain the legislation subsequent to it, and which is yet to be examined.

The Legislature does not appear to have proceeded at that time on any allegation of wrong or neglect on the part of the bridge company; nor did they make any compensation to the latter for thus taking from it the benefits of a discontinuance of the ferry, and attempting to revive half the privileges again in East Hartford. The State court appears to have considered such a repeal, under all the circumstances, as contrary, at least, to the vested rights of the bridge company, and to certain provisions in the State constitution. (See, also, The Enfield Bridge *v.* The Hartford & Springfield Railroad, 17 Conn. 464.)

But, without going further into the history of this proceeding, in

1836, and the decision on it by the State court, it is manifest that the dissatisfaction and complaints growing out of it, or some other important reason, induced the Legislature, in 1841, to repeal the repealing act of 1836, and thus to leave the bridge company once more in the full enjoyment of its former privileges, after the ferry had been discontinued, in 1818.

To this conduct of the Legislature, the plaintiffs in error objected; and, under this writ, ask our decision, whether it does not impair contracts which had before been made with them by the Legislature. In reply, it need only be stated, that we think it does not, and this for the reasons already assigned, why it was competent for the Legislature to pass the discontinuing part of the act of 1818, if it thought proper, and in this did not violate the constitution of the United States as to contracts.

But matters were not permitted to remain long in this position. In 1842 the Legislature proceeded to repeal the act of 1841, and thus sought virtually to restore the ferry to Hartford and East Hartford, as it stood before 1818. It appears to have done this on the complaint of East Hartford, that half of the ferry had been taken away from her without making "any compensation."

It is unnecessary, in relation to this last repeal, to say more than that, like the repeal of 1836, and for like reasons, the State court pronounced it void; and on the ground before explained, we are not called on by this writ to reconsider or reverse that decision.

It follows, then, finally, that East Hartford, in proceeding to exercise the ferry privilege again since 1842, and to the special injury of the bridge company, has done it without legal authority, and should, therefore, be restrained by injunction from exercising it longer.

The judgment below must be affirmed.

## ON GRANTING NEW TRIALS BY THE LEGISLATURE.*

THIS case is an appeal from a decree of the Court of Probate in this county, approving an instrument which purported to be the last will of Nathaniel Ward

It appears, from the copies of the proceedings, and the admissions of the parties, that, on the sixth day of June, A. D. 1806, Ward died; that, in the instrument before mentioned, all his property was devised to Benjamin Merrill, the plaintiff's intestate; that, on the twenty-third day of the same month, Merrill obtained a decree of the Court of Probate, approving and allowing in common form said instrument as the last will of Ward; that Merrill thereupon took and retained quiet possession of said property, till December 28, 1812, when the defendants, being heirs at law of Ward, petitioned the Court of Probate to reconsider, in solemn form, the decree before mentioned, and to disallow said instrument; that, on the 4th of February, A. D. 1813, said court did reconsider, and affirm the former decree; that the defendants claimed an appeal therefrom to the Superior Court, in which the appeal having been entered, all the issues joined between the parties were, at Nov. term, 1813, found against said Merrill; that he then made a motion for a new trial, which, after a full hearing, was refused, and at November term, 1814, final judgment was rendered, that the decree of the Court of Probate be reversed, and said instrument disallowed. Merrill then petitioned the Legislature for another trial; and they, at their June session, A. D. 1817, passed an act, granting to the plaintiff, as administratrix of Merrill, at that time deceased, liberty to reënter said cause in the Superior Court, and there have it re-tried, like common cases of review. Pursuant to that act, the plaintiff served a copy of it on the defendants, which required them to appear in this court, at September term, 1817, and proceed to a new trial of the cause. The names of the parties were at that term entered on the docket, and the defendants appearing, moved the court to quash the proceedings, on the ground that the act of the Legislature was unconstitutional. The cause was continued for argument upon that motion, and is now to be decided.

It involves a question of no small magnitude. For the motion contains a charge, that encroachments have been made upon constitutional rights; and though in form the measures of a branch of the govern-

* Case of Merrill *v.* Sherburne ; tried in Rockingham Co., N. H., Sept. term, 1818. Opinion of the Superior Court of New Hampshire, on the question, — " Has the Legislature a right to grant new trials in any case, and if so, in what cases ? "

ment towards a few individuals only are arraigned, yet in substance those measures affect the interest of all, as the rule of construction adopted to-day may become a precedent to-morrow, and be adduced to vindicate, or oppose, similar conduct towards every member of society. The alarm thus excited induces most people to listen to such charges with great readiness; and it would not be unnatural for courts, in examining these charges, sometimes to fancy the existence of what is only feared.

Perhaps, also, it is inseparable from the structure of the legislative and judicial departments, that jealousies should arise between them as to the exercise of their respective powers. For they were intended, in some degree, to be mutual checks (Miller on Ranks, 287. Fed. No. 47, p. 78); and though thus situated, both ought to rejoice that their own errors can be discovered, and corrected. Yet such are the dispositions of mankind, that collision is often the consequence of these checks, and encroachments are suspected where none are meditated, and when in truth the obnoxious measures were only new exercises of legitimate powers. To detect mistakes in others is likewise flattering to the vanity and ingenuity of some. From these and similar circumstances, therefore, it has happened, that questions of this nature have not always been examined with that coolness and patience which their importance deserved; and that, since the adoption of our constitution, courts of justice, as well as legislative bodies, have furnished some complaints that their jurisdiction has been violated, when those complaints were not founded upon sound principles or respectable precedents. Conscious of the force of these considerations, we have, in the present cause, experienced considerable embarrassment; but duty has compelled us to act, and it hardly need be repeated, that we have attempted to divest ourselves of every feeling, except an earnest desire to perform what duty dictated. It must be admitted, that courts ought to decide, according "to the laws of the land," all cases which are submitted to their examination. To do this, however, we must examine those laws. (Fed. No. 78; 7 John. 494; 3 Cok. 7; 6 Bac. Stat. H.) The constitution is one of them, and "is, in fact, and must be regarded by the judges as a fundamental law." (Fed. No. 78.) It was created by the people, who in our republics are "the supreme power" (Bill of Rights, art. 8); and, it being the expression of their will, their agents, as are all the branches of government (Bill of Rights, art. 8), can perform no act which, if contrary to that will, should be deemed lawful. "To deny this, would be to affirm that the deputy is greater than his principal; that the servant is above his master; that the representatives of the people are superior to the people themselves; that men acting by virtue of power may do, not only what their powers do not authorize, but what they forbid." Their oaths of office, too, prohibit, and the constitution itself, in express terms, prohibits, the Legislature from making "laws repugnant or contrary to the constitution." If, then, there should happen to be an irreconcilable variance between the constitution and a statute, that which has the superior obligation and validity ought, of course, to be preferred; in other words," "the intention of the people ought to be preferred to the intention of their agents. Nor does this conclusion by any means suppose a superiority of the judicial to the legislative power. It only supposes that the power of the people is superior to both; and that, where the will of the Legislature, declared in its statutes, stands in opposition to that of the people, declared in the constitution, the judges ought to be governed by the latter, rather than the former. They ought to regulate their decision by the fundamental laws, rather than by those which are not fundamental." Our confidence, also, in the liberality of the Legislature is such, that, when through inadvertence or mistake they have passed an unauthorized act, we believe that, should the unpleasant task of adjudging it void devolve upon us, they would think the task is performed only from a conviction that the act is in the *clearest* manner unconstitutional, and that our right and duty so to pronounce it are both unquestionable. (Dal. 386; 1 Cran. 175; 4 Mas. R. 1; 5 do. 533; 6 do. 77, 375; 10 do. 302; 11 do. 402; 12 do. 253; 4 John. 75, 80; 8 do. 388; 9 do. 564; 1 Gal. 19.) To determine whether the act which awarded a new trial to the plaintiff was thus unconstitutional, it is necessary to ascertain what was its nature and effect. When Ward died, all his estate descended to the defendants, unless "by him devised to other persons." (Stat. 207.) Merrill claimed that it had been "devised" to him: the defendants questioned it: a controversy commenced; legal proceedings were instituted; and after two hearings on the merits, and after a new trial had been asked and refused, it was adjudged that Ward had made no valid devise of his estate. Being dissatisfied with these decisions, Merrill transferred his application for a new trial to the Legislature. They examined his testimony, and heard counsel. They then, by the present act, enabled him "to enter said cause anew at the Superior Court," and directed "that said cause shall have former trial; and the said court are hereby authorized and empowered, upon said new trial, to affirm or reverse the former judgment, or decree, day in said court, and shall be heard, tried and determined, in said court, upon the pleadings had on the appeal aforesaid, as the said new trial may terminate for or against either party." &c.

This does not empower the court, in their discretion, to grant or refuse a new trial, but directs that "the cause *shall* be heard" again; and thus amounts to an absolute reversal of the judgment in November, 1814, against the motion of Merrill for another trial, and also to an alteration of the judgment on the merits, from a final and absolute judgment, to a judgment which this court might "affirm or reverse," as the said new "trial might terminate for or against either party." Whether, in their inquiries, the Legislature and the court proceeded upon the same or different evidence, doth not change the nature and effect of the act, when stripped of the forms of legislation: because, unless it virtually reversed the judgment which was rendered against the motion of the plaintiff, and altered, as above mentioned, the judgment on the merits, they could be pleaded in bar to the present proceedings, and we should not be justified in holding another trial, and in rendering another judgment in this case, while the first judgments remained in full force.

Such being the operation of the act, it becomes proper to examine,

1. Whether the passage of it was not an exercise of judicial powers.

2. If it was, whether our Legislature are a branch of the judiciary.

3. If they are not, it will then remain to inquire, whether the Legislature, either by special clauses in the constitution, or as a mere legislative body, possesses authority to pass an act containing such provisions as the act under consideration.

1. No particular definition of judicial powers is given in the constitution; and, considering the general nature of the instrument, none was to be expected. Critical statements of the meanings in which all important words were employed would have swollen it into volumes; and when those words possessed a customary signification, a definition of them would have been useless. But "powers judicial," "judiciary powers," and "judicatories," are all phrases used in the constitution: and though not particularly defined, are still so used as to designate with clearness that department of government which it was intended should interpret and administer the laws. On general principles, therefore, those inquiries, deliberations, orders and decrees, which are peculiar to such a department, must, in their nature, be judicial acts. Nor can they be both judicial and legislative; because a marked difference exists between the employments of judicial and of legislative tribunals. The former decide upon the legality of claims and conduct; the latter make rules, upon which, in connection with the constitution, those decisions should be founded. It is the province of judges to determine what is the law upon existing cases; but of legislators to declare what shall be the law in future cases. (6 Bac. Stat. H.; 2 Cran. 272; 7 John. 498.) In fine, the law is *applied* by the one, and *made* by the other. To do the first, therefore,— to compare the claims of parties with the laws of the land before established,— is in its nature a judicial act. But, to do the last,— to pass new rules for the regulation of new controversies,— is in its nature a legislative act; and if these rules interfere with the past, or the present, and do not look wholly to the future, they violate the very definition of a law, as "a rule of civil conduct" (1 Bl. Com. 44); because no rule of conduct can, with consistency, operate upon what occurred before the rule itself was promulgated.

It is the province of judicial power, also, to decide private disputes "between or concerning persons" (Const. 9th page); but of legislative power, to regulate public concerns, and to "make laws" for the benefit and welfare of the State. (Const. 7th page.) Nor does the passage of private statutes conflict with these principles; because such statutes, when lawful, are enacted on petition, or by the consent of all concerned; or else they forbear to interfere with past transactions and vested rights. (2 John. 263; 8 Co. 138. art.; 1 Inst. 176; 2 Cran. 344, 345; 2 Bl. C. 344, 345.) As the Legislature, then, in the act under consideration, adjudicated on a case which had already happened, and had been litigated between individuals, their proceedings must, on general principles, be deemed an exercise of judicial powers. But, regarded in a more particular sense, the character of their proceedings cannot be different.

A legal process had been instituted in a subordinate court,—had been heard, and then, by appeal, carried to a higher tribunal. It had been re-heard in that tribunal, and, after a motion for a new trial was overruled, a final judgment had been rendered, which, by existing statutes, closed the controversy forever. The Legislature then undertake to revise these proceedings: they convene the parties, canvass the evidence, and afterwards reverse, in substance, the interlocutory judgment, and materially alter the effect of the final judgment of this court. If these doings of the Legislature are considered a mere continuation of the former doings of the courts, then, as those former ones were judicial, so are these. But if they are considered as disconnected with the former doings, they are still judicial, on account of their nature and effect. The grant of a new trial belongs to the courts of law, from immemorial usage. The power to grant a new trial is incidental to their other powers. It is a judgment in relation to a private controversy; affects what has already happened; and results from a comparison of evidence and claims with the existing laws. It will not be denied, that the consideration and decision by the Superior Court of the motion for this same new trial was an exercise of judicial power. If so, a consideration and decision upon the same subject by the Legislature must be an exercise of power of the same description; for what is, in its nature, judicial to-day, must be judicial to-morrow, and forever. The circumstance, also, that the Legislature themselves did not proceed to make a final judgment on the merits of the controversy between these parties, cannot alter the character of the act granting a new trial. To award such a trial, was one judicial act; and because they did not proceed to perform another, by holding that trial before themselves, the first act did not become any more or less a judicial one. We apprehend, therefore, that the character of the act under consideration must be deemed judicial. This position will probably be less doubted than the position that our constitution has not confided to the Legislature the power to pass such an act. But that power, if confided, must be exercised by the Legislature as a branch of the judiciary, or under some special provision, or as a mere legislative body.

2. Our next inquiry, then, is, whether they, as a branch of the judiciary, are enabled to exercise it. No article in the constitution can be designated, which, in specific terms, makes the Legislature a branch of the judiciary. Consequently, if it is, it must depend upon inference; and that inference, it is admitted, can be drawn from nothing but the grant of powers to the General Court, and from the 31st and 37th articles in the bill of rights. By that grant they are invested with "full authority to make all manner of wholesome and reasonable orders, laws, statutes, ordinances, directions and instructions, either with penalties or without, so as the same be not repugnant or contrary to this constitution." But nothing is here said of decrees or judgments, or of judicial power. The phraseology is altogether peculiar to legislative subjects. Though styled the "General Court of New Hampshire" (Const. 9; 9 Cok. Pref. 7), they are considered in the first section to be merely "the supreme legislative power." The constitution, then, proceeds to state, not that this General Court shall be a branch of the judiciary, but that they "shall forever have full power and authority to erect and constitute judicatories;" not that they themselves shall hear and try private controversies, but that the "Courts of Record," so constituted, "shall be holden in the name of the State for the hearing, trying and determining all manner of crimes, offences, pleas, processes, plaints, actions, causes, and things whatsoever, arising or happening within this State, or between or concerning persons inhabiting or residing or brought within the same."

As to the 31st article of the bill of rights, it merely provides that "the Legislature shall assemble for the redress of public grievances, and for making such laws as the public good may require." Yet "the grievance" attempted to be redressed by the act under consideration was not a "*public*" one; and, if it were, the obvious meaning of the article is, that such grievances should be redressed by "laws," and not by proceedings which are, in their nature, judgments. The constitution afterwards confers upon the Legislature only legislative power for the purpose of effecting that "redress."

The 37th article is more ambiguous. It declares that, in the government of this State, "the three essential powers thereof — to wit, the legislative, executive and judicial — ought to be kept as separate from and independent of each other as the nature of a free government will admit, or as is consistent with that chain of connection which binds the whole fabric of the constitution in one indissoluble bond of union and amity."

It has been contended, and we with readiness admit, that, from the close of this article, the inference is clear that our constitution did not intend to make a total separation of the three powers of government. The executive was to be united with the Legislature in the passage of laws; and the former was to depend upon the latter for his salary. A part of the judiciary, too, was united with a part of the

Legislature in the trial of some impeachments; and all of the judiciary were made dependent on the executive for appointments, and on the Legislature and executive for the erection of courts, the apportionment of jurisdiction, for compensation, and for removal by address.

But these connections and dependencies are not left to implication; they are all created by subsequent express provisions: and the above article was probably clothed in such cautious language that it might not conflict with those provisions. (Fed. No. 47, Mr. Madison.) It means no more than a similar article in the Illinois constitution, which, after dividing the powers of government, proceeds to say (15 Niles' Reg. 93) "that no person, or collection of persons, being one of these departments, shall exercise any power properly belonging to either of the others, except as hereinafter *expressly* directed and permitted." For, in our constitution, if any one power, not afterwards expressly permitted or properly belonging to one department, could be exercised by it through implication, these consequences will follow: either that no powers need have been expressly permitted, or apportioned, as the whole could, through implication, be exercised by either branch; or that, though some are expressly apportioned, others may be implied and exercised contrary to the *spirit* of what are so apportioned.

As the 37th article, then, declares the general propriety of a separation between the different departments of government, and as it contains no qualifications of that principle which are inconsistent with excluding the Legislature from judicial powers, "properly belonging to another department," no inference from this article can be deduced, that the Legislature were intended to be a branch of the judiciary. In fine, that they were not so intended by this or any other part of the constitution, is manifest from many more circumstances, some of which it may be proper to enumerate.

At the formation of our present constitution, whatever might have been the prior connection between the legislative and judicial departments, a great solicitude existed to keep them, thenceforward, on the subject of private controversies, perfectly separate and independent. (1 Bl. C. Ap. A; Letter of Judges Sup. Court of U. States, April, 1792.)

It was well known and considered, that "in the distinct and separate existence of the judicial power consists one main preservative of the public liberty" (1 Bl. Com. 269); that, indeed, "there is no liberty, if the power of judging be not separated from the legislative and executive powers." (Montesquieu, B. 11. Ch. 6.) In other words, that "the union of these two powers is tyranny" (7 Johnson 508); or, as Mr. Madison observes, "may justly be pronounced the very definition of tyranny" (Fed. No. 47); or, in the language of Mr. Jefferson, "is precisely the definition of despotic government." (Notes on Vir. 195.)

Not a single constitution, therefore, exists in the whole Union, which does not adopt this principle of separation as a part of its basis. (Fed. No. 81; 1 Bl. Ap. 126, Tuck. Ed.; 3 Niles' Reg. 2; 4 do. 400.) We are aware that in Connecticut, till lately, and still in New York, a part of their Legislature exercises some judicial authority. (4 Niles' Reg. 443.) This is probably a relic of the rude and monarchical government of the eastern world; in some of which no division of powers existed in theory, and very little in practice. Even in England, the executive and judicial departments were once united (1 Bl. 267; 2 Hutch. His. 107); and when our ancestors emigrated hither, they, from imitation, smallness of numbers, and attachment to popular forms, vested often in one department, not only distinct, but sometimes universal powers. (2 Wil. Wks. 50; 1 Minot His. 27; 1 Hutch. His. 30; 2 do. 250, 414.)

The practice of their assemblies to perform judicial acts (3 Dal. 386; Calden & wife, *v.* Bull & a.) has contributed to produce an impression that our Legislatures can also perform them. But it should be remembered that those assemblies were restrained by no constitutions, and that the evils of this practice (Fed. No. 44), united with the increase of political science, have produced the very changes and prohibitions before mentioned. The exceptions in Connecticut and New York do not affect the argument; because those exceptions are not implied, but detailed in specific terms in their charters; and this power, also, as in the House of Lords in England, is in those States to be exercised in the form of judgments, and not of laws; and by *one* branch, and not by all of the Legislature. (4 Niles' Reg. 444.) "The entire Legislature can perform no judiciary act." (Fed. No. 47.) It is questionable whether at this day such an act, by all the branches of the British Parliament, though in theory omnipotent, could be enforced. (1 Bl. C. 44; 2 do. 344.) "There is a statute, made the fourth year of King Henry IV., ch. 22, whereby it is enacted that judgment given by the king's courts shall not be examined in the chancery, Parliament, nor elsewhere." (Doctor and Student, dialogue 1, ch. 8.)

Be this, however, as it may, in that country, one great object of constitutions here (Fed. No. 81) was to limit the powers of all the departments of government (Bill of Rights, art. 1, 7, 8, 38); and our constitution contains many express provisions in relation to them, which are wholly irreconcilable with the exercise of judicial powers by the Legislature, as a branch of the judiciary. That clause which confers upon the "General Court" the authority "to make laws" provides, at the same time, that they must not be "repugnant or contrary to the constitution. One prominent reason for creating the judicial distinct from the legislative department was, that the former might determine when laws were thus repugnant," and so operate as a check upon the latter, and as a safeguard to the people against its mistakes or encroachments. But the judiciary would in every respect cease to be a check on the Legislature, if the Legislature could at pleasure revise or alter any of the judgments of the judiciary. The Legislature, too, would thus become the court of last resort, "the superior court," or "supreme judicial" tribunal of the State; and those expressions so often applied to this court in the constitution (Const. art. 7, 9, 22, 20) would become gross misnomers. If our legislators, too, possess such high judicial powers, much consistency cannot exist in the provision, that "upon important questions of law, and upon solemn occasions," they may be advised by the justices of this court, which, on the above principle, is inferior and subordinate. Nor is this all. "Every reason which recommends the tenure of good behavior for judicial officers militates against placing the judiciary power, in the last resort, in a body composed of men chosen for a limited period (Ham. Wks. 255); men, too, not selected for their knowledge of the laws, nor with a view to those other qualifications which fit men to be judges." Nor are our legislators commissioned and sworn in any manner as judicial officers are required to be. Nor can they, like judges, for mal-conduct, be removed by address or impeachment. Because the House themselves are the tribunal to make, and the Senate the tribunal to try, impeachments; and both united are the bodies authorized to present addresses for removals. (Const. 13.) Nor can it easily be conceived that the judiciary are independent of the Legislature to any extent, however small, if the Legislature itself compose a part of that judiciary.

Certain reasons induce us to rest this opinion upon general principles; but, under this point, it may not be unimportant to notice one consideration of a particular nature. The constitution itself seems to declare what tribunals shall exercise jurisdiction over the subject-matter of the dispute between the present plaintiff and defendants. For it says, in express language, that till other provisions are made, the probate of wills "shall be exercised by the judges of probate," and "all *appeals* from the respective judges of probate *shall* be heard and tried by the Superior Court." (Const. 20.) No provisions have since been made which transferred any part of the above power to the Legislature.

In deciding an abstract question like this, it cannot, we apprehend, be material, whether a review is provided in appeals from courts of probate, or whether, after judgment in such appeals, a new trial could be awarded by this court, on petition by the party aggrieved. Because, if all our statutes on reviews and new trials were repealed to-morrow, the Legislature would possess no more authority to exercise judicial powers than they now possess; as their authority was confined and limited by the people at the formation of the constitution, and must continue as it was then until the constitution itself is altered. A different construction would enable the Legislature, if the Court of Common Pleas was abolished, to issue writs and try causes till other courts for that purpose were organized; and if no sheriffs happened to be in office, to proceed also to serve the writs issued by themselves.

3. As our Legislature, then, is not a branch of the judiciary, it only remains to inquire, whether, without being made a branch of the judiciary, they are, either by special clauses in the constitution, or as a mere legislative body, authorized to pass the act under consideration.

The people, being supreme, might, without intending to make the Legislature a branch of the judiciary, have invested them, by some special clause, with that judicial power which was exercised in this act. But no such clause has been found in the constitution; and without such a clause, it would be most unwarrantable to presume that the people intended to confer this judicial power on the Legislature, when all the reasons before mentioned, and the spirit of the people's language in the whole instrument, forbid such a presumption. If our General Court, then, were in any capacity authorized to pass this act, it must have been in that of mere legislators. The legislative power is surely one of the most honorable and useful in all governments. We should be among the last persons inclined to impair its rights. As it emanates more immediately from the people, it should also be ample, in order that the grievances of the people may be redressed; and we entertain no doubt that in this State all its acts of a legislative character, not prohibited by our constitution, should be supported and construed favorably. (7 John. 492; Dash *v.* Vanklack.) But those acts must in *substance* be of a legislative character. Their form is immaterial. They must be *laws*,—must be confined to subsequent occurrences. For the very nature and effect of a new law is a rule for future cases. (7 John. 503; 2 Inst. 95.) They must, too, in general, be rules prescribed for civil conduct to the whole community, and not a "transient, sudden order from a superior to or concerning a particular person." (1 Bl. C. 44.) For every subject of this State is entitled to a certain remedy, by having recourse to the laws (Con. 14); but an act which operates on the rights or property of only a few individuals, without their consent, is a violation of the equality of privileges guaranteed to every subject. It is, also, an interference with existing interests, and prescribes a new rule for the regulation of them, after they have become vested. This is forbidden by first principles. "*Vetant leges sacræ, vetant duodecem tabulæ leges privatis hominibus irrogare, id edin est privilegium.*" (Cicero de. Leg. 3: 19.) Acts of the Legislature, too, which look back upon interests already settled, or events which have already happened, are *retrospective;* and our constitution has in direct terms prohibited them, because "highly injurious, oppressive and unjust." (Bill of Rights, 23d art.) But perhaps their invalidity results no more from this express prohibition, than from the circumstance that, in their nature and effect, they are not within the legitimate exercise of legislative power. For though, under the name of *ex post facto* laws, when "made for the punishment of offences" (Dall. 386; 9 Mar. R. 363; 1 Bl. C. 46), they have long been severely reprobated, because more common in times of commotion, and because they endanger the character and person, as well as the property; yet, laws for the decision of civil causes, made after the facts on which they operate *ex jure post facto*, are alike "retrospective," and rest on reasons alike fallacious. (7 John. 495; 1 Bay. 107; Bac. Stat. 6; 3 Ham. Wks. 254; 7 Ma. R. 385.)

We wish it to be distinctly understood, however, that acts of the Legislature are not within the above prohibitions, unless they operate on the interests of individuals or of *private* corporations. (Trus. Dart. Col. *v.* Woodward.) Nor are they within them when, in an implied or express manner, the parties affected have consented to their passage; as all public officers impliedly consent to alterations of the institutions in which they officiate, provided the public deem it expedient to introduce a change. So all citizens consent to the passage of acts which the constitution in express terms has enabled the Legislature to make, though those acts might otherwise be unjustifiable; because all either aided to form, or, by living under, are presumed to adopt, the constitution. (6 Bac. Stat.; 4 Inst. 1.) Thus the constitution has ratified acts respecting the persons or estates of absentees (Const. 22.), and has empowered "the representative body of the people to take a man's property for public uses." (Const. 3.) Nor can acts of the Legislature be opposed to those fundamental axioms of legislation before particularized, unless they impair rights which are *vested;* because most civil rights are derived from public laws; and if, before the rights become vested in particular individuals, the convenience of the State produces amendments or repeals of those laws, those individuals have no cause of complaint. The power that authorizes or proposes to give may always revoke before an interest is perfected in the donee. Thus the right to prosecute actions in a particular time or manner may, perhaps, be modified or taken away at any period before actions are commenced. (10 Mass. R. 439.) So, also, may be the right of femmes covert to the dower at any period before the death of their husbands; and so the right of the next akin to a relation's estate at any period before the relation's death. But it is questionable whether even these rights, though inchoate, and in mere expectancy, can be taken from one portion of the community, and be left unmolested with another portion. (12 Mass. R. 258.) Be that as it may, however, it is clearly unwarrantable thus to take from any citizen a *vested right;* a right "to do certain actions or possess certain things," which he has already begun to exercise, or to the exercise of which no obstacle exists in the present laws of the land. (3 Dall. 294.) But previous to the passage of the act granting a new trial to this plaintiff, the defendants had become authorized, by the laws of the land, to possess all the estate of which Ward died seized. Every obstacle to the exercise of their rights had been removed or annulled; and whether those rights became vested by Ward's death, or by the final judgment in November, 1814, is immaterial; because both of these events had happened before the passage of this act. (7 John. 494; Burr. 2460.) The defendants being thus situated, the Legislature interfered; not to enact what is in its nature and effect a law, but to pass a decree; not to prescribe a rule for future cases, but to regulate a case which had already occurred; not to make a private statute by the consent of all concerned, but, at the request of one party, to reverse and alter existing judgments; not to promulgate an ordinance for a whole class of rights in community, but to make the action of a particular individual an exception to all standing laws on the subject in controversy. (Mass. R. 396.)

The expense and inconvenience of another trial were also imposed upon the defendants, and all their claims to the property in dispute, which had become indefeasible by the laws then in being, were launched again upon the sea of litigation, to be lost or saved as accident and opinion might afterwards happen to injure or befriend them.

The misfortune of having vested rights thus disturbed is not small, when we consider that, on this principle, no judgment whatever in a court of law is final. "If," says Germaine, "judgment given in the king's courts should be examined in the chancery, before the king's counsel, or any other place, the plaintiffs or demandants should seldom come to the effect of their suit, and the law should never have end." (Doct. and Stu. Dial. 1, ch. 8.) The misfortune, too, is not small, when we recollect, with Mr. Madison (Fed. No. 44), that usually "one legislative interference is but the link of a long chain of repetitions, till the properties of parties are ruined in the contest." (14 John. 73.) "The sober people of America," says he, "have seen, with regret and with indignation, that sudden changes and legislative interference in cases affecting personal rights become jobs in the hands of enterprising and influential speculators, and snares to the more industrious and less informed part of the community." "It is not," says Spencer, J. (7 John. 490), "necessary to inquire whether a Legislature can, by the plenitude of its power, annul an existing judgment. This power I should undoubtedly deny." "A Legislature (3 Ham. Wks. 254; Jefferson's Notes, 195), without exceeding its province, cannot reverse a determination once made in a particular case." The theory of the British nor the State constitutions authorizes the revival of a judicial sentence by a legislative act. (Fed. No. 81.) But it has sometimes been argued, that in case of extreme hardships, Legislatures are always authorized to interfere. The defendants deny this hardship; and though the record shows that, before the application to the Legislature, two trials had been enjoyed, — which is a greater number than the common law generally allows, — and that a motion for another one had also been fully heard and considered, yet all the hardship may be presumed which the plaintiff alleges, and still that could not confer upon one department of government a power which the constitution had withheld. In a case of great State necessity, the Legislature might be warranted in adopting strong measures. But even in that case, it would deserve consideration, whether here they could advance beyond their delegated power. In this country it is not the Legislature who are supreme, but the people; and "there is no position which depends on clearer principles than that every act of a delegated authority, contrary to the tenor of the commission under which it is exercised, is void." (3 Ham. Wks. 230; 1 Bl. 315.) The hardship in this case, however, is, at the most, only a pecuniary one of a mere individual, and, like many other sufferings under the best system, and the best administration of laws, may be remediless. Could perfect justice be always obtained, our institutions would cease to be human. Those evils, therefore, that have already happened, and those rights that have already been lost, and which the existing laws cannot reach, are irretrievable. In such cases, it must be as unwarrantable for the Legislature, as for the executive or judicial power, to interfere in such a manner as to impair interests already vested in particular members of society.

The long usage of our Legislatures to grant new trials has also been deemed an argument in favor of the act under consideration. But that usage commenced under colonial institutions, where legislative powers were neither understood nor limited, as under our present constitution. Since the adoption of that, the usage has been resisted by sound civilians, and often declared void by courts of law. Though no opinions have been published, and though the decisions have been contradictory, yet the following ones appear, by the records, to have adjudged such acts void. (Gilman, *v.* M'Clary, Rock. Sep. 1791; Chickering *v.* Clark, Hills; Butterfield *v.* Morgan, ch. May, 1797; Jenness and a. Ex. *v.* Seavey, Rock. Feb. 1799.) Nor could it be pretended, on any sound principles, that the usage to pass them, if uninterrupted for the last twenty-seven years, would amount to a justification, provided both the letter and spirit of the written charter of our liberties forbid them. That charter is the supreme law of the land to us all; and we know that the sacred regard to the rights of the people which our legislative department have ever evinced will induce them, as readily as ourselves, to conform to the provisions of that supreme law, whenever it is not misapprehended.

But, in the passage of the act granting a new trial to the plaintiff, we are constrained to think that the constitution was misapprehended. The nature and effect of the act was judicial. It was also retrospective. The Legislature cannot pass such an act; and our judgment, therefore, is, that the proceedings in this cause be quashed, and the *parties go without day.*

# DECISION ON THE APPLICATION FOR A WRIT OF HABEAS CORPUS ON BEHALF OF THOMAS SIMS, THE FUGITIVE SLAVE.*

AFTER adjourning the hearing in the petition for a habeas corpus in Sims' case from chambers at the Tremont House to the court-house, Judge Woodbury listened further to Messrs. Dana and Sumner, his counsel, till almost nine o'clock, P. M.

He then remarked, that two grounds seemed to be relied on: one was the badness of the warrant which had been issued against Sims for an assault on Butman when serving another process; and the other was the illegal delay by the marshal, in not having Sims earlier examined by the commissioner on that warrant.

He agreed with the other judges in this city, that where all the facts and documents were before them necessary to a correct decision on the discharge of the prisoner, they might be examined, and the writ not issued, if nothing could result from it but delay and expense, or embarrassment to other proceedings.

Yet, if some facts were wanting,—as here, for example,—what other process had been served by the marshal, on which, also, with this warrant, he held Sims, and whether it was still in the course of being executed, so as to excuse him for not carrying Sims before a commissioner on this, it furnished a good reason to issue the habeas corpus at once, in order that the marshal might return these facts. He could now decide on the validity of the warrant on its face, the first point, as a copy of it was now before him; but he could not decide on the second point, without further and official evidence what other process was in the hands of the marshal against the prisoner, and how it operated, if at all, on the delay.

Where real doubt existed whether the marshal ought not to be required to return more facts, he felt bound to incline in favor of liberty.

The writ must issue.

In about an hour, the prisoner was brought into the court-room, and the return made on the writ, which has before been described.

B. R. Curtis, counsel for the marshal, after reading the return, observed that the marshal would now leave the case with the court,

* Reported for the Boston Daily Bee, and published April 14, 1851. B. R. Curtis, counsel for the marshal; Seth J. Thomas, for the owner of Sims; R. H. Dana, Charles Sumner, and S. E. Sewall, for Sims.

he having no interest in the final decision, except that it should be legal. He would merely add, that, by the Massachusetts statute, those who might be interested in the result were to be notified.

Mr. Dana wished this might be done, and the case delayed; but Woodbury, justice, remarked that he was acting under the acts of Congress, and not the statute of Massachusetts, and should not delay the hearing for this, unless, in the further progress of it, something should appear rendering it fit and reasonable.

He further said, that the case was taken up on Fast-day, a sort of New England Sabbath, to oblige or accommodate the prisoner and his counsel, who considered it so urgent; and was examined thus late, in order to dispose of it that night, and without interfering unnecessarily with other proceedings.

The counsel, however, moved for delay till Saturday, insisting that it was a mistake to suppose they had intended to close the business that night; and the judge consented to allow further time, if anything new was disclosed in the return, or any surprise caused by its contents.

Mr. Sumner said nothing of this kind could be specified; but still further time was earnestly asked, to examine the return, and to call in witnesses to certain facts deemed material.

The judge said he would grant delay, though he feared at much inconvenience to the public business in the Circuit Court, and contrary to what he supposed was the arrangement when coming there; yet, it was right, if more time was really wanted by the prisoner and his counsel for preparation, to indulge them. If anything more, however, can be done before the postponement, it had better be suggested.

Mr. Dana then moved that the marshal be required to state more fully and specifically his reasons for delay in having the prisoner examined under the warrant for assault on the officer.

Judge Woodbury observed, that if the marshal chose to rely on his return as it was, without moving, on his own behalf, for any leave to amend, he should not interfere, unless it appeared, on further examination, that sufficient was not stated to enable him to dispose of the case understandingly.

The further hearing was postponed till three o'clock, P. M., the next day. When that time arrived,

Mr. Sewall, as counsel for Sims, moved the court to appoint a person to serve a writ *de homine replegiando*, issuing against the marshal for Sims, and urged it as requiring immediate attention.

Judge Woodbury advised delay till the writ of habeas corpus was disposed of.

Mr. Thomas then objected to Mr. Sewall acting in this new case as counsel for the prisoner. The commissioner having decided, that forenoon, that Sims was a slave, and having given a certificate and order to send him to Georgia, whence he escaped, he was now under the control and advice of his master and agent; for whom Thomas, and not Sewall, was counsel.

The marshal then had read an additional return, setting out this certificate and decision of the commissioner that day.

Judge Woodbury said that these papers must decide the point that Mr. Thomas now had the better right to appear in behalf of the master and Sims, unless Mr. Sewall objected to the constitutionality of the laws under which the commissioner had acted. If he did, an opportunity would be given to be heard on that point, and it would then be decided.

Mr. Sewall did not wish to go into that argument now, on this motion; and the judge then said, the laws must be presumed constitutional till the contrary was shown or adjudged; and consequently Mr. Thomas had now a right to act on this motion as to the *writ de homine*, rather than Mr. Sewall. But let all take notice, that it did not follow, because Sims was a slave and had a master, that he possessed no rights, or that he might not have a right to proper food, clothing and shelter; to have a wife and children, and religious instruction, and be protected from improper abuse of them or himself, whether by his master or others. Slaves have rights, on many subjects, in the greatest slave States, and are often allowed to try them by writs and courts. And while here, especially, as well as there, it would be scrutinized closely, that no oppression or mal-treatment was practised on the prisoner; and if he really had good grounds for such a writ, no doubt it would and could be issued and served.

But it does not answer to say, as a reason for it, as counsel have urged, that no slavery exists or can exist in Massachusetts. That is true only under her present State laws. For, under the United States laws and constitution, slavery constitutes a part of the representation in the House of Representatives, and the number of electors of President, and the foundation for direct taxation; and when slaves escape to such States as Massachusetts from other States, still *allowing the institution*, as these do, they are still slaves, both by the constitution and the acts of Congress. This was one of the compromises for the Union.

Mr. Sewall rose, and was understood to say that he referred to Massachusetts alone.

Alone! Thank God, Massachusetts yet forms a part of the Union! [Great applause, which was checked by the court.] May she long enjoy its benefits, and long help to enforce its mutual and fraternal obligations. We live under two governments; and owe allegiance to both, as well as derive incalculable blessings from both.

And so far as regards his official duties, connected with one of these, he should uphold it, or perish in the attempt. [Applause.]

Mr. Sumner then moved that an attachment issue against the marshal, for not returning more specifically the date and cause of the arrest and detention of Sims.

The judge observed he supposed this motion was made to ascertain his views as to what must be the construction of the return, concerning these as it now stands, before arguing the question of the discharge. He was willing to state, that on the return, saying he received the warrant of such a date, and served it, he must be presumed to have received and served it on the day of its date. He should hold the marshal to that; and if he did not mean to be so understood, he might ask leave to amend. This would give also to the prisoner the benefit of the longest time of detention, in order to inculpate the marshal most as to the cause of detention, which is the other ground of the motion for an attachment. In the next place, on this return, no cause can be regarded but that appearing now in the existence of a prior process against Sims, which had been under hearing from time to time by adjournments, till since the service of the writ of habeas corpus.

If that, under the circumstances, did not justify the delay, he would stand in fault; but to what extent, and with what consequence, was to be settled hereafter.

The motion was disallowed.

Mr. Sumner, at the close of his argument for the discharge of Sims, proposed to offer some witnesses to prove fraud connected with the criminal process in question, and the use of it in connection with the other process against Sims as a fugitive.

The district attorney, Mr. Lunt, being present, stated that he caused the criminal proceedings to be instituted, and had regulated them thus far, and was responsible for the manner of conducting them.

B. R. Curtis, Esq., in behalf of the marshal, objected to any evidence against his return.

Judge Woodbury observed, that if the counsel for the prisoner could show that there was no foundation, either in fact or law, for the complaint against Sims, but that it had been got up falsely and fraudulently by the marshal, or by others with his consent or connivance, he was inclined to receive the evidence.

It is true that the writ of habeas corpus is a proceeding, in some respects, peculiar in character. It is not like an action between parties, or an indictment on which issues can be made and tried by a jury. He was now hearing it, as if at his chambers, with no jury present, and with none of the paraphernalia of a court, except the officers who had charge of the prisoner.

It was a writ, too, which, though justly sacred with our fathers, and dear to our fathers' fathers, near two centuries ago, was to be acted on by the judge who issued it, and under certain rules which had been, from time to time, wisely established to regulate his discretion. He desired the counsel to point him to a case, during that whole period, where an inquiry like this had been gone into with witnesses, on the hearing of the habeas corpus.

The counsel said he could refer to no such case.

The judge added that the twelve judges of England were, about a century ago, asked by the House of Lords for their opinions on this and other points, and all but two or three thought the evidence inadmissible. But the party could indict the marshal, or sue him for damages, for any falsity in his return or his proceedings, and must resort to that mode of relief against such misconduct. Parliament then passed an act not requiring the receipt of such evidence, on this hearing; but allowing the judge, on affidavits, when he pleased, to ascertain the truth of any material facts or allegations.

Now, though this act may not be binding on him, it was a reasonable act, and he would enforce its principle in the broad discretion which all judges possessed in such hearings, and allow any proof to be given by witnesses which would show any fraud in the charges made in the complaint, or any false and wrongful conduct by the marshal in obtaining it. But it would be quite too remote, collateral and unimportant, here, to inquire whether the effect of this movement might not be to help protect the prisoner from an arrest on another like warrant, issued by a State magistrate on the application of one of his own counsel, and to inquire which was most legitimate or *bona fide*. All things in society were so interwoven and dependent, that it was difficult to perform any rightful act, without some influence or effect on other matters, for which the actor was not responsible, generally.

Mr. Sumner said he had no such evidence to offer as the judge indicated, but asked the discharge of Sims on the proofs and documents now before the court; showing first the warrant to have been bad in form and substance, and showing next an illegal delay in executing it, and one which, by itself, raised a presumption of fraud in the marshal. And, if these failed, he moved that the judge himself now hear and examine the criminal charge against Sims; or, if declining that, admit him to bail upon it.

Judge Woodbury inquired if anything more was desired, on either side, to be said in respect to the habeas corpus. On the reply that there was not, he proceeded to remark in substance as follows:

It is proper to say that the proceeding before me is not an application to discharge from custody of the marshal the prisoner Sims, as a fugitive slave, but the petition for the habeas corpus is confined exclusively to the allegation of his being held by a criminal warrant, and which issued on a complaint for an assault on an officer of the United States while executing legal process; and it asks, merely, that he may be discharged from custody so far as held under that warrant.

The writ of habeas corpus, by which he has been brought before me, is also confined specially to the same inquiry.

There seems, then, on such a collateral question of mere law, little occasion for so vast a crowd, or any high public excitement.

The first objection is to the legality of the warrant on its face. But every professional man knows the difference between what is required in such a warrant, merely like mesne process to bring the party before a magistrate for examination, and a final warrant of commitment in execution of a sentence, or a warrant to search the premises of a suspected person.

The cases cited, where warrants are bad on their face, are all of this last character, and not of the kind like this. They are, too, for defects not existing even in this; such as the want of an oath, when an oath to this appears, or, as in Cranch, the want of any offence for the commitment described at all; whereas, here it is alleged to be the offence of obstructing the complainant in the service of a legal precept, or, as in the case from the Massachusetts Reports, not setting out carefully the premises to be searched, and the name of the owner or person suspected, when here the respondent is accurately described.

But, besides this, the present warrant, after stating what has been suggested, is fuller than most precepts issued merely for an arrest, and much fuller than the old writ for an insulated trespass in all cases to get parties into the king's bench, and then declare against them, and try them on some contract, or other cause of action.

For the trial or hearing is on the declaration or complaint, here as well as in England, and not on the writ. And the warrant to arrest is merely to bring the party in, and then to exercise jurisdiction, and decide on the complaint or not, as that may be sufficient.

Here, in the warrant itself, the respondent is referred to what "is more fully set forth in" the complaint, as the cause for which he is to be arrested and tried. And in the return of the marshal, a copy of the complaint is included, and is conceded to contain every allegation necessary to give jurisdiction to the commissioner, and justify the arrest.

The question on this first objection, likewise, is not one between the complainant, Butman, and Sims, or either of them, and the commissioner; but whether the marshal, an executive officer, is not justified in making an arrest, as required in the precept on this warrant. It seems to me, clearly, that he was.

There is no pretence of want of sufficient cause for such an arrest. The offence stated to have been actually committed is conceded to have occurred; and a Mr. List, said to be one of the prisoner's counsel, is represented, in the argument for him, to have made a complaint that it was a still higher crime, namely, an assault with intent to kill, and for which he is stated to have obtained another warrant from the State authorities. But that it was committed rather against the United States' authorities and the Union, and should be investigated by her commissioner, and the offender arrested by her marshal, is manifest from the fact that it was committed on an officer, or an assistant to one, acting under her laws, while executing one of her precepts, and in order to carry into effect a provision of her constitution and acts of Congress.

That constitution and these laws must be maintained against all violence, or the United States must cease to exist as a government. [Applause, but promptly checked by the officers.] They must be maintained, too, rather by precepts like this, issued by the public officers of the United States, and by the request of their prosecuting officer, than by a complaint and warrant, made before a State magistrate, by one of the prisoner's own counsel, against his own client,—a new kind of professional service, and whether on public or private motives can better be inquired hereafter, when that conduct may be brought in question for other purposes.

This assault on a United States officer, to obstruct him in serving the process of the United States, and issued as to a subject within the cognizance of the United States, was made penal by a United States law, passed the very first year after the United States government went into operation; and Judge Washington, in the Circuit Court, had held it to be a most important provision to the execution of all laws of the United States, and without enforcing which, the administration of justice under the United States constitution was likely to be utterly prostrated.

Why any one of the prisoner's counsel should interfere, and endeavor to turn it into an offence against the State, and punish their own client for it there, when the injured party and the prosecuting officers have not gone there, looks extraordinary, and does not seem entitled to any special encouragement by the authorities of the United States.

The prisoner has a claim to sympathy for thus being harassed by two prosecutions for the same assault, and, indeed, for the offence itself, more than others, if, in his ignorance, others have excited him to it by exhortations to murder the public officers when attempting to arrest and return fugitives to their masters, in conformity to the public laws. [Much sensation in the audience.]

The second ground for claiming a discharge of the prisoner was the delay in taking him before the commissioner to be examined on this criminal complaint, and the exceptionable facts connected with it.

The usual course, in criminal proceedings, was to have an examination follow speedily on arrest, and an unnecessary and injurious delay was censurable.

But that could seldom render the warrant invalid, or entitle the prisoner to an absolute discharge, though it might properly expose the officers who did it to a civil action, at times, or cause an indictment.

In the case cited from Barnwell and Cresswell, the prisoner was not discharged from the criminal arrest.

Mr. Sumner said he did not mean to contend that the warrant thus became invalid, but that, by this and other facts, the arrest would be.

The judge replied, If the warrant still remained in full force, how could the arrest be invalid? It was made in the proper form; there had been no escape since; it was for an offence admitted to have been committed; and the fact of more delay, if illegal, was to be punished collaterally, and no case was cited showing that it alone nullified the arrest.

On the contrary, the whole ground of principle, on which it could be held illegal, failed on the facts set out in this return. When adjudged illegal, it generally had been because the prisoner was thus deprived of his liberty for several days, if held by only that one warrant. But here the return showing an earlier arrest by another process, and a detention under it up to the present time, he had not been imprisoned or detained a single hour by this alone. There was by it, therefore, no imprisonment or injury. In the cases cited, however, he was held in confinement by the warrant alone which was complained of, and thus was injured and imprisoned by it unnecessarily long. That could not be justified. Every case but one in Cowan was of this character; and there one of two precepts was considered null, and adjudged bad, but the other continued good, and he was not discharged.

Now, was the marshal, under these and the other facts, excusable for this delay? The design in issuing the writ was to have before him officially the reason for it, — as it might be justifiable by sickness of the prisoner, magistrate or marshal, or by the wish of the prosecutor and assent of the accused to delay, or the pendency of other prior legal proceedings. It turned out to have been the latter; and, considering the menaces uttered of violence, — considering the array of force and arms around and near us, to prevent a rescue of the prisoner, — it furnishes an unusual and weighty reason not to expose him abroad, in going from office to office, and from one kind of examination to another, to the imminent danger of escape, till the previous one was completed, and till it could be done with safety. The more especially was this prudent when not thereby causing the prisoner's detention, but a prior precept doing that.

But it is strenuously urged that this, being a criminal warrant, should, at all risks, have been examined before the other, which is supposed to be only a civil proceeding. Without inquiring now whether that be merely civil in character, this is not the case of the marshal having both precepts at once, and then serving the civil one first. Such a course might not always be proper. But he had what is called the civil precept first, and served it first; and while serving it, the offence was committed by the prisoner, for which the criminal warrant issued.

It was delivered to him while the examination or trial of the others was going on; and the question left is, whether that inquiry was to be abandoned or suspended, and the prisoner taken before another commissioner, and tried on this, though the district attorney did not desire it who has charge of it, nor, for aught which appears, the officer, Butman, or the commissioner, or even Sims himself.

The cases quoted of rights of property in slave States yielding to the punishment for crimes are generally but decisions that the master must lose his private slave property when the latter is demanded for punishment for crimes committed against the public.

That is far from this case, which relates merely to the mode or form of trying one question first or last, after the civil trial has begun. What is the practice on this daily in the State court near us, and in all other States? Does not the civil trial, pending, go on till closed, before a criminal one is called. Who ever heard of an attorney-general breaking into the midst of a civil trial, and asking a criminal one to be substituted? however proper it might be, when no trial has commenced, to request that the criminal cases have a preference.

In the case of the fugitive Crafts, last November, which has been the topic of so much misrepresentation and mistake, the counsel for the agent of the master (Seth J. Thomas, Esq.), who now sits before us, and cannot but well remember the facts, came to his chambers while the court was not in session; and having failed to find a commissioner who did not prefer to have the Circuit Court examine the case, it being one of the first impressions and the subject-matter a very excitable one, requested that the court would do it. He was informed that a civil cause had been several days on trial, and was likely to continue several more, and could not be broken off without the consent of the parties; but that their counsel would be asked to consent as soon as the court met. The parties declined to give way entirely, as they had many witnesses, and, on one side, belonged to another State; but agreed to suspend the trial an hour, so as to have the papers examined, and a warrant issued, if appearing to be proper. They were accordingly examined, and the warrant issued, pending the other case, but only on the express consent of the parties before the change.

Nor would it have been proper here, any more than there, without some special urgency, and the consent of the parties in the other case. The same rule we have seen applied in criminal as in civil cases, after trials have once been begun.

Both of these leading objections to the warrant and conduct of the marshal failed, therefore, to make out a case which would justify Sims' discharge from the criminal warrant.

But two other motions had been made, this afternoon, which required a few minutes' consideration. One was, that the judge, sitting as he was now in chambers, should hear the case to which the warrant referred when the original complaint was not before him; and when a commissioner could, and doubtless would, discharge that duty, if requested by the complainant or district attorney; and when neither of the latter desired it now; and when the prisoner was brought before him now for another and specific object.

The other motion was to admit him to bail. But that duty belongs to the magistrate before whom he is taken for examination; and no other has a right to interfere, unless refused by him, or bail is required in an unreasonable amount.

Both of these motions are therefore overruled.

He said he could not conclude without expressing the strong reluctance entertained by him to the transaction of such business as this at chambers; and though he consented at last to do it so on the urgent request of the prisoner's counsel, yet he afterwards postponed the hearing to this court-room, in order that justice might be administered in public, and in a place to which all could have full access, so far as accommodations existed.

But at chambers he had no officers for protection or convenience, and hence had ordered none here for that purpose; but those present were a guard over the prisoner, or kind volunteers.

He mentioned this to show how inappropriate, compared with a hearing in court, was the course now pursued, to gratify the urgent desires of the counsel yesterday, rather than being a matter of his own choice. And though, in one sense, he stood defenceless in a vast crowd, under the highest excitement, and felt obliged to decide against the feelings and hopes of many of them, yet he did it without fear as to the result; and was ready to abide the result, while in the path of duty, and conscious that he was administering justice honestly and straightforward, and in the true spirit of the constitution, and in the midst of a community who have been educated to shun violence, and obey and respect the laws. (Bursts of applause, which were immediately checked by the court.)

Perhaps it may be proper to add, that though the prisoner cannot, in the present condition of things, be discharged from this criminal warrant, yet it seems proper, without any imputation on the public officers for their conduct thus far in relation to it, that an examination be had as soon as the public safety and convenience will permit; though it seems competent for the district attorney and the complainant, before an examination, to abandon the prosecution, if they consider it advisable.

Let the prisoner be remanded to the custody of the marshal, as before this writ of habeas corpus issued.

# CHARGE ON THE SLAVERY QUESTION.*

GENTLEMEN OF THE GRAND JURY:

IN the regular administration of the laws, exigencies sometimes arise, when it becomes the duty of the Court to invite your attention particularly to a class or classes of those laws. If any of them have had the misfortune to be forcibly assailed, though by a small portion of the community,— if the public officers, while enforcing them, have been resisted with violence, and this at noon-day, and in the very temple of justice, — it is a breach of the public peace highly flagrant in character, the prostration of everything decorous and orderly, and it furnishes urgent reasons to examine the subject with a care proportionate to the aggravation of the outrage.

It is a part of our constitutional obligations to secure an undisturbed administration of the laws, and shield the community at large from a repetition of riotous disorders, by prompt and exemplary punishment of offenders; and it is due to the peaceable portion of the people to separate from them the guilty, so as not to let all remain under one indiscriminate ban of condemnation.

The circumstances adverted to are supposed to have recently taken place in this circuit; and being of very evil tendency, and exposed to occur again, and in each district of it, if not duly noticed, I shall invite the attention of the Grand Jury in each to the subject; at the same time congratulating those who may reside where nothing of this kind has happened on their good fortune thus far, and the law-abiding principles which their population have evinced. That the active participators in the violence referred to, and those who countenance them, are very few, in so moral and intelligent a community, ought certainly to be believed, unless the latter fail to make a warning example of the guilty. In making such an example, it is true, we can and should be both charitable and just; but, at the same time, without being negligent as to the rights of the government of the whole Union, devolved on our protection in some respects within this region of our common country.

So far, therefore, as the subject of this excitement is connected with restraints on human liberty, it is certainly calculated to cause sympathy, and in some respects to excuse error of opinion. But, while tolerant, as we must be, to all differences of mere opinion, and to free

* Delivered to the Grand Jury for the U. S. Circuit Court, at Newport, July 14, 1851.

discussion, yet, if they end in bad conduct, all must reprobate, and courts of law must punish, that conduct, or become themselves implicated. Indeed, opinions, in a country like this, will be unchained — should rove free as air. Freedom of speech, too, while disconnected with the disturbance of public bodies and the public tranquillity, or with personal slander, or blasphemy, or exhortations to violence, may be wild as the waves. Much of the steam in society here is let off by that vent, as a safety-valve, harmlessly, or without dangerous explosions; but proceed to deeds, to force, to invocations to the actual commission of crimes, to the public desecration of the laws and the destruction of order, and the whole aspect of the case is changed, and punishment must be inflicted, or ruinous anarchy is inevitable.

These last have always constituted a penal offence by the laws of the land; and not by the fugitive slave laws merely, though the enforcement of these seems to have been the immediate occasion for most of the recent excitement and outbreaks.

But, as a matter of fact, whether these laws be defective in form or censurable in operation,— be liked or disliked by many at the North,— is not the great inquiry for you or this Court, on the present occasion. That would be very material for us, if legislators, and convened to discuss a change of those laws. On the contrary, met to enforce them in a judicial capacity, our duty is to ascertain whether, in point of fact, the execution of them by the duly appointed officers has not been resisted by force, and this still advised to be repeated, and therefore should not, by our oaths, our duties, and the safety of society, be condignly punished.

Nor is the question a matter of doubt whether slavery is not generally wrong, since on that point, in New England, there is probably only one opinion. But it is, whether, where this institution is solemnly recognized to exist in some States by the constitution and acts of Congress, and must continue to be recognized, by the restoration of the fugitive, till those States choose to abolish it, or till the constitution and acts of Congress on this point are altered, any individual is justified, and is to be left unpunished, for attacking violently the public functionaries, in order to prevent the due performance, on this matter, of their official obligations?

I would fain believe that many have erred on this from a want of due examination and discrimination, rather than mischievous designs. And I do not, therefore, deem it amiss, on this occasion, among other remarks, to attempt to soften any undue prejudices which might lead to further breaches of these laws, or render grand juries reluctant to punish attacks on them, when committed with brute force.

Looking at the history of slavery in this country dispassionately, there will be found less excuse for error, even of opinion, as to the necessity of some provision on this delicate topic, if the North is to continue at all united with the South; and looking at this, and our imperative obligations at every hazard to sustain the laws till duly repealed, there is still less excuse for error of conduct, for menacing denunciations, and, indeed, such violence as to overthrow order, and, by polluting the very sanctuary of justice with anarchy and crime, strike at the root of all organized society.

It is well known to most of you that, before our Revolution, the parent country had allowed African slaves to be introduced into all the colonies for purposes of labor, and had vindicated the moral right to do it — as has since been done by the celebrated proclamation of the King of Spain in 1817 — on the ground that most of them were already slaves, by capture in war and other calamities; and that, by such a purchase, they were not deprived of liberty, but their existing bondage rendered less severe and less oppressive, and their condition more civilized, humane and enlightened, by Christian principles. But, without upholding the sufficiency of this excuse, it is certain that, when that great crisis arrived, our fathers found the institution fastened upon them, and in several instances against their strenuous remonstrances; and they proceeded, therefore, to do with it what seemed the best in their power, under existing embarrassments. The Union was to be formed. The Union was, if possible, to be made perpetual. Nobody then doubted as to this, or the mutual forbearance and concessions on this delicate subject indispensable to insure cordial coöperation.

Slavery existed then among most of the thirteen Provinces, although the extent of it was much less at the North than the South. Yet, regardless of such differences, all united, heart, head and hand, in opposing the common enemy; and, after the close of the Revolution, all again united in the same way to guarantee their common rights, by a common constitution, and a mutual compromise of opinions as to the continuance of this institution by each, till each in its own independent and sovereign capacity might deem it safe to abolish it. The foreign slave-trade could be provided for without peril or encroachment, its abolition being within the control of the General Government as an affair of foreign commerce. It was, therefore, regulated and virtually abolished, prospectively, in the constitution itself. But the institution of slavery in each State could be regulated only by itself, without making each a slave to the rest; and could not at once and over the whole Union be voluntarily abandoned, without imminent danger to life, liberty and property, of the white population, by letting loose all the terrific furies of fanaticism, combined with extreme ignorance and bad passions.

It happened in this way that the northern States earliest commenced the extinguishment of slavery, the number in bondage there being fewer, and the measure therefore easier, and less exposed to disorder.

And the progress of emancipation, under the inevitable operation of free principles, steadily and quietly advanced south; and, by means of colonization, still more rapidly and safely for all concerned, was on its beneficent march, and was returning to benighted Africa arts and

Christianity, instead of brutal ignorance, barbarism and idolatry, when arrested almost entirely by officious external interference, tending, through servile insurrection thus excited, to cover with carnage and conflagration all the fair fields of the South.

The increased severities, necessary to prevent this and the more seductive appliances interposed to cause escapes, coupled with an unexpected judicial decision against the action of State magistrates on this subject, so augmented the fugitives from labor as to require closer attention to the guarantees which had been provided in the constitution itself, for the security of this kind of property, and the consequent amicable perpetuity of the Union, as connected with it.

Among other things, the constitution had declared, — article 4th, section 3d,— in these words, that "no person, held to service or labor in one State, under the laws thereof, escaping into another, shall, in consequence of any law or regulation therein, be discharged from such service or labor, but shall be delivered up on claim of the party to whom such service or labor may be due." In the opinion of some, this may not, in that great exigency, have been the wisest compromise, to insure the adoption of the constitution, and perpetuate the Union. But our fathers thought otherwise, and inserted this clause by a unanimous vote; and we, ourselves, have voluntarily taken and retained to this moment the constitution, with this clause in it; and, till duly altered, we can neither impair nor repudiate it, even by legislation, and much less by force, without infidelity to our duties and our oaths.

Even earlier than this provision, and in the ordinance of 1787, which is so celebrated for abolishing slavery within its limits, a like provision was introduced to restore fugitives from labor to other portions of the Union.

It deserves special notice, that the principle involved in this restoration, now so severely censured, seems then to have originated with Nathan Dane, the reputed author of that ordinance,— a New England man, and a foe to slavery. In 1789, too, by the provision as to this in the constitution, our fathers did not establish involuntary servitude. As we have just seen, it had for several generations been established here by others. Nor did they undertake to regulate the internal institutions of each other, by interference, founded on their own abstract notions of what was equal or right; but left to each State, in its due sovereignty,— as they should and must,— the regulation of its own domestic concerns, without settling at all the grounds for or against the original legality of such property in men of any color or condition. They merely allowed it to be returned whence it came; and, as the ordinance of 1787 had done before, gave assurance to deliver it up for that purpose. It is to carry out this plain constitutional duty, this provision which we and our fathers acceded to, and have sworn to fulfil, that the two acts of Congress were since passed, which are assailed of late by such severe censure, and which some of the community in this circuit most unfortunately have been invoked, and even *induced*, to resist with unwarrantable violence. But how little ground exists for harsh or inflammatory opinions as to the origin of these laws, and much less for opposition by force and riotous assaults on the ministers of the law while executing them, is very manifest from the whole history of the past, to which we have just adverted.

Without entering into the question of abstract rights, but recognizing the property claimed by others elsewhere, in this class of persons, as is done through various parts of the constitution, and solemnly engaging, as we have, to aid its restoration when escaping, we did only what the fraternal feelings of all lead them to do, without constitutional engagements and oaths, *as to other property;* that is, to aid friends and neighbors in regaining it, if lost, should it escape into our boundaries. And if that property existed in the service of even a *white* minor child, or *white* apprentice, as it often does, it would be no less just and right to assist in its recovery, both at the South and the North, when appealed to by kindred blood and a kindred Union, the hopes of the future, and the common triumph and glories of the past.

These reciprocal duties must also be discharged by deeds, as well as words,— boldly, faithfully, with true loyalty to the Union, and not with evasion or procrastination. For, if the promise is kept only to the ear, and the pledges of the constitution not fulfilled honorably in acts to others, how can we stand erect, as a moral, honest and manly people, or expect that the benefits of that constitution will be continued to ourselves in other respects,— to our numerous privileges under it as to our commerce and rights abroad as well as at home, and in war as well as in peace?

It is due to the occasion, and an act of justice to those who are supposed to be under erroneous impressions on this subject, to consider, beside the prejudices against it, some of the leading justifications which have been set up for the use of tumult and violence against the execution of the constitution and laws concerning fugitives from labor.

Some who resist these provisions attempt to excuse themselves under a very dangerous assumption in all cases for personal assaults, that they are clearly unconstitutional. I am not aware that they have been so pronounced by any judicial tribunal, the final arbiter on most such questions. Nor do I propose, on this occasion, when no parties in interest are before me, to discuss that question. Beside this, a sufficient, and, I have no doubt, satisfactory rule, exists already, for your guide upon it. The Supreme Court and the courts of several of the States, after full argument between parties, have held the act of 1793 to be constitutional; and some of the latter, since the act of 1850 passed, have held the same concerning this; and it is a well-settled principle, too, that all laws are by courts and juries to be presumed and treated as constitutional, till the contrary is shown, or is adjudged by the judiciary. We could not transact business a single day, without such a principle. You have, then, a plain rule, on this topic, for your inquiries and decisions, still leaving all exceptions on this ground hereafter to all parties in interest for further discussion and adjudication, where they may come before the courts for trial. Another objection urged against them is, that they are strange in character, contrary to public opinion at the North, and for reasons like these may be disregarded.

But, if these allegations were true as to their strange or unpopular character, the inference from them, justifying forcible resistance, is neither legal nor defensible.

The chief exception under this head is, that at the hearing to send back a fugitive, no trial by jury is had. But the acts forbid no such trial, nor is the trial for the escape, or for any rights connected with it, required by the law to be without a jury,— but may be with one, wherever and whenever in like cases it is provided by the constitution or the common law. It is left, by the practice under these acts, to be at the place where the escape or offence was committed, as is the usual practice in *all* cases; and the summary hearing to send back there a person escaped has been without a jury at that hearing, since the first records of the common law, and probably in every civilized government of the known world. The acts of Congress, too, if wrong in any respect, are open to any proper modification on this or other points; but there is nothing strange or unusual in them as they now stand. And on the States allowing them — however unpopular in some places, and however open to future amendment — to be executed successfully while the laws remain in force, depends, in my opinion, the continuance of that constitution, and the sacred Union it has created. Public opinion, in a majority, in some large regions may have become poisoned, so as to continue to use violence, and justify it, in resisting the constitution and laws on this subject. If so,— which is not to be believed till demonstrated by results,— it will be difficult, if not impossible, to succeed in punishing the offence throughout; and then the Union will probably ere long fall asunder, and all the horrors of its dissolution must burst on our astonished gaze.

But, if the case be yet only that of a small minority, possessing such views,— if most of those who think badly of the law think as badly of violent resistance,— if a majority intend to offer no forcible opposition (it being so rash and hostile to the whole genius of our institutions, and to the reign of any laws and constitutions on any subject), nor to permit such opposition by others to go unpunished,— there is hope left. The republic will be saved. There still may be embarrassments by unfortunate acts of State legislation, but it is hoped not fatal errors.

It is due to the present non-slaveholding States to say, that no censure can be cast on them for desiring the limitation and extinguishment of slavery. But, when carrying these natural wishes into effect by legislation so far as regards their own States, the difficulty has been for them to act only within their own rightful powers, and not in conflict with the spirit of their duties to the other States, the General Government, and the Union. For, if legislating so as to prohibit any State officer in his private capacity, or in a military station (owing duties, as is often if not always the case, to the General Government as well as the State), from assisting to execute process for the restoration of fugitives, it would transcend all lawful measures in principle. The charitable construction of the existing statutes seems to me, however, to be, that they intend to punish State officers only when acting *as such officers*, and not as citizens; else they would most unhappily come in direct collision with other and permanent acts of Congress, and citizens relying on them, and refusing aid, would find themselves in a most perilous position. Mistakes on this subject sometimes arise from not distinguishing that a State officer, who holds his commission from the State, and is accountable to it, may not be obliged to perform official duties for the General Government, from which he holds no commission; whereas a citizen and officer, as a citizen, owes allegiance and duties to both governments, and neither can exonerate him from what is due to the other; but when each commands, the requisitions of the General Government are highest, or paramount. Indeed, in olden times, the straight-forward good faith of our fathers, it is believed, in every State in New England, imposed an oath on every officer, which is still taken,—however fulfilled by some,—to support the constitution and the Union. I cannot believe, therefore, that the legislative officers of any State have anywhere been so forgetful of fraternal feeling in our fraternal Union, as not only, by legislation, to refuse its prisons for constitutional purposes, and to punish its judicial officers for aiding the General Government, or to punish the owners of fugitives for arresting and regaining their services, but to punish, and understandingly mean to punish, the citizen or militia-man, as such, for obeying the commands of the marshal to assist in the service of judicial precepts. This can hardly be credited as to any State composing a part of this very government and its Union, and, by its Representatives and Senators in Congress, aiding to pass these very laws for marshals, and to appoint and regulate this very marshal in all his official duties, and under the constitution also aiding to discipline, arm and govern, this very militia, and their use to help execute laws when resisted. And how unnecessary or inconsistent would be the provision in the constitution itself to restore fugitives, and in the acts of Congress to hold marshals liable for escapes and rescues, provided they had not the right to command from all citizens necessary assistance! And who compose their *posse comitatus*,—who can they resort to for aid,—but the people of each District or State?—a people who belong to the government of the Union as well as to a State, and who are often operated upon directly and individually by that government. And if each State can in this way legally exonerate its people from obedience to the summons of the marshal, what becomes of the supremacy of the laws of the Union? and how exposed, on this principle, is every sacred and invaluable right enjoyed by you and others, under the wing of our Union! Congress provided, the very first year of its existence, that every marshal "*shall have power to command all necessary assistance in the execution of his duty.*" (1 Stat. at L. 87; 27 section of act of Sept. 24th, 1789.) And if the statute of a State provide that whoever gives this assistance in a slave case shall be punished, a State might just as properly attempt to exonerate its citizens from all obedience to the General Government, — even from serving as militia, on the orders of the president to repel a murderous invasion of your coast, or to help execute the laws against pirates who plunder your cargoes, or murderers of your sons on the ocean, or the wretched felons who wilfully cast away your vessels, or mutiny against your officers, in the lonely wastes of the Atlantic or Pacific.

The only other justification for violent resistance to these laws and the constitution, which has come under my notice, is, that conscience, or a "higher law" than these, disapprove of them.

But, if they do, they will, if enlightened, alike disapprove of sedition, riots, and violence against the laws made by a majority, till repealed by a majority, or till quietly pronounced unconstitutional by the judiciary. It is this compact which must not be violated, or all contracts may be treated with perfidy. It is no justification, that we dislike the compact or laws; else all compacts or laws, disliked, as many are, on one point or another, might be violated with impunity. In such cases in our political system, it is obvious that obedience is a duty, till a majority agree to changes; and an enlightened conscience teaches that, when obedience can be rendered no longer by a minority, they should withdraw from such a compact and government, rather than oppose it with tumult and violence. A distinguished statesman (Bolingbroke) has said that "our obligation to submit to the civil law is a principal paragraph in the natural law." Christianity and the Bible, too, instruct all consciences to obey the existing laws till repealed, unless resorting to a revolution, which is exposed to prosecutions for treason, and never justifiable, except under oppressions intolerable, and not otherwise remediable, — almost impossible in a government like ours, which these opponents have adopted, if not helped to make, in which they are fully represented, and which a majority can peacefully change at the ballot-boxes. How very different is such a case from that between Great Britain and her colonies when our Revolution took place; and how is the ground for any resort to violence wholly overturned, and nothing left to justify rash and bloody insurrection!

Look to another consequence of this doctrine of a *higher* and uncontrolled law to each citizen, in a government of regulated control and fixed laws. Each will then have his own law for everything for himself, — which is the state of nature, with no government but that of the strongest, with a despotism by mere force, with constant war and the miserable anarchy, where, as a sagacious divine once said on another occasion, assassination will become the law with one, robbery the law with another, lust with another, tyranny and unbridled power with others.

Recollect, too, amidst all other considerations, that if these violent courses are insisted on, even to a dissolution of the Union, the abettors of it do not thereby abolish slavery, but leave the South free and independent to perpetuate the institution forever, and gain to the North thereby merely the loss of their trade, and perhaps border wars more atrocious and bloody than the worst of antiquity.

A statement of these things is repeated, in order to place the subject-matter of the recent outrages, and some of the apologies for them, in their true light. And I beg leave to assure you, it is done more in sorrow than anger, and gives quite as much pain to the bench as it can to those who may feel that they have been exposed to reproach merely by the occurrence among them of these forcible outbreaks, in a manner so alien to New England habits and education, and so unlike its usual patriotism and religious respect for law and order, as, by the blessing of Providence, to show on its very face a different parentage.

But, to wipe off entirely any stigma from the mass of the community on this account, it behooves all the innocent, like good men and true, to stand forth in the light of heaven, and, under their duties and oaths to their Maker and their country, to assist in punishing offenders; and thus, it is hoped, preventing a repetition of misconduct so flagrant as in principle to pervert the whole administration of the laws, and overturn the very foundations of social order.

Your attention is next invited to some other offences, connected with those already described, in relation to this unfortunate subject, but which depend on general principles, or on statutes passed long ago, touching other duties to the General Government and its officers; and yet have been trampled on indiscriminately and wantonly, in order to defeat the fugitive slave law, and without any pretence whatever that they are unconstitutional.

These belong to two leading divisions. One is, aiding, abetting, or counselling any act in opposition to the arrest or helping the escape of any prisoner, whether fugitive from labor or not. Another is, an assault or murder committed on a public officer who has a fugitive from labor or any other prisoner in charge; or committed in aiding an escape, or in resisting an arrest by violence.

It is high time the community were undeceived on this subject. The law looks through all devices, and all cobweb disguises, in order to reach real guilt; and though one screens himself by absence, or dares not openly participate in the violence he recommends to others, yet he is often more culpable than the apparent actor in evil, and must be rigidly held answerable for his misbehavior. He is usually well informed, and more responsible in property than his instruments or victims, the ignorant and fanatical. He is often one that, by good advice, would possess great power to influence the masses to sustain law and order; and who, by his more elevated condition in society, is looked up to as a model or oracle, and could thus strengthen the bulwarks of property and good government. Let such men, then, be made to respond to the full extent of their moral and legal delinquencies in these matters; while others, less intelligent, and clearly excited to wrong and misled by them, receive more sympathy. Such ill-starred advisers load the gun which they themselves have not the courage to discharge, but persuade others, less intelligent and responsible, to fire at the public officers; and these others thus become exposed to be shot down by the officers in return, while the advisers keep out of the way, and seek, by physical inaction, to shelter themselves from injury.

Yet every drop of blood thus shed will cry from the ground to Heaven for vengeance on those who advised and urged the wretched fugitives into forcible resistance to the laws. It will be noticed that I speak not now against free discussion of abstract questions, or of men, or measures, or of opinions, retained in the author's desk; nor even of opinions publicly expressed, that violent resistance is lawful, but expressed without advice and solicitation to carry them into effect;—I am not treating of these.

But suppose that some reformer, over-zealous and inconsiderate, exhorts such resistance, and that the butchery of the ministers of the law be actually attempted: it may be advised from the side-walk to a crowd, or in the thronged forum, or even from the profaned pulpit, or behind the press, scattering firebrands and death to the four winds of heaven, and the ignorant or dependent rush forward to do the bloody deed, and on the steps of the very altar of justice. Can we act like rational beings, or uphold law and order a single hour, when thus in tribulation, unless the former are punished, as well as the latter?

Again, as another illustration, that none can fail to comprehend, suppose that your enemy advise and exhort a weak-minded dependant to apply the midnight torch to your dwelling-house; that "wife, children, and sacred home," perish before your eyes, being unable to save anything from the flames except your own life;—is not the exhorter to this punishable for the horrid arson?

I give it to you, then, in charge, gentlemen, as an illustration of this topic, that, by the common law, "if A advises B to kill another, and B does it in the absence of A, (now) B is principal, and A is accessory, in the murder." (4 Bl. 6.) If A, after so advising, is present at the murder, he is even a principal.

This is a part of the great jurisprudence which our fathers acted on, and claimed as their birthright.

Descending into details, the counsel for the government will, of course, advise you, when cases arise, if the offences are so committed, as to manner and place, as not to be open to prosecution before this particular court, whose jurisdiction is in some respects limited. So where an offender cannot be prosecuted as an accessory here, but only as principal, though he may be an accessory at common law, or in a State court.

The other class of offences, by principals rather than accessories, and which are most likely to happen in connection with the fugitive slave law, deserves a little further notice.

Murder is the prominent one; but, under our system of mixed government, it is generally to be prosecuted in the State court, though we have undoubted cognizance of it when committed in any building or place exclusively within the jurisdiction of the United States, as well as on the high seas.

The other offence most likely to occur and be punishable here in the principals is, obstruction or resistance to the service of process, though it may be without killing or murder. This, as early as 1790 (Stat. April 30th), was made punishable by fine not exceeding $300, and imprisonment not beyond twelve months; and is highly penal, independent of any provision in the fugitive slave law punishing a rescue.

No matter if the resistance be to a process from a judge, rather than a court of the United States. Washington, Justice, says (3 Wash. C. C. 137), "If such a resistance is not an offence, for which a person can be prosecuted, it is better that all the criminal law be struck out of the statute-book, as it is there only to show the debility of the government. No man can be brought for trial before the court without process; and if he can resist it with impunity, he cannot be brought at all; and he may resist every law of the United States with safety."

No matter, also, what precept, mesne or final, — no matter what the ground of it, civil or criminal, — no resistance to the ministers of the law, no derogation from its quiet majesty and rule, even by *threats of violence*, much more by blows, are to be tolerated. (1 Stat. at L. 117; U. States *v.* Lovery, 2 Wash. C. C. 169; U. States *v.* Lukins, 3 Wash. C. C. 335.) Men must take heed to their duties, as well as rights. They must, too, weigh well their dangers. Remember that the officers of the law are empowered to resist the attacks of rioters on them, to produce an escape when in the execution of any legal process, even unto death. Every rioter thus places himself out of the protection of the government he is resisting. He becomes an outlaw, and may be shot down with impunity by those he is wickedly assailing. (4 Bl. C. 179, 180; 1 Hale, P. C. 494; 1 Hawk, P. C. 71.)

Little could many of those recently opposing the officers of justice know their own danger, and that their lives had been spared only by the clemency or incredulity of those they attacked; and little did they dream that, if their own attempts at resistance were accompanied by the death of those they opposed, they would probably have to expiate the offence against society and the laws, like wretched felons, on the gallows!

Let all remember, beside this, that, nearly twenty years ago, it was made highly penal by Congress, on general principles, and with no special reference to this subject, for any person, "by threats or favor," to "endeavor to influence, intimidate or impede," any officer of the United States, in any court thereof, "in the discharge of duty," or to attempt, in like way, to impede "the due administration of justice therein."

Though this act looks probably to doings in court as its chief object, yet it may be quite broad enough to cover a case which takes place in a court-room, during an adjournment, with the express design to defeat the due administration of justice, by a rescue of a prisoner, pending his trial. (4 Stat. at Large, 488, act of March 2d, 1831.)

I shall now, gentlemen, part with this unpleasant subject, which, it is hoped, you will believe nothing could have tempted me to discuss, except an imperative sense of official duty. If I have aided you, as I should, in a fair execution of the laws connected with it,—if I have softened any prejudices against those laws, so as to prevent violence, and misrule, and utter disunion,—if I have enabled you to do any more good in your intercourse with society, by placing these laws in their true light, and discouraging the indulgence of such hostility to them as to make good citizens halt or falter in their duty to assist to execute them while unrepealed, and discouraging also philanthropy, however amiable under proper circumstances, if it is to be exercised here at the peril of the public peace, and the expense of others, and the risk of bloodshed and anarchy,—I have accomplished all my intentions, or even hopes. In truth, gentlemen, we all must feel, in our cool moments, without the aid of precedents or labored reasoning, that all constitutional laws passed by the General Government must be enforced, or it ceases to govern,—it is virtually overturned; and the Union connected with it becomes, in principle, dissolved. In such a case, likewise, there is substituted for the sanctity of law and order, when a mob triumphs and goes unpunished, the government of a mob; the sword of justice is wrested from her grasp, and wielded by a mob; the spirit of misrule and rebellion is substituted; the tumultuous violence and anarchy of human passions, freed from legal restraint, and stimulated by plunder or revenge, are substituted; and, though we all may deprecate the necessity of calling on the militia or army to protect the laws, and vindicate their reign, yet they are far safer than the sway of an infuriated mob, and must be invoked to assist in executing the laws, if needed, rather than let the sun of the republic go down in the clouds and blood of rebel insubordination.

In conclusion, gentlemen, feeling, as I am aware you do, that this government was made or adopted by yourselves, and not forced on you by tyranny,—that it must be sustained by yourselves, through a faithful administration of the laws, till a majority choose to alter them, or else the bayonet will be the only other resort against inevitable anarchy,—I improve this occasion to exhort you to continue firm and united in standing by peace, order, the constitution, the laws, and our holy Union.

And, disagreeable as it may be to you or me, if any of our fellow-citizens have, under sudden and misguided impulses, offended against the public safety of everything dear to us, by ruinous attempts — I might almost say *treasonable* attempts — to overturn parts of the constitution itself, as well as some of the laws, and violently obstruct their administration, — painful, if we must visit on them exemplary punishment, — yet it is, in my view, not only indispensable, to secure the sovereign reign of the laws, but to prevent all the beauties and glories of our beloved Union from being scattered in fragments over a ruined country, by the parricidal hands of some of its own children.

# APPENDIX.

# APPENDIX.

---

## NEW HAMPSHIRE *v.* DANIEL H. COREY, ON AN INDICTMENT FOR THE MURDER OF MRS. MATILDA NASH.*

Ere this the jury are undoubtedly aware that they hold in their hands the life of a fellow-being.

Whether that life should be destroyed, or should be left unharmed, is the question to be decided. A question interesting to the public,— deeply interesting to the affectionate wife and tender children of the prisoner,— and, to that unfortunate being himself, the most momentous question this side of the eternal world.

The decision of it would probably soon restore him to all the endearments of life, and extend the brief probation allotted him for repentance and hope; or it will send him at once — sane or insane, guilty or innocent — to meet the solemnities of eternity.

He did not stand there to deny they possessed this alarming power over a fellow-creature,— erring mortals as we all were; though the right to take life in this way had been denied by theologians, jurists, and, indeed, by the established codes of some whole communities. It may be wiser, it is surely safer, to imprison for life. But our laws have not yet abolished capital punishment in all cases; and, consequently, an allusion had been made to this consideration only to warn them that, in a question about taking life from the prisoner,— the very charge against him as to another, — they are in the exercise of a power where any mistake against the accused, whether accidental or designed, can never be corrected after he has passed that "bourn whence no traveller returns,"— a power beyond any other in magnitude they may ever exercise, from their cradles to their coffins.

---

* Argument at the term of the Superior Court of Judicature, holden at Keene, County of Cheshire, on the 1st Tuesday of October, 1830. Reported by Hon. Joel Parker. Verdict, acquittal on the ground of insanity.

Hence, by the principles both of law and common sense, a jury cannot convict of a capital offence unless the guilt is clear; unless a wicked heart is manifested, and the offender has the possession of his mental faculties so as to be a proper subject of punishment, for either reformation or example. Hence, all doubts are to operate in his behalf,— all presumptions are in his favor. And, if a conviction takes place in violation of these principles, the jury themselves become accessory to a judicial murder; they profane their own oaths, in the presence of God, to decide only according to law and the evidence, and the whole trial becomes a mockery and a curse. Admit that an adherence to these principles may sometimes lead to the escape of the guilty. But remember they are the only principles which can shield the innocent. The lives of you — of all of us — depend on their preservation; and it is better that many should escape capital punishment here, if guilty, than that the safeguards of society should all be prostrated. The humblest, as well as the highest, is intrenched around by these principles; and if any are improperly rescued by their operation, they still, not only can be punished hereafter,— but here, even here, they carry about them the worm of conscience that never dies, and commence on earth the sufferings of that hell which the guilty must always endure.

Look at the deplorable condition of the prisoner in another respect, if you do not most solemnly and rigidly adhere to these principles in his favor.

He is poor, ignorant, and almost friendless, and in such circumstances appears before you alone, in a contest with two hundred and fifty thousand people, the whole population of the State; add to this the wealth of the State, its intelligent and active officers, and the alarming fact that you yourselves, as well as the bench, are all, in theory, arrayed against him in aid of the prosecution, or among the prosecutors. This is not mentioned in the tone of complaint, but only of caution. Recollect, also, the prejudices and prepossessions to be guarded against from other sources. All the sympathies and better feelings of our nature have been roused against this wretched being. An aged female was destroyed at noon-day, without provocation. Her afflicted relatives, her own blood, cried for vengeance. Rumor was busy with her thousand tongues, and her ten thousand falsehoods, attempting to mingle even masonry and antimasonry in the boiling cauldron; and, amidst all this excitement, it may be added, more in sorrow than in anger, that the press itself has been affected, and the very types stained with gall.

Is it a matter of surprise, that, under all these circumstances, this miserable man has already been tried and hung at half the firesides in the county?

Do we complain of this? — Far, very far otherwise! On the evidence before them, he has been rightfully hung. On the evidence before the community, they have been rightfully agitated.

On the evidence rumored, you, and all of us, would have been marble-hearted and base, not to have wished his apprehension and trial. It is praise, and not censure, to the community and its officers, that he is before you. He has been rightfully arrested; rightfully immured within the damp walls of a prison, for many months; rightfully arraigned here, and, it is hoped, on the law and the new evidence now before you, and before the public, will be rightfully tried, and rightfully acquitted.

It is consoling, and creditable to humanity, that truth should thus overtake error, however late; that if error should start, as she often does, with the speed of the pestilence, truth should, ere long, follow, like health, with healing in his wings.

This public trial has wisely been provided for by our laws, with a view to correct any delusions, to remove prejudices, and evince to all, as has been evinced to this large audience, the real circumstances of that lamented occurrence which has placed this unfortunate man at the criminal bar of his country. On a little reflection, you will find that, wretched as he is, even he, as well as the deceased, is entitled to some little consideration.

He is, at least, a human being, like the rest of us. He has civil rights, like others; he should be fortified and saved from injustice, by the law, as well as others; he has, likewise, some relatives to suffer, — children to love and protect; and, poor and friendless as he is, in some respects, is blessed with one fellow-being — a wife — who has hung over his destiny like a ministering angel, and endured and performed more to save him than what has immortalized many a heroine of romance. She — they — lament as sincerely as you do the unhappy occurrence which ended in the death of Mrs. Nash.

They ask of you no other treatment of him, under all the circumstances, than you yourselves would expect, in a like case. They only implore you to guard against any hasty or delusive impressions, that might, regardless of strict law and evidence, hurry a being, of the same immortal hopes, and fears, and perils, with yourselves, suddenly and unpreparedly, perhaps, to the bar of his God.

They hold up before you, in the records of criminal jurisprudence, numerous cases where mistakes have occurred, under such excitements, and where juries have thus, themselves, unlawfully imbrued their own hands in blood, and embittered their future lives with the deepest remorse and horror.

This is not the language of mere counsel. History and legal reports are full of cases of the most fatal, deplorable, and irremediable mistakes.

One of the ablest writers on medical jurisprudence expresses his strong convictions that even many insane prisoners — the very case, as we contend, of our wretched client — have, from the subtlety of such complaints, and the precipitancy or prejudice of juries, — that many such have been sent, untimely, wrongfully, barbarously, into the eternal world.

"There is no species of madness" says Marc, "which so much deserves the attention of the physicians, and the jurists, as *mania without delirium*. It has brought to the scaffold many deplorable victims, who merited compassion, rather than punishment." (1 Beck's Med. Jur. 371.)

We know that in this civilized age, and in this humane community, such will be your deliberate impressions, such your mature inclinations; and that, having those cautions which the duty of counsel makes proper, and the excitement of this case demands, we can safely and coolly proceed to the investigation of the principles and facts involved in the issue before you.

Were we not conscious that we could thus proceed, all must see, that little would be the regard you must cherish for the character of your country, as well as for your individual selves, and great would be the reproach over all the civilized world cast upon the noble institution of the trial by jury. The panel would otherwise become a mere sewer, through which should run, and fester, and corrupt, all the passions, prejudices and violence of society, without the purifying and preserving influence of all those glorious principles of equal law which our ancestors bled to secure, which have made our country a name and a praise in the earth, and which are now receiving the imitation of twenty-five millions of freemen in France.

This has helped to restore to their flag the two colors symbolic of justice and truth; and will lead you, from duty as well as pride, to uphold the reputation of all our free institutions, and to publish to the world that the motto of your own State seal — *fiat justitia ruit cœlum* — is not empty verbiage, but a security for the triumph of truth, the administration of perfect justice to the weakest citizen, whatever of clamor or excitement may at first have interposed, to warp and mislead.

This security has hitherto been the boast of American juries,— this is now the glory of a jury trial in every free country; and this leads us, in confidence, to place our lives in your hands, and to ask and hope, for the prisoner,— from God and his country,— a safe deliverance.

He then appealed to the jury in relation to the sanity of mind, and malice aforethought, whether, after the full exhibition of the circumstances attending the transaction, the counsel for the State might not have done well to relieve the unhappy prisoner from any further peril and defence. He did not, as his counsel, expect to be called on to address them. He regretted the necessity. But if, as we were left to infer, public opinion was still unsettled,— if the prosecuting officer still doubted,— it was proper, however painful, to examine the case in detail, and have a verdict pronounced upon its character.

The general ingredients of the crime are,—the killing of a human being, by a person of sane mind, with malice aforethought.

The first inquiry, and one which seemed involved in the very definition of murder, was the sanity of the prisoner.

This was not his sanity at the time of the trial, nor any time precedent to the killing, but at the moment of the supposed offence. In this inquiry, the causes of the alleged insanity were immaterial,—though they would properly come under consideration in another branch of the investigation,—but we now are only to ascertain whether insanity existed on Saturday, the 13th of June.

It would, after the development during the last two days, be hardly too strong to say, that any listener who still retained reasonable doubts that it did exist was open to a suspicion that he himself was, in some degree, insane.

One prominent feature in insanity is, the cherishing opinions and performing acts entirely different from the rest of mankind, in relation to certain subjects.

Now, let me ask each member of the jury if, on the 13th of June, a neighbor had entered his house, and informed him that, at noon-day, and not under the cover of darkness,—that, on a helpless female and a friend, and not on an equal or an enemy,—that, without any previous quarrel or grudge, and not on a dispute and in revenge,—that, in a public highway, before a living witness, and without subsequent flight or concealment,—an attack like this had been made, terminating in death, by a man educated among us, and hitherto of a moral and religious character,—is there one who would not answer at once, "the man must have been insane"?

Under such general considerations and impressions, made by the evidence on the part of the State alone, he did not believe that any human ingenuity could remove all reasonable doubts as to the prisoner's sanity.

With this settled belief, therefore, the case would there have been left by the prisoner's counsel, without calling a single witness, or uttering a single syllable in argument, had it not been an issue of life or death, involving to the accused everything temporal; and had it not been due to him and his relatives, as well as the public, that the truth, the whole truth, and nothing but the truth, should go forth to the world, on this final and interesting investigation. When we descend to particulars for the purpose of deciding on his sanity at the time of the killing, it is indispensable to carry with us correct notions concerning what constitutes insanity.

It may exist from birth, or for only a single day; it may extend to all subjects, or only one; it may arise from physical or moral causes; it may have been induced by an evil or good course of life;—and yet, if it exists, the subject of it cannot be punished for acts committed under its influence. So far as that influence extends, he is not an accountable being: he can neither control his body or his mind by reasonable and moral considerations; he is a mere machine of bones and muscles; and the punishment of such a person, for such an act, can neither reform nor intimidate, and would indicate a species of barbarism and ferocity utterly derogatory to this enlightened age.

Such a person cannot, in the common acceptation of language, possess the other ingredient in murder — malice aforethought. But the acts, to be criminal, must be done under the influence and dominion of malice, instead of insanity; there must have been mind and sense, steeped in wickedness — *mala mens* — *malo animo*. The offender, in this case, must have had a heart deliberately and fatally bent on mischief, and must have done, as the great poet of nature expresses himself on another occasion, to an offender —

> "Thou hid'st a thousand daggers in thy thoughts,
> Which thou hast whetted on thy stony heart,
> To stab at half an hour of my life."

But here existed neither hatred, anger or revenge, before the fatal occurrence; but perfect harmony and esteem.

[Mr. W. here detailed and commented on the cases of Hadfield, of Greenwood and others, to show the nature and operation of partial derangement; and how perfectly rational the subject of this malady might appear on some occasions, and on some particulars, when under the highest degree of insanity upon other occasions and other particulars.]

So inscrutable is this calamity, that the reasoning powers on most subjects often remained in great perfection, but the disorder was evinced, as Locke once remarked, only in the assumption of false premises. It could sometimes be traced to special causes, and sometimes not; but, its existence once shown, the exemption from liability began, whatever may have been the cause, and whether clearly known or unknown. Though physicians cannot always fathom its origin, nor tell what part of the brain, if any part, is affected under its influence, yet certain circumstances, both physical and moral, are found most likely to produce derangement, and certain indications of its existence have been ascertained and settled from the earliest ages. To these we shall refer more fully than might otherwise be necessary, in order that the jury may be satisfied that they are not conjured up for the present occasion, by either the industry or ingenuity of counsel.

[Mr. W. here read from 1 Beck's Med. Jur. 350—375, and the article before cited from Rees' Cyclopedia, on the cause of insanity.]

Thus, we see that the chief physical causes of this malady are hereditary predisposition, paralytic attacks, epilepsy, and injuries on the head,— causes, every one of which, except the second, are clearly proved to have existed in the present case.

The father and sister have been proved, by sundry witnesses not attempted to be contradicted, to have been insane for many years; suddenly changing their appearance and conduct, avoiding society, neglecting their business, cherishing novel and irrational ideas, and treated and watched over by their relatives as if deranged. The epileptic fits are proved likewise, not only by the brother, but by Whitney and Dort, and even by Cummings, one of the swiftest witnesses on the part of the prosecution.

The falls, severe and frequent, are proved by the brother and son; and the last one, combined with excessive physical labor (another physical cause mentioned in the books, and proved by the two young women), we shall attempt to show, by and by, was the immediate precursor of the settled derangement under which, in about nine days afterwards, the deceased was destroyed.

It is an established rule in philosophy, not to seek for new and doubtful causes of certain effects where sufficient ones have already been shown to exist; and it is an equally well established rule in law, not to seek and impute evil causes for acts where innocent ones can be found. But here, though we fix beyond cavil numerous and adequate causes for insanity of a character physical and entirely innocent, the State, instead of contradicting one of them by evidence, compasses heaven and earth to discover proof of some new and criminal cause, like intemperance, or deny entirely the insanity which these causes were so likely to produce, and which we contend they did produce. It was an insanity most manifest and incontrovertible,— not pretended now for the first time, not counterfeited since the killing, but believed the day before the killing by those who examined him; an insanity which, whether breaking out on certain occasions from certain causes at former periods or not, had at least visited its unhappy victim for nine days previous to this lamented event; an insanity, without a particle of evidence that he had, for weeks before its commencement, drank a drop of ardent spirit; an insanity that continued during the whole nine days, without the least proof of intemperance within the time, except on a single occasion, and that the very day after the insanity began, and eight days before the killing; an insanity which, the day before the killing, had become so established and violent as to induce the family to send for medical aid,— and, after the arrival of the physician, and by his advice, to draw up and direct a paper to the selectmen of the town, alleging the derangement of this unfortunate man, and invoking them to interfere and secure him. There can be no mistake about the uncontrollable strength or truth of this last evidence. It remains in writing. It was not made after the occasion, or for the occasion. It admits of neither coloring nor weakening; and, if the public authorities, as was their duty, had seasonably interfered, the calamity which we all deprecate would have been prevented. Delays are emphatically dangerous, in such cases.

[Mr. W. here read, from the American Jurist, the following extract from the Boston Medical and Surgical Journal:]

"We are satisfied that the amount of care bestowed is, in many instances, wholly insufficient, and that great hazards are frequently incurred from indulging the notion that the subjects of this delirium are altogether harmless. There are two rules, in regard to persons in this situation, which ought to be rigidly adhered to: one, that they be never suffered to go abroad alone; and, secondly, that they should never be left in the care of female relatives. That both these precautions are often neglected with impunity, we are well aware; but this by no means disproves the existence of the danger; and the occurrence, in a single instance, of the horrible consequences above related, affords a warning which we hope will not be disregarded." (Am. Jurist, No. 5, p. 19.)

There seems something almost providential in visiting on the family of Daniel Nash the misfortune that might have been averted by his carrying this writing to the selectmen, as he was requested to do, on the morning of the fatal occurrence.

It is unnecessary to dwell longer on the physical causes of insanity, and the evidence, *a priori*, of their existence in our unfortunate client. Had we proved none of them, but still have shown moral causes enough, or had we shown neither, but still have proved plenary indications of insanity at the time of the killing, it would have sufficed. Not only is it difficult to trace out the origin of this disease, but the causes of it may lie dormant for years; the predisposition may remain till the last sands of life, before any accident may occur to call them into activity. The seeds of this, as well as of some other disorders, may lie in the system, like some seeds in the earth, many years, before they vegetate and bear baneful fruit.

In the discovery of the truth in this case, we have received no aid from the prisoner. Whether he be now sufficiently recovered to aid us or not, he certainly has shown no disposition to do it; and though his mind is doubtless in a less excited state than it was a year ago, never has been witnessed greater apathy and indifference than has been shown by him concerning his destiny. Not an individual of this large audience, for the last three days, has evinced so much unconcern; and, to all appearance, even now, punishment would have no more effect upon him than on the beasts that perish. He is much more entitled to compassion and protection than to severity. Even savages shield their lunatics and idiots, from a principle of superstitious reverence, which seems happily ordained as a substitute for civilization; and to indulge the thought, for a moment, that we should be less humane, less charitable, than Indians, would be to stigmatize our people most wrongfully.

Whether, as a cause of insanity, the use of ardent spirit to excess, in some former years, may or may not have operated in some degree in this case, it is neither legal nor reasonable to inquire.

More than half the male lunatics, in many of our hospitals, have been made so chiefly by intemperance. But are they any the less lunatics? and are they any the more to be punished for acts done while lunatics?

Such a doctrine would be most novel and dangerous, and inhuman; and would lead, in every defence of insanity, to an investigation of the cause; and if it was gaming, bad speculations in trade, wrong religious notions, or intemperance, there would in each be error, and hence the insanity no defence in law. Push the argument further, and every adviser to any wrong, whether by precept or example, and which wrong caused insanity, would make the adviser also answerable for every crime, however enormous, committed by the insane person.

In such a complex inquiry, we might all need the pardoning power here, as well as hereafter, to escape condign or capital punishment.

Let us, then, advert a moment to the special indications of a deranged mind, as laid down by the soundest writers; and afterwards review the evidence, to ascertain if any of them appeared at and about the time of the killing of the deceased.

Should we, in the end, find nineteen out of twenty of the usual indications existing here, it is vain to cherish, for a moment, the harsh, the absurd and unlawful notion, that he can be convicted of any crime whatever, whether murder or manslaughter.

[Mr. W. here read from Beck the following extracts upon the symptoms of mental alienation :]

"In many instances, though it is far from being general, pain in the head, and throbbing of its arteries, precede an attack of insanity."

"They abandon their business, and enter into the most extravagant undertakings."

"He becomes angry without any assignable cause; attempts to perform feats of strength, or efforts of agility, which shall strike the beholder with astonishment at his great powers. Many talk incessantly, sometimes in the most boisterous manner; then, suddenly lowering the tone, speak softly, and whisper."

"The commission which they suppose themselves to receive from some superior being is given by the ear; they imagine it is constantly repeated. They are thus, they imagine, urged to its performance, and, in many cases, murder or self-destruction is the unhappy result."

"The *eye* is also diseased. Objects appear bright or fiery, and the organ itself is sparkling and protruded."

"Wakefulness is another symptom, which sometimes precedes all others, and is coëval with pain or uneasiness of the head, or of some other diseased organ; and its degree is determined by the age, habits, situation, and original vigorous or feeble constitution, of the patient."

"It is this discontent of mind that detaches them from their parents and friends, and causes them to hate most those whom they previously cherished with the fondest affection."

"The sufferers are pursued, day and night, by the same ideas and affections; and they give themselves up to these with profound ardor and devotion."

"They often appear reasonable, when conversing on subjects beyond the sphere of their delirium, until some external impression suddenly rouses the diseased train."

"Some are gay, and highly excited, — laugh, talk, and sing, — fancy themselves deities, kings, learned and noble."

"Some patients, when laboring under this form, are excessively irascible, and even, without any apparent cause, are suddenly hurried into a violent passion or fury. It is while laboring under this that they become dangerous to themselves, or to those around them. They will seize any weapon, and strike or injure others or themselves."

"An internal sensation is perceived,— as a burning heat, with pulsation, within the skull, previous to this excitement."

"Probably this is a form of insanity as common as any other. It is also said to be less durable, and to end more favorably." (1 Beck's Med. Jur. 336 to 343.)

Thus you will see that the most conspicuous marks of an insane person are, that the ear is often affected, and strange noises heard; that the eye is protruded and glistening; that the head suffers severe pains; that the attention cannot long be confined; that business is neglected; that suspicions exist of conspiracies; that antipathies are conceived against those before beloved; that wild fancies are formed; that they believe themselves princes or kings; that they are sleepless, irascible, boisterous, profane, inclined to drink, appear like those inebriated, and, in fine, often prove mischievous to themselves or others.

Now, let me ask, have you not, in reality, been listening to the very substance of the testimony, in the present inquiry?

Has not almost every one of this large number of indications of insanity been fully proved, within the last two days?

We leave nothing to conjecture,—we ask nothing from rumor,—we appeal to the evidence delivered in your presence, under the solemnities of an oath to God.

By that, it was shown, beyond contradiction, that, within a fortnight of the fatal transaction, his complaints were frequent of strange pains in his head,—of droppings in it,—"of its feeling like a potash kettle,"—and his wife applied cold water to it, and fears were expressed lest he should become insane, like his father. About the commencement of that fortnight, after severe labor in the woods, he came in, and related that an air-gun had been shot at him, and the ball distinctly heard. Believing falsely, as the ear was disordered, that he heard such a sound, he, on Locke's hypothesis about lunatics, reasoned correctly, from erroneous premises, that it must have been an *air*-gun, as he saw no smoke.

Again, early on the 5th of June, after hard labor in the woods, he came in, and was possessed of the wild fancy that a bee was an angel, with power to carry him to hell; and returned, just at evening, to the woods, with the avowed purpose of chopping all night. Again, he soon imagines that twelve men from Walpole waylay him in the woods, point their guns at him, but are restrained from firing by his angel. It is his wife, too,—the being most dear to him,—the being to whose devoted fidelity and untiring affection he is indebted for his defence and his life, if saved by your verdict,—it is his wife whom he madly believes to have conspired with them to destroy him, and whom, with his affrighted children, he imprisoned the whole of the morning of the fatal day of the killing.

It will not answer to talk of these fancies—these noises heard, and men seen—as mere differences in opinion from mankind at large on religion, on spirits, on other subjects. No! They are the very madness of the moon—the mind diseased.

Again, his delusion about witchcraft might exist theoretically, though such notions have seldom been carried into practice in this country the last fifty years, and never been tolerated by courts or juries since the Salem trials of the seventeenth century. But not only to believe in the existence of witches, but their possession of his cat, and that all cats of a black color were infested the same way; that they must be killed with silver; the offer of money for leave to kill Guillow's, and the actual killing of his own, with such secret loading and care; the darning-needle placed over the cat-hole, and the axe set up edgeways at the crack of the door,—these are circumstances which might make the most credulous doubt. But his idea of spirits went far beyond this. The spirit of an Indian, in the shape of a snake, guarded his mine; and the evening before the killing, by the spirit's advice, he carried boards half a mile, nearly, to cover the spirit up. It assumed a still different shape when it directed him to wear a red, instead of a black waistcoat, on the morning of Mrs. Nash's death. He imagined he saw balls of fire in the air blown up from the infernal regions; that war had broken out with England, and he must march to repel invasion; that he was to pass "*through bloody seas,*" and, strange as all, for a man in his condition, and of his education (whatever might happen to others differently situated), conjectures that he was called forthwith to visit and convert the heathen in the north-east.

In the very midst of all this, the very day before the killing, he fancies he has obtained a new wife, and offers up ardent prayers for her welfare. His eyes assume a wild and glassy appearance. He not only sees gold and silver in common gravel, and talks of importing from Europe refiners and machinery to work his mine,—which some sane men might be deluded to think of,—but he madly sees the gold and silver spread over his rocks and buildings, and even cross into the adjoining farm of his neighbors.

There is, to be sure, some method in his madness, like Hamlet's; for he reasons naturally enough on false principles, and avows that, under such wealth, he has become what the insane Lear once was—a very king.

The morning of the accident, he fastens his cane into the block of wood, and carries it about in triumph. He imagines himself a prince, and proclaims that he has conquered, and forthwith there shall be peace.

Add to all this, gentlemen, his peculiar irritableness; his refusal, at times, to answer common questions; his profanity at one moment, his loud singing and prayers at another; his unusual rapidity in walking; his strange manner of carrying his cane and hat; his entire neglect of business; his extraordinary appearance, throughout, beyond anything before seen, and testified to by one of the most intelligent witnesses for the State,—and you have a combination and a mass of circumstances utterly irreconcilable with perfect sanity of mind. There can be no mistake about this. For, after almost a year and a half, you yourselves see him, even now, before you, with an eye, a complexion, and a manner, which mark strongly the disease, and one of which Haslam states that he found in over two hundred and five out of two hundred and sixty-five patients in Bethlem Hospital. (Cyclopedia, Art. *Mental Derangement.*)

But, gentlemen, could a doubt remain, the absence of all moral motive to kill the deceased,— of any motive to influence a sane mind, — is decisive that he did the act under the dominion of a different and uncontrollable power. I will read an extract taken from Marc, an eminent medical jurist in France.

> "*Moreover, the moral circumstances which precede or accompany crimes generally show whether they are the result of criminal intentions, or derangement of intellect; that is to say, that in a real criminal there is always some motive of personal interest, by which the moral cause of his act may be known.* Thus, a homicide, followed by robbery, cannot be attributed to *mania without delirium.*" (Vide 1 Beck's Med. Jur. 372.)

Here, however, he robbed the unfortunate woman of nothing. He was to gain nothing by her death, in a pecuniary view, by will or inheritance, as in the late assassination in a neighboring State. He had no quarrel to provoke him,—no injury to revenge. They lived in the same neighborhood, in perfect friendship; and worshipped in the same religious society, with united hearts and tongues.

More than all this, to show that the very essence of madness is alone apparent, the deed was committed in public, before witnesses, without any attempt to escape; leaving a part of the gun, well known, on the head of the deceased; retaining the residue in his hand, when taken, hallooing after and threatening to kill the little girl likewise; frothing at his mouth after arrested; and his whole previous character marked with industry, mildness, and public professions of religion.

It would be an insult to your understandings to linger longer on the defence on the ground of insanity, as applicable to the general charge of murder.

But it has been suggested that the prisoner might be convicted of manslaughter, though not of murder; and that this insanity, if caused by drunkenness, immediate or remote, would not exonerate him from the charge of either crime.

Give me leave, however, to say, and to demonstrate, that the sane mind is just as indispensable to the guilt, the wickedness, of one crime as the other; and that he cannot, therefore, be convicted of manslaughter.

[Chief-justice Richardson here remarked, that the Court had considered that subject, and he thought that the jury could not convict of anything but murder; that if the insanity was such as to exonerate the prisoner from the charge of murder, he could not be convicted of manslaughter.]

We are happy to hear that the Court has come to that conclusion; but, as the jury have the law in their hands, we would merely remark further, that a lunatic cannot be convicted of manslaughter, because there is not the evil heart and mind, and the knowledge necessary to constitute the crime. We do not believe that the good sense of the jury would, for a moment, tolerate the position, that a lunatic could be punished to any extent for an act committed under the immediate influence of derangement.

The only remaining position on which a conviction can be properly asked is, that the deed was committed when in a state of intoxication.

We meet this, in the first instance, on the evidence, and not on evil report, by a categorical denial of the fact.

The testimony on both sides shows that he drank nothing whatever on Saturday, the day of the killing; nothing on Friday, Thursday, and indeed for a whole week previous, that anybody can pretend would be likely to produce the least intoxication.

But, if he had, and was deranged before he began to drink, the jury could not convict him. Because drinking to excess is often the consequence of insanity, the want of due control over one's faculties; and would here be the effect, rather than the cause, of his state of mind. Insane people may become intoxicated, also, from accident or inclination, as well as other people, and while intoxicated may do mischief. But, if either the intoxication or the mischief occurred from the *insanity*, it would be absurd to punish them.

But, in the most explicit language, we deny the fact of the least intoxication at the time of the supposed offence; we deny its existence for more than a week previous; and we deny that it had occurred for many months before, except in a single instance, after he had become deranged.

In this denial, we are not only fortified by no proof to the contrary having been adduced by the State, but by positive proof, adduced by ourselves, of his sobriety, and by the decisive circumstance of persons being now present, from many miles around him in all directions, and not one of them being able to implicate him beyond what we have stated. It is not left to conjecture,—they produce everybody from whom they could show it. Even for years previous, his habits of drinking have by no means been proved to be those of a drunkard. In only some half-dozen instances in his whole life, and most of those at trainings, musters, and on such occasions, has he been proved to be intoxicated by spirit, and only once, the year previous, by cider.

[Mr. W. here recapitulated the testimony of each witness as to his condition for eight days before the killing, and showed that on that day neither rum nor cider had been drank; on the day before, only two glasses of wine; on the second day before, only one glass of rum and one draught of cider; on the third day, nothing; on the fourth, nothing, unless a gill of rum testified to by his son; on the fifth, sixth and seventh, nothing, unless perhaps a single draught of cider on the fifth; and on the eighth day previous, after coming from the woods and hard labor, and sustaining a fall from the log and evincing great wildness, drinking the gin sworn to by Day and Thompson.]

The drinking of the gin was the effect, and not the cause, of his insanity. He had evinced a sadly bewildered mind for two days previous, as testified to by the Misses Bingham and Hudson, and for two months or more previous is not proved to have used either spirit, wine or cider.

In this way, the whole charge as to the killing having occurred while in a state of intoxication, or while the fumes of liquor remained in his head, vanishes into thin air.

Almost as little foundation is there for the last position which we have heard advanced to sustain the charge,— that excessive drinking long before the deed had caused the insanity; and, in that event, that he should be answerable, especially if he knew such drinking was likely to derange him.

We are not, here or elsewhere, the apologists of intemperance. We rejoice at the improved and improving habits of our community on this subject. We would lend, rather than oppose, our feeble hand and voice to the cause of reformation. And if an individual, under the immediate influence of liquor, and not otherwise insane, commits mischief, we say, let him respond fully to the violated laws. So, if he drinks or takes opium, like the irritated Malays, with a view "to run a muck," and do all possible mischief, let him be made answerable.

But we are, it is hoped, neither fanatics, inquisitors, or stoics, and would never, in a human tribunal, attempt the vain task of tracing up to first moral causes the origin of any crime, and punishing the remote and ignorant accessories to any small sin for all the heinous consequences in the furthest degree, and till the end of time, and by the highest penalties mortal power can wield.

No human tribunal can thus administer the laws; but must leave all causes and consequences, beyond the most immediate, to the scrutiny, wisdom, and mercy, of that Being who cannot err in judgment.

[He then proceeded to comment on the testimony as bearing on this question of intoxication at this and former periods of his life.]

It must be manifest, then, from all this evidence, that sufficient excessive drinking has not been shown to produce *mania a potu*, or any other *mania*. On the contrary, the probability is infinitely greater that the constitutional predisposition to insanity, the epileptic fits, the falls, and his general temperament of body, having made him more easily to be deranged, he became so from the immediate circumstance of his excessive labor in the woods, about two weeks prior to the killing. Then reason was first seen to be dethroned, then his imagination and actions first became bewildered and wild, and then his opinions and conduct became rather the proper subjects of compassion than of censure and vengeance.

But he protested against the position of the State's counsel in point of law, if the insanity had been produced by habits of intemperance, provided the actual intoxication had entirely ceased at the time of the killing.

[Mr. W. here referred to the case of Drew, in the Circuit Court of the United States,* and read from the Jurist the following extracts, from medical writers, there cited :]

The truth is, that the immunity from punishment results from the insanity itself, and not from the nature of the causes which produced it. (Western Jour. of Med. and Phys. Sciences.)

Would it be said that the action was not excused by his insanity, because he brought that insanity on himself? Such an argument never could be listened to with patience, either within a court of justice or without it. By the late reports of madhouses in England, it will be seen that a very considerable proportion of their inmates have become so from this indulgence. All these, then, are moral agents, and responsible for the crimes they perpetrate, &c. (Boston Med. and Surg. Jour. Am. Jur. No. 5, pp. 15—17.)

But, as the facts here proved had already been shown not to give rise to any question on these points, he said he should dismiss them without further comment. He believed all would now agree that the prisoner was insane at the time of the fatal transaction. That time,

* No principle in criminal law is more universally admitted than that the insane man is not responsible for his acts; that guilt does not attach to the individual who is unconscious of his deeds; that it is the criminal mind, the wicked intent, which makes him the subject of punishment : and yet this principle must be received with some qualification. Voluntary insanity, brought on by indulgence and excess, is no excuse for crime. A homicide committed in the frenzy of intoxication subjects the offender to punishment. And here insanity and its cause must not be confounded. The law discriminates between the delirium of intoxication and the insanity which it sometimes produces. While the drunkenness continues, the person under its influence is responsible as a moral agent, though reason, in the mean time, has lost her dominion; but when the intoxication ceases, if insanity immediately follow as a consequence of the vice, he is in the eye of criminal justice no longer amenable for his acts. This legal distinction in the criminality of acts in relation to insanity and its causes is exemplified in cases of *delirium tremens*, a species of madness which often deprives the sufferer of the power of distinguishing between right and wrong, and which medical writers attribute to frequent intoxication, or the sudden cessation from habitual drinking, or to the combined effect of both upon the system. But, however just the distinction, it does not appear to have been judicially settled, before the decision of Justices Story and Davis, in a late case, which it is the design of these few preliminary remarks to introduce.

At the May term, A. D. 1828, of the Circuit Court of the United States, Alexander Drew, commander of the whaling ship John Jay, was indicted and tried for the murder of his second mate, Charles F. Clark, while upon the high seas. It appeared in evidence, that previously to the voyage during which the fatal act took place, Drew had sustained a fair character, and was much respected in the town of Nantucket, where he belonged. It was proved that he was a man of humane and benevolent disposition, but that for several months he had been addicted to the use of ardent spirits, and for weeks during the voyage had drank to excess; that he made a resolution to reform, and suddenly abstaining from drinking, he was seized with the delirium tremens; and that, while under the influence of the disease, he made an attack upon Clark, and gave him the stab of which he afterwards died.

The first witness who testified in the case was George Galloway, the cooper on board the ship. He stated that he joined the ship in the Pacific Ocean; that he found Capt. Drew to be an amiable man, kind to his crew, and attentive to his business; but that he often indulged to excess in spirituous liquors. During the latter part of August, 1827, he had been in the habit of drinking very freely; that they spoke a ship, from which Capt. Drew obtained a keg of liquor, and after he returned to his own vessel he drank until he became stupefied; that soon after he recovered a little from his intoxication, and ordered the keg with its contents to be thrown overboard, and it was accordingly done. There being now no more liquor on board of and that alone, was the eventful moment on which all the other testimony was to bear. He believed most, if not all, would concur, that the cause of that insanity was immaterial, unless it was the insanity of recent intoxication. He believed that any such cause was rebutted

---

the ship, and none to be procured, Capt. Drew, in two or three days, discovered signs of derangement. He could not sleep, had no appetite, thought the crew had conspired to kill him, expressed great fears of an Indian who belonged to the ship, called him by name when he was not present, begged he would not kill him, saying to himself he would not drink any more rum. Sometimes he would sing obscene songs, and sometimes hymns; would be found alternately praying and swearing. In the night of the 31st of August, Drew came on deck, and attempted to jump overboard; and when the witness caught hold of him, he sank down trembling, and appeared to be very weak. His appearance, the next morning, the witness described to be that of a foolish person.

At seven o'clock in the morning of the first of September, the witness, Capt. Drew, and others, were at breakfast in the cabin, when Drew suddenly left the table, and appeared to conceal something under his jacket, which was on the transom in another part of the cabin. He immediately turned round to Mr. Clark, and requested him to go upon deck; the reply of Clark was, "When I have done my breakfast, sir." Drew said, "Go upon deck, or I will help you," and immediately took from the transom a knife which had been covered over by his jacket, and before another word was spoken by either, he stabbed Clark in the right side of his breast. Clark was rising from his chair at the time the knife struck him, and immediately fell upon the floor. He afterwards rose up, and went upon deck alone. As the witness left the cabin, Drew cocked his pistol, and pointed it at him, and snapped it; but it missed fire. Capt. Drew followed them upon deck, and addressing the chief mate, said, "Mr. Coffin, in twenty-four hours from this, the ship shall go ashore." He was then seized, bound hand and foot, and a guard was stationed over him. His whole demeanor, for some time after, was that of an insane person. He would frequently call upon persons who were not on board, and who never had connection with the ship. Some weeks after, when Drew first appeared to be in his right mind, he was informed of the death of Clark and its cause. He replied that he knew nothing about it; that when he awoke he found himself handcuffed, and that it all appeared to him like a dream. There had not been for months any quarrel or high words between Clark and Capt. Drew.

The second witness was Moses Coffin, the first mate of the ship. Coffin stated that Capt. Drew had been in the habit of drinking, and that it was by the order of Drew that the keg of spirits was thrown overboard. He recounted numerous instances, in addition to those before stated, of frivolous complaints made by Drew of his countermanding his orders, of his fear of being left alone, and his conversation with the imaginary beings by whom he supposed himself surrounded, all going to prove physical weakness and alienation of mind. Though familiar with his habits, the witness had not, before this affair, supposed him insane.

With regard to Clark, the witness dressed his wound, and took care of him. Two physicians at a Spanish port, which they reached soon after, gave it as their opinion that it was not dangerous, and that it would be well in a few days; but Clark himself had said, in describing his complaint to witness, that the wound caused an internal flow of blood. It healed externally before Clark expired.

At this stage of the proceeding, the Court asked the district attorney if he expected to change the posture of the case. He admitted that, unless upon the facts stated the Court were of opinion that this insanity, brought on by the antecedent drunkenness, constituted no defence for the act, he could not expect success in the prosecution. After some consultation, the opinion of the Court was delivered as follows:

Story J. We are of opinion that the indictment, upon these admitted facts, cannot be maintained. The prisoner was unquestionably insane at the time of committing the offence. And the question made at the bar is, whether insanity whose remote cause is habitual drunkenness is or is not an excuse in a court of law for a homicide committed by the party while so insane, but not at the time intoxicated, or under

by the most decisive evidence. His condition now, and since the deed, had not been gone into by physicians, or other witnesses, because that inquiry had been objected to as irrelevant; — we have been ready to meet it, even at this trial. But, should the jury acquit him, it will then become clearly material and relevant, whenever he, or his friends, apply to have him discharged from custody; and the jury, in acquitting him, will have the satisfaction to reflect that he cannot be set at large till the Court are convinced of his having become perfectly sane.

He will be kept, without undeserved stigma to him or his connections, as there would be if sent to the state-prison for even manslaughter. They will have the satisfaction to reflect, that no mistake will be committed, irremediable, and affecting the life of a fellow-being.

They will sustain those sound principles of law which construe all presumptions favorably to the accused, and which inculcate an entire acquittal, whenever reasonable doubts interpose, rather than hurry to eternity a fellow-being, who may have had, at the time of the accident, no more control over his faculties than over the roll of a cataract, or the speed of a tornado.

We repeat our entreaties, that you beware of a mistake, where no correction in time can restore life improperly taken. Beware of an example, which, how soon, God only knows, may be applied to yourselves, or families, or friends.

None of us can boast security against the attacks of the most subtle and deplorable malady of a mind diseased, — none of us have a bond of fate, that soon, overwhelmed by its inscrutable influences, we may

---

the influence of liquor. We are clearly of opinion that insanity is a competent excuse, in such a case. In general, insanity is an excuse for the commission of any crime, because the party has not the possession of his reason, which includes responsibility. An exception is when the crime is committed by a party while in a fit of intoxication, the law not permitting a man to avail himself of the excuse of his own gross sin and misconduct to shelter himself from the legal consequences of such crime. But the crime must take place and be the immediate result of the fit of intoxication, and while it lasts, and not, as in this case, a remote consequence, superinduced by the antecedent exhaustion of the party, arising from gross and habitual drunkenness. However criminal, in a moral point of view, such an indulgence is, and however justly a party may be responsible for his acts arising from it to Almighty God, human tribunals are generally restricted from punishing them, since they are not the acts of a reasonable being. Had the crime been committed while Drew was in a fit of intoxication, he would have been liable to be convicted of murder. As he was not then intoxicated, but merely insane from an abstinence from liquor, he cannot be pronounced guilty of the offence. The law looks to the immediate, and not to the remote cause; to the actual state of the party, and not to the cause which produced it. Many species of insanity arise remotely from what, in a moral view, is a criminal neglect or fault of the party, as from religious melancholy, undue exposure, extravagant pride, ambition, &c. &c. Yet such insanity has always been deemed a sufficient excuse for any crime done under its influence.

The jury, without retiring from their seats, returned a verdict of *not guilty*. The case was conducted for the government by George Blake Esq., district attorney; for the prisoner by Daniel Davis and Francis Bassett, Esquires.

(American Jurist, No. 5, p. 6.)

not become the instruments of death to some of our race. The most learned cannot always discover its approaches, or escape its calamities. The most lofty, and powerful, and good, as well as the humblest tenant of the lowest shed, are equally its victims: from George the III. on his throne, delivered over to his keepers; from the sagacious and witty Swift, in a mad-house; from the beautiful poet Collins, with a mind in ruins; from the amiable and virtuous Cowper, attempting suicide, under its bitter influence,—to the most ignorant and stupid inmate of a lunatic asylum.

Let me conjure you, then, as you value humanity or life, a good name here or happiness hereafter, do not, in a case of any doubt as to the existence of this deplorable disease, add suffering to suffering, calamity to calamity,—hasten away, from time and hope, its wretched victim,—and make him, and all that hold him dear, martyrs to any public excitement, or popular prejudice, however deep or wide. Let it not be forgotten that you yourselves have much at stake, in this decision, as well as he; for, as you are governed by the law and the evidence alone, or by other considerations, you commit perjury of your official oaths, and must answer hereafter, if not here, at the same tribunal with the miserable prisoner before you. But my confidence is unshaken that you will decide as your solemn duties demand, and that, so deciding, he must be acquitted.

Such a course, and such a result, will leave you to sleep quietly on your pillows; and will be approved, it is hoped, when you again meet this unfortunate man, as meet him soon we all must, at the bar of a merciful God!

# ARGUMENT IN CASE OF STATE OF NEW HAMPSHIRE *v.* AMOS AND ABIGAIL FURNALD.*

I APPEAR before the jury in the cause of an unfortunate and wretched child. It is true that this child has now probably found a more able advocate, protector and friend. However forsaken and persecuted here,— though torn from the arms of its mother when only a day old, and hastened, as it was believed, untimely to its grave, in the bud of life, and without any heart of sympathy to smooth its dying pillow,— it is now, I trust, beyond further suffering. But a voice of inquiry and complaint has gone forth loud and wide. All the better and saving principles of our nature have been roused. The child is universally supposed to have been taken off by means most foul and damnable. And if the evidence fully verifies this supposition, though a verdict of guilty can neither restore the child to the hopes and enjoyment of life, nor soften the anguish already endured, yet it can inflict merited punishment on the murderer, and redeem us all from any participation in his crime. Such a verdict is indispensable, to effect these salutary purposes. Whatever has been urged against the severity of our penal code, it is written upon the heart of man, and by the finger of God himself in scripture, that the shedder of innocent blood should die.

At the same time, I invoke you, in the name of the deceased, and by every laudable motive, human and divine, to remember the important consequences which will flow from such a verdict to the safety and character of our population. A deep stain has been imprinted on the State by the inhuman death of this child; and though the indictment is against the prisoner alone and his unhappy wife, not now on trial, yet, if by any ill-timed compassion, or lack of civil courage, the jury shall improperly acquit the prisoner, they become accessories in his guilt, and they fail to vindicate the character of their county, of the State, and, indeed, of humanity, from countenancing one of the most atrocious outrages which ever blackened the annals of our race.

In this view of the prosecution, the fate of the prisoner at the bar, so far as regards himself individually, is a mere drop in the ocean. And though many appeals have been made to the jury for lenity towards him, in consequence of his jeopardy and distress, these last are of trifling consequence, compared with the influence of their ver-

* Amos Furnald, and Abigail his wife, were indicted for the murder of Alfred Furnald, a child of five years of age, 1824.

dict, if wrong, upon the morals and character of living and unborn millions. I agree with the counsel for the prisoner, in the sacredness of their duty,—in the solemnity of the occasion,—but these both speak a language to the jury which forbids the indulgence of any private sympathies, to the injury of the public; and it is hardly necessary to remind them, that God himself has been invoked, since they sat in those very seats, to forsake or befriend them, as they decided this indictment by weakness and compassion, or by the law and the evidence. Should any facts attempted to be proved remain in some degree doubtful, it is admitted that feelings of commiseration may incline the scale to the injured side; or, in other phraseology, to him who *does* rather than to him who *suffers* wrong. If pity, then, is here to be adjured,—if pity is to influence the jury in any portion of their present deliberations,—let me ask, if it be pity for the marble-hearted monster who forced the tender infant from the breast of its mother, and answered her tears and agony with threats of more than savage barbarity? Is it for him who beheld that infant, without yielding it relief or sympathy, perishing slowly for months under the combined effects of cold, nakedness, and famine; and who neither watched over and soothed its departing spirit, nor followed its coffin to the grave? Or is it pity for the deserted, and friendless, and persecuted child, withered and cut down in the morning of life, and by a death the most agonizing which hellish malignity could invent?

The Ugolinos, and other tyrants of the darkest ages, only starved their victims at once; but here the torture lasted for months; and though the prisoner at the bar was without their power to defy vengeance, and hence sought to escape detection by using means less palpable, yet the food given was so little in quantity, that, in connection with its bad quality, and the want of proper clothing and cleanliness, the protracted suffering must have been infinitely more severe, and death equally inevitable.

Another appeal has been made to the jury for favor to the prisoner, on the ground that he stood at the bar, contending with the State, under fearful odds. It was admitted there were fearful odds; but they were against the State, and not against the prisoner. On the one hand, the prisoner, with as many counsel as he chooses to fee, and others assigned to him by the Court,—and then the judges themselves declaring (and that declaration, as all have seen, not a mere form in the present case), that they too were his counsel,—with as many witnesses as he chooses to name, both summoned and paid by the State, with any length of time asked for preparation,—with our charge and witnesses all furnished him beforehand, to meet and impeach, with a right to challenge any number of jurors with cause, and twenty more without cause, and then permitted to cull twelve from the residue,—with the legal presumption on his side of innocence,—with the oft-repeated principle on his side, that he is not to be convicted till every reasonable doubt is removed, and with our natural and accustomed dread of capital punishments, to shelter him from a conviction of murder, upon evidence, which, in some countries, would satisfy a jury without leaving the stand. These advantages, in truth, and improperly, often cause ten guilty to escape, where one innocent person suffers. (Foster's C. Law, 250, 251; Paley's Moral Philosophy, Book 6, Chap. 9.)

On the other hand, the attorney general for the State is absent, and no presumption, or principle, or favor, exists to aid the State, but the naked justice of the charge, and the resistless strength of the evidence. The State, likewise, has no "quirks and quiddities" of the law; no "dos" and "dittos," to reinforce them; nor would the State summon to its aid reproach and contumely, as the unfortunate mother of the child had been abused by the counsel for her betrayer and seducer. Nor would they bring other railing accusations against him as an adulterer — a murderer of his own offspring; though the State sincerely wishes he had come forward, at least, with the face of conscious innocence and fearless integrity, and, as all who are strong in honesty would have done, had met the merits of the case manfully, and, with a trust in Providence and in the good sense of the jury, had not sought by quibbling subtleties to turn aside the arm of justice. Nor will the State upbraid the prisoner with conspiracies and combinations, charges of which have been lavished so profusely upon the Ladds, the solicitor, and some of the respectable witnesses. But the jury will judge from the testimony of Furnald's daughters, and the following facts, from which side these charges could have come with the better grace.

[Mr. W. then went into an examination of the evidence, to show that none of the Ladds, or the solicitor, or Dr. Durkee, had conducted with any impropriety; but, on the contrary, had evinced a scrupulous regard to their duty and the prisoner's rights. While, on the other hand, one, at least, of the prisoner's daughters, and one of his other witnesses, stood totally discredited, if not suborned to perjury.]

Having met these general objections and claims, as well as the unfounded aspersions, uttered by authority from the prisoner, let me entreat the jury not to forget that the State, or, in other words, that the people of New Hampshire have rights at stake in this trial, as well as Amos Furnald. That they not only represent his unfortunate child, and claim for its sufferings, so extreme, unprovoked, and barbarous, some penal atonement, and this from the only tribunal short of God's which can now give redress, but they are anxious to remove from the character of this section of the country every degree of suspicion that the great mass of its population could for a moment tolerate the horrible transaction which has been proved upon this trial. I entreat the jury not to be diverted from the merits of the inquiry, by attempts to settle many irrelevant and delusive points, pressed on their consideration by the prisoner's counsel; pressed, too, as if they were the sole subjects in issue — the alpha and omega of the trial. Whether the prisoner has had a controversy with Jonathan Ladd, or not,—whether this witness has mistaken a month in a date, or that one has been contradicted in the size of a mud-puddle,— the true nature of the charge remains the same, and the evidence in support of it is substantially unimpaired.

The charge is, that the prisoner, between the 1st of February and the 8th of April, 1824, confined Alfred Furnald in a house in Gilmanton, and feloniously produced his death,— not by total starvation, as has been alleged by counsel, but by a neglect to furnish him with "*sufficient* meat, drink, victuals, and other *necessaries*, proper and requisite for" his sustenance.

That such an act, if proved, amounted in law to murder in the highest degree, I shall attempt to satisfy the jury; and that these acts have been committed by the prisoner has, in my opinion, been conclusively proved.

The various authorities as to the definition of murder have been read to you by the solicitor. To constitute murder, there must be malice and a killing; and that killing may be by improper exposure or insufficient food, as well as by poison or the steel. Nor is it necessary that the act should cause immediate death, or be likely to produce death under all circumstances, upon every description of persons. But it is a killing within the eye of the law and of reason, if, considering the age and health of the sufferer, such acts were likely to cause death, and did, in fact, cause it. For all men must be considered as having intended the natural and obvious consequences of their acts. In respect to malice,— when the natural consequences of certain acts are death, malice is, as a general principle, to be presumed against the perpetrator of those acts, and, unless explained and justified, the irresistible inference is, that he could not do such acts without a heart fatally bent on mischief.

[The following authorities on the subject of killing and of malice were then adverted to, and discussed: 1 East C. L. 143, 242, 218, 226; 2 Chitty Cr. L. 478; Foster's Cr. L. 322, 257; 1 Hale Pl. Cr. 428, 431—2; 2 Strange 884, Rex *v.* Huggings; 2 Lord Ray, 1577, S. C.; 1 Hawk. Pl. Cr. 118 page, B. 1, ch. 31; 3 Chitty Cr. L. 524, 533; Kelynge 78, 111.]

The cases adduced, of a harlot exposing her infant, so that it was destroyed by a kite,— of an inhuman son, who carried his sick father abroad against his will, by which he sickened and died,— of overseers of the poor, who removed a pauper from place to place, without nourishment, till it perished; of a jailer, who forcibly carried his prisoner into an apartment where the small-pox prevailed, and of another jailer, who confined his prisoner in a damp room, without proper furniture, so as in both cases to prove fatal to the prisoner,— and of masters who refused suitable clothing, medicine and nourishment, to their apprentices, so as to end in death,— are all analogous, and strongly illustrate the ideas advanced by the State, both as to the killing and malice.

[After sundry other remarks upon this head, he proceeded to show that the evidence in this case removed every reasonable doubt as to all the acts having been committed by the prisoner, which were necessary to constitute murder.]

I. The child was confined as set out in the indictment. The length of time the child was confined is immaterial; but it never left the house, and probably not the garret, on the last three days previous to April 8th, and was in the view of the law confined in the house the whole period from February 1st to its death. The child was carried there by force — had never been seen abroad at a single neighbor's, or on a single visit, or a single day at school; and, considering the natural love of children for exercise and sports, and the fact that Furnald's other children partook in them abroad, and attended school, the jury cannot doubt that this child was restrained to the house, and most of the time to its block, by the commands, threats, and chastisement, of Furnald. At the age of five years, a restraint upon the mind and fears of such a child is as much confinement as walls, or locks, or fetters. If these last are always necessary, infants unable to go abroad, or invalids, or idiots, could never be murdered by neglect.

[The testimony of different witnesses on these facts, and particularly on the absence of the child, and the search for it by the workmen the last three days, was examined at length.]

II. This confinement was by the prisoner, and not by his wife or family, without his knowledge and direction. It was the prisoner who forced the child from its mother, carried it to his house, and menaced it with barbarity. It was he who governed and controlled his family; it was he who had from its birth evinced the most fatal enmity to the child; he, who had cruelly scourged and knocked it down; he, who felt the disgrace and the crime of its existence; he, who fled from justice to the wilderness, after its death; he, who had been admonished by Burleigh and others what would be the fatal consequences of his conduct; and he, who, if not present at other times, was at home most of February and March, and all of April, and would then have ordered medicine and different diet, clothing and lodging, had not his heart been hardened into iron, against the pleadings of nature and of humanity.

III. Was the death of the child caused by this confinement, and the neglect to furnish it with food and other necessaries, such as clothing, cleanliness, and lodging, sufficient and proper for its sustenance? The question is not whether the neglect as to one of these particulars caused its death, or whether a neglect as to all of them would have caused it, had the child, the first of February, been healthy and vigorous; but whether the neglect as to all of them, towards a child of that tender age, and reduced to that emaciated condition, did not hasten it prematurely to the grave. Look first at the feebleness of the child, as testified to by every creditable witness,—and as must be true, whatever the daughters of the prisoner may have been suborned to swear, or how could a child have become, without any intervening disease, the ghastly skeleton it is admitted to have been in April? The child being in such a condition, did not this feebleness require some more nutritious and varied diet than potatoes and potato-skins, and even these in very stinted quantities? Did it not require, till the agonies of death were upon the child in the morning of the 8th of April, a call on some physician, or at least on some neighbor, for nursing and advice? Did it not require stockings and shoes, as much as Furnald's other child of the same age? Did it not require different lodging, and woollen garments, and greater cleanliness? Do not its frozen toes, and diseased head, and indescribable filth, carry a conviction, on this subject, beyond the powers of language? Its cries from cold when a witness was present,—its hunger at a period of life when the stomach craves food often, and of a nutritious character, which hunger was so aggravated as to drive it to feed on leather, and to prolong a famished existence at the swill-pail,—hardly need be added, to show the causes of its constant suffering and decay, till relieved by death. Instead of that extraordinary care and attention which were requisite to the proper sustenance of a child in such a condition, it had not the ordinary quality of food, nor its ordinary variety, nor its ordinary quantity, nor at the frequent ordinary times for children of that age; and the same deficiency existed in respect to clothing, lodging, and cleanliness, coupled with the total want of medicine and nursing.

[The testimony on these points was here detailed, and the supposed deviations from this treatment were argued to have been occasional, and merely with a view to mislead strangers that happened to be present.]

Every appearance after death was in perfect accordance with the hypothesis here contended for. A perfect union of opinion among the medical gentlemen, that they see nothing in the dissection indicating with certainty any other cause of death; but every symptom corresponding with what they would expect when death resulted from these causes. The collapsed state of the abdomen — the emptiness of the stomach and intestines — the small size of the former — the total absence of fat from beneath the skin, and from every portion of the body, are all indications, in the best medical authors, and in reason, of death by insufficient nourishment. (Baillie's Morbid Anatomy, 93; 2 Beck's Med. Jurisprudence, 91.) Most or all of these appearances, it is admitted, may result from certain emaciating diseases, such as those of the liver, of the mesentery glands, of the stomach, &c.; but here the liver was sound, the glands not diseased, and every organ performing its accustomed functions. Here, too, the prisoner would have been alarmed at the deadly change in this wretched child, had that change happened by a secret disease, by some species of marasmus, and not by other causes well known and meditated by him. Hence, no information of illness was given by him to the neighbors, or to its miserable mother; hence, no nurse was employed to attend it,— no physician to relieve it,— no astonishment by him expressed at its death; and hence, conscience, the worm that never dies, goaded him into subsequent flight, and resistance to legal process. Alas! had the miserable mother been notified of its approaching end, and, emboldened by that maternal affection which imparts courage to the most timid animals, had she dared to enter the dwelling of her seducer, and the prison of her child, and gazed upon its living skeleton, she could not have known her son, reduced to such a loathsome wreck of despair, cold, and famine!

"It is a fearful thing to see the human soul take wing, in any shape, in any mood." But to see the healthy bloom of infancy fade by hunger, the buoyant spirit broken down by blows, the heart drooping in solitude and misery, and nakedness and frost joining to change the elastic step of youth into the tottering decrepitude of age; to see the scene closing in stifled groans, in a deserted garret, without a mother's tears or a father's sympathy; and to be hurried to the grave like carrion, with no mourner, or a sigh,— is too horrible for a Christian community ever to endure, without fixing on its author the brand of Cain. Yet this course of treatment not only caused the child's death, but it originated in the most hardened malice. 1st. Because such treatment is consistent with nothing but malice: death was the natural and obvious consequence of it. What other consequence could have been anticipated? A person of adult age, with a constitution of iron, could not be expected to enjoy health, under diet and discipline so unusual and severe. It would require the aid of the invincible mind, of some o'er-mastering passion, or of some all-absorbing principle in religious or political martyrdom, to sustain the body at all, any great length of time, under such a mass of privations. But a child is not a monk, a dervise, or a Brahmin, to undergo the penance of hunger, cold, and the scourge, for weeks and months, with impunity. Of the father and his children, described by Dante, who perished in a dungeon by starvation, the youngest yielded first under his agonies; and their tyrant, like him who immured and chained to the floor the prisoners of Chillon, beheld the oldest and most resolute of heart against oppression live longest, to mock that despotic power, which, with all its myrmidons and wrath, is ever unable to chain the spirit. Youth is most bound up in the senses; it requires more frequent and nourishing diet, and can endure exposure and suffering less firmly, than mature age. The respondent, in this case, was the father of a family, and therefore well knew the wants of children, and the propriety not only of ample food and clothing, but of warm lodging and decent cleanliness. He furnished these necessaries of life to his other children, and must have withheld them here with the full consciousness of the consequences, and with the felonious design to remove from him the living monument of his infamy. He also had abundant means to provide every necessary and comfort for this child, as he did for his other children. He was admonished of the consequences, long before his brutality terminated in the death of his victim; and every person of common sense, as well as the physicians, must be conscious that such an end could not be otherwise than natural, obvious, and, indeed, inevitable, from such cruel privations.

2d. Many of these circumstances, as well as others to be enumerated, not only show implied malice from the act of killing, but they are conclusive to prove malice the most deliberate and express. There is a chain of circumstances and acts, from the day of the birth to the funeral of Alfred Furnald, showing in the prisoner an inveterate hostility to him. The child was of that unfortunate class most exposed by the principles of our depraved natures to suffering and violent death. To protect such children from their mothers, who, when overtaken by disgrace, and anxious to conceal their shame, are often inflamed to madness, our laws, and the English laws, have made extraordinary provisions. But such children are equally, and, in truth, more exposed to the bad passions and profligate principles of the father, whenever he can obtain access to them. To this child, at the age of only twenty-four hours, the prisoner got access,—removed it by violence, and returned it only on condition of soon receiving it again under his brutal power. The history of the first year of its life is calculated to melt a heart of adamant. Again and again torn from the weeping and shrieking mother,—exposed prematurely and in unsuitable clothing to the inclemency of the weather,—threatened, during its subsequent life, with the food and lodgings of a dumb beast! And, when the mother, for fear of her own personal safety, left it for a few months, how soon did it begin to evince, by its appearance, the incipient execution of these barbarous threats! The mother was then driven from it forever. After the interval of another year, while under the care of Mrs. Sanborn, who returned it healthy and active, and who had kept it more from sympathy than reward, the same inhuman treatment was re-commenced, and pursued with deliberation and system until its death. A few detached instances, to save appearances, are the only exceptions; and they must have been few indeed, or its health and life, without any disease, would not have sunk so early and rapidly. The prisoner, doubtless, deemed the child a constant reproach and eye-sore, as well as an expense imposed against his will, by the rigor of the law. To destroy it at once by poison or by blows, would have exposed him to detection, immediate and certain. He therefore resorted to means less palpable, but equally sure. He evinced, by his passionate threats, an intention to break down its health and spirits, by a relentless system of cruelty. He persisted in a course to brutalize its mind, by ignorance the most deplorable; to destroy its social feelings, by driving it from his table, and the society of children of its own age; to make it feed like his swine, without spoon or knife; to subject it to immoderate chastisements; to lodge it in solitude and cold; to clothe it in rags and filth;— and if its nature could not thus alter, and undergo the life of a dog, with which it was threatened, he knew that the child must ere long perish, and thus relieve him from the detested burthen of its maintenance, and put far away such a standing memento of his profligacy. The malice is here the more aggravated, as it was altogether unprovoked by the miserable object of it; the more savage, as it was wreaked upon a helpless being, bound to him in some degree by the ties of nature, and placed under his roof for hospitality, sustenance, and safety; the more ferocious, as it was not sudden or transient, but cherished, with Indian inveteracy, for months, if not years; and persisted in after its effects became sufficiently apparent and horrible to make any heart more penetrable than a fiend's relent.

[The counsel here traced the acts and language of the prisoner, as deposed to by the witnesses, from July, 1821, to April 8th, 1824, all indicating his settled and fatal purpose towards this child, but to bring about its death in such a gradual way, and under such circumstances, as to escape punishment; and the counsel thus attempted to harmonize and reconcile all the testimony entitled to any credit on either side.]

All this is fortified by the apathy of the prisoner during the dying scene, and his subsequent flight and resistance, after discovering that his deportment had not blinded the public, and that an investigation of his behavior towards the child was contemplated. His failure afterwards to attend the funeral was a circumstance in perfect keeping with the rest.

The nauseating filth and vermin which appeared on the body, when undressed for its winding-sheet and coffin, could not have been unknown to him, any more than its ulcerated head; and all would have been prevented or remedied, had they not formed a part of the systematic brutality to be exercised on his innocent victim. The appearances on dissection,— the absence of everything but the mere organs of life, and a fleshless skeleton,— these appearances, also, without any previous disease, or call for medicine, or physician, though one had attended on the prisoner himself within a few weeks,— and last, though not least, the missing toes and joints, attributable to no possible cause but frost and nakedness, and about which no medicine, surgeon, or nurse, had ever been employed,— are all confirmations of the most hardened malice, and confirmations strong enough, one would think, to convince the sternest infidel.

Go home, then, gentlemen of the jury, if you can, after this evidence, acquit the prisoner,— go home and tell the friendless and the poor how they may be threatened, scourged, frozen and starved, and thrust into a garret to die, without punishment on their oppressors, in a country boasting of its humanity, its equal laws, and its impartial justice! Send home again, also, to his former neighborhood, the heartless wretch before you, where his return will carry dismay like the approach of pestilence, and encourage him to repeat these enormities on his other illegitimate offspring, who may chance to fall within his merciless power! Give to all others similarly situated the same humane advice and countenance! But more. Your verdict may secure or invade, ere long, even the hearths and the altars where a still nearer and dearer interest exists.

The things of this world are rapidly passing away, and many of us must soon descend to the same narrow dwelling with Alfred Furnald. Into whose hands our tender offspring may fall, and under what desolate circumstances, it is not given us to foresee. But hand down, if you can, to future juries, sitting on the trial of a destroyer of any of your orphan children, a precedent, that the murder is mitigated, if that destroyer only prolongs their agonies to months, instead of minutes!

Say, if you will, also, to other States and other countries, which your verdict may visit on the wings of the press, that the talk among us, concerning humanity, civilization and Christianity, is merely to keep the promise to the ear; but that, for your single selves, you either fully approve the prisoner's conduct, or feel greater sympathy for him than for his famished child, cut off in the dawn of being by the prisoner's relentless malice, and in a manner the most horrid that imagination can paint!

But pause, ere you do this, one moment longer. Has the character and conduct of Amos Furnald in the course of the present trial, and particularly as respects the testimony of one of his misguided and unhappy daughters,—or has his former life, and particularly his persecution and murder of Alfred Furnald,—entitled him to such high commendation and mercy? Do I err in saying the MURDER of Alfred Furnald? The counsel for the State disclaim every feeling vindictive or unjust towards the prisoner. The searcher of all hearts knows that they wish the prisoner, if innocent, acquitted. But if, on this evidence, there was not murder, Farmer was unjustly sentenced to the gallows, and Cain, himself, was guilty only of manslaughter. The evidence has been heard by this vast audience, as well as by you. It will soon circulate to the four winds of Heaven; the tender years and barbarous treatment of this child cannot be concealed; his utter desertedness at his utmost need, his protracted sufferings, his forlorn and agonized hours, under the roof of that miserable garret, cannot be forgotten; his mutilated and fleshless corpse haunts the imagination, and seems to swell the cry for justice which went forth long since from the recesses of his grave.

I know that from those recesses his emaciated frame cannot be reänimated till the resurrection of the just; but had the mantle of the prophet descended on me, how gladly would I hasten to breathe his dead bones into immediate life! Even *now*, should you meet the gaze of his sunken and imploring eyes, you should look on his cold skeleton hands, raised to the jury as his only human refuge for redress, and you should listen to the pleadings of his bloodless lips!

But go and acquit his destroyer, if you must,—the departed spirit probably hovers over us, to learn your determination. If, like the prisoner, you can still turn a hard heart and a deaf ear to its wrongs, it must reäscend to the God of the fatherless and the forsaken, and hereafter obtain that justice which is now withheld!

In the mean time, it may be well for us all to remember that we, likewise, must ascend to the dread tribunal of the same God; and when there meeting the deceased in judgment, that we must answer his accusing spirit for any dereliction of duty which the recording angel may register against us in the present transaction. And as you then may wish you had now acted, so I entreat you to act; and to say that the prisoner is or is not guilty of the crime whereof he here stands charged.

# CHARGE IN RELATION TO THE SLAVE-TRADE.*

Gentlemen of the Grand Jury:

Having, on former occasions, given some explanations of the different crimes which come within the cognizance of your body, and endeavored to show the great importance of your early and prompt attention towards the punishment of them, I shall now, in those respects, only renew what has before been enjoined.

But there is one of those crimes, before alluded to, concerning which public attention has, of late, been much excited, and prosecutions have been more frequent than formerly.

It therefore becomes proper that the principles applicable to it should be well understood, in order to protect the innocent from costs and expenses growing out of groundless indictments, and, at the same time, to detect real guilt, and hold it up to deserved ignominy before our own countrymen and the civilized world.

I refer to violations of the acts of Congress in relation to the slave-trade.

The history and progress of these acts furnish the best explanations of the intentions of their makers.

Various decisions upon them, by judicial tribunals, during the last twenty years, have served to settle the just construction of them; and, during the present season, I have officially been called on to perform the unpleasant duty of trying an American citizen — one born and educated in New England — for an offence against those acts, which placed in jeopardy not only his property and character, *but his life.*

It was fortunate for the reputation of this section of our country, and the influence of our free institutions, and our social abhorrence of menial slavery, that he appeared, in the end, to a jury of his fellow-citizens, to have scrupulously avoided any interest or participation in making men slaves, by kidnapping, or buying, or transporting, or selling them into bondage.

It was manifest, however, that he allowed his vessel to be chartered by slave-dealers; that she carried merchandise suitable to be sold or exchanged for slaves; that she took passengers on board who had been employed in slave vessels, and others who were purchasers of slaves on the coast of Africa; and that he transported some of those persons, as voluntary and free passengers, to and from the slave factories on that

* Delivered to the Grand Jury of the U. S. District Court, Providence, R. I., November, 1846.

coast; — but, throughout, he received only the ordinary price of freight or passage, and it was stipulated expressly, in the charter-party of the vessel, that nothing illegal, whether in persons or property, should be taken on board his vessel.

It hence became highly important to decide what was and what was not illegal, under such circumstances. Or, in other words, how far, under the existing laws, a person could engage in carrying freight and passengers, connected with the trade in slaves, without making himself amenable to punishment, capital or otherwise, for violating those laws. The results of my inquiries on that occasion, as collected from the language and design of the act of Congress, and the judicial decisions which had before been pronounced on them, I shall now summarily present to your consideration.

You will take them in charge as your guide in respect to any complaints which may be laid before you for transgressions of those acts; and if they shall tend to protect the truly innocent from suffering, and to make signal and just examples of the guilty, my purpose in submitting them to you will be answered.

There are four leading propositions which embody what I consider the law on this subject.

*First.* — Whoever, being an American citizen, receives negroes on board his vessel on the coast of Africa, with an intent to continue them in bondage, being interested in them and in the trade, is liable to be punished as for a capital offence.

*Secondly.* — Whoever, being such a citizen, carries only merchandise in his vessel, but is coöperating with others, who carry slaves in a different vessel of the United States, with the intent to make them slaves, and is transporting the merchandise as a participator in the slave-trade and its gains, is exposed to a like capital punishment.

*Thirdly.* — Whoever is not interested in the slaves, and has not kidnapped or taken them on board his vessel with intent to make them slaves, but merely carries them from one foreign port to another, for others, and for ordinary hire, he is guilty of a misdemeanor under acts of Congress, which punish such conduct with heavy fine and imprisonment; but is not doing what is punished by those acts with death, and the ignominy of piracy.

*Fourthly.* — If such person be neither interested in the slaves themselves, nor engaged, personally, in making others slaves, nor employed in carrying them, knowing them to be slaves, but transports merchandise merely, and that as a carrier of goods for others, to earn freight, rather than coöperate in making or paying for slaves, it is not declared to be an offence of any kind by any of the existing acts of Congress.

All principles can best be illustrated by examples.

Allow me, then, to make these four positions more clear and intelligible to you, by some details of the facts and directions recently given by this court in the case of the Porpoise, commanded by Cyrus Libby, and to whose trial I have just referred.

I do this for another purpose, also; and that is, to apprize you of some of the kinds of *evidence* which are admissible in such cases, and their bearing. Because the proof, in regard to these transactions, is often difficult, — complicated, — in several respects novel in character, and doubtful as to its competency.

Libby was indicted and tried in the Maine district of the first circuit of the United States Court, at an adjournment, in July, of the May term, 1846.

He belonged to Scarborough, in the State of Maine, and commanded the brig Porpoise, a vessel owned by citizens of the United States. He was charged with having received on board said brig, on the 8th of December, 1846, within flow of the tide, at a place called Lorenzo Marquez, on the eastern coast of Africa, a negro called Luez, not held to service by the laws of the United States or either of them, and with an intent to make him a slave.

The defendant was arraigned on this indictment, at an adjourned session of the court, in August, 1845, when the indictment was found; and pleaded thereto not guilty.

The trial came on July 7th, 1846, and, after a full hearing, was committed to the jury on the 16th of that month, under the following rulings; and also the following charge of the court on the various questions of law arising in the cause.

Most of the facts will be stated in the opinions of the court, that are necessary to understand the grounds of the law upon them.

It is sufficient to say here that the Porpoise was proved to belong to G. Richardson, of Gorham, Maine, and to have sailed from Portland in 1842, on a freighting voyage, under the command of Libby, both being American citizens.

He was instructed, when reaching Rio Janeiro, as he did in January, 1843, to report to Knight, Maxwell & Co., as consignees, with authority in them to let her for freight, or sell her at a limited price named in the instructions.

On the 14th of January, 1843, they entered into a charter-party for her with one Franceco, a Brazilian, for one year, and as much longer as was necessary to complete any voyage then begun, at the rate of 900 milreas (about $460) per month, and to carry no persons not free, and no goods illegal in character.

She sailed thence for the eastern coast of Africa the next month, with certain merchandise and free passengers on board, as hereafter described; and while on the coast of Africa, and on her return, was employed in the manner which will be stated in the opinion of the court.

On her return, she was informed against by Johnson, a free colored man on board, who had been severely punished in Africa for taking a boat ashore without leave; and after examination at Rio before the

American minister, consul, and the commander of the American squadron, was sent home by the latter for a breach of the laws of the United States against the slave-trade.

In the course of the trial, the counsel for the government offered evidence in order to show Libby's knowledge and intents in this voyage, — that while on the eastern coast of Africa he had received on board the Porpoise not only the boy called Luez, and the sole one named in the indictment, but another boy by the name of Pedro, who was a slave, and a brother of Luez, and, at another port, another boy, by the name of Guilheme.

And the government proposed to prove, also, some facts which took place on a prior voyage of the defendant in the Porpoise, on the western coast of Africa, under the same general charter-party; and urged the admission of all this for the purpose of showing the knowledge of Libby of the illegal objects of the hirers of the vessel, and of the slave character of the black, Luez, when he was taken on board.

The court ruled that anything done by Libby, or those who chartered the vessel during the voyage, and near the time when Luez was taken on board, might be shown, in order to prove his knowledge and intents; but nothing of a separate and independent character, transacted at a different place, and on a different voyage, and so distant in time as not to bear on this transaction, nor he be likely to come prepared to meet or rebut it on this trial. (See note, 1 Denio. R. 574; The People *v.* Hopson.)

On the same principle, it was ruled that questions could not be asked as to what afterwards became of some of the slaves put on board a vessel called the Kentucky, that sailed to Brazil from that part of the African coast, while Libby was there, unless the government proved first some connection in interest and business between the Kentucky and Libby, or between those slaves and the receiving Luez on board the Porpoise, which is the only charge in the present indictment.

The letters of G. Richardson, the owner, as well as of his consignees, written to Libby before Luez was on board, and giving instructions as to the object and character of the voyage, though objected to by the government as not being competent evidence, were admitted as a part of the *res gestæ*, to show the design with which the vessel was sent from this country, and chartered; and, if believed to be written honestly, and not as a cover or artifice to conceal illegal objects, the jury were instructed they should tend to rebut any improper views in the outset in this voyage of the Porpoise. But if designed to conceal illegal objects, they were an aggravation of the offence. So letters of freedom, or acknowledgments of manumission to Pedro, at Lorenzo de Marks, and to Guilheme, at Inhambane, made before persons styling themselves to be notaries public of the Portuguese government, with their seals annexed, were also allowed to go to the jury, though objected to by the counsel for the United States,* and permission was given to Libby to offer any evidence in his power as to their being genuine, and as to his having possession of them, believing them to be genuine when these boys were received on board. The court said it should instruct the jury that, being under the signature and notarial seals of persons purporting to be notaries public, they might be considered prima facie genuine, without any collateral proof, and were to be presumed to have been executed at the time of their date (1 Beyt on Presumptions, 116), which was before the boys came on board. The court allowed in evidence, to corroborate them and strengthen the probability that they were executed before Libby left the coast, the facts that the paper had the royal water-marks on it, such as is used by the Portuguese public officers there; that it had also the stamps for duties which are affixed there; that it was like other paper, in appearance and texture and marks, which is used there for public purposes; that the name of one of the notaries is the name of a person known to have acted as a Portuguese notary public there on other occasions; that the seal annexed to a passport, connected with one of the documents, is the seal used by the officers of the Portuguese government there; that these papers were lodged with the regular authorities at Rio, when the Porpoise arrived there, and were forwarded here with a certificate on each, by a person purporting to be a Portuguese consul, stating that the notaries signing and sealing were legal officers of Portugal, on the eastern coast of Africa, and were accompanied with translations of all into English, and were so forwarded under the signature of the American consul at Rio, as having been applied for by Libby, the prisoner.

These facts and circumstances were all permitted to go to the jury for their consideration, but under instructions to be given upon them in the charge, that the papers purporting to be manumissions should have no weight, unless, in the end, they believed, from all the testimony, that the accused had them in his possession, or had seen and believed them to be genuine, when he took Pedro and Guilheme on board.

And if he so had them, or so saw and believed, that was sufficient, whether the due execution of the papers was technically proved or not. For, if so believing, he, of course, did not intend to make them slaves, by so receiving and carrying them, since he carried them as free persons, and, for aught which appears, they still remain free.

[Both of them were then in court, nobody claiming them as slaves since they came on board.]

After the evidence was closed, and the counsel on both sides had submitted their views to the jury, the opinion of the court on the

---

* Peake eo 75; 10 Mod. 66; 8 Wheat. 333; Story on Bills, 266 sec.; 10 Pet. Ref. 170; Greenleaf eo 1 Denis, 276.

general principles of law arising in the case was stated, with extended references to the testimony.

The law as laid down, on the main points, was as follows :

The first question, made as to the voyage, by the counsel for the government, is, that it was illegal, on the face of it, to carry such merchandise on freight, from Rio to Africa, as was taken in the Porpoise. But the jury were instructed, that, for aught which had been proved, the voyage of the Porpoise, as planned by the owner, G. Richardson, was an ordinary one, and, on its face, not in violation of any act of Congress. It was under consignment to Knight, Maxwell & Co., for usual employment in carrying freight, or for sale at a limited price.

Next, they were instructed, that the charter-party entered into by the consignees with Franceco for one year for nine hundred milreas, or about $450 per month, to carry any lawful merchandise or free passengers, was, on its face, not a voyage prohibited by any law whatever. Yet all these might be colorable and false.

It was then a further and very important inquiry, whether anything occurred afterwards, and in connection with the voyage, which should alter the legality of it, in the appearance of its legality. For, however lawful in part a voyage might be in its inception, or external features and purports, circumstances might be developed and misconduct occur afterwards, which would indicate it to be entirely unjustifiable.

The Porpoise, in this case, after such instructions and such a charter-party, sailed from Rio in February, 1844, for the eastern coast of Africa, with several passengers on board, who were Brazilians, and some of them agents of Franceco, with a cargo consisting of rum, cotton goods, iron bars, gunpowder, brass rings, &c., being articles such as are in demand on that coast, and such as usually are sold for money, and slaves purchased sometimes with the proceeds; or such as are often exchanged for slaves. The cargo was landed there at different factories, under the direction of Paulo and others, and a launch, which belonged to him.

The Porpoise arriving there in April, 1844, and remaining on the coast till December, 1844, landing the cargo at the places described, tended to show L.'s knowledge of their business; and for the same purpose he was proved also to have gone on shore occasionally, during the time, to get provisions at the factories; sometimes dined there by invitation with Paulo; saw slaves in their yards, and some of the witnesses swear he was present at times, with themselves, when some were bought and branded by Paulo. It was further shown, that he sailed in company from Lorenzo de Marks to Inhambane with a vessel called the Kentucky, and under the control of Franceco and Paulo, and took on board there some of her crew, who were Americans, as passengers, before the Kentucky loaded with slaves under a Brazilian captain and crew, and sailed with them as she did to Brazil.

That the Porpoise and Kentucky hung out lights in the night for each other in going from Lorenzo de Marks to Inhambane, a voyage of sixty or seventy hours; that Libby took on board there one African boy, before named, called Guilheme, and another on his return at Lorenzo de Marks, called Pedro, but both supposed to have the manumission papers before described; and carried no other Africans, unless he knowingly received Luez, as charged in the indictment, and carried him about fifteen miles to Inaak, where he was landed with Paulo and the pilot's crew.

That after Libby's return from Inhambane, he waited, by direction of those chartering the Porpoise, till a slave vessel, the Galafelia, was loaded, and sailed the same day he did for Rio,—but he with no cargo on board the Porpoise, and merely provisions and water and some free passengers, and the two boys, Guilheme and Pedro. Various other incidents and expressions used by Libby were given in evidence to prove his knowledge of the business in which Franceco and Paulo were engaged, and in rebuttal, showing his disapproval of it; and especially the evidence before referred to, in the rulings of the court as to the manumission of Guilheme and Pedro, before he took them on board. In all of these, the court instructed the jury, that the conduct of Libby, on the whole voyage, must be considered legal or illegal according to the real intentions with which he entered upon it, and conducted till its close, accompanied by such acts as Congress has made penal. The law requires both, to constitute a capital crime, intentions to make persons slaves, and such acts as either kidnapping them, or receiving them on board a vessel with such views. For intents without acts, or acts without intents, are insufficient. Where an act is a crime and capitally punished, courts and juries must require very decisive participation in the principal offence by a guilty intent,—more than is necessary to avoid a contract, to recover for what is done or furnished in such a case; though even there it must be clear.

There they must aid and participate in the principal design, or in the illegal acts themselves. (See 1 N. H. R. 165, and cases there cited.)

Without any explanations as to such a voyage, and with such companions and such a cargo as Libby sailed with from Rio to the suspicious coast of Africa, and returning in such polluted company to Rio, it might be entirely justifiable to infer that he was a co-partner in the slave-trade itself with Paulo and Franceco, participating in the slave-trade itself, by receiving Luez on board; profiting by its gains, blackened by its guilt, intending to assist in the confinement of its victims, and coöperating designedly in depriving them of liberty, or in perpetuating such a wretched condition by transporting them in bondage to a foreign country. And if the jury believed this to be his position, after all the evidence and explanation on his part, then it was competent and proper, however painful, to find him guilty of the capital offence charged in this indictment.

It would make him a principal in the trade; and the jury need not trouble themselves about the circumstance that some sections of the act of Congress, like that now under consideration, did not *eo nomine* punish *aiding* and *abetting*, while others did.

Libby's conduct in such case would not be like that of one merely an aider,—an accessory before or after the fact,—or an abettor in it; but would be that of an active participator,—one of the principals,—and equally guilty and equally punishable with other principals.

In short, gentlemen, consider it the law for this trial, that if Libby himself was a coöwner in the slaves, if he embarked in the profits and loss of the slaver's voyage, if he had power and control over the slave cargoes, if he united in the kidnapping or confining, the purchase or the sale of them, he was a principal with the others in both heart and deed; and as such, he can and ought to be punished capitally, under the act of Congress, for receiving any of them on board of the Porpoise.

But, on the contrary, he and his counsel deny all this, and they offer much evidence, and refer to numerous circumstances, to rebut it.

The jury will examine them with care, as it is a case of life and death; and if reasonable doubts as to guilt remain, after examining them, he is entitled to an acquittal under this indictment, however he may be guilty of a different and less crime for carrying slaves for others as a mere carrier, and be liable to conviction under the other indictments now pending against him for such last offence.

Some of the facts relied on by the prisoner are these:

From the charter-party itself, it is insisted to be clear, that Libby had no idea of entering into the transportation or purchase and sale of slaves; that however he may have seen and known the slave dealing of his employers, he conducted throughout in accordance with the contract, adhering to it in substance, and not using it as a cover; going with the intent to take no slaves on board, no persons whom he supposed to be slaves; buying none, selling none, allowing none to touch his vessel or boats, but only those he believed to be manumitted like Pedro and Guilheme, or to be the crews of the African pilot, like Lucz, and which crew it was necessary to have temporarily on board, and to carry whom, while piloting the vessel, was, of course, not within the spirit or letter of the act of Congress.

It was further insisted, that his birth, education, and principles, all preclude the idea he should attempt to violate so important a law of his country. That he had no motive for it, in receiving any increased wages,—no indemnity, no security; nor had his owners any object, to expose their vessel to forfeiture, or he or his crew any inducement to risk their lives and property, as well as character, in such an illegal enterprise,—the freight, to be paid monthly by the charter, being proved to be only an ordinary rate.

On all the facts appealed to in support of this view, connected with those urged by the government to sustain a different view, it was for the jury, and not the court, to decide what was Libby's real object; and, if they believed he received Luez on board knowingly, and supposed him to be a slave, and with intent to make or continue him a slave, they should convict; but if otherwise, acquit of the capital offence.

The court, as before remarked, do not consider this one of those cases where a certain act is made penal, without reference to intent. Because the act of Congress itself makes the intent, the great essence of the offence, as it is, in most cases, of crimes. Without the *malo animo*, — the evil mind, — the guilt to be punished cannot, in a case like this, exist.

It is true that the legislative power may be broad enough to declare certain acts to be illegal, and to punish them, without saying anything about motives.

But no act of Congress has, in terms, made such a charter-party as that of the Porpoise unlawful on its face, though made to slavers, and to carry their goods. Nor has any act prohibited the freight to the coast of Africa, whether as an owner or carrier for others, of rum or gunpowder, or colored cottons, or brass rings, independent of any design to use them by the carrier himself in the slave-trade, or to engage with them himself in its traffic and merchandise.

If we, then, without any express law, were to hold that such a voyage or freight was on its face illegal, we should make the law, rather than expound one already made. It may seem a little singular to this generation, but before 1794 it was not punished as illegal for citizens of the United States to engage even in the slave-trade itself, whether foreign or domestic.

We had, to be sure, while colonies, been obliged to submit to the importation of slaves by the parent country, though under earnest remonstrances of our fathers against it. We had felt its horrors in our own persons,— our sons and daughters taken captives by the savages and held as slaves, and, at times, so sold in the Montreal market, and again and again redeemed, as was Stark himself, the subsequent hero of Bennington, by an agent of New Hampshire.

We have since seen it worse than repeated as to our gallant seamen by some of the barbarians of Africa herself,— by the semi-savages of Algiers and Tripoli,— till we became powerful enough to avenge our wrongs, and prevent a renewal of them. In short, the whole Union, even before the adoption of the constitution, had gradually become convinced that the only mode effectually to extirpate what the northern States considered the curse of slavery, was at an early day to stop the addition to the number here from abroad; not only thus cutting off a large and constant supply or reinforcement, but putting an end to the introduction of new ignorance, new superstitions, new paganism, and allowing the arts of civilization and Christianity gradually to elevate and make more safe the liberation of slaves long remaining here; and when safe, to do it by returning them, more civilized, to enlighten and reform slavery at home in Africa, or by releasing them here, when fit subjects for emancipation,— thus, in time, to terminate the evil throughout and forever.

Seeing and feeling all this, and that slavery itself might thus, in time, safely cease, the prudent framers of the constitution secured a right in it to prohibit the slave-trade into the United States after 1808, with an implied power to prohibit it at once from being carried on abroad by American citizens; and left slavery itself to be abolished here entirely, and as fast as each State should find it expedient and secure to itself. It is from this apparent that the foreign slave-trade with this country was left to each State to legislate for itself till 1808. Accordingly, most of the States, after the Revolution, even at the South, acted promptly for themselves, and prohibited the importation of slaves into their own limits from abroad.

But nothing was done by Congress, under the constitution, in respect to the slave-trade, till an act in 1794 made it penal for Americans to engage in it abroad. No court or jury of the United States could, before that, have inflicted penalties on persons engaged in that trade; nor could they then, by that act, have inflicted them on those engaged in the slave-trade to the United States. Only the judges and juries of each State could enforce their own laws against this trade. It is more emphatically the rule under a government of specified powers, such as the constitution of the General Government, that its officers cannot regard and punish as offences anything not forbidden by the constitution, or by acts of Congress.

The further history of the legislation of the General Government on this subject is very instructive on this point, as also on the peculiar character and proper construction of the particular law the prisoner is now tried for violating, as distinguished from other laws of a kindred but less severe character. Adverting to it, then, for a few minutes, — Congress having made, by that first act, the fitting out of a vessel here for the foreign slave-trade punishable by a forfeiture of the vessel, and two thousand dollars fine, proceeded next, in 1800, six years after, and made any citizen of the United States engaged in that trade liable to double the amount of his interest therein; and, furthermore, they punished with a fine of two thousand dollars, and imprisonment not over two years, the serving in any such vessel by a citizen of the United States.

Next, in February, 1803, Congress, in aid of those States which had voluntarily prohibited the slave-trade into their boundaries from abroad, made it penal to import slaves into them, and forfeited the vessel in addition to imposing a fine for each negro thus introduced.

Again, on March 2d, 1807, Congress, in its eagerness to exercise the constitutional right to prohibit the slave-trade to this country at all after the commencement of 1808, passed a law in advance, expressly forbidding any such importations, under the penalty of forfeiting the vessel, and paying a fine of twenty thousand dollars, and imposing a further fine of five thousand dollars on any person aiding or abetting therein, and subjecting those interested in the slaves themselves to imprisonment as well as fine.

After this, it was not till the treaty of Ghent stipulated for further measures towards the abolition of the trade that, in 1818, an act was passed forfeiting any vessel of the United States engaged in that trade, to or from any place whatsoever; and, furthermore, imposed a fine from one to five thousand dollars, and imprisonment from three to five years.

It punished, in like manner, the transportation from any place abroad of a negro or mulatto not held to service by any of our own laws, and made some other modifications of former acts on this subject. But not content with this moderation for the worst cases, and seeing there were different degrees of turpitude in the mere carrying of slaves, and being engaged on the African coast, or any foreign shore, in the kidnapping of them, or securing them on board, or in decoying or forcing them on board in any way, to make them slaves, Congress, in A. D. 1820, passed an act, declaring the latter offence a piracy, and punishable with death.

This is the act, and not that of 1818, or any prior or milder one, under which the prisoner is now on trial for his life.

But to hold, under this last law, that the mere carrying of cottons or rum to the coast of Africa, without regard to intent, and without meaning to make men slaves, by seizing or carrying them away, is a capital offence, when Congress has not said so, would be a great stretch of judicial legislation. Congress has not done all things on this subject, because it has done some. This has been shown fully in the history of its legislation just sketched to you. So, if one State, for instance, prohibits selling spirits without a license, another does not. But the judges, by construction, cannot punish such sale in the latter State, unless it is prohibited there also. So of the keeping of gunpowder, in large quantities, in cities. So of carrying deadly weapons. They are punishable only by the courts of a State where they are prohibited, and not by the United States courts, unless expressly made penal by some act of Congress or the constitution. If we were to pronounce the carrying such goods as the Porpoise freighted illegal, and a capital offence, without reference to the intent not to be engaged in making negroes slaves, or even carrying them on board, where should we stop?

The whole trade to Africa, by such a system of construction, might be abolished as illegal, and this, too, by the judicial tribunals alone.

That whole trade is all, more or less, in articles suitable to be exchanged for slaves, or sold there, and the money invested in slaves. The owners of the cargoes know this, who carry for themselves, as well as the owners of vessels who carry such articles for others. The whole coast, from the Isthmus of Suez to Algiers and Morocco, and the mouth of the Niger, doubling the Cape of Good Hope, to Cape Inaak, to Mozambique, Zanzibar, and the Red Sea,—the whole is black with slavery, and has been probably since the days of Joseph, who was sold to the Ishmaelites to be a slave in Egypt. And the great export of Africa now—not the only, but paramount one—is slaves; as much as silver is from Mexico, and coffee from Cuba. Slaves are the chief means of payment from the interior for their wants in foreign merchandise, and are universally made, used and sold. The Pacha of Egypt, one of the most enlightened rulers in Africa, though professing to abolish the slave-trade, is believed by travellers to go even beyond this, and to make annual incursions over his Ethiopian borders to fill his armies and household with captive slaves.

And till education and Christianity elevate the African mind—elevate their governments—above the savage practice of making captives in wars slaves, rather than mere prisoners, to be exchanged,—for this is the great seat and source of the evil, and has been in all ages,—I say, till these great principles, with re-colonization and advances in industry and the arts, lead the African people to mitigate the horrors of war as to prisoners, as has been their influence in modern Europe, since our proud British ancestors were sold into bondage in the slave-markets of Rome, and induce them to produce articles enough, independent of slaves, to exchange or sell, to supply their wants in foreign merchandise, nothing but the extirpation of the foreign slave-trade can be at all effective in lessening the evils of slavery in that wretched quarter of the globe.

In regard to the American efforts to break up the foreign slave-trade, and to take away the demand and the market, whether by fleets on the coast, or penal severities inflicted here, the courts of the United States can go, and are disposed to go, as far and as fast as the laws permit. But they cannot go further, without exercising judicial legislation, without usurpation, without infidelity to their oaths.

We are mere agents of the laws, to execute, and not enlarge or add to them. If they reach only to punish carrying slaves, we cannot extend them to punish carrying merchandise. Whenever Congress may choose to go further, and punish, as illegal, the transportation of any merchandise to Africa, whether by its owners or for owners, and those others mere merchants or slave-dealers,—if that merchandise be such as is usually exchanged for slaves, then such a voyage can be treated as illegal; but not till then, unless undertaken with the intent to participate in that trade, and accompanied, before its close, by acts of seizing or receiving on board slaves, knowing them to be such.

So, if Congress should please to go further still, and can do it constitutionally, and pronounce it illegal to carry articles to any slave-holding country,—Brazil or elsewhere,—suitable to be used by slaves, and to thus help sustain the institution or condition of slavery,—whether shoes, ploughs or clothes, of domestic or foreign manufacture,

—or make it penal to bring hither or consume the productions of slave-labor,—whether cotton, or sugar, or tobacco,—the courts of the United States can then, but not till then, punish such acts. These acts are, in the views of some, sinful, and should be denounced as illegal. And England has, of late years, actually imposed a higher and discriminating duty against slave-grown sugar, though allowing it to be imported and used. But recently she has abolished that discrimination, seeing, probably, if it was immoral or inexpedient to consume sugar unless under a higher duty, it was immoral, if not inexpedient, to consume it at all, on account of its vicious origin; and not probably being yet prepared, with some, to hold the use of all articles produced by slave-labor as a culpable participation in its guilt. But let the United States government prohibit the consumption, or purchase, or sale of articles produced by slave-labor, black or white, or the sale of anything likely to be used in the slave-trade,—it will then behoove courts and juries to enforce such prohibitions, if they can do it constitutionally.

But till then we possess no authority, acting on common-law principles, or any subtle distinctions in the metaphysics of moral science, to set up our private opinions and attempt to enforce them, without any legislative warrant from Congress.

A single illustration more on these distinctions, and I have done with them.

It is drawn from a practice common elsewhere, but which, it may well be a cause of gratitude, is less known among ourselves. Two duellists proceed to the field of honor, with their weapons and seconds. The seconds aid and abet, by arranging the terms of the fight, by loading the pistols, and giving orders to fire, and hence are punishable like the principals. But who ever heard that the coachman, or hack-driver, or conductor of the railroad-cars, who aided to carry them or their pistols and balls, was ever indicted as principal, or punished as such? The carriers may have known the intention of the parties to fight, but they had no object beyond their own fare, or common wages, in their customary business of carrying persons and things for hire.

If this was merely the design of Libby, and nothing more, it is clear that he cannot be punished for a capital offence. Something has been said of former decisions bearing on this question, as more or less stringent. The principle involved in Baptist's case (2 Story 240), decided by my eminent predecessor, was the same as that adopted here. The facts there differed from this, as to the commencement of the voyage being more disconnected with the trade itself; but the conduct there afterwards, in taking known and shackled slaves on board, and carrying them from one foreign port to another, was open, reiterated, and far stronger than in the present instance.

Nor am I aware of any decided case, connected with these questions, where the courts of the United States have held doctrines concerning them different from those just laid down.

Take up, then, gentlemen, all the circumstances in the present case, differing as well as similar to that of Battis, and any former decisions. Look at the whole real object and character and conduct of the voyage, and then decide whether the three points are satisfactorily made out or not, which are necessary to convict under this indictment, namely :

1. That Libby was a part of the crew or ship's company of a vessel of the United States.

2. That he received Luez on board the Porpoise about the 8th of December, 1844.

3. That he did it with intent to make him a slave.

I omit repeating to you, gentlemen, any further details under this or other heads, which were gone into in the charge in Libby's case, lest your patience would be taxed too much.

And I conclude with what was said there as applicable to all complaints of a like kind coming before you. That while, on the one hand, you cannot be too anxious to vindicate your country from any imputation of connivance at the illegal traffic in slaves from the African coast, and to punish every offence, satisfactorily proved, against its laws on this subject (this nation being first and foremost in the world to hold up such offences to condign severity of punishment), and solicitous, as we all are, to show every people that no reasonable effort will be spared to sustain the policy of most of the present governments of Christendom to suppress that inhuman traffic, yet you will, of course, abide by your oaths in doing this, and convict the prisoner only if guilty under the laws and the evidence. And you will be happy to find, in any case, if these laws and the evidence justify the conclusion, that one of your own countrymen, charged with this crime, has been so true to the biddings of duty, and so faithful to the laws,— so observant of the honors and character of the place of his birth and education,— as not to pollute his hands with participating in the gain or the turpitude of what in the present age is generally regarded so ignominious, as well as cruel, as the trade in human blood.

# REPORT OF THE COMMITTEE ON THE JUDICIAL DEPARTMENT, MADE TO THE CONSTITUTIONAL CONVENTION, CONCORD, N. H., NOV. 19, 1850.

THE Committee on the Judiciary ask leave to report, that they have carefully examined those parts of the existing constitution which relate to the subject confided to them.

Constitutions being the great fundamental laws passed by the people, should, in our view, not be recommended to be changed, except in matters and to an extent clearly desired by the people. To that extent, so far as ascertainable by us, we have, therefore, considered it our duty to go, notwithstanding the private opinions of some of us differ on several of the matters proposed to be changed. Thus guided in our deliberations, we first considered the alterations which might be proper in the term or tenure of office in our different judicial functionaries. In the present condition of public opinion in the State, a majority of the committee think that this term should be different in most classes of judges from what now exists. It is now, except with justices of the peace, during good behavior. In them, it is only for five years; in order, after that period, to bring their behavior under public consideration, and to reäppoint them or not, as the conduct of each incumbent and as the public interests may appear to require.

We think this provision for a short term of office has operated well in practice, and would, therefore, advise the adoption of a like system as to all judicial officers; though with more hesitancy as to the judges of the Superior Court than others. It is true, that by address to the Governor and Council, or by impeachment, judicial officers can now be removed at any time; but some defects of character, and some kinds of unfitness that may be developed, would seem to be corrected with more delicacy, and with equal if not greater efficiency, by omitting to reäppoint where at limited intervals a reäppointment is made to come under consideration; while the incumbent, by receiving a reäppointment, will obtain one of the most grateful rewards and powerful encouragements to well-doing which belong to public life.

The experience on this subject in this country has not, to the extent originally feared, proved unfavorable to the stability of the judiciary under short terms of office; it being found in practice not unusual to reäppoint, while the incumbent, by good legal acquirements, sound health and close attention to his public duties, seems worthy of it.

On account of this change in the length of the terms of judicial office, and the incumbents coming under review as to fitness so often, we have recommended not to retain longer the disability on account of mere age.

As the judges of the Superior Court are the most important of this class of officers, and would be likely to serve at lower salaries when the term is longer, and would be capable, by more experience in office, to understand better their more difficult and responsible duties, we propose to shorten their terms only to six years, and those of county judges and judges and registers of probate to four years, and justices of the peace, as well as trial justices, to two years.

Another argument in favor of six and four years, rather than five, for the higher judges, and two instead of otherwise for ordinary justices of the peace and trial justices, is the economy of time in electing them at the biennial periods, which seem to be preferred by the convention for electing representatives to the Legislature, and for the stated meetings of the Governor and Senate.

The attention of this committee was next bestowed on some changes in the appointing power as to judicial officers. They are now selected by the Governor and Council; but public opinion seems to us to require that, as a general rule, so many of them be appointed directly by the people as can be without too great expense and loss of time, and as are likely to be sufficiently known to them. It is, too, in our view, the right of the people in republics personally to exercise all official duties, and personally to act in all public affairs. But when this is not convenient, and is very laborious and expensive, except in democracies quite small as regards both numbers and territory, the people have the same right to act by agents for legislation, for executive purposes and judicial, as they have to act individually and directly. And it is a matter of usage not to be changed too greatly and suddenly, as well as of convenience, economy and benefit to themselves, whether, in practice, they appoint at once every agent, or appoint some through the instrumentality of other agents of their own selection. In both cases the people, as they should, control and govern.

Hence, when a class of candidates for office or agencies may reside so remote from some of the community, or be of such a character and profession, as not to be probably well known to most of them, a majority of us think it is for the advantage of the people themselves, both in point of economy and of a wise choice, that such agents be not selected by the people at large and directly, but by a few others of their own choice, less expensively, living nearer and likely to know them better, and under strict accountability to the people for making a good choice. The few thus electing will still be a part of the people themselves; will be by all of them in districts appointed agents for all; and will, by their residence and public standing, be more likely to be better acquainted with the candidates and their peculiar qualifications than the whole people, most of whom have never or seldom seen them, nor heard of them, nor live so near to them as to be able readily to inquire into their fitness.

But when the office is of a mere local and limited character, and the candidates reside near, and are probably well known to that part of the people who may vote for them, any aid of intermediate agents may well be dispensed with. Consequently, as ordinary justices of the peace and trial justices should belong to the town where they officiate, the people of the town—these small democracies, or republics in miniature—are presumed to know the candidates in person, to be acquainted well with their qualifications, and to be able, with ease, economy, safety, and in most respects with benefit to themselves, to elect them directly. Their own judgments, in such cases, are also not so exposed to sinister influences by others, or sudden impulses, and their confidence reposed in the incumbent and his decisions will be greater. Hence we recommend this change in the mode of the appointment of ordinary and of trial justices, except where more than one trial justice in a town is provided for by the Legislature; and then that one of them shall be appointed by the Governor and Senate, in order to attempt to overcome any political bias or error crept in from exciting causes, and to insure in such cases more fully the confidence of all in the fair administration of the laws by these local tribunals.

For reasons similar to what have influenced us to recommend the selection of justices of the peace and trial justices by the people, we advise that all county judges, and commissioners, and judges and registers of probate for each county, be elected by the people of each county, the candidates residing so near to most of them, in our present system of small counties, as to be likely to be generally known or easily inquired about, and their qualifications well ascertained. From the large amount of property adjudicated on by judges of probate, and the great trusts reposed in them, some of us are willing to have their appointment remain as now; but a majority of the committee think that it should come within the general rule as to offices for counties. The judges of the Superior Court, however, acting as they do for the whole State, and not any one town or county, stand differently. They would, by analogy, receive their appointment from the people of the whole State, voting directly for them. Yet, considering that they are not political officers, are not likely to be much known to the people of every town, and that full information as to their qualifications would not usually exist, and could not readily be obtained as to candidates residing in remote sections, we consider it wiser for the people to select them through the Governor and Senate. Such information could more easily be obtained by the latter, if not already existing, as some of the Senate come from every district of the State.

And the people, when generally intelligent, as ours are, would be no more unwilling to have judges selected by agents of themselves, and accountable to themselves, when those agents are so situated as probably to know the candidates better, and procure better judges for the community, than they are to have judges at all to act in administering the laws for the people, rather than themselves attempting to do it in person; or to have agents to *legislate* or execute the laws for them, instead of doing it themselves. The people virtually appoint the judge in both instances, though in one they do it *per se*, in person, and in the other *per aliud*, or by agents. In neither case is the right or competency of the people called in question; but the convenience and economy and intelligence of the representative system is preferred, for the benefit of the people themselves, where the action is to be on matters remote in distance, and operating over a wide area. Why else are the members of this convention, as agents of the people, now deliberating and examining for them? It has probably been for reasons, in part, like these, that no judge of the Superior Court for the State at large has ever, heretofore, been appointed directly by the people of the whole State; and, indeed, the rule has not been very different as to political officers — none acting as State officers at large having been elected by the whole people directly, except the governor; and he may well be an exception, as he is usually a person known to all parts of the State, has usually been before all the people in other eminent offices, and is criticized and his qualifications made known fully to the people through political and party presses.

But it is certainly safer for judicial independence and impartiality, the less a candidate for judge has mingled in party strife, and has been known in the movements of the political world, however proper it may be in a free country, and among a self-governing people, for every citizen to possess decided opinions on all great questions, and in no situation to halt or falter in sustaining them. By the mode we propose, there is, too, introduced a more popular and legislative element in the selection, by the assent of the Senate, than when the assent of a mere Council, as heretofore, was required; and yet more freedom from party interference or party dictation in the judiciary is secured than would be likely to exist in an election wholly popular.

A few words as to precedents bearing on this point. It is a mistake to suppose that the experiment of electing a judge of a Superior Court for the whole State, by the people directly, has been to much extent tried in other States, or tried at all with better success. It is true that many other States have shortened the term of office, as we propose to, and others have elected them by the Legislature — one branch of which we propose to have participate here. But it is believed that, in respect to this class of judges, not over four or five States out of thirty-one have thought it proper to make the experiment of a popular election by the people of the whole State, directly; and the success which has attended it in some of them, in public economy, convenience and useful qualifications of those elected, is considered by many as very problematical. Beside the precedents set, in a large majority of the States, against it, we have our own experience to show whether, in the mode heretofore acted on, and proposed to be still retained as to the Superior Court, the people of this State have not been blessed with as learned and faithful a succession of judges, in their higher courts, as any of the few States who have adopted a different system.

The course we pursue, under the constitution of the United States, — it being the fundamental law on many important subjects for us,— in conjunction with our sister States, throws light on the course of reasoning we have adopted, and is a distinguished precedent for our guide. That constitution, after being in operation over half a century, has never been altered as to the appointment of judges of the Supreme Court by the chief magistrate and Senate, and never made it elective directly by the people of the United States. Nor is this last mode known to have ever been seriously thought of, so strong are the reasons against it, before enumerated, as applicable here, of great distance of the residence of some of the candidates from that of many of the people, and their qualifications so little known to them all personally.

As a precedent, likewise, can any one believe that a selection of those judges by a direct vote of the whole people of the Union would have given to the country a better court?

In respect to the filling of vacancies, which must be very numerous among so many hundreds of offices, by declining to accept, by resignation, removals, and death, and great time and expense required to fill them by the people, we recommend, on the ground of convenience and economy, that they be filled by the appointing power, in each case, permanently; but that, temporarily, in county officers, the judges of the county or commissioners (when no such judges exist) fill the vacancies till town-meetings in the county can, with convenience, be notified and convened; and in case of officers appointed by the Governor and Senate, the former alone fill them till a regular biennial session of the Senate happens.

The subject of the jurisdiction, and mode of proceeding in chancery, has been discussed some, in committee of the whole, in the convention; and we recommend a change only in the latter, believing that the jurisdiction can safely be intrusted to the Legislature, under the limitations of the 20th article of the bill of rights as it has been amended, and of the 90th section of the 2d part of the constitution. It becomes, too, of less importance, under the additional provision which we now recommend; and which is, to make each party file an oath to the truth of his pleadings, and to allow either to have any facts in dispute settled by a jury, and to have the benefit of the testimony of his antagonist on the stand, if he pleases to call him.

The last clause in that 20th article has become unnecessary, by the amendment already adopted by the convention in the former part of it, and by the admiralty jurisdiction over seamen's wages, and transactions happening on the high seas, being, by the federal constitution, transferred to the cognizance of the General Government. We therefore advise that it be stricken out. The only remaining head for consideration, in respect to the judiciary, is the jurisdiction that ought to be confided to the different judicial tribunals.

We propose to leave that to be regulated, from time to time, by the Legislature, as it has been heretofore, and as public convenience may appear to demand, except in respect to justices of the peace, and the new courts by trial justices. Here we advise great and interesting changes. In regard to the jurisdiction of justices of the peace, we propose to transfer all of it, in the hearing of civil causes, to trial justices,—to be fixed by the Legislature, and not exceeding three in each town,—and to invest them with jurisdiction over all civil causes where the amount in controversy does not exceed $50, except cases involving the title to real estate; and leaving to the Legislature, from time to time, to regulate the criminal jurisdiction of both classes of justices, as well as those of the quorum, and those through the State, and the miscellaneous duties of all of them, and the term of office, and mode of appointing the latter classes. We further recommend that, in all cases, civil or criminal, except to bind over for trial elsewhere, either party be entitled to a trial by a jury, before the trial justices of the town where the proceeding is instituted; and that, in all cases, the proceeding shall be instituted in the town where one of the parties resides. We advise, too, that the jury consist of any number, not exceeding six, which the party asking it may desire; and the decision of the jury to be final on all matters of fact submitted to it, and not appealable from by writ of error, or otherwise as to the law, where the sum in controversy is less than ten dollars.

It is conceded that these are great changes in the jurisdiction and trials by local tribunals; but we advise them from a conviction that the existing complaints concerning the delay and expense in the present administration of justice can in this way be mostly cured. There have been several memorials referred to us, asking like changes. And it is a strong commendation of the mode proposed, that it will give redress, in all small disputes, nearer every man's door,—by judges, too, mostly of his own selection,—at much less expense, by cutting off appeals on facts, and yet preserve, unimpaired, the sacred palladium of a trial by jury. It is our belief that the present evils grow out of the present defective judicial system, and not from any omission of duties by the present judicial officers.

It is a remarkable fact, in support of this view, that from the returns made to this convention, by the clerk of the Court of Common Pleas for the county of Belknap, it appears that the whole number of judgments rendered in a given time was 73 under $25, and 60 between $25 and $50; while between $50 and $75 it was only 37, and between $75 and $100 only 14, and only 60 over $100,—making those for less than $50 near twenty per cent. more in number than all above that amount, and from double to treble all between $50 and

$100. In another county, Merrimack, and the only other from which returns are yet obtained and printed, no statement is made of the cases over $100, but those judgments over $50, for 1849, and less than $100, are only about 56 in number, and those under $50 are 153, or nearly treble in number.

In both of these counties, likewise, the cost recovered appears to be nearly as large as the debt in the cases below $25, while in those above its proportion is considerably less.

The evil is thus apparent in the small kind of litigation, and the large costs on it, which cover the dockets of the higher courts, and which must be much diminished by the amendments we propose.

We can devise no mode so likely, in our view, as this, to reach the root of the evils; and, what is most desirable in all amendments of constitutions, to satisfy that community which is to be governed by them.

As a still further check to vexatious litigation, the Legislature, more properly than the convention, could, with public advantage, impose cost in all cases of actions in higher courts, and no recovery had of the amount within their jurisdiction, nor any fair ground existing to expect such a recovery. And so, in case of any appeal or writ of error, without success in reversing the judgment below, in full or in part, the party who carries the case up can be made to, and should, pay large cost.

One subject more deserves some attention, as it is, in one aspect, judicial, and open, in our opinion, to improvement.

There is a clause in the constitution requiring the judges of the Superior Court to give their opinions to the Legislature and governor on questions of law; and we recommend a change, imposing this duty on the attorney-general. He is theoretically the law-officer of the government. A change like this has already been introduced in some other States, and it accords with the constitution and practice of the government of the United States. As the provision now stands, it is often embarrassing to a judicial officer to give an opinion on a question without argument on either side; and which question may be already pending, before him, between private parties, or soon to come before him, and their rights be prejudged without a full and impartial hearing.

Having gone through with the matters technically judicial, where any amendment is proposed by this committee, we would suggest another change in relation to the attorney-general and solicitors of counties. They are so connected with the judiciary that their appointment and term of office ought, in our view, by analogy, to be similar, and the solicitors be elected by the people in their counties, and the attorney-general, for the whole State, be appointed by the governor and senate; and that the former should hold office for the term of four, and the latter six years.

With a view of carrying these various recommendations into effect, the committee advise the passage, by the convention, of the following resolution:

*Resolved*, That the last period or paragraph in the 35th article of the bill of rights, on the term or tenure of judicial office, having been stricken out by the convention, that the 73d article in the 2d part of the constitution, on the same subject, be amended, so as to strike out, after the word *offices*, to the word *provided*, and insert: "If judges of the Superior Court, six years; if judges or commissioners, or judges of probate, registers, and solicitors for counties, four years; and if justices of the peace, or trial justices, two years."

That the word *President*, in this section, be stricken out, and the word *Governor* inserted.

And that there be added, at the close of this section, the following words: "When vacancies occur, in any way, in any of these offices, they shall be filled up, permanently, by the same power which filled the office originally; but that the county judges as to county offices, and the Governor alone as to those appointed by him and the Senate, may temporarily supply the vacancy, till the regular appointing power can conveniently act on the subject."

That in the 46th article, on the subject of the appointing power as to judicial officers, &c., the words *judicial officers*, *solicitors*, *and registers of probate*, be stricken out, and insert, after *all*, *judges of the Superior Court.*

And that there be added, at the close of the section, "And all judicial officers for counties, including judges and registers of probate, and also solicitors for counties, be elected by the people of the respective counties; and all justices of the peace, and all trial justices, by the respective towns in which they reside; except that when more than one trial justice is allowed, he shall be appointed by the Governor and Senate as aforesaid; and that justices of the quorum, and those throughout the State, be appointed, and their duties defined, and term of office limited, as the Legislature may direct."

That in this and all other sections, in respect to judicial officers, the word *Council* be stricken out, and *Senate* substituted.

That in the 74th section, 2d part, the words *justices of the Superior Court* be stricken out, and *attorney-general* inserted in its place.

That the 75th and 78th sections be stricken out, the subjects being substantially provided for elsewhere.

That, in the 77th section, the word *empowered* be stricken out, and the word *required* inserted in place of it; and that the word *trial* be inserted before the word *justices*. Also, strike out *four pounds*, and insert *fifty dollars*. After the word *concerned*, strike out the rest of the section, and insert these words: "The number of said trial justices to be at least one in each town or city, but not exceeding three, to be fixed by the Legislature; and one of the parties before them must belong to the town or city where the justices reside, and each party have the liberty of a trial by jury, not over six in number, whose verdict shall be final on the facts in all cases, and not to be appealed from, or reversed as to the law, in any way, in any case, by a higher tribunal, unless the sum in controversy is larger than ten dollars. The criminal jurisdiction of trial justices, and justices of the peace, and of justices of the quorum, and of those throughout the State, shall be regulated by the Legislature."

That after the word *peace*, in the 94th section, there be inserted, *and trial justices.*

That the 20th article in the bill of rights, relating to the judiciary, stand as it has been amended by the convention, but to strike out all the words after *jury.*

That to the 76th section of the 2d part be added these words: "And they shall provide that, in proceedings in chancery, both parties shall file an oath to the truth of their respective pleadings, and each party possess the right to have the facts in issue tried by a jury, and to use before them the testimony of his antagonist."

# HON. JOSEPH STORY.*

On this occasion, possessing at once so much interest and solemnity, the court would adopt a course similar to that pursued on this subject in another district of the circuit. The gentlemen of the bar might rest assured that the appropriate resolutions just offered should be entered on the records. They have the full concurrence of the whole court. The feelings of regret on account of the lamented decease of Judge Story, and the sympathies evinced towards his family, which had been expressed so widely, were common both to his associates and himself. There was no necessity to repeat the detailed review of the public services and private character of his predecessor, on which others have dwelt so impressively, whose longer and closer intimacy with the deceased rendered it proper that they should enlarge, when the hand of death had interposed to sever that intimacy till the resurrection of the just.

He would add, however, what had been said by him in substance in another part of the circuit, that all of the profession residing within it, and to some extent within the Union,—and, indeed, wherever an enlarged jurisprudence, connected with commercial, constitutional, and national topics, exists,—may well take the liberty to express, what they cannot but feel, a deep sense of the great loss they have sustained. The learning and eloquence which in him near a third of a century adorned this bench, and that of the Supreme Court of the United States, the tomb has closed over forever. You will no longer listen to the tongue that so long and so ably vindicated here the jurisdiction and powers of the General Government; and while, in the decision of private rights, he defended innocence with ardor, and relieved the oppressed by a most liberal exercise of equitable principles, and lost no fit occasion to expose injustice and punish fraud, his motives always had the good fortune to be respected, even by those who differed from him in his judgments.

It is a great consolation, when such men are removed from their elevated sphere on earth, that they have not lived in vain for the future, any more than the past, in respect to their fellow-men. The courtesy and blandness of manner which so strongly characterized him will long be remembered by most of us, as models for imitation.

* At a meeting of the bar of the Circuit Court in New Hampshire, October 8th, 1845, a series of resolutions was adopted, commendatory of the great worth of the Hon. Joseph Story, deceased, lately a judge of this court. They were presented to the court at its opening, at which time this address was delivered.

And his pure life, unspotted as the ermine of the justice he administered,— his unwearied toils in serving his country and profession,— have sown seeds which will long yield to both a rich harvest, and have met with their rewards from grateful millions, which will long encourage our youth, as well as those of more advanced age, to emulate his example. It is fortunate that the records of much of his various labors will survive for the edification of us all. And painful to many as has been the death of one distinguished by so many excellences and so much usefulness, it is a source of gratitude that his efforts were spared to the world so long, and till he accomplished so much; and that the fruits of them can never die, while the law endures as a science, and genius, industry, and ambition, nobly employed, are held in veneration among men.

# INDEX.

## A.



## B.

C.

D.

## G.



## H.



## I.

J.

## N.



## O.



## P.

R.



S.

T.



U.



V.

## W

www.ingramcontent.com/pod-product-compliance
Lightning Source LLC
LaVergne TN
LVHW021147110826
845150LV00005B/1147

* 9 7 8 1 4 2 5 5 4 7 4 7 9 *